Clothing

FASHION, FABRICS, CONSTRUCTION

Clothing

FASHION, FABRICS, CONSTRUCTION

THIRD EDITION

Jeanette Weber

GLENCOE

McGraw-Hill

New York, New York
Columbus, Ohio
Mission Hills, California
Peoria, Illinois

REVIEWERS

Margaret T. Cramer
Family and Consumer Sciences
Turpin High School
Cincinnati, Ohio

Jeannie Frazier
Home Economics/Industrial Clothing
Enterprise High School
Enterprise, Mississippi

Susan Miller
Fashion Merchandising
East Central University
Ada, Oklahoma

Josephine Ploetz
Family and Consumer Sciences
New Prague High School
New Prague, Minnesota

Jean Schack
Custom Garment Making
Palm Bay High School
Melbourne, Florida

Connie Zaenglein
Home Economics Coordinator
Arlington High School
La Grangeville, New York

CONTRIBUTING WRITER

Anne Marie Soto
Fashion and Sewing Specialist
AMS Associates
Teaneck, New Jersey

Glencoe/McGraw-Hill

A Division of The McGraw-Hill Companies

Send all inquiries to:
Glencoe/McGraw-Hill
3008 W. Willow Knolls Drive
Peoria, Illinois 61614-1083

ISBN 0-02-647605-3 (Student Edition)

Printed in the United States of America

4 5 6 7 8 9 10 11 12 13 14   003/046   02 01 00 99 98

Contents

Contents

Contents

Contents

Special Features

Sewing and Serging Handbook

Serging Techniques

Clothes and You

CHAPTER 1

Why Do People Wear Clothes?

After reading this chapter, you will be able to:

- List the reasons why people wear clothes.

- Explain how clothing identifies a person.

- Describe how culture, family, and friends influence clothing choices.

- Discuss the influence of peer pressure and advertising on clothing selections.

Terms to Learn

- *modesty*
- *standards*
- *insignias*
- *status*
- *status symbols*
- *adornment*
- *society*
- *culture*
- *lifestyle*
- *values*
- *peer group*
- *peer pressure*

Have you ever played this game? You are alone in a crowded place. Perhaps you are waiting for your friends to show up, or you are waiting for a ride home. To pass the time, you begin to observe the people around you. You try to guess some things about them, such as where they go to school, what they do for a living, or if they are someone you would like to know.

The clothing that people wear offers many clues about themselves. Some people dress in a certain way so that others will notice them. Other people use their clothing choices as a way to blend in with the crowd.

Why do people wear the clothes that they do? Usually the reasons are complex, even if people make their clothing decisions quickly. Clothing is used to cover the body, to make one feel more attractive, and to communicate with others.

The Reasons for Clothes

People wear clothes for many different reasons. Some of these reasons are physical. You wear clothes for comfort and protection. Others are for psychological and social reasons. Clothes give you self-confidence and express your personality. Clothes also help you identify with other people. Knowing something about the role of clothing helps you to understand yourself and others better.

Protection

In our world, we humans need to protect ourselves from our environment. We do not have a natural protective covering like most animals. The feathers and fur of animals protect them and keep them comfortable. Our skin is uncovered and exposed. We can be easily affected by the elements—rain, snow, wind, cold, and heat. We need to be protected on certain jobs or while participating in sports.

Climate and Weather

If you lived in an environment that was completely controlled for comfort, your clothing needs would be very simple. You would not need to consider the climate or changes in the weather. Large indoor shopping malls, hotel complexes, and many schools come close to such environments.

Even on balmy days or while inside climate-controlled buildings, clothing adds to your comfort. It absorbs perspiration, prevents sudden chills, and acts as a buffer between your body and rough surfaces.

However, it is outdoors under extreme weather conditions that clothing plays its most important physical role. The right garments can insulate your body against extremely hot or extremely cold temperatures.

People who live in severely cold climates keep warm by wearing pants and parkas with fur linings. The fur traps the warm air from their bodies and cre-

Coats, hats, and gloves provide warmth and prevent body heat from escaping in cold weather.

ates a life-saving insulating layer of warmth. Desert nomads keep the harmful hot sun from dehydrating their bodies by covering up with long flowing robes and headdresses. Their clothing actually keeps them cooler than they would be without it.

In areas where the climate is more moderate or where it changes with the seasons, people dress according to the weather. Warm-weather clothes include loose styles and light colors. Cold-weather clothing features multiple layers and heavy or bulky fabrics.

Safety

Clothing also serves to protect your skin from harm or injury. Some sports require protective clothing for safety reasons. Football and hockey players wear helmets and protective padding to help prevent injury during rough play. Soccer players wear shin guards to protect their legs from hard hits by the ball. These protective aids were developed so people could enjoy a sport and reduce the risk of injury.

Some occupations involve dangerous or hazardous situations. Many workers must wear hard hats while on the job. Construction and mill workers wear safety shoes and boots with steel-reinforced toes. Firefighters wear asbestos clothing for added protection. Police officers wear bulletproof vests. Road workers wear fluorescent orange vests so that drivers can see them easily and prevent accidents.

Clothing also offers protection for leisure activities. While hiking through the woods, you may wear long pants and a long-sleeve shirt to avoid insect bites and scratches from the bushes. While sailing, you may wear a life vest in case the boat overturns.

Sanitation

Special clothing and accessories are often worn for sanitation reasons. In factories that produce food and medical products, people wear sanitary clothing, face masks, and hair coverings. This precaution prevents contamination of the products by germs.

In hospital operating rooms, doctors and nurses wear disposable sanitary uniforms, gloves, and face masks. Fast-food workers wear hats or hair nets to prevent their hair from falling into the food they are preparing or serving. These are some examples of how other people protect you by wearing special clothing. Can you think of any other examples?

Clothing and protective padding can help prevent sports injuries. How many protective items are these in-line skaters wearing.

Hard hats and heavy gloves protect these construction workers on the job.

This chef wears a hat, gloves, and special clothing when preparing food products.

Modesty

Modesty refers to *what people feel is the proper way for clothing to cover the body.* Different groups of people may have different standards of modesty. **Standards** are *ethics or customs that are generally regarded as acceptable.* People follow these standards in order to fit in and be accepted by the group or community. Usually you can recognize what is considered modest or immodest because most people dress in the acceptable manner.

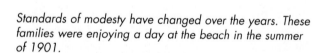

Standards of modesty have changed over the years. These families were enjoying a day at the beach in the summer of 1901.

Standards of modesty may vary from one situation or activity to another. No one would think twice about a young man playing volleyball on the beach without his shirt. However, it would be unacceptable for him to appear shirtless for his math class at school. Clothes that a woman might wear to a fancy party would probably be unacceptable at work the next day.

Standards of modesty differ from one group of people to another. Some women of the Muslim religion wear a long veil that completely covers them when they are in public. Only their eyes show through a small opening in the veil. This is a very old tradition. In other parts of the world, it is acceptable to wear very little clothing, such as only a loincloth.

Modesty standards can change over a period of time. Around the turn of the century, American women wore long skirts. A woman always followed a man when walking up stairs. Why? It was unacceptable for him to see her ankles!

Identification

Clothing can identify people as members of a group. Certain types of clothing, colors, and accessories can represent special occupations or athletic teams. People can show they belong to the same group by dressing alike.

Special clothing is also used for ceremonies and celebrations. This helps to identify a person's role for the occasion.

Uniforms

A uniform is one of the easiest ways to identify group members. Uniforms can provide instant recognition or create a special image for the group.

Members of the police force, fire department, and military wear uniforms so they can be recognized quickly and easily for public safety. Athletic teams wear different colors to identify their team and to tell them apart from their opponents. Different sports have different styles of uniforms. For example, rugby players wear traditional striped shirts and shorts.

Uniforms provide instant recognition. The police officer's uniform helps to identify her in a crowd. The colorful band uniforms identify the members and create an image for the group.

Wrestlers wear tight, one-piece uniforms called singlets. Baseball, football, basketball, and soccer players all have different styles of uniforms.

People who work in service occupations, such as restaurant workers, airline personnel, and hotel staffs, also wear special uniforms. These uniforms help to identify the worker to their customers, as well as create an image for the company.

Insignias

Insignias are *badges or emblems that show membership in a group.* They can be worn on members' jackets or caps. To indicate participation in athletics, a school letter with a sports pin can be worn on a jacket or sweater. Specially designed scarves, ties, or hats can also identify people as members of a particular group.

Styles and Colors

Some occupations require a unique style of clothing that may date back many centuries. Judges wear a traditional black robe in the courtroom. Ministers, priests, and other clergy members usually wear special clothing for conducting religious services. These special robes or shawls visually identify the person's role.

Special styles and colors of clothing are worn for special occasions. Many brides wear a traditional white wedding gown and a veil. Some parents dress babies in long white christening gowns that are passed down from generation to generation. Graduates usually wear long robes and mortarboard hats with tassels to receive their diplomas.

Status

Clothes and other accessories can be used by people to show their level of importance. For example, kings and queens wear crowns to set them apart from the rest of their subjects. Their crowns indicate their **status**, or *position or rank within a group.*

Leaders of marching bands may wear tall fur hats to help them stand out from the rest of the band. Presidents and deans of universities wear special scarves or hoods over their robes during ceremonies to show their rank.

Clothes or other items that offer a sense of status for the ordinary person are called **status symbols**. Usually these items are more expensive or the latest in design. For some people, status symbols can be expensive jewelry or designer clothes.

Decoration

People decorate themselves to enhance their appearance. They wear clothes, jewelry, and cosmetics in hopes of improving their looks and attracting favorable attention. **Adornment**, or *decoration*, helps people to express their uniqueness and creativity.

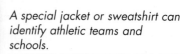

A special jacket or sweatshirt can identify athletic teams and schools.

Traditional caps and gowns identify these happy graduates.

Throughout the world, different people have adorned their bodies in a variety of ways. Some of these methods are still used today. See "Self-Adornment" on this page .

Influences on Clothing Choices

From experience you have learned to wear a coat or jacket when it is cold outside. But why did you choose the particular style and color of your coat or jacket?

Our clothing choices are influenced by many factors in the world around us. Our culture and our family help shape the choices we make. Other influences, such as friends and advertising, may lead us to buy certain styles because they appeal to our emotional needs.

Self-Adornment

Throughout history, people have adorned their bodies in different ways. Cosmetics, paint, and tattoos have been used for decoration, status, and identification.

- Native Americans painted their faces for many reasons. Often it was to protect their skin from wind, sun, snow, or insects. After buffalo-back fat was rubbed on the skin, the paint was applied. Sometimes the designs meant something special. In the Omaha tribes, the leader of a war party painted diagonal lines from the bottom of his eyes to his neck. These lines represented the path of his tears as he cried for a successful battle. Among the Sioux, the first warrior to kill an enemy in battle painted his face black for the victory ceremonies.

- In Japan during the 1660s and 1700s, a type of tattooing called *irezumi* was popular. These highly decorative tattoos covered almost the entire body. Because only the nobles were allowed to wear fine silks, brocades, and gold and silver ornaments, many wealthy merchants decorated their bodies with these expensive tattoos.

- In the Hindu religion, a red mark on the forehead, called a *tilaka,* means that the person has performed the daily prayer ceremony. The mark is made from a red powder and is applied by a priest, family member, or friend.

- For the Karaya people of eastern Brazil, it was an important event when visitors came to their village. Everyone in the village put on red and black face paint as a sign of hospitality and celebration.

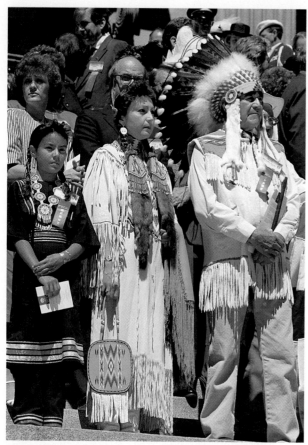

This Native American family is wearing garments that are embellished with beautiful beading, fringe, and other trims. Their culture is also reflected in the soft buckskin clothing, handcrafted jewelry, and feathered headdress.

Many families enjoy wearing the traditional costumes of their culture to celebrate special occasions.

Society and Culture

The society in which we live influences the type of clothing we wear. A **society** is *a group of individuals who live together in a particular area.* The Native Americans are a society of people who have lived in North America since ancient times. A **culture** is *the collection of ideas, skills, beliefs, and institutions of a society at a particular time in history.* Native American culture includes their special styles of art, architecture, clothing, language, religion, and forms of government.

Clothing can be a valuable clue to various cultures. The style of clothing that people wear—the fabrics, the designs, and the colors—can tell you many things about the way that the people think and live.

Look around your classroom at the outfits worn by your classmates. How similar are they? What do you think students in other schools in the United States are wearing? Now think about students in other countries around the world. What might they be wearing in China, Italy, Ghana, Brazil, India, or Australia?

Many students in other cultures are probably wearing outfits very similar to yours. Others, however, may be dressed in quite different styles. These similarities and differences help us to better understand people around the world.

Family

Your family has a strong influence on your clothing needs and choices. The **lifestyle** or *typical way of living*, of a family and its members affects clothing decisions.

For example, where your family lives influences your wardrobe needs. Do you need a heavy coat, mittens, and boots for snowy winter days? If you live in Minnesota, these clothing items are very important. If you live in Florida, your clothing needs are quite different.

The activities you do with your family also influences your clothing needs. A family who enjoys lots of outdoor activities would need different types of clothing than a family who attends many concerts and plays. Think about the various activities that your own family likes to do. Do any of these activities have special clothing requirements?

This family enjoys many outdoor winter activities. Warm clothing and accessories are needed for all the family members.

Many teenagers wear certain clothing styles in order to feel a part of their peer group. What styles are currently popular with your peers?

Every family has its own set of **values**, or *beliefs about what is important, worthwhile, or desirable.* These values influence the clothing choices of family members. In some families, it is important that a new baby have all new clothes. Other families think it makes more sense to borrow baby items from family and friends because infants grow so rapidly.

If physical activity is important to a family, then family members probably own more active sportswear than a family that spends its leisure time watching television or going to the movies. If status is very important to a family, then more of the family's budget may be spent on new clothes and accessories than a family that values practicality.

Sometimes families have to make choices about the clothing needs of family members. Should they buy new shoes for the children or a suit for a parent who has started a new job? Is it more important to get swimming suits and shorts for a week at the beach, or new outfits to wear for a family wedding? At times, families may decide that a certain goal, such as buying a car, is very important. Then it may be necessary for all family members to limit their clothing purchases.

Peer Group

A **peer group** is made up of *people who have a similar background, social status, and age.* Peer groups usually consist of friends, classmates, or job associates.

Most people feel a strong need to fit in with other members of their peer group. Some will even adjust their clothes and habits in order to look and act like others in the group. This similarity creates a sense of belonging.

Appearance may be regulated within the peer group by written or unwritten rules. Certain clothing styles, brands, and colors may be approved or disapproved by the group. Usually there is an "in" way of dressing. Certain accessories may be important to the group. The "right" shoes, boots, belts, hats, or backpacks may be clearly identified.

Sometimes members of the group are expected, and even pressured, to dress in the approved way. This *pressure by the peer group to conform* is called **peer pressure**. Clothing that does not conform to the group's standards may be criticized. The person may be talked about, laughed at, or teased.

Sometimes peer pressure can be gentle and used to help members develop a sense of belonging and togetherness. The group members can benefit from such positive peer pressure.

However, peer pressure can be strong and cruel, forcing people to either conform or be excluded from the group. To resist negative peer pressure, you need to have a clear understanding of your own values and identity.

Advertising

Advertising exists to sell products. Television, radio, newspapers, magazines, and billboards all carry many advertising messages. These can make clothing and accessories look so attractive that you want to buy them.

Advertising can be a source of valuable information. It can tell you about new products on the market. If you need a new coat or pair of shoes, it can help you compare styles and prices before you go shopping. Ads can also tell you which stores carry a particular item and whether it is on sale.

Many advertisements are designed to appeal to your emotions. They create special wants and desires for specific products. These ads can tempt you to buy something you don't really need or something that costs more than you want to spend.

It is important to read, look, and listen carefully to what is said in advertisements. Then you can separate the factual information about a product from the emotional appeal. Advertising should be only one of the many influences on your clothing choices.

Clothing choices can be influenced by the emotional appeal of fashion advertising. Use these ads to gather helpful information and ideas for planning your wardrobe.

Summary

- Clothes provide protection, modesty, identification, status, and decoration.
- Uniforms, insignias, and certain styles and colors can identify people as to occupation, groups, and roles.
- Our clothing choices are influenced by our society, culture, family, friends, and advertising.
- The lifestyle and values of family members affect clothing decisions.
- Peer groups can apply peer pressure to make group members dress in the approved way.

Using Vocabulary Terms

On a separate piece of paper, write the vocabulary term that best fits the definition:

1. People who have a similar background, social status, and age.
2. What people feel is the proper way for clothing to cover the body.
3. Position or rank within a group.
4. Beliefs about what is important, worthwhile, or desirable.
5. Typical way of living.
6. The collection of ideas, skills, beliefs, and institutions of a society at a particular time in history.

Recalling the Facts

1. List the five reasons why people wear clothes.
2. In what three ways does clothing provide protection?
3. Explain how standards of modesty differ from one situation or activity to another.
4. How can clothing identify people as members of a group?
5. What are status symbols?
6. What are two reasons why people adorn their bodies?
7. What is a society?
8. How do families influence clothing needs and choices?
9. What is peer pressure?
10. What is the purpose of advertising?

Thinking Critically

1. **Analysis.** Compare and contrast the type of clothing worn in warm, moderate, and cold climates.
2. **Synthesis.** What might happen if uniforms were no longer worn by people in different occupations? Give examples.
3. **Evaluation.** Why do you think status symbols are popular with many teens?
4. **Analysis.** How is a society different from, yet interrelated to, a culture?
5. **Evaluation.** What do you think are the positive and negative aspects of peer pressure?

Applying Your Knowledge

1. **Reasons for Clothes.** Working in small groups, look through magazines and newspapers for illustrations of people wearing clothing for different reasons. Label the illustrations according to purpose. Create a display.

2. **Styles and Colors.** Make a list of special occasions where special clothing styles and colors are worn. Describe how the clothing identifies various people at each occasion.

3. **Culture.** Imagine that you are a visitor from another planet. Looking at the outfits worn by classmates, write an essay about how students in your community think and live.

4. **Family, Friends, and Advertising.** Make a list of several outfits in your wardrobe that you chose because of the influence of lifestyle, activities, friends, or advertising. For each outfit, describe what influenced your clothing choice.

Making the Connection

1. **Social Studies.** Many cultures have used elaborate forms of jewelry to decorate their bodies. Write a report about the role of jewelry in another culture.

2. **Language Arts.** Describe how clothing standards might vary in different areas or regions of the United States.

What Is a Market Researcher?

Market researchers study the needs and attitudes of consumers. They conduct interviews and surveys to find out what consumers like and dislike about different products. Market researchers also track the type of advertising that people respond to most. They analyze the sale of specific products to identify trends. This information is used by manufacturers to decide what styles, fabrics, colors, and sizes are most likely to sell in various regions of the country.

Try It Yourself

Imagine that you are a market researcher for a garment manufacturer. The company wants to develop a special line of clothes for the teenage market. Conduct a survey of students' likes and dislikes about clothing and accessories. Ask questions about styles, fabrics, colors, prices, brand names, and advertising. What do they like best? What do they need and want? What would appeal the most to teenage customers? Analyze the results of your survey.

Build Your Portfolio

After completing your market research and analysis, write your recommendations for a new line of clothing that would appeal to teens. Include specific information about styles, fabrics, colors, and price range. Suggest a name for the new clothing line, as well as advertising methods that would reach the teen market. Place a copy of your survey results, analysis, and recommendations in your portfolio.

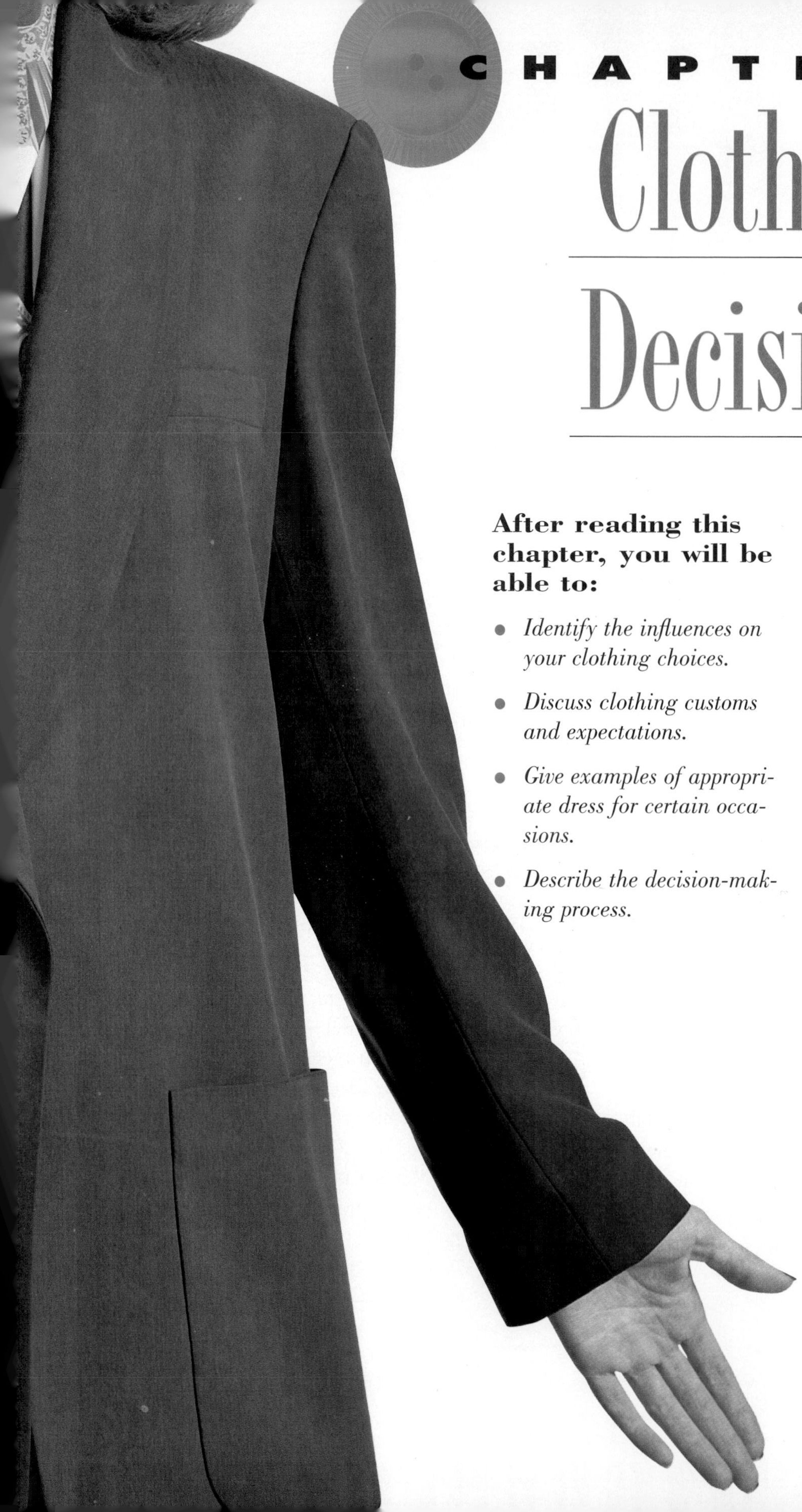

CHAPTER 2

Clothing Decisions

After reading this chapter, you will be able to:

- *Identify the influences on your clothing choices.*
- *Discuss clothing customs and expectations.*
- *Give examples of appropriate dress for certain occasions.*
- *Describe the decision-making process.*

Terms to Learn

- *appropriate*
- *personality*
- *customs*
- *expectations*
- *resources*

Each morning you are faced with a decision. What will you wear today? On some days, the decision will seem easy, and you will reach into the closet for the perfect outfit. On other days, the decision may seem hard, and you will have to think about it. You may even try on several garments until you find the right outfit to wear.

Each time you decide what to wear, you consciously or unconsciously go through a decision-making process. There are many influences on your clothing decisions. You may consider where you are going, what you plan to do, who will be with you, what the weather is like outside, and how you feel that day.

Deciding What to Wear

When you get dressed each day, you undoubtedly think about your plans. What activities are on your schedule for the day? Do you have school, practice for a sport, a part-time job, or a special occasion to attend?

Sometimes you have a wide choice of clothes that you could wear. At other times, the choice may be limited or made for you.

For example, some schools have uniforms or a special clothing code that lists what types of clothes may or may not be worn. Perhaps an employer requires that you wear a uniform or a certain style and color of clothing, such as a white shirt with black or navy pants. In these instances, choices have been made for you. You have fewer decisions to make.

However, when your choices are unlimited, how do you decide what clothes to wear? Suppose your calendar shows three events for today: taking your brother to the park, going to a party with friends, and being interviewed for a job by someone whom you have never met. Would you dress differently for each event?

Probably there are many factors that influence your clothing choices for these occasions. Sometimes you may be uncertain as to which choice would be best. In making more difficult clothing choices, you have to decide what is important to you.

Your clothing choices depend on many things. Some of these include what you plan to do, who will be with you, your mood, your personality, and your values.

What You Plan to Do

On Saturday morning, you may put on your old sweatshirt and comfortable blue jeans. You are planning to clean up your room and then work on a special hobby project. If you have a part-time job in a local store, you may put on a nice sweater and pair of slacks. If you are going swimming with several friends, you may put on your bathing suit under your clothes. The activities that you plan to do have determined what types of clothes to wear. You have chosen clothes that are **appropriate**, or *suitable*, for your activities.

If you are going hiking, shopping, or visiting a museum, you will need to wear comfortable shoes because you will be doing a lot of walking. If you are planning to participate in sports or exercise, you will be most comfortable in clothing that allows you to stretch and move easily.

How do you decide what clothes to wear each day?

Your clothing decisions depend on what activities you plan to do. These teens are wearing clothes that are practical and durable while washing the car.

You also need to think about the weather. Is it going to be cold, hot, or wet? If you are going to be outdoors in cold weather, you need to keep warm. Wearing several layers of clothes, plus a hat and gloves, is best. If it is snowing, boots will keep your feet warm and dry.

On rainy days, be sure to wear something that will keep you dry. A water-repellent jacket, a slicker, a hat, or an umbrella will protect your other clothes. Since leather shoes can be ruined by getting soaked, wear waterproof shoes or boots.

When you dress appropriately for the weather, you will stay warm and dry.

Who Will Be with You

Whom you plan to be with is another important influence on your clothing choice. With your family or best friend, you probably do not worry about what to wear. You feel very comfortable with them. You know that you can relax around your home in your most casual clothes, such as a baggy shirt, ripped jeans, and old worn sneakers.

With school friends, you may want to wear similar types of clothing for certain activities. In some groups, teens will often telephone other members of the group to find out what they plan to wear to school, a party, or a special event. Then they can all dress in the same way.

On other occasions, you may be with people whom you do not know. You might be interviewing for a job or attending a large celebration. On these occasions, you may take extra time to select an outfit that you feel is appropriate for the occasion. You will want to look your best and not have to worry about what you are wearing.

Your Mood

Think about your own wardrobe. Do you have an outfit that you always feel good in when you wear it? Does another outfit always feel comfortable? Almost everyone has favorites in his or her wardrobe. These are the clothes that you turn to and always enjoy wearing.

Your mood often affects your clothing choices. If you are happy and cheerful, you may reach for bright, bold colors. If you are feeling down, you may unconsciously select a darker color. You may even choose a favorite article of clothing that gives you a sense of comfort and security.

Everyone's mood affects personal clothing choices to some extent. As a teenager, your moods may change rapidly as you are growing and changing. Many times you may not be aware of these changes. Sometimes clothes can help change your mood, too. On a day when you are feeling down, wearing a bright color or favorite outfit may lift your spirits a bit.

People enjoy wearing casual clothes when relaxing with friends. When are other appropriate times to wear casual clothes, such as jeans?

Clothes are a good way to express your mood and your personality.

Your Personality

Your **personality** is *the combination of all your unique qualities.* You express your personality through your attitudes, emotions, and behavior. Your personality also directly affects your clothing choices.

Are you outgoing and talkative, or quiet and shy? Are you self-confident or unsure of yourself? Do you like to stand out in a group or blend in? Do you like to be a trendsetter and unique in your clothing selection? Perhaps you prefer a middle-of-the-road approach.

The answers to these questions tell you about your personality. In turn, your personality influences the style of clothing that you prefer. You can learn how to express your personality through the clothes you wear.

Your Values

Have you ever stopped to think how much clothes really mean to you? What values do you take into account when you make clothing choices? Practicality, comfort, wealth, economy, and appearance are examples of values that may have an impact on your clothing choices.

Practical people are concerned with comfort and durability. They want clothes that feel good and wear well over a long period of time. They may or may not concern themselves with current styles.

People who value wealth will select clothing and other material goods that look expensive. Those who value economy will look for special sales and bargains. For others, appearance may be most important. They may sacrifice comfort and practicality to wear the latest up-to-the-minute fashions.

Which values matter the most to you when choosing clothes? By answering this question, you will learn more about your own clothing philosophy.

Menswear: Historical Details

Here are the origins of some details in menswear:

- At one time, buttons on both men's and women's clothing were placed on the left side. Men's buttons were changed to the right side during the Middle Ages. This was done so a man could quickly unbutton his coat with his left hand and draw his sword with his right hand.

- In the middle of the 1600s, men wore a rectangular piece of linen trimmed with lace around the neck. It was tied in a bow or knot. This *cravat* was the forerunner of the necktie.

- Hannah Montague, a blacksmith's wife, noticed that the collars on her husband's shirts needed a daily washing but the bodies did not. She is credited with inventing the detachable collar in the 1820s. By the early 1900s, most men's shirts had detachable collars that could be laundered and starched separately.

- The blazer gets its name from the English ship, the H.M.S. Blazer. Its captain wanted to impress Queen Victoria when she visited the ship in 1837. He had short, double-breasted navy blue jackets with gold buttons made for his crew.

- Before the 1850s, men's jackets, vests, and trousers were made of contrasting colors and fabrics. Then the fashion trend of matching the coat, vest, and trousers began.

- The style of creased trouser legs is credited to Edward VII of England. When he tried on pants that had been folded for some time in a tailor's shop, he liked the slenderizing effect created by the creases. Thus began a fashion detail that still continues.

Clothing Customs

Every society has certain social **customs**, which are *established ways of doing things*. These guidelines or rules may be written or unwritten. Custom has dictated that certain styles of clothing are considered more appropriate than others for certain occasions. For example, jeans are considered appropriate for a rock concert but not for a symphony concert. Wearing dark colors to a funeral shows respect for the family's loss. Wearing a clean, neat outfit to someone's home for dinner shows that you are pleased by the invitation.

In our society, it is traditional to wear certain types of clothing for special occasions and events. Wearing a tuxedo or a formal dress to a prom makes it a special event. At most schools, mortarboard caps and gowns are worn for graduation ceremonies. Children wear costumes when they go trick-or-treating at Halloween. What other types of clothing are worn for special events?

Even though people in our society may dress as they wish in most places, social customs are very helpful. Whether interviewing for a job or attending a funeral, you will find guidelines for what to wear. Following these guidelines will help you feel more comfortable, even if the occasion is new to you.

Expectations and Standards

Many people have certain clothing **expectations,** or *thoughts about what is reasonable or justified* for people to wear. For example, males do not wear skirts in our society. Children are expected to wear clothes that are not too old-looking or mature. Parents may have very definite ideas of how their children should dress for different occasions. Sometimes conflicts occur when a teenager's choice of clothes, hairstyle, or makeup differs from the expectations of parents or others.

Within your own school and community, there may be certain clothing expectations. Your employer, neighbor, customer, or team members may have certain expectations about how you should dress when you are with them. For example, your employer expects a well-groomed appearance. If you have a leadership position within a group, you may be expected to set an example for other members as to how to dress.

Some of these groups have rules about clothing. You may be required to wear a uniform for school, sports, or a job. These uniforms give the members a sense of identification and belonging. When you wear the group's uniform, your actions reflect on the entire group. Thus, wearing the uniform encourages a member's a sense of responsibility to the group.

Other groups may have clothing requirements that are unwritten but understood by the members. For example, members of school organizations may wear a certain type of clothing, such as a special jacket, to a club meeting. Students may wear the school's colors to the basketball game to show enthusiasm and spirit for the team.

Clothing standards differ among communities and among regions of the country. What may be appropriate to wear for an activity in one community may be different in another community. For example, people who live in small towns usually dress more informally than those in urban areas. While suits and ties are the standard for business men in large cities, men in smaller communities can wear a sport coat and slacks. For women, dresses or pantsuits may be the standard for social events in some communities, while casual sportswear can be worn in other communities.

In resort areas, standards are also different. Both men and women may wear brightly colored casual wear for all types of activities. What are the standards for appropriate clothing in your community?

Dressing Appropriately

You can learn what type of clothing is appropriate for different occasions from your own experience and by observing what others wear. You probably have a variety of clothes that you wear to school that are similar to clothes worn by other students. You may wear these same clothes to other activities, such as a party, a football game, or a part-time job.

Some special occasions may need an outfit that is dressier than what you wear to school. These occasions might be a job interview, a fancy party, or a special ceremony.

Job Interview

When you interview for a job, it is important to make a good impression. The way you dress for the interview gives messages to the employer about what kind of employee you might be.

Dress for the interview, not for the job. On the job you might wear blue jeans or a uniform. For the interview, you should wear good clothes, the type you might wear to a special dinner. Dress conservatively. This means no extreme outfits, heavy makeup, or elaborate hairstyles. Choose colors and styles that flatter you and make you feel good.

Before you leave for the interview, make sure that:

• Your clothes are neat, clean, and pressed. There are no loose buttons, ripped seams, or hanging hems.

• Your shoes are polished.

Many employees must wear a uniform or a certain style and color of clothing when working in a restaurant or a store.

- Your hands are clean, including under the fingernails.

- Your hair is clean and brushed.

- You have used a deodorant and, if necessary, a breath freshener.

- You are not wearing strong perfume or cologne.

On the Job

Most offices have certain standards of dress. A business suit and tie have long been the standard outfit for men in many offices. Women are expected to wear a tailored suit or dress. In more informal offices, employees may wear casual wear, such as slacks and sweaters.

Clothing that may be appropriate at a picnic or a dance is unacceptable for most offices. The rule for business attire is to wear nothing extreme—not too tight, too short, too low, too thin, too bold, too fancy, or too bright. This type of clothing is considered inappropriate for the workplace because it distracts others and creates wrong impressions.

With the general trend toward more casual clothing for all occasions, the workplace has also seen a relaxation of certain standards. In the 1990s, some companies have relaxed the dress codes for their employees. The trend began with casual dress on Fridays during the summer months. For example, males were no longer expected to wear jackets and ties to work on Fridays. Women could wear sportswear and flats, instead of tailored outfits and heels. Soon magazines, newspapers, and stores featured casual fashions that were appropriate for office wear. Now the idea of "Friday-wear" has become acceptable even in the winter months in some offices.

Special Occasions

Some special occasions require certain types of clothing. These include going to fancy parties and formal dances, dining in elegant restaurants, and attending weddings, funerals, and other religious ceremonies.

When going to a fancy party, males usually wear a suit and tie, and females wear dressy clothes. A for-

In many offices, employees are expected to wear tailored suits and outfits. This contributes to a businesslike environment.

mal dance may request "black tie." This means a tuxedo for men and formal dresses or gowns for women. With a trend toward more casual clothing, some men are not wearing a tie with a tuxedo or suit. Instead, they might choose a banded shirt or a collarless sweater. High-fashion styles are very acceptable at parties and formal events.

Some fine restaurants require a jacket for men and noncasual clothing for women. These requirements help to create a more formal atmosphere within the restaurant. However, strict dress standards are gradually changing. For example, many restaurants used to insist that male customers wear a tie and jacket. They even kept extras on hand to lend to customers who were not properly dressed. Now very few restaurants require a tie and many no longer require jackets. This reflects the general trend to more casual dressing in our society.

Even casual restaurants may require customers to wear shoes and shirts because of local health laws. If you do not follow these rules, the restaurant has the right to refuse to serve you.

Health laws often require customers to wear a shirt and shoes in order to be served in restaurants.

Some special occasions, such as a prom, call for a formal dress or a tuxedo. Such outfits help make the event more exciting and memorable.

Weddings, funerals, and other religious services have special clothing expectations and standards. For most weddings held in a church, temple, hotel, or club, guests are expected to wear special-occasion clothing. This means dresses or pantsuits for women, and jackets and ties for men. For some ceremonies, long gowns and tuxedos may be expected. At funerals, people are expected to dress conservatively. This means darker colors and tailored styles.

Some religions have special clothing requirements for their services. For example, some type of head covering may be expected. Others may require that the shoulders be covered. For all types of religious services, it is best to dress conservatively.

If you are uncertain as to what to wear for a special occasion, you can ask friends who have been to a similar event. You might also ask your parents or teachers what is acceptable. For a special party, you can call the host or hostess or ask other guests what they plan to wear.

Conflicts over Clothing

Sometimes what you want to wear does not conform to what is appropriate to wear. This may create a conflict with your parents or other authority figures.

When conflicts occur, it is important to be considerate and thoughtful of others. Perhaps it is a special occasion with your parents, grandparents, or other adults. By dressing appropriately, you are showing respect for their feelings and beliefs. At a party or dance, it is important to consider the feelings of your date and friends, too. Appropriate clothing can help to make everyone feel comfortable at a special event.

Clothing Mistakes

You will probably feel more self-confident when you are dressed appropriately. In the "right" clothes, you will feel more relaxed and comfortable, especially if the situation is new for you. Sometimes, however, you may make a wrong clothing choice. When you arrive at an event, you may discover that you are not dressed appropriately. You might be too dressy or too casual.

If this happens, try to forget about it. Concentrate on talking with other people. Get involved in the activity of the event. If you forget about what you are wearing, you will probably enjoy yourself much more. Everyone makes clothing mistakes once in a while.

Decision Making

Each and every day you are faced with choices. Making a decision about something is the process of making up your mind. The process may be simple or complex.

You make many simple and complex decisions that relate to your clothing needs. Unconsciously picking a belt to wear with your jeans is a simple

When dressing for a special occasion, it is important to have consideration for your family or friends and dress appropriately.

decision. Deciding what combination of clothing to wear, what to buy or sew, and what to discard are just a few of the more complex decisions.

As a child, your parent or another adult probably made most of your clothing decisions for you. You may have been given the opportunity to make some choices. Perhaps you selected which outfit to wear on a certain day, or maybe you even participated in the buying process. However, the adult had the final decision in the situation.

As you grow older and assume more responsibility and control over your wardrobe, you will want to develop successful decision-making skills.

The Decision-Making Process

Making the best clothing choices for yourself requires good decision-making skills. Until now, you may have learned whether your decisions were good ones only through the trial-and-error method.

For example, the blue plaid shirt that you bought is one of your favorites. It matches two pairs of slacks, it fits, and the color looks good on you. The brown checked shirt that you bought at the same time does not match anything else in your wardrobe. It fits, but the color is wrong for you. It just hangs in your closet. Through the trial-and-error method, you have discovered that the blue plaid shirt was a successful choice; the brown checked was a poor choice.

If you use the decision-making process, you will get better results in your clothing selections. Making a decision involves five steps:

Step 1: State the situation. It is important to clearly identify the problem or situation. What decision needs to be made? How much time do you have to make the decision? For example, you may want a blazer to wear to a new job that you are starting in two weeks.

Step 2: List the possible options. Think about the various choices you have. You could buy a new blazer now or wait until one goes on sale. Perhaps

you could make a blazer. Does an older brother or sister have a blazer that is no longer worn? Perhaps it could be passed on to you. What other options do you have?

Step 3: Consider the consequences of each option. What are the pros and cons of each one? You will have to consider your choices based upon your own **resources**—your *money, time, and skills.* These factors play a big part in the decision-making process. How much money can you spend for a blazer? Do you have the skill or the time to sew? Do you need a blazer now or can you wait until you find one on sale? How do you feel about wearing a secondhand jacket? It is important to evaluate all of your choices before you make your decision.

Step 4: Select the best option and act on it. Based on your evaluation of each option, which choice is best? When you have selected the route to take, follow through on your decision. The sooner you act on your decision, the sooner the situation or problem will be solved. For instance, you decide to sew the blazer. In this way, you save money and can choose the exact type and color of fabric that you want.

Step 5: Evaluate the results. Take time to evaluate your decision. Why did you make the decision that you did? Did the pros of one option outweigh the pros of another? Was there an important fact, once identified, that helped you to make your decision? In the long run, did you make the right choice? When you evaluated your decision to sew the blazer, you were satisfied. Even though it took almost two weeks to make, it came out beautifully and is very special looking.

Each time you go through the decision-making process, you will improve your decision-making skills. You also will become better prepared to make other decisions.

The
Decision-Making
Process

1 State the situation.

2 List the possible options.

3 Consider the consequences of each option.

4 Select the best option and act on it.

5 Evaluate the results.

REVIEW

Summary

- Your clothing choices each day depend on many things, such as what you plan to do, who you will be with, your mood, your personality, and your values.

- Appropriate clothing for different occasions has been established by social customs.

- Both individuals and organizations have certain clothing expectations and requirements.

- When clothing conflicts occur, it is important to have consideration for others.

- Good decision-making skills can be developed.

- The decision-making process involves five steps: state the situation, list the options, consider the consequences, select the best option, and evaluate the results.

Using Vocabulary Terms

On a separate piece of paper, write the vocabulary term that best fits the definition:

1. All your unique qualities.
2. Money, time, and skills.
3. Suitable.
4. Established ways of doing things.
5. Thoughts about what is reasonable or justified.

Recalling the Facts

1. List five factors that influence your clothing choices.
2. How does your mood affect your clothing choices?
3. How can values influence clothing decisions?
4. Why is it helpful to follow social customs when dressing for certain occasions?
5. How may clothing expectations affect teens at school, on a team, and at a job?
6. How can you learn what type of clothes to wear for a special occasion?
7. List six guidelines for dressing appropriately for a job interview.
8. What should you do if you have dressed inappropriately for an event?
9. List the steps of the decision-making process.
10. Why is it important to evaluate the results of your decisions?

Thinking Critically

1. **Analysis.** Compare the advantages and disadvantages of wearing a uniform to school or to a job.

2. **Synthesis.** Describe the style of clothing that would be appropriate for: a business office, a picnic, a formal dance, a wedding, and a funeral.

3. **Analysis.** Jeans can be worn for many occasions in our society. When might jeans not be appropriate?

4. **Evaluation.** Do you think all companies should relax their dress codes and allow casual wear in the workplace? Why or why not?

Applying Your Knowledge

1. **Favorite Outfit.** Describe an outfit that always makes you feel good when you wear it. Explain possible reasons for your feelings.

2. **Expectations.** Make a list of the various roles that you may have: student, teammate, employee, friend, son or daughter, grandchild. Then explain how the clothing expectations of others affect how you dress for each role.

3. **Job Interview.** Locate illustrations of appropriate and inappropriate clothing to wear to a job interview. Create a classroom display.

4. **Decision Making.** Select a personal goal that is related to clothing or your appearance. Go through the decision-making process. Describe possible options, consequences, and what decision you will make. Explain how you could evaluate the results.

Making the Connection

1. **Language Arts.** Describe what people in your community wear to restaurants, offices, athletic events, concerts, and special occasions.

2. **Philosophy.** Research the *yin* and *yang* personality traits described by Chinese philosophers. Prepare a report on the design shapes, lines, fabrics, textures, colors, and accessories that are associated with yin or yang qualities.

What Is a Fashion Coordinator?

Fashion coordinators work in the fashion office of a retail store. They are responsible for creating the fashion personality of the store. They prepare fashion reports for the store buyers and salespeople. They work with the display artists in selecting and coordinating outfits for window and in-store displays. They also plan the fashion shows presented by the store. This includes selecting the theme for the show, borrowing the clothes from various departments, accessorizing the outfits, hiring the models, and writing the commentary. A fashion coordinator may talk to community groups about fashion trends and present fashion shows for the groups.

Try It Yourself

Imagine that you are a fashion coordinator for a large retail store. You have been asked to plan a fashion show for a local organization. You are to highlight fashion trends and appropriate clothing styles for various occasions. Select a theme for the show and ten outfits that could be worn for different activities and events. For each outfit, write a description of the garment and accessories. Then write the commentary for the show.

Build Your Portfolio

Place a copy of your fashion show commentary, along with illustrations or sketches of each outfit, in your portfolio. If possible, record the commentary on tape or video and place a copy in your portfolio.

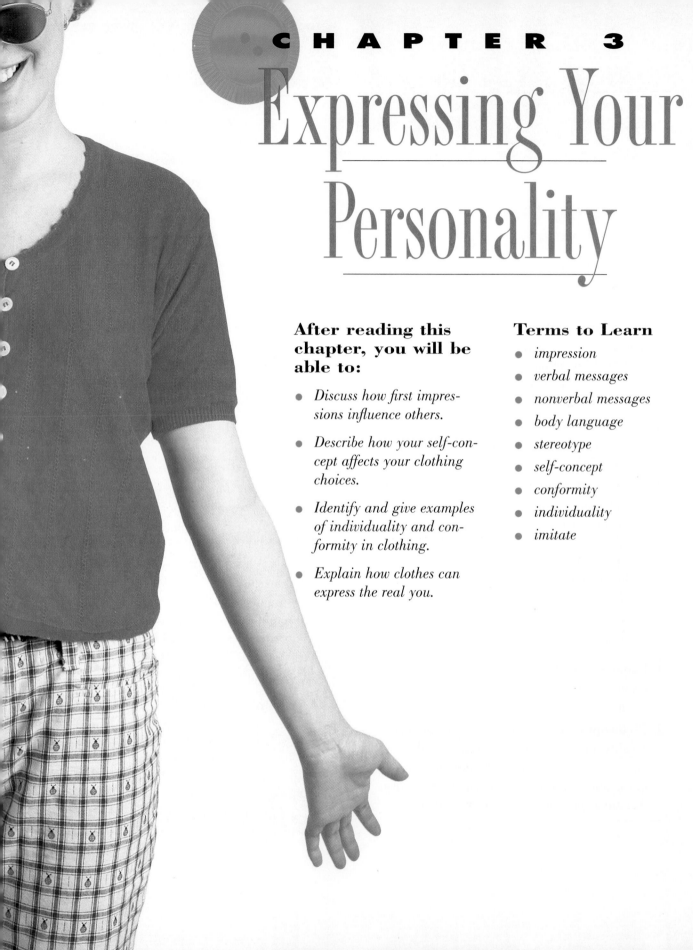

Expressing Your Personality

After reading this chapter, you will be able to:

- Discuss how first impressions influence others.

- Describe how your self-concept affects your clothing choices.

- Identify and give examples of individuality and conformity in clothing.

- Explain how clothes can express the real you.

Terms to Learn

- *impression*
- *verbal messages*
- *nonverbal messages*
- *body language*
- *stereotype*
- *self-concept*
- *conformity*
- *individuality*
- *imitate*

Are you a people watcher? Do you ever sit in a shopping mall or other public place and watch the people pass by? Do you play a guessing game about them based on the way they look? Is the tall, young man in the football jacket an athlete? Is the couple in expensive-looking clothes really wealthy? Could the group in the outlandish clothes be members of a rock band?

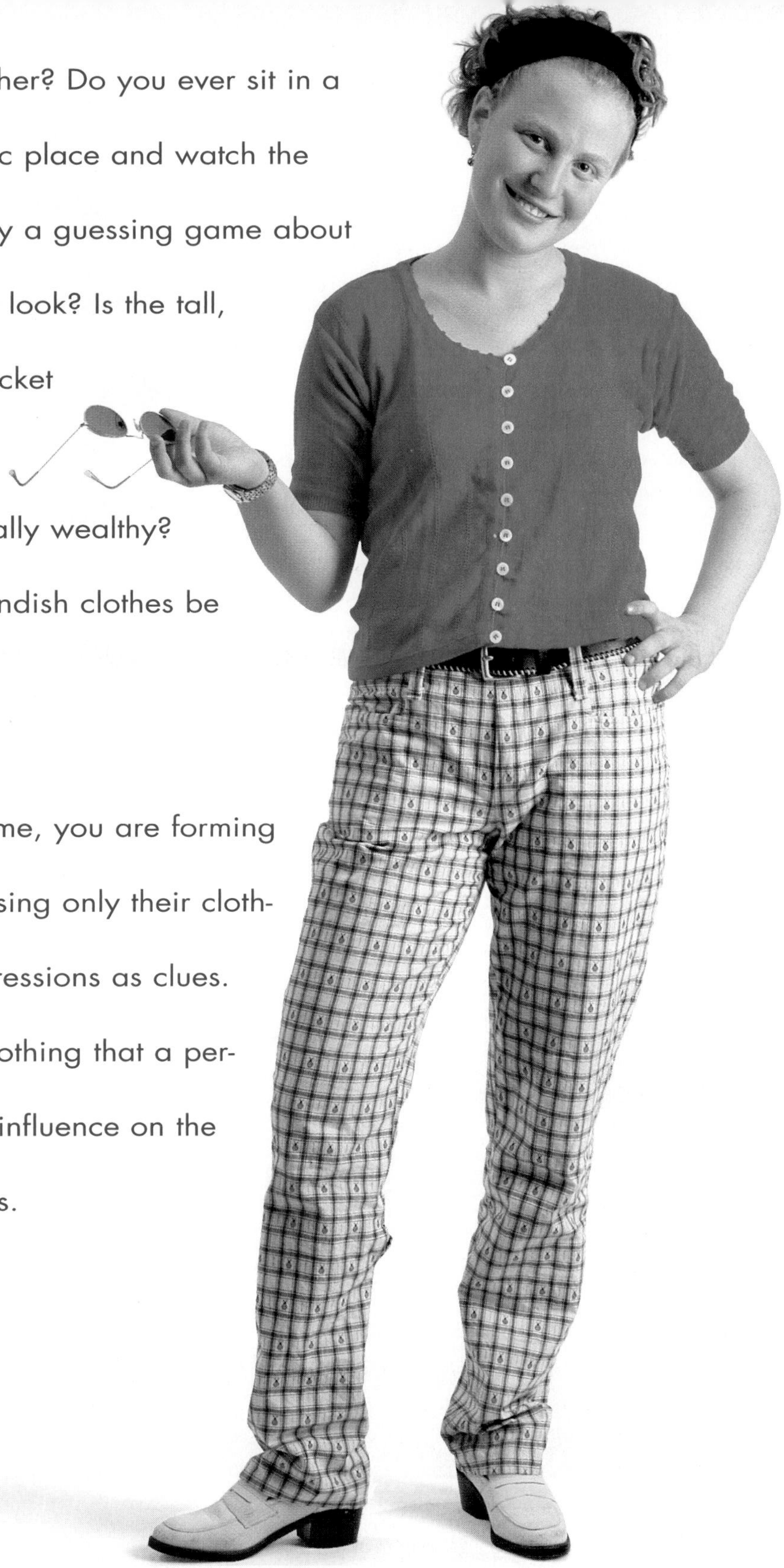

When you play this game, you are forming impressions about people, using only their clothing, body features, and expressions as clues. Of these three factors, the clothing that a person wears has the strongest influence on the image that he or she projects.

Forming First Impressions

When you leave your fingerprints on a glass or mark a piece of paper with a rubber stamp, you have left impressions on the glass and the paper. An **impression** is *an image that is transferred from one place to another.*

Just as you can create impressions with fingerprints or rubber stamps, you can create impressions about yourself. When you interact with other people, you are subconsciously making an impression. When you walk into a room, enter a conversation, or answer a question, you are creating an impression.

When others meet you for the first time, they develop a first impression about you in their mind. First impressions are formed in a very short time, usually less than a minute or two.

How can people form an impression of you so quickly? They observe the way you look and the way you act. Your appearance and behavior provide clues about yourself. Your clothes, body features, expressions, voice, and manners are some of these clues.

Good grooming communicates to others that you care about yourself.

Firts impressions are formed very quickly. What is your first impression of this young man?

Appearance

Often people will notice what you are wearing before they see your face or hear your voice. Clothing is important in making a first impression. The style, color, fit, and neatness of a person's clothes will influence opinions about the person. Because clothes can send out strong messages to others, it is important to understand their impact.

Good grooming gives the finishing touch to an attractive appearance. Step in front of a full-length mirror and take a look at yourself. Check your skin, hair, nails, and teeth. Is your skin clean and healthy-looking? Does your hair shine from being washed and brushed regularly? Are your nails trimmed neatly? Your skin, hair, nails, and mouth all need daily attention for you to look your best.

A person's total look is the combination of the person's general health, grooming, and clothing.

Imagine the identical outfit on two different people. One has dirty hair, a dull complexion, and slumping posture. The other has shiny hair, clean skin, and erect posture. The appearance of each person is totally different. Looking good is much more than just your choice of clothes.

Verbal Messages

Verbal messages include a person's *choice of words and tone of voice*. It is both what a person says and how he or she says it. What verbal clues do you send out? Try hearing yourself as others do. What kind of emotion does the tone of your voice express to others? Anger, joy, and sadness are just a few of the emotions that can be heard when a person speaks.

Verbal messages communicate many things about people. Words can express ideas and feelings clearly, or mask them behind other phrases. People can show politeness or rudeness with their words and tone of voice. How did you sound when you said "Good morning" to someone today? What impression would a teacher or employer have of you if you answered a question with a loud, slurred "Yeah?" or a clear "Yes, Mr. Martinez?"

When you communicate with others, you send both verbal and nonverbal messages about yourself.

TECHNOLOGY

Developing New Tests for Cosmetic Safety

How do you know that your favorite cosmetics and personal grooming products are safe to use? Small animals, such as rabbits, rats, and guinea pigs have been used for many years to test the safety of cosmetic and grooming products. However, many groups have protested the use of animals in product testing.

Now scientists are developing alternative methods for testing the ingredients in products. These alternative tests are called *in vitro*, which in Latin means "in glass." Some of these new tests are now being used; others are in the developmental stages.

- A protein from a certain kind of bean mimics the way the eye's cornea responds to irritants.
- An artificial skin has been developed that lets researchers study how various products and ingredients affect the skin.
- A human cell culture clones itself, reproducing many new cells. These cloned cells will be used to determine if a product will irritate the skin. Scientists can inject the cells with human genes. When a product is tested on these cells, the way the genes react will help scientists determine the type of damage. For example, the product might cause allergies, mutations, or be poisonous.

Scientists are comparing the results of these new tests with known results from animal testing. Both scientists and cosmetic companies agree that alternative tests will eventually replace the testing that is done on animals.

Characteristics

Each person has certain physical, mental, social, and emotional characteristics. The sum of these characteristics is called *personality*.

- **Physical characteristics** make up a person's outward appearance. They include the shape of the body and face, height and bone structure, and coloring of hair, eyes, and skin. People inherit their physical characteristics from their parents and grandparents. Almost all people have some features they like, and some they wish they could change. You might firm up your muscle tone through sports, or trim your waistline with exercise. However, you cannot make yourself taller or shorter, or change the width of your shoulders.

- **Mental characteristics** reflect a person's intellectual self. This self gives a person the ability to think, know, understand, and remember things. Your intellectual self has talents and abilities just like your physical self. These talents can be developed by reading, practicing, studying, and exploring.

- **Social characteristics** describe how a person relates to others. A person might be polite or rude, accepting or judgmental, introverted or extroverted. Most people behave somewhere between the extremes. It is natural to express different social traits with different people, such as with friends or strangers. You can learn skills that will help you to better relate to others.

- **Emotional characteristics** are the ways that a person expresses his or her feelings about everything in the environment. Feelings create emotions, such as love, hate, anger, joy, and sorrow. Emotions can make you laugh or cry, be happy or sad, feel enthusiastic or bored. It is normal to feel all kinds of emotions. How you manage or control your reactions, however, is largely up to you.

Nonverbal Messages

People's actions send **nonverbal messages**, or *communication without words*, to others. If you have ever seen a mime perform, you know that people can communicate with only their face and body.

The way a person acts or behaves toward others shows much about the person. Being polite gives one impression, while being rude implies another. Manners usually have a strong influence on whether someone forms a favorable or unfavorable impression about another.

In addition to actions and behavior, people also send nonverbal messages with their **body language**. This includes *facial expressions, eye contact, posture, position of arms and legs, and even the distance that the person stands or sits from others*. Many feelings and attitudes are expressed, consciously or unconsciously, through body language. Research shows that people form many opinions about others from observing their body language.

Each person is a unique combination of physical, mental, social, and emotional characteristics. You can learn to express your own personality through the clothes you wear.

Body Language

Eye Contact.

Looking directly at another person shows interest, warmth, and self-confidence. Averting the eyes shows disinterest, shyness, or nervousness.

Facial Expression.

The face has many muscles that control facial expressions. A raised eyebrow shows surprise, a frown shows disappointment. A smile is happy and friendly, a downturned mouth is sad. Much of what goes on in a person's mind finds expression in his or her face.

Posture.

An erect, comfortable posture shows self-assurance and a positive attitude. Sloping shoulders and slumping posture give a negative appearance.

Position of arms and legs.

Open and relaxed positions of the arms and hands demonstrate receptiveness and friendliness. Closed and clenched positions show anger, discomfort, and nervousness. Legs planted squarely or comfortably relaxed show that the person is secure in the situation. Tapping the fingers or a foot probably means that the person is bored or impatient with what's going on around her or him.

Distance.

How far a person sits or stands from another person can indicate feelings. Everyone has a "personal space" around them. Coming too close to an individual and invading that space may make the person feel uncomfortable. Close friends usually stand only 6 to 8 inches (15 to 20 cm) apart. Other people stand farther apart but may slowly move closer together to show friendliness.

Accuracy of First Impressions

No matter who they are, people are often judged by first impressions. A teacher meeting a class, the politician on a platform, the entertainer on screen or stage, a speaker in a school assembly, clerks in stores, and receptionists in offices are all making impressions. What have been your first impressions of different people that you have met?

First impressions can affect your judgment of others, just as your own appearance and behavior can affect how others think about you. However, first impressions can be wrong. In all fairness, you must stop and evaluate your impression of another person before you make a quick judgment.

What impression might you make about someone who is wearing a soiled sweatshirt, baggy pants, and dirty shoes? Perhaps the person has a smudged face and messed-up hair. Is the person really sloppy and unkempt, or has he just finished washing a car? Perhaps he has just returned from a five-mile run.

Forming an opinion about a person because of a past association can be inaccurate, too. A **stereotype** is *a simplified and standardized image of a person or group.* It is usually based on some type of characteristic, such as age, gender, or height.

People are often stereotyped by the way they look and by the type of clothes they wear. For example, an unusual hairstyle may make people think that a teen is a rebel. Horn-rimmed glasses may suggest that the person is a serious student. A letter sweater or jacket makes some people think that the wearer excels at sports. These are a few examples of stereotyping through appearance. Can you think of other examples?

Your self-concept affects how you feel about yourself and how others see you.

Self-Concept

Have you looked at a recent photograph of yourself and said "That doesn't look like me!"? Perhaps you have heard your voice on a cassette recording and asked "Do I really sound like that?" The image you have of your appearance or voice didn't match what you saw or heard. *The image you have of yourself* is called your **self-concept**.

Take a moment to think about your "self." You have an outward appearance, plus inner qualities. You have special talents, interests, thoughts, and emotions. You also have certain shortcomings.

Now make a list of your own special qualities. This list will help you discover your self-concept.

The Importance of Self-Concept

A person's self-concept is important for a number of reasons. It influences the way the person feels about himself or herself. It also affects the way others see the person.

A person's self-concept can be positive, negative, or somewhere in between. A positive self-concept helps to make an individual look better. Such a person will project a positive feeling and make others feel good just to be with him or her. For example,

Ashley thinks of herself as a friendly person. Because she greets others in a cheerful and friendly manner, they think of her as friendly and like being around her.

To learn what image you project to others, you can observe their reactions. It also helps to listen to yourself and be aware of how you act. Then ask a relative or best friend about his or her image of you. Is it similar to how you see yourself?

Individuality Versus Conformity

As young people seek their own identity as a person, their self-concept begins to emerge. They begin to get a clearer picture of themselves. They also have a deep need to feel secure about that image.

In order to feel good about themselves, most teenagers seek the approval of others. They identify closely with their peers and want to wear what others in their group are wearing. This provides them with a sense of identity, belonging, and security. It makes them feel accepted and part of the group.

As a teenager's confidence grows, however, there is an awareness of the need to be an individual—not just a carbon copy of others in the crowd. This drive contributes to a conflict. On one hand, there is the strong desire to be part of a group. On the other hand, there is a growing urge to be recognized as an individual in one's own right.

These desires often result in conflicts about what to wear. You may want to dress like your peers in order to feel a part of the group. **Conformity** means *agreeing or going along with current standards, attitudes, or practices.* At the same time, you may feel that you want your clothes to represent you, not everybody else. You want to express your own **individuality** which is *the characteristics that make you unique or distinctive from others.*

If you have a conflict between individuality and conformity, perhaps you can find a middle ground in which you are comfortable. For example, if everyone in your group is wearing a certain style or brand of jeans, you may want to wear them, too. This will help you to feel a part of the group. However, you can express your individuality by wearing a unique shirt or sweater that you like with your jeans.

Even when wearing the same type of clothing that others in the group wear, you can express your individuality through your choice of colors, specific styles, or accessories. You may even start your own trend within the group. Others may like what you are wearing and want to dress the same way, too.

These teens enjoy wearing clothing and accessories that make them distinctive from their peers.

Even though these teens are wearing similar styles, they are expressing their individuality through their choice of colors and accessories.

Expressing the Real You

Have you ever been shopping with friends who say "Try this on! It looks just like you!"? What is the meaning behind this remark? Your friends are trying to say that they know something about you. They have some definite ideas about the kind of clothes that they think matches your personality.

What is your reaction? Do you agree with their selection of clothes for you, or are you amazed that they picked out something that you do not like at all?

Everyone is a highly complex blend of many different personality traits. You can express your personality through the clothes you wear. You can communicate what type of person you are—whether you are outgoing or reserved, a leader or follower, conservative or daring, confident or unsure, plus much more.

Some people have a strong desire to dress exactly like a friend or someone they admire. This may cause them to **imitate**, or *copy*, how the other person dresses. When people try to wear the exact same clothing and hairstyle as another person, they are only a "copy" and not themselves.

Other people adopt extreme styles of clothing to create a false image of themselves. They may dress too old, too young, too extreme, or bizarre. They also are not expressing their real selves.

By trying new colors, styles, and combinations of clothing, you will gradually learn what you like best and what looks best on you.

Some people put too much emphasis on appearance. They spend so much time, effort, and money to look "just right" that other interests and activities are neglected. At the other extreme are people who show no interest in their appearance and clothes. They may always look sloppy or wear the same clothes everywhere. Either too much or too little concern with clothes may limit one's experiences in life.

If the image you project does not reflect your real self, then others will get a false picture of you. You will send mixed messages that are confusing to others and to yourself.

Perhaps you are not sure of your identity and how to present yourself to others. This is a time to look inward and evaluate who you are and who you want to be. You can experiment with your clothes and try new styles, colors, and fabrics. You will learn more about yourself—how you look, how you want to look, and how others see you. You will discover what you like and what is best for you.

Clothes cannot change your personality. However, they can reflect the real you. They also can create favorable impressions that may lead to new opportunities and experiences.

Summary

- First impressions are formed in less than a minute or two and may not be accurate.

- A person's appearance is determined by the person's clothing, grooming, and general health.

- Both verbal and nonverbal messages communicate many things about people.

- Each person is a unique combination of physical, mental, social, and emotional characteristics.

- A person's self-concept influences the way others see the person.

- You can express your personality, individuality, and conformity through your clothing choices.

Using Vocabulary Terms

On a separate piece of paper, write the vocabulary term that best fits the definition:

1. The image you have of yourself.

2. The characteristics that make you unique or distinctive from others.

3. Communication without words.

4. An image that is transferred from one place to another.

5. Choice of words and tone of voice.

6. Agreeing or going along with current standards, attitudes, or practices.

Recalling the Facts

1. List four clues that people use when forming impressions of others.

2. What impact does clothing have on first impressions?

3. Why is good grooming important?

4. What is the difference between a verbal message and a nonverbal message?

5. What is body language?

6. What is a stereotype?

7. Why is a person's self-concept important?

8. Describe two advantages of having a positive self-concept.

9. What is the difference between individuality and conformity?

10. Why should your image reflect your real self?

Thinking Critically

1. **Analysis.** What might be the result of communicating one message verbally and, at the same time, sending a different message nonverbally? Give an example.

2. **Analysis.** What personal characteristics can you change or improve? What characteristics can you not change?

3. **Synthesis.** Give an example of how you can express both individuality and conformity in the way that you dress.

4. **Evaluation.** If you were to interview for a job, what steps could you take to present an accurate first impression of yourself?

Applying Your Knowledge

1. **First Impressions.** From magazines and newspapers, cut out six photos of people who are sending clues about who they are by the clothes they wear. Mount the photos, along with a description of the messages they are sending.

2. **Body Language.** With a partner, demonstrate two identical situations, such as two people meeting for the first time. Use positive body language in one situation, and negative body language in the other. Discuss the impressions created in each situation.

3. **Self-Concept.** On a piece of paper, write how you see yourself. Describe your appearance, voice, talents, interests, social skills, and emotional traits. Then ask a relative or close friend to write how he or she sees you. Compare the lists.

4. **Individuality.** Sketch ways that teens can express some individuality even when wearing the same type of clothing as their peers. Share your ideas with the class.

Making the Connection

1. **Language Arts.** Read an article about "dressing for success" in the workplace. Summarize the information in an oral or written report.

What Is a Display Artist?

Display artists create the merchandise displays in retail stores. The displays are designed to motivate customers to purchase not only the garments, but also the shoes, belts, ties, and other accessories shown with the garments. Display artists design both window and in-store displays. They must plan, build, and arrange each display in an eye-catching manner. The displays must also reflect the fashion image of the store.

Try It Yourself

Imagine that you are a display artist. Sketch an idea for a window display of fashion merchandise. Show how the garments and accessories will be displayed, draped, or hung. Include in your sketch any three-dimensional props that could be added to the arrangement. Write a brief advertising slogan that promotes the fashion image of the store.

Build Your Portfolio

Write a description of how the same fashion message could be promoted with in-store displays and ads. Include sketches of your ideas. Place a copy of your sketches, advertising slogan, and display descriptions in your portfolio.

2. **Drama.** A *mime* is an actor who uses only gestures and actions to imitate others or act out an event. Imagine that you are a mime. Try telling a short story without using any words.

Clothes,
Families, and
Cultures

After reading this chapter, you will be able to:

- *List examples of clothing from various cultures.*

- *Describe what clothes can reveal about a person's occupation, status, values, and beliefs.*

- *Discuss how factors such as location, activities and interests, occupation, and family structure affect the clothing needs of a family.*

- *Explain how family values and priorities influence clothing decisions.*

Terms to Learn

- *heritage*
- *symbol*
- *family structure*
- *priorities*

Suppose you are the director of your school play. The play has a large cast of characters. In order for the play to be successful, the audience must understand a great many facts about these characters in a very short time. How can you accomplish this? One way to do it is to use different costumes.

The costumes you select for each member of the cast can give the audience clues about the character's background, occupation, wealth, and social status. This chapter explores the many things that clothing can tell you about families and their culture.

Your Heritage

The United States is often described as a colorful mosaic. The way we dress today is the result of the influence of the many different people who settled here. Our basic style of dress is inherited from Europe, but many other cultures have contributed special items. For example, the mandarin collar comes from China, and the caftan comes from Africa. Many styles of adornment were contributed by the Native Americans. The turquoise and silver jewelry of the Navajo and Zuni tribes is highly prized.

Heritage is *the body of culture and tradition that has been handed down from one's ancestors*. Each of us has a heritage that is a unique combination of the cultures in which our parents and grandparents were born, the customs that our family has developed, and our own individuality.

Clothes in Other Cultures

Every culture throughout history has something special and unique about its clothing. The style of clothing that people wear—the fabrics, the designs, and the colors—can tell you many things about the way that people think and live.

The ancient Greeks wore gracefully draped garments that reflected the same qualities of beauty, harmony, and simplicity that were valued in art and architecture. French fashion in the eighteenth century had richly embellished fabrics, yards of ribbons and laces, and elaborate wigs. It reflected the complicated manners and life at the court of Versailles.

In the early American colonies, many goods, such as clothing and furniture, were not easily available. If the colonists needed new clothes, they had to

Certain styles of clothing are identified with a particular culture. This family from India wears several traditional styles, such as a sari, a long blouse or coat over pants, and a loose top over a draped garment.

These young girls are wearing richly embroidered garments with Mandarin collars that reflect their Chinese heritage.

spin the yarn, weave the fabric then sew the garments themselves. As a result, their clothes were plain and practical.

Many cultures developed a unique style of dress or national costume. Most of these items of clothing had very practical beginnings.

Ancient Celts in the highlands of Scotland began to weave clan blankets with special plaid patterns to identify each clan. In the sixteenth century, they started wrapping these clan blankets around the body to form a short, belted-on, all-purpose garment called a kilt. The extra fabric was pulled up over the shoulder from the back and pinned in place.

In Middle Eastern countries, where the desert is very hot during the day and very cold at night, the turban became a common item of clothing. It absorbed sweat during the day and insulated the head at night.

In some parts of the world, such as Africa, China, and India, people still wear distinctive native costumes as part of their everyday dress. The African tribal robe, Chinese coat, and Indian sari have changed little over the centuries.

In other parts of the world, national costumes are usually worn only for festive occasions, such as holidays, parades, weddings, and dances. Why do you think this has occurred in different cultures?

Clothes as Symbols

Societies have many symbols. A **symbol** is *something visible that represents something else*. A symbol can represent something that you cannot see, like an idea, a philosophy, or a custom. Clothing is one of these symbols. As a result, clothing can tell you about a person's heritage, gender, occupation, wealth, status, values, and beliefs.

Heritage

Some styles of clothing are identified with a particular area or country. A sombrero reminds us of Mexico, a kimono reminds us of Japan, and a fur parka reminds us of Alaska.

Clothes from Other Cultures

Scotland

China

Mexico

Africa

India

Saudi Arabia

Some fabric designs are also identified with a particular culture. Distinctive plaid fabrics remind us of Scotland. Batik fabric, with its unique designs, is associated with Indonesia. Guatemalans wear ponchos made from a certain type of woven striped fabric.

Although many different cultures developed garments that were similar in shape, each one personalized its clothes by adding unique forms of ornamentation. Traditional Hungarian clothes are decorated with leather. Colorful embroidery designs accent Scandinavian clothing. Hawaiian dress features various colored feathers, arranged in special patterns and sewn to the cloth.

This young woman is wearing a contemporary fashion that is inspired by traditional African garments and fabrics.

Arpilleras

Needlework is one way that a culture records the way its people live. The people who live in the Andes Mountains in South America developed a distinctive type of wall hanging. It is called arpillera (ar-pee-YAIR-ah).

These wall hangings tell stories about important events in the daily lives of their creators. Some arpilleras have pockets in the back to hold written parts of the story.

An arpillera consists of small pieces of cloth cut into shapes and stitched on a background. The edges of the shapes are neatly stitched down, using a simple hand embroidery stitch. Most of the fabrics are plain and brightly colored. The embroidery stitches add pattern and texture. Many of the shapes, such as dolls, musical instruments, and vegetables, are three-dimensional appliqués.

The first arpilleras were made in Chile. Today they are also made in Columbia and Peru. Arpillera designs can also be found on jackets, totebags, and other accessories.

Sometimes you can tell what state or region people are from by their clothing. Where do you think this man lives? What clues does his clothing provide?

Clothing styles can vary within a country. In the United States, you can sometimes tell what region people are from by the way they dress. A Texan often wears cowboy boots with his business suit. People from warm climates, such as Florida and Hawaii, usually wear brighter colors than people from Minnesota. People from large cities tend to wear more formal clothes than people from small towns. Can you think of some reasons for these regional differences in clothes?

Males and Females

In some cultures, it is traditional for males and females to dress very differently. In other cultures, their clothing is very similar. Clothing styles associated with either gender evolve from customs, traditions, religion, work, and leisure activities.

There are places in the world where pants have been appropriate attire for both males and females for many years. Eskimo and Lap men and women wear pants as protection against the subzero temperatures. In the rural areas of many societies, both males and females wear pants as they labor in the fields.

However, pants do not always have to be practical. Some Turkish women wear very full pants in elegant fabrics. Spanish bullfighters and Balinese dancers wear elaborately decorated pants.

In other parts of the world, males wear skirts or long robes just as females do. Arab men wear long, flowing robes to protect them from the heat of the desert. In Africa and the South Pacific Islands, males wear wrapped skirts, called *sarongs*. Chinese and Japanese men have worn silk robes for centuries. Scotsmen still wear kilts for special occasions.

Until recently in our Western society, men always wore trousers and women always wore skirts. Now pants are accepted clothing for both genders.

Occupation and Status

The clothes that people wear can tell something about their occupation and status. Over the centuries, garment styles, quality, and quantity have been a way of distinguishing the nobility from the common person.

In late thirteenth-century France, there was a law that specified the number of dresses and the value of the materials worn by every class of society. Laws limited peasant clothes to certain colors and certain fabrics. At one time, peasants who looked like they were trying to imitate the clothing of the upper class could be fined, imprisoned, or executed.

In some societies, clothes are an indication of a person's social or economic class. In China, the farmers and villagers still wear dark cotton trousers and plain jackets, while many city residents wear clothes that have a Western influence.

Uniforms are also symbols of occupation and status. Think about the police officer's uniform, the

The clothing that people wear can tell something about their occupation. What type of work do these people do?

nurse's cap, the priest's collar, and the chef's hat. Members of the military wear distinctive uniforms. Their status is identified by special insignias on the uniforms. What other examples can you think of?

Today we live in a society where people are usually free to dress as they wish. However, we still have certain standards of dress that are influenced by our occupation. The business suit is out of place on a construction site. Blue jeans are out of place in many offices.

Beliefs and Values

Clothes can reflect the beliefs and values of a culture or a special group. They can be used to identify a person as a member of a religious group. Society's attitudes can strongly influence what type of clothing is appropriate for certain occasions.

Clothing, hats, and other symbols can identify the members of a particular religious group, such as this Hasidic father and son.

Religion

Clothing and jewelry can indicate membership in a particular religious group. People wear crosses, stars, or other religious symbols as pins or necklaces.

Special clothes are also associated with certain religious ceremonies. These include christening gowns for baptisms, veils for weddings and first communion ceremonies, and prayer shawls and robes.

Social Customs

Every society develops its own set of rules for clothes that are appropriate for certain occasions. In our culture, the bride traditionally wears white. In China, she wears red. In our culture, a person in mourning wears black. In other cultures, a person in mourning wears white.

In Western society, it is the custom for men to wear a tuxedo for formal occasions. In the Philippines, men wear a long-sleeved, off-white, embroidered shirt, called a *barong tagalog*, for formal events.

Standards for modesty can be very different. Nearly two centuries ago, women in Napoleon's time wore dresses cut very low in the front but would never expose their shoulders. In contrast, women in Victorian times exposed their shoulders but would never expose their ankles.

In our culture, a bride traditionally wears a long white gown and a veil.

Clothes and Families

Every family has certain clothing needs that are influenced by their culture. A family's lifestyle also influences their clothing decisions. It includes factors such as the family's location, activities and interests, occupation of family members, values, and priorities.

Location

Where your family lives influences clothing choices. People who live and work in colder climates will have different needs than those who live and work in warmer climates. People in northern areas need almost two complete wardrobes—one for winter and one for summer. On the other hand, people who live in the Sun Belt need only warm weather clothes, plus a few jackets and sweaters for cooler days.

Families who live in colder climates need different types of clothing than those who live in warmer climates.

How might the interests and activities of this family influence their clothing choices?

The type of community in which the family lives can also affect its clothing selection. Many people who live in cities need dressier clothes than people who live in the suburbs or in rural communities. The style of clothing worn in urban offices, restaurants, theaters, and at special events may be dressier than in smaller communities. Smaller towns usually have more casual styles of dress for various events.

Activities and Interests

Clothing choices are influenced by how a family spends its time. What are the interests and hobbies of the family members? How do they spend their leisure time? A family that often goes camping would need clothes that are appropriate for the outdoors. A family that spends much of its time at cultural activities, such as concerts and plays, would have very different clothing needs. A family that prefers to stay at home, reading and watching television, would need other types of clothing.

Some activities have special clothing requirements. For example, if a family member takes danc-ing lessons, then a leotard and special shoes or slippers might be needed. Skiers need parkas, boots, hats, and gloves. Family members who jog in the evening or early morning need reflective vests, in addition to their other jogging clothes. Do any of your family members need special clothing for certain activities?

Occupation

Every family member has an occupation. It may be working outside the home, working in the home, or going to school.

A person who wears a uniform or a person who works at home will probably not need as great a variety of clothes as a person who works in an office or a store. A person who works outdoors will have very different clothing needs than a person who works inside. Well-constructed, wash-and-wear shirts in dark colors and rugged fabrics are more suitable for a construction worker than a banker. The construction worker might need only one dressy outfit, but several pairs of heavy-duty shirts and pants. On the other hand, the banker would need several business suits.

A person who is self-employed may need different types of clothes for different occasions. He or she may wear casual clothes when working at home or at a shop, and a business suit when going out to meet a client.

A family member who changes jobs may find that his or her clothing needs change. In some companies, there are different standards of dress for different types of jobs.

A parent who is at home caring for young children needs casual clothes that can be cleaned easily. If that parent takes on a part-time or full-time job, he or she may need different or additional clothes.

Family Structure

Family structure refers to *the number, ages, and relationships of the family members.* A couple with no children and a single person with no family obligations have only themselves to consider when planning their clothing needs. Perhaps their clothing needs only focus on their job and social activities.

If a family has children, then the needs of the children must be balanced with the needs of the adults. Children grow very quickly and outgrow clothing before it is worn out. Older children may be involved in a variety of activities that require special clothes. These may be sports, scouts, 4-H, or special hobbies.

A family with teenage children will have different clothing needs. Clothing for teenagers is usually more expensive than children's clothes. Many teenagers are developing their own tastes and want to be involved in the selection and purchase of their clothes. This may cause conflict between parents and teenagers over the styles of clothing worn and the amount of clothing purchased.

These parents must balance their own clothing needs with those of their children.

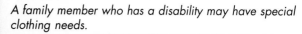

A family member who has a disability may have special clothing needs.

Older family members who have retired will probably find that their clothing needs have changed. Since they now have more leisure time, their clothes will probably reflect this change in lifestyle. Casual clothing may replace business clothing.

A family that includes an elderly member or a member who is disabled will have special clothing needs. Certain styles of clothes may make it easier for the person to dress and undress or to feel more comfortable in their clothes.

Family Values

Many families have certain traditions or customs associated with clothing that they value. Perhaps every family member gets dressed up for special celebrations or holidays. They may wear certain articles of clothing that relate to their family heritage.

Some families place a special value on gifts that are handmade rather than purchased. A scarf that is handknit by a family member is a more valued birthday gift than a more expensive one that is bought in the store.

Some families value easy care in their clothing. They choose fabrics that are washable and require little or no ironing. Other families may value designer labels and the latest fashions. They are willing to pay more money to get these styles.

Family Priorities

A family needs to decide on its **priorities**, or *preferences*. How important to the family is clothing? Do all the family members share this same opinion about the importance of clothing? Which is more important to family members—comfort or style, prestige or economy, time or money?

Some family members may want the latest look in clothes. They like to spend money on many fashionable clothes and accessories. Others may look for comfortable, sturdy clothing that they can wear for work or leisure activities. They are more interested in durability and easy care than in status and prestige.

Many families find that both their time and money are limited, so they need to carefully balance both. To save shopping time, clothing might be purchased through catalogs or stores that have a large selection. To save money, some families may delay clothing purchases until the items go on sale. They may shop in discount and outlet stores. If they have a family member who sews, they can have more outfits for less money.

The decisions that families make about clothing will be influenced by their lifestyle, stage of life, values, and goals. Sometimes conflicts occur over the priorities. Perhaps one family member wants a new outfit for a special occasion, while another family member needs clothes for school or work. These situations should be discussed by the family so that the best decision can be made.

It is important that all family members clearly understand their own responsibilities regarding clothing decisions. They should also understand their spending limitations. Many teenagers use their own money or sewing skills to expand their wardrobes.

REVIEW

Summary

- Every culture has something special and unique about its clothing.

- Clothing styles provide information about the way that people think and live.

- Native costumes are worn everyday in some cultures and for festive occasions in other cultures.

- Clothing can be a symbol of heritage, gender, occupation, status, beliefs, values, religion, and social customs.

- The clothing needs of families are influenced by their location, activities, interests, occupation, family structure, values, and priorities.

Using Vocabulary Terms

On a separate piece of paper, write the vocabulary term that best fits the definition:

1. Something visible that represents something else.

2. Preferences.

3. The body of culture and tradition that has been handed down from one's ancestors.

4. The number, ages, and relationships of family members.

Recalling the Facts

1. Why did the early American colonists wear plain and practical clothing?

2. How did the ancient Celts use clothing to identify each clan?

3. List six styles of clothing that are identified with a particular country or region.

4. What two things can uniforms symbolize?

5. Give two examples how social customs influence clothing.

6. How are clothing choices influenced by where a family lives?

7. Why might changing jobs result in different clothing needs?

8. How do the clothing needs of an adult couple differ from those of a family with three children?

9. Describe two ways that family values influence clothing decisions.

10. What should family members do if they have conflicts over clothing priorities?

Thinking Critically

1. **Evaluation.** Do you think the clothing styles in the United States reflect a variety of heritages? Support your answer with examples.

2. **Analysis.** Compare the clothing styles worn by ancient Greeks, French royalty, and American colonists. What conclusions can you make about how each group thought and lived?

3. **Evaluation.** In the past, women in our society did not wear trousers in public. What factors do you think influenced this tradition and why did it change?

4. **Analysis.** Compare the clothing needs of three families with different family structures.

Applying Your Knowledge

1. **Native Costumes.** Working in small groups, look through magazines and newspapers for illustrations of people in native costumes. Identify the country or region associated with each costume and create a display.

2. **Your Own Heritage.** Research the style of clothing that may have been worn by your ancestors. Write a description of a typical garment and explain how it is special or unique.

3. **Costume Design.** Design a national costume for the United States. Share your design and explanation with the class.

4. **Family Lifestyle.** Looking at your own family, analyze how your family's lifestyle, structure, and values influence the clothing decisions of family members. Write an essay about the clothing needs and choices of family members.

Making the Connection

1. **Social Studies.** Select a culture from the past or present. Research the style of clothing that was or is worn by its people. Describe what you can learn about the culture from the styles, fabrics, and designs of the clothing.

What Is a Fashion Photographer?

Fashion photographers provide fashion photos for ads, magazines, newspapers, catalogs, and promotional materials. Sometimes, the fashion editor or creative director will tell the photographer how to portray the fashions. At other times, the photographer decides how best to create the mood of the photographs. Fashion photographers have individual styles. Some are known for very high-fashion shots; others specialize in capturing a very natural look.

Try It Yourself

Imagine that you are a fashion photographer. Take a variety of "fashion" photographs. Experiment with capturing various looks and moods for the individual fashions. If possible, use both indoor and outdoor settings.

Build Your Portfolio

After your photographs are developed, select the ones that best create the fashion image that you were seeking. Write a description of the techniques that you used to capture the look and mood of the photos. Place the fashion photographs and written description in your portfolio.

2. **Math.** Using information from the chapter, discuss with your family how to prioritize the spending of $500 for family clothing needs. Then list the percentage of the "budget" that each family member could receive.

Fashion Director

Jennifer Bristow is the fashion director for a mid-size chain of specialty stores. "Ever since I was a little girl," says Jennifer, "I have dreamed of working in the fashion industry. I thought I wanted to be a fashion illustrator or a designer, but the responsibilities of fashion director are broader and more challenging. However, I worked in many different areas of retailing before I reached this managerial position."

Education and Training

Jennifer became interested in a fashion career when she was in high school. She took several art and clothing courses, which gave her an introduction to color and design. She also became involved in FHA, the Future Homemakers of America student association. "Through FHA, I learned leadership skills such as running a meeting, planning events, and organizing committees," said Jennifer.

After high school, Jennifer attended the local community college for two years. There she took courses in fashion, art, business, and marketing. She worked at night and on the weekends as a salesperson at a local discount store. This experience gave her an understanding of the various responsibilities of retail employees, from stock clerk to merchandise manager.

Next, Jennifer enrolled in the state university where she received a bachelor's degree in fashion merchandising. As she learned more about the retailing industry, she decided her interests and skills best suited her for a job in fashion coordination rather than sales.

After graduation, Jennifer became a fashion stylist in a buying office. She researched trends

and fashion information for the company's merchandise department. With a lot of determination and hard work, Jennifer gradually climbed the fashion ladder: from fashion stylist to fashion coordinator for a department store, then fashion director for her present company.

Responsibilities

As fashion director, Jennifer has many different responsibilities that utilize her education and experience. Her primary task is to promote the sale of fashion merchandise for her company.

- **Research trends.** Jennifer spends a great deal of time analyzing style, color, and fabric trends. She reads fashion publications, attends market weeks and trade shows, monitors movies and TV, and observes people wherever she goes.

- **Direct fashion promotion.** Stores need a coordinated effort of the merchandising, advertising, and display staffs to promote a fashion look. Jennifer, as fashion director, guides this promotional planning. She seeks the most creative and appealing manner in which to promote the chain's merchandise.

- **Communicate with store personnel.** The fashion director must continually communicate fashion information to many people. These include top management, the buying staff, the sales personnel, and the advertising and display departments. Jennifer attends planning meetings, prepares reports and forecasts, and conducts staff training seminars.

- **Be a spokesperson.** As the chain's fashion leader, Jennifer is often in the position of public spokesperson for the company. She may deal with the press, plan a fashion event with a community organization, or work with other fashion firms.

Knowledge and Skills

Jennifer listed the knowledge and skills she has found to be valuable to her success in the fashion field:

- **Communication skills**—for giving presentations and seminars, discussing issues with management, writing planning strategies and reports, and serving as company spokesperson.

- **Art and fashion knowledge**—for understanding the elements and principles of design, fashion history, fashion terminology, fabric characteristics, and clothing construction.

- **Math skills**—for planning budgets, reading sales reports, comparing research data, and handling expenses.

- **Computer skills**—for writing reports, creating spreadsheets, developing design layouts, doing research, and communicating with colleagues.

- **Business and consumer skills**—for knowing how to manage resources, make decisions, develop marketing plans, and sell merchandise.

- **Leadership skills**—for knowing how to plan, organize, implement, manage, motivate, solve problems, and evaluate.

"When I was going to school, I often wondered whether I would ever use the information I was having to learn in class," says Jennifer. *"I only wish I had known how important certain knowledge and skills would be in my career."*

Clothes and Fashion

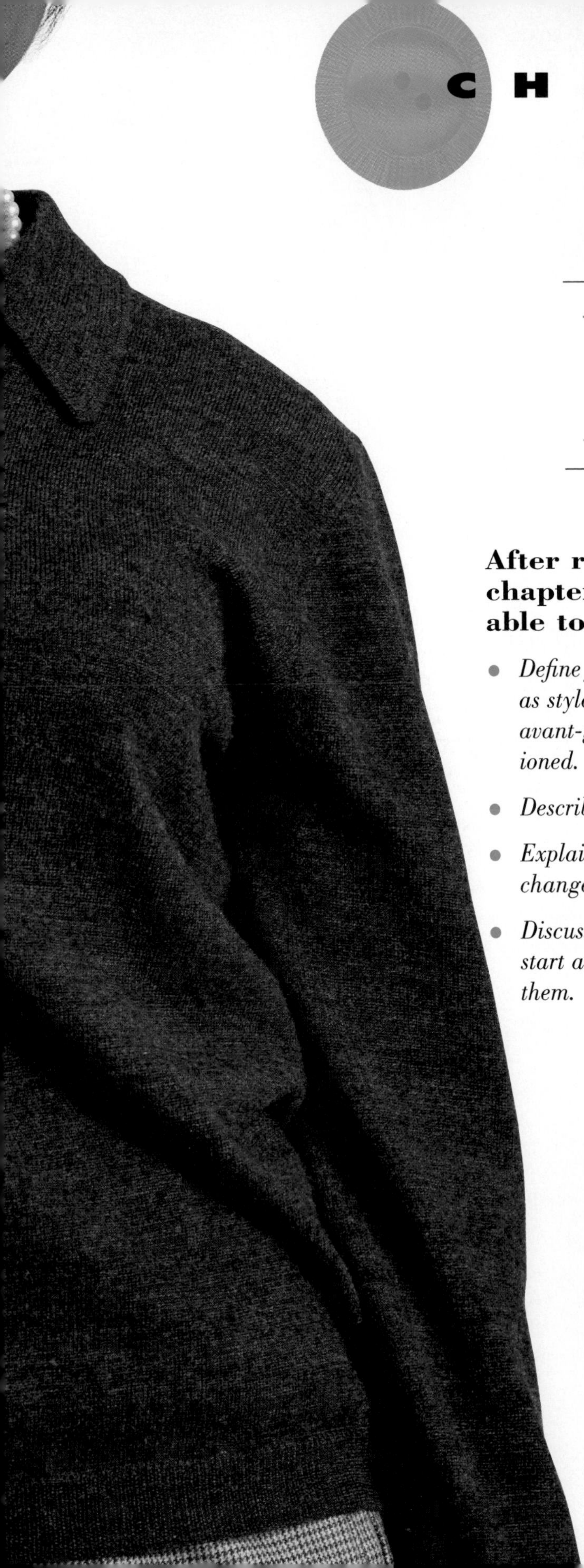

What Is Fashion?

After reading this chapter, you will be able to:

- *Define fashion terms, such as style, classic, fad, avant-garde, and old-fashioned.*

- *Describe a fashion cycle.*

- *Explain why fashions change.*

- *Discuss how new fashions start and what influences them.*

Terms to Learn

- *fashion*
- *style*
- *classic*
- *fad*
- *avant-garde*
- *old-fashioned*
- *retro*
- *trend*
- *economics*
- *technology*

What is fashion all about? Why does the outfit that you couldn't wait to own last year suddenly look "old" to you this year? Why do the clothes in pictures of your mother as a teenager look very old-fashioned, while the clothes in pictures of your grandmother may seem more attractive to you? Why do some fashions seems to last longer than others?

Fashion is constantly changing. When a new style is introduced, it may be considered too strange or daring by most people. As a style becomes popular, it is worn by many people. Then new fashions are introduced, and the style is no longer popular. It looks old and dated. After many years, old fashions may again be considered charming and attractive.

Fashion

Fashion is *the particular style that is popular at a given time.* It is anything that is currently "in." Fashion usually means clothes, but there are fashions in hairstyles, in home decorating, and in the foods we eat. A few years ago, very few people ate yogurt. Now yogurt is very popular and fashionable.

Fashion Terms

Advertisements and articles about fashion contain terms such as *style, classic,* and *fad.* If you understand what these terms mean, it will help you to become a wiser and more informed consumer.

You will be able to select clothes that meet your own needs and wants. You will be able to better evaluate clothing styles as to how long they might stay in fashion.

Style

Style refers to *the shape of a particular item of clothing that makes it easy to recognize.* Straight, A-line, and circular are all styles of skirts. Set-in, raglan, and kimono are all styles of sleeves. Jeans are a specific style of pants. The style of a single-breasted jacket is different than the style of a double-breasted jacket.

Although basic styles remain the same, certain details may change according to fashion. Skirt lengths go up or down, and jackets become longer or shorter. Sometimes jacket lapels are wide; other times they are narrow.

Certain styles of garments are more fashionable at one time than another. Clothes may be fitted or loose, simple or detailed. Shoulders may be wide or narrow. Sleeves or pant legs may be tight or full. A new look may not replace a previous fashion, but merely add another style from which to choose.

Classic

A **classic** is *a traditional style that stays in fashion for a very long time.* The blazer jacket is a classic. Blue jeans are a classic. A tailored shirt and a cardigan sweater are classics. Usually styles that become classic are simpler and less innovative than other styles.

The classic blazer is navy blue. Some years the blazer may feature narrow lapels with metal buttons. Other years the fashion may be wide lapels with navy buttons. However, the blazer style is always classic.

Many other styles have become classics. They include polo shirts, pleated skirts, sweatshirts, trench coats, and tuxedos. These styles have been around for years. What other styles do you think are classic?

These classic styles—a navy blue blazer, tailored shirt, and tan chinos—have been in fashion for many years.

A Fad

A **fad** is a *fashion that is very popular for only a short time*. It can be a color, such as mauve or chartreuse. It can be an accessory, such as rhinestone jewelry or shoes with colorful laces. Fads can also be an item of clothing. Short miniskirts and low-slung baggy pants are examples of a fad. Fads can even be a certain look, such as "punk-rock," "safari," or "grunge."

Fads usually involve less expensive items of clothing or accessories. For example, "pop-it" plastic necklaces and cinch belts were fads in the 1950s. Fluorescent socks and leg warmers were fads in the 1980s. Wearing boxer shorts as outerwear became a fad in the 1990s. Sometimes a fad is rediscovered by another generation. For example, many young people wore mood rings in the 1970s. These rings became popular again in the 1990s.

Many fads, such as wearing slashed jeans or untied shoelaces, are popular mainly with teenagers. Fads help teens express two important needs. The first need is to belong to a group. Many teenagers want to be a part of a group that is special and different from the rest of the world. The other need is to express their own individuality. What fads are currently popular with teens?

A Status Symbol

A status symbol is an item of clothing that gives the wearer a special feeling of importance or wealth. Fashion designers are celebrities today. They put their names, initials, or symbols on the clothes they design to show that the clothes are special. People who wear these clothes are trying to communicate that they are special, too. They also may wear these clothes or accessories to show that they can afford these items.

Past Fashion Fads

1920's

1950's

1970's

Shoe Styles and Customs

Throughout history, fashion has determined the style of men's and women's shoes. The first foot coverings were probably wrappings made of animal fur. The ancient Egyptians, Greeks, and Romans wore sandals made of plant fibers or leather.

People's desire to be fashionable has led to many unusual kinds of shoes. In the 1400s, Europeans wore shoes with an extremely long toe. Some had a chain that fastened the toe to the knee to prevent the wearer from tripping. Shoes once worn in the Orient were set on a six inch wooden stilt. This made it almost impossible for the wearer to walk without support.

Other people have developed special shoes for protection or safety. Fishermen and farmers in The Netherlands wear heavy wooden shoes to protect their feet from dampness. Athletes wear shoes with rubber soles, cleats, or spikes to prevent them from slipping. Some work boots have a special steel section inside the toe for protection against injury.

Various cultures have different customs associated with shoes. In our society, we may take off our shoes at home or at someone else's home when we want to be comfortable. Otherwise, we wear shoes almost everywhere.

In other cultures, removing one's shoes is a mark of respect. In many countries, shoes should always be removed before entering someone's home. This custom is followed in Thailand, Korea, Tahiti, Samoa, Malaysia, Morocco, and India.

In Japan, you should remove your shoes when you enter a restaurant or a private home. It is polite to place them neatly together with the toes pointing toward the door by which you entered. In Indonesia, you should remove your shoes if the home is carpeted or if your host goes shoeless.

In the Middle East, it is considered an insult to sit so your host can see the soles of your shoes. Around the world, visitors are forbidden to wear shoes in Buddhist temples and in Muslim mosques.

Avant-Garde

Avant-garde (ah-vahn-GARD) is a French expression that in the clothing industry means *being ahead of fashion*. These clothes are daring and unconventional. They are considered "far out" and do not appeal to most people. However, some avant-garde features may become popular after a few years.

Some teenagers choose clothing, hair, and make-up styles that are considered avant-garde. These styles call attention to the wearer. Cut-out clothing, green or orange hair, and black lipstick are examples of avant-garde looks.

Old-Fashioned

Old-fashioned is a term that describes *any style that is no longer in fashion*. With today's instant communication, our brain receives a great deal of new information every day. Nothing seems new for very long. A garment can look old-fashioned to us in a very short time. However, the fashion pendulum swings back and forth so that some styles do return. Some examples of this are button-down shirts, skinny ties, V-neck sweaters, and twin sweater sets.

Sometimes an old-fashioned look becomes an important look in fashion. Today the **retro** look, or *styles of an earlier time*, is popular. Clothing styles from the 1940s, 1950s, and 1960s are being shown in current fashions. Some people want to wear the original clothes, not updated versions. Thrift shops and attics are popular sources for such garments.

What criteria do people use to decide when clothing styles are in or out of fashion? There are no specific rules or guidelines to follow. Instead, people's attitudes are influenced by designers, manufacturers, magazines, television, friends, family, and even their local community.

Fashion Cycles

Every fashion has a life cycle. A fashion is born when someone begins to wear it. The person who wears it could be a model in a magazine, a celebrity, or a small group of people with similar tastes. A fashion matures when many people start to wear it. It is old-fashioned when people are tired of it and do not want to wear it anymore.

When the fashion cycle happens quickly, it is a fad. When *the fashion cycle happens quite slowly*, it is a **trend**. In the 1950s, the most popular style of dress had a fitted bodice, a belted waistline, and a full skirt. By the middle 1960s, a loose-fitting, unbelted dress was the most popular style. In the early 1980s, fitted dresses and suits were popular again. By the late 1980s, large, loose-fitting jackets, shirts, and dresses were in fashion. Then, by the middle 1990s, fitted dresses with waistlines and unbelted, body-skimming dresses looked new again.

Men's neckties undergo a similar fashion cycle. In the 1940s, ties were very wide in order to balance the double-breasted suits with wide lapels that were fashionable. In the 1960s, when Ivy League suits were stylish, ties became very skinny. Diagonal stripes were popular designs. As suits with wider lapels again became popular in the mid-1970s, ties got wider, too. In the 1980s they narrowed to a medium width. Stripes, tiny prints, and dark colors were popular. Then, in the early 1990s, ties began to get wider and more colorful. Fabrics featured flowers, cartoon characters, and other bold designs. These changes in width and design happened gradually.

Fashion cycles also occur in trousers and pants. The tops of trousers are sometimes tight across the hips. At other times they have pleats to create added fullness. The width of pant legs can change from wide to medium to narrow, and then back to wide again. Sometimes trouser legs have cuffs and sometimes they are plain. The fashion cycles are ongoing.

Why Fashions Change

Many years ago, fashion changed very slowly. Communication between groups of people took a long time. New production methods occurred gradually. People often wore the same style of clothing for their whole life.

Sometimes a particular style of clothing continued for more than a lifetime. An outfit that was worn

Fashion Cycles

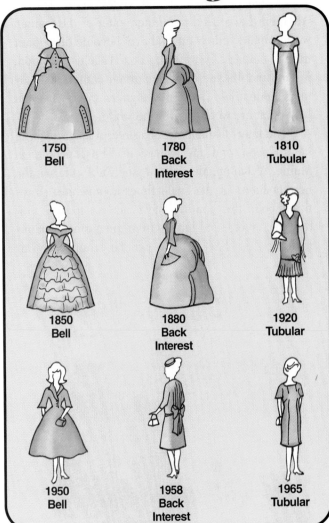

1750 Bell	1780 Back Interest	1810 Tubular
1850 Bell	1880 Back Interest	1920 Tubular
1950 Bell	1958 Back Interest	1965 Tubular

Until recently, three silhouttes were repeated about every 100 years. Now the fashion cycle is much faster.

for special occasions was often handed down from generation to generation.

Today fashion changes quickly. World-wide communication can tell us instantly what people in London, Paris, or Tokyo are wearing. Travel and trade spread fashion and production ideas quickly. Both people and events around the globe can influence fashion trends.

The Fashion Industry

Designers introduce new styles every season. Although Paris used to be the center of the fashion world, many other cities have become important design centers. New York, Los Angeles, London, Milan, and Tokyo are all important centers for garment industries. Today's designers create fashion looks that are worn all over the world.

The latest fashions are featured in magazines, in newspapers, and on television. Thus, people in Maine, Wyoming, Mississippi, and California see the new fashions at the same time. Meanwhile, stores throughout the country have access to the new designs, colors, and fabrics from the garment manufacturers. A "hot" fashion can be shipped by air freight to distant states and countries. Within days, teens around the world are able to wear the same fashion or fad.

Social Trends

Fashion reflects the trends and values of a society. For example, the role of males and females in a society can often be determined by the clothes they wear. As roles change, clothing changes also.

Styles for Women

The role of women in our society has changed dramatically since the 1800s. In Victorian society, women were looked upon as fragile and delicate creatures. The style of clothing reflected and contributed to this belief.

A lady's skeletal structure was believed to be weak. The *corset*, an intricate cage of heavy canvas reinforced with whalebone or steel, was thought to be an absolutely essential undergarment. Victorians believed that it was needed to support the body, as well as provide a fashionable look. This corset was so restrictive that women did, indeed, develop health problems and become fragile.

In addition to the corset, the Victorian lady wore several layers of undergarments. These consisted of at least three petticoats and a hoop skirt. They were worn underneath a long dress that contained up to 20 yards of fabric. When she went out, she added a heavy woolen shawl and a large bonnet. All of this could weigh from 10 to 30 pounds!

Before World War I, women's clothes were designed more for appearance than for practicality. Dresses had long skirts with bustles or crinolines, high necklines, and very full sleeves. During the war, more women worked in shops, offices, and factories, so more practical fashions developed.

After World War I, women did not want to return to their former way of life or dress. Clothes became shorter and less fitted for both comfort and practicality. Some women began wearing slacks for athletic activities.

Designers seek inspiration for new designs from many different sources.

Changing Men's Fashions

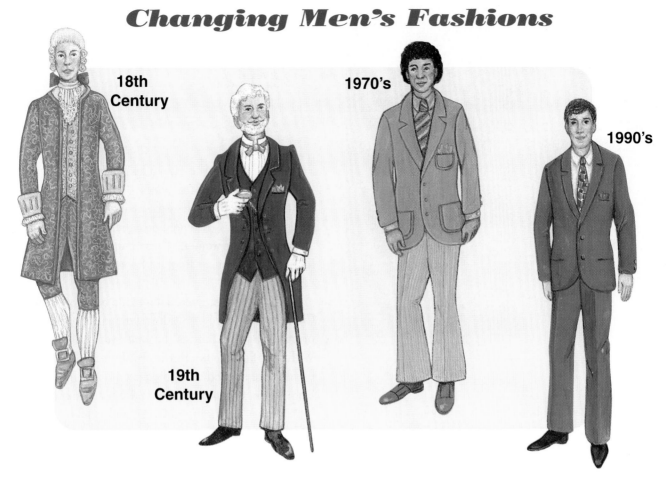

18th Century

19th Century

1970's

1990's

During World War II, many women entered the workforce. They worked in offices and factories, replacing the male workers who were in the armed forces. Slacks and jumpsuits became the standard work apparel for female factory workers. Tailored business suits were worn by female office workers.

Styles for Men

Styles for men have also changed over the years. In the seventeenth and eighteenth centuries, men wore silks, satins, ribbons, and lace. They wore fancy plumed hats over their long hair or large powdered wigs. Some of their garments were more elegant and decorative than women's styles.

By the nineteenth century, men's clothes were plainer. They began wearing trousers instead of knee breeches, and coats were similar to styles today.

In the 1950s, the t-shirt came out from under the dress shirt. This former undershirt was now worn on its own with blue jeans. It has remained a popular style for years.

In the 1960s, many younger men started wearing colorful fabrics and jewelry. Soon men of all ages were wearing shirts in stripes, checks, and many colors with their business suits. Some men grew beards and mustaches and wore longer hair.

Styles for All

By the 1970s, fashions for both men and women were often similar. Blazers, trousers, jeans, trench coats, and tailored shirts were styled the same for everyone. In the 1980s, health and physical fitness became more important for both males and females. Exercise clothes, such as leotards and jogging suits,

Today physical fitness is important to both men and women. Active sportswear is comfortable to wear whether you are exercising or relaxing.

became fashionable to wear even when people were not exercising.

In the 1990s, the fashion trend has been toward more casual clothing. Both males and females are dressing less formally for work, travel, and parties. Blue jeans, sweatshirts, and sneakers are worn by men, women, and children. Knits, denims, flannels, and other casual fabrics are very popular. What do you think this says about our society?

Historical Events

Major historical events can influence fashion. After the French Revolution, France changed from a monarchy to a democracy. Clothes reflected this change, with everyone dressing in simpler styles.

During World War II, there was a shortage of fabric because so many textiles were being used for military uniforms and equipment. As a result, styles became slimmer, and shorter skirts became fashionable. Nylon stockings were almost impossible to get, so women had to wear cotton ones.

After World War II, styles changed radically. People were tired of the clothes they had worn during the war and fabric was easily available again. Christian Dior, a French designer, introduced his "New Look" for women. These clothes featured very full skirts and longer lengths. Soon this style became very popular.

In 1972, President Nixon made a historic trip to China to re-establish trade relations. Soon oriental prints and silk fabrics became very fashionable. With the fall of the Berlin Wall in 1989 and the breakup of the Soviet Union, countries in Eastern Europe are promoting travel and trade. This is creating interest in traditional arts and crafts in these countries.

Economics

A society's economic system can affect how quickly fashion changes. **Economics** refers to *the way that a society produces, distributes, and spends its wealth.*

In United States or Europe, the economic system is a highly industrialized, free enterprise system. In this system, there is a great amount of competition among businesses. You can choose from many different types of stores when you go shopping. There are many different styles of clothes, too. Because so much variety is available, fashion changes very quickly.

In a society such as China, there is little competition. All manufacturers produce similar goods. There is little or no advertising. As a result, fashion changes very slowly because people do not have many choices.

The Desire for Change

Sometimes fashion changes because the events that created hardships pass. People no longer wish to wear clothes that remind them of these events. Sometimes fashion changes because people simply get bored with one type of look.

Since the 1960s, fashion has changed rapidly. There are many theories as to why this is occurring. Probably there is no one single cause. Perhaps fashion is reflecting the many changes that are happening within our society. What do you think?

What Inspires Fashion?

There is a theory in fashion called the "trickle down" theory. It means that a new fashion starts at the top, with a fashion designer or an important personality. Then it trickles down until it is accepted by everyone.

In recent years, however, fashion also "trickles up." This means that a fashion is started by a group of people, often teenagers. Blue jeans are a good example of a trickle-up fashion. When teenagers began to wear them, everyone thought blue jeans were just a fad. Now people of all ages wear them and fashion designers manufacture designer jeans.

What inspires fashion? There are many sources of inspiration and influence. They include designers, media events and celebrities, technology, and groups of people.

Fashion Designers

Fashion designers create the styles of clothes displayed in magazines, newspapers, catalogs, and stores. They decide the type of lines, colors, and fabric for each garment.

Have you ever wondered what inspires a fashion designer? Have you ever wondered why different fashion designers come up with similar ideas at the same time? It is because they are influenced by the world we live in.

Most designers attend art exhibits, study the history of costume, go to the movies, read the newspapers, and travel. They look at the way people around them dress. All of this provides new ideas for new designs.

For example, some designers look at the more casual lifestyles of individuals and families. They promote fashion looks that feature flannel shirts, denim jeans, and barn jackets. Other designers create mix-and-match separates that can be worn for school, work, and leisure activities. Still others are inspired by the new, body-hugging fabrics to produce apparel items such as biker shorts and leggings.

Media Events and Celebrities

A popular movie, a television show, a musical group, or a sports event can all inspire fashions. When the Beatles became popular in the 1960s, young men changed their haircuts and began to wear collarless jackets. In the 1980s, Michael Jackson and Madonna created popular fads in clothing and accessories. The TV series "Miami Vice" popularized loose, unlined jackets for men.

Popular entertainers, such as Madonna, have influenced fashion trends. What famous personalities are inspiring current fashions and fads?

Today actors, models, and sports figures play an important role in fashion. Because people admire celebrities, they often want to wear the same clothes, athletic shoes, or accessories as the celebrities do.

In the 1990s, some fashion models became as well known as the designers whose clothes they modeled. Some of these models entered into agreements with apparel manufacturers to promote moderately priced fashions that bear their names.

Manufacturers often hire sports celebrities to endorse their products. Athletes are featured in advertisements and commercials. Sometimes they make personal appearances for the products.

Names or symbols of athletic teams are popular for jackets, sweatshirts, and caps. Cartoon characters, such as Mickey Mouse® and Minnie Mouse™, decorate all types of clothing for both children and adults. Special events, such as the Olympics® and the World Cup®, always offer special designs as souvenirs. What celebrities or recent events are currently popular with your friends?

Technology

Technology refers to *the way a society uses its scientific knowledge to produce things*. Technology has a great influence on fashion.

In the 1960s something happened that was called the "double-knit revolution." Fabric companies were able to manufacture a great variety of polyester double-knit fabrics. These fabrics were inexpensive to produce. Because they were also washable, they were very popular. However, these fabrics were more suitable to simple straight styles than soft, draped garments. As a result, clothing styles became very simple and straight.

New types of fibers have been developed that look and feel like natural fibers. Unless you read the label, it is difficult to tell what types of fibers are used in today's fabrics. For example, polyester fibers can be knit or woven into fabrics that drape like silk yet cost less and are easier to care for. New dyes and printing techniques have been developed that imitate or improve upon ancient techniques.

Other developments have produced fabrics with new characteristics. One example is the stretch fabrics used for swimwear and exercise wear. Another example is Gore-Tex®, a fabric that can breathe, yet rain and snow cannot penetrate. It is popular with runners, hikers, and skiers.

New technology enables apparel manufacturers to produce garments with specialized characteristics. For example, garments made from Gore-Tex® fabric are waterproof and windproof, yet comfortable to wear. This is because the fabric sheds raindrops on the outside but allows perspiration to pass through from the inside.

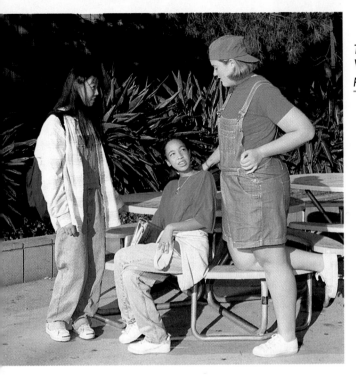

Teenagers have influenced many fashion styles. What current fashions and fads have been popularized by teens?

Groups of People

People, in small and large groups, can influence fashions. With mass communication today, representatives of the fashion industry are able to monitor fashion trends in all parts of our society. They may report a unique style being worn by people in a certain region, or occupation, or age group.

Teenagers are major influences. In the 1980s, they popularized painter's pants, lumberjackets, sweatshirts, and cowboy boots. In the 1990s, frayed and slashed jeans, baggy pants, oversized shirts, and baseball caps become popular.

In 1995, young people began wearing a collarless shirt made of a heavy cotton knit. It has three to five buttons at the neck that can be left open. The style suggests the turn-of-the-century laborer's undershirt. It is also called a Henley shirt, named for a rowing regatta held in England. Some fashion experts have predicted that this shirt style could challenge the popularity of the round-neck t-shirt.

One World of Fashion

In many societies throughout the world, people wear similar styles. The Russian businessman in Moscow wears the same type of suit as the American businessman in New York City. Teenagers in Tokyo, Japan wear the same style of pants and shirts as teenagers in Toledo, Ohio.

Mass communication allows people around the world to get the same information at the same time. We can all watch the same sports events, see the same rock videos, and view the same movies. When new styles appear on the designers' runways, photographs of these clothes are in newspapers and on television stations in a matter of hours around the world. As a result, you can find similar clothing in almost all of the world's big cities.

However, not everyone dresses alike. People who live in underdeveloped areas or in areas that are very hot or very cold may not dress like people from other parts of the world. People of various religions may dress differently, according to their beliefs. Some people continue to dress in styles that are unique to their culture. They may do this all the time because their native clothing is more comfortable. They may wear the clothing only for special occasions to express pride in their heritage. Fashion can be celebrated through the many similarities and differences seen around the world.

Summary

- Fashion is constantly changing.

- Some common fashion terms include style, classic, fad, status symbol, avant-garde, and old-fashioned.

- Every fashion has a life cycle. Some happen quickly, others quite slowly.

- The fashion industry, social trends, historical events, economics, and a desire for change influence and change fashion.

- Fashion is inspired by fashion designers, media events, celebrities, technology, and groups of people.

- Today people wear similar styles around the world.

Using Vocabulary Terms

On a separate piece of paper, write the vocabulary term that best fits the definition:

1. A traditional style that stays in fashion for a very long time.

2. The way a society uses its scientific knowledge to produce things.

3. The particular style that is popular at a given time.

4. A fashion that is very popular for only a short time.

5. The shape of a particular item of clothing that makes it easy to recognize.

6. Being ahead of fashion.

Recalling the Facts

1. What is the difference between a classic and a fad? Give an example of each.

2. What is the difference between avant-garde and retro? Give an example of each.

3. Explain the life cycle of a particular fashion.

4. Why does fashion change quickly today?

5. What can you learn about a society from the clothes that the people wear?

6. How did World War II influence fashion?

7. List four sources of fashion inspiration.

8. How do designers get new ideas for their designs?

9. What is the influence of technology on fashion?

10. Why do many people around the world wear similar styles today?

Thinking Critically

1. **Analysis.** Analyze the fashions that are currently being worn by students. Which ones are classics, fads, avant-garde, retro, or status symbols?

2. **Evaluation.** Why do you think fads are so popular with teenagers?

3. **Analysis.** How has the changing roles of males and females in the twentieth century influenced fashion?

4. **Synthesis.** From the information in the chapter, identify the most important influences on fashion today.

Applying Your Knowledge

1. **Fads and Classics.** Working in small groups, look through catalogs and magazines for illustrations of various types of clothing and accessories. Identify each as a fad or a classic. Mount and label the illustrations on a poster.

2. **Old-Fashioned and Retro.** Look through old yearbooks from your school. What fashions and hairstyles look old-fashioned? Are any styles currently popular with today's teens? Share your findings with the class.

3. **Celebrities.** Look through magazines for photos of celebrities who currently influence fashion. Describe the influence or role of each.

4. **Interviews.** Interview parents or grandparents about the "double-knit revolution" in the 1960s. How did this fabric impact their wardrobes? Write a summary of the interviews.

Making the Connection

1. **Social Studies.** Make a timeline of historical events during the past century, along with major fashion changes for males and females. What conclusions can be made about the impact of historical events and social trends on fashion?

What Is a Fashion Writer?

Fashion writers may write articles for newspapers, magazines, and forecasting services. They describe fashion trends and new developments in textiles. They also interview designers and review fashion collections. Some fashion writers work on promotional publications or advertisements for designers, manufacturers, or retailers. They often work with fashion illustrators and photographers in the planning of sketches and photos to accompany their fashion articles.

Try It Yourself

Imagine that you are a fashion writer. Using information from magazines, newspapers, and store displays, write an article about fashion trends for the teen market. Describe the popular styles, colors, fabrics, and accessories, along with current fads. If possible, have your article published in the school newspaper.

Build Your Portfolio

After completing your article, suggest ways that it could be illustrated with photos or sketches. Then place a copy of the fashion article and illustration suggestions in your portfolio.

2. **Social Studies.** Research the fashion styles worn in various countries. Where do people wear styles similar to ours? Where do they wear styles that are unique to their culture? Describe some of the factors that may account for these similarities and differences.

CHAPTER 6

The History of Fashion

After reading this chapter, you will be able to:

- *Explain how the first clothes were made.*

- *Describe how styles developed from simple, draped garments to complex, tailored ones.*

- *Discuss how trade, economics, political power, religion, and technology affect clothing.*

- *Describe how modern clothes have evolved.*

Terms to Learn

- *tanned*
- *barter*
- *sumptuary laws*
- *cellulose*
- *fashion babies*

When you look at the illustrations in a history book or at an exhibit in a museum, do you ever wonder why everyone's clothes do not look the same? Why do some ancient societies appear to be wearing animal skins, while others are wearing clothes made from fabric?

Why do the clothes from some countries look very similar to the ones worn here in the United States? Why do clothes from other countries look very different? This chapter explores the way clothes and fashions have changed through history.

The First Clothes

Thousands of years ago, people learned to make clothing from the natural resources around them. In many climates, clothing was essential for protection from the cold weather or the blazing sun. Animal skins and hair, plants, grasses, and tree bark were some of the materials used for clothing.

These first clothes were very simple. The daily tasks of providing food, shelter, and clothing did not leave much time to decorate and embellish clothes for everyday wear.

Learning to Sew Leather

In a developing society, the type of clothes that the people wear is determined by the climate and the natural materials available. In prehistoric times, the climate in northern Europe was cold and dry. The warm weather lasted only two or three months a year. Cave drawings from this area show animal skins being used as body coverings.

Untreated animal skins are very stiff and uncomfortable to wear, so primitive people discovered different ways to make the skins soft. Some people beat the skins with stones, while other people chewed the skins to make them soft. Others beat the skins, then wet them, and rubbed them with oil. Much later, skins were **tanned**, or *converted into leather by treating with tannic acid made from tree bark*. With this method the skins stayed soft for a long time.

Some of the first clothing was made of animal skins.

To hold the skins together, holes were punched in the leather. Then sinews, or stringlike tendons from animals, were laced through the holes. With this crude form of sewing, several skins of small animals could be stitched together to form a garment.

Learning to Make Fabric

People in areas with warmer climates, such as Africa and the South Pacific, needed protection from sun and rain. They learned to make garments from the trees and plants around them. Some plants, such as the grasses, could be picked and used right away. Grasses were laced together to form the first woven fabric. It was probably used for mats and baskets rather than for clothing. Parts of plants, such as the bark of the trees, had to be soaked and treated until soft enough to be used as cloth.

The ancient Egyptians lived in a warm climate where plants, such as the flax plant, grew abundantly along the Nile River. Flax was woven into linen cloth. This was styled into simple garments that were suitable for the hot climate of Egypt.

People in colder climates who used animal skins began to cut them for a better fit. As they did this, they found that the wet, matted clumps of animal hair formed a crude version of felt.

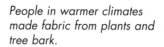

People in warmer climates made fabric from plants and tree bark.

Basic Clothing Styles

Ancient people were much too busy working to stay alive to worry about fashion. Eventually they learned how to live in one place by raising animals and growing their own crops. They then had time to develop other skills and interests. Their spinning and weaving skills developed, and people learned how to shape fabric into a variety of garments.

Because ancient people left visual records, we do not need to guess at what these garments looked like. Drawings of these garments have been found on the walls of caves. Drawings, mummy cases, and actual fabrics have been discovered in the tombs of the Egyptian pharaohs. Surviving sculpture of the Greeks and Romans shows clothing styles of their times. Paintings, religious statues, and illustrated manuscripts show us how people in the Middle Ages dressed.

Draped and Wrapped Garments

The very first draped garment was the animal skin that the cave dwellers wrapped around their shoulders. Later, people took a square or rectangle of fabric and draped, hung, or wrapped it around their body.

The Greeks and Romans draped or wrapped fabric around their body to create simple garments.

Greek himation and chiton

Roman toga

Clothes and Charms

Clothing and jewelry have long reflected people's beliefs in charms and magic. Folktales contain many stories about items that gave the wearer special powers. For example, magic rings and special cloaks were believed to make the wearer invisible.

A primitive hunter would wrap himself in the skin of an animal such as a lion. He believed that he was transferring the skill and the strength of that lion to his own body. The animal skin also helped serve as a disguise for the hunter. It became a magic symbol for a successful hunt.

A necklace of shark's teeth was believed to have an effect on the wearer that was similar to reciting a special prayer or casting a spell. It provided the wearer with all the qualities a fisherman needed to be successful.

Masks and elaborate headdresses have been worn throughout history for many reasons. Some were used to provide magic powers or to ward off evil spirits. Others were worn as a disguise or to tell a story. Most masks had the features of a human being or an animal.

Today people continue to wear special items as charms or disguises for various events. For example, people wear masks and headdresses at Halloween and *carnival,* a period of merrymaking just before Lent. Native American tribes still use masks in harvest festivals. Processions and festivals in India, China, and other countries also include masked people.

Some people wear special jewelry or clothing for occasions where success is important. This might be an athletic event, a test, or an interview. Others carry a symbol, such as a rabbit's foot, to bring them good luck. These items are "lucky charms" for the wearers.

There are examples of draped garments in many cultures. The Romans wore a *toga,* a piece of fabric that was wrapped and draped around the body. It was crescent-shaped with one straight end. It measured 4½ to 5½ yards or meters long.

The ancient Greeks wore a garment called a *himation,* which was a long, rectangular piece of fabric worn as a cloak. It could also be worn with one end draped over one shoulder and the other end draped over the opposite arm. The fabric was nearly 5 yards or meters long. The Greeks also wore a *chiton,* which was a tunic made from two rectangles of fabric joined at the shoulders.

Draping was the quickest and easiest way to make a garment. It often took a long time to weave a beautiful piece of fabric. People did not want to cut it up. Since there were no modern washing machines or irons, it was easier to clean a rectangle of fabric. It could be washed and carefully smoothed out. When it dried, it was neatly pressed.

Today women in India wear a *sari,* which is a piece of silk or cotton fabric 45-inches (115 cm) wide and 80-inches (200 cm) long. One end is tucked into the waistband of a petticoat. Then the fabric is pleated and wrapped around the body, and the other end goes over the head or the shoulder.

Fitted Garments

When primitive people learned how to punch holes in the animal skins and lace them together, they made the first fitted garment. A group of people known as Minoans

The earliest examples of fitted garments were found on statuettes and frescoes from the island of Crete.

lived on the Mediterranean island of Crete before the time of the ancient Greeks. The women wore some of the first recorded examples of fitted garments. They wore full skirts and very tight-fitting jackets with elbow-length sleeves.

Gloves, developed by some of the first cultures that lived in cold climates, are another example of a fitted garment. Trousers were worn by northern invaders who swept into ancient Greece and Italy on horseback.

Today we wear many fitted garments. Slacks, jeans, shirts, suits, and most dresses are fitted garments. They are created by stitching pieces of fabric together.

Combination Garments

Combination garments are garments that have been draped, then cut and sewn so that they hang loosely on the body. Examples of combination garments are the Arabian *kibr*, a hooded robe with sleeves; the Japanese *kimono*; the Hawaiian *muumuu*; and the *caftan* from many cultures.

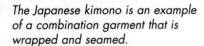

The Japanese kimono is an example of a combination garment that is wrapped and seamed.

Influences on Fashion

As a society becomes more developed, the way that clothes look can become even more important than the protection they provide. In fact, clothing is considered an art form in some societies. When societies begin to trade with each other, they exchange goods and ideas that influence their clothing. Religious beliefs and political ideas also can influence the type of clothing people wear. Technological developments can change the way fabric is made and clothes are produced.

Trade and Economics

Clothing ideas are frequently shared among cultures. Sailors and merchants who established trade with other countries brought back fabrics, yarns, and trimmings. Soldiers who went to war abroad saw how others lived and dressed. Missionaries who went to other lands taught the native people about the European styles of clothing.

When people learned that they could exchange their goods and skills for someone else's goods and talents, they were no longer limited to what was available in their own backyards. Trade between societies was usually done by **barter**, which means *trading without the use of money*. Goods were exchanged, along with ideas and techniques.

For instance, between the eleventh and the thirteenth centuries, the Crusades opened trade routes between western Europe and the Middle East and the Orient. At first, only the fabrics were imported. Those who could pay the price could have garments made from the finest silks, damasks, and thin cottons. Later the production techniques were imported so that the fabrics could be made in Europe.

Trade also helps to balance any excess of some supplies and scarcity of others between societies. For example, people might trade leather for cotton, or tools, or even food.

Politics and Power

For many hundreds of years, kings and queens and their courts set the style. They were the only groups who could afford to change their fashions. When people saw members of the royal court, they copied their style of clothing. However, fashion changes spread very slowly.

During the Middle Ages, a wealthy middle class developed. It became difficult to distinguish a rich commoner from a rich nobleman. Special laws, called **sumptuary laws**, were created. These were *regulations controlling what each social class could wear*. For example, peasant clothes were limited to

For many centuries, kings and queens and their court set the fashion styles. This painting shows Elisabeth d'Autriche, Queen of France in the sixteenth century, wearing an elaborately jeweled gown with a high ruff collar.

certain colors and certain fabrics. Peasants who looked like they were trying to imitate the clothing tastes of the upper class could be fined, imprisoned, or executed.

Until the fourteenth century, European clothes were loose-fitting and draped. People from different cultures wore similar clothes. Around 1350, people started wearing more fitted styles of clothes. From then on, regional differences in garments began to develop in western Europe. Many of these differences reflected the culture within the various countries.

For example, the Renaissance movement in Italy, Spain, and France encouraged elegant styles, extravagant fabrics, and a great amount of decoration. The Reformation movement in Germany, Switzerland, Holland, and England encouraged dark colors, simple styles, and little decoration.

Throughout history, countries with wealth and power have influenced the fashions of other countries. When Spain and Portugal were exploring the New World, their fashions influenced styles throughout Europe. In the seventeenth century, France under the rule of Louis XIV became the most powerful country in Europe. French court dress became the fashionable dress. Since that time, France has been considered a leader in fashion.

In Africa and Asia, societies were not strongly influenced by western Europe. As a result, clothing styles in these countries reflect their own unique cultures. What countries influence clothing styles today?

Religion

Religious beliefs can influence the type of clothing people wear. For example, in the sixteenth century, there were religious groups such as the Society of Friends, the Puritans, and the Amish. These groups believed that religious ceremonies should be very simple. They adopted a very plain style of clothing to show that they did not conform to worldly standards.

The Amish came to America and settled mainly in Pennsylvania and Indiana. They continue to wear clothes that are very similar to the simple clothes their ancestors wore in the 1700s. The Amish do not believe in violence. Because belts and buttons were prominent features of military uniforms in the 1700s, most Amish men still do not wear belts or buttons on their coats.

The Amish continue to wear simple styles and dark colors that reflect their religious beliefs.

Technology

After ancient people settled in one place, they raised certain plants and animals that provided raw materials to make fabrics. For many centuries, natural fibers such as cotton, flax, wool, and silk were used to make garments in homes and workshops.

The Industrial Revolution of the 1700s and 1800s changed the way that goods were made. Power-drawn equipment was invented, and factories were developed. There was a great increase in the amount of fabrics and the number of finished garments that could be produced.

In 1889, a French chemist exhibited fabrics made of "artificial silk" at the Paris Exhibition. These created quite a sensation because they were the first fabrics made of manufactured fibers.

For many years, research scientists in England and Switzerland had experimented with dissolving the fibrous inner bark of mulberry trees. This produced **cellulose**, *the main component of plants such as cotton and flax.* However, the scientists had trouble creating fibers from the dissolved bark. Eventually they tried forcing the solution through fine holes, just as a silkworm does to make silk. This technique successfully produced long fibers or threads. Thus, *rayon* was invented.

Gradually textile chemists developed other manufactured fibers, such as acetate and nylon. This created a new industry that grew rapidly. In 1924, manufactured fibers were only one percent of the total fibers used in fabrics. Today they account for more than 70 percent.

Computers are the newest development in technology. They can be programmed to tell a machine how to weave a fabric. They can analyze a color sample and tell you how to dye a particular fabric so that it matches your sample. Computers can even keep track of a store's inventory and forecast future sales.

The Evolution of Modern Fashion

Many of the clothes that you and your classmates wear are based on styles that were developed in western Europe. The early colonists brought these styles with them when they settled in America.

Until the twentieth century, fashion in both western Europe and the United States was heavily influenced by the rulers of England and France. This changed after World War I when monarchies lost much of their power.

The Eighteenth Century

The 1700s was a time of colonization in America followed by the Revolutionary War. The textile industry was developing in the midst of the Industrial Revolution. In Europe, the late 1700s was the time of the French Revolution.

Fashions for both men and women were elaborate and elegant, with laces, ribbons, and colorful silks. **Fashion babies** were used to spread the fashion news. These were *small dolls about a foot high that were carefully dressed in the latest styles.* Queen Marie Antoinette's dressmaker made the first fashion babies in the 1770s. She dressed them in copies of the French queen's newest clothes and sent them from Paris to London.

Fashion babies, or dolls, were carefully dressed in the latest fashions. They can be seen in museums today.

Dressmakers in London could then see and copy the newest look. The fashion babies then traveled to America. These dolls continued to be the most important form of fashion communication up until the Civil War.

People in the late eighteenth century were very interested in Greek sculpture. In France, commoners began to rebel against the extravagances of the royalty. Many women began wearing loose, flowing muslin dresses based on classical Greek garments. These dresses were very different from the wide skirts, rich fabrics, and elaborate trims worn by the very wealthy. Because these soft dresses had no room for pockets, women began to carry purses.

The Nineteenth Century

The 1800s saw the Civil War as well as expansion of the United States to the West Coast. Clothing styles changed rapidly, too.

During the early 1800s, women wore lightweight, plain gowns with high "empire" waistlines. These gowns were inspired by the French fashions worn by the Empress Josephine, who was Napoleon's wife. Men wore cutaway coats over long, tight-fitting pantaloons.

By the middle of the nineteenth century, dresses were full-skirted and supported by crinolines and hoops. The knee-length frock coat replaced the cutaway coat for men. Many of these garments were modeled after fashions made popular by Queen Victoria of England. France's Empress Eugenie, the wife of Napoleon III, popularized many fashions, such as the bolero jacket, the felt hat, and Scottish tartans.

By the 1880s, full skirts gave way to back bustles. Tailored shirtwaist blouses and suits for women were introduced. Men's fashions featured a shorter coat, the forerunner of today's business suit.

The Twentieth Century

World War I and World War II were immense political events of the twentieth century. In the 1920s, after World War I, women became more active. They wore short, unfitted dresses with long necklaces. They also began to wear garments designed especially for sports. These included wide slacks, known as trousers, and above-the-knee shorts.

Fabric restrictions during World War II resulted in tailored styles with padded shoulders for men and women. After the war, when more fabric became available, dresses had very full, long skirts.

Short miniskirts were in fashion during the 1960s. In the 1970s, the unisex look was very popular. Men and women wore the same styles in the same fabrics and colors. It became fashionable for women to wear pantsuits, styled like men's suits, and neckties. Styles in the 1980s featured broad, padded shoulders. Skirt lengths ranged from long to short. In the 1990s, both men's and women's fashions have become more natural in shape. At the same time, styles range from baggy pants to tight leggings, from oversized shirts to skinny tops. Fashion continues to change.

Early 1700's

1700's

1780's

1750's

1770's

The Evolution of Fashion

Early 1800's

1800's

1850's

1900's

1920's

1930's

Early 1940's

Late 1940's

1940's

1890's

1960's

1950's

1880's

1970's

1980's

Summary

- People first used animal skins, plants, grasses, and tree bark for clothing. Later they learned to weave cloth.

- Early clothing was draped and wrapped around the body.

- Fitted garments were created by stitching pieces of leather or fabric together.

- Over the centuries, fashion has been influenced by trade, economics, politics, religion, and technology.

- Until the twentieth century, fashion was influenced by the rulers of England and France.

- Since World War I, fashion styles have changed more rapidly.

Using Vocabulary Terms

On a separate piece of paper, write the vocabulary term that best fits the definition:

1. Small dolls that were carefully dressed in the latest styles.

2. Regulations controlling what each social class could wear.

3. Trading without the use of money.

4. The main component of plants such as cotton and flax.

5. Converted into leather by treating with tannic acid made from tree bark.

Recalling the Facts

1. How did the climate influence the type of clothes that people wore in prehistoric times?

2. What types of natural materials did people use for clothing ages ago?

3. How do we know what type of clothing people wore in early times?

4. Give examples of the three basic styles of clothing.

5. How did the start of trade between societies influence clothing styles?

6. Until this century, who set the fashion styles?

7. How did the Industrial Revolution change the way that goods were made?

8. Describe how current technology is influencing fashion.

9. What was the purpose of fashion babies?

10. What two political events of the twentieth century had great impact on fashion? How did each event affect clothing styles?

Thinking Critically

1. **Analysis.** Compare and contrast the first types of clothing worn in colder climates and in warmer climates.

2. **Evaluation.** Why do you think most of today's garments are fitted rather than draped?

3. **Analysis.** Compare male and female styles of the 1700s with the styles of today. Are there any similarities?

4. **Synthesis.** Summarize the evolution of modern fashion from the eighteenth century until today.

Applying Your Knowledge

1. **Draped Garments.** With another classmate, design a draped or wrapped garment using a square or rectangular piece of fabric. Demonstrate and model your design.

2. **Combination Garments.** Using catalogs and magazines, find illustrations of current fashions that are variations of the kibr, kimono, and muumuu.

3. **Fashion Babies.** Using pieces of fabrics and trims, dress a small doll in a fashion from a different time period or culture. Describe your doll to the class.

4. **History of Fashion.** Imagine that the local historical society has asked your class to plan a fashion show, "Through the Ages." Working in small groups, plan the fashions to be shown and write the script.

Making the Connection

1. **Social Studies.** On a world map, locate the various countries and areas where fibers or the clothing styles originated. Trace on the map how the various fibers and clothing styles spread to other countries.

What Is a Costume Historian?

Costume historians study the clothing worn by the members of various societies and cultures throughout history. They research clothing styles and evaluate the historical accuracy of garments in costume collections. The collections may be located at museums, universities, or historical societies. Costume historians also keep the collections in good condition and locate additional items of clothing for the collections. They select and arrange the clothing and accessories for any displays at the museum or institution.

Try It Yourself

Imagine that you are a costume historian for a local museum or historical society. Research the clothing styles worn in your region during the past century. Then select five to ten costume styles that would represent the history of fashion in your state or community. Make a colored drawing of each costume. Write a description of the garments and accessories. Select a theme for your costume "display."

Build Your Portfolio

After completing your costume "display," write a short essay about your research of clothing styles. Place a copy of the essay, along with the drawings and descriptions of the costumes, in your portfolio.

2. **Social Studies.** Research clothing styles worn in an African or Asian country. Describe what you learned about the culture from the fashions.

The Fashion Industry

After reading this chapter, you will be able to:

- *Describe some inventions that changed the way fabrics were made.*

- *Evaluate how the Industrial Revolution affected the quality, quantity, and type of clothes available to everyone.*

- *Explain how the fashion industry operates.*

Terms to Learn

- *Industrial Revolution*
- *shuttle*
- *factory*
- *wage*
- *piecework*
- *sweatshops*
- *assembly line*
- *mass-produced*
- *ready-to-wear*
- *lines*
- *fashion merchandising*
- *fashion promotion*

Take a look around you and observe what your classmates and teachers are wearing. Chances are, their clothes were made in many different countries. Some of the jeans may have been made in the United States, shirts may have made in Hong Kong, and shoes may have been made in Spain.

At one time, you could tell where a garment was made by looking at its style. Today the only way to be sure is to read the label inside the garment. Communication and technology have made it possible for the newest styles to be produced around the world.

Evolution of the Fashion Industry

Until the eighteenth century, all fabrics were handwoven and all clothes were sewn by hand. Clothes took many hours of labor to construct. Garments were highly valued and expensive. Wealthy people owned many garments; poor people owned very few. Then a Scottish inventor named James Watt developed the steam engine around 1760 and everything changed.

The Industrial Revolution

Watt's invention began what is now known as the **Industrial Revolution**. The term describes *the changes in society that resulted from the invention of power tools and machinery and the growth of factories.*

Before this time, fabric was woven on a loom by hand. Many people worked long hours to weave a limited amount of fabric. After the invention of power tools and machinery, a few people operating machines could produce many, many yards of fabric. This fabric was used to make more clothes for a greater number of people.

After the sewing machine was invented in the nineteenth century, clothes could be made even faster and cheaper. It became much harder to tell the difference between upper-, middle-, and lower-class people by looking only at their clothes. It was possible for almost everyone, rich or poor, to own more clothes.

The Industrial Revolution also had an impact on the styles of clothing that people wore. Before the Industrial Revolution, an English gentleman's clothes were as elaborate as an English lady's clothes. Both wore light colors and delicate fabrics. However, machinery in the new factories created a lot of dark and dirty smoke. Because of this, middle-class businessmen began to wear darker colors and practical fabrics.

Inventions to Produce Fabric

During the Industrial Revolution, new mechanical processes were invented for use in weaving, spinning, and knitting. The first was the flying shuttle, invented by Englishman John Kay in 1733. A **shuttle** is *an instrument that is used to weave the crosswise threads in and out, back and forth, on a loom.* Until the eighteenth century, the shuttle was moved by hand.

The flying shuttle came with two boxes, one on either side of the loom. When the weaver pulled a stick, the shuttle was released from one box and "flew" across the loom to the other box. Fabrics could now be woven faster, and they could also be made wider.

The next invention, the spinning jenny, was developed in 1767 by James Hargreaves, an Englishman who named it in honor of his wife. Until the Industrial Revolution, yarn was spun by hand on a rod or stick called a spindle. The spinning jenny had eight spindles so that eight yarns could be spun at the same time.

In 1779, the spinning mule was invented. This machine could produce as much yarn as 200 hand spinners. At the time it was invented, it was the largest machine in the world. Englishman Samuel Crompton developed it by combining many of the ideas utilized in the spinning jenny.

The textile industry began to grow in the United States, too. Cotton was already the major crop in the southern states when Eli Whitney invented the cotton gin in 1793. This machine separated the cotton fibers from the seeds. As a result, much more cotton fabric could be produced.

Inventions to Make Garments

While some people were inventing faster ways to make more fabric, others were inventing faster ways to make more garments. The tape measure, the sewing machine, and the paper pattern were invented in the eighteenth century. These inventions made ready-to-wear clothes possible and simplified home sewing.

The Tape Measure

Before the Industrial Revolution, men's clothes were made by tailors. Women's clothes were made by dressmakers or by the women themselves. Each person's measurements were taken by using strips of paper cut to size and then marked as "waist," "shoulder," "neck," and so on. There were no standard measurements or sizes.

Then someone got the bright idea of marking these strips into certain segments, or measurements, and the tape measure was invented. Now there was a universal way to record everyone's measurements. Soon people noticed that a person's chest, waist, and hips were in proportion to each other and that some combinations of measurements occurred more often than others. Using the most common combination of measurements, the concept of sizes was developed.

The Sewing Machine

The sewing machine came next. It was the result of combining the ideas and work of many inventors. In 1790, the first patent was given to Thomas Saint, an Englishman, for a machine that sewed leather.

In 1832, Walter Hunt developed a machine in his shop in New York City that incorporated two new ideas. These were the eye-pointed needle and a locking stitch.

In 1845, Elias Howe, an apprentice watchmaker from Boston, made the first practical lock-stitch machine. It had a needle with an eye near the point to hold the thread. The needle was fastened to a pivoting arm that forced the needle into the cloth. A shuttle held a small bobbin of thread underneath the fabric. The shuttle carried the under-thread through the loop of the upper-thread to form a lockstitch. This is the same type of stitching that is done by today's home sewing machines. Howe's machine could sew 250 stitches per minute. That was five times faster than the fastest hand sewer.

In 1846, Isaac M. Singer, an American, produced a machine that had a straight needle and could sew continuously. By the 1860s, large quantities of ready-made clothes were available. Although the quality was not good, the clothes were inexpensive.

Early sewing machines were operated by foot treadles. The Singer Sewing Machine Company added the first electric motor to machines in 1889.

The Paper Pattern

The paper pattern was an American invention. Very wealthy gentlemen had their shirts made by a shirtmaker. Everyone else's shirts were made at home.

A Massachusetts tailor named Ebenezer Butterick developed a paper pattern that his wife used to make his shirts. Friends and neighbors soon began to buy the patterns.

Isaac Singer developed a more sophisticated sewing machine model that could be mass produced. It led to the development of the apparel industry.

By 1865, the Buttericks had moved to New York and were selling paper patterns by mail to customers from all over the world.

In 1870, James McCall, a tailor and an author of a system for drafting patterns, began to manufacture dress patterns in New York City. For over 50 years, patterns had no printing on them. In 1921, McCalls introduced the first printed pattern, which helped to simplify home sewing.

The Development of Factories

Factories were developed to contain all of these wonderful new spinning, weaving, and sewing machines. A **factory** is *a building or group of buildings in which goods are manufactured.* The first factories were developed in Europe. They were dark, noisy, dirty, unpleasant, and overcrowded places to work. The factory worker was paid a **wage**, *a certain amount of money per hour or per day of work.* Factory owners became very rich, but factory workers stayed very poor.

The plans for all these new machines and factories were carefully guarded secrets. A man named Samuel Slater was responsible for introducing factories to the United States. In 1789, he sailed from England to the United States. Soon after he arrived here, he built a cotton mill in Rhode Island from the plans that he had memorized in England.

Many different textile factories were established in New England. Most of the first factories were located in seaport cities such as New York and Boston. Others were located near railroad lines and rivers. In 1842, the first loom especially designed for weaving silk was set up in a factory in Paterson, New Jersey. Paterson was the silk center of the world until the early 1930s.

Many of these factories were textile mills. Natural fibers such as cotton would be shipped to the mills. There the fibers would be spun and woven into fabric. Then the fabric would be cut and sewn into garments.

At first, a garment manufacturer would employ women who lived close to the textile mills to sew the garments at home. These women did **piecework**, which means *being paid so much per piece or per garment*, rather than being paid by the hour.

Soon factories were established to make garments. These factories were sometimes called **sweatshops**, because they were *dark, airless, uncomfortable, and unhealthy places to work.* Most of the workers were women and children.

The change from hand to machine sewing meant that clothing could be mass-produced in factories.

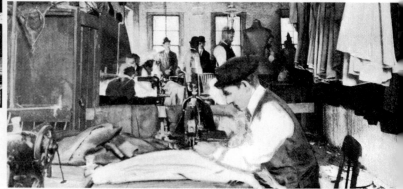

After the Civil War, people started to build textile mills and factories in the South in order to be closer to where the fibers were grown. Then the finished fabric was shipped to factories in the North to be made into garments.

In the early 1900s, Henry Ford developed the idea of the assembly line for the automobile industry. On an **assembly line**, *each worker specializes in a certain task as the product moves along a planned route*. It was soon introduced into other industries, including the garment industry.

Using the assembly line, each garment worker completes a certain part of the garment's construction. On a shirt, for example, one person may stitch the sleeve, another person may attach the collar, another may sew the buttonholes, and another person will put on the buttons. Special sewing machines can be designed for each of these separate tasks.

Almost all of today's clothes are **mass-produced**. This means that *many garments are made at the same time*. The factories where these clothes are made are located in many different cities or countries. Machines do most of the work. Hems are usually machine-made. Even buttons can be sewn on by machine. As a result, garments can be made faster and cheaper than ever before.

Marketing and Selling Clothes

Once people developed ways to make clothes faster and cheaper, they looked for ways to sell them more efficiently. People working in factories were becoming a new middle class. Merchants realized that these people had some money to spend on clothes.

There were also pioneers, miners, and sailors who needed simple, durable clothing. They could not wait for a tailor to make up a garment. Catalog and mail-order selling became a popular way to reach all these people.

The Stores

Dry goods stores were common in the days when everyone's clothes were made by tailors, dressmakers, or at home. At first, these stores sold fabric, thread, and ribbons. Then some stores began to sell the mass-produced clothing that was made in the factories.

These stores expanded and carried so much merchandise that all shirts were sold in one area, all trousers in another, and so on. By 1850, the department store was born. A large store in Boston was the first one to use special marketing techniques such as "sales" and "specials." The method spread quickly.

Ready-to-Wear

In 1825, the first men's clothing factory was established in the United States. Its specialty was making sailors' suits. Because men's clothing was easy to sew and did not change in style very often, the market for ready-to-wear for men grew very quickly. The term **ready-to-wear** means *clothing made in advance for sale to any purchaser*.

In the 1850s, women who could afford to do so were still wearing clothes made by dressmakers from expensive fabrics. Because women's fashions changed frequently and were difficult to sew, the first ready-to-wear items were simple capes and shawls. Later, garments that would not go out of fashion quickly, such as robes, underwear, and petticoats, began to be manufactured.

In the 1890s, young women who worked in factories and offices began to wear a style called the Gibson Girl look. It was named after illustrations drawn by Charles Dana Gibson, an American artist. These simple

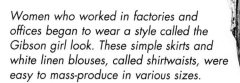

Women who worked in factories and offices began to wear a style called the Gibson girl look. These simple skirts and white linen blouses, called shirtwaists, were easy to mass-produce in various sizes.

The textile industry produces fibers and fabrics for many products. These include home furnishings, accessories, tools, sports equipment, and tea bags.

Today's Fashion Industry

The fashion industry includes anyone who is involved in the making or selling of garments and accessories. It includes textile and apparel manufacturers, as well as people from the retail and communications industries.

The Textile Industry

The textile industry is made up of fiber and fabric producers. It is one of the oldest and largest industries in America.

The largest percentage of the total fiber used in the United States goes into clothing. The remaining fibers are used for home furnishings and industrial uses. It may surprise you to learn that the covering on a tea bag, the strings on a tennis racket, the napped surface on a paint roller, and even the artificial turf on the football field are all textile products.

From Fiber to Fabric

The textile industry begins with the people who produce the fibers. Farmers grow the plants that provide the cotton fibers. Ranchers raise the sheep that provide the fleece for wool. Scientists work for chemical companies that develop and manufacture fibers. All of these fibers are eventually spun into yarns.

Mills take the yarns and convert them into fabric. Designs are dyed, printed, knitted, or woven into the fabric in endless variations. Fabrics are treated with special finishes, such as wash-and-wear or stain-repellent finishes, that increase the fabric's performance.

Finished fabric may be sold to a designer or manufacturer who cuts and sews it into finished

skirts and tailored white blouses, called *shirtwaists*, were easy to manufacture in proportioned sizes. Soon many more styles of clothing were manufactured for women. By 1900, New York City had about 475 shirtwaist factories that employed over 18,000 workers.

Computers are used throughout the textile, apparel, and merchandising industries. They can tell a machine how to weave fabric, analyze colors to dye fabric, forecast sales, and keep track of inventory.

products such as shirts, towels, curtains, or even automobile seats. Fabric is also sold to fabric stores where you can buy it by the yard and sew it into whatever you wish.

Today's Locations

For years, the South has been the center of textile manufacturing, as well as research and development. Textile mills tend to be located near small urban communities. Many of the industry's related businesses, such as design, sales, and market research, are in the Northeast. In fact, most of the major textile companies have sales and marketing offices located in or near New York City.

The Apparel Industry

The shirt you just bought because the style is really "in" this year, the special clothing you wear for playing sports, and even the gloves you wear to keep your hands warm are all products of the apparel industry. It is also known as the *garment industry* or the *rag trade*.

The "heart" of the garment industry is in New York City. Most of the major manufacturers have

design and marketing offices there. Los Angeles has become the headquarters for the garment industry on the West Coast.

Although many manufacturing facilities are located in these two urban areas, you will find individual manufacturers located in many other cities, suburbs, and small towns throughout the United States. Cities such as Chicago, Dallas, Denver, and Atlanta have developed *apparel marts*. These are special markets or centers where manufacturers have showrooms and sales offices.

Apparel marts are located in several major cities in the United States. This is the Apparel Mart in Dallas, where buyers can visit the showrooms of many manufacturers and place orders for new merchandise.

From Design to Customer

The fabric designer selects the weaves, patterns, prints, and colors for new fabrics.

2 The textile manufacturer produces the fabrics.

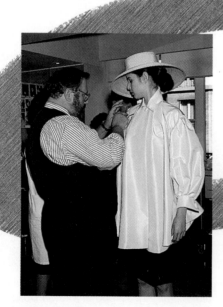

3 The apparel designer creates a new "look" by designing the shape, choosing the fabric, and adding the details.

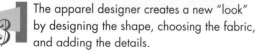

4 The sales rep shows sample garments to store buyers and takes orders.

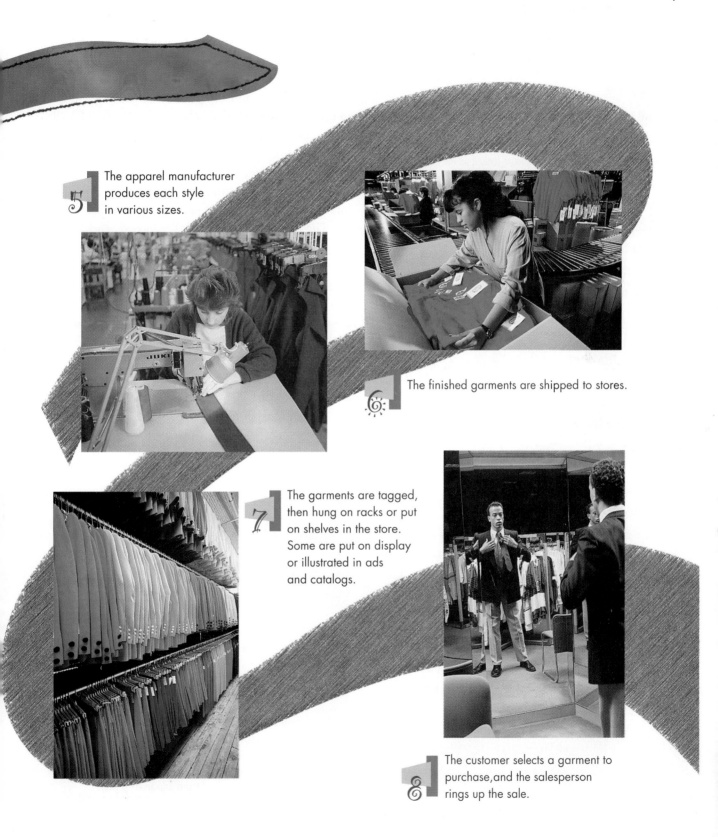

5 The apparel manufacturer produces each style in various sizes.

6 The finished garments are shipped to stores.

7 The garments are tagged, then hung on racks or put on shelves in the store. Some are put on display or illustrated in ads and catalogs.

8 The customer selects a garment to purchase, and the salesperson rings up the sale.

From Paris to Peoria

Most designers introduce their latest collections at by-invitation-only fashion shows. Until recently, only those who were invited could see how a designer's fashions looked on the models and on the runways. Everyone else had to wait until photographs of the collection appeared in the newspapers and fashion magazines.

Today the latest collections can be seen immediately after the shows have been presented:

- Computer web sites and on-line fashion magazines make it possible for consumers to download pictures from a fashion show that just took place on another continent. New "walk around" technology allows consumers to go behind the scenes to a model's fitting session. It is possible to spin the model around on the computer screen  so that the designer's clothes can be viewed from any angle.

- Cable television networks send cameras and reporters to record the fashion shows. The tapes, along with interviews with the designers, are broadcast to viewers all over the world.

- Many designers produce their own video tapes of their fashion shows. Retailers show these videos in the stores, next to the designer's clothes. The consumer can see a detailed picture of the clothes, accessories, hairstyles, and makeup that are part of the designer's current fashion "look."

How It Operates

Most manufacturers produce two **lines**, or *collections*, of clothes per year. These lines are produced at least six months ahead of a season. Clothes shown to the retail buyers and the press in the spring will be in the stores in the fall. Clothes shown in the fall will be available in the stores the following spring.

Small firms usually specialize in one or two categories of apparel in a certain price range. Large firms may produce garments under many different labels in several different price ranges.

The apparel industry is fast-paced, constantly changing, and very complex. It is also a very risky business. Ideas about what is fashionable can change very quickly from season to season and are very difficult to predict. Although some companies have been in business for many years, others go in and out of business almost overnight. Manufacturers can make a large profit one season because their line is "hot" and sells very well. If they guess incorrectly about what will sell in the next season, they could lose a great deal of money.

Many apparel manufacturers are headquartered in New York City. They have their designers and showrooms located in the garment district, centered on Seventh Avenue. Racks of garments are rolled from place to place.

The Role of the Unions

At one time, the average garment worker labored 10 to 12 hours per day, six days per week. The wages were so low that workers often took extra work home to do at night and on Sundays. Conditions in the first garment factories were so bad that workers began to organize into unions.

Labor unions were formed to obtain better working conditions, better pay, and benefits such as medical insurance, sick pay, and vacation pay for the workers. The unions worked hard to get laws passed that would give their members these things. As a result, American garment workers are among the best paid in the world. Their wages allow them to maintain an average standard of living. However, many manufacturers have chosen to have their clothes made in other countries where the cost of labor is cheaper.

Many American garment workers belong to the Union of Needletrades, Industrial, and Textile Employees (Unite). It was formed in July 1995 when the International Ladies' Garment Workers' Union (ILGWU) and the Amalgamated Clothing Workers of America (ACWA) merged. Unite now represents 355,000 garment workers. It puts a union label in every item that is made by its members. The union has sponsored an advertising campaign to remind people to look for the union label, which shows that the clothes were made in America.

Fashion Merchandising and Promotion

Goods are produced by the textile and apparel manufacturers. Then these goods are sold to the retailer who sells them to you, the customer. **Fashion merchandising** involves *all phases of buying and selling clothes and accessories.* People who work in fashion merchandising present these goods in an attractive and pleasing way. They highlight items that are very new and in fashion, or show new ways to wear familiar styles. They may work for manufacturers or retailers. The aim of fashion merchandising is to get you to buy new clothes and other fashion items.

Fashion promotion includes *all efforts made to inform people about what is new in fashion and to convince them to buy it.* These are the people who are responsible for the "look" of fashion magazines, advertisements, catalogs, and fashion shows.

A wide variety of job opportunities exist within the fashion industry. The road from fibers to fabrics to garments to stores requires many steps and millions of employees. You will learn more about the fashion industry in Unit 7, The Workplace.

Fashion malls contain a wide variety of stores that offer many different types of merchandise. Today malls have become the major retail source for many communities.

REVIEW

Summary

- The Industrial Revolution in the eighteenth century enabled fabrics and garments to be made faster and cheaper.

- Many different inventions contributed to the growth of the textile and apparel industries.

- Mass-produced clothing, or ready-to-wear, created a need for new ways to market and sell clothes.

- Today's fashion industry includes textile and apparel manufacturers, retailers, and communications specialists.

- There are many steps in the process of creating a garment, from producing the fibers to selling the finished item to a customer.

Using Vocabulary Terms

On a separate sheet of paper, write the vocabulary term that best fits the definition:

1. Clothing made in advance for sale to any purchaser.

2. Each worker specializes in a certain task as the product moves along a route.

3. The changes in society that resulted from the invention of power tools and machinery and the growth of factories.

4. Being paid so much per garment.

5. All phases of buying and selling clothes and accessories.

Recalling the Facts

1. Describe how fabrics and clothes were made before the eighteenth century.

2. How did the Industrial Revolution affect the production of fabrics and clothing?

3. Explain how each of the following inventions increased fabric production: flying shuttle, spinning jenny, and spinning mule.

4. What contribution did each of the following people make toward the development of the garment industry: Elias Howe, Isaac Singer, Ebenezer Butterick, and James McCall?

5. Where were the first textile factories located in the United States?

6. What is an assembly line?

7. How did the marketing and selling of clothes change over the years?

8. What is the major function of the textile industry and the apparel industry?

9. What was the role of the unions in the garment factories?

10. Where are the textile and apparel industries located today?

Thinking Critically

1. **Analysis.** Compare the production of fabric and clothing before and after the Industrial Revolution.

2. **Analysis.** What factors determined the location of the early textile factories?

3. **Evaluation.** What are the advantages of producing garments on an assembly line?

4. **Synthesis.** Describe the process of creating a garment, from fiber production to retail sale.

Applying Your Knowledge

1. **Textiles.** List eight to ten textile items in your home that are not clothing or home furnishings.

2. **Inventions.** Choose an inventor mentioned in the chapter and research his life. Summarize your findings for the class.

3. **Unions.** Research and write a report on the history of the ILGWU or ACWA. How did salaries, benefits, and working conditions in garment factories prior to the unions compare with those afterwards?

4. **Fashion Industry.** Working in small groups, make a lists of textile companies and apparel manufacturers that are located in your town or state. What types of jobs do they offer? Compile a class listing for future reference.

Making the Connection

1. **Social Studies.** Identify current issues, such as foreign imports, that are a concern to workers in the textile and apparel industries.

2. **Career Education.** Interview a person who works in some aspect of the fashion industry. Ask about job responsibilities, likes and dislikes, educational background, and experiences.

What is a Sewing Machine Operator?

Sewing machine operators assemble fabric pieces into garments. They operate high-speed, industrial sewing machines that are designed for specialized tasks. Each sewer handles only one or two parts of a garment, such as the seams, collar, sleeves, or zipper application. Then it is passed along to another person on the assembly line who completes the next one or two steps of the production. By the end of the assembly line, the garment is completed. Sewers who complete any hand sewing of garments are called *finishers*.

Try It Yourself

Imagine that you are a sewing machine operator on an assembly line. Using a serger or a conventional sewing machine, make several samples of various construction techniques, such as seams, hems, collars, and buttonholes. Keep a record of the time it takes to make each sample. Does your speed and accuracy improve after you have done the same task repeatedly?

Build Your Portfolio

Write a report about operating a sewing machine using assembly line techniques. Include an analysis of any differences in time and accuracy for each of your samples. What are the advantages and disadvantages of doing the same operation repeatedly? Would you want to work on an assembly line? Why or why not? Place a copy of your report, along with the construction samples, in your portfolio.

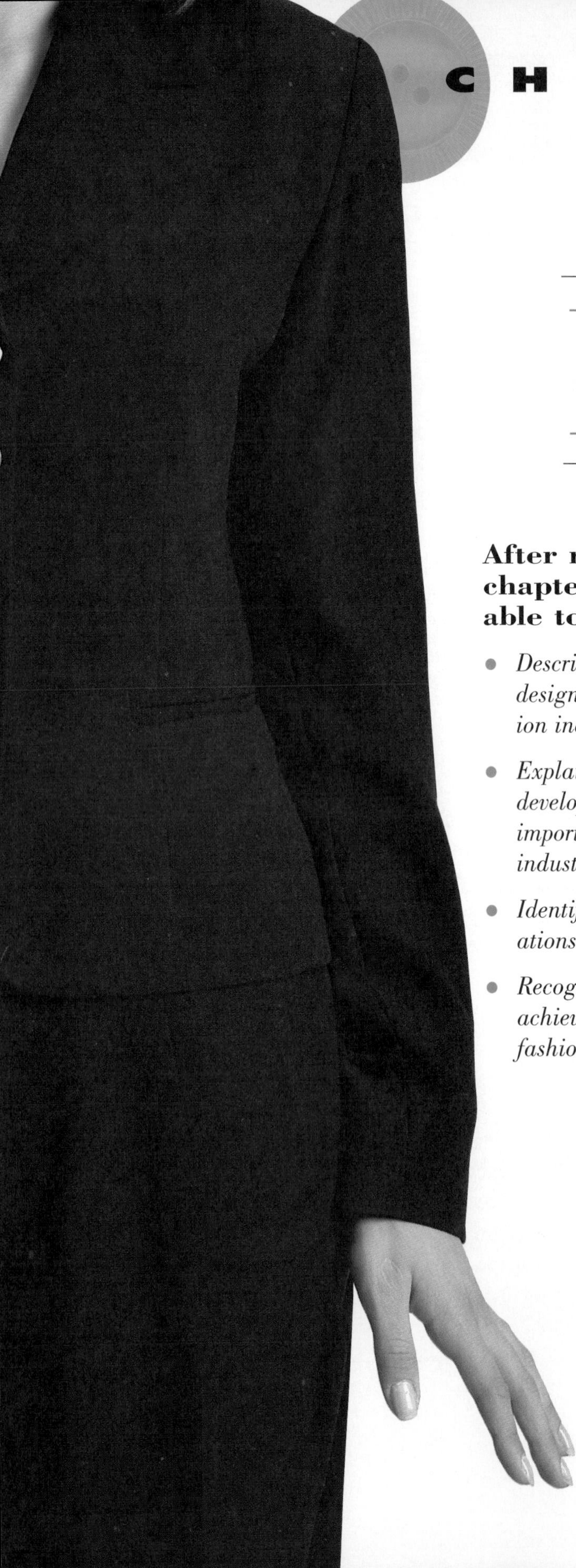

CHAPTER 8

Fashion Designers

After reading this chapter, you will be able to:

- Describe the fashion designer's role in the fashion industry.

- Explain how haute couture developed and why it is important to the fashion industry.

- Identify some trade associations and publications.

- Recognize the names and achievements of famous fashion designers.

Terms to Learn

- collection
- couture
- haute couture
- couturiers
- croquis
- draping
- atelier
- pret-a-porter
- licensing
- royalty

Many of us think of fashion designers as people who lead very glamorous lives. We imagine them surrounded by beautiful people, gorgeous fabrics, and wealthy customers. What we do not see is how hard they work.

To be successful, fashion designers must understand design principles, fabrics, and construction techniques. They must be able to come up with new ideas on a regular basis. They must also understand their *target market*—those who are likely to buy their designs. After all, if no one wants to buy a designer's clothes, the designer will soon be out of business.

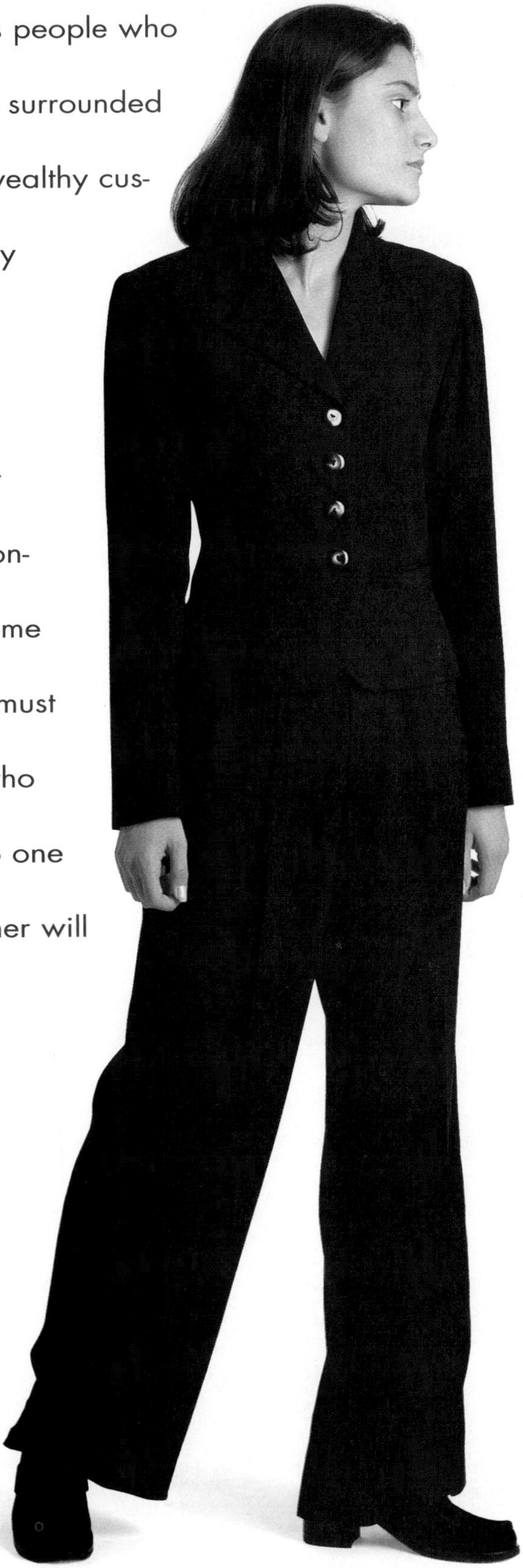

Role of Fashion Designers

A fashion designer develops original ideas for clothing or translates other people's ideas into clothing for a particular market. The designer is constantly on the lookout for new ideas. He or she is inspired by many things, such as travel, movies, theater, art exhibits, historical clothing, and the work of other designers.

Being a fashion designer is a high-pressure job. He or she works against many deadlines to develop fresh, new ideas for a collection that must please many people. A **collection** is *the clothes produced by a designer for a specific season.*

The fashion reporters must like the collection enough to write about it. The retailers must like it enough to buy the clothes for their stores. The customers must like the clothes enough to purchase them from the stores. There is a saying in the garment industry that "a designer is only as good as his or her last collection."

A designer turns out at least two collections a year, and sometimes three or four. Some designers have several lines or collections. These lines might be designed for different types of customers, such as a menswear line and a women's line. Perhaps the lines are for different price ranges, such as haute couture and ready-to-wear.

History of Haute Couture

Couture (koo-TOOR) is the French word for *dressmaking*. The dressmaking industry that creates *the most fashionable, expensive, and exclusive designer clothing* is called **haute couture** (oht koo-TOOR). The word *haute* is French for "high" and also an expression meaning high-class or fancy.

Designers create their haute couture collections for fashion-conscious customers. The clothes are original designs that are made mostly by hand and custom-fitted for each customer.

Haute couture began in Paris several hundred years ago. Do you remember the fashion babies discussed in Chapter 6? They played a role in the history of haute couture. In the 1770s, the French dressmaker Rose Bertin started sending fashion babies to London. These dolls were dressed in detailed copies of Queen Marie Antoinette's latest clothes. Dressmakers in London used these dolls to duplicate the style, the fabric, and the construction techniques of the original garments.

Other **couturiers** (koo-TOOR-ee-ays), or *designers who make fashionable, custom-made clothes,* copied this idea. They began to send dolls to potential customers around the world. Early American dressmakers studied these dolls to copy the original French designs and to learn French construction techniques. This practice continued until newspapers and fashion magazines became an important method of fashion communication.

Charles Worth was a young Englishman who started his design career in London. In 1845, he went to Paris to work for a firm that specialized in fabrics and shawls. Thirteen years later, he opened his own highly successful fashion house. He had many wealthy and important clients, including Empress

Hubert de Givenchy has been a leading French designer for many years.

influential in the fashion industry. These include New York, Milan, Rome, Florence, London, and Tokyo.

Designer Collections

At one time in haute couture fashion, each garment was specifically designed for the client who would wear it. Today a designer presents a collection of clothes. The client orders from the collection. Then the garment is custom-made to exactly fit the purchaser's measurements.

Paris has been an international fashion center for hundreds of years. Couture designers have located their businesses in "fashion houses."

Eugenie and the court of France's Second Empire. Worth was the first designer to present gowns on live models. He was the first to sell sample gowns to be copied in the United States. He was the first designer to market a perfume under his own name. Because of these and other innovations, Worth is considered the father of haute couture.

Until World War II, everything that was important in fashion started in Paris. During World War II, many of the Paris fashion houses had to close. Retailers and fashion-conscious customers in the United States began to pay more attention to talented American designers. These included Claire McCardell, Norman Norell, and Charles James. After the war, French designers such as Coco Chanel, Christian Dior, and Cristobal Balenciaga helped Paris regain its place of importance.

Today fashion designers in the United States, Italy, England, and Japan have established couture houses. As a result, many cities also have become

Most designers present two major showings of their collections a year.

Apparel Design by Computer

Computer-Aided Design (CAD) systems are rapidly changing the way apparel designers work. Traditionally the designer would create free-hand sketches of his or her designs. Then the designer or a skilled sample maker would convert these sketches into actual, three-dimensional garments. This process could take hours or even days. If the designer did not like the finished results, the process would start over again.

With a CAD system, the designer can create a three-dimensional drawing directly on the computer screen. The process begins with a *digital,* or on-screen, three-dimensional dress form. This dress form can be designed so that it corresponds to the proportions and measurements of the designer's master pattern size.

Using special computer technology, new designs are sketched directly onto the digital dress form. The dress form can be turned around so that the designer can make adjustments on the front, back, and sides of the garment. Fabric and color can be added so that the garment on the computer screen looks as close as possible to an actual sample.

If the designer wants to make changes on the original garment, it takes only a few minutes to create variations on the computer. The designer can see how different collar or neckline shapes look on the garment. He or she can also see how the garment would look in different colors or fabrics.

After the design is finalized, the computer can convert the garment design into flat pattern pieces. Seam allowances and other construction details are added. With this information, the computer can then compute how much fabric will be required to make the garment and how much it will cost to produce it.

The design process begins with the designer's idea. A *rough preliminary drawing*, called a **croquis** (kro-KEY), is prepared. Next, the fabric is draped on a live mannequin or a dress form. The process of **draping** means *arranging fabric into graceful folds or attractive lines*. Then the fabric pieces are sewn together by a sample maker and modeled by the design house's couture model. The garment may be revised many times until the designer is satisfied that it can go into the collection.

Many construction techniques are still done by hand in the *designer's workroom*, or **atelier** (at-el-YAY). The fabrics are the finest ones available. They are often one-of-a-kind fabrics that have been created exclusively for the designer. A simple dress can cost thousands of dollars. There are very few people in today's world who can afford true couture fashions.

Twice a year, couture houses in Paris present fashion shows. Retailers, the fashion press, celebrities, and wealthy private clients attend these by-invitation-only events. Similar but smaller events take place in Milan, Florence, and Rome. Fashion collections are also shown in New York, London, and Tokyo.

These shows are very elaborate events. This is where the designer can be as imaginative as possible. Some of the clothes that appear on the runway are purely fantasy. The designer includes them to attract attention and to get the fashion press to write about his or her collection.

Designer Ready-to-Wear

At one time, everyone in the fashion world eagerly awaited the Paris collections. American manufacturers would send representatives overseas to attend the fashion shows. Then the representatives would rush back to America and copy the designer originals they saw on the runways. These ready-to-wear copies were mass-produced in factories and shipped to stores as soon as possible.

In time, talented American designers began to produce expensive, ready-to-wear clothes with a distinctly American point of view. Many fashion leaders began to appear in clothes by American designers. The Paris fashion houses soon realized that they would need to find some other ways to make money. They decided to do the same thing the Americans were doing. They created their own ready-to-wear collections.

Now the French haute couture fashion houses also present two **pret-a-porter** (PRET-a-por-TAY), or *deluxe ready-to-wear*, collections per year. These clothes are more practical and are not quite as expensive as the couture line. The fabrics may not be quite as unique. There is very little, if any, hand-sewing. It is the pret-a-porter collections, as well as the other business ventures such as fragrances and accessories, that earn money for the couture fashion houses.

Today many European couture designers sell their pret-a-porter clothes in major department stores

Most department stores have special departments that feature clothing by various designers.

in the United States and other countries. Some have opened their own boutiques in New York City and other cities. These specialty stores carry the latest ready-to-wear collections of the designers. Top designers in New York, Milan, and other cities also hold showings of their ready-to-wear collections. These may be held in hotels, museums, tents, or the individual designers' showrooms. Many of these showings are sponsored by large design or industrial groups. They may last for a week or more. Retail buyers place their orders, and the press reports the new fashion directions of each designer. Thus, clothes by top American designers are sold in Paris, London, Rome, and other cities around the world.

To help promote their fashion industries, many other cities hold special fashion fairs and exhibitions. Some focus on sportswear, menswear, or children's wear. Others promote specialties such as knits, silks, tweeds, beading, or leather goods. You can find smaller fashion centers in Los Angeles, Chicago, Dallas, Montreal, Hong Kong, Madrid, Florence, Rome, and Israel. Today, talented designers of clothing and accessories can be found in cities around the world.

Today many designers have their own boutiques in major cities throughout the United States. In New York City, many boutiques are located on Madison Avenue.

Licensing

In the fashion world, **licensing** means *giving legal permission to use your name to promote a product*. In return, the person is paid a fee and *a percentage of the profits*, called a **royalty**. The licensee is the manufacturer who buys the rights to the name. The licensor is the person or company who sells the name. Common licensors include fashion designers, celebrities, sports figures, and cartoon or other fictional characters.

Fashion designers have licensed their names to everything from perfume to automobiles. Beauty products, accessories, and home furnishings are particularly popular. In some cases, the designer makes suggestions about the product and approves designs done by someone else. This is often someone who technically understands the final product better than the designer. In other cases, the designer is responsible for the actual product design.

Licensing of moderately-priced items has enabled many more customers to buy designer products. It also has become a major source of profit for fashion designers and couture houses all over the world.

Many designers have licensed their names for use on a wide variety of products.

Role of Fashion Organizations

It is important for everyone in the fashion industry to be informed about fashion trends all over the world. Trade associations and trade publications help spread information about the fashion industry.

Trade Associations

A trade association is an organization of manufacturers, designers, retailers, or other people involved in a particular industry. In the United States, there are many trade associations that have something to do with the fashion industry. These include apparel and accessory trade associations, such as the Men's Fashion Association of America (MFA). There are also retail trade associations, such as the National Retail Merchants

Some designers create commercial patterns. This enables consumers to make their own designer apparel.

Association (NRMA). The textile industry also has trade associations, such as the American Textile Manufacturers Institute (ATMI).

There is a special organization in France that represents and markets the entire couture industry. It is called the *Chambre Syndicale de la Couture Parisienne.*

In the United States, many fashion designers belong to the Council of Fashion Designers of America (CFDA). Twice a year, this group organizes a special week in New York City when designers show their new collections to retailers and to the fashion press. In 1985, the organization established the CFDA awards to recognize designers who have made special contributions to the fashion industry. Prior to the CFDA awards, the Coty American Fashion Critics' Awards were presented annually to the most creative and outstanding designers of womenswear, menswear, and accessories.

Another important group of awards are the Tommy Awards, which are sponsored by the

Fashion magazines and trade publications contain information about the fashion industry.

American Printed Fabrics Council. The Tommy Awards recognize fashion designers and manufacturers for the best printed fabrics.

Another important trade organization in the fashion industry is The Fashion Group. It is an international professional organization of women executives in fashion and related fields. Several times each year, The Fashion Group puts together special reports for its members on the American ready-to-wear collections and the European pret-a-porter and couture collections. The Fashion Group also sponsors an annual Night of Stars. This event honors people who have made important contributions to the fashion industry.

Trade Publications

A trade publication is a magazine, newspaper, newsletter, or book that prints information about one specific industry. The most important trade publication in the fashion industry is *Women's Wear Daily.* This newspaper covers all aspects of the women's fashion industry. People who are interested in the menswear and textile industry read *DNR (Daily News Record).*

The Council of Fashion Designers of America (CFDA) honored the menswear designer, Tommy Helfiger, at their 1996 awards.

Famous DESIGNERS

Callet Soeurs (French couture house, 1895–1935). Fashion house founded by three sisters and considered one of the greatest dressmaking establishments of its time; famous for delicate lace blouses, richly embroidered floral patterns, and the use of chiffon, georgette, and organdy.

Adolfo (American designer, 1929–). Born in Cuba; known for elegant knit suits that are inspired by Chanel's famous tweed suits; Nancy Reagan, as First Lady, was often photographed in Adolfo's clothes.

Giorgio Armani (Italian designer, 1936–). Known for unconstructed jackets, finely tailored menswear, and women's suits with menswear details; credited with reintroducing linen to menswear and women's wear.

Cristobal Balenciaga (French couturier, 1895–1972). Born and raised in Spain; a major influence from end of World War II until he retired in 1968; trained many other designers, including Courreges, Ungaro, and Givenchy; innovations included narrow rolled collars that are higher in front, evening gowns with a slight train, patterned hosiery in heavier fibers, and cocoon coats.

Geoffrey Beene (American designer, 1927–). Designs beautiful, couture-quality clothes; also licenses many products, including shoes, gloves, hosiery, eyewear, home furnishings, and perfume.

Bill Blass (American designer, 1922–). Known for classic sportswear in menswear fabrics, elegant mixtures of fabrics, and glamorous evening clothes; licenses many products, including automobiles and chocolates; received Coty Hall of Fame Award in 1970.

Pierre Cardin (French designer, 1922–). Born in Italy and worked for Schiaparelli and Dior before opening own couture house in 1950; first Paris couturier to sell his own ready-to-wear; first designer to license his name and once held over 500 licenses.

Bonnie Cashin (American designer, 1915–). One of the first American designers not influenced by Paris couturiers; known for comfortable country and traveling clothes, such as hooded jersey dresses, ponchos, and soft, knee-high boots; also designed costumes for the theater, ballet, and movies.

Gabrielle "Coco" Chanel (French couturiere, 1883–1971). Perhaps the most famous of all French couturiers; her many contributions include slacks for women, the classic "little black dress," and suits with boxy, collarless jackets trimmed in braid. The House of Chanel continues today under the direction of Karl Lagerfeld.

Liz Claiborne (American designer, 1930–). Born in Belgium and raised in New Orleans; designed for Johnathan Logan for sixteen years before beginning own company; known for her dresses, coordinated sportswear, and petite lines; also licenses many accessories.

Andre Courreges (French designer, 1923–). Called the "space age designer" because of his forward-looking designs made of all white fabrics and accessorized by white tights and white boots; introduced industrial zippers in clothing and jumpsuits with an astronaut look.

Oscar de la Renta (American designer, 1932–). Born in the Dominican Republic; known for elegant, feminine daywear and for evening wear that features luxurious fabrics, such as taffeta, organza, and tulle; has also designed the couture collection for the House of Balmain in Paris.

Christian Dior (French couturier, 1905–1957). In 1947, introduced "The New Look" which featured a closely fitted bodice and long, full skirt; created inner construction methods to shape dresses in the H, A, or Y silhouette. After Dior's death, Yves Saint Laurent headed the House of Dior; today it is headed by Marc Bohan.

Perry Ellis (American designer, 1940–1986). Known for young, adventurous clothes, natural fibers, neutral colors, and handknitted sweaters for men and women. After his death, the Council of Fashion Designers of America began the "Perry" award to recognize new design talent.

Mariano Fortuny (Italian designer, 1871–1949). Known for long, delicate, pleated gowns that were inspired by Greek statues; his unique pleating technique remains a mystery.

Jean-Paul Gaultier (French designer, 1952–). Began as an assistant to Pierre Cardin; designs unusual, controversial, and expensive ready-to-wear clothing for a younger market; inspired by street fashions to create overly tight garments and unisex styling.

Rudi Gernrich (American designer, 1922–1985). Known in the 1960s for daring clothes, such as topless swimsuits and see-through blouses, as well as knit minidresses and knee-high leggings patterned to match tunic tops.

Hubert de Givenchy (French designer, 1927–). Worked for several French designers, including Schiaparelli; known for simple, elegant designs that were worn by his favorite movie actress, the late Audrey Hepburn; his many licensing agreements include hosiery, eyewear, sportswear, and home furnishings.

Halston (American designer, 1932–1990). Known in the 1970s for his ultrasuede dresses and suits; popular designer for many celebrities, including Elizabeth Taylor and Liza Minelli.

Edith Head (American designer, 1899–1981). Costume designer who won eight Oscars; designed movie wardrobes for such screen stars as Grace Kelly, Mae West, Paul Newman, Robert Redford, and Elizabeth Taylor.

Charles James (American couturier, 1906–1978). Raised in Chicago but operated dressmaking salons in London and Paris; also ran a custom-order business; considered an equal by the top Paris couturiers.

Betsey Johnson (American designer, 1942–). Known for funky, youthful fashions that have a sense of humor, such as a vinyl slipdress, a dress with loose grommets at the hem, and the "Basic Betsey"—a limp, clinging T-shirt dress in many lengths.

Donna Karan (American designer, 1948–). One of the most successful designers today; has own design firm and specializes in simple, well-made sportswear; first designer to popularize the body suit; has many licensed products, including shoes, jewelry, hosiery, and eyewear; her DKNY line is a popular department in many stores.

Rei Kawakubo (Japanese designer, 1942–). Creates asymmetrical designs, often by tearing or slashing cotton, linen, or canvas fabric; her favorite colors are black and gray; shows pret-a-porter collection in Paris; operates Comme de Garcons boutiques in Japan, U.S., and Europe.

Kenzo (French designer, 1945–). Born and educated in Japan; known as a trend-setting French ready-to-wear designer; his garments are a happy combination of textures and patterns, usually based on traditional Japanese clothing.

Calvin Klein (American designer, 1942–). Famous for creating Calvin Klein jeans; designs simple, sophisticated sportswear with architectural lines; uses natural fabrics, mostly in earth tones; has created controversy over his daring advertising campaigns.

Christian Lacroix (French designer, 1951–). Opened own couture and ready-to-wear business in 1987; introduced dresses with fitted tops and short bubble skirts for a special evening look; occasionally designs costumes for the ballet and theater.

Karl Lagerfeld (French designer, 1939–). Born in Germany; designs garments under his own name and for the House of Chanel; designs furs for Fendi; designs shoes for Mario Valentino and Charles Jordan.

Ralph Lauren (American designer, 1939–). Famous for his Polo line of menswear; also designs womenswear, children's clothes, home furnishings, accessories, and cosmetics; designs are influenced by the American West and an idealized version of traditional English apparel and decor; owns his own company and many of the stores that bear his name.

Claire McCardell (American designer, 1906–1958). Considered the top all-American designer in the 1940s and 1950s; specialized in the "American Look," which were practical clothes designed for the average working woman; used sturdy fabrics such as denim, gingham, and wool jersey; introduced bareback summer dresses, bolero jackets over halter dresses, and ballet slippers as streetwear.

Mary McFadden (American designer, 1936–). Known for hand-painted tunics that are influenced by the symbols of ancient cultures; garments feature luxurious fabrics, pleating, braid and rope trim, and hand-painted silks.

Issey Miyake (Japanese designer, 1938–). Worked as an assistant to Givenchy and Geoffrey Beene; has own design business in Tokyo and also shows in Paris; his work combines Japanese fashion attitudes with the exotic fabrics that he designs.

Isaac Mizrahi (American designer, 1961–). Worked with Perry Ellis and Calvin Klein before starting own business at age 26; designs young, inventive clothes in unexpected colors and fabrics for women and men; occasionally designs costumes for the ballet. In 1995, Mizrahi was the subject of *Unzipped*, a popular movie documentary about the fashion industry.

Claude Montana (French designer, 1949–). Recognized for leather fashions, as well as bold, well-defined silhouettes and broad, exaggerated shoulders for men and women.

Norman Norrell (American designer, 1900–1972). Sometimes called "the American Balenciaga" for the precise tailoring and timeless elegance of his clothes; remembered for many designs, including trouser suits for town, slinky sequined sheaths, and sweater tops with luxurious skirts. He was the first designer elected to the Coty Hall of Fame, and was founder and president of the Council of Fashion Designers of America.

Paul Poiret (French designer, 1880–1944). Considered the father of the French fashion industry and one of the greatest designers of all time; banished the corset and introduced the hobble skirt, turbans, and kimono tunics in the early 1900s; many French artists designed his fabrics.

Mary Quant (English designer, 1934–). In the mid-1950s, London was the center of the fashion world and Quant was its most important designer; credited with starting the Mod Look, featuring miniskirts, hiphugger pants, body stockings, and hot pants; now designs for other companies.

Yves Saint Laurent (French designer, 1936—). Worked for Christian Dior and, after Dior's death, became head of the House of Dior at age 21; known for many designs, including the trapeze dress, pea jackets, Mondrian dresses, coat dresses, the safari look, and Russian-inspired designs; opened a series of pret-a-porter boutiques called *Rive Gauche*; his many licenses are often identified by the initials YSL.

Elsa Schiaparelli (French couturiere, 1890–1973). Considered one of the most creative and unconventional couturiers of the 1930s and 1940s; first to design fitted sweaters with collars, bows, and other details knitted in; introduced the color "shocking pink"; loved unusual details, such as brightly colored zippers and musical purses.

Willi Smith (American designer, 1948–1987). Started own firm, WilliWear Ltd., at age 28; designed youthful clothes for men and women in a style he described as "real clothes."

Emanuel Ungaro (French designer, 1933—). Born in France to Italian parents; worked for Balenciaga and Courreges; early designs were structured and ultramodern; known today for soft, body-conscious designs.

Valentino (Italian designer, 1932—). Shows couture collection in Rome and pret-a-porter collection in Paris; many of his clothes and accessories have his signature initial V marked in the seams or incorporated into the design.

Gianni Versace (Italian designer, 1946–1997). Designed menswear and women's wear collections under own name, as well as costumes for the opera and ballet; dressed many famous celebrities and entertainers.

Madeleine Vionnet (French couturiere, 1876—1975). Considered one of the three greatest couturiers, along with Chanel and Balenciaga, of the 20th century; famous for bias-cut dresses, handkerchief hems, cowl and halter necklines, and art deco embroideries.

Charles Frederick Worth (French couturier, 1826—1895). Known as the father of haute couture; in 1858, opened own fashion house, which remained the most important fashion house in Paris for 50 years; dressed many famous women, including Empress Eugenie of France and Empress Elizabeth of Austria; his perfume, *Je Reviens*, is still sold today.

Summary

- Fashion designers create two or more collections a year, which must appeal to retailers, reporters, and customers.

- Haute couture began in Paris several hundred years ago.

- After World War II, fashion designers established couture houses in the United States, Italy, England, and Japan.

- Couture fashions are constructed mostly by hand and are very expensive.

- Many current designers present ready-to-wear collections and license their names to products.

- Trade associations and publications provide information about the fashion industry.

Using Vocabulary Terms

On a separate piece of paper, write the vocabulary term that best fits the definition:

1. Deluxe ready-to-wear.

2. Clothes produced by a designer for a specific season.

3. Rough preliminary drawings.

4. The most fashionable, expensive, and exclusive designer clothing.

5. Giving legal permission to use your name to promote a product.

6. Designers who make fashionable, custom-made clothes.

Recalling the Facts

1. Name five things that inspire designers.

2. How many collections might a designer produce per year?

3. What does the term *haute* mean?

4. Who is considered the father of haute couture?

5. Name six major cities that are influential in the fashion industry.

6. Why are couture fashions so expensive?

7. What is the difference between a ready-to-wear collection and a couture collection?

8. What do many cities do to promote their fashion industries?

9. Why do fashion designers license their names to various products?

10. What is the most important trade publication in the fashion industry?

Thinking Critically

1. **Analysis.** What does the statement "a designer is only as good as his or her last collection" mean?

2. **Synthesis.** Describe the creation of a couture fashion for a designer's collection.

3. **Evaluation.** Which do you think is more important for a fashion house today: couture collections, ready-to-wear collections, or licensing agreements? Explain your answer.

4. **Analysis.** In what way did each of these past designers influence the fashion world: Balenciaga, Chanel, Dior, Fortuny, McCardell, Norell, and Worth?

Applying Your Knowledge

1. **Designers.** Research a famous fashion designer. Write a report about the designer's life, fashion designs, and influence. If possible, include illustrations of the designer's fashions.

2. **Fashion Designs.** Look through a high-fashion magazine for a style that would not be worn by most people. Then suggest ways that the fashion look could be modified to have greater appeal.

3. **Licensing.** Using magazines, newspapers, and visits to stores, make a list of various products that are promoted by fashion designers, celebrities, and sports figures.

4. **Trade Publication.** Read *Women's Wear Daily* and report on the designers and fashion trends that are discussed in the publication.

Making the Connection

1. **Foreign Language.** Using information in this chapter, Chapter 9, and fashion publications, make a list of French terms used in the fashion industry.

2. **Art.** Do "rough" pencil sketches of several original fashion designs.

What Is a Fashion Designer?

Fashion designers develop original ideas for clothing for a particular market. They might design women's, men's, or children's clothes. Many concentrate on a specific type of clothing such as sportswear, swimwear, lingerie, bridal gowns, or shoes. Two or more times a year, they must produce a collection of 50 to 70 items. Besides creating the actual designs they must select fabrics and trims. They also work with the sample makers, production people, and marketing people. Top designers are involved in all aspects of a fashion's creation—from searching for new ideas to establishing prices to meeting with buyers and clients.

Try It Yourself

Imagine that you are a fashion designer. Select a target market and create sketches of various garments for your "collection." For each sketch, recommend specific fabrics, trims, and colors. If possible, attach small swatches of actual fabrics and trims to the sketches. Using muslin or other inexpensive fabric, drape one of your designs on another student.

Build Your Portfolio

After creating sketches of your "collection," place copies in your portfolio. Include a description of your target market, the price range of your clothing line, and marketing suggestions. If possible, include a photo of the design that you draped on the "model."

The Language of Fashion

After reading this chapter, you will be able to:

- Identify various styles of dresses, skirts, necklines, collars, and sleeves.

- Name some shirt, pants, jacket, and coat styles that are popular for men and women.

- Explain how some styles got their names.

- Discuss how new designs can be created by changing one part of a garment, such as the length.

Terms to Learn

- *sheath*
- *shift*
- *princess*
- *cowl*
- *lapel*
- *set-in sleeve*
- *raglan sleeve*
- *kimono sleeve*
- *culottes*
- *jumpsuit*
- *blazer*
- *cardigan*

Suppose you are looking for the perfect outfit for a special occasion. You have a picture in your mind of exactly what you want it to look like. Unfortunately, you are having trouble finding it in any store. You are not very good at sketching, and you cannot find a photograph of a similar outfit. How can you explain what you are looking for?

Clothing Styles

Clothing styles change from season to season. Some changes happen because designers introduce new ideas. When Christian Dior introduced his "New Look" shortly after World War II, women stopped wearing slim, knee-length dresses almost overnight and started wearing ones with a fitted bodice and a long, very full skirt.

Other style changes happen because people get tired of wearing the same clothes the same way. For example, decorated blue jeans may be very popular one year. The next year, everyone wants to wear plain jeans.

Not every fashion detail is used by designers every season. A certain type of collar may appear on many garments one year but look out-of-date the next year. Garment parts are continually being put together in new ways. Often, new names are given to styles that have been worn in years past. For example, mid-calf pants have been known as toreador pants, pedal pushers, clam diggers, gaucho pants, capri pants, and cut-offs.

Certain styles may be popular for a long time, but the way they are worn may change from season to season. For example, a vest can be worn under a jacket or as the outer layer over a jacket. It can also be worn over a shirt or without a shirt. In the 1960s, the traditional menswear vest was an important part of the businessman's conservative three-piece suit. At the same time, denim, patchwork, and leather vests were popular items of apparel for young people who did not want to be part of the traditional establishment.

If you can recognize fashion details and terminology, you will be a more informed consumer. It is also interesting to understand the origins of many of today's common clothing styles.

As you read about the various styles and fashion details, refer to the illustrations throughout the chapter. A special dictionary of fashion terminology is located at the end of the chapter.

Dress Styles

Dresses have been the main item of female apparel in the Western hemisphere for centuries. Until the eighteenth century, a dress was called a *robe* or a *gown*.

Some dress styles have no waistline or horizontal seam. Three classic styles without waistlines are: the **sheath**, *a close-fitting dress that is shaped by darts*; the **shift**, *a loose-fitting dress*; and the **princess**, *a close-fitting, flared dress that is shaped by seams*. Additional styles without waistlines include the A-line, the tent, and the coatdress.

Other dress styles feature a bodice and skirt joined together at, above, or below the natural waistline. These styles include the empire, high-waist, dropped waist, blouson, and shirtwaist. A two-piece dress consists of a matching skirt and separate top.

- The chemise is another name for the shift. It is inspired by the dresses of the 1920s.

- The A-line dress was introduced in 1955 by Christian Dior.

- The empire style, featuring a high waistline, was named after a dress popularized by Empress Josephine of France in the early 1800s.

Neckline Styles

A neckline refers to the area around the neck and shoulders. Before the twentieth century, garments from the same period all had similar necklines. Today fashion features many different types of necklines in a season.

- The jewel neckline got its name because it is a high, round neckline that makes a good background for necklaces and pins.

- The crew neckline is a high, round neckline finished with a knit band.

- The cowl neckline is usually part of a dress or blouse that is cut on the bias to make the neckline drape better. The word **cowl** means *softly draped, hoodlike*. It was originally a hooded garment worn by monks.

Dress Styles

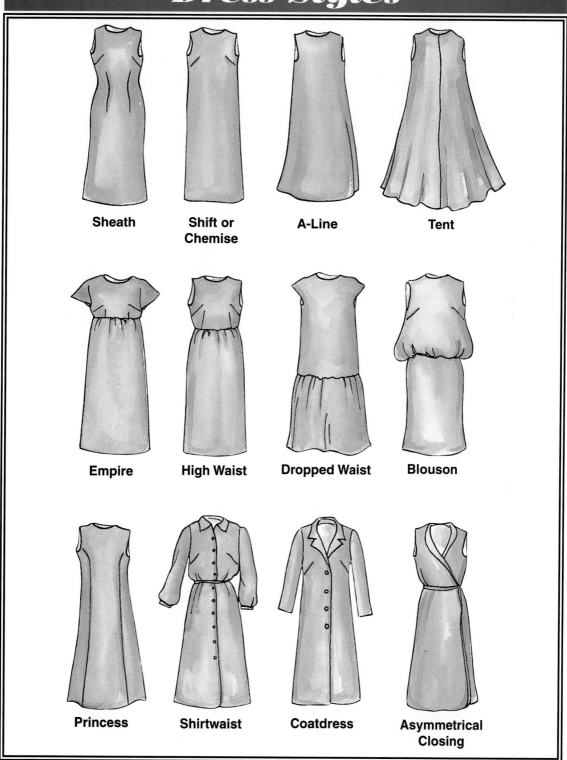

Sheath	**Shift or Chemise**	**A-Line**	**Tent**
Empire	**High Waist**	**Dropped Waist**	**Blouson**
Princess	**Shirtwaist**	**Coatdress**	**Asymmetrical Closing**

Neckline and Collar Styles

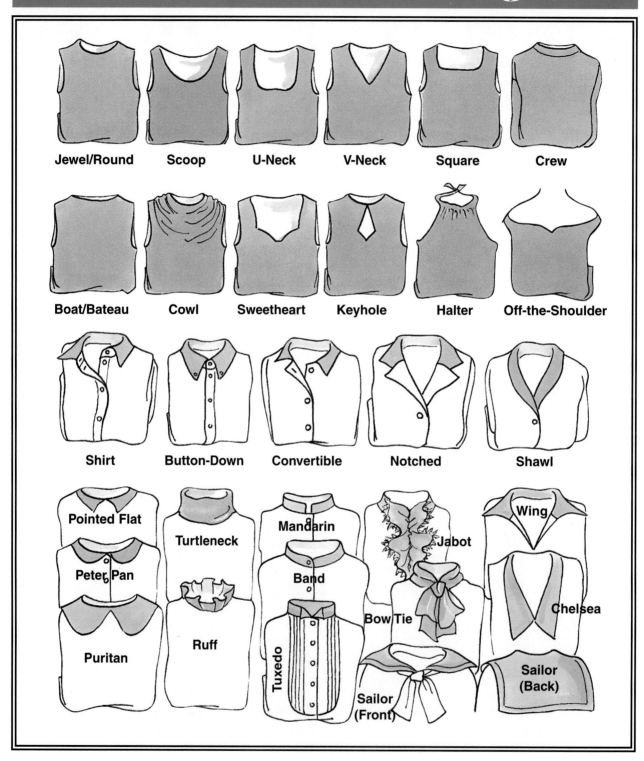

Jewel/Round   Scoop   U-Neck   V-Neck   Square   Crew

Boat/Bateau   Cowl   Sweetheart   Keyhole   Halter   Off-the-Shoulder

Shirt   Button-Down   Convertible   Notched   Shawl

Pointed Flat

Turtleneck

Mandarin

Jabot

Wing

Peter Pan

Band

Bow Tie

Chelsea

Puritan

Ruff

Tuxedo

Sailor (Front)

Sailor (Back)

- The bateau neckline's name is the French word for *boat*.

- The sweetheart neckline is moderately low and heart-shaped in the front.

- A halter neckline consists of a sleeveless front held in place at the neckline with a drawstring or a band. The shoulders and back are bare.

Collar Styles

A collar is a separate piece of fabric that is attached to the neckline of a garment. It can be small or large, stand-up or fold-over, soft or stiff. Most collars are permanently attached.

The classic collar styles include the shirt collar, the button-down collar, the convertible collar, the notched collar, and the shawl collar. Some collars are joined to a **lapel**, *the front part of a shirt or jacket that is folded back on the chest*. A lapel may have a point, such as in a notched collar. It may also be a continuous part of the collar, such as a shawl collar.

Some collars are temporarily attached with buttons, snaps, hook and loop fasteners, or basting stitches. These are called *detachable collars*. They can be removed for cleaning or to change the look of the garment.

- The Peter Pan collar is a small, flat collar with rounded corners. Its name comes from the costumes designed for the play *Peter Pan*, which was written by James M. Barrie in 1904.

- The Chelsea collar is named for the Chelsea section of London where it first became popular.

- The sailor collar is copied from the collars on a sailor's uniform. It is also called the *middy collar*.

- The tuxedo collar has turned-down points. For formal occasions, a tuxedo collar is worn with a bow tie.

- The Puritan collar is copied from the styles worn by the Puritans in the sixteenth century.

- The ruff collar has a small, stand-up ruffle. It is a softer version of the stiff, white ruffs that were worn by men and women in the late 1500s and early 1600s.

- The jabot collar is a small standing collar with a lacy, ruffled, or pleated trimming, called a *jabot*, attached at the front.

Sleeve Styles

Primitive clothing had sleeves that were cut with the garment in one piece. In the Middle Ages, the set-in sleeve became popular. Today we wear many different types of sleeves.

- A **set-in sleeve** is *joined to the garment by an armhole seam that circles the arm near the shoulder*.

- A **raglan sleeve** has *a front and back diagonal seam that extends from the neckline to the underarm*.

- A **kimono sleeve** is *cut in one piece with the front and the back of the garment*. Then it is sewn together along the outer arm and the underarm.

- A dolman sleeve is narrow at the wrist and wide at the underarm. It is a variation of the kimono sleeve.

- The puff sleeve is also called the *baby doll* sleeve. This type of set-in sleeve is popular for babies' and children's clothes.

- The leg-of-mutton sleeve was very popular in the Victorian era. It got its name because, from the side view, it looks like a leg of lamb.

- The angel sleeve is any type of long, flowing sleeve.

Shirt Styles

The term *shirt* is usually used to describe a piece of clothing that is more tailored than a blouse.

- A dress shirt is a traditional man's shirt that was originally designed to be worn with a suit and a necktie.

- A sport shirt is a casual shirt that is designed to be worn without a necktie.

- The polo shirt is a knit shirt that looks like the ones originally worn by polo players in the 1920s.

- The Hawaiian shirt is a sport shirt made from floral prints in tropical colors. It is also called an *aloha shirt*.

Sleeve Styles

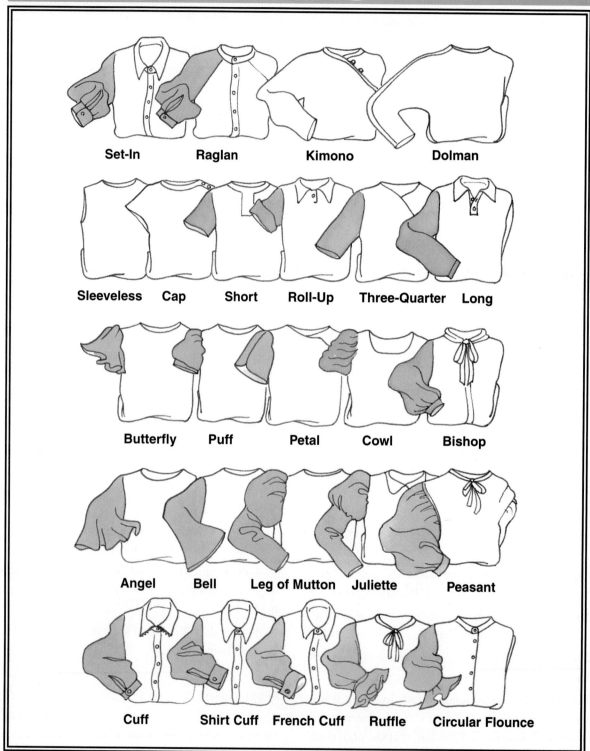

Set-In **Raglan** **Kimono** **Dolman**

Sleeveless **Cap** **Short** **Roll-Up** **Three-Quarter** **Long**

Butterfly **Puff** **Petal** **Cowl** **Bishop**

Angel **Bell** **Leg of Mutton** **Juliette** **Peasant**

Cuff **Shirt Cuff** **French Cuff** **Ruffle** **Circular Flounce**

Shirt Styles

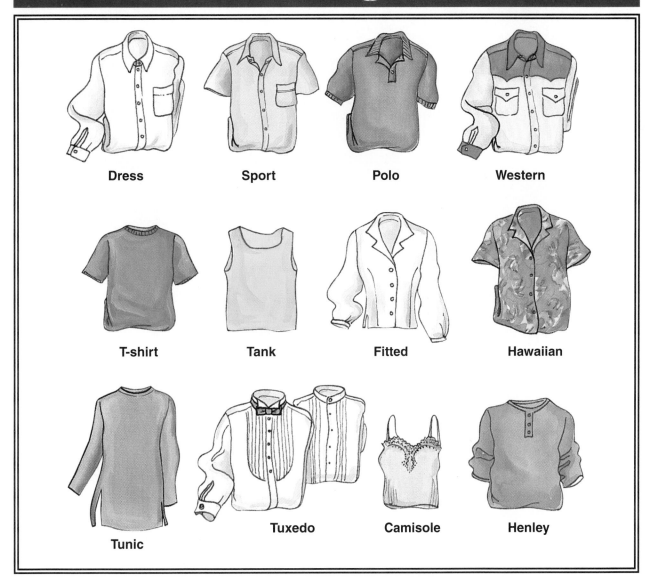

Dress　　**Sport**　　**Polo**　　**Western**

T-shirt　　**Tank**　　**Fitted**　　**Hawaiian**

Tunic　　**Tuxedo**　　**Camisole**　　**Henley**

- A tuxedo shirt has a pleated front and a small wing collar or a banded collar.

- A tank top is similar to a man's undershirt. Its name comes from the type of bathing suit that was worn in the first indoor pools. These pools were originally called *tanks*.

- A tunic is a loose-fitting top that is hip-length or longer.

Skirt Styles

Today a skirt is described as a separate piece of clothing that can be worn with any style of top. However, from medieval times until the eighteenth century, dresses were usually made with separate skirts and bodices. In the 1870s, women began to wear tailored suits with separate skirts and jackets.

Skirt Styles

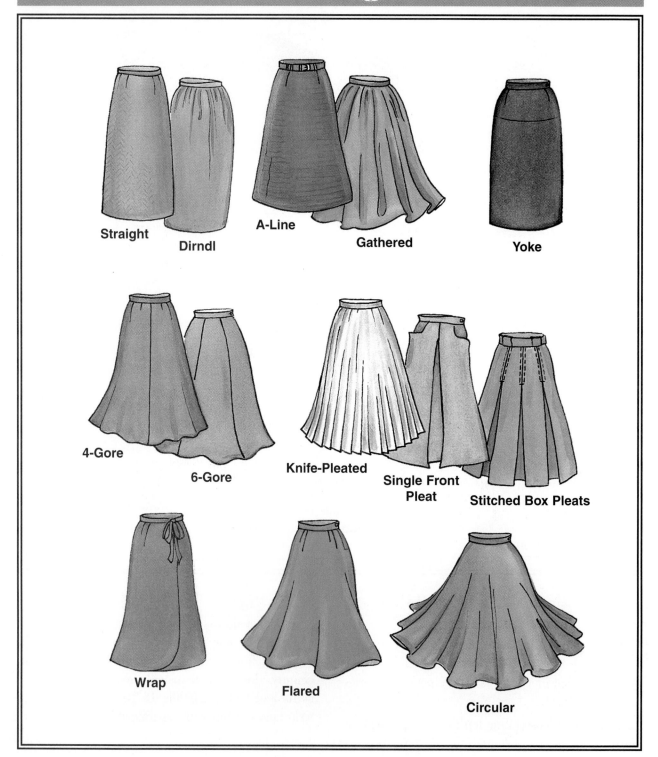

Straight

Dirndl

A-Line

Gathered

Yoke

4-Gore

6-Gore

Knife-Pleated

Single Front Pleat

Stitched Box Pleats

Wrap

Flared

Circular

Pants Styles

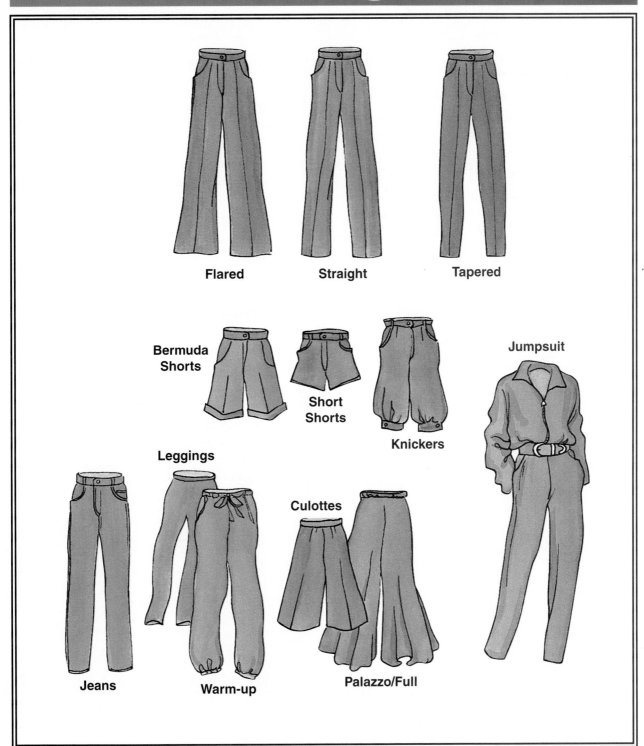

Flared

Straight

Tapered

Bermuda Shorts

Short Shorts

Knickers

Jumpsuit

Leggings

Culottes

Jeans

Warm-up

Palazzo/Full

Skirts can be straight, flared, or full. They are shaped by darts, gathers, pleats, or seams. Straight skirts often have an opening in the back seam or a pleat to allow for movement.

- A dirndl skirt is a straight skirt with extra fullness that is gathered at the waistline.

- A gored skirt is created from shaped sections, called *gores*. It fits at the waistline and flares out at the hem. The most common styles are four-gored and six-gored skirts, although it can be made from as many as twenty-four sections.

- A wrap skirt wraps around the body and fastens with buttons or ties. A kilt is a pleated wrap skirt that was originally worn by men in Scotland.

Pants Styles

In ancient times, pants were worn by Persian and Anglo-Saxon men. However, the term *pants* was not used until the late 1800s. At that time, it meant outergarments worn by men and boys. Today pants are worn by both males and females in our society.

Pants styles vary in length as well as in width. They can be short or long, full or fitted. Although the waistline usually falls at the natural waistline, it can also be higher or lower. Pants that have a close-fitting waistline at the hip, rather than the waist, are called *hiphuggers*.

- Flared pants are wider at the hem than at the knee. Those that form a wide flare from the knee down are called *bell-bottoms*.

- Straight pants are the same width from knee to hem.

- Tapered pants are narrower at the hem than at the knee.

- Bermuda shorts are above-the-knee pants named for a type of shorts worn as streetwear by men on the island of Bermuda.

- **Culottes** are *pants that are cut to look like a skirt.*

- Leggings are close-fitting knitted pants.

- Palazzo pants are long, wide culottes. They are sometimes called *pajama pants*.

- Warm-up pants are knit pants with an elastic or drawstring waist and ribbing or elastic at the ankles.

- A **jumpsuit** is a *one-piece garment that combines a bodice and pants.*

Jacket and Coat Styles

The word *coat* comes from the English word *cloak*, which was a large piece of fabric. It was wrapped around the body over other clothing to keep the wearer warm. The term *jacket* comes from the old French word *jaquette*, which means little coat. Today a jacket usually means an outer layer of clothing that is hip-length or slightly longer or shorter. A jacket can be worn as the outer layer or under a coat.

Jackets and coats can be either *single-breasted* or *double-breasted*. A single-breasted garment has one row of buttons down the center front opening. A double-breasted garment has a wider front overlap and two rows of buttons.

Single-breasted jackets have one row of buttons. Double-breasted jackets have two rows of buttons and a wider overlap

Jacket and Coat Styles

Blazer

Double-Breasted

Boxy

Fitted

Vest

Tuxedo

Cardigan

Bolero

Chanel

Safari

Bomber/
Varsity

Windbreaker

Parka

Pea

Poncho

Trench

Polo

Chesterfield

Wrap

Cape

Traditional African Fashions for Today

Traditional African garments are finding their way into contemporary fashion apparel. Here are a few of the most popular garment styles:

- **Bou bou** is a long robe. It was originally a garment worn by older women. Today French-speaking women in West Africa wear it as an everyday outfit.

- **Ad'eze** is a caftan that is draped and gathered in the front below the waist, creating a butterfly effect. The wearer's figure is concealed so it is hard to tell if she is slim or full-figured. The ad'eze was originally worn by daughters of kings. Its name comes from the Igbo word for princess.

- **Dan shiki** is a caftan originally worn by men of royal descent. The name is a variation of the Hausa expression, *Dan Sar'ki* or "Son of a King." The caftan was popularized by drummers of the Gen-gen or animal-skin talking drums. It is made from a rectangle of fabric that is sewn together at the sides, leaving deep armhole openings.

- **Agbada** is an outfit that consists of a loose-fitting, t-shaped caftan, called a *buba*, and drawstring pants, called *sokoto*. In the Yoruba language, *agbada* means "sweeping." The original version was a very full garment worn only by kings. In fact, the Hausa people call the longer type *babanriga*, which means "outfit for the father." Today the slimmed-down version is often worn by men in the sub-Sahara region of Africa.

- The **blazer** is a *classic, sold-color jacket that may be single- or double-breasted*. It was first worn in England during the 1890s. These original single-breasted blazers were deep red or red-and-white striped.

- A **cardigan** is *a collarless jacket or sweater that buttons down the front*. It is named after the 7th Earl of Cardigan, who added an extra layer of warmth to his military uniform in 1854.

- The bolero jacket is copied from the jackets worn by Spanish bullfighters.

- The tuxedo jacket is a semi-formal jacket with a satin collar. It is named after the country club in Tuxedo Park, New York, where it was first worn.

- The chesterfield coat was named after the 6th Earl of Chesterfield, who was a fashion leader in the mid-1800s. This type of coat usually has a black velvet collar.

- The trench coat is an all-purpose coat made of water-repellent fabric. It got its name because it was worn by British military officers during World War I.

- The pea coat is copied from the hip-length coats worn by sailors.

Garment Lengths

In the past, women wore all of their skirts at the same length. Until World War I, the fashionable skirt length was floor length. During the 1920s, knee-length was popular. In the 1930s, skirts fell to calf-length. During World War II, when fabric was in short supply, they rose to knee-length. In the 1960s, a variety of fashion lengths were introduced—mini, midi (mid-calf), and maxi. Since then, many different lengths have been popular at the same time.

Like skirts, pants can be all different lengths. Fashion dictates which pants styles are the most popular and how they are worn. For example, in the late 1960s and early 1970s, short shorts were called *hot pants*. Fashionable young women wore them with tights for all types of occasions. Today short shorts are worn as sportswear.

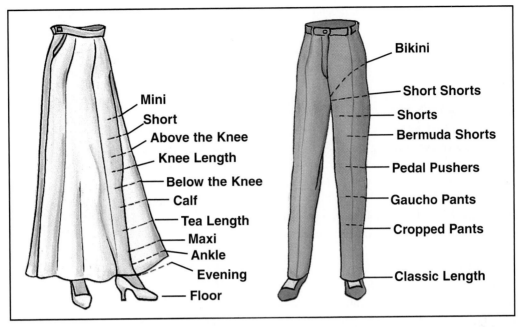

Skirts and pants can be almost any length, depending on fashion and personal preference. What lengths are currently popular in fashion?

The Vocabulary of Fashion

This list of fashion terminology includes terms used to describe the silhouettes, styles, and details of clothing design. Included are some French terms that have become part of the fashion vocabulary.

A

A-line Dress or skirt resembling the shape of an A.

appliqué (ap-luh-KAY) Fabric design that is stitched or glued to another fabric or garment.

ascot Broad neck scarf tied so one end falls over the other; originally worn at racetrack in Ascot, England.

B

bateau (ba-TOH) Wide neckline that follows curve of collar bone; French for "boat."

bell-bottom Pants that are narrow through the hips, then form a wide flare from the knee down; popular during 1960s.

bell sleeve Full sleeve, flaring at lower edge like a bell.

Bertha collar Cape-like collar that extends from neckline to over the shoulder.

bias-cut Garment made from fabric cut on the bias, usually clinging.

bishop sleeve Sleeve that is full in the lower part and held by a band at wrist.

blazer Classic solid-color jacket that may be single- or double-breasted.

blouson Bloused effect created by gathering the bodice fullness and letting it fall over the waistline seam.

bodice Portion of garment from neckline to waistline.

bolero Short jacket that is open in front and ends above waist; Spanish origin.

bomber jacket Short jacket, often leather, with collar, side pockets, cuffs, and waistband; adapted from Navy flight jacket.

box jacket Straight, loose-fitting, beltless, single- or double-breasted jacket.

bustier (boos-TEE-AY) Close-fitting, strapless top, usually with boning to give it shape.

button-down Collar with buttonholes on the points that button onto the shirt front.

C

caftan Long, robe-like garment with long sleeves.

camisole Lingerie-like top with narrow shoulder straps.

cape Outer garment without sleeves that closes at the neck and hangs over back and arms.

cap sleeve Short sleeve just covering shoulder, but not underarm.

cardigan Collarless jacket or sweater that buttons down the front.

Chanel suit Classic suit with a straight skirt and short jacket, which is often edged with braid; created by French designer Coco Chanel.

chemise (shuh-MEEZ) Dress styled like a loose slip or long undershirt; also known as a shift.

chesterfield Semi-fitted, beltless coat with flap pockets and a contrasting velvet collar.

chevron V-shaped stripes.

circular Skirt that forms a circle when laid flat; smooth across the hips and full below.

coatdress Dress with front closing that is styled like a coat.

convertible collar Collar that can be worn either buttoned at neck or open to form notched lapels.

cowl Soft, bias-cut neckline draped in the front or back of the garment.

cravat Piece of fabric or a scarf tied around the neck; forerunner of men's necktie.

crew neck Round neckline that fits close to base of neck and common on sweaters; originally on sweaters worn by rowing crews.

cropped pants Pants that end just above the ankle.

culottes Pants that look like a skirt.

cummerbund Wide sash worn around the waist.

D

detachable Removable, specifically collar, cuffs, or dickey.

dickey Detachable shirt front that gives the illusion of a blouse or turtleneck; eliminates bulk under garment.

dirndl (DURN-duhl) Skirt with a gathered waist and curved side seams that eliminate some fullness at the hips.

dolman sleeve Large sleeve cut in one piece with body of garment, tapering to fit closely at wrist.

double-breasted Front closing that overlaps enough for two rows of buttons.

dress shirt Short- or long-sleeved shirt with a collar that is usually worn with a suit and tie.

dropped shoulder Armhole seam placed around upper arm, rather than at edge of shoulder.

duffle coat Boxy, knee-length coat of coarse, sturdy fabric and fastened with wooden toggles.

dungarees Sturdy work pants with curved front pockets, front zipper, and reinforcements at stress points.

E

empire (em-PEER) Dress with high waistline placed just below the bust; originated in French empire period.

epaulet (EP-ah-let) Shoulder tab usually secured with a button; originally on military uniforms.

evening shirt Long-sleeved shirt with wing collar and starched front for formal attire; also known as a tuxedo shirt.

F

fichu (FISH-oo) Sheer triangular scarf that goes around the shoulders and is tied in front.

fitted shirt Shirt with curved seams that make it hug the body.

flap Shaped garment piece attached at only one edge.

flare Portion of garment that spreads out or widens.

flounce Wide, decorative ruffle.

fly front Garment closure that has an overlapping fold of fabric to conceal zipper or other fastening.

four-in-hand Necktie that is tied with a slipknot, allowing the ends to overlap vertically.

French cuff Double cuff formed by folding back a wide band at end of sleeve; usually fastened by a cuff link.

full-fashioned Knitted garments, such as sweaters, that are shaped by increasing or decreasing stitches.

G

gaucho pants Pants with fitted hips that flare to middle of calf at hem; inspired by South American cowboys.

godet (goh-DAY) Triangular piece of fabric inserted into lower edge of skirt for flare.

gore Tapered section of garment that is wider at lower edge.

gusset Fabric piece inserted at underarm of fitted kimono sleeve to give extra room for movement.

H

halter Sleeveless, backless bodice held by a band around neck.

harem pants Soft, full pants that are gathered above the ankle.

Hawaiian shirt Tropical print shirt with notched collar, button front, and short sleeves.

henley shirt Collarless knit shirt with three to five buttons at front neck opening; from rowing regatta in Henley, England.

hip-hugger pants Pants that sit on the hipbone rather than on the waist.

J

jabot (zha-BOH) Lacy, ruffled, or pleated trimming attached at neckline and extending down front of bodice; originally worn by men.

jeans Pants originally made of cotton denim with front and back yokes, front zipper, front and back pockets, and straight or flare leg.

jewel Simple round neckline at base of neck.

jodhpurs Riding pants that are full and loose from hip to calf, tight-fitting from calf to ankle, and worn tucked inside boots.

jogging suit Sweatshirt-styled top and loose-fitting pants gathered at waistline and ankles.

jumper Sleeveless, one-piece garment consists of low-cut bodice attached to skirt and worn over a blouse or sweater.

jumpsuit One-piece garment that combines bodice and pants; updated version of the industrial coverall.

K

keyhole Round neckline with wedge- or teardrop-shaped opening at front.

kick pleat Pleat used for ease in a narrow skirt.

kilt Short, pleated skirt with unpleated panel in front, usually plaid; originally from Scotland.

kimono sleeve Style of sleeve that is cut in one piece with bodice.

knickers Loose pants that are gathered below the knee into a snug band.

L

lapel Facing on front part of garment that folds back to form continuation of collar.

leggings Close-fitting pants, usually of knitted or stretch fabric.

leg-of-mutton Sleeve that is full and puffed from shoulder to elbow, then tightly fitted from elbow to wrist; named for triangular shape of leg of mutton.

lumberjacket Short, heavy, double-breasted jacket, usually made of wool plaid.

M

mandarin Small stand-up collar that hugs neck; Chinese origin.

middy Slip-on blouse with sailor collar, low waist, and long sleeves.

mini Hem length falling at mid-thigh.

N

Nehru jacket Straight, boxy jacket with set-in sleeves, buttoned front, and stand-up collar; popularized by Nehru, former prime minister of India.

Norfolk jacket Single-breasted, hip-length, belted jacket with patch pockets, yoke, and box pleats in front and back.

notched lapel Lapel with V-shaped space between it and the collar.

O

off-the-shoulder Neckline that extends over the arms and below the shoulder line.

overalls Loose pants with a front panel that extends over the chest and is held in place by shoulder straps; originally made in sturdy fabrics for farmers and railroad workers.

overcoat Warm, heavy coat worn over other clothing.

P

pants suit Woman's suit consisting of a jacket with coordinating pants, instead of a skirt.

parka Hooded jacket with down, fleece, or fiberfill for warmth; Inuit or Eskimo origin.

pea coat Hip-length, double-breasted jacket of heavy woolen fabric, usually navy; originally worn by sailors.

peasant sleeve Full sleeve set into a dropped shoulder and gathered onto a wristband.

pedal pushers Slim pants that end just below the knee.

peplum Flared, hip-length tier attached at waistline of a dress, blouse, or jacket.

petal Sleeve or skirt with overlapping fabric that resembles flower petals.

Peter Pan collar Flat collar with round corners; adapted from costume worn by Peter Pan in play of same name.

pinafore Sleeveless, apron-like garment worn alone or over a dress; often has ruffles at the shoulder.

placket Garment opening that is fastened with buttons, zipper, snaps, or hooks and eyes.

pleats Folds of fabric that are usually pressed or stitched in place to add fullness to a garment.

plunge Neckline that dips low in front.

polo coat Single- or double-breasted coat of camel's hair or similar fabric, often with a back belt.

polo shirt Short-sleeve knit shirt with ribbed collar and ribbed trim on sleeve.

poncho Rectangular piece of fabric with no seams and a hole in the center for the head.

princess Close-fitting, flared dress or coat that has no waistline; fit is achieved with seams instead of darts.

puff sleeve Set-in sleeve that is gathered at the shoulder for fullness.

Puritan collar Wide, flat, round collar similar to those worn by the Puritans.

push-up sleeve Close-fitting sleeve worn pushed up to, or above, the elbow rather than at its full length.

R

raglan sleeve Style of sleeve that has a diagonal seam in front and back, extending from the neckline to the underarm.

reefer Princess-styled coat that can be single- or double-breasted.

roll-up sleeve A long sleeve that is rolled to desired length, usually just above elbow.

ruff Stand-up, circular collar that is gathered or pleated; originated in Europe during sixteenth and seventeenth centuries.

S

safari jacket Lightweight jacket with lapels, four pockets, epaulets, and belt; originally worn by sportsmen on safari.

sailor collar Collar that is broad and square in back, and tapers to a V in front; originally worn by sailors.

scoop Deep neckline cut to shape of U.

set-in sleeve Style of sleeve that is stitched into a regular armhole.

shawl collar One-piece collar and lapel that curves from the back of the neck down to the front closure of a garment.

sheath Close-fitting dress with no waistline seam that is shaped by darts.

shift Loose-fitting dress with no waistline seam; also known as a chemise.

shirt cuff Cuff that fits snugly around the wrist, fastens with a button, and has a placket opening to allow the cuff to slide over the hand.

shirtwaist Dress with front closing that is styled like a man's shirt; also called a shirtdress.

shorts Pants that end anywhere from the top of the knee to the top of the thigh.

single-breasted Center front closing with one row of buttons.

ski jacket Warm but lightweight jacket with zipper front, usually made of water-repellent nylon and interlined with down or fiberfill for warmth; originally designed for skiers.

slicker Loose, waterproof coat, usually made of vinyl; originally worn by fishermen.

slit Long, narrow opening in garment.

smock Loose shirt or jacket with front and back yokes, collar, patch pockets, and cuffed sleeves.

sport jacket Man's jacket, often checked, striped, plaid, or tweed, worn over contrasting trousers.

sport shirt Short- or long-sleeved shirt worn with casual attire; can be brightly colored, patterned, or novelty fabric.

sportswear Garments meant for informal or casual wear.

spread collar Collar on a dress shirt that is not a button-down collar.

stole Long scarf wrapped around the shoulders.

suit For men: a garment consisting of a jacket, trousers, and sometimes a vest. For women: a jacket with a skirt or pants and sometimes a vest.

surplice (SUR-plis) Bodice with one side wrapping over the other side.

sweatshirt Loose, long-sleeved, collarless pullover of soft, absorbent fabric; worn during athletic activity for warmth.

sweetheart Neckline with a high back and a low-cut front with two curved edges resembling the shape of a heart.

T

T-shirt Plain, short-sleeve shirt with a crew or V-neck.

tab Small flap, usually attached to a collar or shoulder.

tail coat Men's formal coat, usually black or white, with long tails in back.

tank top Unfitted, sleeveless top with a deep U-neck.

tiered Garment made with rows of ruffles or flounces, layered one on top of another.

top coat Lightweight overcoat.

train Extended part of garment, usually a wedding dress, which trails at the back.

trench coat Raincoat, usually double-breasted, with a military collar, epaulets, pockets, belt, and a strap near the bottom of each sleeve; originally worn by English officers in World War I.

tunic Loose-fitting top that is hip-length or longer; worn over a skirt or pants.

turtleneck High turnover collar that hugs throat.

tuxedo Single- or double-breasted semi-formal jacket with a notched or shawl collar (usually satin); worn with matching trousers, evening shirt, bow tie, and cummerbund; named after country club at Tuxedo Park, NY.

V

V-neck Neckline shaped in front like the letter V.

varsity jacket Short, snap-front jacket with collar or neckband, cuffs, waistband, and slash pockets; may have sleeves of a different color and have team and player names; also called a baseball jacket.

vest Close-fitting, sleeveless garment stopping at waist or hips; can be v-neck or crew neck, buttoned front, pullover, or buttonless.

W-Y

western shirt Tapered shirt with yoke front and back, pointed collar, two patch pockets with flaps, and snap closure on front placket, pocket, and cuffs.

windbreaker Short jacket with front zipper and elastic waistband and cuffs; usually made of poplin or nylon with a water-repellent finish.

Windsor knot Wide, triangular knot for tying a four-in-hand necktie.

wing collar Stand-up collar with front edges or corners folded down; worn for formal or evening dress.

wrap Dress, skirt, or coat that wraps around the body and fastens with snaps or hidden closure; usually secured with ties or belt.

yoke Fitted portion of a garment, usually at shoulders or hips, with rest of garment hanging from it.

Knowing fashion terms will help you understand garment descriptions in ads and catalogs.

REVIEW

Summary

- Certain clothing styles may be popular for a long time, but the way they are worn may change from season to season.

- You will be a more informed consumer if you can recognize fashion terms and details.

- Classic dress styles without waistlines include the sheath, shift, and princess.

- There are many styles of necklines and collars.

- Three basic sleeve styles are the set-in sleeve, raglan sleeve, and kimono sleeve.

- Shirts can be fitted or loose, dressy or casual.

- Both skirts and pants can vary in length and amount of fullness.

- Jackets and coats can be single- or double-breasted.

Using Vocabulary Terms

On a separate piece of paper, write the vocabulary term that best fits the definition:

1. The front part of a shirt or jacket that is folded back on the chest.

2. Sleeve that is cut in one piece with the front and back of the garment.

3. Sleeve with a front and back diagonal seam extending from neckline to underarm.

4. A close-fitting dress that is shaped by darts.

5. A close-fitting, flared dress that is shaped by seams.

6. Pants that are cut to look like a skirt.

Recalling the Facts

1. Name two reasons why clothing styles change from season to season.

2. What style of dress features a high waistline?

3. What style of neckline is cut on the bias so it will drape better?

4. What is the distinguishing feature of a shawl collar?

5. Name the collar style that has turned-down points and is worn for formal occasions.

6. What is a set-in sleeve?

7. Where does the name *tank top* come from?

8. What is a gored skirt?

9. What is the difference between flared, straight, and tapered pants?

10. What is a cardigan?

Thinking Critically

1. **Analysis.** Compare the location of a waistline in various styles of dresses.

2. **Synthesis.** What geometric shapes are created by different styles of necklines?

3. **Analysis.** What styles of sleeves are currently in fashion?

4. **Evaluation.** In the past, skirt lengths were all the same. Why are so many different lengths popular today?

Applying Your Knowledge

1. **Current Styles.** Working in small groups, look through magazines and catalogs for styles of garments that are currently in fashion. Mount the illustrations on posters and label the styles.

2. **Terminology.** Go through your own wardrobe and list the various styles of your garments. How many different styles of garments, necklines, collars, and sleeves can you identify? Share your list with the class.

3. **Garment Lengths.** Different lengths of skirts and pants have had various names over the years. Looking at the illustrations on page 145, make a list of the names you are familiar with and another list of the names you do not know. Do any of the lengths have "new" fashion names?

4. **Designing.** Choose four different collar and sleeve styles. Create different styles of shirts or blouses with various combinations of the collars and sleeves. How many different designs can you create? Which ones do you prefer? Show your designs to the class.

Making the Connection

1. **Language Arts.** Look at the various clothing styles in the chapter and brainstorm "new" names for at least 10 styles.

What Is a Fashion Illustrator?

Fashion illustrators specialize in drawing clothing on the human figure. These illustrations are usually drawn in a stylized manner. For example, the figures are taller, with longer arms and legs, and have more elegant faces than real life drawings of people. Fashion illustrators must be able to indicate different types of fabrics through the use of shading and texture. Many develop a distinctive style of illustrating that helps to convey the fashion look.

Try It Yourself

Imagine that you are a fashion illustrator. Working from a magazine photo, create a stylized drawing of a fashion model. Use shading and texture to show the type of fabric and trim on the garment. If desired, sketch in some type of exotic background.

 ### Build Your Portfolio

Write a description of how you tried to stylize your fashion drawing. Do you think it is harder to create a stylized illustration or a real life drawing? Place a copy of your fashion illustration, the original photo, and the essay in your portfolio.

2. **Social Studies.** Research the clothing styles from a different time period. Write a report, using the correct terminology to describe the styles and fashion details.

Model

You may have seen her photograph in mail-order catalogs or store ads. Tanisha Jones is a professional model in a mid-size city. Says Tanisha, "Success in modeling depends on your physical appearance, persistence, and a willingness to work hard. Although few people become the high-fashion, glamorous models you read about, there are opportunities for modeling in stores, manufacturers' showrooms, and catalogs."

Education and Training

Growing up, Tanisha was always interested in fashion. She joined 4-H and learned how to sew. When she was a freshman in high school, she participated in the 4-H Dress Review. Everyone had to model an outfit that they had made. Tanisha enjoyed sewing, but she enjoyed the modeling experience even more.

During high school, Tanisha worked part-time for a small clothing store. When the store put on a fashion show for a local charity, she was asked to model. "After that," says Tanisha, "I modeled for several more charities, even though they couldn't pay me. It was great experience! The more I did it, the more comfortable I became in front of an audience. And when I couldn't model, I volunteered to be a dresser backstage. That way I got to know some of the professional models and asked them for advice."

Shortly after high school graduation, Tanisha had a few simple photos taken of herself, including a head shot. Then she made appointments at three modeling agencies. The first two turned her down, but the third one was interested in repre-

senting her. During the next year, Tanisha did some runway modeling and informal modeling for several stores. However, she continued to work part-time in the clothing store.

Finally Tanisha got the break she had been dreaming about: a chance to work as a print model for a large mail-order catalog. Slowly she began to get more and more bookings. Other assignments have included showroom modeling, fashion shows, informal modeling, and even "parts" modeling. For example, her hands and legs have been photographed for catalogs, newspaper ads, and product packaging.

Tanisha has been modeling for almost 15 years. Although she still loves it, she is beginning to think about her next career. "Most models are very young," said Tanisha. "Although there is more work now for mature models than there used to be, I'm not sure I can count on it. So I've enrolled in college part-time, and I'm taking some business courses. I'm looking forward to my next career."

Responsibilities

Before going on a interview, Tanisha tries to find out what the client is looking for so she can present herself appropriately. Her major responsibility is to make the clothes look as attractive as possible.

- **Maintain her appearance.** Tanisha is tall and slim. To maintain her size 8 figure, she takes a weekly ballet class and works out regularly at a fitness center. She watches what she eats and tries to get plenty of sleep.

- **Keep up with fashion trends.** Sometimes Tanisha works as a showroom model. For this type of job, she must supply shoes to go with the outfits and apply her own makeup.

- **Be flexible.** Most fashion photography is done six months ahead. Tanisha has posed in a bathing suit on a beach in the middle of winter and in a winter coat on a sweltering summer day. She has to create a certain "mood" for the camera in spite of the actual situation.

- **Handle rejection.** Even successful models don't always get the job. Tanisha has had to learn to be objective about her looks, without sacrificing her feelings of self-worth.

Knowledge and Skills

Tanisha views herself as a salesperson who uses the following skills and knowledge every day:

- **Communication skills**—for talking with her agency, discussing fashion looks with photographers and art directors, and promoting herself to prospective clients.

- **Creativity**—to change the way she looks through makeup, hairpieces, and body movements.

- **Math and business skills**—for keeping financial records of her earnings and expenses.

- **Relationship skills**—for being pleasant, patient, and cooperative with people who may be very demanding and difficult to get along with on the job.

"Even though I am self-employed," says Tanisha, *"I am represented by a modeling agency. It has a catalog, called a head book, which contains photos of all the people the agency represents. I must supply my own photos and pay a fee to be in this book. In addition, the agency's fee is 20 percent of what I earn on every booking."*

Art
and
Design

CHAPTER 10

Understanding Color

After reading this chapter, you will be able to:

- *Explain how colors convey different messages.*

- *Define the language of color.*

- *Develop color schemes that work well together.*

- *Choose colors that compliment your coloring and body shape.*

Terms to Learn

- *hue*
- *primary colors*
- *secondary color*
- *intermediate color*
- *complementary colors*
- *value*
- *tint*
- *shade*
- *intensity*
- *color scheme*

What would our world look like in shades of gray? Would it seem dull and depressing to you? Try to imagine sitting down to a meal with all gray food. Would you enjoy wearing clothes that were only black, white, and gray? You can visualize the change to a completely gray world when you compare a black and white movie on television to one in color.

Color definitely makes a difference in our lives. We see it in the sky, ocean, grass, and flowers. Color adds appeal to our food, clothing, homes, and schools. It attracts our attention through posters, magazines, movies, and television shows. It provides beauty, warns us of danger, and even affects our mood.

Choosing Colors for You

Color is one of the elements of design used to create clothing, artwork, furniture, toys, homes, and offices. The other elements are line, shape, space, and texture. Knowing how to use these elements can help you look your best.

Color is the design element we usually notice first. It can be bold and exciting or subdued and quiet. You can use color to accent or play down certain areas of your body. You can create illusions of height and size. Color can be used to emphasize a special feature such as the color of your eyes. Some people with blue-gray eyes appear to have very blue eyes when they wear a blue shirt. You can learn to use color to your advantage.

How do you choose the best colors for you? It is helpful to study the messages and language of color. Then you will understand how to select colors that compliment your personal coloring and body shape.

The Message of Color

Colors convey many messages. They act as symbols and communicate feelings. Some colors suggest coolness while others appear hot. Some fade into the background while others stand out. Optical tricks can even cause us to see color that is not there.

Color and Symbols

A stoplight at a busy intersection sends messages without words. Red means stop, yellow means caution, and green means go. Without these symbols traffic would quickly jam up.

Think of the colors associated with special holidays or celebrations—orange and black for Halloween, red and green for Christmas, and red, white, and blue for the Fourth of July.

Colors are also associated with the flags of different countries and the uniforms of athletic teams. What are the colors of your favorite professional football, basketball, or baseball team? What are your school colors?

Our language is rich in expressions about color. You can "see red" when you are angry, and "feel blue" when you are sad. "In the black" means that you are making a profit, while "in the red" means that you owe money. A "gray day" and "green with envy" are two more common phrases that use colors. Can you think of any others?

You can learn how to select colors that compliment your personal coloring and body shape.

Color Symbols

Colors have different symbolic meanings in different cultures. In our culture, white symbolizes innocence, faith, and purity. Baptismal outfits, first communion dresses, and bridal gowns are traditionally white. In China, brides wear red garments which symbolize joy and permanence.

Black can be sophisticated and formal in our culture. Tuxedos and velvet gowns are traditionally black. It can also represent mystery, evil, and death. A person in mourning usually wears black. However, the people of India wear white clothing to mourn the dead.

During the Roman Empire, toga colors were used to distinguish a person's career. Blue signified a philosopher, white a soothsayer, black a theologian, and green a doctor. Those of noble birth could wear purple and gold, while the lower classes wore somber colors.

At one time, the only way to get purple dye was to extract it from the glands of a mollusk that was found on the coast of Asia Minor. Because this dye was rare and difficult to obtain, it was very expensive. Wearing purple garments became the sign of a very wealthy person. In some societies, only royalty was allowed to wear purple. Over the centuries, the color purple has come to signify royalty, wealth, and power.

Each of these photos have special color messages. What do these colors suggest?

159

COLOR ILLUSIONS

Ray of light

Red
Orange
Yellow
Green
Blue
Violet

Light is the source of all color. When a ray of light passes through a glass prism, it forms a band of colors called a spectrum. The colors of the spectrum blend into each other. Each color has its own wavelength, or rate of energy. The longest wavelength produces red; the shortest, violet.

We see an object in a specific color because light is reflected from that object. When light strikes a red apple, the red wavelength is reflected; all other wavelengths are absorbed. A yellow banana reflects only the yellow wavelength. White objects reflect all wavelengths so white is the absence of color. Black is the combination of all colors because all wavelengths are absorbed.

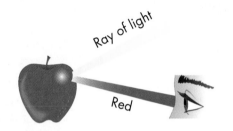

Ray of light

Red

Warm colors tend to advance and dark colors tend to recede. Glance quickly at the two circles. Which seems larger? The yellow one appears to advance and gives the illusion of being larger. However, both circles are the same size.

Complementary colors can create an afterimage. Stare at the center of the flag for about thirty seconds. Then look at a sheet of white paper. You will see an image of the flag with its proper colors.

VIBRATION
HARD TO READ

When two colors of equal brightness are used together, they seem to vibrate. Your eyes have trouble focusing because each of the colors are fighting for your eyes' attention.

Color and Temperature

Colors suggest temperatures that are associated with nature. Red, orange, and yellow look like fire and sunlight. Blue is the color of deep waters, clear skies, and ice. Green represents grassy lawns and shade trees. Violet is seen in the shadows of a cool evening or the sparkle of snow.

Such associations make us seek cool, crisp colors on a hot day. Blues, blue-violets, and greens are considered cool colors. Warm colors make us feel more comfortable in colder weather. Reds, oranges, and yellows are considered warm colors.

Designers and artists consider these qualities when choosing colors. There are usually more cool colors—blues, blue-greens, and greens—in spring and summer clothes. In fall and winter, colors turn more to warm colors—red, orange, gold, and brown.

White and black, which are neutral colors, also suggest temperatures. White reflects the sun's rays and helps to keep the wearer cool. People in warm climates generally wear white or light-colored garments. Black, on the other hand, absorbs light and heat. Dark colors are worn more frequently in the winter and in colder climates.

Color and Movement

Colors can create illusions of movement. Look around the room and notice which colors stand out. Warm colors tend to advance, or move toward you. Cool colors tend to recede, or move away from you.

This is why warm colors are used to attract attention. Yellow traffic signs and emergency vehicles are easy to see. Orange safety vests and hunters' clothing are highly visible. Red flags and flares call attention to danger zones.

Warm colors are widely used in advertising and package design. Bright reds and yellows attract your attention to product logos and labels. Next time you are in a store, notice what colors are used for product labels.

Color and Mood

You may reach for a red or yellow sweater on a dreary day to help brighten your mood. Reds, oranges, and yellows express excitement and stimulate action. They encourage us to be cheerful. Blues, greens, and violets have a subduing effect. They give a sense of calm and relaxation. These feelings and qualities are important when planning colors for a home or office, as well as for clothing.

Fast-food restaurants are decorated with bright, cheerful colors, which invite you to order and eat more food. Shades of blues and greens are used in places where a feeling of restfulness is desired. Doctors' offices and hospitals are now decorated in these colors instead of sterile white.

Color can also imply levelheadedness and confidence. The typical business suit is deep blue, which indicates professionalism. If a red tie is added, what effect might it create?

You probably have one or more favorite colors. Do you know why? Do you receive compliments when you wear it? Does it make you feel happy and cheerful?

Think about colors and how you feel about them. If you could buy a whole new wardrobe, what colors would you choose?

Colors suggest various emotions. When do you like wearing bold, bright colors or dark, dull colors?

The Language of Color

Have you ever owned a box of crayons or paints that contained more names of colors than you could remember? As a child, it was fun to use all of them and fill up a page with a truly original color mix.

Learning about color offers a challenge. remembering their names is not as important as learning how to combine them in creative, yet pleasing, color combinations.

The Color Wheel

Colors are called hues. A **hue** is *the name given to a specific color*, such as pink or green. To understand the relationship of one color to another, it is helpful to use a color wheel.

The three **primary colors** are *red, yellow, and blue*. All other colors are made from a combination of these three basic colors. The three primary colors form the points of an equal-sided triangle on the color wheel.

A **secondary color** is created by *combining equal amounts of two primary colors*. Blue and yellow make green. Red and yellow make orange. Red and blue make violet, which is often called purple.

If a *primary color is combined with a secondary color*, an **intermediate color** is created. Blue combines with green to make blue-green. Red combines with orange to make red-orange. Using the color wheel, what other intermediate colors can you make?

Complementary colors are *colors that are directly opposite each other on the color wheel*. Red and green are complementary colors. What are the other complementary colors on the color wheel?

Color Variations

On a color wheel, the colors are very bright and vivid. However, the majority of colors are not bold or intense. Most colors that you see around you are lighter, darker, or softer than the hues on the color wheel.

Value describes *the lightness or darkness of a color*. Every color has a wide range of value, from very light to very dark. For example, red can go from a very pale pink to a dark burgundy.

Value is created by adding white or black to the pure color. A **tint** is *a color combined with white*. The light pastel colors of pink, mint green, and baby blue are tints. A **shade** is *a color that is darkened by the addition of black*. Navy blue is a shade of blue, and brown is a shade of orange.

Intensity is *the brightness or dullness of a color*. Blue can be a strong vivid blue or a dull gray-blue. Both tints and shades can be bright or dull. For example, pink can be very soft and pale, or fluorescent bright.

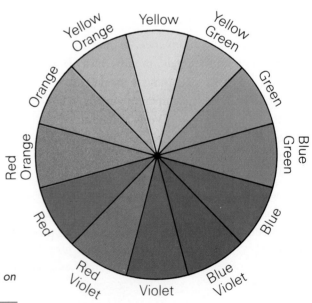

Find the primary, secondary, and intermediate colors on the color wheel.

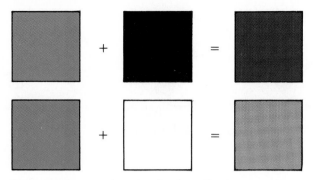

Tints are colors combined with white. Shades are colors darkened by of black.

The intensity of a color varies with the amount of color pigment in it. Bright colors are very color-intense. Colors referred to as jewel tones, such as emerald green and ruby red, are examples of high-intensity colors. Dull colors are less intense and softer. They have been dulled by adding their complementary color or black. Khaki green and beige are two examples.

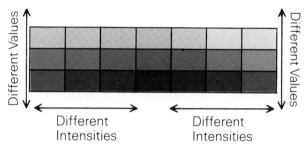

Color values range from very light to very dark. Color intensities range from very bright to very dull.

Neutral colors are those with an absence of true color pigment. They include white, black, and gray, which is the combination of white and black. Tints and shades of beige are often considered neutrals; they are not true neutrals because they have a yellow or green base.

Color Schemes

A **color scheme** is *the way you use a color or combination of colors when planning an outfit or decorating a room.* Some modern artists use a random mix of colors very successfully. However, they have an understanding of color and the subtle differences between the many values and intensities. This method does not usually work for the amateur. Instead, it is better to follow one of several time-tested color schemes as a guideline.

Monochromatic

Mono is the prefix meaning one. *Chromatic* refers to color. Thus a monochromatic color scheme uses the values and intensities of just one color.

In planning a monochromatic color scheme, you can choose values that have either a lot of contrast or very little contrast between them. For example, you might wear a pale blue shirt with navy blue slacks. This will create strong contrast between the upper and lower halves of your body. Or you might choose a sweater that is only a shade lighter than the slacks. This combination has little contrast and creates a more continuous look.

Analogous

An analogous color scheme is the use of two or more colors that are next to each other on the color wheel. For example, yellow, yellow-orange, and orange are analogous colors. A blue-green shirt with blue shorts is an outfit using analogous colors.

When using an analogous color scheme, the colors will blend better if they are close in value and intensity. Red and red-violet are more harmonious than pink and red-violet, even though pink is a tint of red. Pink and pink-lavender would mix well.

Complementary

A complementary color scheme combines colors that are direct opposites on the color wheel. Examples are red and green, and orange and blue.

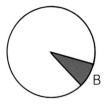

Monochromatic

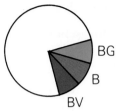

Analogous

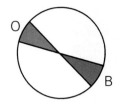

Complementary

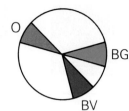

Split Complementary

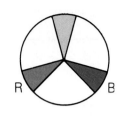

Triad

When complementary colors are used together in equal intensity, a very bold color scheme is created. The colors emphasize each other. Wearing an outfit of two bright complements will call attention to you.

A softer effect can be obtained by using different values and intensities. Try pairing up pink and forest green, instead of red and green. Choose a rust and navy plaid, instead of orange and blue.

Another method is to use one of the complementary colors as an accent. A yellow blouse with violet trim, or a red tie with a narrow green stripe are also complementary color schemes.

Split-Complementary

One color used with the two colors on either side of its direct complement make up a split-complementary color scheme. This color scheme is more common and easier to wear then a complementary color scheme. The color combinations are less bold.

You will often find a split-complementary scheme used in a plaid or print fabric. A blue and green plaid with an accent stripe of red-orange within the plaid is an example.

Triad

Three colors that are of equal distance from one another on the color wheel create a triadic color scheme. Orange, violet, and green is one example. The primary colors of red, blue, and yellow is another. A triadic color mix of bold, bright colors would be more difficult to wear than one of softer, duller colors.

Accented Neutral

Since neutrals have no color, they combine well with other hues. When a color is matched with white, black, or gray, it is considered an accented neutral color scheme. The accent color is used in smaller amounts to brighten up the neutral color.

The accent color often serves as a center of interest in an outfit. The eye is drawn to it, making it more noticeable than the other parts of the outfit. A man wearing a gray suit might accent it with a yellow tie or a blue handkerchief.

Selecting Your Best Colors

Which of the many hues of the color spectrum are for you? Do you choose the warm reds, oranges, and yellows, or the cool blues, blue-violets, and greens? Some color experts say that everyone can wear every color, as long as it is the right value and intensity.

When selecting colors for your wardrobe, consider your personal coloring and your body shape. The right values and intensities of a color will compliment your coloring and flatter your body shape.

It is always best to evaluate colors in natural light, because other types of light can alter color. For example, incandescent light might add a touch of yellow, while fluorescent light adds blue. Some light bulbs are "soft pink" and add a subtle pink tone to colors. Natural sunlight, though, reflects the true colors of an object.

Your Personal Coloring

Your personal coloring consists of the color of your skin, hair, and eyes. It becomes the basis for choosing the colors of your clothing and accessories.

Personal coloring can change. Your hair color may darken as you grow older, or you may change its color. Your skin may tan or darken in the summer.

Skin Tones

Skin tones vary widely, from pale white to cream to olive to ebony black. However, all skin tones have either yellow or blue *undertones*. These are subtle traces of color seen through the skin. To determine the color of your undertone, look at the skin on the inside of your wrist. If possible, compare it with other people's to see the difference between warm and cool undertones. Skin with a more yellow, gold, or peach cast has warm undertones. In contrast, skin with a blue or pink trace has cool undertones.

Analyzing Colors

To find out which colors look best on you, compare various colors to your personal coloring. Do this by looking in a mirror and holding colors underneath your chin. The colors can be clothing, pieces of fabric, or even colored paper. Remember to use natural daylight rather than artificial lighting if possible. Have one or more friends or relatives help you with your evaluation.

As you hold up various colors, watch for changes in your eyes and face. Does your face look more red or yellow with certain colors? If you have dark skin, do some colors make it look darker? Does the color seem to overpower you or enhance you?

A good color will accent your eyes or hair and seem to give them sparkle. Your complexion will look healthy and glowing. Your face will appear softer and any laugh lines or circles under your eyes will be less noticeable. In contrast, another color may cause your eyes to lack luster and your face to appear hard and sad. That color is not one of your best colors.

Often you need to switch colors back and forth to determine their effect. Do you look better in bright, clear colors or softer hues? Are cool colors or warm colors more flattering? For example, do you look better in clear red, blue-red, or orange-red? Is your best green an olive green, a blue-green, or a true green? Is pure white or ivory more attractive for you? Your best colors will create a healthy look for you.

Your Body Shape

Colors can create illusions about the way you look. They can be used to make you look taller or shorter, larger or smaller.

If you look at two identical size cubes, one white and one black, the black one will look smaller. Why? White reflects light and makes objects look larger. Black absorbs light and makes objects look smaller.

Size

Advancing colors can emphasize your size. If you want to look larger, choose light colors, warm colors, and bright colors. Receding colors, in contrast, can minimize your size. If you want to look smaller, choose dark shades, cool colors, and dull or soft colors. Compare two outfits in the same style, one in bright red and the other in a soft, burgundy shade. What illusion is created by each color?

You can use these color guidelines to help emphasize or camouflage certain body areas. If you want to accent your broad shoulders, what colors would you choose for a shirt or a sweater? If you want to de-emphasize your hips, would you wear a pair of white or brown pants?

Height

Wearing one or more colors that are close in value and intensity will help to make you look taller. An unbroken block of color from the neckline to the hem gives a taller illusion.

Wearing sharply contrasting colors, either in hue or in value, will make you look shorter. A bright red shirt and bright blue pants will cut your height. The same is true when you wear a light colored top with a dark shade below. The broken blocks of color create a shorter illusion.

Emphasis

Color can be used as an accent or center of interest. Wearing a collar in a contrasting color moves the center of attention away from the body and toward the face.

If you have a slim waistline, you might emphasize it by wearing a belt in a bright, contrasting color. If you want to hide your waistline, however, wear a narrow belt in the same color as your dress, skirt, or pants. Do not make it the center of attention.

Your Personality

In addition to complimenting your coloring and body shape, your best colors should make you feel good. These are colors that you like. When you wear them, you receive compliments on your appearance. Plus, it is fun to wear colors that make you feel special.

Colors can help make you look taller or shorter, larger or smaller. What illusions do these outfits create?

Use color as an accent or center of interest. This colorful scarf draws attention toward the young woman's face.

SEASONAL COLORS

One system of color analysis uses the four seasons to categorize people according to color types: Winter, Spring, Summer, Autumn. Your season is determined by the color of your skin, hair, and eyes. Seventy-five percent of all individuals have blue undertones in their skin and fall into the seasons of Winter and Summer. Note the differences in the seasonal colors, especially the greens, blues, and reds. Winter's greens are true or icy, and Summer's are blue-green. Spring has clear yellow-greens, while Autumn has both yellow-greens and earthy greens. Winters and Summers can wear blue-reds, while Springs and Autumns look best in orange-reds.

	WINTER	SUMMER	SPRING	AUTUMN
SKIN	**Blue undertones:** Fair, beige, rosy, ivory, olive, brown, black	**Blue undertones:** pale to deep rosy beige, often translucent and/or freckled	**Gold undertones:** ivory, peach, pink, medium beige, or brown	**Gold undertones:** ivory, peach, coppery beige, or golden black; often freckled
HAIR	Light to dark brown with red highlights: charcoal, black, or silver gray	Blonde, dark brown, sometimes black	Golden to strawberry blonde, or brown with gold highlights	Copper to brown to blonde with gold or red highlights; sometimes black
EYES	Deep in color with gray rims around the iris	Blue to gray to green with white flecks, soft brown, golden brown	Blue to violet to hazel with white flecks	Green to blue with aqua over gray
COLORS	Blue-based colors, clear true colors, vivid or icy colors, black, white	Soft colors with blue undertones, pastels, dusty colors	Medium to light colors with yellow undertones	Strong but dusty colors with yellow and orange undertones, earthy shades

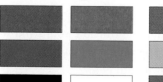

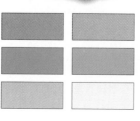
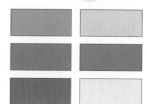

Summary

- Colors convey many messages. They act as symbols, suggest temperature and movement, and influence moods.

- The three primary colors can be combined to create all other colors, or hues. Every color has many different values and intensities.

- Color schemes help you combine colors that work well together. Some common color schemes are: monochromatic, analogous, complementary, split-complementary, triad, and accented neutral.

- When selecting your best colors, you should consider your personal coloring and your body shape.

Using Vocabulary Words

On a separate piece of paper, write the vocabulary word that best fits the definition.

1. The name given to a specific color.
2. Created by combining equal amounts of two of the primary colors.
3. The lightness or darkness of a color.
4. Colors that are combined with white.
5. Colors that are directly opposite each other on the color wheel.
6. The brightness or dullness of a color.

Recalling the Facts

1. List eight examples of colors used as symbols.
2. What are warm colors and cool colors? What moods do they express?
3. What is meant by advancing or receding colors?
4. Name the primary colors. What combinations make the secondary colors?
5. What is the relationship between tints and shades?
6. Why are some colors more intense than other colors?
7. Define the following color schemes and give an example of each: monochromatic, analogous, split-complementary, and accented neutral.
8. When choosing colors for your wardrobe, what two factors should you consider?
9. What are the two undertones that skin tones have?
10. What types of colors could you choose to make you look taller?

Thinking Critically

1. **Analysis.** Think of three different moods that could be created with color. What colors could you select to express each mood?
2. **Analysis.** Compare the visual effects of wearing the same outfit in high-intensity, bright colors and in low-intensity, dull colors.
3. **Synthesis.** What one illusion would you want to create about the way you look? How could you accomplish it with color?

4. **Evaluation.** Of all the color schemes described in the chapter, which one do you think would be the easiest to use when coordinating an outfit? Which would be the most difficult to use? Why?

Applying Your Knowledge

1. **Color Schemes.** Select four outfits in a fashion magazine or catalog that appeal to you. Identify the color scheme used for each outfit. Then describe the specific hues, values, and intensities of each color scheme.

2. **Skin Tone.** Evaluate your skin color for either blue or yellow undertones. Cut out a 2-inch (5 cm) circle from a white sheet of paper and place it over the skin of your inner lower arm. Compare your skin undertone with other classmates. Do you have cool (blue) or warm (yellow) undertones?

3. **Personal Colors.** With another classmate, evaluate your best colors. Use colored paper, swatches of fabric, or actual garments. What colors do each of you look best in? Would you be considered Winter, Summer, Spring, or Fall? Demonstrate the different effects to the class.

Making the Connection

1. **Art.** Using water-based paints, create a tint, a shade, a dulled intensity, a secondary color, and an intermediate color from a primary color.

What Is a Color Consultant?

Color consultants advise clients on the best colors to wear. They use color analysis techniques to determine which colors are most flattering for their client's personal coloring. Most provide color swatches to use as guides when shopping for clothing or fabrics.

Try It Yourself

Imagine that you are a color consultant. Analyze a friend's or family member's coloring in natural daylight. Use the chapter information and library resources on color analysis. Begin by looking for blue or yellow undertones in the skin. Drape colored fabric or paper around the person's neck and shoulders to determine which hues, values, and intensities are best.

Build Your Portfolio

After completing the color analysis, create two sets of an information packet. Include a written description of the person's coloring, the color category he or she fits in, and colors that best enhance his or her appearance. Gather small swatches of these colors and mount them on a pocket-size card for easy reference. If you wish, you may include photographs or a videotape of the color analysis session. Give one packet to your "client." Place the other in your portfolio.

2. **Science.** Color blindness, or *daltonism*, is not being able to tell all colors apart. Prepare a written or oral report on color blindness and how people can be tested for the condition.

CHAPTER 11

Understanding Design

After reading this chapter, you will be able to:

- Define the elements of design.

- Demonstrate how to use lines, shapes, and spaces to create fashion illusions.

- Describe how fabric textures and patterns can affect your appearance.

- Use the design elements and design principles to create the look you want.

Terms to Learn

- *elements of design*
- *line*
- *shape*
- *space*
- *texture*
- *silhouette*
- *principles of design*
- *balance*
- *proportion*
- *emphasis*
- *rhythm*
- *harmony*

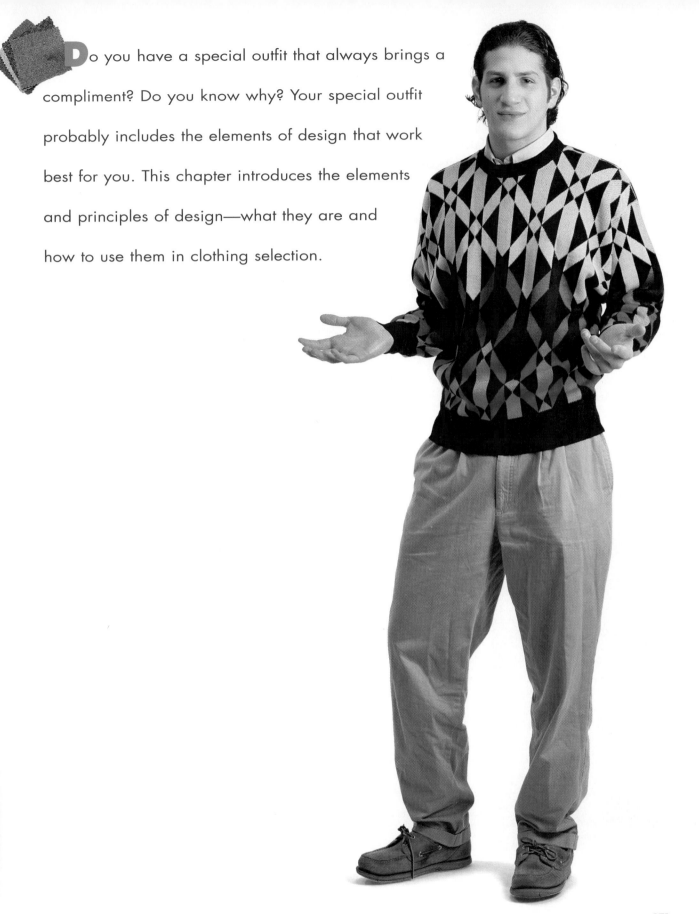

Do you have a special outfit that always brings a compliment? Do you know why? Your special outfit probably includes the elements of design that work best for you. This chapter introduces the elements and principles of design—what they are and how to use them in clothing selection.

The Elements of Design

If a designer studied in Europe or Japan, he or she learned the same language of design as someone who studied in the United States. Artists, architects, interior designers, and fashion designers all use the same basic ingredients to put together their creations.

These building blocks are called the **elements of design**. They include *line, shape, space, texture, and color*. Designers learn how to combine the elements of design within an object to create a finished project.

• A **line** is *a series of points connected together to form a narrow path*. You may have studied "lines" in a math class. Lines divide areas into shapes and spaces.

Describe each of the design elements in this outfit: line, shape, space, texture, and color.

• **Shape** is *the outline, or silhouette, of an object*. Look at the objects around you—they all have an outer shape. What is the shape of your classroom chalkboard, your living room sofa, and your pants or skirt?

• **Space** is *the area inside the shape, or outline, of an object*. It may be divided by lines. How many panels is the chalkboard divided into? How many cushions are on the sofa? How do the seams of your pants break up its space?

• **Texture** is *the surface characteristics, or feel, of an object*. The chalkboard feels hard and smooth. Your sofa may be soft and nubby. Touch the fabric of your clothing. Does it feel soft or crisp, smooth or fuzzy?

• **Color** is *the hue, value and intensity of the light reflected by an object*. You learned about the importance of color in the preceding chapter. Now let's look at the other elements of design.

Understanding Line

Line is the most basic element of design because it divides areas into shapes and spaces. Line can also give direction, or a feeling of movement, to a design. Individual lines can be straight or curved.

Straight Lines

Straight lines are divided into three types: vertical, horizontal, or diagonal.

• *Vertical lines* go up and down on a garment. They generally give you a taller, more slender look. They have a feeling of strength, dignity, and formality.

• *Horizontal lines* go across on a garment. They can give a shorter, wider look. They tend to create a feeling of stability and restfulness. However, the spacing and width of horizontal lines can affect the feeling they create.

• *Diagonal lines* move at an angle on a garment. They add movement and excitement to clothing. The effect of diagonal lines depends upon whether the lines slant in a more vertical or horizontal direction. Zigzag diagonal lines create the most excitement.

Straight lines can also suggest a certain style. Such lines have a crisp look and are usually used in classic or conservative designs. Most men's and women's business suits have crisp vertical and horizontal lines at the shoulders, sleeves, pockets, cuffs, and hems.

Diagonal lines are dramatic and more trendy in nature. They are often seen in high-fashion clothes and sportswear.

Curved Lines

Curved lines can be circular or gently waved. They can move in a vertical, horizontal, or diagonal direction.

Curved lines add softness and roundness to a garment. They also create a more casual image. A western-style shirt with a curved seam across the chest and back has a more casual look than a tailored shirt.

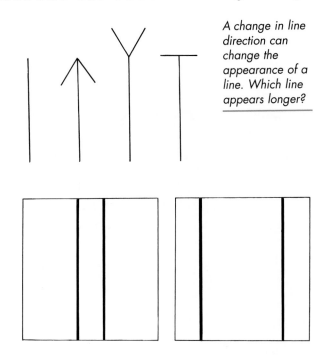

A change in line direction can change the appearance of a line. Which line appears longer?

A change in the location of lines can change the apparent size of an area.

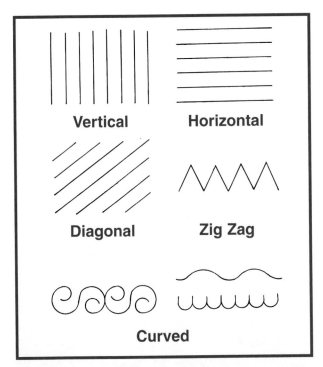

Lines can be straight or curved. They can go in many different directions in clothing.

Lines and Illusions

Illusions can make things appear quite differently than they actually are. In fashion design, illusions cannot make people disappear, but they do create a bit of magic. You can use them to emphasize, minimize, or camouflage your body shape.

In order to create positive illusions with lines, you must understand how they work. Look at the illusions shown above. These are created by the direction in which the eye moves when looking at the lines and the shapes created.

How can you use optical illusions in fashion? Our eyes naturally follow the dominant line. In a garment, this line may be a center seam, a waistline, a curved neckline, or a bold stripe. Whatever it is, it will have the most influence on the total look of a garment or outfit.

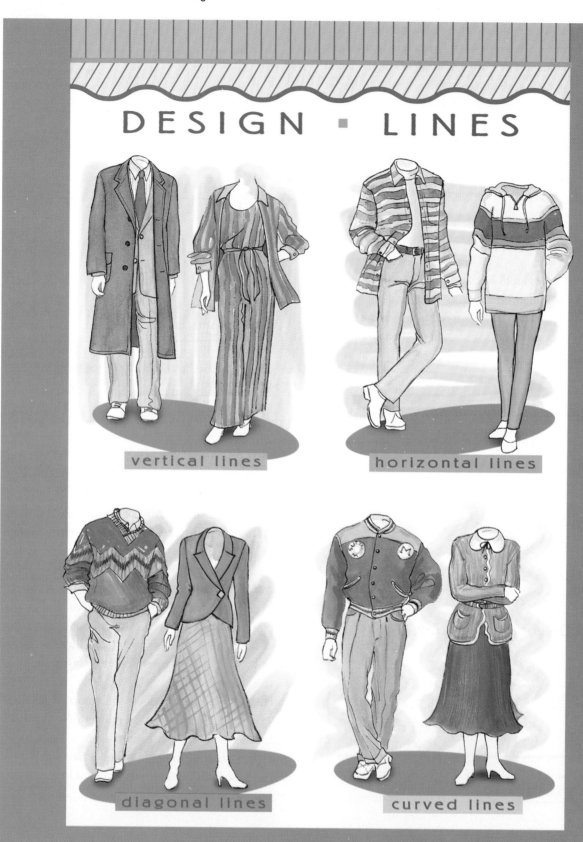

DESIGN · LINES

vertical lines

horizontal lines

diagonal lines

curved lines

Vertical lines lead the eyes up and down. They create the illusion of more height and less width. Thus, you can use vertical lines to create a taller, thinner look. To do this, keep the lines long and unbroken. Narrow panels, raised collars, and V necklines emphasize the vertical look.

Horizontal lines move the eyes from side to side. They give the illusion of more width and less height. For a shorter, wider look, use horizontal lines. They can add width to shoulders, chest, or hips. Wide collars, full sleeves, and large pockets help to widen the effect. Two-piece outfits and contrasting belts also cut the body with a horizontal line.

In some instances, the thickness of the lines and the amount of space between the lines affect the illusion. Widely spaced vertical stripes may give the impression of added width. The eye moves sideways across the lines. With widely spaced horizontal stripes, the eye moves up and down instead of sideways.

Vertical lines give an illusion of height. Horizontal lines give one of width.

Fashion Shapes

Study the **silhouettes**, or *outer shapes*, of your classmates' clothing. If you cannot see the shapes quickly, try squinting at them. When you squint at an object, you can see its outline or shape more easily. How many different garment shapes can you identify? Is one shape more common than the others?

Are any classmates wearing skirts or pants that are straight and narrow, flaring and bell-shaped, or full and rounded? Can you tell where their actual waistlines are?

Most clothes are one of four basic shapes: natural, tubular, bell, or full.

- The *natural shape* is one that follows your body's outline. Clothes of this shape are close to the body and emphasize your natural waistline. This shape is the most classic.

- The *tubular shape* is rectangular with vertical emphasis. The dominant lines go up and down. Usually the waistline is not defined. A T-shirt dress, straight-leg pants, and a tailored business suit are examples of tubular shapes.

- The *bell shape* combines both vertical and horizontal lines in a silhouette. A-line skirts and dresses, flared pants and jackets, and capes are all bell shapes.

- *Full shapes* have more horizontal and curved lines than do the other shapes. Gathered skirts and dresses, full sleeves, and pants with wide legs are examples of full shapes.

Fashion trends influence which shapes are in style during a fashion season. Usually silhouettes change gradually from year to year, but occasionally a whole new shape is introduced by fashion designers. Styles may suddenly swing from full to tubular if a "new look" is promoted by designers, magazines, or stores.

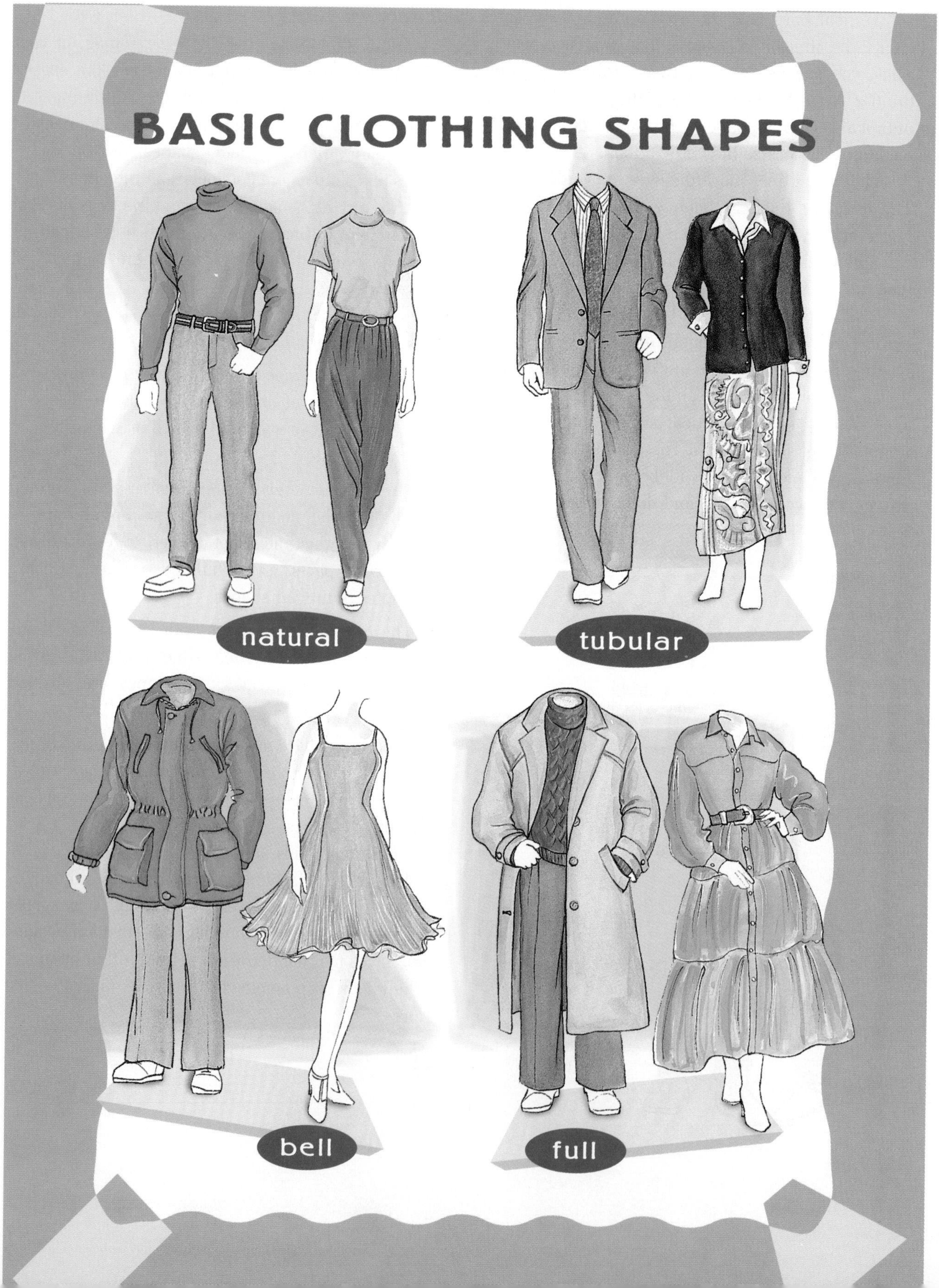

BASIC CLOTHING SHAPES

natural

tubular

bell

full

Filling in a Silhouette

Silhouette is the outer shape or outline of a garment.

Structural lines are formed by sewing the different parts of a garment together. They include seams, darts, tucks, gathers, pleats, necklines, armholes, waistlines, and hems.

Decorative lines are created by adding trims, such as braid, edgings, lace, and buttons, to a garment.

Fashion Spaces

The area inside the shape of your garment is just as important as the silhouette. The lines created within this area by seams and trims divide your garment and you into inner spaces.

These internal lines can be either structural or decorative. Both can create strong illusions. The bolder the lines are, the more emphasis they will create. When choosing a garment to buy or sew, be sure to note where the structural and decorative lines fall on your body.

For example, pants or skirts with a fitted yoke will emphasize your hipline. Do you want emphasis here? Usually, the fewer the lines within a garment, the less attention they will attract. You can use lines, shapes, and spaces to create the illusions and effects that you want.

Fabric Texture

Fabric selection plays an important role in the final look of a garment. Imagine a favorite shirt. How would it look if it was made of a heavy wool plaid, a crisp striped cotton, a soft nubby knit, or a shiny satin? Each result would be totally different!

All of those fabrics differ in one important characteristic—texture. Just as color and line can create different illusions, so also texture can make you look taller, shorter, larger, or smaller.

Textures and Illusions

The texture of a fabric is caused by the type of its fiber, yarn, construction, and finish. The texture determines how the fabric feels, looks, and moves when it is worn. Fabric texture can be soft or crisp, smooth or nubby, and dull or shiny. Each texture creates a different impression.

Fabrics by Computer

From the design process to the actual knitting and weaving, computers have changed the way the textile industry operates. Design and production steps that once took many weeks now take only hours with the aid of computers.

Before Computer-Aided-Design (CAD) systems, the design process was time-consuming. First, a new fabric design was carefully drawn on graph paper. Next, a sample was hand-woven. If the designer wanted to change the colors, yarns, or weaving pattern, a new sample would be created.

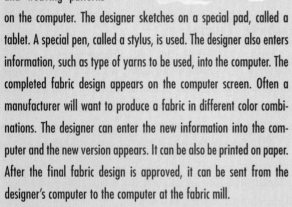

Today a fabric designer can experiment with changes in colors, yarns, and weaving patterns on the computer. The designer sketches on a special pad, called a tablet. A special pen, called a stylus, is used. The designer also enters information, such as type of yarns to be used, into the computer. The completed fabric design appears on the computer screen. Often a manufacturer will want to produce a fabric in different color combinations. The designer can enter the new information into the computer and the new version appears. It can be also be printed on paper. After the final fabric design is approved, it can be sent from the designer's computer to the computer at the fabric mill.

Some advanced CAD systems can duplicate up to 16 million colors. Special equipment analyzes an existing color and identifies the formula for reproducing that color in a variety of yarns and fabrics.

Computers can also determine how much it will cost to produce each version of a fabric. They can estimate the quantities of raw materials, such as yarns and dye, that will be needed to produce the desired amount of finished fabric

- *Soft or clingy fabrics*, such as jersey and chiffon, hug the body and emphasize any figure irregularities. However, when draped into soft silhouettes, these fabrics can be very flattering to most body shapes.

- *Moderately crisp or stiff fabrics*, such as corduroy and denim, stand away from the body just enough to conceal figure faults.

- *Extra-crisp fabrics*, such as taffeta and vinyl, may create a stiff-outer shell and make the body seem larger.

- *Smooth fabrics* with a dull finish do not seem to create illusions about size and shape. Some examples of smooth fabrics are flannel, broadcloth, gabardine, and wool jersey.

- *Nubby or bulky fabrics* add dimension and can make you appear larger. Fabrics such as widewale corduroy, mohair, and heavy tweeds look best on a slim to average figure of medium to tall height.

- *Dull fabrics* absorb light and tend to make a figure look smaller. Flannel, denim, and gingham all have dull surfaces.

- *Shiny fabrics* reflect light and give an impression of added size. Some shiny fabrics are satin, polished cotton, nylon, and vinyl. Sequined and metallic fabrics also have shiny surfaces.

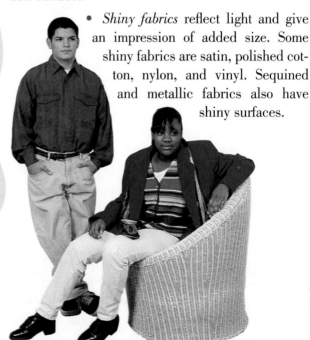

Look closely at the clothing worn by these young people. How many different textures can you name?

Fabric Patterns

Large Print

Small Print

Subtle Print

Vivid Print

Large Plaid

Small Plaid

What illusions do these fabric patterns create? Which would be best for a small person?

Fabric texture can also help create different moods. Rough, bulky fabrics give a more casual appearance. Delicate and glittery fabrics look more formal. However, do not be afraid to mix textures within an outfit. Years ago, fashion had "rules" about mixing different types of fabrics. Today all types of combinations are possible from velveteen and tweed, to denim and satin.

Fabric Patterns

Pattern designs on fabric are created by color, lines, shapes, and spaces. They come in an endless variety—stripes, plaids, geometrics, florals, scenics, borders, and many others. The designs can be large or small, even or uneven, light or dark, spaced or clustered, muted or bold. All will affect how a fabric will look on you.

Fabric patterns, just like fabric texture, can create illusions in design. Small prints in subdued colors usually decrease apparent size. Large, overall designs increase size. Widely spaced motifs will also make you seem larger. Prints with large curves give a feeling of added roundness and size.

When selecting striped or plaid fabrics, follow the basic theory of line and illusion. Identify the dominant stripe of the fabric. If you cannot identify it easily, try the squint test. As you squint at the fabric, note which stripe you see first. This will be the dominant one. Placement of this stripe is important. How will it divide up the space within your garment? Is it vertical, horizontal, or diagonal?

Where on the body do the stripes fall? For example, a bold horizontal stripe across the hipline or waistline will make either look larger. What happens when the stripes meet at the seams? Do they match horizontally or vertically? Do they *chevron*, or form angles, at the seams?

Select prints, stripes, and plaids that are *in scale*, or in proportional size, with your own body size. Small designs look best on the small to average person, but they look out of place and lost on a large figure. On the other hand, large designs are best worn by the average to tall person as these designs can overwhelm a small figure.

179

The Principles of Design

How can you successfully combine all of the elements of design—line, shape, space, texture, and color—in clothes so they will look good on you? The **principles of design** are *artistic guidelines for using the various design elements within a garment*. These principles include balance, proportion, emphasis, rhythm, and harmony.

Balance

Balance is *how the internal spaces of a shape work together*. The area of a design may be broken up by structural lines, trims, fabric pattern, texture, or color. Balance can be symmetrical or asymmetrical.

• *Symmetrical balance* is the division of space within a garment into equal parts. A simple skirt with a center front seam is an example of symmetrical balance. Another example is a simple shirt with a center front closing. Both the left front and the right front of each garment are the same. Symmetrical balance usually has a more formal or tailored look.

• *Asymmetrical balance* is the unequal division of space within a garment. A wrap skirt that has an off-center opening is an example of asymmetrical balance. A shirt with a bold pocket design on only one side is another example. Although the space is divided unequally, it can be balanced by adding design details, color, or accessories to the other section. Asymmetrical balance has an informal or exciting look.

Proportion

Proportion is *the size relationship of each of the internal spaces within a garment to one another and to the total look*. The most pleasing proportions are those that are unequal. For example, a garment split exactly in half by a belt or horizontal seam is usually less attractive than one that is divided unevenly.

Clothing should also be in proportion or scale to your own size. If you are short or small-framed, avoid large, overpowering details such as wide lapels and collars or huge pockets and bows. If you are tall or large-framed, avoid tiny details. If the parts do not relate well to one another or to yourself, they are said to be *out of proportion*.

Balance

Which outfits show symmetrical and asymmetrical balance?

Proportion

How do the different jacket lengths affect the proportion of this outfit?

The selection of accessories also involves an understanding of proportion. Ties, belts, jewelry, hats, handbags, shoes, and boots are available in a wide range of shapes and sizes. Be sure that the accessories you choose are in proportion to your outfit and to you.

Emphasis

Emphasis is *the focal point, or center of interest, of a garment.* In fashion design, emphasis should highlight your best features and draw attention away from your figure faults. Emphasis can be accomplished with line, design details, color, texture, trims, or accessories. For example, a colorful belt would emphasize a waistline. A contrasting collar would focus attention on your neckline. A bright tie or shiny buttons could be a center of interest.

Well-planned emphasis will lead the eye quickly to the center of interest. Poorly planned emphasis confuses the eye so that it does not know where to focus. What happens when wide, contrasting trim outlines all the edges of an outfit?

Wearing many busy, contrasting fabrics at one time tends to confuse the eye. Fewer details create a focal point in a garment.

Emphasis

Rhythm

Rhythm is *the flow of the lines, shapes, space, and texture of a garment.* The flow should gently carry the eye from one area of the garment to another. Good rhythm is apparent when all of the lines of an outfit work well together. For example, a curved pocket compliments the curve of a jacket hem. A pointed shirt collar repeats the point of a jacket lapel. Conflicting lines, such as curved seams and striped fabric, help to break the rhythm of an outfit.

Rhythm can also be achieved through repetition. Rows and rows of ruffles have rhythm. There is rhythm in a gradual change of size or color. Unmatched stripes and plaids can destroy the rhythm of an outfit. The breaks in the fabric pattern along the unmatched seamlines upset the natural rhythm of the fabric design. Jagged or jerky lines are seldom attractive.

Harmony

Harmony is *the pleasing arrangement of all parts of a garment.* Harmony is achieved when the design elements work well together. The colors, lines, shapes, spaces, and textures look like they belong together. The total result also should be harmonious with you—your size and shape, your coloring, and your personality.

Harmony

Which outfit has a more harmonious appearance?

Putting It All Together

Each of us has body characteristics that we cannot change. They help to make each of us look unique. Some of us may have wide shoulders, narrow hips, or a bit more waistline than we would like. The key to improving your appearance is learning how to select clothing that brings your total look into balance. You can use your knowledge of the design elements and the design principles to enhance the way you look.

Design Equation		
Use These Design Elements	**According to These Principles**	**To Create**
line	balance	
shape	proportion	
space +	emphasis =	good design
texture	rhythm	
color	harmony	

Body shapes

Bodies come in many different shapes. These shapes are influenced by your height, size, and proportions. By identifying your own body shape, you can learn how to emphasize your best features.

Two people of the same height and weight may look very different because of their frame. This is the skeletal structure of the bones. It may be small, medium, or large. A person with a larger frame will appear bigger than a person with a smaller one.

People who are the same height can have different body proportions. Some may have a long torso and short legs, while others have a short torso and long legs.

Body proportions also determine the silhouette of your body. This is the relative width of your shoulders, waist, and hips. Some of the most common body shapes are:

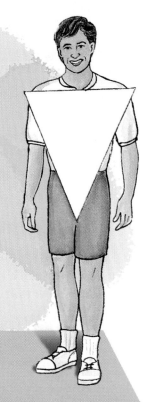

Triangle shape has narrow shoulders and wide hips.

Hour-glass shape has a small waist with chest and hips that are approximately equal in size.

Rectangle has shoulders, waistline, and hips that are approximately the same size.

Inverted triangle has wide shoulders and small hips.

Summary

- The elements of design include line, shape, space, texture, and color.

- You can create optical illusions with lines to emphasize, minimize, or camouflage your body shape.

- Most clothes are one of four basic shapes: natural, tubular, bell, or full.

- Fabric textures and patterns can make you look taller, shorter, larger, or smaller.

- The principles of design include balance, proportion, emphasis, rhythm, and harmony. They are the guidelines for using the various design elements.

Using Vocabulary Terms

On a separate piece of paper, write the vocabulary term that best fits the definition:

1. Line, shape, space, texture, and color.

2. Outer shape of a garment.

3. Focal point or center of interest.

4. Size relationship of each of the internal spaces within a garment to one another and to the total look.

5. Surface characteristics, or feel, of an object.

6. How the lines, shapes, space, and texture of a garment work together.

Recalling the Facts

1. Name the five elements of design. Explain how each one contributes to the look of an outfit.

2. What are four types of lines used in design? What look or feeling does each one create?

3. Explain how illusions can be created by lines.

4. Describe the four basic shapes, or silhouettes, of clothing.

5. What is the difference between structural lines and decorative lines in a garment?

6. How can texture create different illusions? Give three examples.

7. List the five principles of design.

8. How do the elements of design and the principles of design work together?

9. What is the difference between symmetrical and asymmetrical balance?

10. How could you create a focal point of a garment? Give examples.

Thinking Critically

1. **Analysis.** Compare the feeling or mood created by straight lines, curved lines, and diagonal lines.

2. **Evaluation.** What basic shape of clothing do you think is currently in fashion?

3. **Analysis.** Compare and contrast the impressions created by the following fabric textures: clingy, stiff, smooth, and bulky.

4. **Synthesis.** Which principles of design do you think are most important in designing a garment? Explain your reasoning.

Applying Your Knowledge

1. **Lines.** Collect illustrations of clothes that have vertical, horizontal, diagonal, and curved lines. Use felt-tipped pens to highlight the dominant lines. Describe the effect of the line direction on each garment.

2. **Decorative Lines.** Find an illustration of a simple garment. Describe how decorative lines can be added to change the garment's look.

3. **Textures and Patterns.** Collect fabric swatches with different textures and design patterns. Divide into two groups: fabrics that are best for taller or larger-framed people, and those for shorter or smaller-framed persons. Can any fabrics be worn by both groups?

4. **Proportion.** With another classmate who is taller or shorter than you, demonstrate the principles of proportion. Try on jackets or sweaters of different lengths. Discuss how proportion affects each person's appearance.

5. **Design.** Examine your school and surroundings for the elements and principles of design. Describe how these elements and principles affect the appearance of the objects you see.

Making the Connection

1. **Music.** Clap your hands to the rhythm of different pieces of music. Count out the beats to show the repetition of each rhythm. Is the rhythm ever broken?

2. **Social Studies.** Research clothing shapes from the 1920s to the 1970s. What was the popular silhouette of each decade? What part of the body was emphasized? What design lines created that emphasis?

What Is a Stylist?

Stylists translate other people's ideas and put them together in a way that looks fresh and original. They can work for a textile or apparel manufacturer. A fabric stylist may recommend new color combinations and print designs. A fashion stylist may create a less expensive adaptation of a famous designer's fashion.

Try It Yourself

Imagine that you are a fabric or fashion stylist. Create a new adaptation of a fabric or garment design by changing the color combinations, print designs, or garment details. Be sure to use the principles of design as you work with the design elements.

Build Your Portfolio

After creating your new fabric or garment design, write a description of its lines, shape, space, texture, and color. Explain how each of the design principles have been used to create the new design. Place your design and written description in your portfolio. If possible, include a copy of the original design that you adapted.

Illustrator

"**W**hen I graduated from art school," says Greg Farrell, "only a few artists and illustrators were using computers. Now almost everything I do is on the computer." Greg is both a fashion artist and a technical illustrator. He creates elegant sketches of people wearing beautiful clothes. He also creates precise drawings that accompany craft and sewing instructions.

Education and Training

Greg was always interested in art and in how things were put together. When he was eleven, he and his friends spent the summer building a treehouse. In high school, he took both fine art and industrial arts courses. During summer vacations, he worked for a small construction business.

Greg then enrolled in a small technical college with a well-respected graphic arts department. During his college years, Greg won several awards in student art competitions. He also put his art skills to many different uses in the college's theater group. He designed the programs, painted scenery, and designed and sewed costumes.

After graduation, Greg worked in the advertising department of a large department store. The store's newspaper ads featured his illustrations of everything from toasters to tailored suits. When the store was bought by a large national chain, the advertising department was eliminated. After a few months of unemployment, Greg secured a position at a medium-size advertising agency. When the agency installed a computer system, he received "on the job" computer training. Soon Greg was

using the computer to design everything from fashion ads to web pages for the Internet. When the agency merged with a larger one, Greg's job was eliminated. He decided to use his skills and contacts to become a freelance illustrator.

Today Greg has many clients scattered all over the country. These include a pattern company, a publishing company that specializes in craft books, a mail-order clothing business, and the advertising agency that used to employ him. He communicates with them by fax, overnight mail, e-mail, and modem.

Responsibilities

As an illustrator, Greg works on a wide variety of projects for different clients. His primary responsibility is to create illustrations that meet his clients' needs.

- **Produce fashion and technical illustrations.** Greg must create illustrations that capture the "look" or details that his clients are seeking. When he does fashion illustrations, he sometimes hires a model to pose in the garments. Because he created costumes in college, he knows what garments look like in their various construction stages. Clients seldom need to correct his illustrations or explain things to him more than once.

- **Meet deadlines.** Often Greg has to work evenings and weekends to meet his clients' deadlines. Because he has worked in an advertising agency, he understands their needs, concerns, and problems.

- **Keep accurate records.** Being self-employed, Greg is responsible for paying state and federal income taxes every three months. Greg also keeps track of all the expenses involved in running his business. These include art supplies, computer equipment, and telephone charges.

- **Learn latest technology.** Greg attends seminars and computer shows to keep himself up-to-date on changing computer technology. He is also a member of a large user's group that has several SIGS, or special interest groups that share information and ideas.

Knowledge and Skills

Greg has found that he uses a variety of skills and knowledge on every project:

"I love being my own boss," says Greg, "but sometimes working alone can be lonely. So I communicate with special interest groups via my computer. One is a group of artists and illustrators, and another group are small business owners. The people I've met through these groups are part of my support network."

- **Computer skills**—for preparing illustrations, keeping accurate records, and communicating with clients.

- **Art and fashion knowledge**—for interpreting fashion looks, using design elements and principles, and creating original illustrations.

- **Business and marketing skills**—for maintaining mailing lists, sending promotional brochures to potential clients, and keeping records of accounts.

- **Sewing skills**—for preparing technical illustrations of sewing and crafts projects.

- **Math skills**—for sending out bills to clients, paying expenses, and keeping financial records.

- **Communication skills**—for discussing illustration ideas with clients, describing design details, and interpreting clients' wishes.

Fabrics

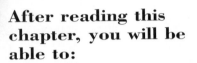

Fibers

After reading this chapter, you will be able to:

- *Describe the fiber characteristics needed for use in fabrics.*

- *Identify the different classifications of fibers.*

- *Explain how manufactured fibers are made.*

- *List the various fibers and describe their characteristics.*

Terms to Learn

- *fiber*
- *tensile strength*
- *resilient*
- *abrasion*
- *pill*
- *absorbent*
- *natural fibers*
- *manufactured fibers*
- *generic name*
- *luster*
- *trade name*

ray or unravel a scrap of any fabric until you find a single thread or yarn. Now untwist the thread or yarn so that you can pull out one hairlike unit. It will be so fine that you can scarcely see it. That is a fiber.

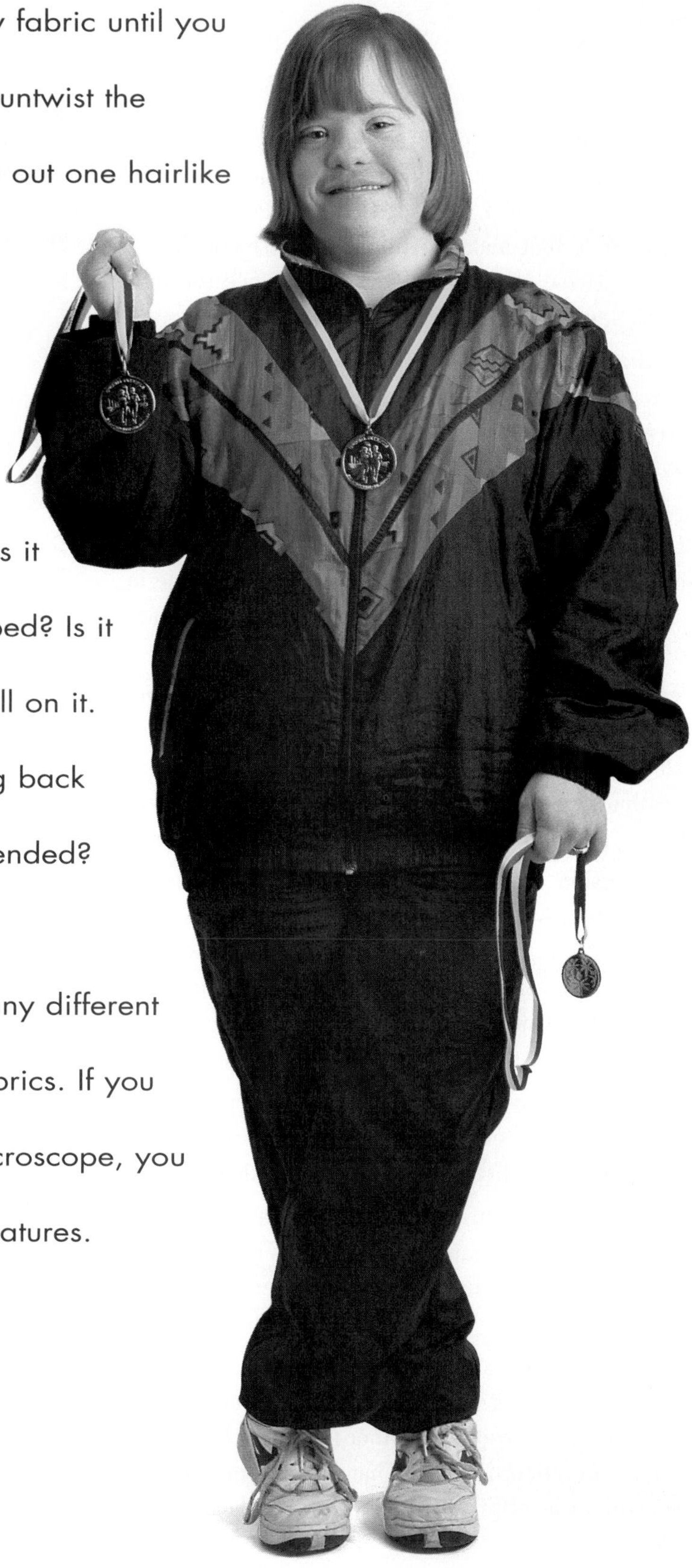

Take the fiber you have pulled out and examine it closely. Is it long or short? Is it straight or crimped? Is it dull or shiny, smooth or coarse? Pull on it. Does it break easily? Does it spring back when stretched, or does it stay extended?

These are just a few of the many different characteristics of fibers used for fabrics. If you would look at the fiber under a microscope, you would see even more identifying features.

Fiber Characteristics

A **fiber** is *the basic unit from which fabric is made*. However, not all fibers can be made into fabrics. A fiber must have certain characteristics, or properties, that make it suitable to be made into a fabric. These characteristics will influence the fabric's appearance and performance.

- **Strength.** Is the fiber strong enough to be made into fabric? Different fibers have different **tensile strengths**, or *the ability to withstand tension or pulling*.

- **Durability.** Is the fiber resistant to wear and decay? Durability refers to how long you will be able to wear or to use a particular garment or item. The fabric in a prom dress is usually not as durable as the fabric on an upholstered couch.

- **Resiliency.** Is the fiber **resilient**, or *able to spring or bounce back into shape after crushing or wrinkling?* The fibers in a wool carpet may flatten underneath a piece of heavy furniture. However, they will spring back into shape when the carpet is steamed.

- **Abrasion resistance.** Will the fiber resist abrasion? **Abrasion** is *a worn spot that can develop when fibers rub against something*. This can occur on the inside of a collar where it rubs the back of your neck. Some fibers can **pill**, or *form tiny balls of fiber on the fabric*. This affects the appearance of the garment.

- **Wrinkle resistance.** Fibers have different characteristics that affect wrinkling. Polyester is very wrinkle-resistant, but cotton and rayon wrinkle easily.

- **Shape retention.** Will the fiber retain its shape after wearing or cleaning? Some fibers stretch when the garment is worn; others shrink when exposed to water or heat.

- **Absorbency.** Is the fiber **absorbent**, or *able to take in moisture?* Some fibers, such as cotton and wool, are very absorbent. Other fibers, such as polyester and nylon, are not. That is why you can dry yourself faster with a terrycloth towel made from 100

Different fibers have different characteristics that influence the appearance and performance of fabrics. These wool fibers may be used in warm sweaters, durable coats, or resilient carpeting.

percent cotton than one made from a cotton and polyester blend.

- **Wicking.** This term refers to a fiber's ability to draw moisture away from your body so the moisture can evaporate. The wicking ability of some fibers makes up for the fact that they are not very absorbent.

- **Washability.** Can the fiber be washed or must it be dry cleaned? This characteristic determines the type of care that a fabric requires.

Types of Fibers

To make it easier to understand the various fibers and their characteristics, fibers are grouped according to their source or origin. **Natural fibers** are *fibers that come from natural sources, such as plants and animals*. Other fibers are the result of scientific experimentation and development. These "test tube" fibers are called **manufactured fibers**. They are *fibers made from substances such as wood pulp, petroleum, natural gas, air, and water*.

Fibers are also classified by name. Each fiber has a **generic name**, which indicates *a general classification of fibers of similar composition.* Cotton, wool, nylon, rayon, and polyester are examples of generic names. The Textile Fiber Products Identification Act requires that the generic name of a fiber be listed on the label of all textile products.

Natural Fibers

Natural fibers come from plants and animals. Cotton, flax, and ramie are plant fibers. They are made from cellulose, which is a fibrous substance found in plants. Wool and silk are animal fibers that are made of protein. Wool comes from sheep, and silk is spun by silkworms. Other animal fibers include specialty fibers such as cashmere and angora.

Cotton

Cotton comes from the *boll*, or seed pod, of the cotton plant. After the seed pods are harvested, the cotton fiber is separated from the seeds and processed. Under a microscope, a cotton fiber looks like a twisted ribbon. Some types of cotton plants produce seed bolls with fibers as long as 2 inches (5 cm). These are known as long staple fibers and are used for fine quality cotton fabrics.

The cotton boll bursts open to expose the fluffy white cotton fibers. The cotton is then plucked off the plant by a mechanical picker.

Discovering Natural Fibers

Flax is a tall, slender plant that grew plentiful along the Nile River. The Ancient Egyptians wove it into linen fabric that was light, cool, and easy to launder. This type of fabric was particularly suitable to their climate. Pieces of linen have been found in Egyptian tombs that are more than 4,000 years old.

The Sumarians, who lived in the valley of the Tigris and Euphrates Rivers, learned to make fine woolen cloth over 5,000 years ago. They were great traders who exported it to other parts of the world. The Romans introduced sheep into Spain in 150 B.C. and crossbred them with the African ram. This produced merino sheep, which are valued for their fine wool.

Cotton was probably first made into cloth by people who lived in the areas known today as Pakistan and northern India. In the fourth century B.C., the armies of Alexander the Great introduced cotton to northern Africa. The Nile Valley in Egypt became a center for raising the cotton plant. Soon Egyptian cotton surpassed Indian cotton in quality. Cotton was introduced into Europe during the Crusades. When the Spanish conquistadors arrived in the New World, they found fine cotton textiles in Peru, Mexico, and the southwestern part of North America.

Written records from China dating as far back as 2640 B.C. talk about growing silk. For centuries, the Chinese kept the process of making silk, called *sericulture*, a carefully guarded secret. Punishment for revealing the secret was torture and death. In the East, this knowledge was eventually smuggled into Japan via Korea. It was smuggled into the West by monks, who hid the little silkworms in their bamboo canes.

Cotton is strong, absorbent, and comfortable to wear even in hot weather. It does not cling or pill. Cotton can be washed in high temperatures and with strong soaps or detergents. It accepts dyes very easily.

However, cotton wrinkles easily and can shrink. It is not resilient or elastic. It also mildews easily and is flammable. Special finishes can be applied to cotton fabrics for wrinkle resistance, shrinkage control, mildew resistance, and flame retardance.

Cotton is used in a wide variety of fabrics for both clothing and home furnishings. It is made into shirts, sweaters, dresses, jeans, underwear, socks, and even baby diapers. Household uses range from towels to sheets to upholstery. Cotton is often combined with other fibers.

The Seal of Cotton is the registered trademark of Cotton Incorporated for 100% cotton products.

The stalks of the flax plants furnish long fibers that are made into linen fabric. The flax fibers can be separated from each other by soaking the stems in chemically treated water.

Flax

Flax is the name of the fiber that comes from the inside of the stem of the flax plant. Under a microscope, a flax fiber looks like a bamboo pole. When flax is made into fabric it is called linen.

Flax is stronger than cotton and is very absorbent. It is lint-free and dries more quickly than cotton. It can be washed, bleached, and ironed at high temperatures without scorching.

However, flax is not very resilient and wrinkles easily. Thus, linen fabric is often used for garments with a wrinkled or unpressed look. The fiber can shrink and be damaged by mildew.

Linen fabric is used for both clothing and home decorating items such as towels and tablecloths. It can be soft and lightweight for a handkerchief, crisp and smooth for a suit, or thick and heavy for draperies. To reduce its natural tendency to wrinkle, linen is often given a wrinkle-resistant finish.

Ramie

Ramie comes from the stems of China grass that is grown primarily in Southeast Asia. It has a natural silk-like **luster** or *gloss or sheen*. When seen under a microscope, ramie is very similar to flax.

Ramie is one of the strongest fibers known. It is very resistant to insects and mildew. However, it is stiff and brittle, with poor elasticity and resiliency. As a result, ramie is usually combined with other fibers such as cotton or flax. It is used in sweaters, knitted tops, shirts, placemats, and upholstery.

Wool

Wool comes from the fleece of sheep. Wool from sheep that are less than eight months old is called lamb's wool. The quality of the wool depends on the breed of sheep and the climate in which the animal was raised. Sheep are sheared once or twice a year.

Wool is a comfortable, durable, and versatile fiber. If you look at a wool fiber through a microscope, you will see that it is covered with scales. It also looks wavy and crimped. Wool fibers trap air which in turn prevents the loss of body heat. This

The Wool Bureau has the Woolmark label to identify pure new wool fabrics.

After sheep are sheared, the fleece is washed and carded to remove impurities and straighten the fibers.

Wool is used for coats, suits, slacks, sweaters, socks, blankets, carpets, and other items. All-wool fabrics made from fibers that have never been used before are labeled "pure wool" or "virgin wool." "Recycled wool" is fabric made with fibers that have come from previously-made wool fabrics. Wool can also be combined with other fibers.

Silk

Silk is formed when silkworms spin their cocoons. The silk fiber is one continuous filament that can be as long as one mile. The cocoons are harvested before the silk moths emerge. If a moth breaks through the wall of its cocoon, the single filament would be broken into many shorter fibers.

Under a microscope, silk looks like a glass rod with an irregular surface. This surface texture provides its superb luster.

Silk feels very soft and smooth. It is strong, yet lightweight and comfortable to wear. Silk has elasticity and resists wrinkling. It is absorbent, drapes easily, and can be dyed in brilliant colors and prints.

Silk is usually dry cleaned, but some silks can be hand washed. Strong soaps, bleaches, perspiration, deodorants, and high ironing temperatures can weaken or discolor silk fabrics.

Silk is used for a variety of fabrics for both clothing and home furnishings. It can range from lightweight sheers to heavy, textured fabrics. Lingerie, scarves, ties, dresses, and wedding gowns may be made of silk fabrics.

Silkworms grow by eating mulberry leaves. When fully grown, they spin a cocoon. After two or three weeks, the cocoon is unwound by hand or machine to collect the silk thread.

helps you to feel warm in cold weather. The overlapping scales help to shed raindrops, yet wool absorbs moisture from the air or body and still feels dry.

Wool is resilient. The fiber is very springy or elastic and returns to its original shape and size after being stretched. That is why wrinkles and creases will hang or steam out easily. Wool wears well and resists abrasion. It is naturally flame-resistant, so a wool blanket can be used to smother a fire.

When heat and moisture are applied to wool, the scales spread and soften slightly. This is called felting. If the fabric is rubbed or pressed hard, the scales interlock and the fabric mats and shrinks. Thus, most wool fabrics should be dry cleaned or washed carefully by hand in cold water. To prevent felting, washable wool fabrics have been treated with a special finish or blended with other fibers such as nylon.

Wool also can be damaged by moths, carpet beetles, and other insects. Special finishes can be applied to wool for moth resistance.

Characteristics of Natural Fibers

Fiber Name	Advantages	Disadvantages	Care
 **Cotton**	Extremely versatile Strong and durable Comfortable and soft Absorbs moisture Does not cling or pill Dyes easily	Not resilient or elastic Wrinkles unless treated Shrinks in hot water unless treated Will mildew Flammable	Easily laundered at high temperature Can be ironed at high temperature
 **Flax**	Stronger than cotton Comfortable Absorbs moisture Durable Lint-free Dries quicker than cotton	Not resilient Wrinkles easily Shrinks unless treated Will mildew Hard-to-remove creases	Easily laundered Can be ironed at high temperature
 **Ramie**	Silk-like luster Very strong Very resistant to insects and mildew	Stiff and brittle Poor resiliency Poor elasticity Best when combined with other fibers	Washable
Wool 	Very versatile Provides warmth Durable Very resilient Resists wrinkling Absorbs moisture Resists abrasion Naturally flame resistant	Damaged by moths and other insects Shrinks and mats May pill Absorbs odors	Usually dry cleaned Sometimes washable Iron at low temperature
 **Silk**	Natural luster Strong yet lightweight Smooth Absorbs moisture	Weakened by sunlight, perspiration, high iron temperature May yellow with age May waterspot	Usually dry cleaned Sometimes washable Iron at low temperature

Specialty Animal Fibers

Specialty animal fibers come from goats, rabbits, camels, and llamas. These fibers include angora, alpaca, cashmere, camel's hair, mohair, and vicuna. They are usually expensive because they are not available in large quantities. Their characteristics are similar to those of sheep's wool.

These specialty fibers may be used alone or with sheep's wool to produce softness or luster effects. Dry cleaning is usually recommended for these fibers.

Rubber

Natural rubber is made from a latex, a milky liquid that comes from rubber trees. It is used to waterproof coats, hats, boots, gloves, and aprons. It can provide elasticity for waistbands and support garments. It also is used as a backing for rugs and for recreational items. However, spandex, a manufactured fiber, has many more advantages in fabrics than rubber.

Manufactured Fibers

Manufactured fibers come from substances such as wood pulp and petroleum. Chemical engineers transform these substances into fibers with specific characteristics. There are two basic types of manufactured fibers:

• *Cellulosic fibers* are produced from wood pulp with a minimum of chemical steps. The three cellulosic fibers are rayon, acetate, and triacetate.

• *Noncellulosic fibers* are all other manufactured fibers. These are made from carbon, hydrogen, nitrogen, and oxygen molecules. The molecules are linked together into long chains called polymers. The illustration on page 199 explains this process.

In many publications and advertisements, you will see manufactured fibers referred to as *man-made fibers*. Sometimes the term *synthetic* is used, although not all manufactured fibers are produced from chemicals.

Since the first manufactured fiber was produced in the United States in 1910, a total of 22 generic manufactured fibers have been developed. Not all of them are currently produced. Each generic fiber differs significantly in its chemical composition.

Today fiber research is focusing on changing manufactured fibers to improve their performance. These variants are sometimes called second- and third-generation fibers. Fibers can be engineered to produce fabrics with specific qualities, such as elasticity or flame resistance. Many of the manufactured fibers resemble natural fibers but have improved performance and care properties.

Just like natural fibers, each manufactured fiber has a generic name. However, fiber companies also have a **trade name** for each manufactured fiber they produce. These names are *registered as trademarks and are protected by law*. No other company can legally use the same name for the same type of product. For example, polyester is a generic name for a manufactured fiber. Its trade name may be Dacron®, a DuPont product; Kodel®, an Eastman product; or Fortrel®, a Celanese product.

Rayon

The first manufactured fiber was rayon. It is a cellulosic fiber, made primarily from wood pulp. Rayon can be produced in many different variations for different end uses.

Rayon, like cotton and linen, is absorbent and comfortable to wear. It is soft, drapes easily, and has a nice luster. Rayon dyes well and can be printed with bright designs. Some rayon fabrics are washable, but most fabrics must be dry cleaned.

Rayon wrinkles easily and can shrink. It is also weak when wet and can be weakened by long exposure to light and high temperatures. However, special finishes can be applied to improve all of these performance qualities.

Rayon is used in a wide variety of clothing and household fabrics. It is often used for blouses, shirts, and linen-like fabrics. Rayon can be combined with most other fibers.

Acetate

Acetate is also a cellulosic fiber. Thus, some of its characteristics are similar to those of rayon. It is absorbent and dries faster than rayon. It can be dyed and printed, but special dyes must be used.

Acetate has a silky appearance. It can be soft or crisp and drapes well. It is resilient and holds creases well. Acetate is also resistant to shrinking, moths, and mildew.

Because acetate is heat-sensitive, it must be ironed at low temperatures. It also can be dissolved by acetone, which is contained in nail polishes and polish removers. It may cling to the body unless treated with an antistatic finish.

Many different types of fabrics are made from acetate. Some common ones are satin, taffeta, and silk-like fabrics. Usually acetate fabrics are dry cleaned, but some may be washed, depending on care instructions. Acetate is frequently blended with other fibers.

Triacetate

Triacetate and acetate have many similar properties. Both are drapeable and have a silky feel. Both are resilient and hold creases well. They also have a low resistance to abrasion.

However, triacetate is not as sensitive to heat as acetate. This allows triacetate fabrics to be permanently pleated because the fibers can be heat set. Triacetate also is stronger and more shrink resistant than acetate. It is easily laundered.

One of the unique characteristics of triacetate is that white fabrics stay white better than most other fibers. It is used in light to heavyweight fabrics that usually have a crisp finish.

Nylon

Nylon was introduced in 1939 as a "miracle fiber" because of its excellent strength, elasticity, and washability. Made from petroleum chemicals, it was the first noncellulosic fiber.

Nylon is very strong, lightweight, and lustrous. It is resilient and does not stretch or shrink. It also can be blended with many other fibers.

Because nylon does not absorb moisture well, it can feel uncomfortably warm in hot weather and cool in cold weather. It also collects static electricity, unless specially treated.

Nylon is easy to wash, quick drying, and needs little or no pressing. However, it may yellow or gray after a period of time. Some nylon fabrics absorb and hold oil stains. Because it is heat-sensitive, it must be ironed at low temperatures.

Nylon is a very versatile fiber with many consumer and industrial uses. It is used in lingerie, pantyhose, swimsuits, outerwear, carpets, tents, and car tires.

Polyester

One of the most widely used manufactured fibers on the market is polyester. It is a strong, high performance fiber that is used alone or blended with many other fibers.

Polyester has excellent resilience and outstanding wrinkle resistance. It does not stretch or shrink. It also washes easily, dries quickly, and needs little or no pressing.

Polyester fabrics retain heat-set creases and pleats better than other fabrics. When combined with other fibers, polyester adds strength and wrinkle resistance.

Polyester is not very absorbent. Thus, 100 percent polyester fabrics may feel hot and uncomfortable in warm weather. Recent developments have improved its moisture absorbency properties.

Some polyester and polyester-blend fabrics have a tendency to pill. Polyester also attracts and holds oil-based soil unless the fabric is pretreated with a soil releasing agent.

Polyester fibers are used in a wide range of textiles that can look like cotton, silk, or wool. Both woven and knitted fabrics in a variety of weights are used for clothing and home furnishings. One of polyester's most common uses is blending with cotton for easy care shirts, blouses, pants, sheets, and tablecloths.

The Process of Manufacturing Fibers

Raw materials can be cellulose (wood chips) or chemical polymers. It is changed to a thick, syrupy liquid by dissolving in a solvent or melting with heat.

The liquid solution is extruded (forced) through a spinneret, a metal plate with tiny holes similar to a shower head. Each hole forms one fiber. The fibers can be thin or thick, depending on the size of the holes. Different shapes of holes (round, oval, three-sided) create different fiber characteristics.

After emerging from the spinneret, the liquid hardens into a long filament. Some go into a chemical bath where they become solid(wet spinning). Others go into warm air where the solvent evaporates and the fibers harden (dry spinning). Those that have been melted pass through cool air to harden (melt spinning).

Next, the filaments are stretched to align the molecules and increase strength and elasticity.

Some filaments are twisted into yarns onto spools. Others are cut into short lengths for spinning into yarns later.

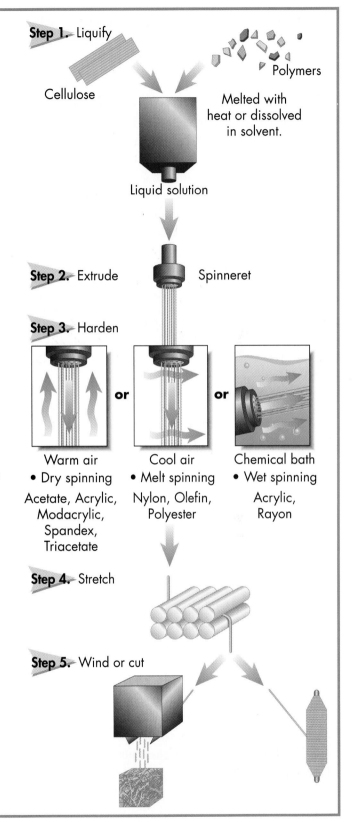

Step 1. Liquify

Cellulose

Polymers

Melted with heat or dissolved in solvent.

Liquid solution

Step 2. Extrude — Spinneret

Step 3. Harden

Warm air — or — Cool air — or — Chemical bath
• Dry spinning — • Melt spinning — • Wet spinning
Acetate, Acrylic, Modacrylic, Spandex, Triacetate — Nylon, Olefin, Polyester — Acrylic, Rayon

Step 4. Stretch

Step 5. Wind or cut

199

Polyester also is used as fiberfill in parkas, jackets, and comforters. It is warm and lightweight. Unlike down, it remains fluffy even when wet.

Acrylic

Acrylic is a soft, resilient fiber that resists wrinkling. It has high bulking power and offers warmth without added weight. It is often substituted for wool because it has similar characteristics but is washable and nonallergenic. Acrylic fibers have good resistance to sunlight. Because of this, they are suitable for curtains, draperies, and upholstery.

Some acrylic fabrics will pill or collect static electricity. They may hold oil-based stains. They are heat-sensitive and should not be dried or ironed at high temperatures.

Acrylic fibers are used in sweaters, wool-like fabrics, carpets, blankets, and upholstery fabrics. They can be washed or dry cleaned.

Modacrylic

Modacrylic fibers share many of the characteristics of acrylic fibers. They are often used in pile fabrics, fake furs, children's sleepers, and even wigs.

Olefin

Olefin is strong, lightweight, and quick drying. It has good resistance to abrasion, perspiration, soil, and mildew. Hard-to-remove stains, such as ink and grease, can be easily removed from olefin fibers.

However, olefin is sensitive to heat and light. It does not absorb moisture and is difficult to dye.

Polypropylene (pawl-ee-PRO-pah-leen), a type of olefin fiber, is used in a variety of outdoor garments and exercise wear. It does not absorb moisture and will wick perspiration away from the skin. Therefore it keeps the body warm and dry in cold or damp weather. Skiers and runners like its wicking properties for shirts, underwear, and socks.

Olefin also is used in upholstery fabrics, indoor-outdoor carpeting, and disposable diapers. Industrial apparel, such as protective garments, can be made from olefin fibers.

Aramid

Aramid fibers have exceptional strength and heat and flame resistance. Even at high temperatures, these fibers maintain their shape and form. They also are very resistant to abrasion.

Aramid fibers are used in protective clothing, such as fire fighters' apparel, race-car drivers' suits, and lightweight bullet-proof vests. Aramid is also found in radial tires, cables, aircraft furnishings, and other industrial products.

Spandex

Spandex is an elastic fiber with excellent stretchability and recovery. Even after repeated stretching, it still retains its elasticity. Because it is resistant to sunlight, perspiration, oil, and abrasion, this fiber has replaced rubber in most clothing uses.

Using high temperatures when washing or machine drying this fiber can cause it to discolor and lose some of its stretching power. It also can be damaged by chlorine in bleach and in swimming pools.

Spandex can be covered with other yarns or left uncovered. It is used in elastics, underwear, swimwear, and active sportswear.

Metallic

Metallic fibers can be added to fabrics, primarily for decoration. They can be made entirely of metal, or they can be combined with plastic. Metallic fibers are used in dressy fabrics, accessories, and industrial products.

Glass

Fiberglass is a fiber produced from glass beads. It has outstanding heat resistance and nonflammability. It is strong, yet can break because it is brittle. It is nonabsorbent and water repellent.

Fiberglass is not suitable for clothing. However, it is used in draperies, insulation, and in some boat hulls and sports car bodies. The newest use of fiberglass is in fiber optics for communication lines.

Characteristics of Manufactured Fibers

Fiber Name and Trade Names	Advantages	Disadvantages	Care
Acetate *Chromspun®, Estron®*	Silk-like appearance; soft and drapeable; dries quickly; resistant to shrinking, moths, mildew	May wrinkle; low abrasion resistance; heat sensitive; damaged by acetone	Usually dry cleaned; iron at low temperature
Acrylic *Acrilan®, Creslan®, Orlon®, Zefran®*	Soft, warm, wool-like; lightweight; wrinkle resistant; resistant to moths and sunlight	May pill; may accumulate static electricity; heat sensitive	Dry cleaned or laundered; iron at low temperature
Aramid *Kevlar®, Nomex®*	Exceptional strength; exceptional heat and flame resistance; resistant to stretch and abrasion	Not absorbent	
Modacrylic *SEF®*	Soft and warm; resilient; resists abrasion; resists flames; fast drying; resistant to moths, mildew, sunlight	Very heat sensitive; may accumulate static electricity	Dry cleaned or laundered; iron at very low temperature
Nylon *Antron®, Cantrece®, Crepeset®, Cumuloft®*	Very strong; resilient; lustrous; dries quickly	May yellow or gray; heat sensitive; low moisture absorbency	Easily laundered; iron at low temperature
Olefin *Genesis®, Spectra®*	Unique wicking properties; strong and lightweight; quick drying; resistant to abrasion, soil, mildew, weather, and perspiration	Does not absorb moisture; heat sensitive	Washable; iron at low temperature
Polyester *Dacron®, Fortrel®, Kodel®, Trevira®*	Excellent wrinkle resistance; strong; resistant to abrasion; dries quickly; blends well with other fibers; retains heat-set pleats and creases	Absorbs oily stains; low absorbency of moisture	Easily laundered; needs little or no pressing
Rayon *Beau-Grip®, Courtaulds Rayon®, Zantrel®*	Soft and comfortable; high moisture absorbency; drapeable	May wrinkle or shrink unless treated; may mildew	Usually dry cleaned; sometimes washable
Spandex *Lycra®*	Excellent elasticity and recovery; stronger and more durable than rubber; lightweight; resistant to body oils	Damaged by chlorine bleach; damaged by heat	Washable
Triacetate *(not currently produced in U.S.)*	Can be permanently pleated; wrinkle resistant; shrink resistant; crisp finish	Heat sensitive (but not as much as acetate)	Easily laundered

REVIEW

Summary

- A fiber is the basic unit from which fabric is made. It should be strong, durable, and have some resiliency.

- Natural fibers come from plants and animals. They include cotton, flax, ramie, wool, and silk.

- Manufactured fibers are made from substances such as wood pulp, petroleum, natural gas, air, and water. They include rayon, acetate, nylon, polyester, acrylic, spandex, and others.

- Each fiber has a generic name. Manufactured fibers also have a trade name.

- Each fiber has specific characteristics that affect a fabric's appearance and performance.

Using Vocabulary

On a separate piece of paper, write the vocabulary term that best fits the definition:

1. Ability to withstand tension or pulling.
2. Gloss or sheen.
3. Ability to spring or bounce back after crushing or wrinkling.
4. A general classification of fibers of similar composition.
5. Ability to take in moisture.
6. Fibers that come from plants and animals.

Recalling the Facts

1. List five fiber characteristics and explain how each one can influence a fabric's appearance and performance.

2. In what two ways can fibers be classified? Give examples of each.

3. List four natural fibers. What are two advantages and disadvantages of each fiber?

4. Why are cotton fabrics and wool fabrics comfortable to wear?

5. What is sometimes done to natural fibers to improve their performance and care?

6. What is the difference between a generic name and a trade name for a fiber?

7. Explain the purpose of a spinneret in the manufacturing process of fibers.

8. What characteristics do nylon and polyester have in common?

9. What manufactured fiber can be a substitute for wool?

10. Identify two advantages of each of the following fibers: polyester, rayon, aramid, and spandex.

Thinking Critically

1. **Evaluation.** Which fiber characteristics do you think are most important for clothing? Why?

2. **Analysis.** Compare the characteristics of wool and silk. In what ways are they similar and different?

3. **Analysis.** Recommend the type of fibers you would choose for a sweater, a shirt, a swimsuit, and a pair of jeans. Explain your choices.

4. **Synthesis.** Summarize the process of manufacturing fibers.

Applying Your Knowledge

1. **Fiber Usage.** Look through catalogs and write down the names of the fibers listed. Also note which fibers are listed most frequently. Are they natural or manufactured fibers?

2. **Fibers and Fabric Care.** Look through the clothing in your own wardrobe. Using the garment labels, list the names of the fibers on each garment label and the recommended method of care. Summarize your findings.

3. **Fiber Characteristics.** Working in small groups, research the properties of a fiber. Create a commercial or a rap song about the characteristics and uses of the fiber.

Making the Connection

1. **Science.** Examine yarns under a microscope to identify the characteristics of the fibers.

2. **Social Studies.** Research the importance of the production of natural fibers in various countries. Has production increased or decreased over the past twenty years? What impact, if any, has this had on each country's economy?

What Is a Textile Chemist?

Textile chemists create and improve fibers, dyes, and finishes. They also help develop special tests to see how a new fiber or finish will perform. Today fibers can be modified for special purposes, such as greater comfort, reduced clinging, improved flame resistance, or easier dyeability.

Try It Yourself

Imagine that you are a textile chemist. Gather a variety of fabric swatches to analyze. First, look at the appearance of each fabric and feel its surface. Next, remove a yarn from each swatch. Untwist the yarn until you have a small sampling of fibers. Examine the physical characteristics of each fiber, using a microscope or magnifying glass. Record your observations.

Research how to perform a burning test and an acetone test to identify fiber content. In the burning test, the character of the flame and manner of burning, the odor, and the quantity and kind of residue help determine the general type of fiber. Acetate fibers react to organic solvent acetone found in some fingernail polish removers.

Build Your Portfolio

Mount each fabric swatch on a piece of paper. Record your observations of the fabric's appearance and feel, the fiber's physical characteristics, and the data from the burning test and acetone test. From your analysis, record the fiber content of each fabric. Place the analyses in your portfolio.

Fabrics

After reading this chapter, you will be able to:

- *Explain how yarns are formed.*

- *Describe the characteristics of woven fabrics made by different weaving techniques.*

- *Identify the characteristics of knitted fabrics.*

- *Give examples of fabrics made by other methods.*

Terms to Learn

- *yarns*
- *staple fibers*
- *filament fibers*
- *ply*
- *texturing*
- *blends*
- *weaving*
- *knitting*
- *warp yarns*
- *filling yarns*
- *selvage*
- *pile*

Try this experiment: From a small ball of cotton, loosen several fibers. Carefully pull the fibers from the ball. Tug them, noting how strong they are. Now twist them with your fingers as you pull. Notice how much stronger the twisted yarn is, compared to the loose fibers.

All fabrics begin with fibers. However, the fibers must be held together in some manner to create fabrics. For most fabrics, the next step is to spin the fibers into yarns. Then the yarns must be interlaced or looped together to create the fabric.

Yarns

Most fabrics are made from **yarns** that have been created from *fibers twisted together or laid side by side*. The fibers that make up the yarns may be natural, manufactured, or a combination of both. Much of the beauty, texture, performance, and variety of fabrics is due to the difference in the yarns.

Fibers are classified according to their length. They can be either staples or filaments.

- **Staple fibers** are *short fibers that are measured in inches or centimeters*. All natural fibers, except silk, are staples. Manufactured fibers can be cut into staple lengths to give fabrics the appearance of cotton, linen, or wool.

- **Filament fibers** are *long continuous fibers that are measured in yards or meters*. Silk is a filament. Manufactured fibers also are filaments, unless they have been cut.

Types of Yarns

Yarns can be made from one type of fiber entirely or from different types of fibers. Two or more yarns can then be twisted together to create a yarn's texture and color. The varieties are almost limitless.

A yarn made of staple fibers is called a *spun yarn*. The fibers are twisted together to form a single yarn that is long enough for weaving or knitting. Yarns made of staple fibers are more irregular and fuzzier than those made of filament fibers. The short ends of the fibers create a rough surface on the yarns.

A yarn made entirely of filament fibers is called a *filament yarn*. Filament yarns are smoother and more lustrous than spun yarns.

A *monofilament yarn* has only one strand. Nylon sewing thread and fishing line are monofilament yarns. When two or more filaments are combined during the manufacturing process, a *multifilament yarn* is formed.

Most yarns are formed by twisting two or more single yarns together. This forms a ply yarn. The word **ply** refers to *the number of yarn strands twisted*

Types of Yarns

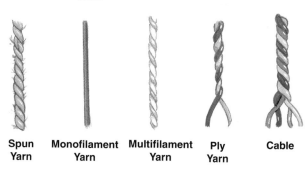

Spun Yarn   **Monofilament Yarn**   **Multifilament Yarn**   **Ply Yarn**   **Cable**

together. Yarns can be two ply, three ply, or more. Several ply yarns twisted together form a cord or cable.

Now take a look at several different yarns. Those used for knitting or embroidery are good examples. How many plies does each yarn have? How tightly are they twisted? The amount of twist affects the yarn's appearance, feel, and behavior.

- *High-twist yarns* are firm, strong, dull in texture, and relatively fine in size. However, too tight a twist can weaken the yarn.

- *Low-twist yarns* are softer, weaker, more lustrous, and less compact than high-twist yarns. Multifilament yarns with a low twist are used for soft, lustrous fabrics.

Novelty Yarns

Novelty yarns are made from two or more yarns that are not alike in type or size. They are used to manufacture fabrics with unusual textures and colors.

Novelty yarns often have loops or different thicknesses. This can be created by twisting a filament yarn that is thin and shiny with a spun yarn that is thick and fuzzy. Sometimes three yarns are used. One of the yarns is used as the base yarn, another creates the decorative effect, and a third acts as a tie or binder.

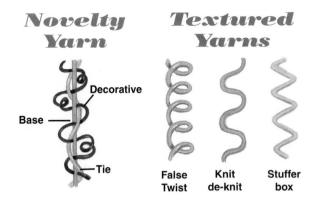

Novelty Yarn

Decorative

Base

Tie

Textured Yarns

False Twist

Knit de-knit

Stuffer box

Textured Yarns

Filament yarns made of manufactured fibers can be permanently set into ripples, waves, zigzags, or various twists. This gives the yarns different textures and increases stretchability. The **texturing** process *uses chemicals, heat, or special machinery to turn the straight, rod-like filaments into coiled, looped, or crimped yarns.*

The texturing process increases the yarns' bulk, giving a softer feel to the finished fabric. It also increases the stretch and recovery of the yarns. Textured yarns have improved wrinkle resistance and wash-and-wear properties.

Adding bulk to filament yarns helps to overcome some of the disadvantages of the fiber's original characteristics. For example, textured filament yarns have more space between the filaments than regular filament yarns. Thus, fabric made of textured yarns

has more breathability and is more comfortable to wear. The texturing process also helps to prevent static buildup in the fabric.

Blended Yarns

Yarns can be engineered to obtain the best qualities of different fibers. **Blends** are created when *different fibers are combined into one yarn.* Natural fibers can be combined, such as wool and silk. Manufactured fibers can be combined, such as nylon and acetate. A natural fiber and a manufactured fiber can also be combined, such as cotton and polyester.

Fibers are usually blended to improve fabric performance. A very common blend is polyester and cotton. The cotton offers comfort, softness, and absorbency. The polyester adds strength, wrinkle resistance, shrink resistance, mildew resistance, and quick drying.

Fibers can also be blended for appearance. An angora fiber may be added to wool to give more texture and softness to a sweater. Silk may be included for shine or luster.

Different fibers are often blended together to form fabric that has the best characteristics of each fiber.

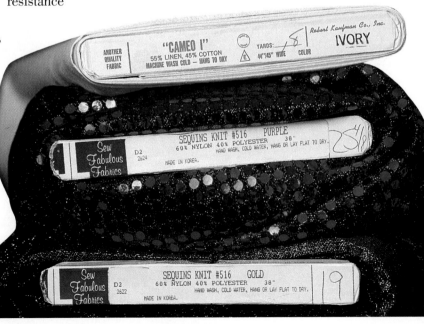

Fabrics

Some types of fabrics are easily identified by their construction. You can recognize terrycloth by its loops. Velvet has a raised surface, while corduroy has rows of cut threads. Satin has a shiny look produced by its special type of weave.

The two most common methods of fabric construction are weaving and knitting. **Weaving** is done by *interlacing two sets of yarns at right angles to each other.* **Knitting** is a method of *looping yarns together.* A few fabrics are made by other methods.

Fabric Characteristics

Fabric characteristics are those traits that distinguish one fabric from another. These include type of construction, texture, hand, and weight.

- **Type of construction** refers to how the fibers or yarns are joined together. They can be woven, knitted, interlocked, fused, bonded, twisted, or looped together.

- **Texture** is how the surface of a fabric looks and feels. It can be smooth, rough, dull, shiny, nubby, fuzzy, or a combination.

- **Hand** refers to how a fabric handles and feels. It can be described as soft, firm, crisp, stiff, or drapeable. You can learn how a fabric behaves by draping it over your hands.

- **Weight** is determined by the yarns and the type of fabric construction. Fabrics can range in weight from very light to very heavy.

Woven Fabrics

Weaving is done by interlacing lengthwise and crosswise yarns on a loom. The *yarns that run the length of the fabric* are called **warp yarns**. These yarns are usually the stronger of the yarns used and are positioned on the loom first.

The *crosswise yarns* are known as **filling yarns**. They are woven or interlaced into the warp yarns, following a specific pattern.

Along both edges of woven fabric, there is a **selvage**. This is a *self-edge formed by the filling yarn when it turns to go back in the other direction.* The selvage is usually a little stiffer and firmer. It will not ravel.

There are many, many variations of woven fabrics that are used for clothing and home furnishings. They range from very lightweight, open-mesh fabrics to heavy, firm, tightly woven fabrics. If you examine a woven fabric closely, you can see how it is woven.

The three basic weaves are the *plain weave*, *twill weave*, and *satin weave*. Almost all woven fabrics are some type or variation of these three basic weaves.

Basic Weaves

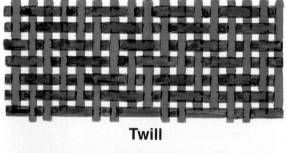

Plain

Twill

Satin

Plain Weave

The plain weave is the simplest of all weaves. The filling yarns pass over and under each warp yarn. The yarns alternate in each row to form an even, balanced weave. Plain weave fabrics have no right or wrong sides unless they are printed or finished differently. The yarns can be tightly or loosely woven.

Some examples of plain weaves are muslin, voile, broadcloth, percale, taffeta, and crepe. Plain weave fabrics are used for shirts, handkerchiefs, and sheets.

A *ribbed weave* is a variation of the plain weave. The rib is created by using filling yarns that are thicker than the warp yarns. Poplin and faille are ribbed fabrics.

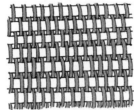

Ribbed Weave

A *basket weave* is another plain weave variation. Two or more yarns are grouped side by side in each direction and woven as one. Oxford cloth is a basket weave.

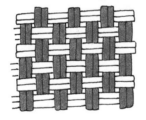

Basket Weave

Twill Weave

A twill weave is recognized by parallel diagonal ridges on the fabric surface. In a twill weave, filling yarns pass over and under one or more warp yarns. Each successive row shifts to the right or left to give the diagonal line.

Twill weaves are firmer, heavier, and more durable than plain weaves. Denim, chino, and gabardine are examples of twill weaves. Twill weaves are often used for strong, sturdy work clothes.

Satin Weave

A satin weave has yarns that float on the surface to give it a luster or shine. Either the warp or the filling yarns pass over four to eight yarns at a time. The long floats appear on the right side of the fabric.

The satin weave creates a smooth surface with lots of sheen. However, satin weaves can snag easily. Satin fabrics are used for blouses, evening wear, and bed linens.

Pile Weave

A pile weave creates *a raised surface of loops or yarn ends*. This surface is called **pile**. The weaving process uses three sets of yarns. The extra yarns are brought to the fabric surface as loops. The loops are left uncut for terrycloth. They are cut to form velvet, velveteen, velour, or corduroy. The back of the fabric can be a plain, twill, or satin weave.

The surface loops of velvet and velveteen can be sculptured when cut to form a decorative surface texture. In most corduroy, the pile yarn is woven in a striped effect to create the rows. The width of the pile can range from narrow pinwale to widewale corduroy.

pile yarns

warp yarns

filling yarn

Pile Weave

Other Weaves

Various patterns or designs can be woven in fabric by changing the way that the yarns are interlaced. Small geometric designs are woven by means of a dobby attachment on the loom. Bird's-eye and honeycomb are two examples of a *dobby weave*.

Large, elaborate designs can be produced by the *Jacquard weave*. Special looms are used to produce the intricate designs and combinations of weaves. Some examples are brocades and damasks, which are used for table linens.

The Weaving Process

Whether fabric is woven on a small hand loom or huge computerized loom, the process is the same. A set of warp yarns is wound onto the *warp beam* at the back of the loom. Each yarn is passed through one or more frames called *harnesses*. Each harness holds one set of yarns in place. Then the warp yarns are stretched over the weaving frame.

The filling yarn is wound around a *bobbin*. It is placed in a container called a *shuttle*. The shuttle draws the filling yarn over and under the warp yarns.

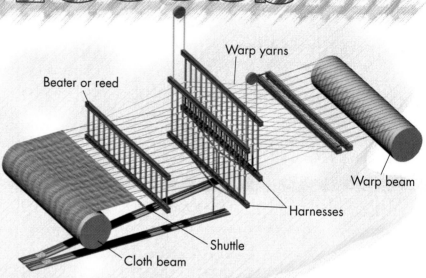

When the harness is lifted, a space is created called the *shed*. The shuttle with the filling yarn passes through this shed. After the harness is lowered, the new row is pushed into place with the *beater* or *reed*. This tightens the weave. To weave the next row, a second harness is raised. The shuttle is passed back through the shed to the original side. This row is then pushed into place. The weaving continues back and forth from edge to edge. The *cloth beam* holds the finished fabric.

High-speed computerized looms can produce over 100 yards of fabric per hour. The shuttle is replaced with a stream of water or an air jet to carry the filling yarn across the fabric at very high speeds. The yarn travels as fast as 200 miles per hour. The harnesses and beaters on these looms move faster than the eye can follow.

The direction that yarns run in a woven fabric is called the *grain*. The warp yarns form the *lengthwise grain*. The filling yarns form the *crosswise grain*. The *bias grain* runs diagonally across the fabric. *True bias* has the greatest amount of stretch.

The two long edges are called the *selvage*. They are formed when the filling yarns turn and go back the other way.

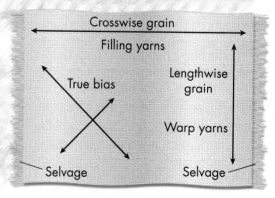

In a *leno weave*, the warp yarns cross and twist between the filling yarns. This produces open or sheer fabrics with good stability because the filling yarns cannot shift. Leno weaves are used to make open weave curtains and draperies, thermal blankets, and netting.

Leno Weave

Knit Fabrics

Knitting is done by pulling loops of yarn through other loops of yarn to create interlocked rows. One yarn can form the entire fabric or garment. The stitches, or loops, can be varied to create different textures and patterns.

Knitting machines can duplicate hand knitting stitches and patterns. Some knitting machines produce knitted fabric, either flat or tubular. Other machines knit the item, such as socks and pantyhose, directly.

A knit fabric has a lengthwise and crosswise direction, the same as a woven fabric. In a knit, the lengthwise rows of stitches are called *wales*. The crosswise stitches are called *courses*. A knit usually has a greater degree of stretchability in either the lengthwise or crosswise direction.

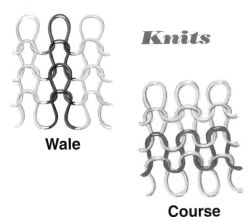

Knits

Wale

Course

Because of their stretchability, knits move with the body. As a result, they are comfortable to wear. Knits are easy to care for and do not wrinkle easily. They can be made in a variety of fibers, weights, and types of construction.

Weft Knits

Weft, or filling, knits are made with only one yarn. When you knit by hand, you are making a weft knit. Weft knits can be made on either a flat knitting machine or a circular machine, which produces tubular fabric. Most weft knits have two-way stretch in both the lengthwise and crosswise directions. However, they can get lengthwise "runs" from broken threads because of their single yarn construction.

Weft Knit

The various types of weft knits include:

• *Plain knits* are the most common type of weft knits. They are sometimes called *jersey*. The front and the back sides have a different appearance. The right side has vertical wales; the wrong side has crosswise courses. Hosiery, t-shirts, sports shirts, dresses, and sweaters can be plain knits.

• *Purl knits* are the same on both sides. They have crosswise courses like the wrong side of a plain knit. Purl knits stretch in both the lengthwise and crosswise directions. They are used for sweaters.

• *Rib knits* have vertical ribs or columns of stitches that alternate on the front and the back. Rib knits are used as neck, wrist, and bottom bands on sweaters and jackets.

• *Double knits* are made with two yarns and two sets of needles. The loops are drawn through from both directions. A double knit is heavier, firmer, and sturdier than other knits. It will not run or ravel. Double knits can be used for a variety of garments.

Warp Knits

Warp knits are made with several yarns on flat knitting machines. The fabric is constructed by looping the multiple warp yarns so that they interlock. Thus, each loop is made up of two yarns. The fabric is usually run-resistant.

Warp Knit

• *Tricot knits* have very fine vertical wales on the right side and crosswise courses on the back. They are used for lingerie, underwear, shirts, and dresses.

• *Raschel knits* may have an extra yarn stitched in to produce a textured or patterned design. Open and lacy knits can be created.

Other Fabric Constructions

There are several other types of fabric construction besides weaving and knitting. Fibers, yarns, and fabric can be joined together by heat and moisture, adhesives, bonding agents, or stitching.

Nonwoven Fabrics

Nonwoven fabrics are made by interlocking the fibers with heat and moisture or with an adhesive substance. Felt is made by applying heat, moisture, and pressure to wool fibers. It depends on the natural ability of wool fibers to shrink and lock together to form a mat. Felt is used primarily for hats, craft projects, and industrial uses.

Nonwoven

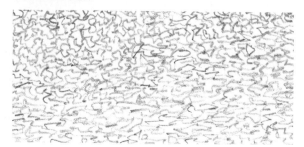

Manufactured fibers can be joined or fused together using an adhesive or bonding agent. These types of nonwoven fabrics are used for sew-in and fusible interfacings, disposable surgical gowns, and disposable diapers.

Nonwoven fabrics do not ravel or fray. They are flexible and have good shape retention. However, they may have weak areas and may tear easily. Most nonwoven fabrics are inexpensive to produce.

Stretch Fabrics

Stretch fabrics are woven or knitted fabrics that have been constructed to stretch more than they normally would. Stretch fabrics are made of yarns that have increased stretchability. These fabrics use textured yarns or yarns that have been wrapped around an elastic core. Spandex or rubber can be used also.

Stretch fabrics can be designed to stretch in the warp direction, the filling direction, or in both directions. Two-way stretch fabrics are especially desirable for swimsuits, exercise wear, and active sportswear.

Bonded and Laminated Fabrics

Fabrics can be bonded to another fabric, vinyl, clear films, or rubberized coatings. This can be done to give more body to the fabric or to create a special surface. Simulated leather has vinyl bonded to a woven or knitted base. Rubberized coatings can be added to fabrics for water repellency.

Stretch fabrics are used in many types of garments. They provide comfort because the fabrics are able to "give" and stretch with the body.

Laminated fabrics have a layer of foam between an outer fabric and a backing fabric. This may be used to give additional warmth to outerwear.

Many bonded or laminated fabrics cannot be dry cleaned. Instead, they should be wiped off or washed gently.

Laces and Nets

Laces and nets are made by twisting or looping threads or yarns together. Special machines can make very intricate lace designs for use in garments and home furnishings.

Quilted Fabrics

Quilted fabrics consist of two layers of fabric with a batting between them. The three layers of fabric can be held together with machine stitching in a decorative pattern or in rows.

Pinsonic quilting is a method of holding the layers of fabric together without any stitching. Instead, the fabric is quilted by heat fusion. This method has no stitching threads that can break. However, holes can develop in the fabric at the point of the heat fusion. Pinsonic quilting is used for bedspreads, mattress pads, and placemats.

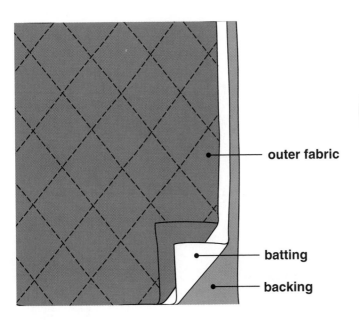

outer fabric

batting

backing

AROUND THE WORLD

What's In a Name?

Etymology is the study of the history of a word. Here is the history of the names of some of the fabrics we wear today:

Cashmere is a different way of spelling Kashmir, a region in northern India and Tibet. Fabric made of wool from the wild Kashmir goat was first fashioned into shawls.

Corduroy, in French, is *corde du Roi* or "cloth of the king." A Frenchman imported the fabric from England. He hoped that people would want to buy it if they thought it was associated with royalty.

Denim got its name from the phrase *de Nimes*. This means "from Nimes," the French town where the fabric was first made. This very strong fabric was worn by sailors and fishermen. The indigo dye used was the only dye that resisted the effects of the sun and saltwater. To save money, the warp yarns were dyed blue but the filling yarns were left white. Many of today's denims are still made this way.

Lamé comes from the French verb *laminer*, which means "to flatten." The first lamé fabrics were made from pure silver or gold that was flattened into strips. Today the threads used may be all metal, metal wound around a core yarn, plastic-coated metal, or metal-coated plastic.

Madras fabric comes from the Madras region in India. It is made from fine cotton on hand looms and dyed with vegetable dyes.

Tweed is derived from the Scottish term *tweel*. Some people think that an English merchant misread the name when placing an order and called the fabric tweed. Another theory is that the fabric was named after the Tweed River, which runs between Scotland and England.

Fabric Dictionary

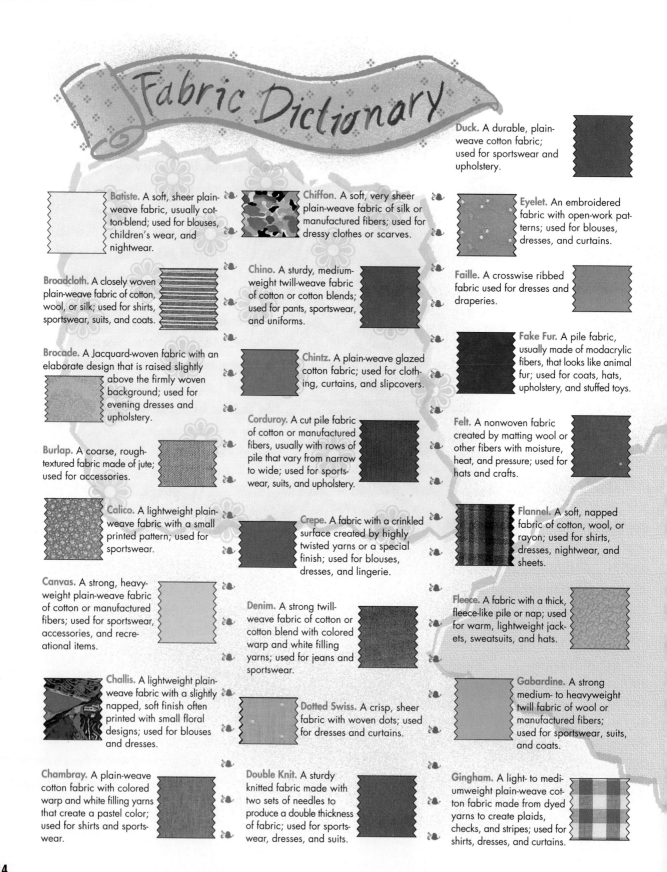

Batiste. A soft, sheer plain-weave fabric, usually cotton-blend; used for blouses, children's wear, and nightwear.

Broadcloth. A closely woven plain-weave fabric of cotton, wool, or silk; used for shirts, sportswear, suits, and coats.

Brocade. A Jacquard-woven fabric with an elaborate design that is raised slightly above the firmly woven background; used for evening dresses and upholstery.

Burlap. A coarse, rough-textured fabric made of jute; used for accessories.

Calico. A lightweight plain-weave fabric with a small printed pattern; used for sportswear.

Canvas. A strong, heavyweight plain-weave fabric of cotton or manufactured fibers; used for sportswear, accessories, and recreational items.

Challis. A lightweight plain-weave fabric with a slightly napped, soft finish often printed with small floral designs; used for blouses and dresses.

Chambray. A plain-weave cotton fabric with colored warp and white filling yarns that create a pastel color; used for shirts and sportswear.

Chiffon. A soft, very sheer plain-weave fabric of silk or manufactured fibers; used for dressy clothes or scarves.

Chino. A sturdy, medium-weight twill-weave fabric of cotton or cotton blends; used for pants, sportswear, and uniforms.

Chintz. A plain-weave glazed cotton fabric; used for clothing, curtains, and slipcovers.

Corduroy. A cut pile fabric of cotton or manufactured fibers, usually with rows of pile that vary from narrow to wide; used for sportswear, suits, and upholstery.

Crepe. A fabric with a crinkled surface created by highly twisted yarns or a special finish; used for blouses, dresses, and lingerie.

Denim. A strong twill-weave fabric of cotton or cotton blend with colored warp and white filling yarns; used for jeans and sportswear.

Dotted Swiss. A crisp, sheer fabric with woven dots; used for dresses and curtains.

Double Knit. A sturdy knitted fabric made with two sets of needles to produce a double thickness of fabric; used for sportswear, dresses, and suits.

Duck. A durable, plain-weave cotton fabric; used for sportswear and upholstery.

Eyelet. An embroidered fabric with open-work patterns; used for blouses, dresses, and curtains.

Faille. A crosswise ribbed fabric used for dresses and draperies.

Fake Fur. A pile fabric, usually made of modacrylic fibers, that looks like animal fur; used for coats, hats, upholstery, and stuffed toys.

Felt. A nonwoven fabric created by matting wool or other fibers with moisture, heat, and pressure; used for hats and crafts.

Flannel. A soft, napped fabric of cotton, wool, or rayon; used for shirts, dresses, nightwear, and sheets.

Fleece. A fabric with a thick, fleece-like pile or nap; used for warm, lightweight jackets, sweatsuits, and hats.

Gabardine. A strong medium- to heavyweight twill fabric of wool or manufactured fibers; used for sportswear, suits, and coats.

Gingham. A light- to mediumweight plain-weave cotton fabric made from dyed yarns to create plaids, checks, and stripes; used for shirts, dresses, and curtains.

Jersey. A smooth, lightweight knit; used for dresses, shirts, sportswear, and underwear. Matte jersey has a dull surface.

Lace. A decorative, openwork fabric; used for fancy blouses, dresses, trims, curtains, and tablecloths.

Madras. A plain-weave cotton fabric in plaid, checks, or stripes with noncolorfast dyes that bleed for a faded look; used for sportswear.

Muslin. A firm plain-weave cotton fabric in a variety of weights; used for dresses, sheets, and draperies.

Net. An open-mesh fabric formed by twisting yarns together; used for evening dresses, veils, and curtains.

Organdy and Organza. A crisp, sheer plain-weave fabric; organdy is made from cotton, organza from silk or rayon; used for dressy clothes and curtains.

Oxford Cloth. A medium-weight basket-weave or plain-weave fabric with colored warp and white filling yarns; used for shirts.

Percale. A firm, smooth plain-weave fabric of cotton or cotton/polyester blend that is similar to muslin but woven of finer yarns; used for shirts, dresses, and sheets.

Piqué. A mediumweight fabric in a dobby weave with small geometric designs, such as bird's eye and honeycomb; used for dresses and children's wear.

Poplin. A mediumweight finely ribbed fabric that is slightly heavier than broadcloth; used for sportswear and dresses.

Sailcloth. A very strong, durable cotton fabric originally used for sails; now used for sportswear.

Sateen and Satin. A smooth, shiny fabric woven in a satin weave; sateen is made from cotton, satin from silk or acetate; used for blouses, dresses, evening dresses, and draperies.

Seersucker. A plain-weave cotton or cotton-blend fabric with puckered stripes; used for summer suits and sportswear.

Shantung. A plain-weave fabric of silk or manufactured fibers with a nubbed surface; used for dresses, suits, and draperies.

Suede Cloth. A woven or knitted fabric with a napped finish that looks like suede; used for coats, jackets, and upholstery.

Taffeta. A crisp plain-weave fabric that has a sheen and rustles when it moves; used for dressy clothes and bows.

Terrycloth. A woven or knitted pile fabric that has uncut loops on one or both sides; used for robes, beachwear, and towels.

Tricot. A drapeable warp knit with fine vertical wales on the front and crosswise ribs on the back; used for shirts, dresses, and lingerie.

Tulle. A fine, lightweight net; used for bridal veils and formal gowns.

Tweed. A sturdy fabric made from wool or wool blends in a plain or twill weave with a nubby surface; used for jackets, suits, skirts, coats, and upholstery.

Velour. A soft woven or knitted fabric with a thick pile surface; used for coats, sportswear, and casual wear.

Velvet and Velveteen. A lustrous cut pile fabric; velvet is made of silk or manufactured fibers, velveteen of cotton; used for jackets, dressy clothes, robes, draperies, and upholstery.

Vinyl. A woven or knitted fabric coated with vinyl to look like leather or rubber; used for coats, rainwear, and upholstery.

Voile. A soft, very sheer plain-weave fabric similar to organdy and batiste; used for blouses, dresses, and curtains.

CHAPTER 13 REVIEW

Summary

- Fibers are spun into yarns. Then the yarns are interlaced or looped together to create fabric.
- Yarns can be textured for added softness, stretchability, and wrinkle resistance.
- Blended yarns can offer the best qualities of two or more fibers.
- The two most common methods of fabric construction are weaving and knitting.
- Types of weaves include: plain, twill, satin, and pile weaves.
- The two basic types of knits are weft knits and warp knits.
- Special fabric constructions include nonwoven fabrics; laces and nets; and stretch, bonded, laminated, and quilted fabrics.

Using Vocabulary Terms

On a separate piece of paper, write the vocabulary term that best fits the definition:

1. A self-edge formed by the filling yarn when it turns to go back in the other direction.
2. A raised surface of loops or yarn ends.
3. Yarns that run the length of the fabric.
4. Long continuous fibers that are measured in yards or meters.
5. The number of yarn strands twisted together.
6. Different fibers combined into one yarn.

Recalling the Facts

1. What is the difference between yarns made of staple fibers and those made of filament fibers?
2. What is a novelty yarn?
3. List four advantages of using the texturing process on filament yarns.
4. Why are fibers blended? Give examples of two blends and their advantages.
5. Define the term *hand* as it relates to fabric.
6. In woven fabrics, which yarn is usually the stronger? Why?
7. Describe each of the three basic weaves: plain, twill, and satin.
8. How is a pile weave created?
9. What are the wales and courses in a knit fabric?
10. How are nonwoven fabrics made?

Thinking Critically

1. **Analysis.** Compare the advantages and disadvantages of woven and knitted fabrics.
2. **Synthesis.** There are many types of woven fabrics. What common characteristics do they all share?
3. **Analysis.** How are weft knits and warp knits alike? How are they different?
4. **Evaluation.** If you were to purchase a new shirt or blouse, which type of fabric would you prefer? Why?

Applying Your Knowledge

1. **Weaving.** Re-create the three basic weaves using thin strips of paper to represent the yarns.

2. **Fabric Construction.** Use a magnifying glass to analyze the fabrics worn by you and your classmates. Record the different weaves and knits that you find.

3. **Fabric Types.** Collect a variety of fabric swatches. Identify each by name of fabric and type of weave or knit. Mount each swatch on an index card, along with its label. Create a bulletin board display.

4. **Fabric Selection.** If you were to design an outfit for each of the following people, what types of fabrics would you use: an infant, a teenager, a doctor, a construction worker, a person in a wheelchair? Describe each outfit and give reasons for your fabric choices.

Making the Connection

1. **Math.** Compare the stretchability of several knitted and/or stretch fabrics. Record your findings in the form of a bar graph.

2. **Science.** Cut three 4 inch by 4 inch samples of different types of fabrics. Soak one swatch of each fabric in hot water and one swatch in cold water for several minutes. Dry flat. Soak the third swatch in warm water and dry in a dryer. Compare shrinkage and wrinkle resistance of the samples. What conclusions can you make from your observations?

What Is an Engineer?

Engineers are involved in many aspects of textile manufacturing. They develop new equipment, keep it in good running condition, and measure its performance and effectiveness. An industrial engineer improves production methods. A mechanical engineer develops and maintains the plant's equipment. An electrical engineer is responsible for the plant's electrical and cooling systems.

Try It Yourself

Imagine that you are an engineer for a fiber or fabric manufacturer. Research the manufacturing process involved in producing fibers or fabrics. Then write a report on the type of equipment, raw materials, and production techniques used in textile manufacturing. Include, if possible, the type of experience and training needed to operate the equipment.

Build Your Portfolio

After completing the report, place a copy in your portfolio. In addition, use the Fabric Dictionary on pages 214-215 to create a fabric file. Mount fabric swatches on index cards and label with the fabric name and description. Use the fabric file as a reference for other portfolio projects.

Finishes

After reading this chapter, you will be able to:

- *Explain the dyeing process.*

- *Describe various printing techniques.*

- *Explain how a fabric's texture can be changed.*

- *Identify the finishes that can improve a fabric's performance.*

Terms to Learn

- *finishes*
- *gray goods*
- *dyes*
- *colorfast*
- *printing*
- *nap*

When fabric first comes from the loom, it looks nothing like the finished fabric that you will see as a shirt, jacket, or towel. Many of the fabrics have no color—they are gray or off-white. The warp yarns may have been stiffened to withstand the strain during weaving. The fabric may be limp, or fuzzy, or dull, or very shiny.

How then are fabrics transformed into beautiful, colorful, and comfortable materials that you want to buy and wear? The answer is finishes.

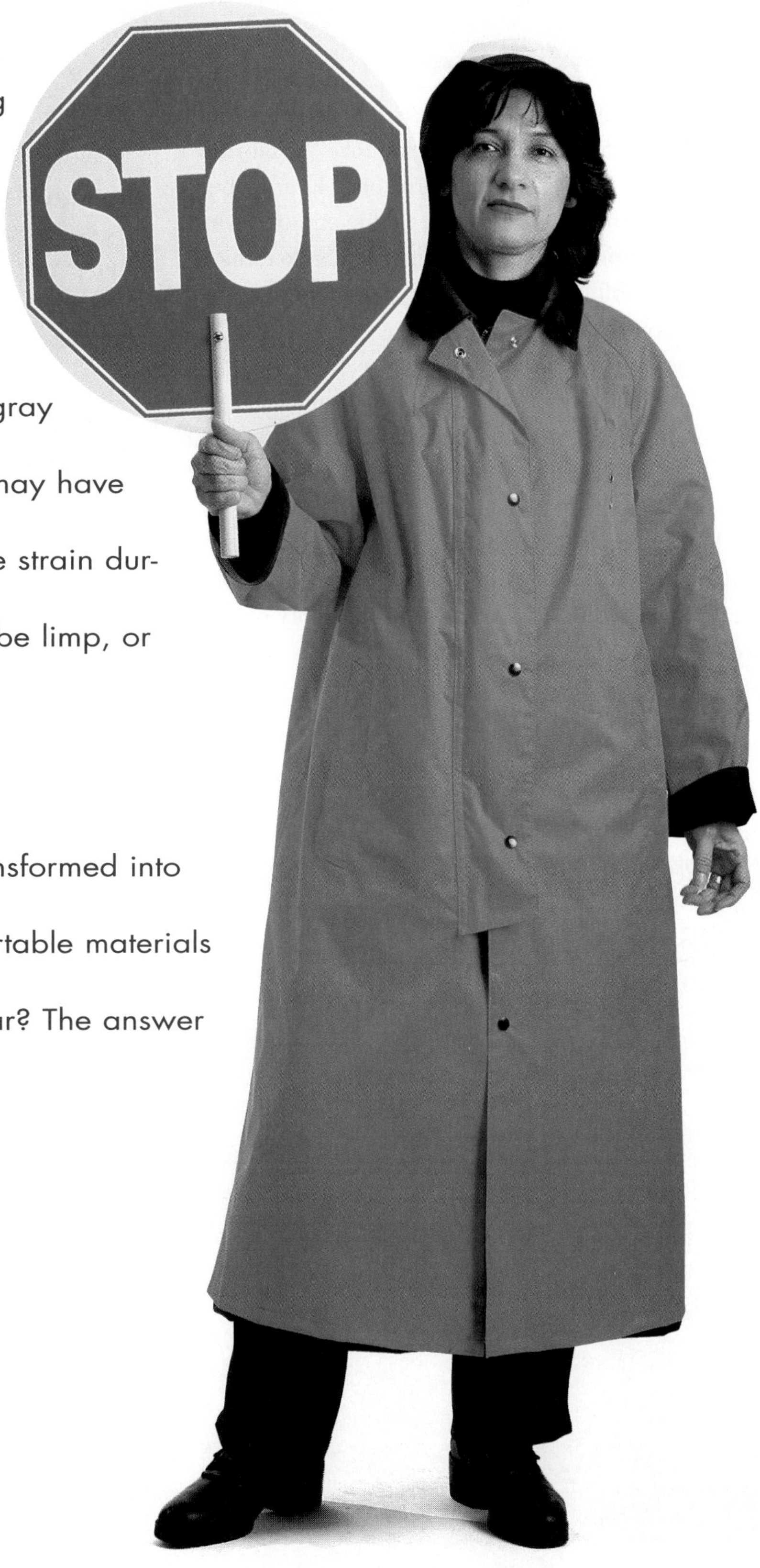

Finishing Processes

Finishes are *any special treatments that are applied to fabrics*. They can improve a fabric's appearance, texture, and performance. Every fiber and type of fabric has certain desirable and undesirable characteristics. Finishes can be added to reduce the undesirable characteristics or to improve the desirable ones.

Some finishes are added to create a specific design, such as a stripe or a print. Other finishes offer a softer, firmer, or smoother hand. Many finishes are used to add a specific property or quality to the fabric, such as wrinkle resistance.

Fabric finishes may be permanent or temporary. Permanent finishes last throughout the life of the fabric. Temporary finishes may last through only one or two cleanings.

Color and Design Finishes

When *fabric first comes from the loom*, it is called **gray goods**. It must be cleaned to remove any oils, resins, gums, or soil that would prevent the finish from penetrating the fabric. Manufacturers then alter the appearance of gray goods by dyeing or printing the fabric.

Dyeing Textiles

Dyes are *compounds that penetrate and color fibers*. They can be used to color the entire fabric or to create special designs on the fabric. For centuries, natural dyes were obtained from plants, insects, shellfish, and minerals. The first synthetic dye was discovered by accident in 1856. Then a whole new industry developed for textiles.

Textile colorists are constantly seeking better dyes for different fibers and blends. Today they use computers to develop exact formulas for dyeing different fibers a certain color.

There are five different methods of dyeing:

• **Stock dyeing.** Natural fibers can be dyed before being spun into yarns. This permits the spinning of tweed and multicolored yarns.

• **Solution dyeing.** Dye is added to the chemical solution before it is forced through spinnerets. The color becomes a permanent part of the manufactured fiber.

• **Yarn dyeing.** Yarns are dyed before they are woven or knitted into fabric. This method is used for plaids, checks, and stripes.

These yarns are being dyed before they are woven or knitted into fabric. Today most dyes are mixed by computer to produce uniform colors.

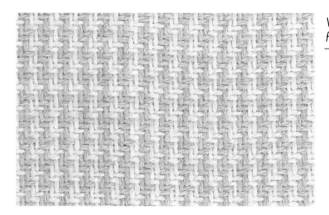

What method of dyeing do you think was used for this fabric?

This textile lab technician is testing the colorfastness of various dyes.

- **Piece dyeing.** Fabric is dyed after being woven or knitted. Manufacturers can store undyed fabric and then dye it a specific color, according to their orders.

- **Product dyeing.** The fabric is cut and sewn into the finished product. Then the entire garment or item is dyed, according to orders.

Colorfastness

The term **colorfast** means that *the color in the fabric will not change.* It will not fade from washing, from chlorine in a pool, or from exposure to sunlight. The fastness of a color depends on the type of dye, the chemical structure of the fiber, and the method of application.

Most dyes are not colorfast to everything. Some may be more affected by washing, dry cleaning, sunlight, or perspiration. Some may *crock*, or rub off onto your skin or other clothing.

It is important to read the label or hangtag for information about colorfastness. You cannot tell how fast a color will be by looking at the fabric.

Manufacturers select dyes that are most suitable to the fiber content and the intended use of the fabric. Colorfastness to washing is important for children's clothes and sportswear. Fastness to sunlight is important for draperies, upholstery, and carpets. Swimwear needs to be colorfast to sunlight, washing, and chlorine.

Some fabrics, however, are designed to fade or bleed. Some denim jeans are meant to lighten when washed. Madras, a woven plaid fabric, is meant to bleed so the plaid becomes softer and less distinct.

Printing Textiles

Fabrics can be printed in a variety of ways. **Printing** involves *transferring color to the surface of a fabric to form a pattern or design.* Some printing methods are very old techniques that are still used by crafts people today. However, the textile industry uses high-speed electronic machines for textile printing. Some specialty fabrics, such as scarves and evening gowns, may be printed by hand.

Four of the most common printing methods include roller, screen, rotary screen, and heat transfer. Other methods, such as tie dyeing, are discussed in the Sewing and Serging Handbook.

- **Roller printing.** The roller printing press contains circular rollers, or printing plates, one for each color of the desired design. Each roller is chemically etched with its colored part of the pattern, leaving high and low areas on the rollers. The raised sections of the roller pick up the desired color. The fabric is printed as it passes through the press and makes contact with the raised sections of each roller. The different areas of color will coincide to form the completed design.

  Two variations of roller printing include discharge printing and resist printing. In *discharge printing,* some of the dye is bleached or chemically removed to create a white design on a colored fabric. In *resist printing,* the fabric is printed using a dye-resistant chemical. Then the fabric is dyed. The printed area resists the dye and remains uncolored.

- **Screen printing.** A fabric or metal mesh screen is stretched on a frame. The design is traced onto the screen. Then all of the areas not included in the design to be printed are blocked out with a special coating. The color is then pressed through the screen onto the fabric, using a squeegee or roller. A separate

Fabric patterns can be designed by computer and automatically programmed into the printing press.

screen is used for each color of the design. Large designs, such as those often used in home furnishings fabrics, can be printed using this method.

- **Rotary screen printing.** This method combines the advantages of roller printing and screen printing. The rotary screens, made from metal foil, are less costly than the printing plates. It is a faster method than flat screen printing.

- **Heat transfer printing.** This method is used for transferring designs, insignias, and words onto fabric. The design is printed in reverse with heat sensitive dyes on paper. When the paper pattern is placed face down on the fabric and heat is applied, the design is transferred to the fabric.

Transfer printing uses heat to transfer a design from paper to fabric.

Texture and Performance Finishes

A fabric's texture and hand can be improved with finishing processes. Finishes also are used to improve the performance of fabrics.

Types of Texture Finishes

Most fabrics have some type of finish applied to improve surface texture and hand. These finishes may also help to improve the comfort or performance of the fabric.

- **Calendering.** Fabric passes between two heated rollers that smooth the fabric and improve the luster.

- **Glazing.** A resin is applied during calendering to produce a high polish or glaze on the surface of the fabric. Chintz is a glazed fabric.

- **Napping.** Rotating wire brushes are used to raise the short fiber ends of staple yarns to create a *soft, fuzzy surface* called **nap**. It appears different when viewed from different directions. Flannel is a napped fabric.

- **Lustering.** Fabric is treated with heat and pressure to add luster.

- **Beetling.** Cotton or linen fabrics are flattened to fill out the weave and add luster.

- **Delustering.** Fibers or fabrics are treated with chemicals to reduce their gloss.

- **Embossing.** Fabrics are given a raised design on their surface by being calendered with rollers engraved with the design.

- **Ciré.** A super glossy finish is obtained by applying wax or some other substance before calendering. Ciré nylon is sometimes used for lightweight jackets.

- **Moiré.** A watered or wavy pattern is obtained by calendering two layers of fabric slightly off-grain. Moiré fabric is used for evening wear.

- **Sizing.** Starches or resins are added to the fabric for extra body. Sizing is usually only a temporary finish.

From Fibers to Finished Fabrics

Natural fibers, such as cotton and wool, come from plants and animals. Manufactured fibers, such as rayon and polyester, are made from wood pulp, natural gas, or petroleum.

Fibers are twisted together to form yarns. They may be made of natural fibers, manufactured fibers, or a blend of both.

Yarns are woven or knitted together to create fabric. In woven fabrics, the yarns are interlaced at right angles to each other. Knitted fabrics have one or more yarns looped together.

Finally, fabric is finished to improve its appearance, texture, and performance. It can be dyed or printed with one or more colors. Its surface can be made smooth, crisp, or fuzzy. It can be treated to resist wrinkles, stains, fire, water, mildew, or moths.

Types of Performance Finishes

Sometimes a fabric's performance is a result of the fibers that are used. However, many different types of finishes can be applied to fabrics to increase their performance. Some of these finishes can be diminished or destroyed by improper care of the fabric. Be sure to read the care labels carefully and follow the manufacturer's recommendations.

- **Crease resistance and wrinkle resistance.** These finishes help fabrics to resist wrinkling and to recover more rapidly from wrinkling caused by normal wear. Wrinkles tend to flatten or disappear when the garment is hung up.

- **Durable press.** The fabric can be washed and dried by machine and will need little or no ironing. The fabric will resist wrinkling during wear, and the garment will maintain its shape, pleats, and creases.

In many advertisements and articles, you will see the term *permanent press* used. Fabric experts prefer the term *durable press*. This means that with proper care the fabric or garment will perform as expected. However, if care instructions are not followed, some wrinkling may occur. The word *permanent* implies that wrinkling can never occur.

- **Shrinkage control.** Shrinkage should only be minimum, even after repeated launderings. It does not guarantee that no shrinkage will occur. The term *Sanforized*® is an assurance that the fabric will not shrink more than one percent in washing. Washable wool fabrics have been treated so they will not shrink when laundered as directed on the label. If a fabric is preshrunk, then some shrinkage process has been applied.

- **Mercerization.** This is a caustic soda treatment used on cotton, linen, and rayon. It gives the fiber added strength and luster.

- **Stain and spot resistance.** These finishes help fabrics to repel water- and oil-based stains. They are often used on table linens and upholstery fabrics, in addition to clothing.

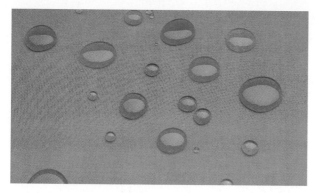

Fabrics treated to resist water, stains, and spots are often used for sportswear and upholstery.

- **Soil release.** This makes it easier to remove soil and oily stains from durable press fabrics and manufactured fibers during laundering.

- **Water repellent and waterproof.** These finishes are designed to help keep the fabric and the wearer dry. Water-repellent fabrics have been treated to resist water, but eventually they will become wet. The fabric remains *porous*, which means that air and water can pass through. The finish may need to be renewed when the garment is dry cleaned.

  Waterproof fabrics have been coated or treated so that no water will penetrate. The fabric has been made nonporous and thus may be uncomfortable to wear. New microporous waterproof finishes have been developed that allow body moisture to escape while not allowing water to penetrate.

- **Antistatic.** This prevents fabrics from clinging.

- **Flame-retardant.** This helps to reduce flaming and burning in fabrics that have been exposed to a flame or high heat. It is used on children's sleepwear and other clothing. Special care may be needed to maintain the finish.

- **Antibacterial.** This checks the growth of bacteria and perspiration odors.

- **Mildew resistance.** This resists the growth of mildew and other molds.

- **Moth resistance.** This repels moths and other fiber-eating insects.

Textile News

The textile industry is constantly working on ways to produce new fibers, as well as to improve the fibers we already have. Here are some exciting developments.

Until recently, silk was the finest fiber known. Now there are microdenier fibers, or microfibers. These fibers are the result of a process that can take manufactured fibers and spin them until they are twice as fine as the finest strand of silk. These polyester, nylon, rayon, or acrylic microfibers can be used alone or blended with natural fibers. Many microfibers are wind-resistant and water-repellent. They are lighter in weight, softer, and more comfortable than coated or laminated waterproof fabrics. This makes them particularly popular for outerwear garments, such as raincoats and windbreaker jackets.

Lyocell is sometimes described as a new natural fiber. Like rayon, it is made from wood pulp. The difference is that lyocell is processed with a recyclable, nontoxic dissolving agent. Fabrics made from 100 percent lyocell are machine-washable and biodegradable. They also have the softness of silk, the strength of polyester, and the absorbency of cotton. Because the manufacturing process is slow and expensive, garments made from lyocell are expensive. Tencel® is one of the trademark names for this fiber.

Some cottons, such as Biocotton®, are being organically grown without toxic pesticides and herbicides. Cotton can also be grown in colors right on the cotton plant. This "naturally colored" cotton comes in soft, pale colors. It is considered environmentally friendly because there is no need to use chemicals to process the colors.

CHAPTER 14 REVIEW

Summary

- Finishes are applied to fabrics to improve their appearance, texture, and performance.
- Some finishes are permanent; others are only temporary.
- Fabrics can be dyed or printed, using various methods.
- Some finishing processes, such as napping and embossing, improve the texture and hand of a fabric.
- Other finishing processes, such as wrinkle resistance and shrinkage control, improve a fabric's performance.
- Some finishes can be diminished or destroyed by improper fabric care.

Using Vocabulary Terms

On a separate piece of paper, write the vocabulary term that best fits the definition:

1. The color in the fabric will not change.
2. A soft, fuzzy surface.
3. Any special treatments that are applied to fabrics.
4. Fabric that first comes from the loom.
5. Compounds that penetrate and color fibers.
6. Transferring color to the surface of a fabric to form a pattern or design.

Recalling the Facts

1. List three benefits that a fabric finish can provide.
2. What is the difference between a permanent finish and a temporary finish?
3. What are the five different methods of dyeing fabrics?
4. What type of colorfastness would be most important for swimwear? children's clothes? draperies?
5. Name the four most common printing methods.
6. List three types of texture finishes that can add luster or glaze to a fabric.
7. What are two types of performance finishes that can reduce wrinkling?
8. What is the difference between waterproof and water repellent?
9. What does the term *Sanforized*® mean?
10. What are four types of resistant finishes that can be added to fabrics?

Thinking Critically

1. **Analysis.** Compare and contrast the five different methods of dyeing. Give an advantage of each method.
2. **Synthesis.** If you could develop a new fabric finish, what would it be?
3. **Analysis.** What is the difference between the terms *durable press* and *permanent press?* Why do you think the term *permanent press* is frequently used in ads?

4. **Evaluation.** Which three performance finishes do you think are most important for consumers? Explain your reasoning.

Applying Your Knowledge

1. **Fabric Finishes.** Look through catalogs for various types of fabric finishes. Make a chart that identifies the finishes and the trade names given for them.

2. **Dyeing and Printing.** Collect samples of various types of fabrics. Identify which samples have been dyed and which have been printed.

3. **Colorfastness.** Dip unwashed fabric samples into hot water. Analyze each swatch for any color loss. Which colors were more likely to fade or bleed?

4. **Designing.** From a large note card, cut out a "shirt." Choose its fiber content, the probable dyeing or printing method used, and the texture and performance finishes that were applied. Describe your shirt to the class and explain the reasons for your choices.

Making the Connection

1. **Art.** Print your own design on a t-shirt or fabric, using screen printing or block printing. For block printing, you can carve designs out of wood or firm vegetables, such potatoes, carrots, or turnips.

What Is a Computer Programmer?

Computer programmers develop the information systems that enable a computer to perform various tasks. Information systems are also called programs or software. Computers are widely used in the textile industry, from designing fabrics to controlling the equipment used to produce, print, and finish fabrics.

Try It Yourself

Imagine that you are a computer expert. Use some type of computer program to create an original design, write a report, or analyze data on a spreadsheet. Experiment with the many different types of functions that the program provides. For example, create different versions of your design or add special features to your report.

Build Your Portfolio

Print out a copy of your design, report, or analysis to place in your portfolio. Write a description of the various computer functions that you used to create your project. Add this to your portfolio.

2. **Science.** Test the water repellency of different types of rainwear, including umbrellas. Using an eyedropper or small measuring spoon, place droplets of water on the different fabrics. Record how long it takes for any water to be absorbed.

Textile Chemist

Amy Chang is a textile chemist who works in the research department of a major consumer magazine. She evaluates everything from blue jeans to pantyhose. "This is the perfect job for me," says Amy, "because it combines my interest in science with my love of fabrics. When I graduated from high school, I didn't know that jobs like this existed!"

Education and Training

Amy remembers how excited she was when she received a chemistry set for her eleventh birthday. It was a gift from her uncle, who was a pharmacist. In high school, math and science were her favorite subjects. Her favorite clothes were treasures she found in antique shops and second-hand stores. She also learned to sew.

Early in her junior year, Amy went to a college fair. There she met a university representative who told her about a very exciting chemistry and biology program. With her uncle's encouragement, Amy applied and was accepted. After college, she was hired by an oil refinery to work in their engineering department.

While working at the oil refinery, Amy began to combine her interest in chemistry with her interest in fabrics. She went back to school to get a master's degree in textile chemistry. She started to write technical articles for textile journals and spinning and weaving magazines. "At first," said Amy, "it was hard to get editors interested in publishing what I had to say. Like many engineers, I didn't have good writing skills." To improve these

skills, she took writing classes at the local community college.

Amy began to sell her articles. It encouraged her to take her career in a new direction. She accepted a job as the technical director for a carpet care trade association. She was responsible for helping carpet cleaners with the basic science of stain removal. She also wrote a monthly column for the association's newsletter. Ultimately Amy was offered her present job: textile project leader for a major consumer magazine.

Responsibilities

The magazine's editor, along with a special committee, decides what products will be tested. Then it is Amy's responsibility to develop the rating system and to supervise the testing staff.

• **Develop testing standards.** Amy decides what standards will be used in evaluating each product. When her staff was evaluating blazer jackets, for example, they looked at the overall appearance, construction details, fabric, lining, buttons, ability to withstand wrinkles, and condition of each garment after several cleanings.

- **Develop budgets.** Before any testing begins, Amy must research how much the project will cost. Then she presents a budget to the magazine's publisher for approval.

- **Copywriting.** When the testing is completed, Amy writes the consumer article that appears in the magazine.

- **Supervise staff.** Amy is responsible for supervising her staff members. She also uses independent laboratories and consultants to test some products.

- **Continuing education.** Amy belongs to several professional organizations, including the American Association of Textile Chemists and Colorists. These organizations help her stay up-to-date on the latest developments in her field. Her employer allows her to attend conventions, seminars, and workshops.

Knowledge and Skills

Here is a list of the knowledge and skills that Amy has found to be valuable:

- **Science and textile knowledge**—for developing testing standards, analyzing data, and evaluating outcomes.

- **Math skills**—for preparing budgets and computing test results.

- **Communication skills**—for writing reports and magazine articles, developing testing criteria, making presentations at staff meetings, and interacting with management and coworkers.

- **Computer skills**—for keeping track of testing projects, analyzing test results, and writing reports and articles.

- **Management skills**—for supervising staff members and working with outside consultants and laboratories.

"All the math and science courses I took in high school made my college courses easier. However, I thought a scientist didn't need to worry about the language arts. But I was wrong. I wish I'd paid more attention in my English classes and maybe gotten some experience writing for the school newspaper."

You and Your Wardrobe

Developing a Wardrobe Plan

After reading this chapter, you will be able to:

- *Explain the benefits of a wardrobe plan.*

- *Expand your wardrobe by creating new clothing combinations.*

- *Evaluate your present wardrobe to determine your clothing needs.*

- *Develop a personal wardrobe plan.*

Terms to Learn

- *wardrobe plan*
- *economical*
- *versatile*
- *inventory*
- *prioritize*

Suppose you are going to drive across the country. You are starting your trip in Boston and want to end up in San Francisco. How will you get there? You could just point your car westward and hope that you eventually reach San Francisco.

However, it would be a lot easier if you got a map and planned your route before you left Boston. That way you could avoid wrong turns, drive on better roads, and arrive in a shorter time.

Putting your wardrobe together with the aid of a wardrobe plan is just like driving with a road map. It is the fastest and most efficient way to get the best results.

What Is a Wardrobe Plan?

A **wardrobe plan** is *a guide for buying and maintaining the clothes and accessories that are appropriate for you and your lifestyle.* You should review your plan each season. It should be flexible enough to change as your needs, wants, and lifestyle change.

A wardrobe plan has several purposes:

- **To help you make better use of items that you already own.** As you develop your plan, you may find new ways to combine the clothes that are already in your wardrobe.

- **To help you decide what you need to add to your wardrobe.** You will be able to determine whether a pair of black wool slacks or a pair of denim jeans is a more useful addition to your wardrobe at this time.

- **To serve as a guide for future additions.** You will be able to determine which items are wearing out or beginning to look dated. This will give you a head start on knowing what you will need to add next season or next year.

Use Everything You Own

The easiest way to expand your wardrobe is to think of ways to use all of your clothes. It is also the most **economical**, or *inexpensive*, method because it does not cost you any money.

Try New Combinations

Perhaps you are in the habit of always wearing the same sweater with the same pair of pants. Now you have a chance to try out new combinations. Take a look at the coordinated outfits that you already own. Separate them into individual pieces, such as pants, skirts, shirts, sweaters, and jackets. Now see if the pieces from one outfit will mix and match with the pieces from another outfit. Many clothes are very **versatile**, or *able to be worn or combined in a variety of ways.*

Experiment with new color mixes. Some seasons, unusual color combinations, such as turquoise and orange or purple and red, are very fashionable. Perhaps you always wear your beige sweater with your tweed slacks. Try combining the slacks with another color, such as bright blue or red.

Experiment with new fabric combinations. The jacket from a corduroy suit can be worn with a variety of other fabrics. Some seasons, combining more than one print in an outfit is fashionable. Checks might be worn with stripes, and prints with plaids. However, the patterns and colors must be carefully combined to create an outfit that is pleasing to the eye. In other seasons, they may be out-of-fashion.

Wardrobe planning will help you make better use of the clothes you already own. It also will help you decide what you need to add to your wardrobe now and in the future.

How many different outfits can you put together from each of these wardrobes?

Try New Uses

Perhaps you can think of new ways to wear the clothes that you already own. You might be able to wear a favorite flannel shirt as both a shirt and a shirtjacket. The turtleneck that you always wear with blue jeans could be worn with slacks and a sweater for a dressier look. The vest that you usually wear under a jacket might be worn over a dress or a top. A sundress might double as a jumper. A change of accessories might transform an outfit from casual to dressy.

Try belting a large, loose-fitting jacket to create a slimmer look. Substitute a tie or a scarf for a belt. Tuck pants into boots. Layer tops in a different order. Look at fashion ads for additional ideas.

This plaid shirt can be worn in several different ways. Can you think of other combinations?

Make a Wardrobe Chart

Working with a wardrobe chart will help you make better use of what you already own. It will also help you determine if you have too many of one type of clothes and not enough of another. In addition, a chart will show you what you need, so that you can plan your clothing purchases.

On the left-hand side of the chart, list all of the different types of items that are in your wardrobe. These may be pants, shirts or blouses, skirts, sweaters, jackets, dresses, coats, and accessories.

Across the top of the chart, make columns in which to describe the garment, your evaluation, and the action you plan to take. See an example of a wardrobe chart on page 237.

To evaluate your wardrobe and its possibilities, follow these three steps:

1. Take inventory of what clothes you have.

2. Evaluate each garment.

3. Decide on your action.

Step 1: Take Inventory

If you were a store owner who needed to know exactly what merchandise was available in the store, you would take a physical **inventory**. This means that *all of the merchandise would be counted*, whether it was on racks, in bins, under the counter, on shelves, or part of a display. Then you could decide what should be added to the store's inventory.

You need to do the same thing with your wardrobe. Start by organizing your clothing by type. For example, put all of the pants together and all of the shirts or blouses together. Then you can see how many you have of each type and what colors they are. Record all of your clothes on your wardrobe inventory chart.

Set aside a day when you will have enough time to take everything out of your closet and drawers, and then put all of the items back again. It is best to take your clothing inventory at the beginning of each season or school year. You will be able to take a fresh look at what you own. At the end you may be tired of your clothes.

Wardrobe Inventory Chart

My Clothes	Description	Evaluation	Plans
Shirts/blouses	3 white 1 plaid 1 stripe	good button missing frayed	sew button buy 1 shirt
Pants	1 black 1 blue	don't like good	keeping for emergency
Jeans	3 pairs	2–love! 1–too short	cut off for shorts
Skirts (female)			
Dresses (female)			
Suits			
Jackets/blazers	1 navy blazer	good shape	
Sweaters	2 crewneck 1 turtleneck	like–ok old, stretched out	buy new one
Coats			
Casual/t-shirts	4 t-shirts 3 knit	comfy 1 faded	replace
Shorts	1 blue 1 tan	ok ripped seam	sew seam
Athletic wear	2 swimsuits sweatsuit	fine getting old	look for sale
Sleepwear			
Underwear			
Socks			
Shoes/boots	1–athletic 1–dress 1–boots	wearing out ok love!	need new pair
Hats/gloves			
Belts	1 black 1 brown	great too small	give away
Ties/scarves			
Jewelry			
Other			

Step 2: Evaluate Each Garment

Next, you need to evaluate each item in your wardrobe. If you are like most people, your wardrobe contains some clothes that you like a lot and wear frequently. It also has clothes that you seldom or never wear.

Ask yourself why you like and enjoy wearing some clothes and not others. Your answers to these questions will give you guidelines for making future purchases:

- Do I like wearing the garment?
- Does it go with other clothes in my wardrobe?
- Does the garment fit well?
- Does it need to be repaired?
- Have I outgrown the outfit?
- Is it worn out?
- Do I simply not like it anymore?

Record your evaluation of each garment on your wardrobe inventory chart.

Step 3: Decide on Your Action

The third step in wardrobe planning is to decide what action you need to take. Take a look at your wardrobe chart. Do any of your clothes need to be repaired or remodeled? If so, set aside some time to sew on buttons, repair rips, or shorten hems. For clothes that you plan to recycle, decide if you could give them to someone else. If not, find a use for the fabric.

You also have to decide what you need to purchase. If you have outgrown or worn out a major item, such as a coat or a pair of boots, you will need to replace it. You may need new clothes for a part-time job or a special activity. Your wardrobe chart can help you identify the clothes you need.

Record your action plans on your wardrobe inventory chart.

Evaluate each garment in your wardrobe. Decide whether you will keep it or whether it needs to be repaired, revised, or recycled.

Evaluate
Your Wardrobe

Remain

Clothes that you like and wear often.
Why do you like and enjoy wearing these clothes? Is it the style, the fabric, the color, or the type of care that they require?

Repair

Clothes that need to be repaired.
These clothes have a button missing, a rip in the seam, or a loose hem. Take time to repair these clothes so you can enjoy wearing them again.

Revise

Clothes that you seldom wear.
Could you wear the item in new combinations with other clothes in your wardrobe? Could a simple alteration improve the fit? Could the style or trim be changed to give it a new look?

Recycle

Clothes that you never wear.
This category includes clothes that you have outgrown, worn out, or never liked. If the garment is still wearable, pass it along to others. If it is no longer wearable, recycle the fabric into projects or household uses.

When evaluating your wardrobe, try sorting your clothes into four different categories: remain, repair, revise, and recycle. Then after you repair or revise a garment, re-evaluate it as an item that can remain in your wardrobe.

Write Down Your Wardrobe Plan

A wardrobe plan is a helpful guide for future additions to your wardrobe. It can help you to choose new clothes that you need and can wear with outfits already in your closet.

Write down the specific items that you need to add to your wardrobe. These should include items that are replacements for clothes and shoes that you have outgrown or worn out. It also should include items that would fill in any gaps in your wardrobe inventory.

Consider Your Needs and Wants

Making a wardrobe plan involves both needs and wants. As a student, your clothing needs are influenced by what is considered acceptable attire at your school. At many schools, students have flexibility as to what they can wear. Jeans, t-shirts, pants, skirts, and sweaters are all worn. Other schools have dress codes that prohibit the wearing of certain types of clothing or accessories to class. Some schools require their students to wear uniforms.

If you have a part-time job, you may need different clothes than those worn to school. Some places, such as fast food restaurants, provide special uniforms. Others may require that you wear a certain style of shirt, a jacket, or a suit.

Wants are usually created by emotional needs. You may want a special item because wearing it will make you feel attractive, confident, slimmer, taller, or shorter. It may be a status symbol for you, making you feel important. Perhaps you want an item because it will help you to conform and fit in with the crowd. On the other hand, you may want it because it will help you to stand out from everyone else and express your individuality.

Many decisions are based on a combination of needs, wants, and values. Buying a new pair of jeans may meet a need because you have outgrown your current ones. It might also be a want because you would love to have the exact style of jeans that your friends are wearing. Your values can help you decide what is more important to you. Should you purchase the expensive pair of designer jeans that your friends are wearing? Or should you buy a pair of regular jeans that are currently on sale and use the savings for something else?

You should write down the specific items you need to add to your wardrobe. Then prioritize which additions are most important.

Prioritize Your Wardrobe Additions

You should **prioritize**, or *rank*, which additions to your wardrobe are most important. Then you will know which items to buy or sew first. For example, if you have outgrown or worn out an item that you need, that should have top priority.

Then you can consider the clothes that you would like to add to your wardrobe. Perhaps one new garment could enable you to coordinate several other outfits. For example, a new shirt could go with several skirts or pants, as well as your jacket. It could also be combined with two of your sweaters.

Your wardrobe plan can also include some items that you want because they are fun, exciting, or up-to-date. However, it is important that you first meet your clothing needs. Then you can add the extra wants that you desire.

The best additions to your wardrobe are clothes and accessories that will satisfy both your needs and your wants. You will enjoy wearing these items time and time again.

If you value easy care, would this shirt be a good addition to your wardrobe?

AROUND THE WORLD

Regional Dress

Although we are becoming one world of fashion, there are still differences in the way people dress in different parts of the country. Sometimes a style of clothing that is identified with a particular region becomes very fashionable. This usually happens because an actor in a popular movie or television show dresses this way. For a while, it seems that people in all parts of the country are wearing that regional style.

- In many Western states, it is common to see cowboy boots and hats worn with business suits as well as blue jeans.

- In Florida and other warm, tropical climates, bright colors are particularly popular. This is because pastel colors tend to look weak and pale in the bright sunlight.

- In Hawaii, men wear aloha shirts for almost all types of occasions. These are loose fitting, short-sleeved shirts in bright tropical prints.

- In large cities, such as New York, Chicago, London, and Paris, black is always a fashionable color for women's clothes.

- A bolo tie is a type of Western neckwear made from heavy, round braid. It has metal tips on the ends and fastens with a metal slide. Men in the West and Southwest wear bolo ties with both sports shirts and business suits.

- In resort communities, sportswear is worn for many activities other than sports. Thus, people may wear skiwear, tennis outfits, golf attire, or swimwear throughout the day.

- Clothing styles in large cities are usually more tailored, darker in color, and dressier than styles worn in smaller towns. Casual clothing may be appropriate for most occasions in suburban and rural communities.

Summary

- A wardrobe plan will help you make better use of items that you already own. It will also help you decide what you need to add to your wardrobe.

- Using the clothes you own in new combinations and new ways can help expand your wardrobe.

- The first step is to take an inventory of your wardrobe.

- Evaluate each garment as to whether it should remain or be repaired, revised, or recycled.

- Using your wardrobe chart, decide what action you need to take.

- Prioritize the clothes you want to add to your wardrobe.

Using Vocabulary Terms

On a separate piece of paper, write the vocabulary term that best fits the definition:

1. Able to be worn or combined in a variety of ways.

2. Rank.

3. A guide for the clothes and accessories that are appropriate for you and your lifestyle.

4. A count of all the merchandise.

5. Inexpensive.

Recalling the Facts

1. What are three benefits of making a wardrobe plan?

2. How can mixing and matching extend your wardrobe?

3. Describe how to take an inventory of your wardrobe.

4. Name the four categories that you can use when evaluating each garment.

5. Why is it beneficial to repair clothing as soon as possible?

6. What are two things you could do with clothes that you never wear?

7. What is the third step in wardrobe planning?

8. Why should you write down your wardrobe plan?

9. Why should you consider your needs and wants when making a wardrobe plan?

10. Why should you prioritize new additions to your wardrobe?

Thinking Critically

1. **Evaluation.** Give some advice to a friend who says "I never have anything to wear!"

2. **Analysis.** Analyze some of the reasons why you like and enjoy wearing certain clothes.

3. **Synthesis.** What might happen if a person tried to make a wardrobe plan without taking an actual inventory of the clothes he or she already owned?

4. **Evaluation.** Make a list of the activities in which you participate the most. Do you think that most garments in your wardrobe are suitable for these activities?

Applying Your Knowledge

1. **Wardrobe Chart.** Make your own wardrobe chart. Take an inventory of your clothes and evaluate each garment. Then decide what action you need to take with your clothes.

2. **Mix-and-Match.** List five garments in your wardrobe. Describe two or three new ways to wear each one.

3. **Repair, Revise, Recycle.** Bring to class one clothing item that needs to be repaired, revised, or recycled. Show your item to the class and discuss what action to take with the item.

Making the Connection

1. **Math.** Research the cost of having minor alterations or repairs made by a dressmaker or tailor in your community. How much money could you save if you could do the work yourself?

2. **Art.** Select two neutral colors, such as black, white, navy, or beige, for the basic garments of a wardrobe. Using drawings or illustrations, show how other color combinations can be created with the addition of various accessories.

What Is a Wardrobe Consultant?

Wardrobe consultants counsel individuals on how to update and revise their wardrobes. Their clients may be seeking a more fashionable or professional image. Such clients may lack the time or the fashion knowledge to evaluate their own wardrobes. A wardrobe consultant will evaluate a client's present wardrobe, demonstrate how garments could be coordinated for new looks and uses, and recommend new additions to the wardrobe. Some wardrobe consultants have written books about wardrobe planning techniques.

Try It Yourself

Imagine that you are a wardrobe consultant. Your "client" is a recent college graduate who has taken a job in a professional office setting. He or she needs help in projecting a more professional image in the workplace. Plan a wardrobe for your client that would meet his or her current needs and be within a moderate budget.

Build Your Portfolio

After completing the wardrobe plan for your "client," create a visual and written description of each outfit. Describe how the garments could be accessorized to enhance his or her appearance. Include the approximate cost of each outfit. Gather the illustrations, written descriptions, and costs into a "Personalized Wardrobe Plan." Place a copy of the wardrobe plan in your portfolio.

CHAPTER 16

Clothing
Choices

After reading this chapter, you will be able to:

- *Explain factors that influence clothing choices.*

- *Develop a spending plan.*

- *Discuss alternatives to buying new clothes.*

- *Describe various resources for expanding a wardrobe.*

Terms to Learn

- *budget*
- *fluctuate*
- *analyze*
- *vintage*
- *customize*
- *creativity*

You may think that everyone who works in the fashion industry has closets full of clothes and wears a different outfit every day. However, people in the fashion field cannot spend all of their money on clothes. They must make choices, just like everyone else.

You might be surprised to learn that the favorite work outfit of several famous fashion designers is blue jeans and a turtleneck. Some of the best dressed people in the fashion industry limit their wardrobe to a few simple garments that can serve as a backdrop for eye-catching accessories.

As you put together your wardrobe, you have many clothing choices. Be sure to make the choices that are best for you.

Making the Best Choices for You

Perhaps your wardrobe plan indicates that you need a blue shirt. It sounds like a simple purchase. However, you probably will shop carefully to find the "right" style, color, and fabric. That is because there are many factors affecting your clothing choices. These include your lifestyle, activities, personality, values, and resources.

These factors help determine your preference for certain styles, colors, and fabrics. They also can help you make decisions about versatility, care, and price.

Styles, Colors, and Fabrics

Most people want to wear clothes that look good on them. If the design lines flatter your body shape, you will probably wear the garment often. If the color is becoming to your hair and skin tone, you will enjoy receiving compliments from others.

Knowledge of fibers and fabrics also will help you to evaluate garments. Should you choose the wool slacks or the cotton corduroys? Would the woven rayon shirt or the polyester knit shirt be best? Do you prefer underwear that is 100 percent cotton, a cotton blend, or 100 percent nylon?

Fabric knowledge also helps you to know what to expect when caring for your clothes. Can the sweater be washed? Does the shirt require pressing? Must a dark color be washed separately? Will the fabric shrink?

Sometimes, in order to make a final decision, you will need to decide which characteristics are more important to you. For example: If you are looking for a dressy garment, you may have to sacrifice washability. If you are looking for a garment that is very comfortable, you may not find it in your favorite color.

Versatility

Versatility is an important consideration when making clothing choices. A small wardrobe can appear to be much larger if it contains items that can be worn for different types of occasions or activities.

Everyone is unique. Base your clothing choices on your own coloring, body shape, personality, and lifestyle.

You should evaluate the color and design of each outfit. This will help you decide which one is the most flattering to you. Also read the garment labels for fiber and fabric care information.

These high school students must wear a white shirt and tan or navy pants to school. Would a school dress code make your wardrobe choices easier?

What activities do you participate in the most? A well-planned wardrobe is one in which most garments are suitable for your regular activities. For example, jeans may be worn for school, parties, sports events, or just getting together with friends. A suit jacket or blazer may be suitable for dances and special occasions.

When you are making clothing choices, think about whether you can wear the item for more than one type of occasion. Think, too, about whether it will go with other clothes that are already in your wardrobe.

Price

The price of an item is another important consideration. A garment that costs more than you can afford is not a wise purchase. Later on in this chapter, you will learn how to develop a spending plan. You will also learn about alternatives to purchasing new garments.

These teens have chosen shirts and sweaters that can be worn with a variety of other clothes.

Developing a Spending Plan

A spending plan will help you to spend your money wisely. In order to develop your plan, you and your family will need to agree on some guidelines. Who pays for what? Are you responsible for earning all, some, or none of the money you spend on clothes? Does someone else in the family have to approve your clothing purchases? Are you responsible for your own laundry, dry cleaning, and clothing alterations?

Once you have answered these questions, there are four steps to establishing a **budget**. This is *an estimate of income and expenses for a given period in the future.*

Step 1: Determine Your Income

Before you can plan your spending, you must know how much money will be available. Most planning periods cover one year. If you receive a paycheck or allowance monthly, estimate your income for each of the 12 months. If you receive a paycheck or allowance weekly, estimate your income for each of the 52 weeks.

Your income might **fluctuate**, or *go up and down.* During some weeks or months, your income is greater than at other times. Maybe you receive money as gifts for your birthday or holidays. Perhaps you earn money by selling handcrafted items, babysitting for families, or working in a local store. You may work part-time for a company only at certain times of the year or when the employer needs you.

If your income fluctuates, make two estimates of your yearly income. Figure out how much money you are sure you will make. This is the amount you can plan to spend on essentials. Then estimate the largest amount of income that you could have. This is the amount you might have to spend on the extras.

Step 2: Keep a Record

The next step is to keep a careful record of how you are currently spending your money. Every day for a one- or two-month period, record everything that you buy. Write down the date, what you bought, where you bought it, and the cost of each item or service. This will be easier to do if you get a small notebook that you can carry with you. At the end of this time, you can determine the average amount that you have spent.

Step 3: Plan Your Expenses

Your spending record will help you analyze how you spend your money. To **analyze** means *to examine carefully and in detail so as to identify causes, factors, and possible results.*

Group your expenses into as many different categories as you feel will be useful. You will probably have a category for:

A spending plan will help you plan for your clothing and other personal expenses.

- Food, including snacks.
- Entertainment, including movies, videos, CDs, and sports events.
- Clothing and accessories.
- Personal items, such as grooming products and haircuts.
- Savings.

Depending on your particular needs, interests, and hobbies, you might include other categories. This might include transportation, music lessons, sports equipment, or craft supplies.

Next, determine the average amount that you spend for each of these categories per week, per month, and per year. Check to see that these all add up to an amount that is equal to, or less than, your estimated income.

Evaluate where your money is going. Are you really spending it on the things that are the most necessary and important to you? Teenagers tend to spend their money on food, transportation, entertainment, clothes, and personal items.

A smart money manager always has a category for savings. A good goal is to save at least 10 percent of your income. Then you will always have some money set aside for unexpected expenses.

Write down the names of each of the categories in your plan. Then list how much money you expect to spend in each of these categories. This list is your spending plan. Remember that if your income or needs change, you will have to revise your plan.

Step 4: Manage and Evaluate Your Plan

A spending plan will not be helpful unless you stick to it. It requires self-control. You must be aware of how much you are spending each day and stay within the limits that you have set.

Evaluate your plan regularly to be sure that it is meeting your goals. If it is not, then you should adjust your plan to better meet your new needs or priorities.

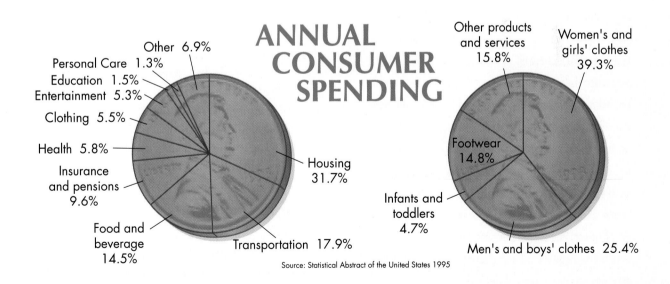

ANNUAL CONSUMER SPENDING

Other 6.9%
Personal Care 1.3%
Education 1.5%
Entertainment 5.3%
Clothing 5.5%
Health 5.8%
Insurance and pensions 9.6%
Food and beverage 14.5%
Transportation 17.9%
Housing 31.7%

Other products and services 15.8%
Women's and girls' clothes 39.3%
Footwear 14.8%
Infants and toddlers 4.7%
Men's and boys' clothes 25.4%

Source: Statistical Abstract of the United States 1995

249

Modern Interpretations of Old Crafts

Craft techniques have been reinterpreted using the sewing machine and the overlock machine. A project that used to take many days to complete can now be finished in a few hours.

- **Heirloom sewing** or **French hand** sewing is the term for decorative techniques used by Victorian seamstresses. Strips of fabric and delicate lace were joined with almost invisible hand stitches. The fabric strips were embellished with embroidery, pintucks, and hemstitching. They could also be gathered along the edges to create puffing strips. It took 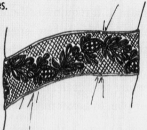 many hours to complete a garment using these techniques. Today these delicate seams can be stitched on the conventional or overlock machine. Built-in embroidery stitches and special needles, such as the twin needle and the wing needle, are used to decorate the fabric strips.

- **Sashiko** is a quilting technique that comes from Japan. Geometric patterns and designs inspired by nature are hand-stitched in heavy white thread on dark blue or black cotton fabric. Machine-stitched versions are done with a long, straight stitch and a heavy rayon or cotton machine embroidery thread.

- **Cutwork** or **Richelieu embroidery** is a type of decorative stitching that comes from Italy. The designs usually consist of flowers and leaves. Originally the edges of the designs were finished with a hand embroidery stitch. After the embroidery was completed, parts of the background fabric were cut away. For today's machine version, the open areas are cut away first. Then a stabilizer is put underneath the fabric. The cut edges are finished with a narrow machine zigzag stitch, and the stabilizer is removed.

Consider the Alternatives

Does your wardrobe plan seem to be in conflict with your spending plan? Most of us may not have enough money to buy everything we want. However, that does not mean we have limited resources.

There are many different ways to add items to your wardrobe. Here are the alternatives:

- Purchase, either new or used, some of the things that you need.
- Sew new garments or restyle garments that you already own.
- Share or trade clothes with a relative or friend.
- Rent clothes for a special occasion, such as a prom or wedding.

Buying

Buying offers you the advantage of trying on a finished garment to see if it is right for you. You can evaluate the style, quality, and fit before you make your final decision. Buying can be a fast and easy alternative. However, it is the most expensive alternative in terms of money.

To help your money go farther, you can buy previously owned clothes at second-hand stores, thrift shops, antique stores, and flea markets. These clothes are usually less expensive than similar new garments. If you like **vintage** clothes, *classics from the past*, you might want to wear these clothes as is. You could also redesign them so they look more up-to-date. These stores can also be an interesting source for old fabrics, trims, and linens that can be made into garments.

Sewing

Sewing offers many advantages. It usually saves you money. It also gives you the opportunity to express yourself creatively. You can sew clothes in the size, color, and style that you want. You also can make accessories to match.

Expanding Your Wardrobe

There are many different ways to add items to your wardrobe.

You can use your sewing skills to **customize,** or *modify according to individual preference,* purchased clothes. Shortening a hem or taking in a seam can result in a garment that fits you perfectly. You can also replace buttons, add trim, or change the entire style of a garment to give it a new look.

Sharing and Trading

You might consider sharing or trading clothes with a family member or friend. Instead of investing in a new outfit for a special occasion, sharing is a good alternative. Trading clothes with another person gives both of your wardrobes a new addition at no cost to either of you.

Renting

Renting clothing is an option that has traditionally been used for special occasions. Caps and gowns are rented for graduation. Tuxedos can be rented for school dances, weddings, and other formal events. In some large cities, there are shops that rent formal clothing for females as well as for males. Uniforms and costumes can also be rented.

Using Your Resources

Your choice of alternatives will depend on your resources. Resources include how much money you have to spend, your shopping and sewing skills, the time you have available to shop or sew, and your ability to be creative. An older brother, sister, or cousin who will hand clothing down to you is also considered a resource.

Money

If you think you do not have enough money for the clothes in your wardrobe plan, there are several things you could do. You could decide to do without a few items. Perhaps you really need only one new shirt instead of the three that are on your list.

You could shop for multipurpose garments. For example, if you need both a winter coat and a raincoat, you might shop for a raincoat with a zip-out lining. You could also re-examine the garments that are already in your wardrobe. Perhaps you can discover new ways to mix-and-match them to create new outfits.

If you do not already work part-time, you could get an after-school or summer job. You could also offer some type of service to people in your community. Then you would have more money to spend on the items in your wardrobe plan. Remember, however, that a job involves commitments of time and energy. Certain jobs also require additional clothes or special outfits.

Skills

You can make the money you have go farther by developing shopping and sewing skills. These skills can help you stretch your clothing dollars.

By reading and listening to advertisements, you can lean how much things cost. Then you will be able to recognize a bargain when you see it. You also can learn how to evaluate your selection before you finalize the purchase. Buying clothing on sale or at a store specializing in lower prices can result in added savings.

One way stretch your clothing dollar is to buy the items that you need when they are on sale.

Anyone can learn to sew. You can begin by learning simple skills such as sewing buttons or stitching a hem. You can progress to easy-to-sew projects such as a t-shirt, shorts, backpack, or pillow. As you develop your skills, you can advance to making a shirt or jacket. You can also make gifts for others or items for your home. However, sewing projects do take time and a certain amount of skill.

If you are not interested in sewing a complete garment, you can save money by learning how to make simple repairs and fitting adjustments. You also can expand your wardrobe by repairing or updating garments that you no longer wear.

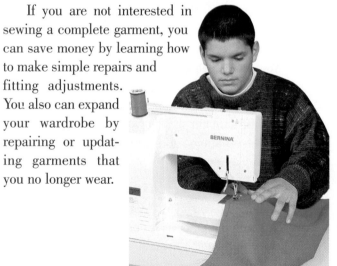

Use your sewing skills to make a new outfit or update an old one.

By using a variety of resources, you can have outfits that look good for many types of occasions.

Flea markets and second-hand stores are often good sources for inexpensive accessories. For a special occasion, family members or friends might be willing to lend you what you need.

Making some of your own accessories is another solution. You could braid leather or decorative cord to make a belt. You could sew a canvas bag instead of buying one. Hair ornaments are easy to make from fabric, ribbons, and braid left over from other projects. Attractive jewelry can be made from everything from beads to modeling clay. Check out the craft area in your local bookstore or library for ideas. Some craft stores provide free instructions and offer classes.

Time

Is your time limited because of commitments to school, work, family, or other activities? If so, a well thought-out wardrobe plan is essential. You probably do not have time to shop "just for fun." You need to know exactly what you are looking for before you go into a store or mall.

If you like to sew, you can save time by choosing simple styles and easy-to-sew patterns. Set aside some time during school vacations to make new outfits. Save any handsewing, such as hems and fasteners, to do when you are watching your favorite television program.

Creativity

Use your creativity to change the look of your outfits. **Creativity** is *the ability to use your imagination and make something original or unique.* You could mix-and-match garments for new combinations. You could decorate garments with fabric paint or trims. You can also add accessories to create new looks.

Accessories can create a new look for an outfit. Most accessories are less expensive than a new garment.

Summary

- When making clothing choices, consider style, color, fabric, versatility, and price.

- A spending plan can help you spend your money wisely.

- Budget planning includes four steps: determine your income, keep a record of your spending, plan your expenses, and manage and evaluate your plan.

- Consider various alternatives when adding items to your wardrobe. These include buying, sewing, sharing, trading, and renting.

- Using resources such as money, skills, time, and creativity, you can manage your spending plan effectively.

Using Vocabulary Terms

On a separate piece of paper, write the vocabulary term that best fits the definition:

1. The ability to use your imagination and make something original or unique.

2. An estimate of income and expenses for a given period in the future.

3. To modify according to individual preference.

4. To examine carefully and in detail so as to identify causes, factors, and possible results.

5. Go up and down.

6. Classics from the past.

Recalling the Facts

1. What are two benefits of knowing about fibers and fabrics?

2. Why is versatility an important consideration when making clothing choices?

3. List the four steps in establishing a spending plan.

4. How can you determine your income if it fluctuates from week to week?

5. Why should you keep a record of all the money that you spend for one or two months?

6. Why should a spending plan be evaluated regularly?

7. List four different options for adding items to your wardrobe.

8. What are three advantages of being able to sew some of your clothes?

9. What two skills can help you stretch your clothing dollars?

10. List three resources that you can use when you have limited money for clothing.

Thinking Critically

1. **Analysis.** Explain how versatile clothing can make a wardrobe appear much larger.

2. **Evaluation.** Do you think budget planning is important? Why or why not?

3. **Analysis.** Compare the following methods of acquiring clothing: buying new, buying used, sewing, sharing, trading, and renting. What are the advantages and disadvantages of each?

4. **Synthesis.** Summarize ways to trade one resource for another in clothing choices.

Applying Your Knowledge

1. **Making Choices.** Look through catalogs for outfits that appeal to you. Analyze the style, color, fabric, versatility, and price of each garment. Decide if you would have to make any sacrifices of characteristics or qualities.

2. **Spending Plan.** Develop a personal spending plan. Determine your income, keep a record of your spending for one month, and analyze your spending. Then set up expense categories, including one for clothing. List how much money you expect to spend for each category. Be sure to evaluate your plan regularly.

3. **Creativity.** With a partner, brainstorm ways to use creativity to change the look of your outfits. Share your ideas with the class.

Making the Connection

1. **Math.** Look through a pattern book for an easy-to-sew pattern with an estimated sewing time. Compute how much it would cost for the pattern, fabric, and notions. Compare the time and cost for sewing the item with that of purchasing a similar ready-to-wear item.

2. **Language Arts.** Write an essay about how your clothing choices are influenced by your lifestyle, personality, values, and resources.

What Is a Consumer Education Specialist?

Consumer education specialists provide product information for consumers. They write articles, brochures, and pamphlets. They answer consumer letters and telephone requests. Some specialists appear on television and radio programs. Others represent companies at trade shows, speak at meetings and conventions, or help train sales staff. Consumer education specialists often spot consumer problems or identify needs that are not being met. This information helps companies improve or develop new products.

Try It Yourself

Imagine that you are a consumer education specialist. You have been asked to write a newspaper article about how to make the best choices when adding items to a wardrobe. Include information about important considerations, alternatives to buying new items, and the various resources available to the consumer. Develop helpful guidelines for consumers to follow. Include an eye-catching title or headline for your newspaper article.

Build Your Portfolio

After completing your newspaper article, place a copy in your portfolio. Then summarize the information in a script for a public service announcement (PSA) that could appear on radio or television. If possible, make a tape or video of the PSA and place it or the script in your portfolio.

CHAPTER 17

Clothing Care

After reading this chapter, you will be able to:

- *Explain how to care for clothing on a routine basis.*
- *Give examples of the information on care labels.*
- *Choose the best method for cleaning a garment.*
- *Describe how to store clothing.*

Terms to Learn

- *laundering*
- *ironing*
- *pressing*
- *dry cleaning*
- *solvent*

Have you ever had a white shirt turn pink in the wash? Perhaps your new sweater was two sizes smaller when you took it out of the dryer? Have you been ready to leave for a party only to find that your outfit was stained or ripped? All of these problems resulted from improper care of fabrics and clothing.

If you are like most people, you would rather buy and wear clothes than care for them. However, proper care of your clothing will save you both time and money in the long run.

Routine Care

It helps to have some type of routine schedule for your clothing care. This means setting aside specific time to do different tasks, such as doing your laundry, hand washing a sweater, or mending a hem.

Learning about clothing care will help you save money. You can learn how to remove spots and stains to save on cleaning bills. Proper care also will help clothing last longer. When a garment is ruined through improper care, it costs you money to replace it.

Every time you wear a garment, take a few seconds to check it over before you put it away. This should become a part of your daily routine.

Check for Soil, Spots, and Stains

Does the garment need to be laundered or dry cleaned? Light-colored fabrics show soil and stains clearly, so you can evaluate them easily. However, dark-colored clothes also need to be cleaned regularly. If you allow fabrics to get too dirty, they will be more difficult to clean.

Check the garment for any spots or stains. It is best to remove these as soon as possible. A quick rinse with cold water helps remove many stains from washable fabrics. The longer a stain remains on a fabric, the harder it will be to remove. See the *Stain Removal Chart* on page 259.

Take time to check your clothes before putting them away.

Clothes that need to be washed should be placed in the location that you or your family uses for dirty clothes. Then they will not be overlooked when laundry time comes. Clothes that are not washable should be taken to a dry cleaner as soon as possible.

Some garments may not need to be washed or dry cleaned, but they do need to be freshened before wearing again. Hang a woven garment where the air can circulate around it. This will help to remove any odors that the fabric has picked up from either the air or your skin. Knitted garments, such as a sweater, can be draped over a chair.

If the garment has picked up any dust, lint, or animal hair, it can be gently brushed to remove the substance. Use a special clothing brush, lint brush, or a specially designed roller with an adhesive surface.

Check for Repairs

Has a button popped off? Has the hem come loose? Has a small rip appeared in a seam? No matter how careful you are with clothes, small repairs are often needed.

Plan to repair the garment as soon as possible. Otherwise, the rip may become longer, or the entire hem will fall down. If you do not set it aside, you may forget about the needed repair until you want to wear the garment again. Then you may not have the time to do it.

If a garment needs repair, take a few minutes to restitch a button or hem. Then it will be ready to wear again.

Stain Removal Chart

- Always remove a stain before laundering a garment. Hot water and heat can set a stain, making it very difficult to remove later.

- Most water-based stains, such as juice and soft drinks, can be removed by water. Oil-based stains, such as grease and lipstick, must be treated with a stain removal product.

Blood	Soak in cold water as soon as possible for 30 minutes or longer. Launder. For dried stains, apply an enzyme presoak or rub detergent on stain. Wash using bleach, if safe for fabric.
Chewing Gum, Candle Wax	Harden by placing in freezer or rubbing with ice cube. Scrape off with dull knife or fingernail. For wax, place between paper towels and press with warm iron. Sponge remaining stain with prewash stain remover or cleaning fluid. Launder.
Chocolate	Scrape off; then apply a prewash stain remover or rub detergent on stain. Wash using bleach, if safe for fabric.
Cosmetics	Rub detergent into area or use a prewash stain remover. If stain is stubborn, sponge with cleaning fluid. Launder.
Grass	Rub detergent into area or use an enzyme presoak. Then wash using bleach and hottest water possible for fabric.
Grease, Oil	Scrape off or blot with paper towels. Use a prewash stain remover or rub detergent into area. Launder. If stain remains, sponge with cleaning fluid and rinse.
Ink	Spray with hair spray or sponge with rubbing alcohol. After a few minutes, blot with paper towels. Repeat if necessary. Rub detergent into stain and wash. Or use a prewash stain remover; then launder. (Some ballpoint, felt tip, and liquid inks may be impossible to remove.)
Mildew	Launder using chlorine bleach, if safe for fabric. Or soak in oxygen bleach and hot water, then launder. (Heavily mildewed fabrics may be permanently damaged.)
Nail Polish	Sponge with nail polish remover (do not use acetone on acetate fabric) or cleaning fluid. Rinse and launder. (Nail polish may be impossible to remove.)
Paint	Do not let paint dry. For latex paint, rinse in warm water and launder. For oil-based paint, sponge with turpentine or mineral spirits and rinse with water. Launder. (Once paint is dry, it cannot be removed.)
Perspiration	Use a prewash stain remover, or sponge fresh stain with ammonia. For old stain, sponge with white vinegar and rinse. Rub detergent into stain and wash in hottest water possible for fabric.
Soft Drinks	Sponge or soak in cool water. Launder.

Many repairs can be done in only a few minutes with hand sewing. Restitching a loose button, snap, or hook and eye takes only a few stitches. It is easier to re-anchor a loose fastener than to wait until it comes off completely.

Put Clothes Away

Get into the habit of putting your clothes away in a closet, drawer, or shelf. This will help to prevent wrinkling and save you from pressing clothes before you want to wear them again. Also you will be able to locate them easier and faster when you know exactly where they have been placed. Resist the temptation to toss your clothes on your bed or on the floor.

Most woven garments should be hung on hangers. For jackets and any clothes that might be marked or creased by the narrow metal hangers, use plastic or wooden hangers that are a little wider. These will better support the shoulder area of the garment. Loosely knitted garments should be stored flat to prevent them from stretching out of shape.

Reading Care Labels

The Care Labeling Rule is a U.S. regulation that requires permanent care labels to be placed in all textile clothing. The label must be permanently attached and remain readable for the life of the garment.

The manufacturer is required to list only one method of safe care on the care label. For example, the label must list directions for either machine washing or hand washing or dry cleaning. The manufacturer does not have to mention any other method that may be used safely.

The labels must provide specific information about the method of care. For example, a label recommends washing as a care procedure. That label must also tell you the washing method, the safe water temperature, and the method and safe temperature for drying. If ironing is needed, the temperature for ironing must be included. If chlorine bleach is not safe to use, then a warning must be added.

Here is the general information provided on care labels:

- **Washing.** "Machine wash" means that you can wash and dry the garment by any method at any temperature — hot, warm, or cold. Otherwise the label will indicate the appropriate wash cycle, such as delicate or gentle, and temperature to use. It must specify hand washing if needed.

- **Drying.** "Tumble dry" means that the garment can be dried in a tumble dryer at the specified setting — high, medium, low, or no heat. Otherwise the label will indicate "Line dry" or "Dry flat."

- **Ironing.** If ironing is needed, even for a touch-up, the label must say so. If it is not safe to use the hottest setting, then the label must indicate "Warm iron" or "Cool iron." A label that states "Do not iron" means that even the coolest setting could be harmful to the fabric.

- **Bleaching.** You can assume that it is safe to bleach the fabric if the label does not warn against it. If only chlorine bleach is harmful, the label will state "Use only nonchlorine bleach when needed." If all types of bleach are harmful, the label must warn "No bleach."

- **Dry Cleaning.** If the label says "Dry clean only," a garment may be dry cleaned by any method, including a coin-operated machine. Any specific warning concerning solvents or steaming must be given when necessary.

Choosing the Proper Method of Care

Garments can often look the same but need very different care. The type of fiber, fabric construction, finishes, color, interfacing, lining, and trims determine what care method is listed on the garment label.

Many garments can be machine washed and dried safely. Others need to be washed by hand and line dried. Non-washable garments require dry cleaning. The care label on the garments will tell you which method to use.

- **Method.** Only the washing or dry cleaning method listed on the label has been checked for safe use.
- **Temperature.** If no temperature is mentioned, it is safe to use any temperature or setting — hot, warm, or cold.
- **Ironing.** If no ironing instruction is given, it should not be necessary to iron the fabric.
- **Bleach.** If bleach is not mentioned, any type of bleach may be used when needed.
- **Warnings.** If no warnings are given, you do not need to make adjustments to the care methods listed on the label.

Laundering Clothes

Different types of fabrics need to be laundered by different methods. **Laundering** means *washing fabric by hand or by machine with a soil removing product.* For best laundering results, follow the guidelines in this section. Then your clothes will maintain their original appearance, color, size, and shape. They will also last longer. See pages 262-263 for *How to Launder Your Clothes.*

Sorting Clothes

You must first decide what clothes can be washed safely together. Errors in sorting can ruin clothes. For example, colored dyes can permanently stain white fabrics. Water that is too hot can shrink certain fibers. Refer to the care labels for recommended procedures.

First, group together all of the clothes that can be machine washed at the same temperature. Set aside the clothes that must be hand washed.

Read the care labels to determine what clothes can be washed together. Then you can sort the clothes by fabric, color, and amount of soil.

Next, separate the clothes by color. In order to prevent any bleeding of colors, all dark colors should be washed together. Many white fabrics, especially those made from manufactured fibers, will pick up color even from colorfast fabrics. The white fabrics may become dull and gray after repeated washings, so wash them separately.

Then, consider the amount of soil on the garments. Heavily-soiled clothes should be washed separately because they need a longer wash cycle. They also can dull other fabrics because lightly-soiled items pick up the extra soil from the wash water.

Finally, consider the type of fabrics being laundered. Some fabrics create lint, such as terrycloth towels and fuzzy sweatshirts. They should not be washed with fabrics that might attract lint, such as corduroy, velveteen, and durable press finishes. It is a good idea to turn lint-producing fabrics inside out in order to reduce the lint pickup by other fabrics. Delicate fabrics should be separated from bulky items to prevent any tangling and tearing of the delicate clothes.

How to Launder Clothes

1 **Read care labels.** Refer to the care label for how each garment can be laundered.

Machine
Wash Warm
Do Not Bleach
Line Dry
Cool Iron

2 **Remove any stains from fabrics before laundering.** Apply liquid detergent or a paste of powdered detergent and water to the area. Or use a special laundry stain remover in liquid or spray form.

3 **Sort clothes.** Group fabrics by recommended washing method and water temperature, color, type of fabric, and amount of soil.

4 **Select laundry products.** Add soap or detergent according to the machine's manual — it may be added before or with the clothes.

bleaches

soaps and detergents

fabric softeners

starches

stain removers

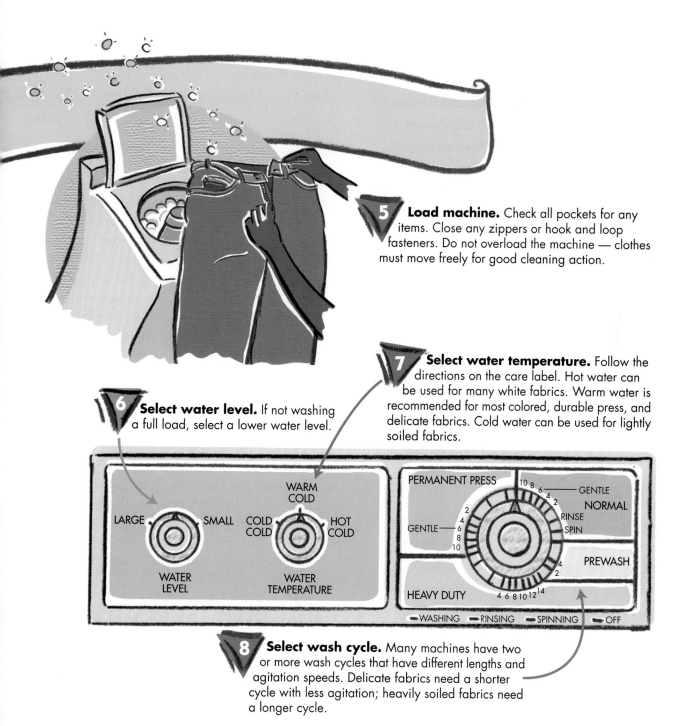

5 **Load machine.** Check all pockets for any items. Close any zippers or hook and loop fasteners. Do not overload the machine — clothes must move freely for good cleaning action.

7 **Select water temperature.** Follow the directions on the care label. Hot water can be used for many white fabrics. Warm water is recommended for most colored, durable press, and delicate fabrics. Cold water can be used for lightly soiled fabrics.

6 **Select water level.** If not washing a full load, select a lower water level.

8 **Select wash cycle.** Many machines have two or more wash cycles that have different lengths and agitation speeds. Delicate fabrics need a shorter cycle with less agitation; heavily soiled fabrics need a longer cycle.

Color Loss in Fabrics

Have you had a pair of blue jeans suddenly fade after they had been washed three or four times? Did you ever purchase a garment that was labeled "Wash Before Wear"? Have you ever seen a silk shirt that lost its color in some places but not in others?

These problems are the result of unstable fabric dyes that fade, run, or rub off under certain wearing or laundering conditions. These conditions can be a long soaking time, hot water, chlorine or non-chlorine bleach, stain removal products, or abrasion.

- New fabrics generally have some excess dye that may come off during the first wearings or washings. If the label says "Wash Before Wear," it is a good idea to follow these directions. Otherwise the color may rub off onto the other clothes that you are wearing. Always wash dark or bright colored clothing with similar colors. This will prevent any excess dye from transferring to other fabrics during laundering.

- Some dyes, especially the blue dyes that are used for cotton denim, come off where the fabric rubs against other things. This is why your blue jeans may lose their color along the seamlines and garment edges. If the jeans rub up against the washing machine's agitator post during laundering, streaks may appear where the color has rubbed off. Some manufacturers recommend that jeans be turned inside out before washing.

- A garment's care label may tell you that you can use non-chlorine bleach. However, if you accidentally splash or pour the bleach directly onto the garment, discolored spots may appear. To avoid this problem, add the detergent and bleach to the washing machine as it fills with water. Then add the dirty clothes.

After sorting, you may have several piles of items. These might be dark colors, light colors, whites, delicates, towels, and sheets.

Machine Washing

Fabrics can be washed in water temperatures that range from very hot to cold. Hot water gets fabrics the cleanest and offers sanitizing benefits. However, water that is too hot can shrink some fabrics. Warm water is recommended for many fabrics, especially those with manufactured fibers and durable press finishes. Cold water does not have much cleaning power, but it helps save energy. It can be used for delicate fabrics and lightly soiled clothes. Follow the directions on the care label of the garments to select the proper water temperature.

Many machines have two or more wash cycles. The cycles, such as normal and gentle, may be programmed for different lengths of time and agitation speeds. For example, a delicate cycle is shorter than a regular cycle and has less agitation. Some wash cycles also may be programmed for different rinse temperatures—warm or cold. A knit or durable press cycle has a cold rinse to help prevent wrinkling.

Do not load too many fabrics into the machine. They must be able to move freely for good cleaning action. Overloading also causes extra wrinkling. For best results, distribute the fabrics evenly around the agitator of the machine. Mix small items with large items to provide good washing action. For most machines, you can adjust the water level according to the size of the wash load.

Hand Washing

Hand washing is best for woolens, silks, and other delicate fabrics. It can also be used for single items that need to be washed separately.

Pretreat any spots and stains before washing. Use the water temperature listed on the care label.

Hand washing is recommended for woolens, silks, and other delicate fabrics. Soak the garment, gently squeeze to clean, and rinse. Roll the garment up in a towel to remove excess moisture.

• *Detergents* work well in either hard or soft water. All-purpose or heavy-duty detergents are suitable for all washable fabrics. Light-duty detergents are designed for hand washing delicate or lightly soiled items. Some detergents contain color-safe bleaching agents or fabric softeners.

• *Prewash soil and stain removers* help dissolve or lift out stains before washing. They work well on oil-based stains such as cooking oils, cosmetics, and motor oils. Stain-removal products are available in spray, liquid, stick, or aerosol form.

• *Enzyme presoaks* are used for soaking clothes to remove stains and soils prior to washing. They are effective in breaking down protein-type stains, such as blood, egg, meat juice, milk, and baby formula.

Add the laundry product and agitate or swish the water until dissolved. Then add the garment to the water and gently squeeze to clean. If necessary, let it soak for 15 minutes or longer to remove any stains. Do not scrub or wring delicate fabrics.

Rinse the garment in cool or cold water until the water is clear. Then roll it in an absorbent towel to remove as much water as possible.

Selecting Laundry Products

Soaps and detergents are cleansing agents designed to remove soil from fabrics. They can be granules or liquids. Other laundry products have different purposes. Whatever the type or brand, be sure to read and follow label directions to achieve the best results.

• *Soaps* are mild and work best in soft water. When used in hard water they react with the minerals to form a sticky white soap curd.

Read the directions for the recommended amount of detergent. The amount depends on your type of washer and size of wash load.

• *Bleaches* remove stains, whiten and brighten fabrics, and destroy bacteria. Chlorine bleaches are the most effective but cannot be used on all fabrics. Nonchlorine or oxygen bleaches are mild and can be used on both whites and colors.

• *Fabric softeners* make fabrics feel softer and reduce static electricity. Liquid fabric softeners are added to the final rinse. Special nonwoven sheets can be used in the dryer.

• *Water softeners* help remove from hard water the mineral deposits that prevent thorough cleaning.

• *Starches, fabric finishes, and sizings* are used to give body to fabrics and make ironing easier.

• *Disinfectants* destroy bacteria on fabric and may be used when there is an illness in the family.

Drying Clothes

Some clothes can be dried by machine. Others should be hung up or laid flat to air dry. Always check the care label for drying instructions.

Many automatic dryers have different temperature settings or specific cycle settings. Manufactured fibers should be dried at a lower temperature than cotton or linen. Heavier fabrics will take longer to dry than lightweight fabrics. A durable press cycle uses no heat at the end of the cycle; this cool-down time reduces wrinkling. The air fluff cycle should be used for rubber and plastic items.

For best results, do not overload the dryer since this slows down drying time, increases wrinkling, and decreases fluffiness. Durable press fabrics should be removed and hung up as soon as the dryer stops to prevent any wrinkling. Do not dry lint-producing fabrics with other types of fabrics. Be sure clothes are completely dry before putting away in a closet or drawer. Always clean the lint filter after each load.

Ironing and Pressing Clothes

Wrinkles can be removed from fabrics with heat, moisture, and slight pressure. Ironing and pressing are two methods of smoothing away fabric wrinkles. **Ironing** is done with *a back and forward motion of the iron*. It should always be done in the lengthwise or crosswise direction of the fabric to avoid stretching the fabric. **Pressing** is accomplished by *raising and lowering the iron from one area to the next*.

As soon as the dryer stops, remove the clothes and hang them up. This helps to prevent wrinkling.

Be sure to point out any spots or stains on the garment so the dry cleaner can treat them.

Different fibers have different sensitivity to heat. Many manufactured fibers have sensitivity to heat and should be ironed at lower temperatures. Cottons and linens are not as heat sensitive and require higher temperatures to effectively remove wrinkles. Most irons have several temperature settings that are labeled with the names of fiber types such as rayon, wool, cotton, and linen.

Dry Cleaning Clothes

Dry cleaning is *a process that uses special liquids containing organic solvents to clean fabrics.* A **solvent** is *a substance used to dissolve another substance.* Clothing is placed into a machine that resembles an automatic washer. The solvent is released and agitated with the clothing to remove soil. Then the solvent is spun away, and the clothing is tumbled or air dried until all traces of the solvent are gone. Steam pressing restores creases and pleats.

Always point out any spots or stains to the dry cleaner. If you know the cause of the stain, be sure to mention it. Dry cleaners have special cleaning products that make it possible for them to remove some stains that you cannot remove at home. Some cleaners also do minor repairs.

Coin-operated dry cleaning is faster and costs less than professional dry cleaning. Although the machines remove most soil, the clothes do not get special spot removal or pressing.

Storing Your Clothing

Organize your storage space to keep your clothes neat and easy to find. Arrange the closet, shelves, and drawers to the best advantage. Store off-season clothing where it will keep clean and dry.

Closet and Drawers

Group similar clothing together in your closet. It will be easier to find your blue shirt if it is among the shirts, instead of hidden between other types of clothes. By hanging similar lengths together, there will be space underneath to place shelves or baskets to hold other items in the closet.

Store the same type of items together in drawers or on shelves. For example, have specific drawers for your socks, underwear, and t-shirts. Keep all of your sweaters together on a shelf. Use a tray on top of a chest or dresser to hold small items, such as a watch or jewelry.

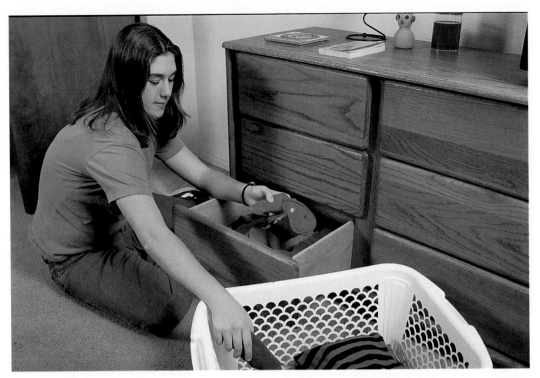

Store your clothes in a closet, in drawers, or on shelves. Group similar items together so they are easier to find.

Here are some practical storage tips:

• Multiple shirt, skirt, and pants hangers enable six garments to be hung on one hanger.

• Small hooks can be used to hang belts, necklaces, and chains.

• Shoe bags can be hung on a door to hold shoes, rolled-up belts, scarves, clothes brush or roller, shoe polish supplies, hangtags, or the extra buttons and yarns that come attached to garments.

• Plastic or cardboard boxes can be used to store folded items and accessories on shelves.

• Various sizes of baskets can hold hats, jewelry, scarves, gloves, and grooming supplies.

• Low boxes or metal chests can be used under the bed to store out-of-season or seldom-worn clothes.

Seasonal Storage

If you live in a seasonal climate, you may want to store off-season clothing in large garment bags, boxes, or chests. Always store clothes and accessories that are clean. Soiled fabrics attract moths and other insects that will eat holes in fabric. Moths are particularly fond of oil-based soils on wool clothing.

Do not store clothing or fabrics in damp places where they might be subject to mildew. If mildew grows on your clothing, it can stain or deteriorate the fabric and be difficult to remove. Drape leather or fur items with a piece of fabric. Do not place in plastic bags. They need to be stored where air can circulate.

ORGANIZE YOUR CLOSET

3. Luggage can be kept on hard-to-reach top shelves.

4. Decorative boxes store out-of-season clothing.

1. A tie rack on the door holds ties, belts, and scarves.

2. A shoe bag stores not only shoes but also socks and underwear.

5. Two rods, one below the other, double the hanging space.

6. T-shirts and sweaters fold easily into wire or plastic baskets.

7. Longer garments can hang in a narrow space with shelving at top and bottom.

8. Small cubicles keep shoes organized.

REVIEW

Summary

- Learning about clothing care can help you save money.

- Every time you wear a garment, check it for soil, spots, stains, and needed repairs.

- Permanent care labels on garments list the recommended care method to use.

- Laundry procedures include sorting clothes, pretreating stains, choosing laundry products, and selecting water temperature and machine cycles.

- Follow fabric guidelines for hand washing, drying, ironing, and pressing.

- Point out any spots or stains to dry cleaners.

- Organize your storage space to keep your clothes neat and easy to find.

Using Vocabulary Terms

On a separate piece of paper, write the vocabulary term that best fits the definition:

1. A substance used to dissolve another substance.

2. A back and forth motion of the iron.

3. Raising and lowering the iron from one area to the next.

4. Washing fabric by hand or by machine with a soil removing product.

5. A process that uses special liquids containing organic solvents to clean fabrics.

Recalling the Facts

1. Why should you learn about clothing care?

2. What should you check for after you have worn a garment?

3. Why should stains be treated quickly?

4. Why should you put clothes away after wearing them?

5. Name five categories of information that are provided on care labels.

6. What is the first step you should do when laundering clothes?

7. What four factors should you consider when sorting clothes?

8. Why should you not load too many fabrics into a washing machine?

9. What can you do to help prevent wrinkling of clothes dried in an automatic dryer?

10. Why should clothes always be clean and dry when stored?

Thinking Critically

1. **Analysis.** Compare advantages and disadvantages of washing clothes in cold and hot water.

2. **Synthesis.** Summarize the steps to follow when washing clothes.

3. **Evaluation.** Why do you think a manufacturer is required to list only one method of safe care even if other methods may be used safely?

4. **Evaluation.** If the care label is missing on a garment, how would you decide how to clean the garment?

Applying Your Knowledge

1. **Stain Removal.** Working in small groups, apply different types of stains to various fabrics. Using the Stain Removal Chart, experiment with different methods of removing the stains.

2. **Laundry Products.** Research the different types of laundry products available in a local store. Create a chart listing the type, purpose, and price of each product.

3. **Storage Organizer.** With a partner, design a closet organizer that would appeal to teens.

4. **Closet Organization.** Take photos of your closet before and after organizing it. Write a summary of what you did to better organize your storage space.

Making the Connection

1. **Language Arts.** Write a booklet on "Laundry Tips" that would be helpful for students.

2. **Science.** Soak red fabric that is not colorfast with white or light-colored fabrics. Once the red color bleeds, test whether washing, bleaching, or stain-removal products can restore the original color of the other fabrics.

What Is a Dry Cleaner?

Dry cleaners may clean garments right in the store or send them to a central location for processing. Because a general cleaning will not remove certain stains, many stains must be specially treated before the clothes are cleaned. Care must be taken with some fabrics so as not to discolor or damage the fabric. The clothes must then be sorted by fiber content, color, and type into groups that can be cleaned together. After the clothes go through the cleaning process, they are pressed with a commercial steam iron or other equipment. Some dry cleaners also provide a repair and alterations service.

Try It Yourself

Imagine that you are a dry cleaner. You must have knowledge about fabrics, finishes, dyes, trims, and stain removal techniques. Using information from the text and library sources, create a chart on various fabrics and trims that require special cleaning techniques. Why are these fabrics difficult to clean? How might delicate trims and buttons be handled? What types of stains and discolorations might not be removed? Are there any fabrics that should not be dry cleaned?

Build Your Portfolio

Write a report about fabrics that might require special care during the dry cleaning process. Include a copy of the report, along with the fabric chart, in your portfolio.

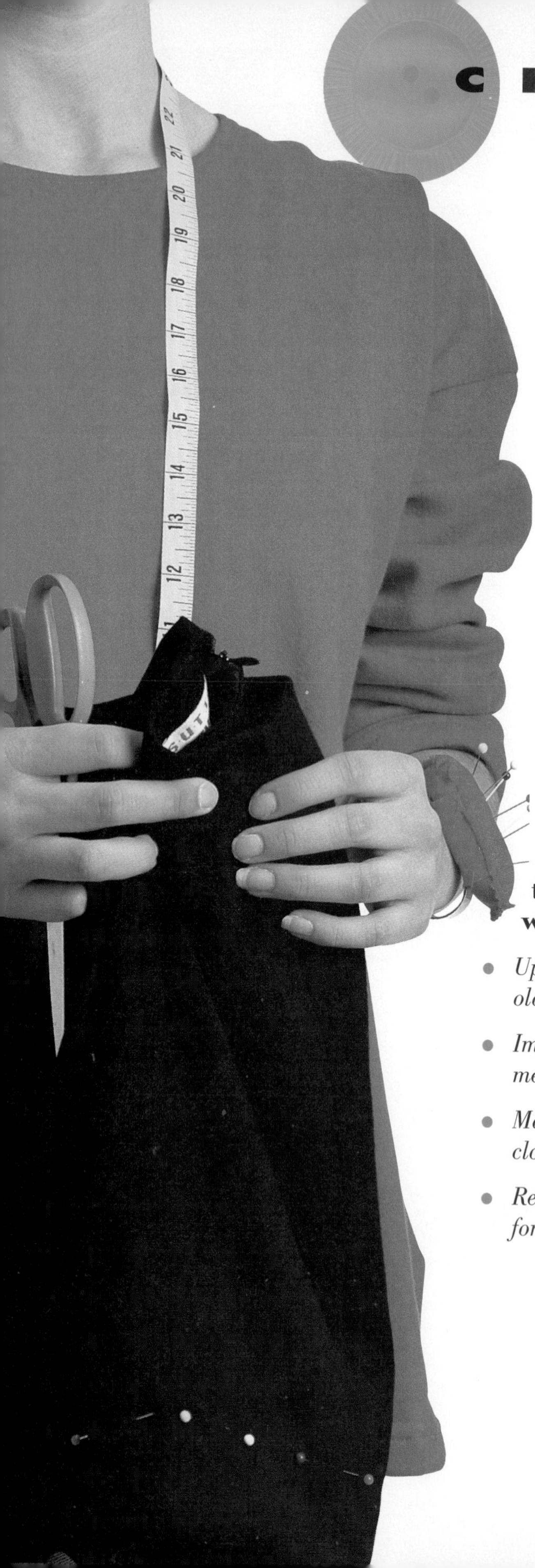

CHAPTER 18

Redesign, Repair, and Recycle

After reading this chapter, you will be able to:

- *Update the fashion look of older clothes.*
- *Improve the fit of a garment.*
- *Make simple repairs on clothing.*
- *Recycle clothes and fabrics for new uses.*

Terms to Learn

- *redesign*
- *recycle*
- *consignment store*
- *patchwork*

What do you do with clothes that you no longer wear? Redesigning, repairing, and recycling are three methods you can use to maximize your clothing wardrobe. They help you to get the most from your clothes and your clothing dollar.

So the next time you look at something that you no longer wear, think about it. How could you put this item back into use for yourself or someone else?

Redesigning Clothes

To **redesign** is to *change an existing garment to better meet your needs.* You can change the style, fit, or color of a garment. Redesigning can be a simple adjustment of the hem length or an update of the total look of the garment.

Redesigning is a very practical method of expanding your wardrobe. It helps you to get the most from what you already have. By making only minor changes, you may be able to achieve the current fashion look. Thus, you can get added wear out of your clothes.

Redesigning also offers you the opportunity to be creative. You can give your clothes a unique look that expresses your individuality. Redesigning can save you money. By using your time and skills, you can expand your wardrobe with very little cost.

You can redesign a garment by changing the fit, style, or trim. What are some design options for this garment?

Changing the Style

Fashion changes from time to time. It may be from season to season or year to year. These trends influence the shape of clothes.

Often you can redesign older clothes to give them an updated look. Hemlines can be shortened and sometimes lengthened. A loose-fitting jacket can be taken in to look more fitted. A full-cut dress may be belted at the waist or hips for a more controlled look. Flared pants legs can be turned into straight legs.

You can also change the entire style of a garment to give it a new look. Cut off long pants to make shorts. Make a short-sleeved shirt from a long-sleeved one. Remove the sleeves of a jacket and turn it into a vest. Shorten a coat to make a jacket.

Before you begin any redesign project, work out the steps and solutions. For example, be sure that you leave enough fabric for a hem or cuff before cutting off pants legs. Before you take out the sleeves of a jacket, plan how you will finish the armholes of the new vest.

Adjusting the Fit

How a garment fits affects both your appearance and comfort. Are your black pants so long that they hang down over your shoes? If so, you may seldom wear them because you know they do not look right. Perhaps a waistband is so tight that your pants are uncomfortable to wear. Moving the hook or button over just a little bit may give you the added comfort that you need.

Most minor fitting problems can be corrected with some time and basic sewing skills. For major problems, it may be best to have a dressmaker or tailor alter the garment for you.

Length Adjustments

Most garments can be shortened but not always lengthened. Plain hems can be measured, refolded, and restitched. Cuffed garments require extra planning and construction steps.

To shorten a hem, mark the new hem length. Remove the old stitching and fold up the fabric along

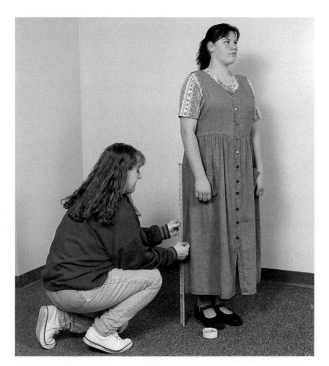

When adjusting the length of a garment, have someone else mark the hem for you. You should stand still, and the person doing the marking should move around you.

width adjustments can be made at the side seams of the garment. The amount to be adjusted is distributed equally between the two side seams.

To take in a garment, or make it smaller, you will stitch the new seam within the garment itself. To let out a garment, or make it larger, you will stitch the new seam outside the original seam in the seam allowance. Therefore, it is extremely important to check the width of the seam allowances to be sure that there is enough fabric to stitch a new seam.

Some ready-to-wear garments have seams that are trimmed and finished to ¼ inch (6 mm). With such a narrow seam allowance, you would not be able to make the garment wider.

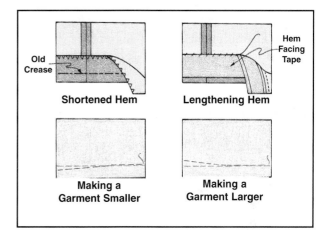

the new hemline. It may be necessary to trim the hem allowance. Most hems should be no wider than 2 to 3 inches (5 to 7.5 cm) in width. A too-wide hem can add bulk and result in a hem that is uneven and too obvious. Hemming techniques are discussed in the Sewing and Serging Handbook.

To lengthen a hem, first check if there is enough fabric to create the added length. If not, you may be able to add wide hem facing tape on the inside of the garment edge to complete the hem. Sometimes the crease in the old hemline is impossible to remove. One solution is to cover the original hemline with trim or several rows of machine stitching. However, this method often looks like it is a cover-up instead of being part of the garment design.

Width Adjustments

Adjusting the width of a garment is often more complicated than adjusting its length. Most minor

Updating Colors

Redesigning clothes through the use of color can open up many alternatives for your wardrobe. You can quickly change the mood or look of an outfit by adding or subtracting colorful accessories or trims. Aim for a well-coordinated, balanced look. One well-selected color is usually better than a combination of several colors in a garment.

Adding Accessories and Trims

A new belt, scarf, tie, buttons, or jewelry can create a new look for an old outfit. Check the fashion magazines to identify the newest trends in colors and

Decorative trims can add color or create a new look for garments.

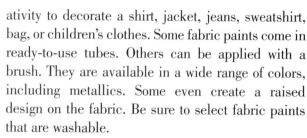

accessories. This season, a bright red belt may make the right accent. For another season, natural-colored accessories, such as a tan rope belt, may be the important look.

Decorative trims can add a touch of color or create a new mood for a garment. Lace can add a romantic feeling to clothes. Rickrack gives a more casual look. Braids and ribbons can be tailored or dressy. Embroidery and appliques can create very colorful accents.

You must also consider the overall effect of the trim on the garment. You might want to add two rows of trim instead of one, or you can repeat the trim at the hem of the sleeve, as well as at the bottom of the skirt. An applique on both patch pockets may look better than on one. Experiment by pinning the trim in place before you attach it permanently.

Painting or Dyeing Fabric

Fabric paints can be used to create colorful designs on clothing and accessories. Use your cre-

Use fabric paints to make colorful designs on clothing, accessories, and gift items.

ativity to decorate a shirt, jacket, jeans, sweatshirt, bag, or children's clothes. Some fabric paints come in ready-to-use tubes. Others can be applied with a brush. They are available in a wide range of colors, including metallics. Some even create a raised design on the fabric. Be sure to select fabric paints that are washable.

Another alternative is to change the color entirely by dyeing the fabric. Fabric dyes are available in liquid and powder forms. Read the instructions on the package carefully. Some fibers will dye better than others. When dyeing fabrics, it is important to follow the step-by-step directions exactly. Otherwise the dye may not be permanent, and the color may fade when you wash the garment.

Repairing Clothes

Simple repairs or replacements can often improve the quality of a new or an old garment. These repairs include restitching hems and seams, changing buttons, adding snaps or hooks and eyes, and mending small holes. Usually each takes only a few minutes to do.

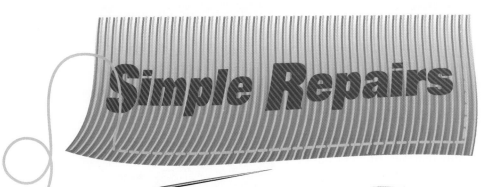

Simple Repairs

• **Stitch a ripped seam.** Restitch a seam by machine or hand, using a small backstitch. Overlap ends of stitching for added strength. If seam is in an area that receives extra stress, such as the underarm or crotch seam, use a double row of stitching 1/8 inch (3 mm) apart.

• **Mend a tear.** A straight tear can be mended by stitching back and forth across the tear to hold the torn edges together. Begin and end stitches about 1/4 inch (6 mm) beyond the tear.

• **Patch a hole.** A patch can be applied by hand stitching, machine stitching, or fusing. Trim away any frayed threads from around hole. Cut out a patch of fabric, slightly larger than the hole. Pin patch to inside of garment; fold in edges of patch and stitch in place. On outside, turn under edges of hole and slipstitch to patch. For added strength, topstitch around patch on outside of garment.

To fuse a patch, cut patch the exact size of hole. Position fabric wrong side up on ironing board. Place patch on top of the hole. Cover area with a piece of fusible web and then a piece of firmly woven fabric. Press from wrong side to fuse patch in 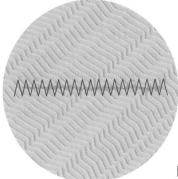 place. Iron-on patches or mending tape also can be used. Following package directions, press patch to the fabric.

• **Fix a snag.** Knitted or loosely woven fabrics often get snags, or loops of fabric pulled out. Use a small crochet hook, snag fixer, or needle threader and insert through the fabric directly under the snag. Grasp snag with hook and pull back to underside of fabric. Smooth out any puckers by gently stretching fabric in the direction of the pulled thread.

Restitching Seams and Hems

Restitching a seam or a hem is an easy way to improve quality. Sometimes stitches break, creating openings in the seam or a sagging hemline. You can repair the stitches with machine or hand stitching.

The hem in a new garment sometimes puckers or pulls. This may be visible on the right side of the garment. To make it look better, remove the old stitches and restitch the hem. Be sure that your stitching does not show on the outside. See the Sewing and Serging Handbook for instructions.

Replacing Buttons and Fasteners

Changing buttons can upgrade a new garment or add life to an old one. Sometimes manufacturers use inexpensive buttons to help keep the cost of clothes down. Old buttons sometimes fade after many washings or cleanings. Replacing these buttons will improve the appearance of a garment.

Sometimes snaps or hooks and eyes on ready-to-wear clothes are not stitched securely. You can restitch these fasteners quickly by hand. You can also add a snap or hook and eye at a neckline, front closing, or waistband. This will help hold the fabric together more securely or smoothly. Refer to the Sewing and Serging Handbook for sewing methods.

Mending or Covering Areas

Small tears and holes in fabric often can be mended with tiny stitches. A patch can also be applied underneath a hole by fusing or stitching.

Sometimes just one area of a garment becomes worn or frayed. The rest of the garment is in excellent condition. For example, frayed elbows of a sweater, jacket, or heavy shirt can be covered with oval patches. To mend, topstitch or fuse the patch to the area. Use contrasting fabric such as leather, suede, corduroy, or flannel.

You can hide the worn edge of a sleeve or pants leg. To do this, apply a row of trim, fold-over braid, or bias binding to the worn edge. Patches can be stitched or pressed to the inside or outside of a pants leg to reinforce the knee or cover a hole. Stubborn

By changing the buttons on a garment, you can improve its appearance or change its look.

stains that cannot be removed can also be hidden with appliques or trim.

Recycling Clothes

To **recycle** means *to reclaim items for another use.* You can recycle clothes by passing them along to others or by making something new out of them. Recycling helps to prevent waste by extending the life of either the garment or the fabric. Something that you no longer need could exactly meet the needs of someone else.

Recycling clothing helps to save resources. Fabrics are made from either natural or manufactured fibers. Recycling helps to conserve not only the sources of these fibers but also the energy used to manufacture the fibers and fabrics.

Recycling also helps families to save money. You can pass a garment along to another family member at no cost. You can utilize old fabrics for new projects at no cost. You can sell clothing at garage sales, bazaars, flea markets, and consignment stores. A **consignment store** is *one that will pay you a percentage of the selling price after the store sells your clothes*. In turn, you can buy clothing at these locations for a lower price than you would pay for new clothing.

Passing It On

Wearable clothing can be handed down to a younger brother, sister, cousin, or neighbor. You can also pass it along to a friend. Sometimes friends will have a clothing swap. Your best friend may have always admired a red sweater that you no longer wear. You might trade it for a shirt or lightweight jacket that your friend no longer likes. Now you each have added to your wardrobe without spending any money.

Your usable, but unwanted, clothing can be passed on to someone less fortunate. You can donate it to religious groups or other charitable organizations. They help families that have lost their belongings in fires, floods, or other disasters. Check in your area for organizations that accept used clothing.

Finding Other Uses

If clothing is no longer usable, you can recycle the fabric. Make an accessory item, clothing for children, or a patchwork project. Some old fabrics can be used for cleaning.

You can recycle fabrics to make accessories, placemats, pillows, quilts, and stuffed toys. Even small pieces of fabric can be used in patchwork designs.

Passing garments along to a younger sister or brother is an easy way to recycle clothing that you no longer wear.

279

From Plastic Bottles to Parkas

Discarded items that once crowded our landfills are now being converted into fashion apparel:

- **EcoSpun®** is a fiber made from recycled plastic soda bottles. Empty bottles are collected and crushed in a process called *densifying*. Then they are ground, washed, and melted into a gooey substance. Poly-fibers are extracted from this substance. The fibers can be woven into fabrics that resemble everything from wool to cotton to fleece. The fibers can also be blended with other natural or manufactured fibers.

- **Reused Denim®** is the trade name for a fabric made from 50 percent new cotton fibers and 50 percent reclaimed cotton denim. The reclaimed denim comes from scraps remaining after new denim fabric is made into jeans and other apparel items.

- **Sturdy hiking boots** and **canvas shoes** are made from 17 to 75 percent recycled materials. These materials include tires, plastic soda bottles, coffee filters, polystyrene cups, and diapers. Several manufacturers are offering these. At least one manufacturer encourages consumers to turn in their worn shoes. These shoes are ground into granulated rubber, which is used for many things including athletic tracks. It can also be made into fabric fluff for cushion stuffing and home insulation.

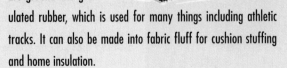

Accessories

Be imaginative. What accessory could you make from an old pair of jeans? How about a sturdy back-pack made from one of the pants legs? An old sweat-shirt could be turned into a vest or a pillow.

Do not forget other fabrics in your home. A table-cloth that is badly stained could be transformed into a set of placemats. A colorful old towel can make a carry-all for the beach.

Children's Clothes

Many children's clothes can be made from used fabrics. For example, create a corduroy jumper from an old skirt or a quilted robe from a larger robe. Shorts, pants, jackets, shirts, and dresses all can be made from used fabrics that are in good condition. Many children like the feel of such fabrics because

Young children love to "dress up" in old clothes, hats, jewelry, and shoes. Keep them in a large box or trunk so they are easily available for creative play.

they are softer and more comfortable than new fabrics. It is the same for adults who choose to pay a premium price for prewashed jeans.

Old clothing can also be used for playing "dress up." Children love to have clothes that they can use for all types of creative play. A box of old clothes is an excellent source of costumes for parties, Halloween, and class plays at school.

Patchwork Projects

Patchwork is *a method of sewing together small fabric shapes to create a new, decorative piece of fabric.* Patchwork quilts have been used for centuries. Today, patchwork can be used for a variety of projects, including pillows, wallhangings, placemats, tote bags, and stuffed toys.

Patchwork clothing, such as vests, jackets, belts, and aprons, can be created by using a variety of patchwork designs. You can get ideas from craft books or magazines for planning patchwork projects.

You can be very creative in your fabric choices, combining colors and prints that blend or contrast. However, do select fabrics that are firmly woven and compatible in care. Since the pieces of fabric will be stitched together, it is important that they wear and clean in the same way.

Several different fabrics have been used to create this colorful appliquéd vest.

Household Use

Clothing that is worn or damaged may be still good enough for other uses. For example, what do you use to dust your furniture? Every family needs some household rags for cleaning. Small pieces of fabric can be used for dusting and wiping. Larger pieces of fabric can be used to cover the floor when painting, sanding, or staining. Old towels, sheets, and other household fabrics can also be used in these ways.

Save fabrics that are absorbent, such as 100 percent cotton or cotton blends. Be sure to remove all buttons, zippers, snaps, hooks and eyes, or other fasteners. These may scratch the surfaces that you clean. You may want to cut off any trims or bulky areas, such as pockets, to make the fabric easier to handle.

You can also use items such as pantyhose for stuffing toys and pillows. Buttons, fasteners, and trims can be saved for use on future projects.

Finally, fibers can be recycled for use in padding and in paper. Some organizations collect old clothing and fabrics for such recycling. By recycling clothes and fabrics, you can help save both personal and natural resources.

Many organizations collect old clothing and fabrics for recycling.

REVIEW

CHAPTER 16

Summary

- You can redesign an outfit by changing the style, adjusting the fit, or updating the colors.
- Simple repairs can often improve the quality of a garment.
- It takes only a few minutes to restitch hems and seams, change buttons, add snaps or hooks and eyes, and mend small holes.
- Recycling can reclaim items for another use.
- You can recycle clothes by either passing them along to others or using the fabric for accessories, children's clothes, patchwork projects, or household rags.

Using Vocabulary Terms

On a separate piece of paper, write the vocabulary term that best fits the definition:

1. To reclaim items for another use.
2. To change an existing garment to better meet your needs.
3. A method of sewing together small fabric shapes to create a new, decorative piece of fabric.
4. A store that will pay you a percentage of the selling price after it sells your clothes.

Recalling the Facts

1. What are three benefits of redesigning clothes?
2. When redesigning a garment, what are three changes that you could make?
3. How could the style of a garment be updated or changed?
4. What must you check about the fabric before lengthening a hem or letting out a seam?
5. How can you use color to change the mood or look of an outfit?
6. Name three repairs or replacements that can improve the quality of a garment.
7. What can you do to hide a worn or frayed area of a garment?
8. What are three benefits of recycling clothes?
9. What could you do with wearable clothing that you no longer want?
10. If clothing is no longer usable, how could it be recycled?

Thinking Critically

1. **Analysis.** In what ways are redesigning and recycling related?
2. **Synthesis.** How might you redesign a jacket that is outdated?
3. **Analysis.** Compare receiving "hand-me-downs" from relatives to purchasing used clothing from a consignment store. What are the advantages and disadvantages of each?

4. **Evaluation.** If you had lots of money, would you consider redesigning or recycling your clothes? Explain your answer.

Applying Your Knowledge

1. **Redesigning.** Choose one item from your wardrobe to redesign for yourself or for another family member. Explain what steps or techniques you will use.

2. **Repairing.** Practice making the following simple repairs on fabric: restitch a seam, sew a button, repair a hem, sew snaps, mend a small tear, sew a hook and eye, and patch a hole.

3. **Recycling.** Make a list of organizations that recycle clothing. Explain their policies for collecting and distributing the clothing.

3. **Dress-up Clothes.** Collect old clothing, accessories, and jewelry for a dress-up box. Donate to a child care center, nursery school, or preschool program in your community.

Making the Connection

1. **Art.** Create a new look for an old t-shirt by tie-dyeing the fabric, using fabric paints, or adding decorative trims.

2. **Social Studies.** Pioneer women created patchwork designs for quilts that are famous as a uniquely American craft. Research the history

What Is an Alterations Specialist?

Alterations specialists make alterations and repairs to clothing. They must have a knowledge of fashion, as well as clothing construction. They repair ripped seams and hems, adjust the length and fit of garments, and repair tears and holes in fabric. In addition to doing alterations, some will custom-make garments for customers. These specialists are usually called dressmakers or tailors.

Try It Yourself

Imagine that you are an alterations specialist, dressmaker, or tailor. Look through old magazines, catalogs, and pattern books for an illustration of a garment that needs a fashion update. Describe how you could change the style of the garment. Then explain the steps that you would follow to achieve the updated look. Using a sewing and alterations book, locate various types of adjustments that you would need to make on the garment. Identify which alterations would be easy to do and which would be complex.

Build Your Portfolio

 After completing your plans for updating the garment, place a copy in your portfolio. Include a sketch of the *before* and *after* designs. Add the list of different types of alterations to your portfolio, too.

of various patchwork designs, such as Log Cabin, Lone Star, and Dresden Plate. Report your findings to the class.

Public Relations Director

Steve Lark works for a large sportswear manufacturer. "In high school I was always organizing something," says Steve. "I was manager of the basketball team. I ran for student council. I helped organize my town's annual Earth Day clean up." So it is no surprise to his former classmates that Steve is a successful public relations director, who is involved in everything from fashion shows to foot races.

Education and Training

Like many people, Steve didn't have a particular career in mind when he headed for college. He had a liberal arts major and took additional courses in business and communications.

After graduation, Steve worked as a junior account executive for a large public relations firm. He wrote press releases and made follow-up phone calls to television and newspaper reporters. He learned how to write pitch letters to convince them to run feature stories about the firm's clients. He did anything necessary to help make a press event run smoothly. He made coffee, ordered food, addressed invitations, and wrote name tags. There were long hours and low pay, but the reward was excellent training in public relations.

Eventually Steve was promoted to senior account executive. He was given complete responsibility for a group of clients that included a toy manufacturer. Steve organized a program that donated teddy bears to the local children's hospital. Then he convinced a major fashion magazine to use the bears as props for a fashion spread. At a party for the magazine's advertisers, Steve met the president of a sportswear manufacturer. Steve tried to convince the president to hire his public relations agency. Instead, the president offered Steve a job.

"It was a big decision," said Steve. "I moved 3,000 miles to a city where I didn't know anyone. But I knew it was an opportunity that was too good to turn down. I have never regretted my decision."

Responsibilities

During Steve's five years with the sportswear company, it has grown from a small manufacturer to a multi-million dollar business. As the company has grown, Steve's responsibilities have increased.

- **Develop media campaigns.** It is Steve's job to know what is going on in the communications media and to use that knowledge to promote his company's products. When the company launched a line of clothing for preschoolers, Steve planned special events and organized a media campaign.

- **Oversee celebrity endorsements.** A popular basketball star endorses their products, and a special line of clothes carries the star's name. Steve personally oversees any public appearances this athlete makes on behalf of the company.

- **Create product visibility.** Thanks to Steve's efforts, the company's clothing regularly appears in fashion magazines. When a TV talk show began featuring audience makeovers, Steve arranged for his company's clothes to be used on the show.

- **Be a spokesperson.** Steve is the public voice for the company. He talks to the business media about the company's financial health. He talks to the consumer press about current fashion trends.

- **Develop a budget.** Steve develops a yearly expense budget for his department. It includes salaries, travel, photography, and special events, such as the 10K charity race that his company sponsors each year.

- **Supervise staff.** There are five people on the public relations staff. Steve is responsible for hiring, supervising, and evaluating their performance.

Knowledge and Skills

Steve listed the knowledge and skills that he has found important for public relations:

"I can talk to anyone one-on-one, but speaking to large groups always made me nervous. A high school speech class calmed some of my fears. After I joined the sportswear firm, I worked with a communications consultant who taught me how to look comfortable in front of the television camera."

- **Communication skills**—for writing press releases, talking to reporters, promoting products, meeting with coworkers, and appearing on television.

- **Interpersonal skills**—for interacting with all types of people, from major sports celebrities to reporters from small newspapers.

- **Computer skills**—for keeping track of promotional projects and special events, writing press releases and reports, and maintaining a data base of contacts.

- **Math skills**—for preparing budgets and keeping financial records.

- **Creativity**—for conceptualizing promotional ideas and special events.

- **Management skills**—for supervising staff, planning and organizing events, solving problems, and evaluating results.

Shopping

CHAPTER 19

Gathering Information

After reading this chapter, you will be able to:

- Explain the difference between an information ad and an image ad.

- Identify different types of media used in advertising.

- Analyze the information printed on labels and hangtags.

- Discuss ways that comparison shopping can help you to gather information.

Terms to Learn

- information ads
- image ads
- media
- sales promotion
- mandatory
- trademark
- logo
- warranty
- comparison shopping
- impulse

As you glance through a magazine, many advertisements for new products compete for your attention. They have a new and exciting look. The colors and styles are fresh and appealing. Suddenly, almost everything you have been wearing seems to be old. You dream of going out and buying a whole new wardrobe!

Advertisements in magazines, newspapers, catalogs, and on television constantly tempt us to buy. None of us can afford to replace all of our clothes every few months. Yet, when we do decide to buy, these ads can be a source of helpful information.

Advertising

The purpose of advertising is to sell something— either a product or a service. Advertisements can appear in magazines, catalogs, and newspapers. They can be seen or heard on radio or on television.

Advertisements can be sources of information and ideas. However, they also can tempt us to buy something we really do not need or something that is too expensive for our budget. Advertising appeals to many different emotions. Some ads are designed to appeal to our dreams and fantasies. Others appeal to our desires to win the approval of others or to have the "very latest." Ads may tap our desire for adventure or our desire for individuality.

Information or Image

There are two basic types of advertising. One type provides you with information. The other type promotes an image.

• **Information ads** are those that *tell you many details about the product*. They will describe the style and the fabric. They will include the size range, price, fiber content, care, name and location of the store, and brand name. By reading these ads carefully, you can compare products without having to go from store to store. Some ads provide more complete information than others. For example, stating that the fabric is "50% cotton/50% polyester" is more informative than saying that the fabric is a "cotton blend."

• **Image ads** are *designed to appeal to your fantasies, to make a fashion statement, or to promote a designer's or manufacturer's name*. These ads are usually very visual. Most of the ad is devoted to illustrations or photographs. Although image ads give little information about the actual product, they can provide ideas for styles, colors, and fabrics to add to your wardrobe. You can learn about new fashions and get ideas for new ways to wear clothes you already have.

Advertising can be a source of information about new products, fashions, stores, and prices.

Chambray Shirt

Soft, prewashed fabric sets this chambray shirt apart from the everyday. Double-needle stitching at the sides, underarms, and pockets shows the quality you've come to expect. 100% cotton in blue, red, and green.
Sizes: M, L, XL, XXL
Machine wash and dry.
Made in the USA. $36

Compare these two ads. What information does each provide?

Spring
Attitudes

Yordy's Department Store

The Advertising Media

Advertising is designed to give us a message. **Media** are *the means used to communicate messages to a large number of people.* Radio, television, and computers are electronic media. Magazines, newspapers, and catalogs are examples of print media. Each has certain requirements and limitations that affect the format of the advertisements.

• **Radio and television.** Most radio and television ads are only 30 seconds or 60 seconds long. Because of this, they usually do not give much information. The ads are short and splashy. Their aim is to capture your attention and make you remember the product or the company name. Most television ads are image ads.

• **Magazines.** Most magazine ads are used to create an image of a certain product or brand. They usually have a large photograph or illustration and contain some information about the product. Most ads do not tell you how much the product costs or where you can buy it.

• **Newspapers.** Except for special ads in large Sunday newspapers, most newspaper ads are black and white photographs or drawings. Newspaper ads appeal to the same desires as magazine ads. However, they usually include more information. These ads explain where to buy the product, what hours the store is open, what sizes are available, and how much the product costs.

• **Catalogs.** Many stores and manufacturers send out catalogs to potential customers. Most catalogs contain color photographs of the products. They also include information about styles, fabrics, colors, sizes, and price. The items can be ordered by phone or by mail without having to visit a local store.

Mail-Order Shopping

Catalog shopping may seem like a new idea, but it has been around a long time. In the late 1700s, Benjamin Franklin published a catalog offering approximately 600 books. In the early 1800s, New Englanders could purchase sporting equipment and supplies through mail-order catalogs. In the late 1800s, Montgomery Ward and Sears, Roebuck began publishing catalogs that offered everything from thread to tractors. Most of their customers lived on farms and in small towns.

When the automobile became popular in the 1920s, most mail-order businesses opened retail stores. Families living on farms and in small towns could travel to larger towns and cities to shop. Many people thought that the days of successful mail-order companies were over. However, that has not proved to be true.

Today more than 6,000 mail-order catalogs and offerings are published every year. Some businesses have both a mail-order division and one or more retail stores. Some department stores have catalogs that offer merchandise that is not available in their stores. Other businesses are mail-order only.

Mail-order companies are located throughout the country. Many have toll-free 800 numbers and fax numbers that make it easy for customers to place orders at any time of day or night. Product information is computerized so the customer service representative who answers the phone can give detailed information about the products. Express mail services can often guarantee that customers will receive their orders within 24 hours.

Catalogs usually provide lots of information about products. However, you have to pay handling and shipping costs when ordering by phone or mail.

• **Home-shopping shows and infomercials.** These are television shows that concentrate on selling products. The shopping channels provide some product information but also focus on the product's image. The infomercials are usually 30-minute advertisements that present detailed information about the product. Many follow the format of television talk shows. Some may feature celebrities promoting the product. All of these shows provide a toll-free 800 number so viewers can order the product.

• **Computers.** Some consumers are able to view merchandise on their computers through special computer services. They can read descriptions and compare features and prices before placing an order via the computer.

• **Promotional articles.** A magazine or newspaper will often have promotional articles on certain subjects. For example, an article may describe the newest styles or how to plan your wardrobe. Many of the products mentioned in the article may also be advertised in the paper or magazine. There is nothing dishonest about this. Just remember that what you are reading may be a *biased* or slanted article.

• **Billboards and posters.** These forms of advertising are found along the highway, on buildings, or on the

Both home shopping shows and infomercials urge viewers to order a product by calling a toll-free number.

sides of a bus. You see these ads for a very short time, so the message is brief and bold.

- **Fashion shows and demonstrations.** These are both *very subtle forms of advertising* that are sometimes called **sales promotions**. Fashion shows give you the opportunity to see the product in person on a model. Remember that a garment may not look the same on you as it does on a professional model, who is usually very tall and slim. Demonstrations show you how to use a product such as cosmetics. Most cosmetic demonstrations give you the opportunity to try out the product on your own skin.

The Influence of Fashion

Because fashion is an industry, its main purpose is to stay in business by selling more clothes and accessories. In order to do this, fashion must change constantly. Every season there are advertisements that describe the "new looks."

A new style may be introduced, last for several years, and then fade away. The best shopping strategy is to purchase a style that is near the beginning, rather than at the end, of its fashion life.

Read, look, and listen carefully to what is said about the new fashions. You will soon be able to tell the difference between a fashion that will be around for a long time and a fad that will quickly fade from popularity.

Look for some key words that are used to describe a new style. If words and phrases such as "latest," "newest," "direct from Paris," or "the BIG news is..." are used, the style may not be fashionable for long. If words like "classic," "traditional," or "always in fashion" are used, you know it is not a fad.

There is nothing wrong with buying something because it is new or classic, a fad or a status symbol. You should, however, know what you are buying and why you have decided to buy it.

Labels and Hangtags

Advertising will not provide all of the information you need to know about a product. Other information comes from carefully reading the labels and hangtags that are attached to the garment. These will give you information such as fabric content and care instructions.

At one time the clothes that everyone wore were made from natural fibers. The most common fibers were cotton, wool, silk, and linen. People knew what to expect from these fibers and how to take care of them.

Then the world of modern chemistry appeared, creating fibers with names such as nylon, polyester, acrylic, and spandex. People did not know what these were or how to care for them. Clothes were marked and advertised in such a way that consumers often thought they were buying one thing and ended up with something quite different.

In 1958, Congress approved the the Textile Fiber Products Identification (TFPI) Act. The purpose of this law is to protect consumers against misbranding or false advertising concerning the fiber content of any textile product. Similar laws have been enacted by Congress to cover products made from wool and from fur.

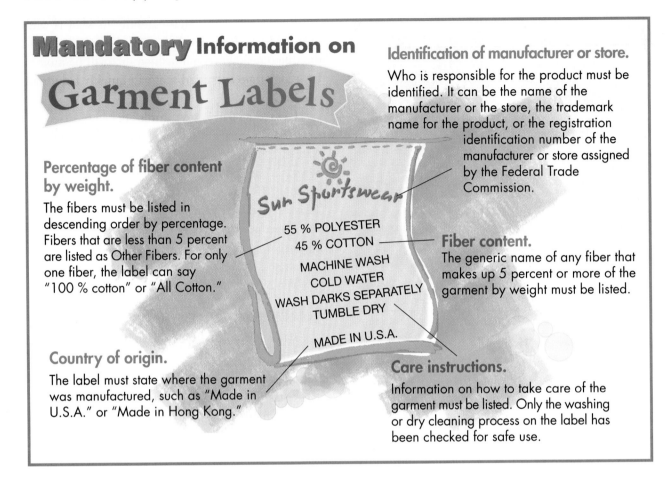

Mandatory Information on Garment Labels

Identification of manufacturer or store.

Who is responsible for the product must be identified. It can be the name of the manufacturer or the store, the trademark name for the product, or the registration identification number of the manufacturer or store assigned by the Federal Trade Commission.

Percentage of fiber content by weight.

The fibers must be listed in descending order by percentage. Fibers that are less than 5 percent are listed as Other Fibers. For only one fiber, the label can say "100 % cotton" or "All Cotton."

Fiber content.

The generic name of any fiber that makes up 5 percent or more of the garment by weight must be listed.

Sun Sportswear
55 % POLYESTER
45 % COTTON
MACHINE WASH
COLD WATER
WASH DARKS SEPARATELY
TUMBLE DRY
MADE IN U.S.A.

Country of origin.

The label must state where the garment was manufactured, such as "Made in U.S.A." or "Made in Hong Kong."

Care instructions.

Information on how to take care of the garment must be listed. Only the washing or dry cleaning process on the label has been checked for safe use.

Mandatory Information

Every garment must now have one or more labels that give the consumer specific information. This information is **mandatory**, or *required by law*. These labels should be attached to the garment in places where they are easy to find. Usually, this is at the center back of a garment—at the neck of a shirt, sweater, or blouse, and at the waist of pants and skirts. Sometimes you will find them in the inside lower front seam of a jacket or in the side seams of lingerie.

These labels can be glued, sewn, printed, or stamped on the fabric. They can even be attached to the outside of the garment. The labels must be attached so they will not come off until you, the purchaser, decide to take them off. If the garment will remain in a package until after it is sold, the fiber content label can be affixed to the package only.

According to the TFPI Act, five pieces of mandatory information must appear on garment labels:

1. Fiber content.
2. Percentage of fiber content by weight.
3. Identification of manufacturer or store.
4. Country of origin.
5. Care instructions.

Every garment that you buy must have a label containing required information. It usually is stitched or glued to the garment. One or more hang tags may also be attached to the garment.

Voluntary Information

Garment labels and hangtags may include additional information that is voluntary, given freely and not regulated by law. Some of this information may be included on the permanent labels in the garment. Others may be on hangtags that are attached with a strip of plastic, string, thread, or a safety pin.

• **Size.** The size may be included as part of the garment label, printed on a small separate label, or printed on a hangtag.

• **Trademarks** or **brand names.** Hangtags and labels can serve as mini-advertisements for the product name or trademark. A **trademark** is *a symbol, design, word, or letter that is used by manufacturers or retailers to distinguish their products from those of the*

competition. Trademarks are registered and protected by law so that no one can use someone else's trademark. Hangtags and labels can also be used to promote the name of the fiber, finish, manufacturer, or store. Sometimes the information is in the form of a **logo**, or *symbol*.

Hangtags may provide additional information about fabrics, finishes, and warranties.

The "Made in the U.S.A." hangtags help consumers easily identify American-made products.

warranties. The Monsanto Company issues a wear-dated warranty. It guarantees that the consumer will receive a refund or a replacement garment if the original garment does not provide normal wear for a specific period of time.

- **Union label.** This tells you that the garment was made in the United States by people who belong to the Union of Needletrades, Industrial, and Textile Employees (Unite). This union was created in 1995 by a merger of the International Ladies' Garment Workers' Union (ILGWU) and the Amalgamated Clothing Workers of America (ACWA).

Stores usually attach separate hangtags to garments with information that is important to the store's inventory control. This usually includes size, price, stock number, and department number.

Comparison Shopping

Have you and your friends ever gone shopping "just to look"? Then one of you decides to buy a belt or a scarf. The next thing you know, everyone has bought something.

- **Warranty** or **guarantee.** A **warranty** is *a pledge or assurance that the product or fabric will meet certain standards.* A few organizations, such as the International Fabricare Institute, maintain testing laboratories that issue warranties or seals of approval. These pledges guarantee that the product will live up to the standards set by that particular laboratory. Some manufacturers also issue their own

Be sure to compare the quality, design, and price of several items before you buy. You can gather valuable information from the labels and hangtags.

When shopping, take care not to make sudden or impulsive purchases. Too often these are for items that are not needed or cost too much.

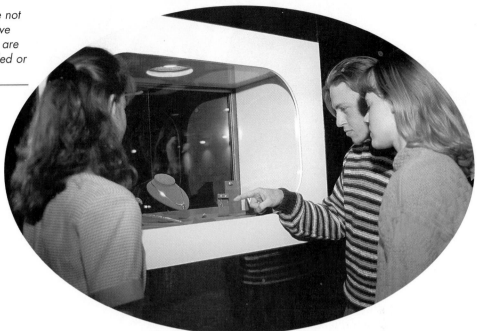

Shopping can often lead to many **impulse**, or *sudden*, purchases. Store displays are specifically designed to catch your attention. An entire outfit is often displayed, complete with accessories, so that you are tempted to buy everything, rather than coordinating one new item with items already in your wardrobe. This is how our closets fill up with fads, "good buys," and a variety of accessories that we do not really need.

Shopping may be an activity among your friends. If so, it is useful to learn how to recognize a good bargain and fair prices. You can do this by **comparison shopping**. This means *to look at quality, price, and design to compare value.*

Begin comparison shopping at home. Read, watch, and listen to advertisements and study catalogs. Then, once you are in a store, you will be able to compare the merchandise with the information you already have.

Examine the quality and take note of the price. Read the labels and the hangtags. They are valuable sources of information concerning the manufacturer, the fiber content, cost of the garment, and much more.

Becoming an educated shopper makes it easier to "just look" and not buy when you are in a store. However, you may occasionally want to buy something just to make yourself feel good. It is a way of giving yourself a treat. Learn to recognize these impulse purchases for what they are. Restrict them to small, inexpensive items, such as a scarf, a belt, a lipstick, or a pair of socks.

It takes effort to gather information about products and services before making a purchase. However, the results are worth it. You will have a better-looking wardrobe that satisfies your needs and wants without putting a strain on your budget.

Summary

- There are two basic types of advertising. One provides information; the other promotes an image.

- The advertising media include radio, magazines, newspapers, and catalogs.

- Products are also promoted through home-shopping shows, infomercials, computers, promotional articles, billboards, posters, fashion shows, and demonstrations.

- Labels and hangtags provide valuable information such as fabric content and care instructions.

- Comparison shopping helps you to recognize good bargains and fair prices.

Using Vocabulary Terms

On a separate piece of paper, write the vocabulary term that best fits the definition:

1. A pledge or assurance that the product will meet certain standards.

2. Looking at quality, price, and design to compare value.

3. A symbol, design, word, or letter that is used by manufacturers or retailers to distinguish their products from those of the competition.

4. The means used to communicate messages to a large number of people.

5. Type of ads that appeal to people's fantasies.

6. Required by law.

Recalling the Facts

1. What is the difference between an information ad and an image ad?

2. What type of ads usually appear on radio and television?

3. How do ads in magazines and in newspapers differ?

4. What type of information can be found in catalogs?

5. What is the purpose of home-shopping shows and infomercials?

6. Why should you purchase a style that is near the beginning of its fashion life?

7. What is the purpose of the Textile Fiber Products Identification Act?

8. List the five pieces of information that must appear on garment labels.

9. What are four additional types of information that may be included on garment labels or hangtags?

10. How can comparison shopping help you?

Thinking Critically

1. **Analysis.** What are some advantages and disadvantages of using catalogs to shop?

2. **Evaluation.** There are many types of advertising media. Which ones do you think are most effective in reaching the teenage market?

3. **Analysis.** How can labels and hangtags help you make smart clothing choices?

4. **Synthesis.** What might happen if fiber content and care instructions were not mandatory on garment labels?

5. **Evaluation.** Are there circumstances when shopping alone is preferred over shopping with a group of friends? Explain your answer.

Applying Your Knowledge

1. **Information and Image Ads.** Find examples of clothing ads in magazines, newspapers, and catalogs. Analyze the ads for the amount of information provided and the appeal to emotions and desires. Explain why you think each ad is effective or not.

2. **Media.** Working in small groups, select one type of media in which to advertise. Create a clothing ad suitable for that media and present it to the class.

3. **Labels and Hangtags.** Check the labels and hangtags on various types of clothing in a store. What information is listed? Where are the labels and tags located on the garment? Share your findings with the class.

4. **Comparison Shopping.** Using two or more catalogs, comparison shop for clothing and accessories. Make a chart to compare design, quality, and price of each item.

What Is a Copywriter?

Copywriters write the words used in print ads, catalogs, and radio and TV commercials. These words are called *copy*. Copywriters must provide information about the product and make it sound attractive and appealing so people will want to buy it. Usually copywriters must do this in as few words as possible.

Try It Yourself

Imagine that you are a copywriter for one of the following: an advertising agency, a retail store, or a mail-order catalog. Select a clothing or accessory item for a particular type of customer. Then write copy about it for both an information ad and an image ad.

Build Your Portfolio

After writing the copy for both types of ads, describe the type of customer you were trying to reach. Analyze how you approached both projects and which one you found more difficult to write. Place the copy for both ads your portfolio, along with your customer description and project analysis.

Making the Connection

1. **Language Arts.** Create a hangtag for a garment that includes both mandatory and voluntary information about the garment.

2. **Math.** Using catalogs, newspapers, and/or magazines, list the prices of similar types of merchandise, such as jeans, t-shirts, or shoes. What is the difference between the highest and lowest prices?

Shopping— Where, When, How

After reading this chapter, you will be able to:

- *Identify the types of stores where clothing can be purchased.*

- *Discuss the advantages and disadvantages of catalog shopping.*

- *Explain the different types of store sales.*

- *Compare the various ways to pay for purchases.*

Terms to Learn

- *boutique*
- *chain*
- *outlet*
- *overruns*
- *irregulars*
- *seconds*
- *money order*
- *layaway*
- *C.O.D.*
- *finance charge*

The idea of "going shopping" sounds fun. However, have you ever spent a whole day running from store to store and accomplishing nothing? The stores were crowded, your feet hurt, and nothing looked right.

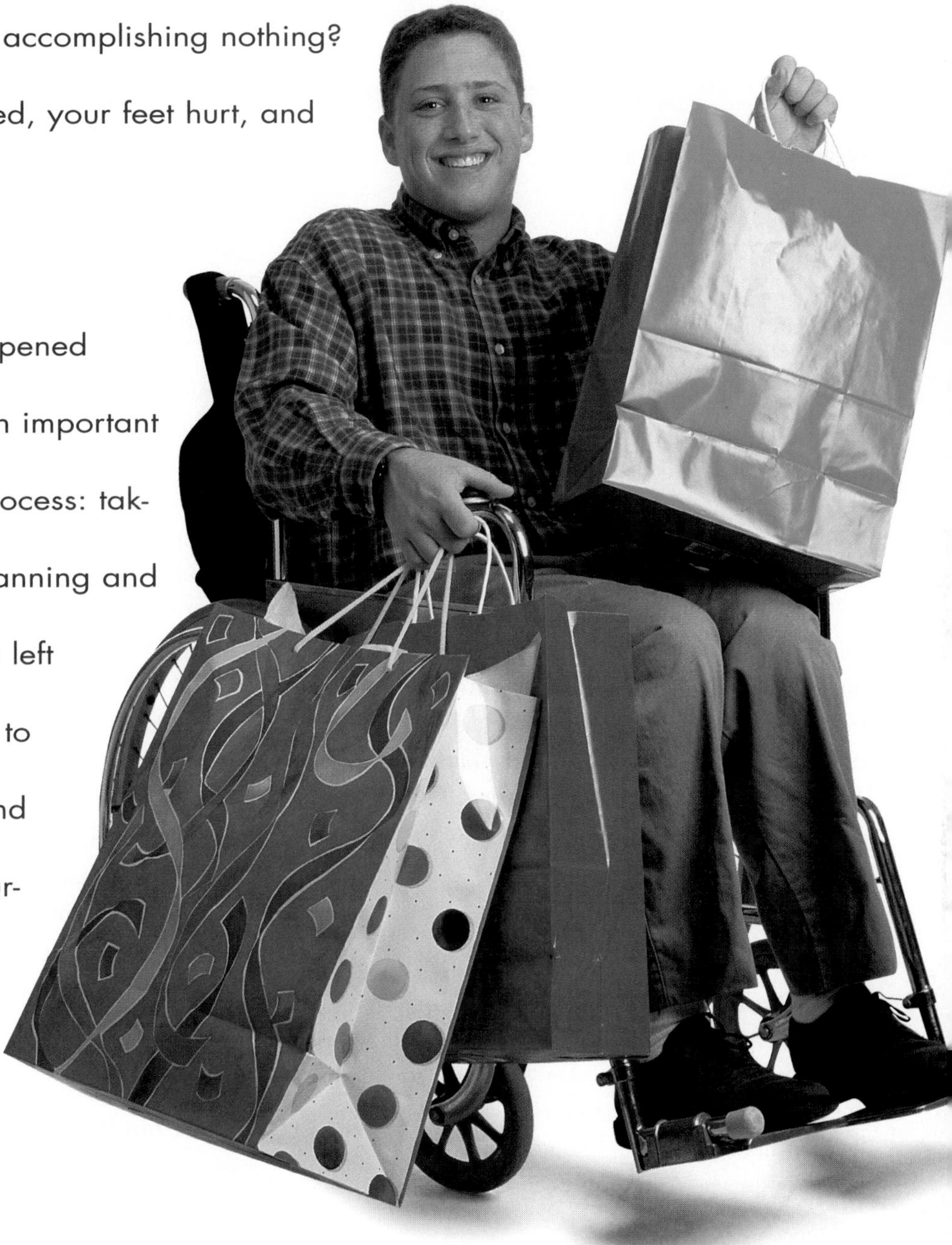

This probably happened because you omitted an important step in the shopping process: taking time to do some planning and preparation before you left home. Deciding where to shop, when to shop, and how to pay for your purchases will make the process smoother.

Where to Shop

First, you should decide what you plan to buy and where you plan to shop. You may have many choices in your area, such as a department store, a specialty store, or a discount store. Perhaps you could order the item through a catalog or even purchase it secondhand at a thrift shop.

Go Prepared

On a piece of paper, list each item of clothing that you plan to purchase. Should a new sweater be a cardigan or a pullover? Should it be blue, like your old one, or would another color work better with your wardrobe? Next, decide how much you want to pay for each item. Then you will be less tempted to exceed your budget.

Now number your list in order of importance. You will want to shop for the most important items first, while you are still fresh and full of energy.

Dress appropriately for the item you are looking for. If you are shopping for a sport coat, wear slacks and good shoes. Jackets will look different with these clothes than with blue jeans and sneakers. If you are buying a fancy dress, bring shoes that are the same height as the ones you plan to wear.

If you are trying to buy something to match an item, either wear or bring it with you. Colors are difficult to match from memory.

Types of Stores

There are many types of stores from which to choose. They may differ in type of merchandise, special services, and prices. For example, some stores specialize in certain price ranges—low, medium, or high. Other stores offer a range of prices within each category.

Department Stores

Department stores are large stores that carry a wide selection of many different types of merchandise. This merchandise is grouped into departments, or areas, according to the specialty.

For example, clothing departments may be organized by size and gender, such as the Men's Department, the Boys' Department, the Petite Department, and the Teen Department. They can also be organized by fashion and price categories, such as "Designer," "Better Dresses" or "Budget." Some may have special departments, such as "Career."

Department stores carry many brand-name items. Some have manufacturers make items exclusively for them. Then the stores put their own name on the items. This is known as private labeling.

Department stores carry many other things besides clothing and accessories. They can sell cosmetics, appliances, sporting goods, electronic equipment, luggage, and housewares. They also offer special services, such as gift wrapping, deliveries, restaurants, cleaning and alteration departments, beauty salons, repair departments, a bridal registry, interior decoration services, and fashion consultations. The cost of these services is added to the price of the merchandise.

Most department stores mail out their own catalogs throughout the year. They usually have their own credit cards. They also honor national credit cards.

Specialty Stores

A store that carries only a limited range of merchandise is known as a specialty store. It may specialize in clothing for a particular group of people, such as children's wear, women's clothes, menswear, or petite or large sizes. Some carry a particular type of merchandise, such as skiwear, hats, tuxedos, or bridal gowns.

A **boutique** is *a type of specialty store featuring very fashionable or unique designs that are higher priced*. Boutiques appeal to customers looking for designer clothes, a special "look," or unusual items.

Some specialty stores are small stores, owned by one person or a few people. The atmosphere and the service may be more personalized than in other stores. Often the salesperson is the owner or manag-

stores focus on lower-priced clothing and accessories. They usually carry some brand-name items, as well as little-known or private label brands.

Discount stores have changed over the years. When they first became popular, these stores had merchandise piled high on tables. There were very few salespeople, no dressing rooms, and long lines at the registers. You had to pay for everything in cash. If you knew how to shop for quality merchandise, you could get some very good bargains.

Today, many discount stores are similar to other types of stores. Clothing is hung on racks. There are window and floor displays, as well as dressing rooms. Most accept checks and major credit cards, although you may not be able to exchange or return items that you purchase.

Specialty stores carry a particular type of merchandise, such as children's clothes, active sportswear, or shoes.

er. Other specialty stores are a part of a **chain**, a *group of stores that are owned and managed by a central office.* All of the stores in a chain carry similar items, have similar prices, and look very much alike.

Most specialty stores accept national credit cards. If you return an item, some will not give you a cash refund. Instead, they will give you credit toward another item in the store.

Discount Stores

Discount stores usually have lower prices than department or specialty stores. Many are chains and are located in plain, large buildings with low overhead. They are self-service and have check-out counters just inside the store exits. Most discount

Factory outlets and discount stores may offer good bargains on merchandise. However, you need to shop carefully and check for any flaws.

All of these services mean that prices may not be discounted as much as they used to be. It is best to do some comparison shopping to see if you are truly getting lower prices.

Outlet Stores

A factory or manufacturer's **outlet** store *sells only the brands of merchandise that are produced by the manufacturer or the factory that owns it.* Some outlet stores are located next to the factory. Others are located in malls that consist solely of factory outlets.

Most outlet stores are self-service and do not offer any special services. They can offer lower prices because the clothing comes directly from the factory.

The clothing sold in outlets usually is one of three types:

• **Overruns** are *excess merchandise* created when a manufacturer produces more of a certain style than can be sold to stores. This merchandise is usually first quality.

• **Irregulars** are *garments that do not pass inspection because they have a small imperfection.* It might be a pull in the fabric, an uneven color, or a mislabeled size. These are flaws that will not affect the wear of the garment.

• **Seconds** are *garments with more serious flaws.* One sleeve may be longer than the other, or the buttonholes may be sewn in the wrong place.

Most outlets now take credit cards. However, many do not allow you to return anything that you buy.

Thrift Shops

Thrift shops are stores that carry secondhand or used clothing and household items. They may be owned by an individual or by an organization, such as a church group or a charity.

Some of the clothing in thrift shops may have been worn many times. However, if you look carefully, you may find garments that are almost new, particularly party clothes or special one-of-a-kind items.

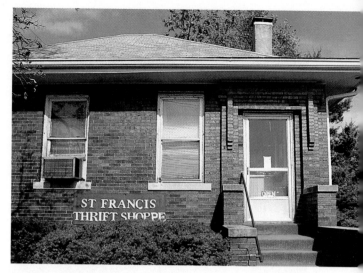

Thrift shops carry inexpensive, secondhand clothing. They are often good sources of retro fashions.

The clothing in these stores is very inexpensive. Most thrift shops are self-service. They do not give credit, and they do not let you return the clothes you buy. This helps keep the prices low.

Catalog Shopping

Catalog shopping is one of the fastest growing industries in the country. Many people find that they can save time by ordering merchandise from store and mail-order catalogs. Often they are able to choose from a greater selection of products or to find items that might not be available in local stores. They also can take their time choosing the items they want when they have the time to shop.

There are many advantages to catalog shopping:

• Ordering is convenient because you can shop at home, without spending time and money on transportation to stores.

• Items are shown and described in detail, including styles, fabrics, colors, sizes, and prices.

• Selection can be greater than in local stores.

• Orders can be easily placed using a toll-free 800 number and a credit card.

- Often you can place orders at any time during the day or night.

- Most returns can be made with no questions asked.

There are also several disadvantages to catalog shopping:

- A shipping charge is usually added to the price of the purchase.

- Since you cannot try on the garment, you may not get a proper fit.

- Colors and details may not be clear in the illustration, so you may not know exactly what the garment looks like.

- If the catalog does not have a toll-free 800 number, you have to pay for a long distance call.

- You have to wait for your order to be delivered.

- To return or exchange an item, you have to repackage and mail it. Often you must pay the return shipping cost.

Catalog shopping offers a great selection of merchandise. Many consumers like the convenience of shopping by phone from home.

Always read the catalog carefully before ordering to familiarize yourself with the merchandise. Look for easy-fitting styles and Petite-Small-Medium-Large-Extra Large size ranges, rather than numbered sizes which may require a more accurate fit. Be aware of shipping and return policies so you know when to expect delivery and how to return products, if necessary.

You can pay for merchandise ordered from a catalog by credit card, check, or money order. Never send cash through the mail with your order. If it is lost or stolen, you will have no proof that you sent it. Keep a record of your order. Merchandise must be shipped within 30 days, or you can cancel the order and obtain a refund.

Other Shopping Sources

Other shopping sources include bazaars and fairs, television, and personal selling. To shop successfully using these sources, you must be aware of prices and quality. You should know what a similar item would cost in a department store, specialty store, discount store, or catalog.

Bazaars and Fairs

Bazaars, flea markets, and craft fairs are becoming more and more popular. Usually, many different people rent booths in a large area and sell merchandise. The booths can be located outdoors in a parking lot or field, or indoors in a school, shopping mall, church, or club. Bazaars and flea markets sell used clothing or new merchandise that has been purchased directly from a manufacturer. Craft fairs usually feature handcrafted clothing and accessories.

Garage sales and tag sales may be held by one or more families. They may sell used clothing, hats, shoes, purses, and jewelry at very low prices.

Just because something is being sold at a low price does not make it a good bargain. Take your time and inspect any item before you purchase it. You must pay cash, and you cannot return what you buy. Craft fairs that offer higher-priced items usually accept credit cards or checks.

Shopping Electronically

The television set and the computer are offering new ways of shopping for consumers:

Craft shows and fairs can be good sources of unique, handcrafted items.

- **Television shopping.** Individual television programs and even entire channels are devoted to presenting merchandise for sale. Viewers can order by calling a toll-free 800 telephone number. They can even ask questions "on air" and talk to the hosts about their personal experiences with the product. Because products are shown on screen for only a limited amount of time, many consumer purchases are made on impulse.

- **On-line shopping.** Consumers who subscribe to an on-line computer service have access to electronic shopping areas. Information about the products or services offered can be called up on the computer screen. If you want to order something, you type in the information that is requested. For example, you might need to specify size and color, as well as provide your credit card number and shipping address. This information is sent electronically to the retailer's computer. Then the retailer ships the merchandise to you.

- **CD-ROM shopping.** Instead of getting a lot of catalogs in the mail, you can order CD-ROM disks that contain catalogs from many different companies. Usually the disk is free, but you must pay a small charge for shipping and handling. When you insert the CD into the appropriate disk drive, the information on the disk is transferred to your computer. With a click of the mouse, a catalog can be opened on-screen, and you can browse through its pages. When you are ready to place an order, you can contact the company by mail, electronic mail, telephone, or fax.

Television Shopping

Certain television channels have home shopping programs which show and describe the merchandise for sale. A host usually urges the viewers to order the items by calling a toll-free 800 number shown on the television screen. After receiving your credit card number, the merchandise is then sent to you.

Television shopping can be very easy and convenient. However, home shopping shows and infomercials use many methods to promote impulse buying. Always stop and evaluate your wardrobe needs and budget before ordering.

Personal Selling

Personal selling is done through showings or parties in homes. Items such as clothing, jewelry, and cosmetics are shown to individuals or groups. A sales representative takes orders from customers and arranges for the items to be delivered later.

Merchandise sold through personal selling is usually of high quality. However, it may be higher priced than similar items available in stores. Sometimes customers feel pressured, because of the party atmosphere, to order items they may not need.

When to Shop

Although new merchandise arrives all of the time, stores have several major selling seasons when the majority of new things appear. Such seasons for clothes are spring, fall or back-to-school, and Christmas or holiday. Stores begin to promote spring clothes in February, fall clothes in July, and Christmas items by the beginning of November.

If the latest fashions are important to you, then you will probably want to buy new clothes at the beginning of the season. This is the time when stores have the best selection of the newest merchandise. If getting a good price is more important to you than having the latest styles, you will probably want to wait until the stores have sales.

Special Sales

Most stores have many sales during the year. If you need a new item but can wait for a little while, you might be able to buy it on sale. Traditionally, winter coats are reduced for Columbus Day Sales in October. Bathing suits and other hot weather clothes go on sale right after the Fourth of July. Many items go on sale after Christmas so that the stores can make room for new spring merchandise.

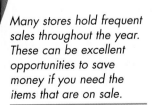

Many stores hold frequent sales throughout the year. These can be excellent opportunities to save money if you need the items that are on sale.

When an item is put on sale, it is offered at a lower price than the usual retail price. This is done for a variety of reasons. The store may be trying to entice customers to come and shop. Perhaps the garments are damaged or the styles are discontinued. The store may have gotten a lower price from the manufacturer and is able to pass the savings on to customers.

Stores use different terms to describe various types of sales.

- **Holiday sales** are timed to match a special day, such as Election Day or Washington's Birthday. Many people do not have to work or go to school on these days and are free to shop. Stores often create their own holiday sales, such as an Anniversary Sale or a Founder's Birthday Sale. Holiday sales are a tradition for many stores. The customers know that the store has the same sale at the same time every year.

- **Pre-season sales** are held at the beginning of a season to entice customers to buy early. A store might advertise a special pre-season sale for fall clothing to encourage customers to come into the store in August. After the sale, prices return to the regular retail price. A pre-season holiday sale might be held in November to promote early Christmas gift buying.

- **Special purchases** are items that a store has bought from a manufacturer at a special price. The store then passes the savings along to customers. A manufacturer may offer a lower price to stores that buy very large quantities of merchandise. It may also occur when a manufacturer is discontinuing a style or has many items left over that were not sold to other stores.

- **Clearance sales** occur when a store wants to move out merchandise to make room for new stock. They also are held when a store decides to no longer carry particular items. Clearance sales are sometimes called end-of-season sales.

- **Inventory sales** occur once a year when a store takes inventory. This is done by counting all items for sale to compare it to the store's written stock records. Some stores have sales before inventory time so there are fewer items to count. Other stores have sales right after they have taken inventory, when they know exactly what merchandise is in the store.

- **Going-out-of-business sales** occur when stores have lost their lease or have gone bankrupt. Usually, all of the merchandise in the store must be sold.

Sales Tips

To judge if a sale is valid, here are a few guidelines to follow:

- **Be familiar with the price and quality of the same or similar merchandise.** Just because a store marks an item as "Sale," it does not necessarily mean it is a good bargain.

- **Check the item for flaws.** Is it a little flaw that either will not be noticed or can be easily mended? If it is a big flaw, will it interfere with how the garment is worn? The label "As Is" on an item means that you are buying seconds or irregulars.

- **Think about how often you will wear the item.** Ten percent off the price of a garment you will wear many times can be a better bargain than 30 percent off on a garment you will seldom wear. A bargain is not a bargain if you never wear it.

- **Many sales are final.** Merchandise marked "Final Sale" cannot be returned or exchanged. Always check store policy before you buy.

How to Pay

There are many ways to finance your purchases. If you understand the advantages and disadvantages of each method, you will be able to choose the ones that are best for you. With some methods, you pay money before you receive the merchandise. With other methods, you "borrow" the money, receive the merchandise, and pay later. No matter which method you choose, you still need money in the end.

Cash Purchases

In addition to actual cash, cash purchases include using a check, money order, debit card, layaway, and C.O.D. These methods of payment enable you to control your expenditures because you cannot spend more money than you have.

- **Cash.** Cash is often the simplest and quickest way to pay for a purchase. All stores take cash. If you pay cash, you can spend only as much money as you have. There are no extra finance costs for paying cash, like there are when you use credit. On the other hand, you take the chance of losing cash or having it stolen.

- **Check.** A check authorizes a store to withdraw a specified amount of money from your bank account. An advantage to paying by check is that you do not have to carry a large amount of cash with you.

Before accepting your check, stores will usually ask for proof of who you are. Several pieces of identification, such as a driver's license or a credit card, will identify you. Some stores, however, will not accept checks. They may have had bad experiences with people who wrote checks for money they did not have.

- **Money Order.** A **money order** is a *form stating that money is to be paid to the person or store named on the form.* It is similar to a check and can be purchased from a post office or a bank. The purchaser pays the face amount plus a service charge. Money orders are used by people who do not have a checking account and want to send a payment through the mail.

- **Debit Card.** When using a debit card, the store deducts money electronically from your bank account. The cash transaction between the store and bank is done entirely by computer. You keep a record of each deduction so you can check that the bank records of your account are accurate. Some debit cards are called check cards.

How to Pay for a Purchase

1 Cash is accepted at all stores and is simple and easy to use.

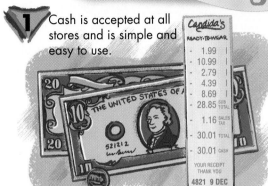

2 When writing a check, write clearly in ink. Be sure to keep an accurate record of the amount of the check, name of the store, and date of purchase.

3 Credit cards can be used to purchase items on credit now, then pay for them later.

When paying with a debit card, money is deducted from your bank account and transferred to the store's account via computer.

4 A layaway plan includes a written agreement with the store. It lists the amount to be paid every week or month until the item is fully paid for.

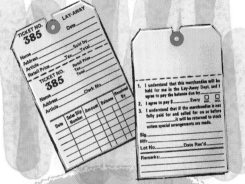

5 A C.O.D. purchase must be paid for when the merchandise is delivered.

6 A money order is similar to a check and can be sent through the mail.

• **Layaway.** With a **layaway** plan, you give the store *a small down payment to reserve an item for you*. The store holds, or lays away, the garment so no one else will buy it. You then pay the store a certain amount of money each week or month until the total amount is paid. After the store has received full payment, plus a service charge, the item is yours. Layaway purchases can be a good way to pay for an item you would not use immediately, such as a winter coat that you see in August. However, the store has the interest-free use of your money during the weeks or months that you are paying for the garment.

• **C.O.D.** This stands for *cash on delivery*. When the package arrives, you give the money for your purchase to the delivery person, who may be a mail carrier or a representative of a shipping company. Some C.O.D. purchases have special requirements, such as a minimum purchase amount. Often there is a delivery charge. Many stores will not ship C.O.D. because of problems associated with finding someone at home to make the payment.

Credit Purchases

When you buy on credit, you borrow money against your ability to pay in the future. Credit or charge cards can be issued by a bank, such as MasterCard or Visa; by a local store; or by a credit card company, such as American Express or Diner's Club.

Before a bank, store, or credit card company will give you a card, you will be asked to fill out an application form. Information such as how much money you earn, what bank accounts you have, and what other charge cards you own will indicate if you are a good credit risk. In order to have a credit card in your own name, you must be 18 years of age or older. Some stores and credit card companies will let younger teenagers use their parents' credit cards, provided that permission has been given.

Sometimes a bank, store, or credit card company specifies a credit limit, also called a line of credit.

This is the maximum amount the customer can owe on the credit card account at any one time.

Advantages and Disadvantages of Credit

Purchasing items on credit can be easy and convenient. Here are several advantages to using credit:

• You can buy merchandise now and pay for it later.

• There is no need to carry large amounts of cash.

• You usually do not have to show identification, as when paying by check.

• Expensive items, such as a coat or boots, can be purchased without having the available cash.

• You can order items by telephone without having to send a check or money order.

• Returns are easy because a credit is simply made to your account.

• When the statement arrives, you can write one check or money order to pay for several purchases.

However, there are also disadvantages to buying on credit:

• It is easy to spend more money than you have or can possibly pay back.

• You may buy on impulse, ending up with items you do not need or cannot afford.

• You might limit your shopping only to stores which accept credit cards.

• If monthly bills are not paid in full, you usually have to pay a finance charge.

• Extra charges may be added for late payments.

• Some credit cards have an annual fee of $25 or more.

• Your credit card or number can be stolen and used by others.

• Late or missed payments can result in a poor credit rating.

There are many ways to pay for clothing purchases. Each has certain advantages and disadvantages.

Finance Charges

In return for taking a chance on your ability to pay, a store or bank usually has a **finance charge**. This is *the cost imposed for the use of credit*. It may be 1½ percent of your monthly bill, for an annual percentage rate of 18 percent per year. The maximum rate is controlled by state law.

A finance charge is applied only if you do not pay the full amount of your bill within a specified time. This time is usually 25 to 30 days after the billing date. If you make only a partial payment, a finance charge will be added to your next month's statement. You must pay a minimum amount, usually 10 percent of the total, each month. When a balance is carried over from month to month, finance charges add up quickly.

According to the Truth in Lending Law, you must be given the following information in writing by the credit card issuer:

- Cost of the finance plan in dollars and cents.
- Percentage of interest charged each month.
- Annual percentage rate.

Monthly Statement

Each month you will receive a statement that tells you about the status of your account. This statement will list:

- Charges made since the last statement.
- The amount of the last payment.
- Any credits or returns.
- The amount of the previous bill.
- The amount that is owed on the current bill.
- The billing date.

In addition, the statement includes any finance charges, information on the finance rates, and the line of credit.

Billing Problems

What happens if you do not agree with the charges on your bill or you have a problem with the merchandise? The Fair Credit Billing Act contains the following provisions relating to monthly statements and credit purchases:

- You must notify a creditor in writing about an error in your statement within 60 days. The creditor (which is the bank, store, or credit card company) must respond within 30 days to your inquiry and must resolve the problem within 90 days.

- You do not have to pay the amount in question until the problem is resolved.

Credit Card Safety

When using a credit card, always take care to prevent loss or theft. Be sure your card is returned to you after each credit purchase. Keep a record of your credit card number. If your credit card is lost or stolen, notify the bank, store, or credit card company immediately.

CHAPTER 20 REVIEW

Summary

- You should plan your shopping before you leave home.
- There are many types of stores, including department stores, specialty stores, discount stores, outlet stores, and thrift shops.
- Other shopping sources include catalogs, bazaars, fairs, television programs, and personal selling.
- Most stores hold various types of sales throughout the year.
- There are many ways to pay for purchases—cash, check, money order, debit card, layaway, C.O.D., and credit card.

Using Vocabulary Terms

On a separate piece of paper, write the vocabulary term that best fits the definition:

1. Garments that do not pass inspection because they have a small imperfection.
2. Store that sells only the brands of merchandise that are produced by the manufacturer or the factory that owns it.
3. A form stating that money is to be paid to the person or store named on the form.
4. Type of specialty store featuring very fashionable or unique designs that are higher priced.
5. Cost imposed for the use of credit.
6. Cash on delivery.

Recalling the Facts

1. List at least three things you should do to prepare to shop.
2. What is the difference between a department store, a specialty store, and a discount store?
3. List four advantages and four disadvantages of catalog shopping.
4. How can you pay for merchandise ordered from a catalog?
5. Name three other shopping sources besides stores and catalogs.
6. Can you always return or exchange merchandise purchased "on sale"?
7. Explain the following types of payments: check, money order, layaway, and C.O.D.
8. What is the difference between a credit card and a debit card?
9. List at least six disadvantages of buying on credit.
10. What should you do if you have a problem with a credit card bill?

Thinking Critically

1. **Analysis.** Compare and contrast the different stores in your community. How do the types of merchandise, prices, and services differ?
2. **Synthesis.** Why is it important to carefully check "sale" merchandise before buying?
3. **Evaluation.** Explain this statement: Just because an item is on sale does not mean it is a good bargain.

4. **Analysis.** Compare the advantages and disadvantages of various ways to make purchases: cash, check, credit card, debit card, layaway, money order, and C.O.D.

Applying Your Knowledge

1. **Stores.** Visit three different types of stores in your community, including a thrift shop. Compare three similar items in each store. List any differences in quality and price for each item. At which store would you purchase each item? Explain your reasons.

2. **Television Shopping.** Watch a home-shopping program on television. Describe the merchandise for sale and the techniques used to encourage viewers to purchase the items. What are the advantages and disadvantages of television shopping?

3. **Credit.** Create a poster or bulletin board display that promotes the responsible use of credit.

Making the Connection

1. **Math.** Obtain an application for a credit card. Read the information given about the card. What is the annual finance charge? If you did not pay the monthly bill in full and had a balance of $200, how much interest would you be charged? If you had the same finance charge added to each month's statement, what would be the total for a year?

What Is a Personal Shopper?

Personal shoppers are a special type of salesperson. They offer fashion advice and select merchandise to meet the needs of individual customers. A personal shopper may accompany a customer around the store, helping to select clothing and accessories from various departments. Personal shoppers also handle mail and telephone requests from customers.

Try It Yourself

Imagine that you are a personal shopper. Using catalogs, select several outfits for a male and for a female customer who have specific needs and a moderate budget. Accessorize the clothing with belts, ties, scarves, jewelry, shoes, or other items. Create an itemized list of the garments, including prices.

Build Your Portfolio

Write a description of each customer and their needs. Mount illustrations of each outfit, including accessories, on paper. Describe how the various items could be mixed-and-matched to create different looks, if possible. Place the illustrations, descriptions, and itemized list of items and prices in your portfolio.

2. **Language Arts.** Interview four friends or relatives about their favorite places to shop. What advantages are mentioned about each store or other shopping source?

313

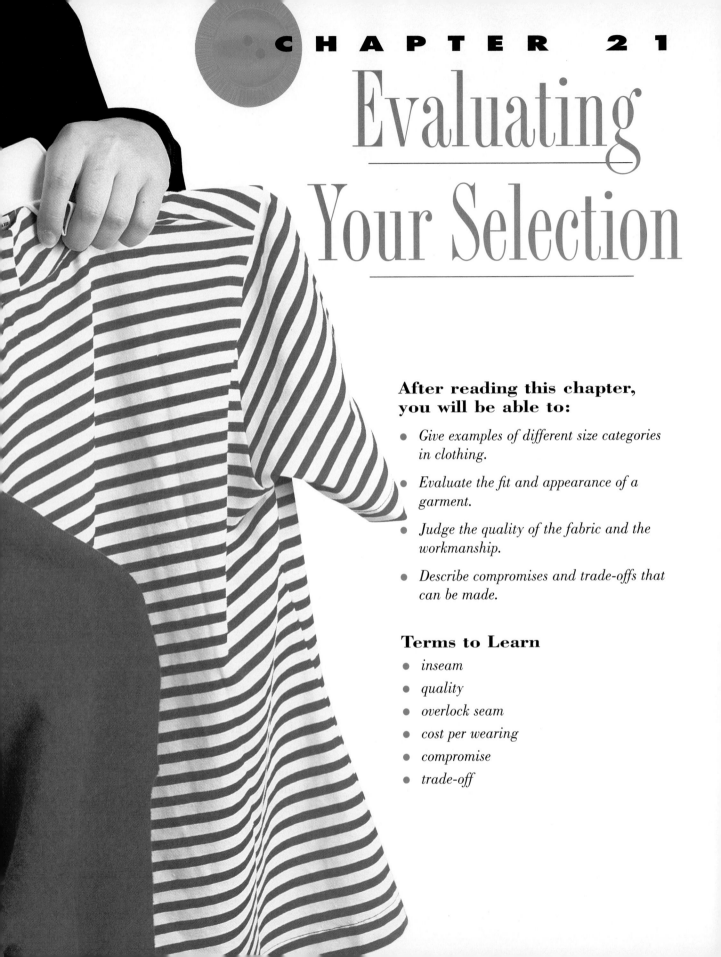

Evaluating
Your Selection

After reading this chapter, you will be able to:

- Give examples of different size categories in clothing.

- Evaluate the fit and appearance of a garment.

- Judge the quality of the fabric and the workmanship.

- Describe compromises and trade-offs that can be made.

Terms to Learn

- *inseam*
- *quality*
- *overlock seam*
- *cost per wearing*
- *compromise*
- *trade-off*

Since your earliest school days, teachers have been grading your work. Grades have appeared on tests, book reports, and term papers. Each grade was the result of the teacher's evaluation of many things, such as the quality of the information you wrote, how well your report fulfilled the assignment, and how the material was presented.

When you are thinking about buying something, you can do the evaluating. Give it a grade based on how well it rates on your personal evaluation scale. The item that gets the best grade is the one you should buy.

Questions to Ask

Imagine that you are in the sportswear department of a store, surrounded by racks and racks of garments. How do you decide which garments to try on? Once you have tried some of them on, how are you going to know which choices are good ones for you at this time in your life?

When a garment catches your eye, stop and ask yourself some questions:

• Where does it fit into my personal wardrobe plan?

• Does it go with anything else in my wardrobe?

• Do I need to buy new accessories in order to wear the item?

• Is the price within my budget?

• Is the garment worth what it costs?

• What type of care does it need?

• How does it fit me?

• Do I really need this item?

Clothing Sizes

Did you ever have the experience of buying something in a hurry without trying it on? When you got it home, you found out it did not fit—even though it was the size you usually wear! Did you think that you had suddenly lost weight, grown taller, or that the garment was mismarked? Most likely, it was none of these things.

How a Size Can Differ

Each ready-to-wear manufacturer has its own standard size measurements. A size 10 from one manufacturer may fit differently than a size 10 from another manufacturer. In fact, you might find that you wear a smaller size in more expensive clothes and a larger size in less expensive clothes.

The standard size measurements used by a manufacturer may be influenced by production costs. If the manufacturer cuts a size 10 garment so that it is a little bit smaller, production costs are reduced. A manufacturer is cutting for

When shopping for clothes, take time to evaluate fit, quality, care, and price before making your final decision.

Only by trying on a garment can you determine how it actually fits and looks on you.

mass production. Therefore, reducing the size by even 1 inch (2.5 cm) of fabric per garment can save hundreds of yards of fabric and hundreds of dollars. This is one way that manufacturers can sell at a lower price. For example, a size 10 dress that sells for $40 will probably be much smaller than a size 10 dress that sells for $150.

Thus, it is essential that you try on every garment before you purchase it. Even if you already own several garments from that manufacturer and are satisfied with the way they fit, the style of a garment can change how it looks and feels on you.

Size Categories for Females

Female clothing has sizes or numbers that represent a combination of body measurements, body proportions, and height. Adult size categories include Misses (even-numbered), Juniors (odd-numbered), Petites (P), and Women. Special Teen departments carry sizes for the developing preteen and teen figure. Girls sizes are for preteens who have not begun to mature.

Skirts and pants are sold by size or by the waist measurement. A size 25 pants means that it has a 25-inch (65 cm) waist measurement. Sweaters, t-shirts, and other loose fitting garments can be sold in petite or extra-small, small, medium, large, and extra-large sizes.

Size Categories for Males

Male clothing comes in Men's, Teen Boys', and Boys' sizes. Special sizes have also been developed for Tall Men, Short Men, Stout Men, Husky Boys, and Slim Boys.

Jackets and suits are sized by chest measurement and length. A size 38 means that the jacket will fit a man with a 38-inch (96.5 cm) chest. A size 38-Short means that the jacket will be 2 inches (5 cm) shorter than the standard size 38. A size 38-Long is for a taller man with longer arms.

Pants are sized by the waist measurement and the inseam measurement. The **inseam** is *the inside leg measurement, from the crotch to the hem edge of the pants.* Size 28/31 has a 28-inch (71 cm) waist and a 31-inch (79 cm) inseam.

Shirts are sized by the collar size and the sleeve length, such as 14/32 (36/82 cm). The collar size is the measurement of your neck, plus ½ inch (1.3 cm). The sleeve length is measured from the base of your back neck, across the shoulder, around the outside of your slightly bent elbow, to the wrist bone.

Many shirts, sweaters, and casual jackets are available in small, medium, large, and extra-large sizes. Some clothing is described as having a relaxed

Size Categories for Females

Category	Sizes	Proportions
Teen Girls	7-14	For girls whose figures are beginning to mature
Petite	2P-18P	For short females under 5'4" in height with a small body structure
Junior	3-15	For females with a trimmer, shorter-waisted figure
Misses	4-16	For females with a developed figure and average proportions
Women's	18-60	For females with large proportions
Tall	6T-20T	For females over 5'8" in height
Extra-Small (XS) or Petite (P)	2-4	
Small (S)	6-8	
Medium (M)	10-12	
Large (L)	14-16	
Extra-Large (XL)	18-20	

Size Categories for Males

Category	Sizes	Proportions
Teen Boys	14-20	For boys of average build
Slim Teen Boys	14S-20S	For boys of slender build
Husky Teen Boys	14H-20H	For boys of heavier build
Men's	30-48 (chest measurement)	For males who are fully developed, height 5'7" to 5'11"
Short Men	30S-48S	For males under 5'7"
Tall Men	34T-48T	For males over 5'11"
Small (S)	34-36	
Medium (M)	38-40	
Large (L)	42-44	
Extra-Large (XL)	46-48	

fit. This means larger through the chest, wider arm-holes, and more room in the thigh and seat areas of pants.

Evaluating Fit

No matter what size is marked on the label, the only important factor is how the garment fits you. When you try on a garment, be sure to look at yourself in a full-length mirror. Look at both the front view and the back view. Are there any wrinkles and bulges that indicate a poor fit?

Many people buy their clothes a little bit snug with the idea that it will make them look slimmer. The opposite is true. Too-tight clothing can make you look pounds heavier.

Always check the appearance and fit of an outfit in front of a full-length mirror.

At one time, the only way to have a garment made exactly to your measurements was to make it yourself or have a dressmaker or tailor make it for you. Today computers provide the technology for a new type of custom sewing, called mass customization.

A garment can now be modified at the factory to match the measurements of individual customers. Here is how mass customization works:

1. A customer visits the store and picks out a garment. The salesperson identifies the garment on the computer, and enters the customer's measurements. The garment appears on the screen. Depending on the program, the customer can make changes in fit, fabric, or color.

2. The computer sends instructions to a computerized fabric-cutting machine at the factory. When the garment is cut out, special bar codes are attached to the pieces. These bar codes keep track of the individual orders during production.

3. The customized garment is sewn, dyed, and finished along with other individualized and mass-produced garments. Special scanning equipment separates customized garments from mass-produced ones.

4. The customized garment may be shipped to the store or directly to the customer.

A mass-customized garment is more expensive than a mass-produced one. Because it takes several weeks to manufacture a customized garment, it cannot be purchased and worn immediately. However, people who do not fit into standard sizes or those who want a perfect fit will benefit from mass-customized garments.

Fitting Checkpoint

Proper fit is important for both appearance and comfort. Here are some basic fitting guidelines to follow:

1. **Collar or neckline** should fit close to the neck without binding or gapping.
2. **Armhole seam** should lie at edge of shoulder, unless designed otherwise.
3. **Chest and back** should fit smoothly with room for movement; closing should not pull or gap.
4. **Sleeves** should be loose enough to raise arms and long enough to cover wrist bone when arm is bent.
5. **Buttons and buttonholes** should not pull or strain as you move.
6. **Jacket or coat** should fit comfortably over other garments.
7. **Waistline or waistband** should feel comfortable without pulling or binding; tops can be tucked in.
8. **Hip area** should skim body smoothly without pulling or forming extra folds; crotch should not wrinkle or bind.
9. **Zipper** should open and close smoothly.
10. **Pleats and gathers** should hang vertically and unbroken.
11. **Pants legs** should fall straight from hipline without wrinkles.
12. **Hemlines** should be parallel to the floor, meet evenly at openings, and be the right length for your body proportions and current fashion.

Steps to Take

Use the following steps to evaluate a garment. If the garment passes all of these tests, it fits well and will be comfortable to wear.

1. **Stand straight to check the overall appearance.** Notice how the seams, hem, and special design features look. (See Fitting Checkpoints on page 320.)

2. **Try the stretch test.** Bend your arms in front of you at shoulder height. Shirts, jackets, dresses, and blouses should be roomy enough so you can do this without any strain across the shoulder blades. Sleeves should not ride up and become uncomfortably short.

3. **Raise your arms straight up over your head.** The armholes should feel comfortable. Jackets and coats should not feel tight in the shoulder area. Blouses, shirts, and sweaters should not come untucked. When you lower your arms, dresses should fall back in place comfortably, with little pulling and tugging.

4. **Sit down.** Make sure the garment does not strain and pull at the hip, stomach, or thigh area when you sit. Pay attention to the waistline of pants and skirts. It should remain slightly loose and comfortable and not gap at the center back.

5. **Stand up and bend over as if to touch your toes.** You may not plan on doing aerobic exercises in your clothes, but you might have to lean over to pick something up or tie your shoes. Even formal party clothes can be subjected to some fairly strenuous dancing.

Evaluating Quality

The price you pay for a garment is not necessarily an indication of its **quality**, or *superior characteristics*. Many other factors can influence the price, such as the number of details, the trim, the brand name or the designer's name, and the store where it is being sold. A high-priced garment can be of poor quality; a low-priced garment can be of high quality. Quality in a garment means two things: good fabric and good workmanship.

Fabric

Here are some guidelines for evaluating the quality of the fabric:

• **Examine the fabric.** Is the color even throughout the garment? If there is a design printed on the fabric, are the colors printed so that they appear in the right place? Are there any snags or pulls? Have little pills, or balls of fiber, begun to form on the surface of the fabric?

• **Crush a corner of the garment in your hand to see if the fabric wrinkles easily.** This will indicate how much the garment will crease or wrinkle during wear. It will also show if the fabric will require pressing. If the fabric is a stretchable woven or knit, pull on it to see how much it stretches. Does it return to the original shape?

• **See if the garment is cut with the fabric "on grain."** A garment that is cut with the fabric on grain will look better and wear longer than one that is cut off-grain. Seams will hang straight without twisting to

To know if a fabric wrinkles easily, squeeze the fabric tightly for a few seconds and then release.

one side. The hemline will hang evenly. If the garment is cut off-grain or the fabric is printed off-grain, the design lines of a plaid or a stripe will not match.

- **Evaluate if the fabric is suitable for the way you plan to wear the garment.** A fragile fabric, such as a chiffon, would not be a good choice for a shirt that you planned to wear for sports activities.

Workmanship

Quality workmanship means careful sewing and using appropriate techniques. For example, if the fabric is loosely woven and frays easily, the garment should be lined or the seams should be finished. Look for these features in checking on the workmanship of a garment:

- **Stitching should be even and secure, in a color thread that matches the fabric.** Avoid garments that are sewn with clear nylon thread. The heat of an iron could easily melt it.

- **Plaid or stripe designs should be matched throughout the garment.** Check that the plaid or stripes match at the garment's center and side seams. The design should also match at the collar, pockets, and bands.

- **Seams should be smooth, flat, and unpuckered.** There should be no ridges showing on the outside of the garment.

Examine the stitching to see if it is even. The seams and hem should be smooth, even, and unpuckered.

- **Check the seam allowances on the inside of the garment.** If the fabric ravels, the seam allowances should be finished to prevent fraying. They should be at least ½ inch (1.3 cm) wide unless the garment is made with narrow overlock seams. An **overlock seam** is *a special combination of stitches that joins the fabric and finishes the edges in one operation.* Overlock seams are used on many woven and knitted garments.

- **Darts should point to the fullest part of the body.** Darts should be pressed smooth and flat, with no puckers. There should not be a "dimple" at the tip of any dart.

- **Facings should lie smooth and flat against the body.** When you look at the garment from the outside, the facings should not show.

- **A collar should have smooth curves and sharp corners.** It should cover the neckline seam, and the edges should lie flat so that you do not see the undercollar. The collar area should be finished nicely on the inside so you can wear the collar open as well as closed.

- **Fasteners, such as as buttons, snaps, and hooks and eyes, should be securely sewn in place.** Make sure the zipper opens and closes easily, and the stitching is neat and secure. Buttonholes should be sewn with tight, even stitches. They should be large enough for the button to slip through easily, but not so large that the garment will unfasten while you are wearing it.

- **Trims should be sewn on securely.**

- **The hem should be straight and even.** The hem stitches should not cause the garment to pull or to pucker. In fact, the stitches should be invisible from the right side of the garment, unless the hem is top-stitched in place. Look at the hem allowance on the inside of the garment. It should be an even width and stitched along the edge if the fabric ravels.

- **Give the garment a final check for imperfections.** Look for any spots, grease marks, lipstick stains, lost

Before buying a garment, check carefully for any spots or stains. Look also for any missing buttons or belts, broken zippers, or small rips in the garment.

belts, broken belt loops, or small rips. Be careful about buying a garment that is damaged. A garment that is marked "As Is" cannot be returned if the spot does not come out. If you ask, a store may try to remove a spot or stain for you.

Evaluating Care

The type of care that a garment requires can be an important factor in your decision to buy. Can the garment be washed or will it need to be dry cleaned? Does the fabric have to be ironed? Some fabrics require more routine care than others.

Light-colored fabrics show soil more easily than dark colors. For example, a white jacket or coat would require more frequent cleaning than a dark brown or navy jacket.

Specific information about washing, drying, bleaching, and dry cleaning are included on the permanent label attached to every garment. Also check the garment label or hangtag for any fabric finishes that affect care.

Here are some factors that influence garment care:

Evaluating Shoes

Shoes have both a number and a letter size, such as 7A or 9½B. The number refers to the length of the foot. Shoes are numbered in full and half sizes. The letter refers to the width of the foot. A very narrow size would be AAA. A very wide size would be EEE.

Here are some guidelines to use when shopping for shoes:

- **Shop for shoes late in the day.** Make sure you have walked around for several hours. Feet swell during the course of the day. You want to try on shoes when your feet are the largest so they will always be comfortable.

- **Have your feet remeasured every time you buy shoes.** Be sure that both feet are measured because no one has two feet that are exactly the same size. Always buy the size that fits the larger foot. If necessary, you can use pads or innersoles to improve the fit on the smaller foot.

- **Buy shoes according to fit, not size.** Sizes differ from manufacturer to manufacturer. One brand's size 9 shoes may not be the same as another brand's size 9. Never buy shoes that feel too tight or too small. No matter what the salesperson may tell you, your feet should be comfortable without having to "break in" shoes.

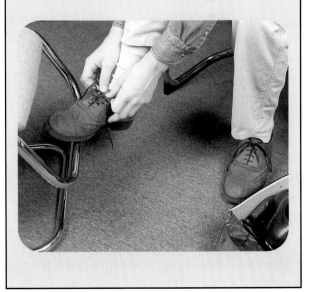

323

• **Washability.** Is the garment machine or hand washable? Over a long period of time, dry cleaning bills may add up to more than the cost of the garment. Do you have the time and space to hand wash and dry different garments? Although it is easy to hand wash a sweater, will you set aside the time to do it?

• **Stain- and spot-resistance.** Is the fabric resistant to stains and spots? Some fibers absorb stains, but special finishes can help the fabric to repel the stain or to release it during cleaning. Coats, jackets, and children's clothes often have these special finishes.

• **Wrinkle-resistance.** Will you have to iron the fabric every time it is washed? Will you have to press the garment before every wearing, or will the wrinkles hang out after a short time? Fibers have different characteristics that affect wrinkling. For example, polyester is very wrinkle-resistant, but cotton and rayon wrinkle easily. Special finishes, such as durable press, can improve the wrinkle resistance of fabrics.

Evaluating Price

On your evaluation scale, a garment gets extra points if it is priced within your budget. That makes it a good value. However, do not be tempted into buying something just because the sign says "SALE." A more expensive garment may be a better investment than a less expensive one. Why? The cost of care and cost per wearing could make it a better value in the long run.

Cost of Care

Your clothing investment consists of more than just the purchase price of a garment. The cost of care should be added to the price as well. How much it costs to take care of a garment depends upon two things:

• How often you will have to clean the garment.

• How much that method of cleaning costs in terms of money and time.

Generally, dry cleaning costs are much higher than laundry costs. A jacket may cost several dollars to dry clean, but only pennies to wash.

The method of cleaning that you prefer depends upon your values. For some people, hand washing is easy and convenient. Others prefer only machine washable items. If time is scarce or laundry equipment is not available, then dry cleaning may be preferable in spite of the cost. A garment that needs to be pressed each time you wear it will cost more in terms of time than a garment that does not wrinkle.

Cost per Wearing

Also think about how much the garment costs versus how many times you are going to wear it. Increasing the number of times that you wear a garment reduces the average **cost per wearing**, making it a good choice. This is determined by *adding cleaning costs to the purchase price, then dividing by the number of wearings.* For examples, see Cost per Wearing on page 325.

When making your clothing decisions, do not just think about the initial cost of a garment. You must also consider its usefulness. The more often you use it, the greater is its value to you.

Do not be tempted into buying something you do not need just because it is on sale.

Cost per Wearing

You are considering buying a jacket that costs $50. Since it can be worn with many outfits in your wardrobe, you expect to wear it 40 times during the year. It will require dry cleaning twice, at a cost of $3 each time.

Purchase price	$50.00
Cost of care	+ 6.00
Total investment	$56.00 ÷ 40 = $1.40 cost per wearing

A sweater you would like to buy costs only half as much as the jacket, and it is washable. Laundry costs will only be 50 cents. However, the sweater coordinates with only one outfit that you have, so you will wear it about 10 times during the year. Although the sweater is less expensive than the jacket, the actual cost per wearing will be greater.

Purchase price	$25.00
Cost of care	+ .50
Total investment	$25.50 ÷ 10 = $2.55 cost per wearing

Compromises and Trade-Offs

It is not always possible to find clothes that look good, fit well, have high quality, cost the right amount, and are compatible with your needs and wants. Fortunately, there are some compromises and trade-offs that you can make. A **compromise** is *a settlement or give-and-take between two points.* A **trade-off** is *an exchange of one thing for another.*

The one thing you absolutely cannot compromise on is fit. If the garment requires more than a simple alteration to make it fit properly, it is not a good buy. Changing a hem length or moving a button would be considered simple alterations. The only exceptions are tailored garments, such as suits and trousers. These may need minor alterations by the store's tailor or dressmaker.

Options to Consider

• **Trade quantity for quality.** Purchase one expensive, well-made shirt or pair of shoes, rather than two cheaper and perhaps not as well-made items. Limit your wardrobe to just a few colors so that everything you purchase will coordinate. Instead of a different pair of shoes for every outfit, you may need only several pairs.

Limit your purchases of the latest fads to inexpensive accessories or items on sale. In this way you can update your wardrobe, but still have enough money for your basic wardrobe needs.

• **Improve the quality of the garments you buy.** Seams can be restitched. You could repair a ripped side seam or reinforce a pants seam. Threads that are hanging can be clipped off or pulled through to the inside with a needle.

Hem lengths can be changed to make them more flattering or more fashionable. Shortening a garment is usually no problem. However, if the garment needs to be lengthened, check to be sure there is enough fabric and that the original fold line will not show once the garment is let down.

Loose trims can be repaired. Missing buttons, snaps, and hook and eyes can all be replaced. Sometimes replacing cheap buttons with ones of better quality can improve the whole appearance of a garment.

• **Use your sewing skills to make garments.** Then you can end up with a better quality garment in exactly the style and color that you want. You will probably save money and may even save time. In any event, you will be proud to wear a garment that is the result of your own skills and talents.

Your final decision should be based on the evaluation of many factors—style, color, fit, quality, care, and price—plus your personal needs, wants, and values. By asking questions and answering them honestly, you will make wise clothing selections.

REVIEW

Summary

- Before purchasing a garment, you should evaluate it as to fit, quality, care, price, and whether it fits into your wardrobe plan.

- Different size categories are available for both males and females.

- When trying on a garment, move about to check the fit.

- You should evaluate the quality of both the fabric and the workmanship.

- When evaluating the price of a garment, also consider the cost of care.

- Some compromises and trade-offs can be made, such as trading quantity for quality or using your sewing skills.

Using Vocabulary Terms

On a separate piece of paper, write the vocabulary term that best fits the definition:

1. An exchange of one thing for another.

2. Purchase price of a garment plus cleaning costs, divided by number of wearings.

3. Superior characteristics.

4. The inside leg measurement, from the crotch to the hem edge of pants.

5. A special combination of stitches that joins the fabric and finishes the edges in one operation.

Recalling the Facts

1. What are at least five questions that you should ask yourself when buying a garment?

2. Why do sizes differ from one manufacturer to another?

3. What do the two sizes, such as 14/32, represent on a man's shirt?

4. Why should you stretch and bend when trying on clothes?

5. What characteristics should you check when evaluating fabric quality?

6. List at least eight features to check when evaluating the workmanship of a garment.

7. What three factors influence garment care?

8. How is cost per wearing determined?

9. Describe three options to consider when making a compromise or trade-off in clothing.

10. What clothing factor should never be compromised?

Thinking Critically

1. **Analysis.** How can you know which clothing choices are best for you?

2. **Evaluation.** What information can you use to help judge the fabric quality of a garment?

3. **Synthesis.** Suggest ways that a person could improve the appearance or quality of a jacket.

4. **Evaluation.** Explain the accuracy of this statement: Price is not an indication of quality.

Applying Your Knowledge

1. **Size Categories.** Look through catalogs for descriptions of size categories. Do the sizes differ from one catalog to another? Are any special size categories included?

2. **Sizes.** Using a tape measure, record the measurements of your waist, chest, and hips. Females should take their back measurement from neck to waist. Males need to measure the neck, arm, and inseam. Compare your measurements with the sizing charts in a pattern catalog. Is the recommended pattern size the same as your usual ready-to-wear size?

3. **Evaluating Quality.** Look at several garments in different price ranges in a store. Evaluate the fabric and workmanship of each garment. How does the quality differ? Are the best fabrics and workmanship always on the more expensive garments? Share your evaluation with the class.

Making the Connection

1. **Math.** Determine the cost per wearing of two outfits, each with a purchase price of $60. One must be dry cleaned (check dry cleaning costs). The other is machine washable (25 cents for laundry costs). Each will be worn ten times.

2. **Language Arts.** Write a skit about one or more people who are evaluating the fit, fabric, and workmanship of garments in a store.

What Is a Sales Associate?

A sales associate is another term for a salesperson. Sales associates are responsible for selling merchandise to customers. They also create an image of the store by the way they handle customers' questions and requests. Although many people are involved in retail operations, sales associates are the ones who deal directly with the customers.

Try It Yourself

Imagine that you are a sales associate in a clothing store. Ask other classmates to role play "customers" who may be impatient, rude, questioning, or uncertain. Be pleasant and courteous to each customer. Use good communication skills to answer their questions, handle their requests, and help them make decisions. Encourage but do not pressure customers to buy.

Build Your Portfolio

Write an essay about your experiences in dealing with the different types of "customers." What emotions did you have when dealing with those who were rude or unpleasant? How difficult was it to remain friendly and courteous? List the communication techniques you used. What additional skills would help you be a more successful sales associate? If you have worked as a salesperson in a store, also include your "real life" experiences. Place a copy of the essay in your portfolio.

Shopping for Others

After reading this chapter, you will be able to:

- *Identify important considerations when shopping for friends and family members.*

- *Select suitable clothing for children.*

- *Choose appropriate clothing gifts for older adults.*

- *Describe the special clothing needs of pregnant women and people with disabilities.*

Terms to Learn

- *fine jewelry*
- *costume jewelry*
- *maternity clothes*
- *disability*

Have you ever had the experience of buying someone a gift of clothing that you liked so much that you wanted to keep it for yourself? Yet, after you gave it as a gift, you never saw the other person wear it. Did you stop and ask yourself why? Perhaps the style, the color, the size, or something else about it was not suitable for that person.

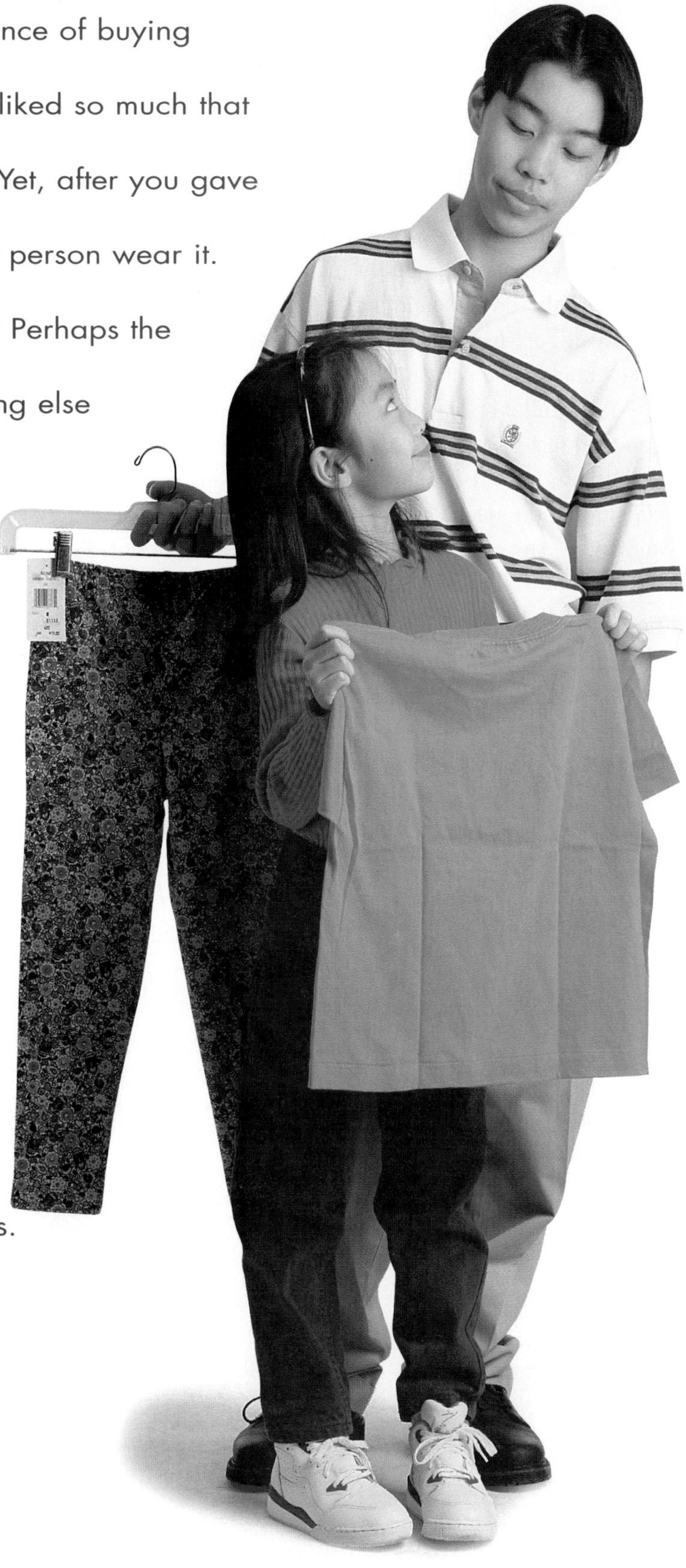

Shopping for others means that we must forget about what pleases us and think about the other person. In order to make successful purchases, we need to have some knowledge about others' wants and needs, as well as observe their preferences of styles and colors.

Shopping for Friends and Family

Sooner or later, you will find yourself shopping for a friend or another member of your family. Just as no two members of a family have exactly the same taste in foods, no two family members will need or want exactly the same clothes.

Even best friends do not have exactly the same taste in clothes. Although many groups of friends dress in similar styles, each member of the group has personal tastes and individuality.

When you are shopping for others, you should consider their needs and wants, styles and colors, and sizes. Any clothing gift that you purchase should be returnable if it is the wrong size or the receiver wants a different color. There should be no problem exchanging or returning it. Just be sure to keep the sales receipt.

Different Needs and Wants

Before shopping, think about the other person's needs and wants. By being a careful listener, you may pick up clues to the person's desires. You may hear comments such as, "I sure wish I had a new belt to go with these pants" or "I need to get a new shirt to replace my old blue one."

Lifestyle, Interests, and Hobbies

Sometimes you have no clues to a person's clothing needs, or you may want to purchase a gift that will truly be a surprise. Then you must consider the person's lifestyle. Clothing needs are influenced by one's occupation and activities. Even the type of community where the person lives has an influence.

Some of the best gifts take into consideration the person's interests or hobbies. Such a gift shows that you have thought about the person's real interests and taken the time to find a gift that is suited just for him or her.

Family members of all ages need clothes that are suitable for their lifestyle, interests, and activities.

Some interests have very obvious clothing needs. For example, a swimmer might want a new beach towel. A tennis player could use a racquet cover, or a jogger could use a new pair of running shorts.

Other hobbies may have clothing needs that are not so obvious. A gardener would appreciate a special pair of garden gloves or a wide-brimmed sun hat. A person who bakes or makes pottery might like a sturdy, washable apron.

Physical Condition

The person's physical condition can be a factor in selecting the right type of clothing. A blouse with lots of tiny buttons would not be suitable for a grandmother who has arthritis. When a family member breaks an arm or a leg, clothes that are very easy to get in and out of will be needed. During pregnancy, a woman needs clothing that allows for her expanding shape. Parents of infants and toddlers appreciate clothing that is easy to put on and take off.

Styles and Colors

You should always consider other people's tastes in clothing and accessories. What styles do they like to wear? Are they interested in the latest fashions and fads, or do they prefer more traditional styles? If the gift is greatly different from the person's taste in clothing, it may never be worn.

Make a note about other people's favorite colors. You might also want to write down the colors of some of the basic items in their wardrobe, such as their coat or favorite sweater.

It is particularly nice to give friends or relatives a gift that coordinates with something they already own. For example, you could choose a scarf that matches their coat, or a shirt to be worn with their sweater.

However, you do not have to limit your selection to duplicates of clothing that the person already wears. Sometimes, a gift that is just "a little bit different" is greatly appreciated. Perhaps you see another side to the person's personality. Maybe the person needs just a little encouragement to wear a certain style or color.

Sizes

It is important to know the sizes of the people you are shopping for. If the garment is the wrong size and has to be returned, you will be wasting valuable time—either your time or the other person's time.

Selecting Jewelry

A piece of jewelry is always a thoughtful gift, whether you are treating yourself or someone else. There are two basic types of jewelry—fine jewelry and costume jewelry.

Fine jewelry is *made with superior workmanship from gold, silver, or platinum and may contain precious and semiprecious stones.* Diamonds and emeralds are examples of precious stones. A garnet or a turquoise is a semiprecious stone. Because fine jewelry is expensive, the designs are usually very classic.

Costume jewelry is *made of nonprecious metals, often set with imitation stones, and relatively inexpensive.* It also can be made with plastic, leather, wood, beads, or other materials. Some costume jewelry is designed to look like fine jewelry. Instead of real gold or silver, it is made from a metal that is plated or coated with gold or silver. Semiprecious or fake stones are used in place of precious ones.

Keep a small index card in your purse or wallet that lists family members' sizes. Check from time to time to see if any sizes have changed.

Accessories, such as scarves, jewelry, ties, hats, and bags, are popular gift items because they can be worn by all sizes. Even many belts and socks are available in "one size fits all."

Your Resources

Price is an important consideration when you are shopping for others. If you are buying someone a present, do not spend more than your budget will allow. Extravagant gifts usually make the receiver feel uncomfortable. The fact that most accessories are small does not mean that they are always inexpensive. It is possible to spend more money for a leather bag than for a coat.

Consider sewing or making a gift instead of buying it. A gift that is crafted or sewn can be designed for the person's specific tastes or interests. In addition, the recipient will appreciate the gift because you put your own time and talents into creating it.

Selecting Clothes for Children

More growth and change occur in a person's body during the infant and toddler years than at any other time in our lives. Infants who can only lay in their crib and kick soon learn to roll over and to crawl. Then they learn to stand, to walk, and eventually to run and climb.

Children have clothing needs that are very different from adults. However, society did not always recognize these different needs. Until the 1900s, children were dressed like miniature adults. They wore scaled down versions of the dresses, suits, hats, shoes, and stockings that their parents wore.

Today children's wear is a separate and very important part of the clothing industry. Clothes are specifically designed to meet the special needs of children: comfort, freedom of movement, safety, and room for growth. Children's clothing should also be easy to put on and take off and easy to care for.

Comfort and Wearability

Because children like to crawl, run, and climb, their clothes should be comfortable and allow for lots of movement. Look for fabrics that are soft and pleasant to touch, not rough or scratchy. Babies, in particular, have sensitive and delicate skin. Outfits should fit loosely—neither too large or too small. Pants legs that are too long can cause a child to trip and fall. Tight neckbands, sleeves, and waistbands can bind and chafe.

Children's Sizes

Children's clothing sizes are classified according to body size and weight. The three common size groupings are *Infants, Toddlers,* and *Children's.*

- **Infants** are sized either by weight or by age. Some clothes are labeled by a weight range: *8 to 10 pounds* or *12 to 18 pounds.* Others are marked by age in months: *6 months, 9 months, 12 months, 18 months,* or *24 months.*

- **Toddlers** sizes have a T with the number: *2T, 3T,* and *4T.* Size is based on chest, waist, and height measurements. Toddlers sizes include extra room to accommodate diapers.

- **Children's** sizes are represented by the numbers *2, 3, 4, 5, 6,* and *6X.* They are also based on chest, waist, and height measurements. Children's sizes are designed for young children who are taller and more slender than toddlers. They do not include a "diaper allowance."

Children's clothes should be selected by the child's weight and measurements, not by the child's age. Most children fit best in sizes that are larger than their actual age. For example, for a baby's first birthday, purchase an *18 month* or *24 month* size outfit. A two-year-old toddler will probably wear a size 3T or a size 4T.

One-piece outfits are very popular for infants and toddlers. These simple styles provide freedom of movement without restriction. They fit easily over diapers. Overalls and one-piece dresses that hang from the shoulders are also popular. When shopping for overalls, look for shoulder straps that crisscross in the back. This design keeps the straps from sliding off the shoulders. Shoulder tabs on shirts are another good way to keep up straps.

Infants and young children grow very quickly. They grow taller much faster than they grow wider. Therefore, look for garments with deep hem allowances that can be lengthened easily. Shoulder straps should be extra long so the buttons can be adjusted as the child grows.

Children's clothes should be able to withstand the wear and tear of active play. Fabrics should be tightly woven or knitted. Denim, corduroy, broadcloth, and firmly knitted fabrics are all good choices. Special features, such as reinforced seams or reinforced knees, will help extend the garment's life.

Safety

It is very important to think about safety when buying clothes for children. Because infants and young children like to put things in their mouths, be careful of loosely sewn buttons and trims that the child could swallow. Avoid garments with flowing sleeves or long hemlines. These could easily get caught during play, and the child could get hurt.

As a result of the Flammable Fabrics Act, all children's sleepwear must be treated with a special flame-retardant finish. This helps to prevent the fabric from burning quickly if accidentally ignited. It does not mean that these garments are fireproof. Be sure to follow the care label instructions for laundering flame-retardant clothing.

Color and Texture

Have you ever wondered why young children are so fond of toys like teddy bears? It is because these toys are warm and comforting to cuddle and touch. The same thing is true about clothes. Children like clothes that have texture. They particularly like fabrics that are soft and pleasant to touch, such as corduroy, flannel, terrycloth, cotton velveteen, and quilted fabrics.

Most children prefer bright, bold colors, especially the primary colors. In fact, red and yellow are

Children like clothes that are comfortable, bright, and colorful. Be sure that any buttons or trims are securely stitched. Choose outfits that are easy to care for and have room for growth.

From Market to Mall

A shopping mall may seem like a very modern concept, but the idea has been around for centuries. In the Middle East, the first malls were called bazaars. One of the largest of these ancient malls, The Grand Bazaar, still welcomes shoppers. It was built in Istanbul, Turkey in 1461. Today it covers several roofed-over city blocks. It contains more than 4,000 stores, plus stalls, mosques, restaurants, storage rooms, and coffeehouses.

Until the 1950s, most stores in the United States were located in or near the center of towns. When parking near these central shopping areas became a problem, some towns opened downtown parking garages. However, some shopping center developers had a better idea. They began to build "strip centers" in the suburbs and outlying areas of towns. By the 1960s, the trend became large, enclosed shopping malls. The malls provided convenient shopping for an increasingly automobile-oriented society.

Today the largest mall in North America is the West Edmonton Mall in Canada. According to the *Guinness Book of World Records*, it is also the largest mall in the world. It encloses 5.2 million square feet, making it one million square feet larger than the Mall of America in Minnesota. The West Edmonton Mall includes more than 800 stores and more than 100 places to eat. Other attractions include an 18-hole miniature golf course, an indoor water park with beaches and a wave-making machine, movie theaters, a zoo, an amusement park, and a hotel.

Infant's clothes should be easy to put on and take off. Look for gripper snaps on the inside leg seam so diapers can be changed easily.

the first two colors a baby can recognize. Bright colors tend to stimulate children. They are also "safe" colors because they make children more visible on dark nights or rainy days. Pale or light colors will show dirt more quickly than medium to dark colors.

Ease of Dressing

Have you ever struggled to get a pullover shirt on an infant? If so, you will understand how important it is that a child's clothes be easy to put on and take off. Baby's and toddler's diapers and clothing are changed several times a day. Pants should have gripper snaps on the inside leg seam so diapers can be changed easily. One-piece garments that fall from the shoulders, and shirts and sweaters that button up the front or on the shoulder all make it easier to dress the child.

When children are learning to dress themselves, select clothes that make it easy for them to manage.

Toddlers take great pride in learning to dress themselves. Garments with large neck and armhole openings are the easiest for them to handle. Pants with elastic waistlines are easier to pull up and down for toilet training than pants with shoulder straps. Large buttons and snaps, hook and loop tapes, and zippers with oversize pull tabs are good choices. Tiny buttons, laces, and hooks and eyes are usually too complicated for the toddler to manage alone.

Look for design features that help children identify the front of a garment from the back. For example, a pocket or applique design on the front of a shirt can help a child know how to put on the garment cor-rectly. Buttons and zippers on the front of an outfit are much easier for a child to open and close than those on the back.

Easy Care

Clothes that are easy to care for may not be important to the child, but they will certainly be appreciated by the parent. Some children go through a stage where they develop a particular attachment to a favorite item of clothing. Everyone is happier if it is something that can be cleaned easily and returned quickly to the child.

Because small children lead active lives, their clothing requires frequent laundering. Certain stains, such as grass, formula, and some foods and juices, will need special treatment.

When you are buying a child's garment, check the hangtags and labels carefully for fabric and care information. If you are sewing the garment, read the label on the end of the fabric bolt. Look for words such as "permanent press," "soil retardant," "stain repellent," "colorfast," and "shrink resistant."

Selecting Maternity Wear

Around the fourth month of pregnancy, a woman may need to start wearing looser-fitting, nonrestric-tive clothing. Oversized shirts and sweaters, wrap skirts, stretch pants, and loose-fitting jackets can provide the adjustability and comfort she needs.

As the pregnancy progresses, an expectant moth-er would appreciate special items that accommodate her body's changes. **Maternity clothes** are *clothes suitable for wear by pregnant women.* Maternity tops and dresses have pleats, gathers, or extra fullness in the front to provide for the woman's expanding shape. Maternity pants, shorts, and skirts have an elasti-cized panel across the front, along with an expand-able waistband. Maternity clothing is sized the same as a woman's regular clothes. Designers add the full-ness needed for the increased weight.

Most women wear maternity clothes for only four of five months during the second half of their pregnancy. Thus, they need maternity clothes for only one or two seasons of the year. For example, fall into winter or spring into summer.

Many women borrow maternity clothes from friends. Garage and rummage sales and thrift and consignment shops are other sources of inexpensive clothing. Pattern companies also offer dressy and casual designs for pregnant woman.

After the baby is born, some maternity clothes can be restyled to get more wear per clothing dollar. For example, dresses that are worn loose during pregnancy can be belted to create a new look.

Selecting Clothes for Older Adults

Many older adults become involved in new activities and hobbies after retirement. They may need new outfits for sports, travel, or volunteer activities. Others may have less need for new additions to their wardrobe. Their activities may be restricted, or they already may have enough clothes.

However, all older adults, regardless of their age or their lifestyle, have a need for the psychological lift that a new item of clothing provides. A colorful sweater, a warm robe, or a pretty pin for a jacket lapel might be a good choice for an older relative. Look for a tie or scarf in a print that matches the person's hobby. Perhaps you can find a bird print for a bird watcher, a stamp design for a stamp collector, or a floral pattern for a gardener. Museum gift shops and specialty stores are good places to shop.

Needs and Values

When you are shopping for older adults, select articles of clothing that reflect their needs and values, not yours. Unless the person has made a special request for something that is "in fashion," avoid buying anything that is a fad. Observe the person's wardrobe carefully. Choose a style and color that is harmonious with items that the person already owns.

Maternity clothes provide extra fullness to accommodate the changes in a pregnant woman's body.

Physical Concerns

Did you ever notice an elderly person wearing a jacket or sweater on a warm day? Many people develop poor circulation as they get older. Lightweight clothing that can be layered on or off is particularly appreciated. Warm slippers, flannel shirts, and cardigan sweaters are other good choices.

Many older adults are affected by arthritis in their arms or hands. They may have difficulty manipulating small buttons or reaching a back zipper. Clothing that is easy to slip into, such as pull-on pants and slip-on shoes, are useful.

A Thoughtful Gift

An older person may be particularly appreciative of a gift you have made yourself. Most older adults have developed a special regard for the time and effort it takes to make something. They are often more touched by a handmade gift than a younger person would be.

Selecting Clothes for People with Disabilities

Almost everyone is disabled at some time in his or her life. A **disability** is *some type of condition that hampers a person in some way.* We usually think of a disability as a permanent handicap that is the result of a birth defect, an illness, or an accident. However, a disability can also be temporary, such as a broken arm or a broken leg. Some older adults become disabled as a result of declining health.

A person with a physical disability may be restricted in his or her physical movements. This person might be in a wheelchair, wear a cast or a brace, use crutches or a walker, or have limited functioning of some parts of the body. People with special needs often find that many common clothing styles are uncomfortable or too confining for them.

Older adults may like a gift of casual clothes that they can wear for a favorite activity or hobby.

Clothing Requirements

Clothing for people with disabilities should be sturdy because restricted movements can put great strain on certain areas of the garment. Garments with an elasticized waist or no waistline at all will be more comfortable for people who must sit for long periods of time. People who use crutches often have problems keeping their blouse or shirt tucked in. Overblouses, shirts with long tails, or long loose-fitting sweaters are good solutions.

People with disabilities want to be as self-sufficient as possible. This may mean being able to dress with little assistance or being able to take care of their own wardrobe. Washable, easy-to-care-for clothes are appreciated. Garments that wrap and tie or that fasten in the front are easier to put on and take off than other styles. Choosing clothes that are one size larger can provide added comfort and ease of dressing.

Choosing the Right Fabric

Select fabrics that are both easy to clean and comfortable to wear. Washable fabrics that require little or no ironing are the best choice. Printed fabrics do not show stains or soil as easily as solid colors. Fabrics should be colorful and attractive. People feel better about themselves when they are dressed attractively.

Since many people with physical disabilities are confined in one position for long periods of time, comfortable fabrics are a necessity. Avoid choosing heavy fabrics. They are too bulky and uncomfortable. Instead, choose two or more layers of lighter-weight clothing for warmth. Stretch and knitted fabrics offer some stretchability for added comfort. Avoid clingy fabrics that tend to reveal casts and braces. Do not choose a scratchy fabric that may irritate the skin.

Customizing a Garment

If you have sewing skills, there are many things you can do to make clothes more comfortable to wear. For example, crutches and braces often rub against a garment. The extra strain on the fabric causes the garment to tear or wear out quickly. You might reinforce the areas of strain by adding a fabric patch or fusing an extra layer of fabric to the inside of the garment.

People with disabilities need comfortable garments that enable them to be as independent as possible.

A person wearing a leg brace or a cast may have trouble getting a pant leg on over the cast. People with acute arthritis or restricted movement often find buttons difficult to handle. A minor styling change or an easier type of fastener can make dressing much easier.

People who are visually impaired need help in matching and identifying colors. You might try stitching small thread knots to the inside of the garments. One knot could mean red, two knots blue, and so on. Such special customization of garments can help others maintain their independence.

Customizing Garments

Simple clothing alterations can provide comfort and self-sufficiency for people with disabilities.

• **Hook and loop tape.** This tape has tiny hooks on one strip and loops on the other. It can be pressed together and pulled apart very easily. Use in small pieces to replace snaps or buttons. Use in longer strips to replace a zipper or provide an adjustable closing. Apply at seam of pants or sleeve to permit easier dressing over a cast or brace.

• **Elastic.** Insert elastic at waistlines to help keep garments in place. Or add a casing with a drawstring or elastic to make skirts and pants more comfortable.

• **Buttons.** Use large, flat buttons and enlarge the buttonholes for easier fastening. Sew on buttons with elastic thread at cuffs and other openings to eliminate unbuttoning.

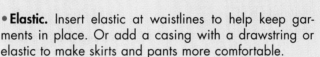

• **Large hooks.** Replace small hooks and eyes with large metal hooks and bars or special coat-size hooks and eyes. For an adjustable waistline, sew on two bars to accommodate weight changes or provide added comfort.

• **Zipper pulls.** Fasten a large ring or a ribbon loop to the zipper pull to make it easier to grasp and pull up or down.

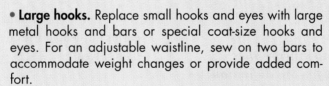

• **Additional zipper.** Add a zipper at the shoulder seam to allow the garment to be pulled over the head more easily. An extra-long zipper can be inserted in the inseam of pants.

REVIEW

Summary

- When shopping for others, you should consider the other person's needs, wants, and personal preferences, as well as your own resources.

- Gifts that are crafted or sewn are particularly appreciated by others.

- Children's clothes should be evaluated for size, comfort, wearability, safety, ease of dressing, easy care, color, and texture.

- Maternity clothes accommodate the body changes that occur during pregnancy.

- Both older adults and people with disabilities want clothing that meets their special needs of comfort and fit.

- You can use your sewing skills to customize garments for a person with a disability.

Using Vocabulary Terms

On a separate piece of paper, write the vocabulary term that best fits the definition:

1. Some type of condition that hampers a person in some way.

2. Jewelry made of nonprecious metals, often set with imitation stones, and relatively inexpensive.

3. Jewelry made with superior workmanship from gold, silver, or platinum and may contain precious and semiprecious stones.

4. Clothes suitable for wear by pregnant women.

Recalling the Facts

1. List at least four factors that should be considered before buying clothing for another person.

2. Why are accessories good gifts for others?

3. Why might a person appreciate a handmade gift over a purchased one?

4. What are the three size groupings for children's clothing?

5. What safety factors should you consider when buying clothes for children?

6. What design features in children's clothing aid ease of dressing?

7. What are some inexpensive sources of maternity clothing?

8. What health factors may influence the clothing needs of older adults?

9. What types of fabrics are most suitable for persons with restricted movement? What fabrics are not suitable?

10. How could you customize clothing to make it easier for people with disabilities to dress themselves?

Thinking Critically

1. **Analysis.** What are some possible results of purchasing clothing for others without considering their needs and wants?

2. **Evaluation.** What guidelines would you use to decide whether a clothing item is a suitable gift for another person?

3. **Synthesis.** Write a poem or story about one or more toddlers trying to dress themselves.

4. **Analysis.** How are the clothing needs of children, older adults, and people with disabilities similar? How are they different?

Applying Your Knowledge

1. **Gifts.** Make a list of gifts that you could buy or make for a friend or relative. Consider the person's interests and hobbies, likes and dislikes, favorite colors and styles. Show your list to the person and ask them to evaluate your choices.

2. **Children's Clothes.** Using catalogs and magazines, analyze children's clothing for ease of dressing, safety, comfort, wearability, and care. Create a classroom display.

3. **Reference Cards.** Fill out index cards with information about family members and friends. Include sizes, favorite colors, interests, and hobbies. Use as a reference when buying gifts.

4. **Handmade Gifts.** Bring to class a handmade item that you have given or received. Discuss the advantages and disadvantages of making gifts for others.

Making the Connection

1. **Math.** Calculate the cost of a gift item that you could make and compare it to the cost of a similar one that you could purchase.

What Is a Craftsperson?

Craftspersons are skilled artisans who create items mostly by hand. Some spin and dye yarns to weave their own fabrics. Others specialize in knitting, crocheting, quilting, lacemaking, or needlepoint. Some handcrafted items are decorated with original designs in paint, embroidery, or beadwork. Many accessories, such as jewelry, belts, bags, scarves, hats, and mittens, are also handcrafted.

Try It Yourself

Imagine that you are a craftsperson. Using the textbook and library resources, research a specific craft. Then learn the basic skills and create a simple project. Keep a record of the time it takes to finish the project, along with the cost of all materials and supplies.

Build Your Portfolio

After completing your crafts project, write a summary of your experiences. Then identify how and where you could reach potential customers. Determine what you would have to charge for each handcrafted item in order to make a profit. Place a photograph or the actual project in your portfolio, along with your written summary and analysis.

2. **Health.** Contact a nursing home or a rehabilitation center to learn what items of clothing are needed by persons who are elderly or have disabilities. Where can these garments be purchased? What is the cost of specialized garments?

Consumer
Rights and
Responsibilities

After reading this chapter, you will be able to:

- *Explain how shoppers can help keep the costs of products down.*

- *Give examples of industry and government regulations that protect the consumer.*

- *Describe the consumers' responsibilities in getting the most satisfaction from purchases.*

- *Explain what to do when a product does not live up to expectations.*

Terms to Learn

- *hidden costs*
- *kleptomania*
- *consideration*
- *toxic*
- *standards*
- *arbitration*

At one time, a sweater that you bought in a store did not have any labels or hangtags. You could not tell what fibers the sweater was made from, or whether to wash or dry clean it. If you took a chance on washing the sweater and it shrank, it was your loss. Fortunately, this situation does not exist any more. Today consumers are protected by rules and regulations.

Consumer Behavior

Your behavior as a shopper can affect the price of clothing. Someone must pay for cleaning and repairing clothes that are damaged by careless customers. Someone must pay for items that are stolen by shoplifters. Someone must pay for the salaries of store personnel who spend their time handling customer exchanges and returns. These *expenses for customer carelessness, theft, and returns* are known as **hidden costs**. The cost is passed on to you, the customer, in the form of higher prices.

Damaged Merchandise

If a seam is ripped, a hem is torn, or a garment has stains on it, the retailer will have to lower the price of the garment. Another example is an outfit with a missing belt that is placed on sale. It may be cheaper, but finding a new belt may cost you more in time and energy than you have actually saved on the price of the garment. In addition, the retailer will raise the price on other items in the store in order to make up the difference.

Here are a few guidelines to help you be a considerate shopper when you try on clothes:

• Do not try to squeeze into a garment that is too small for you. This is how zippers are broken, buttons lost, and seams ripped.

• When pulling a garment over your head, be careful makeup does not stain the fabric.

• Always take off your shoes when trying on any garment. The garment you step into will stay clean, and you will not get your shoe caught in the hem.

• Be careful that your jewelry does not snag the fabric.

• Do not remove any labels, hangtags, or price tags. It costs the store time and money to replace them.

• Do not let a garment fall on the fitting room floor where it might become wrinkled and dirty. Put it back on the hanger with any belt or other accessory.

• Do not leave any garments in the fitting room. Return them to the salesperson or checker.

Be a considerate shopper. When examining clothes, return them to the proper rack or shelf. When trying on garments, take care not to damage any items.

Shoplifting

Shoplifters are responsible for the fact that retailers in North America lose over $10 million worth of merchandise every day. Shoplifting is a crime that can result in a stiff fine, legal supervision, a jail sentence, and a police record that lasts a lifetime.

People shoplift for many reasons. Some people shoplift because they cannot afford to buy some of the things that they need or want. Other people shoplift because of peer pressure from within a group involved in this illegal behavior. A few people shoplift as a result of a personality disorder called **kleptomania**. They have *an abnormal and persistent impulse to steal*.

Whatever the reason, shoplifting is stealing. It costs everyone money. The store that loses merchandise because of shoplifting must raise its prices. The higher prices cover the cost of the stolen items, plus the costs of higher insurance premiums, security guards, television monitors, and security systems.

Because shoplifting has been increasing and retailers cannot afford to absorb the losses, many stores no longer take a lenient attitude toward shoplifters. Additional security guards, as well as increased security systems, are used to apprehend shoplifters. Hidden cameras are used to survey shopping areas. Merchandise is often electronically tagged. These large tags can only be removed with special equipment at the cashier's desk when you pay for the item. Small tags may be hidden in a pocket or seam allowance. If someone tries to take an item out of the store with one of these tags still attached, a special alarm goes off.

Exchanges and Returns

Another hidden cost is the extra expense a retailer may have to absorb if you return an item many days or weeks after it was purchased. When this happens, the returned item may have to be put on sale because the selling season is over or the store does not have any more items like it.

Always exchange or return items promptly. Some stores have a limit of seven or ten days from date of purchase for returns. You will save yourself time, energy, and money if you shop carefully. Be sure of sizes and colors before you buy. Check for fit, evaluate quality, and compare prices to avoid making exchanges and returns.

Stores use a variety of security systems, such as cameras and sensor tags, to deter shoplifting.

TECHNOLOGY

Paying the Price for Shoplifting

Shoplifting is a crime that costs everybody money. Store owners must raise their prices to cover the costs of goods that "disappear" from their stores. Retail industry experts estimate that every consumer in America pays $300 extra per year to make up for shoplifting losses.

Many new devices have been invented to deter and prevent shoplifting:

- **Electronic article surveillance** refers to the heavy plastic security tags that are attached to garments and other merchandise. The tag must be removed by the cashier. Otherwise, special sensors at the store's exits will set off an alarm. With some versions of this tag, a nonwashable ink spreads over the garment if the tag is improperly removed. Another type of tag beeps and sets off an alarm if anyone tries to tamper with it.

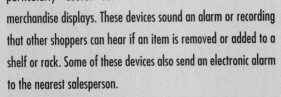

- **Weight sensor devices** are a special type of electronic surveillance that is particularly useful for merchandise displays. These devices sound an alarm or recording that other shoppers can hear if an item is removed or added to a shelf or rack. Some of these devices also send an electronic alarm to the nearest salesperson.

- **Closed circuit cameras** hang from the ceiling, fit into rack lighting, and are hidden behind wall panels. A special type of mannequin has a camera hidden behind her glass eyes. She also has a microphone behind her nose that allows the store's security personnel to eavesdrop on conversations.

Be sure to understand the store's policy on returns, exchanges, and refunds.

Showing Consideration

Shopping often brings out the worst in people because they are tired, rushed, or frustrated in their search for items. However, being rude or discourteous toward salespersons or other customers never solves the problem. Instead, try to show **consideration**, which is *thoughtfulness, or helpfulness toward others* whenever you are shopping.

Always be pleasant to a salesperson when describing what you are looking for. If you must complain about an item or service, state the problem clearly and firmly but never yell. Wait in line for your turn for a dressing room or to pay. If other customers try to cut in line ahead of you, tell them nicely that you are ahead of them. If you are with a group of friends, try not to block the aisles or talk and laugh too loudly.

Consumer Rights

In 1962, President John F. Kennedy delivered a special consumer message to Congress. It was brought about because of mounting problems that consumers were having with certain goods. President Kennedy's message was the inspiration for new legislation and amendments to existing legislation, all designed to protect the consumer. Other consumer rights were later added by President Richard Nixon and President Gerald Ford.

Legislation established six basic rights for all consumers:

- **The right to safety.** To be protected against the manufacturing and selling of goods that are hazardous to one's health, life, or limb.

- **The right to be informed.** To be protected against false advertising, labeling, or highly misleading information about products, and to be given the facts needed to make a good choice.

- **The right to choose.** To have as much access as possible to a variety of goods and services at a reasonable price.

- **The right to be heard.** To be assured that consumers' interests will get a sympathetic hearing by the government and that the laws protecting consumers' rights will be enforced.

- **The right to redress.** To have corrected any wrong done to the consumer in the marketplace.

- **The right to consumer education.**

Government Regulations

Federal, state, and local legislation has been passed to protect consumers. Federal laws cover all consumers. State and local legislation varies in coverage. Many of these laws and regulations are designed to help you know exactly what you are buying and to give you a better, safer product.

Some federal laws and regulations relate to fibers, fabrics, and textile products. Others provide financial protection.

- **Textile Fiber Products Identification Act** specifies that fiber content and percentage, manufacturer, country of origin, and care information must appear on the labels of textile products.

- **Care Labeling Rule** specifies the type of care information and the wording to be used on permanent care labels attached to garments and other textile products.

- **Wool Products Labeling Act** states that the manufacturer must identify the type of wool, fiber content, and country of origin. The manufacturer must also indicate whether the wool is new or recycled.

- **Fur Products Labeling Act** states that the manufacturer must indicate the type of fur, its English name, its country of origin, and whether the fur has been dyed or otherwise altered.

- **Flammable Fabrics Act** prohibits the sale of fabrics that burn faster, easier, and more intensely than other fabrics. This law helped develop the standards for children's flame-retardant sleepwear. These standards also apply to fabric sold by-the-yard that is intended for use in children's sleepwear and apparel. There are also flammability standards for rugs, carpets, and mattresses.

- **Hazardous Substances Labeling Act** protects consumers from the use of **toxic**, or *poisonous*, substances in products. For example, lead is highly poisonous. It can be dangerous to young children who put many things in their mouths. Therefore, all paints and surface coatings used in children's wear, such as painted t-shirts and athletic jerseys, must be free of lead.

- **Consumer Credit Protection Act** requires that institutions, such as banks, credit card companies, and retail stores, clearly explain all of the terms of a credit agreement. They also provide protection if someone steals your credit card and uses it to make any purchases in your name.

Children's sleepwear must be flame-retardant. These standards are covered by the Flammable Fabrics Act.

• **Consumer Product Warranty and Federal Trade Commission Improvement Act** requires that all warranties be written in clear and simple language. They must be posted on, or close to, the product when you purchase it.

Industry Standards

Although federal legislation does require that manufacturers make products that meet certain standards, many retailers and manufacturers set up their own quality standards that go beyond what is required by law. **Standards** are *specific measurements or models to which similar products are compared.*

Sometimes these quality control tests are conducted on behalf of a manufacturer who wants to make certain claims about the product. Sometimes they are conducted for a retailer who wishes to double-check the claims made by the manufacturer.

Some very large companies have their own laboratories for product testing. Others use the services of an independent testing company. A group of manufacturers in an industry may also get together to establish standards of its own.

For example, the pattern companies worked together to establish a set of body measurements for each pattern size. All of the major pattern companies now use these standard sizing measurements when they produce their patterns.

Consumer Agencies and Organizations

Some government agencies are responsible for enforcing laws that affect consumers. Private consumer groups are organized by interested citizens at the national, state, and local levels. They may focus on certain consumer issues of interest to their membership.

• **Federal Trade Commission**, or FTC, has a Bureau of Consumer Protection. It handles consumer problems relating to advertising, price fixing, credit, and fraud.

• **Office of Consumer Affairs** recommends consumer protection and education to the president of the United States.

• **Food and Drug Administration**, or FDA, enforces laws and regulations for cosmetics as well as for food and drugs.

• **United States Postal Service** handles complaints about mail-order shopping.

• The **Better Business Bureau** is an organization formed by businesses. Members promise to abide by strict business standards. In turn, the Better Business Bureau helps to settle customer complaints against its members through voluntary **arbitration**. This is *the settlement of a dispute by a person or panel that listens to both sides and issues a decision.*

The telephone book is a good place to find the listing for a consumer agency or organization.

Understand Store Policies

It is your responsibility as a consumer to understand the store's policies before you purchase an item. If you are using a layaway plan or a credit card, be sure that you have read and understood the terms for payment.

Find out about the store's return policy. It should be posted in the store. If you cannot find it, ask. Can you return the item? How long after you have bought it? Will you get cash or credit?

Save the sales receipt, all hangtags, and any warranties that come with your purchase. The sales slip is your proof of where you bought the merchandise and how much you paid for it. If you must return the item for any reason, you will need to show the sales slip. The warranties and hangtags will give you valuable information about the performance of your purchase.

Consumer Responsibilities

To be a smart consumer, you cannot rely on government regulations, industry standards, and consumer groups to guarantee that all of your purchases will be wise ones. You are the only person who can know your own personal needs and wants.

Research the Product

It is the manufacturer's and the retailer's responsibility to provide information that is clear and accurate and not misleading. It is your responsibility to read that information before you purchase an item. In many cases, you will not want to rely only on what the manufacturer claims or the salesperson tells you. You will want to do some research on your own.

Ask friends and relatives for their recommendations. Go to the library and look in *Consumer Reports*. It is a magazine that specializes in providing information and advice about many consumer goods and services.

Be sure to save the sales receipts and any hangtags or warranties that come with your purchases.

Act in Good Faith

If there is something wrong with your clothing purchase, return it promptly to the store for credit, exchange, or cash refund. When you do this, you should act in good faith. This means you should not expect the store to take back merchandise if you have not followed the instructions on the care label. For example, a sweater's care label says "Dry Clean Only." If you wash it, it is your fault if the sweater shrinks.

Good faith means that you should have reasonable expectations about the wear and performance of a garment. If your new bathing suit fades after two wearings, it is reasonable to return it. If it fades after two months of frequent wear, it is not reasonable to return it.

Complain Effectively

You have a right to expect that the item you buy will perform properly. An umbrella should not leak. The heel should not come off your shoe the first time you wear it. If there is a problem with any item that you have purchased, do not be shy about making your complaints heard. If you approach the problem in a direct and mature manner, your chances of receiving satisfaction are greatly improved.

Whether complaining in person or in writing, always provide the following information:

• A clear explanation of the problem including how the product or service is defective.

• The name and address of the store where the item was bought or the service was arranged, and the purchase date.

• Specific information, such as style number, catalog number, order number.

• The steps you have taken to resolve the problem.

• What you believe should be done about the problem.

• Your name and address.

If you act in good faith, your complaint will usually be resolved. After all, stores and manufacturers do not want unhappy or dissatisfied customers. For more information, see How to Complain Effectively on page 351.

If you have a problem with a purchase, explain it politely to a salesperson, a manager, or a customer service representative.

HOW TO COMPLAIN EFFECTIVELY

1 Go to the store where you purchased the merchandise. Bring the item and sales receipt with you. Explain your problem politely to the salesperson, department manager, or store owner. Some stores have a Customer Service Department. If the problem is not solved...

2 Write a letter to the store. Address the letter to the store owner, store president, or head of the Customer Service Department. Enclose photocopies of your sales receipt. Never send the original documents. If the store does not give you satisfaction...

3 Contact the manufacturer. Write to the manufacturer's Customer Relations Department. Enclose a copy of your letter to the store and a copy of the sales receipt. If the problem still remains unsettled, write directly to the company president. You can obtain a company's address from reference books at the public library. If the problem is still not resolved...

4 Contact a consumer protection agency for advice. Look in the telephone book under the name of your city, county, or state for government agencies. Call the Better Business Bureau or local Chamber of Commerce. Contact the consumer reporter or action line at a local newspaper or radio station. If the manufacturer or retailer does not like bad publicity, it may force them to deal immediately with your complaint.

SMALL CLAIMS COURT

5 Obtain legal assistance. Contact a lawyer or a legal service for serious problems. Less serious complaints can be settled in a small claims court where you present your own case before a judge.

REVIEW

6. Settlement of a dispute by a person or panel that listens to both sides and issues a decision.

Summary

- Damaged merchandise, shoplifting, exchanges, and returns are extra expenses for retailers that can increase prices.

- Legislation has established six basic rights for all consumers.

- Some laws and regulations cover the labeling and safety of textile products. Some manufacturers and retailers have set additional standards of quality.

- A variety of government agencies are responsible for enforcing consumer laws.

- Consumers have certain responsibilities. These include researching the product, understanding store policies, acting in good faith, and complaining effectively.

Using Vocabulary Terms

On a separate piece of paper, write the vocabulary term that best fits the description:

1. An abnormal and persistent impulse to steal.

2. Poisonous.

3. Expenses for customer carelessness, theft, and returns.

4. Specific measurements or models to which similar products are compared.

5. Thoughtfulness or helpfulness toward others.

Recalling the Facts

1. List at least five guidelines for trying on clothing in a store.

2. How does shoplifting affect the prices that you pay for merchandise?

3. How long should you wait before exchanging or returning an item?

4. List the six consumer rights guaranteed under law.

5. What does the Textile Fiber Products Identification Act specify?

6. What type of clothing products are covered by the Flammable Fabrics Act?

7. List at least three government agencies that enforce consumer laws.

8. Why should you save sales receipts, hangtags, and warranties?

9. What procedures should you follow when making a complaint about a product?

10. What information should a letter of complaint contain?

Thinking Critically

1. **Evaluation.** If you were a store owner, how might you lower the hidden costs created by customers?

2. **Analysis.** Explain what each of the six consumer rights means.

3. **Synthesis.** Summarize the four main responsibilities of consumers.

4. **Evaluation.** Why do you think a well-written complaint letter usually resolves a consumer problem?

Applying Your Knowledge

1. **Research a Product.** Choose a consumer item that you would like to buy if finances permitted. Use consumer magazines, catalogs, and visits to retail stores to research the item. Which brand and model would you buy? Why?

2. **Consumer Publications.** Working in small groups, make a list of publications and sources of information that are helpful to consumers. Compile the listings and submit it for publication in the school newspaper.

3. **File Folder.** Set up a file folder or box where you can save sales slips, hangtags, and warranties for items that you have purchased. Be sure to write the name of the item on each piece of information that you save.

Making the Connection

1. **Language Arts.** Using the guidelines in the chapter, write an effective complaint letter about a garment or accessory item.

2. **Science.** Under teacher supervision, test several samples of fabrics for flammability.

LOOKING AHEAD TO CAREERS

What Is a Laboratory Technician?

Laboratory technicians test the performance of fibers and fabrics. These tests can measure characteristics such as fiber strength, colorfastness, stretchability, shrinkage, wrinkle resistance, and water resistance. Some tests may be conducted on the fibers or fabric; others on the finished garment. Laboratory technicians often analyze textile products to see if they perform according to the claims made by the labels and hangtags.

Try It Yourself

Imagine that you are a textile laboratory technician. Select a fabric that has a specific finish, such as wrinkle resistance. Cut four or more large fabric swatches. Retain one as an "original." Using different laundry methods, test the performance of the fabric by comparing the laundered swatches to the original. Be sure to label each sample. Analyze your findings.

Build Your Portfolio

After completing the fabric tests, mount and label each fabric swatch. Place in your portfolio, along with the analysis of your tests. Be sure to indicate whether or not the fabric performed according to the expectations stated on the label or hangtag.

Include at least one fabric that is intended for children's sleepwear. If possible, retest the samples after repeated launderings.

Menswear Buyer and Store Owner

In his work, *John Pershing wears two hats. He is the menswear buyer for a small chain of specialty stores. He also is co-owner of these stores. "As an industry, retailing is changing rapidly. Off-price retailers and large department store chains have made it harder and harder for small stores to stay in business. I must pay careful attention to who my customers are and what they want. Then I can offer them the best possible value and service."*

Education and Training

When John first went to college, he thought he would become an engineer. Early in his sophomore year, he changed his mind and switched to liberal arts. He got his first job in the fashion business a few months after graduation. While looking for a job, he did some research at the library on local companies. He found a newspaper article about a growing company that manufactured men's dress shirts, sports shirts, and neckwear. John said, "During my interview, somehow I managed to convince the owner of the company that I wanted to work for him no matter what. I started in the warehouse as a neckwear picker. This meant that I took the orders, pulled ties, and delivered them to the shipping department. In a few months, I moved out of the warehouse and eventually worked my way up to head of the neckwear division."

When the neckwear division was sold to another company, John became a sales representative for a firm that manufactured men's shirts. After five years, one of John's customers offered him a job as the menswear buyer for a chain of small specialty stores.

When the owner was ready to retire a few years later, he approached John about buying the business. Although John didn't have enough money of his own, he found an investor and borrowed the remaining money from the bank. Now he is co-owner of several stores.

Responsibilities

As co-owner, John employs a store manager for each store, an accountant, and buyers/managers for the gift, accessories, and children's departments. Because he really enjoys buying, John has continued his responsibilities of menswear buyer.

- **Know the customers.** John spends about 20 hours a week on the selling floor. He believes it is important to interact with customers so he can better understand their needs, wants, and preferences.

- **Understand the trends.** Fashion and lifestyle trends affect the clothing choices of customers.

When office dress codes became more relaxed, customers began to buy more casual clothes and fewer dress shirts, suits, and ties.

- **Shop the market.** John is always on the lookout for new products and styles for his customers. He visits an apparel mart regularly. Twice a year, he attends a major apparel show where vendors from all over the world exhibit.

- **Advertise and promote the stores.** To be successful, a business must develop advertising and promotional plans. John works with the advertising managers of local newspapers and employs the services of a small public relations firm.

- **Manage the business.** Although buying is John's major responsibility, he meets regularly with his co-owner about the status of the business. Together they make major decisions about staffing, cost controls, advertising, promotions, renovations, and expansion.

Knowledge and Skills

As a buyer and retailer, John has listed the knowledge and skills that he uses on a regular basis:

- **Fashion knowledge**—for choosing merchandise that will attract customers to the stores and increase sales.

- **Math skills**—for understanding the sales and inventory reports, establishing prices, determining profits and losses, and keeping financial records.

- **Business and marketing skills**—for making decisions, managing employees, planning advertising and promotional campaigns, and arranging store layouts.

- **Consumer science knowledge**—for understanding consumer needs, wants, attitudes, and concerns in order to provide better merchandise and services.

- **Communication skills**—for interacting with customers, employees, vendors, and other service providers.

- **Computer skills**—for tracking sales, maintaining inventory control, processing orders, and keeping track of financial records.

"The computer is a great tool because it tells me what is selling. But it won't tell me if there is something missing that the customer wants to buy. I can only learn this by talking with the customers who come into our stores. Since Saturdays attract the most customers, I make sure I am in the store almost every Saturday."

The Workplace

Fashion Design and Production

After reading this chapter, you will be able to:

- *Explain the designer's role in creating the fashion look of fabrics and garments.*

- *Discuss how new fibers and methods of production are developed.*

- *Identify various jobs in the production and manufacturing areas of the textile and apparel industries.*

- *Identify the responsibilities of marketing experts and sales representatives for selling the finished products.*

Terms to Learn

- *stylist*
- *forecasting service*
- *knock-offs*
- *converters*
- *contractors*
- *pattern grading*
- *marketing*
- *market research*
- *sales analysis*

Do you have a good eye for details? Do you like to tinker with machinery? Do you have a good sense of line, design, and color? These are only a few of the many talents and interests that can lead you to a career in design and production in the textile and apparel industries.

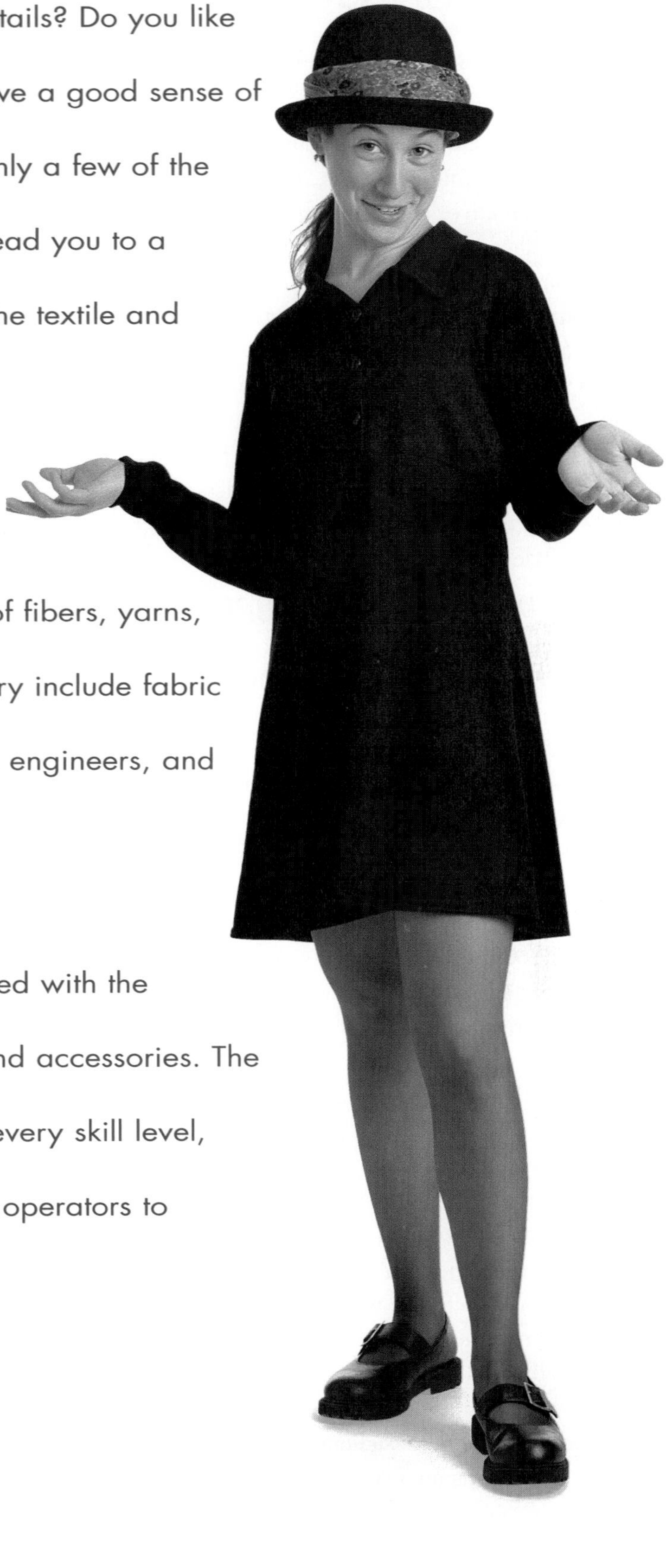

The textile industry is involved in the development and production of fibers, yarns, and fabrics. Jobs in the textile industry include fabric stylists, machine operators, chemists, engineers, and computer programmers.

The apparel industry is concerned with the design and production of clothing and accessories. The industry offers job opportunities for every skill level, from stock clerks to sewing machine operators to designers.

Careers in Design

A designer is a person who is creative enough to have new ideas and practical enough to know how to turn those ideas into a product. Designers must be artistic and creative. They also must have a knack for knowing—ahead of time—what customers want in clothing or home fashions.

A **stylist** is a *designer or consultant who is responsible for determining the look of a product.* Stylists take their own or other people's ideas and put them together in a way that looks fresh and original.

Designers and stylists are employed by both textile and apparel manufacturers. They also work for services that predict trends in colors, fabric textures, garment styles, and accessories.

Fabric Designers and Stylists

Are you interested in new things? Are you interested in new ways of doing familiar things? Do you have a talent for combining colors in fresh and attractive ways? Are you interested in the technical methods of production? If so, you may be interested in a career as a fabric designer or stylist.

A *fabric designer* works very closely with the research department of a textile company to develop new weaves, patterns, prints, and colors. A fabric designer should have the ability to predict trends very far in advance. Fabric designers are working today on fabrics that will appear in the stores one to two years from now. Clothing designs are often inspired by the new fabrics that are created by fabric designers.

In some companies, the fabric designer and the fabric stylist are the same person. In other companies, a *fabric stylist* spots trends by visiting stores, talking to research people, and traveling to other parts of the world to see what is selling there. The stylist then reports back to the textile designers with recommendations for color combinations and print designs.

Today most fabric designers and stylists develop their fabric designs on a computer screen. They can

The textile industry produces fabrics for many items other than clothing, such as these colorful hot air balloons.

Forecasting services provide information about color trends, fabric designs, and clothing styles.

quickly experiment with different yarns, weaves, and color combinations. After the design is approved, it can be sent directly from the designer's computer to the computer at the fabric mill.

Have you ever wondered how clothing and accessories by different manufacturers are produced in coordinating colors each season? Many fabric and apparel manufacturers, as well as retailers, work with **forecasting services**. These services *predict color, fabric, and fashion trends* two or more years in advance. The forecasting services have highly skilled stylists who develop special reports, color cards, fabric swatches, and illustrations for their clients.

Both fabric designers and fabric stylists must have good art and computer graphics skills. They also must understand the technical aspects of fabric construction. The best source of training is a specialized two-year technical school or a four-year college.

Apparel Designers and Stylists

Do you like to work with fabric? Are you constantly looking for ways to change your personal clothing to give it a new "look"? Do you have a talent for sketching? Are you a good observer of how other people live and dress? If so, you may be well suited to a career as an apparel designer.

An *apparel designer* develops original ideas for clothing designs. A designer is inspired by many things, such as travel, movies, theater, art exhibits, historical clothing, and the work of other designers.

Being a fashion designer is a high pressure job. He or she works against many deadlines to develop fresh, new ideas for a collection of garments that must please many people—fashion reporters, retailers, and customers.

Not all apparel designers work in a situation where they develop completely new ideas for clothing. Some designers, also known as *fashion stylists*, translate other people's ideas into clothing for a special market within a specific price range. For example, a well-known fashion designer may introduce a new and innovative design that is very expensive to produce. Then another apparel manufacturer may have its fashion stylist produce a similar design at a moderate price. Many more customers are able to buy these *less expensive copies*, or **knock-offs**.

The stylist has many design options. The original design might be made in silk; the stylist could choose polyester. The original design might have twelve very rare buttons; the stylist could use eight less expensive ones. The original design might have a jacket that was lined; the stylist could make an unlined jacket.

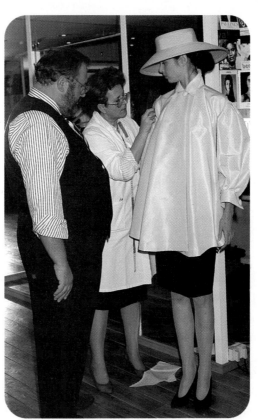

This couture designer is checking the style and fit of a garment for his next collection. His sample maker has translated his original design into a garment that is being fitted on a live model.

Some apparel designers sketch their fashion ideas on paper. Others create a design on the computer, enabling them to see instantly how different details change the look of a design.

If you are interested in a career as an apparel designer or a fashion stylist, you will need special training in a two-year or four-year technical school or college. There you will learn sketching, computer graphics, draping, pattern making, and sewing skills.

Do not expect to get a job as a designer right away. Most designers and stylists begin their careers in positions such as sketcher, sample maker, or design assistant. This may mean duties such as picking up pins when you first start. Most aspiring designers work many years for many different companies before they make it as a successful designer.

Careers in Research and Development

The research and development areas are the backbone of the textile and apparel industries. These are the people who develop new fibers, new weaves and patterns, new dyes, and new quality-control tests. They also develop the equipment to make it all happen.

A career in research and development requires a four-year college degree in chemistry, physics, or one of the engineering fields. Many research and development people also obtain a master's or a doctor's degree in their field.

Chemists and Lab Technicians

Textile chemists are responsible for creating new fibers, new dyes, and new finishes. A textile chemist may work alone, as part of a team, or as the manager of a team of researchers working on a special project. A textile chemist must be patient and accurate. He or she must have a creative mind and a talent for problem solving. New fibers and finishes are the result of the textile chemist's work.

After a new fiber or a new finish is discovered, tests are developed to see how the new product will perform. A *laboratory technician* works with the tex-

Textile chemists help develop new fibers, fabrics, and finishes.

tile chemist to develop and carry out these tests. The tests include how well a new fiber will take and keep a particular dye, how strong a fiber is, and how it will react to special finishes.

Engineers

Someone must develop new equipment, keep it in good running condition, and measure its performance and effectiveness. The engineers who do this are a very important part of the research and development area.

An *industrial engineer* makes sure that all of the operations in the plant are running smoothly and efficiently. He or she develops procedures for testing the efficiency and measuring the costs of existing equipment and methods. An industrial engineer constantly tries to develop better production methods while maintaining the company's standards of quality.

A *mechanical engineer* is responsible for maintaining and developing the plant's equipment and machinery. The industrial and the mechanical engineer often work together to improve production methods.

An *electrical engineer* is responsible for the plant's general operating systems. This includes the electrical and the cooling systems.

An *environmental engineer* is responsible for pollution control systems that reduce the amount of pollution a textile facility gives off. He or she must make sure the company follows all environmental laws and regulations that deal with water, air, and solid waste.

Careers in Manufacturing and Production

The manufacturing and production areas of both the textile and apparel industries offer a wide variety of job opportunities. Although some jobs require technical or college degrees for advancement, others do not require any education beyond high school.

Textile Manufacturing

Textile mills manufacture fibers, yarns, and fabrics. They are involved in the processes of spinning, weaving, knitting, dyeing, and finishing.

Textile mills need skilled *machine operators* for the many pieces of equipment that prepare and spin the fibers into yarn, weave or knit yarns into fabric, and apply the required finishes. *Quality control experts* are also needed. These people are trained to carefully examine the finished products for flaws. *Skilled mechanics* are needed to work with the mechanical engineers to keep all of the machinery in top running condition.

Most of the workers in a textile mill are paid an hourly wage. At some mills, the workers are expected to join a union.

Textile **converters** are *companies or individuals who buy or handle fabric for finishing*. They anticipate fashion trends and serve as middle agents between finishing plants and apparel manufacturers.

Many steps are involved in the production of fabrics. Today most pieces of equipment are controlled by computers.

Quality control is vital in both textile manufacturing and apparel production. This inspector is using a magnifying glass and tweezers to correct a minor flaw in a garment.

Producing a Garment

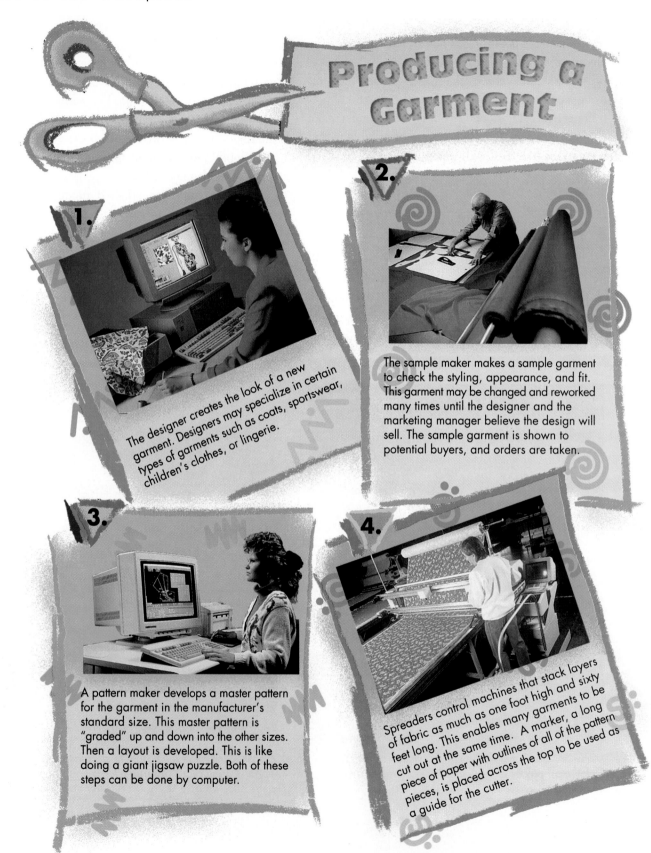

1. The designer creates the look of a new garment. Designers may specialize in certain types of garments such as coats, sportswear, children's clothes, or lingerie.

2. The sample maker makes a sample garment to check the styling, appearance, and fit. This garment may be changed and reworked many times until the designer and the marketing manager believe the design will sell. The sample garment is shown to potential buyers, and orders are taken.

3. A pattern maker develops a master pattern for the garment in the manufacturer's standard size. This master pattern is "graded" up and down into the other sizes. Then a layout is developed. This is like doing a giant jigsaw puzzle. Both of these steps can be done by computer.

4. Spreaders control machines that stack layers of fabric as much as one foot high and sixty feet long. This enables many garments to be cut out at the same time. A marker, a long piece of paper with outlines of all of the pattern pieces, is placed across the top to be used as a guide for the cutter.

5.
Cutters operate machines that cut through up to 100 layers of fabric, depending on the fabric thickness. Sorters number the pieces and gather them into bundles.

6.
Sewers operate specialized industrial sewing machines. Each sewer handles only one or two parts of a garment. Finishers complete any hand sewing, if necessary.

7.
Pressers iron the garments.

8.
Inspectors check the finished garments. Stock clerks and shipping clerks handle the inventory, packing, and shipping of the garments to retail stores.

Computer Integrated Manufacturing

Computers are rapidly changing the way that clothes are produced. Computer Integrated Manufacturing (CIM) is the term for a manufacturing process that uses computers for almost all steps of the production process. There are three parts to the CIMsystem:

- **Computer Aided Design (CAD)** is the first computer program used in the CIM process. Using CAD, a garment is designed directly on a computer.

- **Computer Aided Manufacturing (CAM)** programs automatically convert the CAD program's three-dimensional sketch into a flat pattern. The computer then grades this pattern into the desired sizes. It can also develop a cutting layout, called a *marker*. The computer checks the fabric grainlines, the direction of the nap, and even matches plaids. A high-speed machine, called a *plotter*, prints the marker on paper. The marker is placed on the top of a stack of fabric. A computer controls the knife that cuts through all the layers of fabric. The computer can adjust the speed of the knife to match the thickness and number of fabric layers.

- **Computerized robotics** make up the third part of the CIM system. Robots and sewing machines form a computer-operated assembly line. Garments are stitched together using a series of computer-operated sewing machines. Each machine is programmed to sew a specific part of the garment. Robots are located between the machines. These robots fold, align, or reposition the fabric and move it on to the next sewing machine.

Apparel Production

Some apparel manufacturers do all of their own production work in their own factories. Others hire **contractors**, *companies or individuals who specialize in sewing certain types of garments for a certain price*. They may be located in the United States or in other countries, such as India or Korea. Contractors produce the garments according to the manufacturer's designs and specifications.

After a new garment is designed, patterns must be created for all of the different sizes in which the garment will be produced. **Pattern grading** is *the art of converting a pattern from one size into many other sizes*. Pattern measurements change from one size to another, and the shape of the neckline curve is different for every size. Pattern grading used to be done entirely by hand. Today, most garment manufacturers use computers for pattern grading.

Computers also are used for pattern layouts. All of the pattern pieces must fit onto the smallest amount of fabric possible. When a manufacturer is producing many hundreds of garments, a savings of just a few inches of fabric per garment can add up to a lot of money.

Most apparel production is done by workers on an assembly line. Each sewer does only one task, such as stitching the seams, collar, or buttonholes. Even hems, buttons, and fasteners are stitched by specialized machines. Bundles of garment parts are passed from one worker to another on the assembly line. In more automated factories, the garment pieces are moved by a conveyor system from one work station to the next. By the end of the assembly line, the garment is completed.

Some production workers are paid an hourly wage. Others are paid by piecework, which means being paid for the number of sleeves they sew or buttons they attach. Training is given on the job or through a vocational school program. Many apparel production workers belong to the Union of Needletrades, Industrial, and Textile Employees (Unite).

Careers in Marketing

Marketing is concerned with *all of the various ways to advertise, promote, and distribute a product.* People with jobs as market researchers, sales analysts, advertising and promotion specialists, and sales representatives all have careers in marketing. Marketing plays an important role in both the textile and apparel industries.

Market Research and Analysis

How much is the customer willing to pay? Is it important that the garment be washable? What blends of fibers do consumers like best? What fabric finishes are most desired? Should the line include shirts that coordinate with the pants? What colors will sell best in different parts of the country? How can a manufacturer predict how many garments to make?

In order to run a successful business, a manufacturer should know something about the market and be able to answer questions like these. That is where market research and sales analysis come in.

Market research is *the study of consumer needs and attitudes.* If a manufacturer is considering hiring a well-known designer to develop a special line of clothes, the market research department might conduct a survey. They could find out which customers would want to buy designer clothes and what "names" would appeal to them. Market research can also track the type of advertising that people respond to most.

Sales analysis is *the study of what has sold in the past in order to predict what will sell in the future.* A careful analysis of sales can give a manufacturer information about what styles, colors, and sizes have sold best in different sections of the country. Sales information can also help companies organize their production and shipping schedules so goods are in the stores when the customers want to buy.

Both textile and apparel manufacturers use sales analysis to help develop new products. This information is also helpful when planning how to spend money on advertising.

A career as a *market researcher* or a *sales analyst* requires a college degree that includes courses in marketing and statistics. A graduate degree in business is often helpful.

The sales representative is the company's link with customers. This sales rep is showing her company's line of new fabrics to the owner of a fabric store.

Sales Representatives

A sales representative sells a company's products to its customers. He or she may work for a fiber, fabric, or apparel manufacturer. For example, a fiber company employs sales reps to sell its fiber to manufacturers, who will convert it into fabric. The fabric manufacturer hires sales reps to sell its finished fabric to apparel manufacturers. Apparel manufacturers, in turn, have sales reps to sell their finished garments to retail stores.

Sales reps are an important communication link between the manufacturer and the marketplace. They report back to the manufacturer with information such as market conditions, requests for future products, and activities of the competition.

There are two types of sales representatives. *Manufacturer's sales reps* work exclusively for one manufacturer. *Independent sales reps* work for several different firms that do not manufacture competing products. An independent sales rep might represent a button company, a fabric company that makes lace trim, and a fabric company that makes velvet.

It is important for sales reps to be able to get along with all types of people, and to have a neat and pleasant appearance. They should have good communication skills and math skills. Many sales reps travel extensively. They may be away from home a few days or several weeks at a time. Some people find such a schedule exciting, but others find it lonely.

Most sales reps are paid a salary, plus a percentage of every sale. Thus their income can vary from year to year, depending on how much they sell. A college degree is helpful, but not necessary, for a sales career.

Careers in Computers

More and more jobs that were once done by hand are now accomplished faster and easier by computers. People with knowledge of computers are in great demand in many industries. *Computer programmers* are needed to develop the information systems, also called programs or software, that enable the comput-

Computers are used in design, research and development, manufacturing, production, and inventory control. Both computer programmers and skilled technicians work in all industries.

er to perform various tasks. *Technicians* skilled in operating and repairing computers are needed in all areas of the textile and apparel industry.

Computers in Research and Development

The painstaking job of developing a new fiber, a new dye, or a new fabric weave is made much easier by the use of computers. A computerized piece of equipment, for example, can analyze a color and determine the formulas that will exactly reproduce the color in a variety of yarns and fabrics. Another machine has been developed that applies complex patterns to fabrics by using thousands of tiny dye jets individually controlled by a computer.

Complicated designs can be developed for patterned fabrics, laces, and embroideries. Using sophisticated computer programs, looms can be set up and threaded in minutes rather than hours. Computer graphics can even show the designer or the researcher what the finished design will look like without the need for an actual sample.

Computers in Manufacturing and Production

Before manufacturing begins, computers can help garment manufacturers determine the cost of a finished garment. Computers can even help them decide what changes need to be made in order to produce the style at a price the customers can afford.

Some manufacturing steps, such as pattern grading and developing the cutting marker, can be done faster and easier with the aid of the computer. The machines that cut out the garment pieces can also be operated by a computer. Even sewing machines can be computerized. They are custom-designed to perform a specific function, such as sewing collars, embroidering, or tucking. With the help of a computer, these machines can sew faster and adapt quickly and easily to a change in fabric, stitch length, or type of stitch.

Computer-operated robots can move garments along the assembly line from one spot to another. They can even pick the finished garments off the assembly line and organize them for packing and shipping.

Computers in Business

Both manufacturers and retailers use computers in the day-to-day operations of a business. Computers can keep track of inventory, maintain accounting records, analyze sales and store files, and keep accurate lists of suppliers. Computers with word processing programs have replaced the typewriter in most offices.

Many stores have their cash registers linked to a computer system. When a sale is rung up, that item is automatically deducted from the store's inventory list. The sales information can be electronically transferred to the manufacturer's computer. The manufacturer will know instantly which goods are selling in the marketplace.

If you are interested in a career in computers, you could take a specialized computer program at a vocational school or community college. Some large companies provide their employees with computer training. However, they usually prefer to hire someone with a college degree in business, mathematics, or computer science. More and more people who have jobs as designers, chemists, writers, or market researchers cannot work effectively without computer skills.

Jobs in Design and Manufacturing

Fabric Designer	Quality Control Expert	Inspector
Fabric Stylist	Mechanic	Stock Clerk
Apparel Designer	Sample Maker	Shipping Clerk
Fashion Stylist	Pattern Maker	Contractor
Textile Chemist	Spreader	Market Researcher
Laboratory Technician	Cutter	Sales Analyst
Industrial Engineer	Sorter	Manufacturer's Sales Rep
Mechanical Engineer	Sewer	Independent Sales Rep
Electrical Engineer	Finisher	Computer Programmer
Environmental Engineer	Presser	Computer Technician
Machine Operator		

Summary

- Designers and stylists develop original ideas or translate other people's ideas into new designs and styles.
- Textile chemists, lab technicians, and engineers work in the area of research and development.
- Many different types of production and manufacturing jobs are available in textile mills and the apparel industry.
- Marketing jobs include market research, sales analysis, and sales representatives.
- People with computer skills are needed in all areas of the textile and apparel industries.

Using Vocabulary Terms

On a separate piece of paper, write the vocabulary term that best fits the definition:

1. Companies or individuals who specialize in sewing certain types of garments for a certain price.
2. A designer or consultant who is responsible for developing the look of a product.
3. The art of converting a pattern from one size into many other sizes.
4. Less expensive copies.
5. All of the various ways to advertise, promote, and distribute a product.
6. The study of consumer needs and attitudes.

Recalling the Facts

1. What is the difference between a designer and a stylist?
2. Why do manufacturers and retailers use forecasting services?
3. Name two skills that are important for both fabric designers and fabric stylists.
4. Why are engineers an important part of research and development?
5. What is the role of contractors in the apparel industry?
6. Describe the assembly line method of constructing a garment.
7. Name at least six job categories involved in the production of clothing.
8. What information can market research provide to manufacturers?
9. What are two skills that are important for sales reps?
10. Describe two uses of computers in each of the following areas: research and development, manufacturing and production, and business.

Thinking Critically

1. **Analysis.** Describe at least five modifications that could be made in a "knock-off" garment to make it more affordable.
2. **Synthesis.** Summarize the steps required in the production of a shirt—from fiber to fabric to finished product. Indicate where the process is influenced by research and development and by marketing and sales.

3. **Evaluation.** Would you prefer being paid an hourly wage or being paid by piecework? Explain your choice.

4. **Analysis.** Compare the skills needed for careers in design, research and development, and marketing. What are the similarities and differences?

Applying Your Knowledge

1. **Knock-offs.** Working with another classmate, examine photographs of expensive garments in fashion magazines. Brainstorm how a "knock-off" of each garment could be made.

2. **Computers.** Using a computer program that has design capabilities, create different types of designs that could be used for fabrics or apparel. Experiment with changing colors, shapes, and patterns. Print out your designs.

3. **Assembly Line.** As a class, select a sewing project that could be produced on an assembly line. Identify specific jobs for each student, from design to quality control. Then set up the assembly line and produce the items.

Making the Connection

1. **Technology Education.** View a CAD demonstration at school. Discuss its application in the textile and apparel industries.

What Is a Sales Representative?

Sales representatives work for fiber, fabric, and apparel manufacturers. They sell the company's products to its customers, who might be a fabric converter, an apparel manufacturer, or a retail store. Some sales reps work exclusively for one company. Others may represent several different firms.

Try It Yourself

Imagine that you are a sales representative for a fabric company. Your job is to sell the company's fabrics to apparel manufacturers. Decide what type of fabrics are in the line and the type of clothing for which they could be used. Using information in the unit on fabrics, make a list of the special features and benefits of your company's fabrics. Ask other students to play the role of the president or designer of an apparel firm. Your role is to convince each "president" or "designer" to purchase your fabrics.

Build Your Portfolio

After completing the role-plays, write an essay about your sales experiences. Describe the communication skills that you used, as well as the emotions you experienced as you tried to "close" a sale. Was it easier or more difficult than you had imagined? Why? Place a copy of your essay, along with the list of the special features and benefits of the fabrics, in your portfolio.

2. **Art.** Using a basic body shape for either a male or female, sketch several apparel designs.

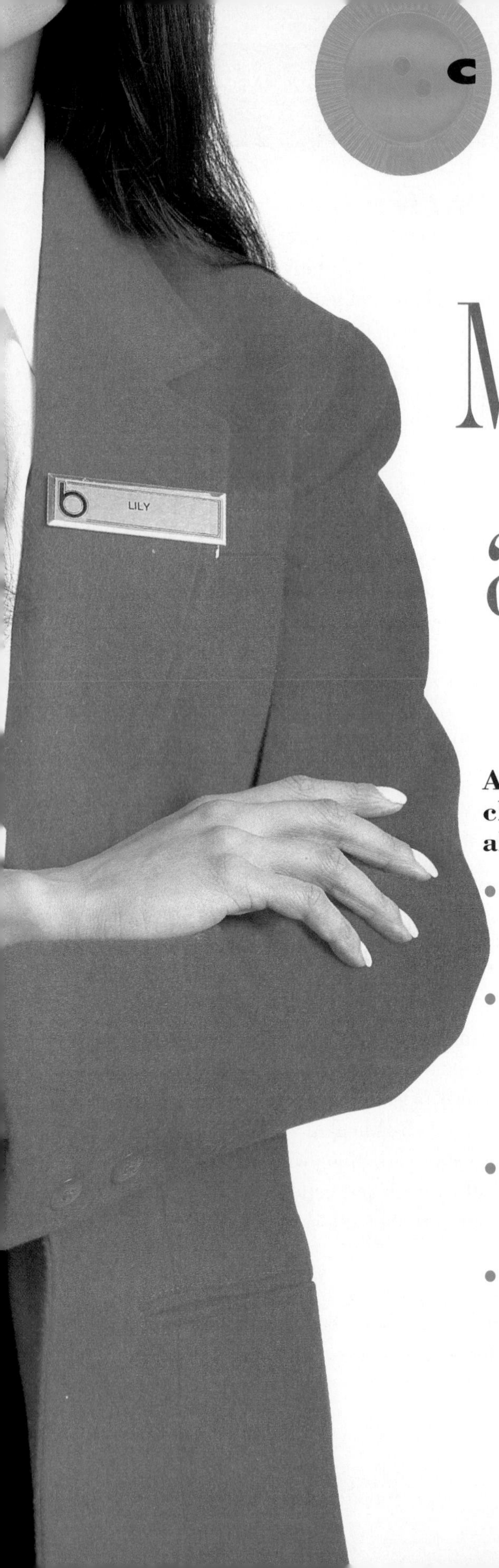

Fashion Merchandising and Retailing

After reading this chapter, you will be able to:

- Describe the responsibilities of salespersons and stock clerks in retail stores.

- Explain the role of a buyer, merchandise manager, and fashion director in choosing the items that are available in a store.

- Discuss how retail advertising and display can create an image for a store.

- List other job opportunities in store operations and service industries.

Terms to Learn

- *merchandising*
- *wholesale*
- *retail*
- *branch*
- *retailing*
- *commission*
- *market*

Whether you live in a large city, a small town, or somewhere in between, it is possible for you to have a career in retailing. Retail stores come in all sizes, from small operations where the owner manages the store and does the buying, to large department stores with hundreds of employees who all have specialized jobs.

Retailing offers many job opportunities in buying, selling, advertising, display, and store operations. A career path may lead from stock clerk to salesperson to buyer to merchandise manager.

There are other career opportunities in the service industries that are concerned with the care and repair of apparel. These include dry cleaners, laundries, and alteration and repair services.

What Is Merchandising?

Merchandising includes *all of the decisions that go into the selling of a product*. These decisions include what to sell, how to sell it, who to sell it to, and what price to charge. Merchandising includes many stages of planning.

Clothing and accessories must be ordered from manufacturers at **wholesale**. This means *the sale of goods in quantity for resale*. Styles, fabrics, colors, sizes, and prices must be selected. Then the merchandise must be displayed, advertised, promoted, and sold to customers. **Retail** selling means *the sale of goods in small quantities to consumers*.

Retail Store Organizations

Most department stores have one or more branch stores. A **branch** is *a separate operating division of a store that is overseen by the main, or flagship, store*. A branch may be located near the main store, in a suburb, for example, or faraway in another state. Branch stores are often located in shopping malls where they serve as an *anchor*, which is a store that attracts many customers to the mall.

The merchandising decisions for all of the branches are made in the main store. Buyers, working out of the main store, purchase goods for both the main store and the branches. A buyer then works with a department manager in each branch to determine what sizes and colors will sell best in that branch. Advertising and promotional themes are also developed in the main store and used for all of the branches.

A chain is a large retail company with stores in many cities and towns all over the country. Chains have headquarters or home offices where all of the merchandising decisions are made, but they do not have one main store. Chain stores may not carry exactly the same goods in all of their stores. Because they have so many stores, chains can afford to buy some goods only for stores in certain regions.

Specialty stores carry one particular type of merchandise, such as children's clothes, shoes, or lingerie. Specialty stores can be owned by an individual or group of individuals, or be part of a chain.

Boutiques are a type of specialty store. Instead of carrying one type of merchandise, they carry a variety of merchandise that is carefully chosen to appeal to a particular type of customer. A store that carries expensive designer clothes, one that carries trendy young fashions, and one that specializes in maternity clothes for working women are all examples of boutiques. Some boutiques are part of a chain, but most are individually owned.

Careers in Retail Selling

A job as a salesperson or a stock clerk is a good way to begin a career in **retailing**. This is *all of the activities connected with the direct selling of items to consumers*. As a salesperson or a stock clerk, you will learn how a store operates from "the ground up." This knowledge is a valuable basis for all retailing jobs.

It is possible to get both full-time and part-time work as a salesperson or stock clerk. Many stores are open in the evenings, as well as on Saturdays and Sundays. This provides flexibility for full- or part-time employees. Many high school students work after school, on weekends, and during the summer. Most stores provide on-the-job training.

Most salespeople and stock clerks are paid an hourly wage. Sometimes, a salesperson is paid a minimum salary, plus a **commission**, or *percentage of the purchase price on every sale*.

Employees of a retail store are usually entitled to an employee discount. This means that they are able to buy items in the store at a lower price than the customer pays. Most stores put a limit on the use of the discount. This limit is usually based on a percentage of the employee's salary.

A successful salesperson is very familiar with the store's merchandise and enjoys working with people.

Salespersons

A *salesperson* is a very important employee in a store. He or she is the person directly responsible for selling the merchandise to the customer. If you are helped by a pleasant, courteous salesperson who is familiar with the store's stock, you will be much more likely to make a purchase.

Even if the store does not carry what you need, you will probably think well of the store and return another time. If a salesperson is rude, unpleasant, or lazy, you will probably go to another store the next time you need to buy something.

A *personal shopper* is a special type of salesperson. He or she selects merchandise to meet the needs of individual customers. A personal shopper may accompany a customer around the store, helping to select items and giving fashion advice. Merchandise may also be selected for mail and telephone requests.

A salesperson should enjoy working with people and make a real effort to become familiar with the store's merchandise. He or she should always be helpful and pleasant when assisting a customer.

A salesperson needs good communication skills. Sales involves both listening and talking to customers. For example, a customer reports that something is wrong with an item in stock or requests an item that the store does not carry. A salesperson should listen carefully and then communicate this information to the manager or buyer.

Math skills are also important. Salespersons ring up sales on cash registers or computers, give receipts, and sometimes handle credits and exchanges.

Stock Clerks

Stock clerks provide the behind-the-scenes support to salespeople. When new merchandise arrives in the store, it goes straight to the store's receiving room. All of the items are carefully counted and recorded, and then checked against the packing slip and a copy of the buyer's order. Any damaged merchandise is set aside for the buyer to examine and possibly return to the manufacturer.

Next, the new merchandise is tagged. A sales tag, which has the price, inventory number, and any other information the store needs, is attached. A security tag may also be attached. This is removed by the cashier or salesperson when you pay for your purchase.

TECHNOLOGY

Quick Response

The garments that you purchase in a store usually have a bar code printed on the price tag. This bar code provides the retailer with a lot of important information, such as style, color, and price. It is also the basis for a system known as Quick Response, which simplifies the reordering process.

When a garment is purchased, a scanner is used to transfer information from the bar code to the computer. This information is electronically sent to the clothing manufacturer and the textile manufacturer. The computer also keeps track of how many items are sold. When the inventory in the store gets low, the computer alerts buyers and others that it is time to reorder. Because the clothing and textile manufacturers have been receiving information all along, they are able to produce and ship immediately.

A stock clerk unpacks new merchandise, checks delivery records, attaches price tags, and delivers the merchandise to the proper department.

A special type of software is an important part of many Quick Response systems. It is called PDM, or product data management. PDM is an electronic filing cabinet that contains a complete record of a garment. This includes the style, fabric, color, and price. It also includes the directions and illustrations for assembling the garment.

PDM maintains lists of people who need to be informed if any change is made regarding the production of the garment. For example, if a retailer wants to change something about the garment's design, the change is recorded on a computer and placed in the electronic filing cabinet. Then the PDM system automatically sends an electronic mail notice of this change to those who need to know. This could be the pattern maker, the production planning department, and the purchasing department. PDM is faster and more accurate than placing a phone call, sending a fax, or making a photocopy.

Then the tagged merchandise is delivered to the proper department to be hung on racks, displayed on counters, or put on shelves. All of this is the responsibility of the stock clerk.

The stock clerk, along with the salesperson, is responsible for keeping the displayed merchandise neat and tidy. Garments that have been tried on by customers must be put back on hangers, zipped and buttoned, and rehung on the racks. Other items must be replaced on shelves and counters.

A stock clerk should be conscientious, careful, and reliable. Math skills are very important for this position. A career path can lead to becoming *head of stock* for a large department or an entire store.

Careers in Buying and Merchandising

Do you like planning for the future? Are you interested in both business and fashion? Do you like a lot of responsibilities and challenges? Are you creative and do you pay attention to details? Can you predict what people will want to buy six months from now? If you can answer "yes" to these questions, a career in buying and merchandising may be for you.

A job as a buyer, merchandise manager, or fashion coordinator includes many glamorous aspects. Many buyers and merchandise managers travel frequently, both in the United States and to foreign countries. They meet interesting people and work in a fast-paced environment. Some people find this very exciting. Others find it tiring and do not like to be away from home so much.

Buyers, merchandise managers, and fashion coordinators work long hours. They are often expected to be at the store in the evenings, on weekends, and on some holidays. Remember, stores are often the busiest when everyone else is not working. Since they are paid a weekly salary, rather than an hourly wage, they do not receive overtime pay. They also have to prepare many reports and budgets.

Buyers, merchandise managers, and fashion coordinators are expected to dress well. If you enjoy fashion, that can be exciting. However, when you start your job as a buyer and you are not making very much money, a large percentage of your salary may be spent on clothes. To compensate for this problem, many stores give a larger employee discount to buyers than to salespeople or stock clerks.

Retail Buyer

A *buyer* is responsible for selecting and purchasing the clothes and other items that are sold in one or more stores. They may work out of a main store or a buying office.

Buyers are always planning for the future. Right now, they are purchasing the clothes that will be in their stores six months from now. Success on the job depends on how well the buyer can predict what customers will want to buy many months from now.

In order to accomplish this, buyers do a great amount of research. They read fashion magazines and fashion publications that predict new styles and trends. A buyer travels to market several times a year. **Market** is *the place where designers' and manufacturers' showrooms are located*. A buyer who works for a large store or group of stores may travel to market at least once a month. Some buyers travel overseas several times a year to purchase new and unusual merchandise from foreign countries.

A buyer is responsible for selecting and purchasing the items to be sold in a store.

Although buyers plan very far ahead, they must still pay careful attention to what customers are purchasing in their store today. This is how buyers decide which sizes to order, which colors will sell best, and what type of customer their store attracts. Customers may be conservative or fashion-conscious, young or older, concerned about price or conscious of designer names.

Today many stores have sophisticated computer systems that can tell a buyer, on a moment's notice, how well a particular style is selling. These systems can predict, based on early sales figures, how many of an item the store can expect to sell. This helps the buyer to keep track of the inventory and to know when to reorder an item.

The buyer decides when to put old stock on sale in order to make room for new merchandise. It is also the buyer's responsibility to keep the salespeople informed and excited about new merchandise. Many buyers have regular meetings with the sales staff to acquaint them with new merchandise, to share fashion information, and to get feedback about merchandise on the selling floor.

Some stores have a resident buying office in New York City or Los Angeles. The office provides the store buyers with information on fashion trends and wholesale markets.

Part of a buyer's time is spent researching the market, selecting merchandise, and working with the salespeople. The rest of the time is spent on paperwork. A buyer must keep track of what is selling, check inventory records against buying orders, and determine how much money is left in the budget to buy new merchandise. Some stores have *assistant buyers* who place orders for merchandise and help supervise the sales staff.

In order to become a buyer, you must have a college, junior college, or fashion merchandising degree. In addition, buyers must have a keen eye for fashion, good math skills, and a lot of energy. They also must be able to get along well with all kinds of people. Most department stores and chains have special training programs for buyers.

Merchandise Manager

A *merchandise manager* oversees the operation of several departments within a store. Usually, the departments are somehow related. For example, one merchandise manager may be responsible for all of the men's departments. Another merchandise manager may supervise the expensive designer departments or the sportswear departments. Another manager may be responsible for all of the accessory departments, such as jewelry, scarves, handbags, hats, and luggage.

Each merchandise manager has several buyers reporting to him or her. The merchandise manager coordinates the departments to make sure that they do not compete with one another. For example, both the sportswear buyer and the dress buyer might want to carry the same type of two-piece dress in their departments. The merchandise manager resolves issues such as this so that each department retains its special image.

The merchandise manager assists the buyers in developing budgets and establishing prices. Often the merchandise manager accompanies a buyer on buying trips. This is particularly important when the buyer is new to the job.

The merchandise manager checks that the sales and promotional events in each of the departments relate to the overall activities of the store. A buyer may be promoted to a merchandise manager.

Fashion Director and Fashion Coordinator

Every store has a fashion personality, or an image, that it presents to its customers. The *fashion director* and staff of *fashion coordinators* are called the Fashion Office. They are responsible for seeing that everything the store does reflects this fashion personality.

It is the fashion director's job to be the person with the most knowledge about upcoming fashion trends and to share that knowledge with everyone in the store. The opinions of the fashion director determine what the store sells and how the store looks. The buyers consult with the fashion director before they go to market. The advertising department consults with the fashion director when it develops an ad. The display department works with the fashion director when it is planning displays.

The fashion director is also the store's representative to those people who make and report fashion news. These people include designers, manufacturers, and fashion reporters.

In order to become a fashion director, you must have a flair for fashion. Fashion directors are expected to look very fashionable. A fashion director should be very objective. He or she must be able to evaluate the importance of a trend, whether or not he or she personally likes it. A degree from a two- or four-year program that emphasizes business and fashion is important.

There are many career paths to becoming a fashion director or fashion coordinator. You could begin as an assistant in the fashion office or the promotion department and work your way up. You could start as an assistant buyer or work at a fashion publication.

The fashion director works with many departments to create the store's image. Here she is meeting with a copywriter and a graphic artist, who are preparing ads for the store.

Careers in Sales Promotion

Do you like to write? Do you have a flair for drawing? Do you have a talent for putting things together in pleasing but unusual combinations? Do you challenge the notion that there is just one way to do something, preferring instead to do things differently each time? If you can answer "yes" to any of these questions, you should explore the possibility of a career in sales promotion.

There are many ways to promote the sales of a product. Eye-catching window displays are designed to make people stop and notice the store. Other displays inside the store are planned to attract your attention to certain merchandise. Clever words and illustrations make a store's advertisements stand out from all of the others. Catalogs bring the store's merchandise into customers' homes.

All of these activities require the talents of many different people. Although each person has special responsibilities, they must all work closely together to promote the store and its merchandise.

Retail Advertising

A store's advertising does not just "happen." There are three different areas of responsibility that must all work together to produce the advertising—the advertising director, the copywriter, and the graphic artist.

The *advertising director* develops an advertising plan for the store. The plan includes any newspaper, radio, and television advertisements that the store will run. The advertising director determines where these ads will appear, the size of each ad, when and how often they will run, and how much money will be spent. The director also plans the design of the store's catalogs.

The advertising director works with the fashion director to develop the "look" of the ads and catalogs. He or she works with the copywriter and the artist who will actually design the layouts. The director also works with the buyers to make sure the store will have the merchandise featured in the ads and catalogs.

Just like the fashion director, no one becomes an advertising director right out of school. A two-year or four-year college degree is usually required. Courses in English, business, and advertising are valuable. Then, the person must get some on-the-job experience in a junior position with an advertising agency or the advertising department of a retailer or manufacturer. Many advertising directors began their careers as copywriters.

A *copywriter* must have a real flair for writing. A good ad is one that makes the product sound as attractive as possible and also gives information about the product. A copywriter has to do this in as few words as possible.

In order to become a copywriter, you need good communication skills. You should enjoy writing, understand grammar, and be well read. Although some education after high school is helpful, it is not always necessary for a beginning job. If you hope to advance to a management position, such as advertising director, a college degree may be necessary.

A *graphic artist* draws the illustrations for newspaper and magazine ads. Some artists work directly for the store. Besides doing artwork for advertisements, they may design posters, inserts for charge account bills, and special invitations. Other artists are self-employed and sell their work to several different stores.

The advertising department plans the store's advertising and promotional campaigns. The department works with the fashion director and buyers to create the desired "look" for the store's ads.

In order to become a fashion artist, you must take specialized art courses. These courses should include figure drawing, fashion illustration, and perspective. Graphic artists also need excellent computer skills, since many ads are created on the computer.

Retail Displays

The way a store's windows are decorated and how merchandise is displayed within the store are both forms of advertising. A store displays each garment in an eye-catching manner. It hopes that you will want to buy not only the garment but also the shoes, the belt, the scarf, and any other accessories shown with it. All of these displays are the work of the *display director*.

The display director works very closely with the fashion director to make sure that the displays reflect the fashion image of the store. The fashion office checks that each garment is shown with the right accessories. The display director also works closely with the advertising department. Very often, a store will feature the same merchandise in its ads, windows, and in-store displays. This gives the fashion message greater impact.

Large stores may employ a display director with a staff of many designers. Smaller stores may have only one *display designer*. He or she is responsible for planning, building, and arranging the store's displays.

A display designer must be very imaginative and creative. He or she must be able to draw or sketch ideas, and then be able to translate those ideas into three-dimensional objects. Garments must be draped and hung in a pleasing manner. Accessories and props must be added to the display to form an attractive arrangement.

In order to become a display designer, you should take courses in art and design, such as fashion illustration, perspective, and color. A high school degree is required. After that, most of what a display designer needs to know comes from on-the-job training. You might begin as an assistant in the display department of a large store. A job as a salesperson in a small store or boutique might give you an opportunity for some on-the-job display experience.

Display designers create the merchandise displays in the store windows and throughout the interior of the store.

Careers in Store Operations

There are many people needed behind the scenes to help make a retail store run smoothly. At the top are the store *executives*. These include the president, vice presidents, and store managers. They have climbed the career ladder by developing outstanding management, decision making, and leadership skills.

A retail store needs people to work in its *administration* and *human resources* departments. Some of these jobs require people with college degrees in business, finance, and personnel. Other jobs are *clerical* or general assistant positions that require a high school degree and some business skills.

Customer service representatives handle customer complaints, merchandise returns, and billing questions. Often the person who comes to a customer service representative is upset. How he or she is treated may make the difference between keeping or losing a customer for the store.

Maintenance workers help keep the store neat, clean, and in good physical condition. *Security workers* protect the store against shoplifters. They are also on call to handle any emergencies, such as a shopper who is taken ill or an accident that occurs in the store.

Careers in Service Industries

The retail service industries include dry cleaners, laundries, and alteration and repair services. These services can be located in a separate store or as part of another store. For example, a dry cleaner may offer a repair and alteration service, or a dry cleaner and a laundry may be combined into one store.

Dry Cleaners and Laundries

These service stores can be individually owned or part of a chain of stores. If the dry cleaner or laun-

A dry cleaner must be very knowledgeable about fabrics and stain removal methods. Industrial pressing equipment is used to steam out any wrinkles.

dry is part of a chain, garments are usually sent from all of the various store locations to one central plant for dry cleaning.

Individually owned stores often advertise that they do their cleaning "on premises." This means that the garments are cleaned right in the store. Prices in such a place may be a little higher, but if a belt or a button is missing from a garment, it is usually easy to find because the garment never left the store.

To work as a *dry cleaner* or *laundry worker*, you must have some knowledge about fabrics and how to operate the equipment. You will need a high school or vocational school education and some on-the-job training.

Alteration and Repair Services

Alteration and repair services include *dressmakers* and *tailors*. Some dressmakers and tailors will custom-make garments for you in addition to doing alterations. Others specialize only in alterations and repairs.

To become an alteration and repair specialist, you must have good sewing skills. You also need a knowledge of fashion in order to alter garments so they do not look out-of-date. Clothing construction courses in high school or at a vocational school are a necessity.

Many department stores, specialty stores, and dry cleaners employ one or more alteration and repair specialists. These stores are good places to get on-the-job training. You might begin by doing simple jobs, such as hems and replacing buttons, and progress to more complicated alterations.

Many tailors and dressmakers prefer to go into business for themselves. They become self-employed. Chapter 27 describes many types of opportunities for self-employment.

Some dressmakers and tailors will make custom-made garments. Others specialize in alterations and repairs.

Jobs in Merchandising and Retailing

Salesperson	Fashion Coordinator	Human Resources
Personal Shopper	Advertising Director	Customer Service Representative
Stock Clerk	Copywriter	Maintenance Worker
Head of Stock	Graphic Artist	Security Worker
Department Manager	Display Director	Dry Cleaner
Buyer	Display Designer	Laundry Worker
Assistant Buyer	Executive	Dressmaker
Merchandise Manager	Administration	Tailor
Fashion Director		

REVIEW

Summary

- Merchandising includes all the decisions that go into the selling of a product.

- Retail store organizations include department stores and branches, chain stores, specialty stores, and boutiques.

- Salesperson and stock clerk are entry-level jobs in retailing.

- Buyers, merchandise managers, and fashion directors are responsible for selecting merchandise for the store.

- Sales promotion jobs include advertising director, copywriter, graphic artist, display director, and display designer.

- Many behind-the-scenes jobs are needed to help a retail store run smoothly.

- Retail services include dry cleaners, laundries, and alteration and repair services.

Using Vocabulary Terms

On a separate piece of paper, write the vocabulary term that best fits the definition:

1. A separate operating division of a store.

2. A percentage of the purchase price on every sale.

3. All of the activities connected with the direct selling of items to consumers.

4. The place where designers' and manufacturers' showrooms are located.

5. The sale of goods in small quantities to consumers.

6. The sale of goods in quantity for resale.

Recalling the Facts

1. What is the difference between a department store and a chain store?

2. What are two skills that a salesperson needs?

3. What are the responsibilities of a stock clerk?

4. Describe how buyers can use computers in making decisions.

5. What education and training is needed to become a buyer?

6. Who is responsible for developing the fashion personality or image of a store?

7. Why is it necessary for the advertising director, fashion director, and buyers to work together?

8. List the skills needed to become a copywriter, a graphic artist, and a display designer.

9. Name at least five behind-the-scenes jobs in a retail store.

10. What skills do dressmakers and tailors need?

Thinking Critically

1. **Analysis.** What career advancement is possible for a person with successful sales or stock clerk experience?

2. **Analysis.** Make a list of the advantages and disadvantages of being a buyer or merchandise manager. How do the jobs compare?

3. **Evaluation.** Why do you think the jobs of a salesperson and a customer service representative are so important in retailing?

4. **Synthesis.** There are many types of jobs in retailing. What common characteristics do they all share?

Applying Your Knowledge

1. **Stores.** Categorize the stores that sell clothing or accessories in your community as: department store, chain store, specialty store, boutique. Discuss the differences and benefits of each.

2. **Salespersons.** Write two scripts about a salesperson waiting on a customer. In one, describe a salesperson's friendly, pleasant manner. In the other, depict an unpleasant and rude attitude. Have classmates act out the scenes.

3. **Sales Promotion.** Working in small groups, create a sales promotion plan for a store. Select a theme and an advertising slogan. Then design special ads and merchandise displays that could be used throughout the store.

Making the Connection

1. **Language Arts.** Imagine that you have moved to a new town. Write an essay about how you would determine where to shop.

What Is a Buyer?

Buyers are responsible for selecting and purchasing the items that are sold in a store. They must predict new styles and trends, as well as monitor current sales. Buyers make many decisions about styles, colors, sizes, quantities, and prices. They also must keep track of inventory, order new merchandise, put old stock on sale, and supervise the sales staff.

Try It Yourself

Imagine that you are a clothing buyer in a store. You want your store to carry the latest styles and fads for your teenage customers. You are about to purchase new merchandise that will not be in the store for another six months. Predict a clothing item that you think will be very popular a year from now. Sketch or describe the outfit or item. Include information about possible colors, fabrics, and prices.

Build Your Portfolio

After completing your sketch or description, place a copy in your portfolio. Include the information about colors, fabrics, and prices. Then write a short essay about why you think this item will become popular with teenage customers. Place this in your portfolio, too.

2. **Art.** Using the elements and principles of design, create a window display of clothing or accessory items. If possible, set up an actual display in a school showcase.

Fashion Promotion and Education

After reading this chapter, you will be able to:

- *Explain the purpose of fashion promotion.*

- *Compare the roles of an editor, writer, art director, illustrator, photographer, and model in the communications industry.*

- *Explain how publicity differs from advertising.*

- *List the types of educational careers in the textile and clothing fields.*

Terms to Learn

- *client*
- *copy*
- *portfolio*
- *publicity*
- *public relations*
- *certification*
- *vocational training*
- *seminar*
- *curator*

Suppose you have just invented the world's most practical jacket. How is anyone going to know you have this wonderful product? If you find ways to let your potential customers know about this exciting product and how to use it, then your chances for success are much greater.

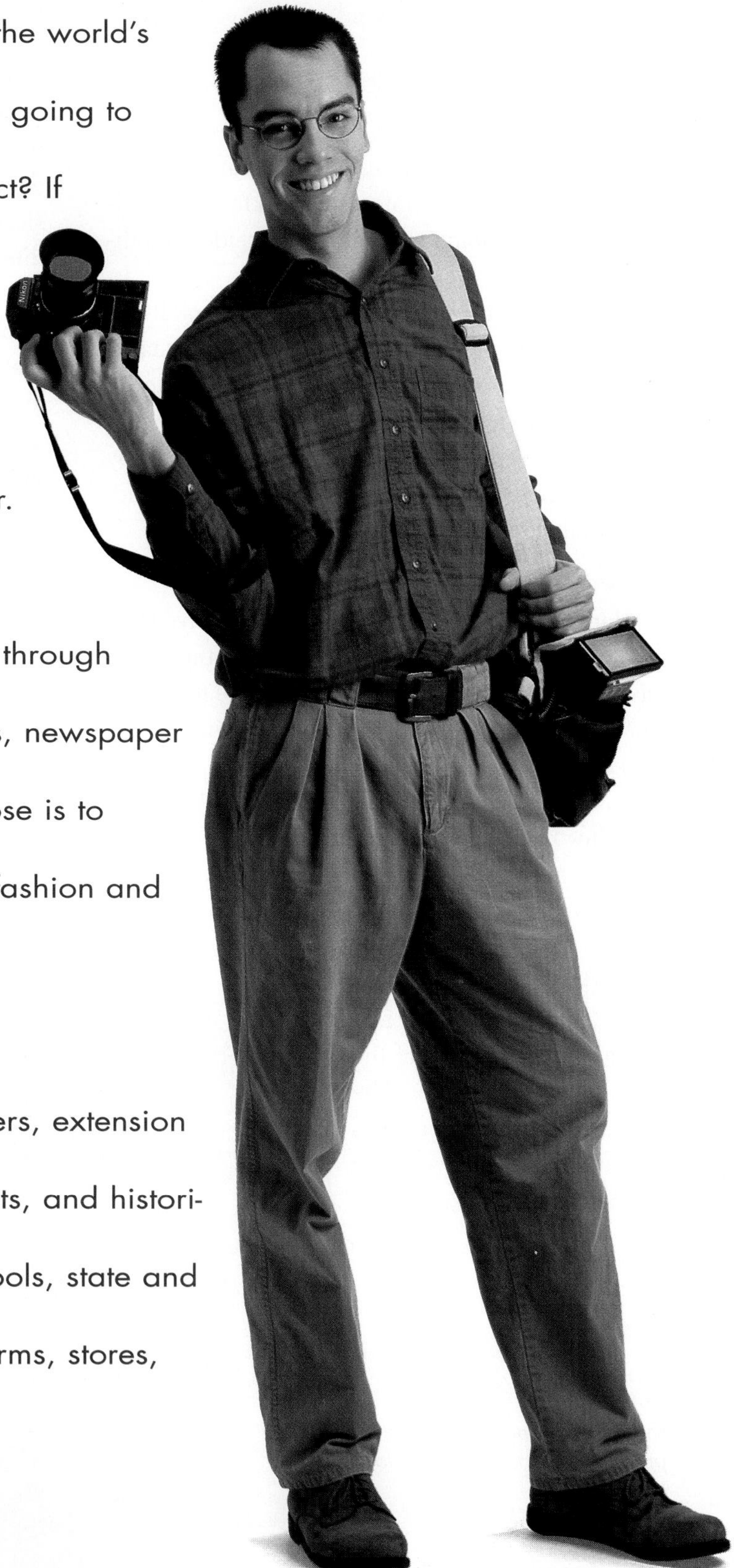

Fashion promotion can be done through advertising, photography, magazines, newspaper articles, and fashion shows. Its purpose is to inform people about what is new in fashion and to convince them to buy it.

Education careers include teachers, extension agents, consumer education specialists, and historians. These people may work for schools, state and federal government, manufacturing firms, stores, museums, and libraries.

Fashion Promotion

The field of fashion promotion includes all of the activities conducted by a designer, manufacturer, or retailer to get the public interested in a fashion product or service. Fashion promotion is considered indirect selling.

There are many ways to promote a product. It can be done through advertising, catalogs, fashion magazines, videos, television shows, newspaper articles, displays, booklets, fashion shows, and special events. These promotional methods are used by advertising agencies, fashion publications, manufacturers, and stores.

Advertising Agencies

Many manufacturers and stores do not have their own advertising department. Instead, they will employ an outside advertising agency. The manufacturer or retailer will be the agency's **client**, or *customer*. One agency will have many clients. Sometimes these clients have similar needs; sometimes they have very different ones.

Many people are involved in preparing an advertising campaign for a client. The *account executive* is the link between the advertising agency and the client. He or she works closely with the merchandising and marketing departments of the manufacturer or store. The account executive manages and oversees the advertising account.

The *creative director* plans the overall advertising campaign and must approve each step of the creative process. He or she works with the *art director* to develop the ads for magazines, newspapers, television, radio, or outdoor billboards. In turn, the art director works with the copywriter and the graphic artist to complete the final designs. The art team may also work together to design any supporting materials that accompany the products for sale. These may be logos, hangtags, packaging, leaflets, or brochures.

Creative directors and art directors must be imaginative, creative, persuasive, and enthusiastic in order to "sell" their ideas to a client. They must be organized and able to work under tight deadlines. Good communication skills are essential. Most art and creative directors are college graduates. They have taken courses in advertising, business, communication, writing, and art. They may advance to an advertising director.

Fashion Publications

Fashion and consumer magazines want to attract more readers and more advertisers. Fashion promotion is very important in helping the magazine to do this.

Many people are involved in preparing an ad campaign for a client.

Magazines carry both fashion articles and ads for their readers to enjoy. Editors, writers, illustrators, and photographers all work together to create these stories for the magazine (more about these careers later). The ads are created by advertising agencies or the advertising departments of manufacturers and retailers.

Fashion magazines may also have a special promotion department that researches and publishes fashion trend reports. These reports predict the styles, colors, and fabrics that the magazine's readers will be wearing next season. The reports are developed as a service to the magazine's advertisers.

Have you ever noticed a listing in a fashion magazine of a special event cosponsored by the magazine and several retailers? Events such as make-over sessions, career programs, or wardrobe coordination seminars may be held in stores around the country. These events are organized and presented by the magazine's fashion promotion department.

The *promotion director* is responsible for developing and planning special events. He or she must be very creative and highly organized. Most promotion directors start as a copywriter or an assistant in the promotion department.

Manufacturers

Many large fiber and fabric companies and apparel manufacturers employ *fashion promotion specialists*. These specialists are concerned with any project that involves the company's fashion image. They may work closely with the advertising department or advertising agency to develop the fashion look of the ads. They may share their knowledge of what is going on in the fashion market with the design and production departments.

Fashion promotion specialists also serve as the company's representative to the fashion press and appear on television. They may provide press releases and fashion photographs for publication.

Most fashion promotion specialists are college graduates in fashion merchandising, communica-

tions, or business. Courses in fashion, design, writing, speaking, art, and business are beneficial.

Retailers

Stores may have special theme promotions, such as "Our Birthday Celebration" or "Spring in January." These events are put together to attract more customers to the store. Fashion shows, personal appearances by designers, and in-store demonstrations may be organized as a part of these events.

It is the promotion director's job to make sure that the store is organized and ready for each event. This might mean ordering staging for a fashion show, hiring caterers for a luncheon, finding clowns for a parade, or arranging for a store full of tulips in January. In addition, the promotion department is responsible for details, such as organizing publicity, sending invitations, and notifying other departments in advance about these events.

This fashion promotion specialist helps plan special promotions for a clothing manufacturer.

Careers in Fashion Communication

Fashion writers, editors, illustrators, photographers, and models are all involved in communicating the fashion message. This message can be communicated by advertisements, catalogs, magazine and newspaper articles, or radio and television programs.

Fashion Writer and Editor

There are several different kinds of fashion writers. An *advertising copywriter* may write advertisements for newspapers, magazines, radio, or television. He or she may work for an advertising agency or for a store.

Some fashion copywriters also write copy for catalogs. However, a slightly different style of writing is required. The term **copy** refers to *words and sentences that will be used.* Advertising copy is written to make you interested enough in the product to come into the store. Once you are in the store, the salesperson will answer any questions you may have. Catalog copy is written so you will get enough information about the item to order it without having to go to the store. A *catalog copywriter* must be more precise and detailed when writing catalog copy.

There are other jobs for fashion writers besides that of a copywriter. Some large newspapers employ a *fashion reporter*. A reporter may write articles about fashion trends and clothing care, interview designers, and review fashion collections.

Magazines have editorial departments that put together the stories you read in the magazine. The *fashion editor* assigns these stories to various *fashion writers*. The fashion editor also develops and supervises any photography that accompanies the story. Many fashion editors begin their careers as fashion writers.

The two most important talents for a fashion writer are excellent writing skills and an endless curiosity. A college degree in journalism can be very helpful. Courses in English, art history, fashion

Copywriters must write detailed descriptions of the garments shown in a catalog.

design, and retail marketing will give the fashion writer extra insight into the areas that he or she is writing about.

Fashion Illustrator

A *fashion illustrator* specializes in drawing the human figure. Fashion illustrations are usually drawn in a stylized manner. This means that the figures are taller, with longer arms and legs, and have more elegant faces than real-life drawings of people. The fashion illustrator must also be able to use texture and shading to indicate different types of fabrics.

Fashion illustrations are used in advertisements, catalogs, pattern envelopes, posters, and anywhere that fashion art is needed. To be a fashion illustrator, you will need to take special art courses, including figure drawing and fashion illustration. Courses in fashion and textiles are also helpful.

A fashion illustrator specializes in drawing fashions on the human figure.

Fashion Photographer

The *fashion photographer* is a very important person in the world of fashion communication. Just as every fashion illustrator has his or her own style, every photographer has his or her own style, too. Some photographers may be known for their natural-looking photos. Other photographers may be known for a very decorative style.

Sometimes the photographer is asked to translate the ideas of the fashion editor or the art director into a photograph. At other times, the editor or the art director gives the photographer only a very general idea. It is the photographer who then creates the mood of the photograph.

Some photographers have special training under experienced photographers. Others learn by reading and doing. Courses in art and photography are always helpful.

AROUND THE WORLD

The Language of the Kimono

The literal translation of the kimono is a *thing* ("mono") *to wear* ("kiru"). Once, kimonos were the common dress of most Japanese. Today they are worn mostly for ceremonial occasions.

To the Western eye, all kimonos look very similar. However, the Japanese recognize some very subtle, but important, differences:

- Colors are chosen to blend with the seasons. For example, accepted kimono colors for the months from November to February are referred to as *ume-gasane*, or "shades of the plum blossom."

- The design of the fabric is important, too. A kimono with a cherry blossom design would not be worn in the fall or winter. It would only be appropriate to wear it in the spring, when the cherry blossoms are in full bloom.

- In contrast to Western-style clothes, all kimonos have the same basic shape. They also are a standard size that can be worn by any man or woman, regardless of height or weight. The person who wears the kimono uses his or her skill in wrapping and padding to create its form and adjust its size.

- According to Japanese tradition, you can tell if a woman is single or married by her kimono. For example, if the sleeves are wide and flowing, the wearer is single. The *obi*, or wide sash that is worn around the waist, is worn lower on the body if the wearer is married. If a woman is married, the collar opening at the back of the neck is rounded into the shape of the letter U. If she is single, it is shaped to look like the letter V.

There are two types of models. *Photography models* pose for advertisements, catalogs, and the fashion pages of newspapers and magazines. *Runway models* wear clothes in fashion shows produced by designers, manufacturers, or retailers. Some models do both runway and photography work.

Fashion photographers may work at a designer's fashion show, in a studio, or outdoors on location.

Some models do runway work in fashion shows for a live audience. Others work in the showrooms of designers or manufacturers. Photography models pose for the pictures used in catalogs and ads.

Many aspiring photographers begin with a job as an assistant to an established photographer and learn as much as they can from that person. Others pursue photography on a part-time basis until they get enough assignments to support themselves. Meanwhile, they are developing a **portfolio**, or *collection of their work* to show to prospective clients.

Photo stylists work for photography studios or advertising agencies. They book models, obtain garments and accessories, handle props, and help prepare for photo shoots. A stylist must have a good sense of color, fashion, and photography.

Fashion Model

Did you ever look at a beautiful or handsome face smiling at you from a magazine cover and think how glamorous it must be to have a job as a model? That glamorous image is the result of a lot of hard work.

Many people who have a pretty or handsome face may want to model, but it takes much more than that. A photography model must photograph well. All models must have a certain type of figure or body shape and must wear clothes well. A runway model must have the type of posture and graceful walk that makes clothes look attractive as the model moves.

Models must have plenty of stamina. They may spend hours in front of a camera, often under hot lights, or be required to change clothes very quickly many times during a fashion show. Models must also have a certain talent for acting. If a photographer is shooting bathing suits on a cold beach in January, the models must be able to make you believe that it is a warm and sunny July day!

Above all, models must have the certain "look" that advertisers and fashion editors want. This "look" could be athletic, or sophisticated, or romantic, or youthful. This "look" can change from season to season.

The largest modeling agencies are located in New York, Chicago, and Los Angeles. They are constantly on the lookout for new talent. Other agencies in smaller cities are looking for models for local photography or fashion shows.

There is a lot of competition for modeling jobs. Even the most successful models usually last only a few years. Either younger or better looking models come along, or their special "look" is no longer needed.

Careers in Fashion Publicity

Fashion advertising in magazines, in newspapers, on radio, and on television must be paid for by the advertiser. **Publicity** is *any information that brings attention to someone, something, or some event.* It is usually gained free of charge. Publicity may be newspaper articles about a product or store event. It could be the showing of a designer's new collection on a television show or in a fashion magazine.

Some large companies have their own **public relations** department. This means *all of the actions used to promote goodwill with the public.* Other companies hire special public relations agencies, sometimes called PR firms, to handle these activities.

A *publicist* or PR agent prepares press kits, which are distributed to fashion writers, editors, and reporters across the country. These kits include information and photos about a company's product or a designer's collection. The company hopes the writers will include the information and photos in their articles.

Public relations agencies also hold press conferences for fashion editors and writers. These may be elaborate parties or shows that promote a new collection, product, or service. The goal is to get as much publicity as possible through various news media.

Publicists need lots of imagination and creativity, plus excellent communication skills. Most have a degree from a two- or four-year college.

Public relations agents use many methods to promote a product or a service.

Careers in Education

When you think of a career in education, you probably think of the teachers in your school. However, there are many others. You could be a college professor, an adult education teacher, a teacher at a sewing school, or an extension agent. You might also work for a museum or university as a costume historian or textile restorer.

The requirements and responsibilities of each of these careers are different. However, they all share several common traits. An educator should know the subject thoroughly, have a desire to share that knowledge, and be an effective communicator.

Teacher

Have you ever thought about how your teachers became teachers? They have a degree from a college or university. They have taken education courses in order to be certified as a teacher. That means that they have a teaching license. **Certification**, or *official approval*, is required for teachers in all public schools and most private schools. Teachers in many states take courses every five years to renew their certification. In some states, teachers must take competency examinations.

Fashion and clothing courses in high school are taught by a *family and consumer sciences teacher*. At one time, clothing courses focused only on sewing techniques. Today, they usually cover a wide variety of topics, such as clothing needs, fashion, color and design, clothing selection, fibers and fabrics, clothing care, and careers. Some middle school programs also include information about fashion, fabrics, and construction.

Vocational training provides *instruction in a particular occupation*. It teaches you a skill or group of skills that will prepare you to get a job in a particular field. You might take a vocational course in industrial sewing or apparel production. A vocational school might offer courses in textile design, pattern making, draping, fashion illustration, or computer programming.

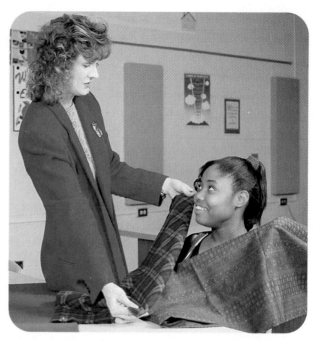

A classroom teacher can work at a middle school, high school, vocational school, college, or university.

A *vocational teacher* often has some work experience in the industry. In most states, the teacher is expected to have a college degree or a vocational certificate offered through state universities.

In order to teach on the college level, you must have both an undergraduate degree from a four-year college and a graduate degree. A *college professor* is a teacher who has done additional, specialized research or study in a chosen field and has received a master's or doctor's degree. In addition to teaching clothing, textiles, or fashion merchandising classes, college professors are expected to do research and write articles for scholarly publications.

Adult education courses are taught in the evenings at the local high school, adult education center, or community college. They focus on topics such as color selection, clothing construction, or sewing crafts. Teaching adult education can be a lot of fun. Students take the courses because they are interested in the subject and really want to learn.

An *adult education teacher* usually is someone who has a great deal of knowledge, skill, and experience in a particular field. A college degree is usually not required. Most jobs are only part-time.

Fabric and sewing machine stores may sponsor their own sewing classes. A *sewing class teacher* can teach courses in one store or in several different stores. Sometimes the teacher conducts a series of classes taught over several weeks. The classes may be on a subject such as serging techniques. At other times, he or she may teach a short one- or two-hour **seminar**, or *workshop*. It usually is on a very specific topic, such as "Fitting Pants."

A sewing class teacher must be a highly skilled sewer and be able to communicate those skills to other people. It is not necessary to have a college degree. The teacher may be paid according to the number of students or the number of hours spent teaching.

County extension agents work with 4-H groups. These teens are learning sewing skills so they can make some new garments for their wardrobes.

Extension Agent and Specialist

The U.S. Department of Agriculture has a division called the Cooperative Extension Service. It has state offices in every state and local agents in almost every county. The *county extension agents* develop information on a wide variety of topics, such as nutrition, housing, agriculture, and clothing. They write material for leaflets and newspapers. They work with 4-H and other youth groups, homemaker groups, and other local organizations. They may have their own radio or television program. Many county extension agents have degrees in family and consumer sciences.

Almost every state has an *extension clothing specialist*, who is affiliated with the state's land-grant university. The extension clothing specialist develops a wide variety of programs on textile and clothing topics and trains county extension agents. In addition, the extension clothing specialist prepares bulletins and pamphlets, conducts workshops, and may teach college courses and do consumer research.

The requirements to become a state clothing specialist are the same as for college educators. Some business or teaching experience may be considered an asset.

Consumer Education Specialist

There is often much more to be learned about a product and its uses than can be included in the copy for an advertisement, a catalog page, or a hangtag. Many companies employ *consumer education specialists* to teach people, in an informal way, about the product. Fiber and fabric companies, apparel manufacturers, pattern companies, sewing machine and sewing equipment manufacturers, and some large retail chains employ consumer education specialists.

A career as a *consumer education specialist* includes a wide range of responsibilities. A pamphlet on clothing care, a letter from a pattern company, and a quilting demonstration in a store may be the work of a consumer education specialist. A specialist may represent his or her company at trade shows, speak at meetings and conventions, and help train sales staff. Some specialists make radio and television appearances.

Consumer education specialists pay attention to what consumers are saying and report back to management. The specialists can often spot a problem or identify customer's needs that are not being met. This information helps the company develop or sell new products.

Consumer education specialists must have a college degree, preferably in family and consumer sciences, and good communication skills. He or she should be able to write well, speak effectively, and have a pleasing appearance. Courses in consumerism, public speaking, and journalism are helpful.

Costume Historian and Textile Restorer

A *costume historian* learns about the history of societies and cultures by studying the clothing worn by its members. A *textile restorer* repairs and reconstructs damaged textiles that have historic or artistic value. The historian and restorer may work closely together on projects.

A costume historian might work for a museum or a university as the **curator,** or *person in charge of a collection.* A costume historian might also work for a historical preservation society such as Colonial Williamsburg. He or she selects clothing items that are historically accurate, helps keep them in good condition, and locates additional items for the collection.

A textile restorer cleans, mends, and reconstructs items such as tapestries, historic costumes, or intricate handmade laces and trims. A museum, university, or historical society might employ a textile restorer full-time or just for a particular project. Textile restorers also work for fabric companies that specialize in restoration work. These companies work with clients all over the world.

In order to become a costume historian or a textile restorer, a college degree is required. A master's degree or some specialized coursework is also necessary. Courses should include art, history, sociology, textile science, fabric construction, and clothing construction.

A consumer education specialist often gives product demonstrations at workshops, conventions, and trade shows.

This costume historian is selecting clothing for a special exhibit in a local museum.

Jobs in Fashion Promotion and Education

Account Executive	Fashion Writer	College Professor
Creative Director	Fashion Illustrator	Adult Education Teacher
Art Director	Fashion Photographer	Sewing Class Teacher
Promotion Director	Photo Stylist	County Extension Agent
Fashion Promotion Specialist	Photography Model	Extension Clothing Specialist
Advertising Copywriter	Runway Model	Consumer Education Specialist
Catalog Copywriter	Family and Consumer Sciences Teacher	Costume Historian
Fashion Reporter	Vocational Teacher	Textile Restorer
Fashion Editor		

REVIEW

Summary

- Fashion promotion includes all the activities conducted by a manufacturer, retailer, advertising agency, or fashion publication to get the public interested in a fashion product or service.

- Careers in fashion communication include fashion writer, editor, illustrator, photographer, and model.

- Companies use public relations departments or agencies to develop publicity about their products or events.

- Teachers, extension agents, and consumer education specialists help educate the public.

- Costume historians and textile restorers help people learn about clothing of the past.

Using Vocabulary Terms

On a separate piece of paper, write the vocabulary term that best fits the definition:

1. All the actions used to promote goodwill with the public.

2. The words and sentences used in advertising or catalogs.

3. Person in charge of a collection.

4. Instruction in a particular occupation.

5. A collection of work to show to prospective clients.

6. Customer.

Recalling the Facts

1. List at least six methods that can be used to promote a product.

2. What is the role of an account executive in an advertising agency?

3. What people may work as a team in an advertising agency to develop an ad? What skills do they need?

4. What is the role of a promotion director at a fashion magazine or a store?

5. Name two talents that a fashion writer should have.

6. What training is needed for a career in fashion illustration or photography?

7. What are some of the demands that make modeling such hard work?

8. Name at least four places where a person could teach a fashion or clothing course.

9. What is the role of a county extension agent?

10. What two jobs require an interest in history?

Thinking Critically

1. **Evaluation.** Why do you think fashion illustrators draw in a stylized manner? What effect does this have on the consumer?

2. **Analysis.** How might being bi-lingual and knowledgeable of other cultures be helpful in fashion promotion careers?

3. **Evaluation.** Some fashion models have become famous personalities in our society. Why do you think this has happened?

4. **Synthesis.** Give an example of a situation that could embarrass a company if a consumer education specialist did not spot it and report it to management.

Applying Your Knowledge

1. **Fashion Ad.** Create an ad for a fashion product or service. Write the copy and illustrate it with a drawing or photograph.

2. **Fashion Magazines.** Look through fashion magazines for ads and promotional articles. Analyze them for appeal and information provided. Which ones do you like best? Why?

3. **Education Courses.** Obtain a listing of the fashion and clothing courses offered in your area. Contact the vocational school, community college, adult education program, county extension office, and fabric stores.

4. **Interviews.** Interview two teachers at your school. Ask what they like and dislike about the teaching profession. What type of degrees and certification do they have? How did they become interested in the profession? Summarize your interviews in a report.

Making the Connection

1. **Language Arts.** Read *Women's Wear Daily* for one or two weeks to identify current fashion trends. Then write a "Fashion Trend" report.

What Is an Educator?

Educators are involved in teaching and training others. They are considered specialists in educational methods, theories, and problems. They work at all levels of education. Educators have an indepth knowledge of their field. As teachers, they are able to communicate that knowledge to others.

Try It Yourself

Imagine that you are a teacher. Plan a clothing or sewing lesson to teach to middle school students. Prepare a lesson plan, stating the objectives you want to achieve. Outline the teaching strategies you will use, such as discussions, demonstrations, questions, and hands-on activities. Develop some illustrations or samples to show the students. Be sure to plan an interesting way to begin and end the lesson. Decide how you could measure the performance or achievement of the students. If possible, teach your lesson to a small group of classmates or middle school students.

 ### Build Your Portfolio

Place a copy of your lesson plan, along with the illustrations and samples, in your portfolio. If you were able to actually teach a group of "students," write an essay about your teaching experience. Add it to your portfolio.

2. **Communications.** Working in small groups, create a fashion video using live action, still photos, and music. Show video to the class.

After reading this chapter, you will be able to:

- *Identify the types of businesses that entrepreneurs have.*

- *Describe management techniques used by small businesses.*

- *Explain the steps involved in merchandising and marketing a product or a service.*

- *Discuss the advantages and disadvantages of being an entrepreneur.*

Terms to Learn

- *entrepreneur*
- *profit*
- *distributor*
- *freelance*
- *mail-order*
- *direct mail*
- *target audience*
- *spreadsheet*
- *regulations*
- *self-motivated*

graphic artist, a sewing school teacher, a fashion photographer, and a copywriter are all examples of people who might be self-employed. This means that they work for themselves. They sell a product (photographs or fashion layouts) or a service(teaching sewing or writing ads) to many different customers.

Some people who are self-employed own a store or sell items that are manufactured by other people. Others make their own line of products or run a mail-order business.

There are both benefits and risks to owning and managing your own business. For many people, their life-long dream is to become an entrepreneur.

Types of Businesses

An **entrepreneur** (AHN-trah-prah-NUR) is a *person who organizes and manages his or her own business.* If there are any risks—such as not making enough money to cover costs—the entrepreneur must take the responsibility. On the positive side, the entrepreneur gets to keep any **profit**. This is *the amount of money left over after all of the expenses have been paid.*

A person who is in business for himself or herself can have almost any type of business. Many entrepreneurial businesses are small businesses. They may be so small that the owner is the only employee or so large that the owner employs many people. Just remember that every large business started as a small business!

Every business sells something. What you sell could be an item that you make, or it could be a service that you perform. How you conduct your business depends on the size and the type of business you have.

The owner of this small business helps customers select yarns and needlework supplies. She also teaches classes on knitting, embroidery, and needlepoint.

Small Business with a Store or Office

Many small businesses, in particular those selling goods and services provided by other people, are located in a store or an office. Your goal might be to own a laundry, a gift shop that sells handcrafted items, or be a **distributor** of fabrics or sewing supplies. This is a *person or firm who sells a line of merchandise within a given territory.*

Some other examples of stores include a boutique, a fabric store, an alterations and repair shop, a yarn and needlework store, and a store that specializes in recycled clothing. An office might be needed for a service that employs several people, such as a design office or a mail-order business.

The entrepreneur who begins this type of business must be prepared to put in long hours at the store or office, particularly when the business is just beginning. A new store usually requires the constant attention of its owner. It often takes time for the owner to find and train a store manager that he or she has complete confidence in.

In-Home Business

Many successful entrepreneurs began their businesses in their homes. Some people work out of an extra room or their basement. Others work at a corner of their kitchen or dining room table. The home workspace could be a desk with a computer. If you always meet your clients or customers in their office, you may need only enough space to keep records, write reports, and make telephone calls in your home.

Many sewing alterations and custom dressmaking businesses can be conducted successfully from the home. You would need space for your sewing machine and sewing equipment and a place where customers can try on their garments.

402

A wardrobe consultant who meets with clients at their homes or at a store might maintain office space at home. A cosmetic representative or fabric representative who sells through visits or parties at other people's homes would need at-home office space. A fashion illustrator or copywriter might also choose to work at home, since he or she usually meets clients at their offices.

Many people who work at home do **freelance** work. This means *selling work or services without receiving a regular salary from one employer*. Many writers, artists, and consultants are freelancers. They are hired by companies to do special projects such as illustrations, articles, books, or reports. They may be paid by the hour or by the project.

Many parents with small children like to work at home. This arrangement lets the parent be near the child while still earning a salary. It solves any child care problems if a child gets sick. It also provides the flexibility in working hours that families with small children often need.

This woman has her own custom dressmaking and alterations business. She has set up a worktable, sewing machine, ironing board, and fitting area in one room of her home.

TECHNOLOGY

Creating a Home Office

Some home offices are equipped with the latest technology—a computer, printer, modem, photocopier, and fax machine. Others have only a table or desk. No matter how elaborate or simple, an office should be well organized.

- **Desk or other work surface.** It should be large enough to meet your needs. A desk does not have to be new, expensive, or even a real desk. Two small file cabinets with a board or door across the top provides a good work surface and space for storage.

- **Comfortable chair.** It should provide good back support. If you need to move between a desk and a computer station, consider a chair with wheels. You will also need a comfortable chair for any clients.

- **Good lighting.** It is very important to be able to see what you are doing. Position a computer monitor so overhead lights, lamps, and sunlight from nearby windows do not create glare on the screen. Clamp a small lamp in place above a sewing machine. It will provide extra light and won't get in the way when you sew.

- **Storage.** Think creatively. Storage can be anything from an extra closet to file cabinets to book shelves. Cardboard boxes can be painted or covered with fabric. For small items, use containers with lids. For example, paper clips, beads, or drawing pencils can be stored in plastic margarine containers or tennis ball tubes.

- **Walls.** Use the walls to display and store frequently used items. A bulletin board will display messages, important phone numbers, and notes. Cup hooks and mug racks can hold scissors and tape measures.

403

Some people, however, find that working at home is difficult. There can be many distractions. Small children may interrupt frequently, even when there is someone else to supervise them. Friends may call to chat. It takes self-discipline to work at home.

The successful home-based entrepreneur will not be distracted by household chores that need to be done or by an invitation to go shopping. Working at home can also be lonely. Some people prefer working and sharing ideas with others in a workplace setting.

Small Manufacturer

Many small manufacturing businesses begin as an at-home operation. If the business grows, the owner could decide to move into a separate factory or workroom.

Different types of products can be manufactured at home. These include accessories such as scarves, hats, belts, and children's clothing and toys. Items for the home, such as pillows, wallhangings, picture frames, and quilts, are other successful products.

You do not need to make the entire item. You might decorate, customize, or personalize a product that someone else manufactures. You might make craft kits that the customer finishes.

There are many different ways to sell products, whether they are manufactured at home or in a factory. One way is to manufacture a quantity of the item and have stores sell it for you. You sell the items to the stores at a wholesale price, the price a retailer pays a manufacturer. The store now owns the items and can sell them at any retail price it wishes.

Another method is to sell the items on consignment. The store will display the items but will not pay you for them until the items are sold. After the items are sold, the store owner and the manufacturer each get a percentage of the price. If the items do not sell, the manufacturer does not make any money and must take back the goods. Crafts and special one-of-a-kind garments are often sold on consignment.

Craft fairs are another way to sell products. Many organizations sponsor these fairs. Sometimes you pay a fee for your booth and keep all of the profits you earn. At other times, you give the organization that runs the fair a percentage of your sales. Some retailers attend craft fairs to find new and unusual items to carry in their stores.

Mail-Order Business

Suppose you have designed and made a special line of bibs for babies. Instead of selling the bibs through local stores, you might advertise in magazines that are read by the parents of new infants. You could keep a small inventory of bibs on hand and make more as you receive orders.

This entrepreneur sells her handcrafted clothing and accessories at local craft shows and fairs.

A mail-order business can send direct mail pieces, such as a brochure or a catalog, to potential customers.

A growing business requires careful record keeping, inventory control, and cost analysis. This entrepreneur keeps his financial records on his computer.

A **mail-order** business is one that *takes orders and ships goods through the mail*. Many mail-order businesses send out **direct mail** pieces, which are *advertising matter sent to large numbers of people*. A direct mail piece can be anything from an elaborate catalog to a simple letter with a sketch of the item. One of the advantages of direct mail is that you can send information to a **target audience**, *a very specific group of potential customers*.

Suppose you designed and made a special knapsack for bikers. If you obtained a list of all of the people in your area who belong to a bicycle club, you could mail information directly to them. There are companies that sell or rent such lists to mail-order businesses.

Small Business Management Techniques

In order to be a successful entrepreneur, you must learn to do more than create a product or offer a service. You must learn how to manage your business.

Good recordkeeping is essential to a well-run business. A personal computer is very helpful for keeping accurate financial records. A **spreadsheet**, *a specialized software program used for financial planning*, simplifies the task.

You must know what your costs are in order to set your prices and make a profit. Some costs, such as rent, the price of materials, and the cost of advertising, are easy to determine. Other costs, such as the time you put into the business, are more difficult to determine. Every entrepreneur should include his or her personal salary as part of the cost to run a business.

Entrepreneurs must also abide by local, state, and federal **regulations**, or *laws*. You can get this information from the local county clerk's office, the town's building inspector, and the local department of public health.

As a business grows, it is not necessary for the owner to do all of the recordkeeping. Many entrepreneurs hire an accountant, and sometimes a lawyer, to work for them for a fee. These fees become part of the entrepreneur's costs to run the business.

Regulations

- **Protecting your business name.** If you do business under a name other than your own, you should protect it by registering it. You can register the name in your county and your state. Then no one else can call their business by the same name as you do.

- **Labeling.** Both large and small manufacturers must comply with government regulations regarding product labeling. Garment labels must include information such as fiber content and care requirements.

- **Sales tax.** Many states have a sales tax on certain items. If you sell any of these items directly to the public, you must collect the sales tax from your customers and pay it to the state. This must be done whether the product is sold by mail order, at a craft fair, or through your own store.

- **Licenses.** If you are planning to manufacture certain products or provide certain services, you may be required to purchase a license. For example, in some states you need a license to make and sell certain kinds of stuffed items, such as toys and quilts.

- **Zoning laws.** People cannot decide to build a dry cleaning store any place they want, or to set up a manufacturing operation in the basement of a house. Most communities have zoning laws that set aside certain areas as *commercial areas* for businesses, and others as *residential areas* for houses and apartments. There are even zoning laws that restrict some areas to certain types of businesses or certain types of housing.

Often a person who is very creative will go into business with a partner who is business-oriented. Each person can handle the parts of the business that match his or her talents. The creative person might design the product, write the advertising, and handle the public relations. The business-oriented person might keep records, set prices, and work with the wholesalers, retailers, and sales representatives.

Merchandising

The product or service you sell and the way you merchandise it is very important to the success of your business. Merchandising includes all of the decisions that go into the selling of a product. These decisions include what you will sell, how you will produce it, where you will sell it, and what price you will charge.

Market Research

Have you ever heard the expression "an idea whose time has come"? Market research will help you decide if the time and place are right for your idea.

Large companies spend many thousands of dollars on market research. They conduct elaborate consumer surveys. They keep sophisticated records of their own sales and their competitors' sales. They are continuously looking for a consumer need that is not being filled. In contrast, a small business usually does not have thousands of dollars to spend on market research.

If you are thinking about starting a business, do the necessary research. Find out if there is a need for your product. Is your idea one that everyone could use or would it be of interest to only a very special market? How would you reach that special market? Talk to some of the people who might be your potential customers.

Determine who the competition is and how much it charges. Look in the Yellow Pages of the telephone directory. Check the advertisements in the local newspaper. Visit area stores to find out how much they are charging for similar items or services.

If you are thinking of designing and making a special item, you could visit local craft fairs to see what items sell best. Are people buying items for children, for the home, or for themselves? Are they most interested in items that are knitted, crocheted, quilted, beaded, or handsewn? Are people willing to pay what you would have to charge in order to make a profit?

Think about how the product or service you offer might be just a little bit different from the ones already on the market. Will it be less expensive, personalized, of better quality?

Production

Another important decision is how you will produce your product. Are you going to produce one-of-a-kind originals or many copies of the same item? Because it takes longer to produce each individual item, one-of-a-kind products are usually more expensive than mass-produced items.

Do you have enough time to personally make every item you are going to sell? Do you need to have a group of people to work with you? To help you decide, you could determine how long it takes you to complete one item and how many hours a week you can devote to it. Then divide the number of hours by the time it takes for each item. That will tell you how many items you can complete each week before you need to hire someone else.

Perhaps you have designed a very special pillow. Several stores have given you very large orders. How will you meet their delivery date? You could try to produce them yourself or you could get a group of friends together to help you mass-produce them. A group working on an assembly line can produce many more pillows than if each person did one pillow from start to finish.

Here is how the assembly line might work: You could choose the fabric and the colors. Another person could cut out the pillows. The next person could sew the seams. A fourth person could clip the corners, trim the curves, and turn the pillows right side out. A fifth person would stuff the pillows, and a sixth person could handstitch them closed.

In order to determine production costs, you will need to know how much you will pay for raw materials. These are items such as fabric, thread, zippers, yarn, needles, beads, and other trimming. You also will need to determine how much you will pay yourself or someone else to produce the item.

Then you will have to decide what you are going to do about packaging and shipping the product. Will it need labels? Will it need hangtags? Will it need a special package or wrapper? Even if you are selling at craft fairs, you will probably find that people expect some kind of bag in which to put their purchases. All of these expenses go into the total cost of producing a product.

Quality Control

It is very important, particularly in a new business, to maintain standards of quality. You do not want a reputation as a person who sometimes does shoddy work or sells inferior merchandise. Customers expect a certain level of quality. If you disappoint them, the result will be no more business.

Many new businesses fail because they expand too rapidly. In order to meet the demand for their product, they sacrifice quality for quantity. Sometimes it is better to limit the amount you produce or the number of customers you handle until you have carefully examined ways to expand your business.

This entrepreneur personalizes items for customers by embroidering monograms or unique designs on the fabrics.

Marketing

Marketing is concerned with all of the ways to advertise, promote, and distribute a product. Some businesses use only one method, such as direct mail, to market a product. Others use a combination of techniques, such as selling some items on consignment, some at craft fairs, and some through ads in carefully selected publications.

Selling

Many entrepreneurs act as their own salesperson. Some entrepreneurs do not have time to call on customers, so they hire someone else to do the selling. Other entrepreneurs use the services of an independent sales representative. The sales rep carries a variety of products from different manufacturers and calls on the types of stores that would sell the products.

Freelance photographers and artists often use agents to get work for them. This leaves the photographer or artist free to create. The agent makes money by receiving a commission on every job. Many modeling jobs are also booked through agents.

A dressmaker might advertise for customers and also have people referred by the local fabric store. An alterations expert might develop a business arrangement with a specialty clothing store and still maintain his or her own customers.

Advertising and Promotion

Advertising is used to attract customers. It should be purchased carefully to get the most orders for the cost. Many communities have newspapers, directories, bulletin boards, and direct mail services that offer reasonable rates for local advertising.

Promotion is a form of advertising that you do not pay for. The local newspaper could write an article about your business, or an organization might mention your business in its newsletter. A store referring its customers to you also is promotion. Promotion is particularly important for a new business that does not have a large advertising budget.

Advertising and promotion should be an important part of any business. You want to let people know that you exist. You want to inform not only potential customers but also those who can help you spread the word to other potential customers.

Success as an Entrepreneur

Becoming an entrepreneur may seem like a very attractive idea. If you are looking for a very small business that will help you earn extra money, it can be fairly easy to start one. If you are looking for a business that will support you full-time, that is much harder. More than 90 percent of the small businesses that are started each year do not succeed. That is because people do not do their homework. It is important that you learn all you possibly can about a business before going into it full-time.

Develop the skills you need to run a business: decision making, recordkeeping, marketing, production, computer technology, and management. Learn about taxes, advertising, insurance, licensing, and zoning regulations. Start small, maintain

When you own your own business, you must promote your skills or products to potential customers. This photographer is showing his portfolio to an art director at an advertising agency.

control, build a reputation—then expand. Most businesses fail because of bad management, not because of bad ideas.

There are many organizations that will give you advice and assistance. The Small Business Administration and the local Chamber of Commerce are just a few of them.

Advantages and Disadvantages

There are many advantages and disadvantages to being an entrepreneur. You should examine them carefully to decide if this is the career path for you.

For most people, the major advantage is that you are your own boss. No one tells you what to do, how to do it, or what hours to keep. You are the one who makes the decisions. You must, however, be the type of person who is **self-motivated**. This means that you *do not need direction from other people in order to work and do a good job.*

Another advantage is the satisfaction that comes from developing a product or a service that people want or need. Entrepreneurship also provides the opportunity to take risks. For many people, this means a feeling of excitement that might not come from working for someone else. Another major advantage is that you will be financially rewarded if you are successful.

The disadvantages of being in business for yourself include an uncertain income. You cannot depend on a regular salary to pay your expenses.

You will need money for start-up expenses. If the money does not come from savings, you will have to take out a loan. Then you will have to pay interest charges, in addition to other expenses. You must be prepared for unexpected events and emergencies. If you get sick, who will run the business and how will you pay your bills?

Another disadvantage is that most entrepreneurs work longer hours than people who work for someone else. This is particularly true when the business is just getting started. In addition, there is always the risk of failure.

This couple own their own business. They enjoy the many challenges and rewards of designing, producing, and selling their own line of clothing.

Know Yourself

Before you decide to become an entrepreneur, ask yourself some questions:

• Do I get along well with other people? (If your answer is "no," stay away from service-oriented businesses.)

• Do I have initiative?

• Do I have self-confidence?

• Am I willing to take risks?

• Can I handle stress and pressure?

• Why am I going into business? Is it for fun, for profit, or for self-fulfillment?

Evaluate your talents and skills as well as your goals and ambitions. Start with a product or skill that you already know and do well. You can always expand your business to include other products or services as you develop additional skills.

As an entrepreneur, you are the one making the decisions. As a result, you get to take all of the credit when things go well. You also get to take all of the blame when things go wrong. All of the joys, problems, and decisions belong to you alone.

Summary

- An entrepreneur can have a business in a store, office, factory, workshop, or at home.

- Products can be sold to stores at wholesale or placed on consignment. They also can be sold at craft fairs or by mail order.

- Good recordkeeping is essential for managing costs and profits.

- Both large and small businesses must comply with many regulations.

- Entrepreneurs must decide what to sell, how to produce it, where to sell it, and how to advertise and promote it.

- There are both advantages and disadvantages to running your own business.

Using Vocabulary Terms

On a separate piece of paper, write the vocabulary term that best fits the definition:

1. Selling work or services without receiving a regular salary from one employer.

2. A specialized software program used for financial planning.

3. A person who organizes and manages his or her own business.

4. Advertising matter sent to large number of people.

5. Not needing direction from other people in order to work and do a good job.

6. Amount of money left over after all the expenses have been paid.

Recalling the Facts

1. List at least five examples of businesses that could be started by an entrepreneur.

2. What are four fashion-related businesses that could be operated in a private home?

3. In a mail-order business, how can potential customers be reached?

4. What are at least three expenses that must be paid before a business makes a profit?

5. Name five regulations that may affect a small business.

6. What is market research?

7. Why is quality control so important to business success?

8. What is the difference between advertising and promotion?

9. Why do most businesses fail?

10. What are the advantages and disadvantages of being an entrepreneur?

Thinking Critically

1. **Analysis.** Compare running a business in your home to having it in a separate location. What are the advantages and disadvantages of each?

2. **Evaluation.** Do you think you have the interest and skills to be an entrepreneur? Why or why not?

3. **Evaluation.** If you were to start your own business, what would you like to do?

4. **Synthesis.** Using the information in the chapter, write a plan for what you should do before starting a small business.

Applying Your Knowledge

1. **Work and Family.** List ways that a person with an in-home business could successfully manage work and family responsibilities.

2. **Business Management.** Working in small groups, select a textile product that could be made and sold at your school. Estimate the cost of materials, marketing and other expenses. Determine a selling price for the product in order to produce a profit.

3. **Market Research.** Think of a product or service that you could produce. Research your community to see if there is a potential market. Is there any competition? If so, how could your product or service be different? Share your research with the class.

Making the Connection

1. **Business Education.** Use a computer software program for business procedures. Work with a spreadsheet, a database, or with graphics in the processing of information.

What Is a Small Business Owner?

Owners of small businesses sell many types of goods and services. The business may be located in a store or an office. For example, a small store owner might sell children's clothes, jewelry, fabrics, or craft items. Other store owners provide services, such as dry cleaning, shoe repair, or alterations. The owner of a mail-order business might need office space for a few employees. All of these small business owners are considered entrepreneurs.

Try It Yourself

Imagine that you want to open a small store in your town. Using the chapter information, decide what you will sell, where your store will be located, how you will advertise and promote your store, and whether you will need to hire any employees. Research what local and state regulations you would have to meet before you could open your store. Write an ad or publicity release about your "Grand Opening" that could be published in the local newspaper.

Build Your Portfolio

After completing your research, write an essay about how you would establish and operate a small business. Place a copy in your portfolio, along with your ad or publicity release about the store's "Grand Opening."

2. **Language Arts.** Brainstorm a service that teens might be able to provide in your community. Create a flyer promoting the new business that could be distributed in the community.

Finding the Job for You

After reading this chapter, you will be able to:

- *Evaluate your talents, interests, and skills.*

- *Identify the education and training needed for various career paths.*

- *Describe the process of finding a job.*

- *List characteristics that help on-the-job success.*

Terms to Learn

- *apprenticeship program*
- *application form*
- *references*
- *resumé*
- *cover letter*
- *job interview*
- *reliable*
- *punctual*
- *courteous*
- *flexible*

High school is the time to explore your own interests and talents. Careers that may have interested you in the past do not always match the skills you are developing now. There may be careers that you have not even discovered yet that would suit you perfectly.

Vocational courses and part-time jobs can help you learn more about different career clusters and career paths. This information can help you as you decide whether you will need additional education or training after high school.

No matter what your future career may be, it is important to develop the school-to-work skills that are necessary for job success. These are skills you can start developing now—and use in whatever career you choose.

Know Yourself

The first step in finding a job that fits you is to find out who you are and what interests you. Take the time to really think about the classes you take. What subjects do you do well in? What subjects are difficult for you? Are there some classes you enjoy even though you must work hard?

Think about how you spend your leisure time. What activities are satisfying to you? Do you like group activities or activities you do alone? Do you get along with all types of people?

What talents do you have? Can you sew? Do you take great photographs? Have you decorated your room in a unique and attractive way? Did you sell the most boxes of cookies or candy for your school or scout troop? Perhaps you have a special gift for selling. Remember that no one is "average" in everything. There are always some things you do very well.

Develop Your Interests and Skills

After you have identified some of your interests and skills, you can begin to develop them. Suppose you are interested in fashion and you like to draw. It would be a good idea to take as many art and clothing courses as you can. Begin with the courses offered in your school.

Next, find out if any fabric stores or art museums in your area offer special courses on Saturdays or after school. Visit art exhibits and read about these subjects. Learn as much as you can about line, design, and color. Where could this lead you? Fashion illustrator, costume historian, fashion designer, and fashion coordinator are just a few of the jobs that require knowledge of clothing and art.

Think about other high school courses. The skills you develop in math, science, and language arts can help you perform better in any job. For example, all employees need good communication skills to communicate with customers, employees, or coworkers. Computer skills are needed by employees at every level. Decision making, critical thinking, and problem solving are important job skills that can

The skills you learn in school, such as communication skills, will make you a more successful employee in the workplace.

be learned in school. See School-to-Work Skills on page 415.

After-school activities also help you learn and grow. If you are interested in writing, volunteer to work on the school paper or yearbook staff. Many people, at some point in their careers, have to make presentations to a group. It could be a small group of workers or a large group of consumers. Any experience you can get in front of an audience, such as debating or acting in the school play, will help you later.

Get Part-Time Experience

Part-time jobs can give you a taste of what it is like to work full-time in a particular field. If you think you might like a career in retailing, get a part-time or summer job as a salesperson or stock clerk. You will learn how a store functions, as well as the rewards and challenges of running a store. You will have the opportunity to learn something about the type of people who choose careers in retailing.

If you want a career in communications, you might try to get a part-time job at the local newspaper. If you would like to become a designer, think about working for a local manufacturer or tailor to learn about clothing design and construction.

Remember that volunteer work can be just as valuable a source of experience as a job that pays a salary. Think about being a guide at a local art museum, teaching younger children how to sew, or helping a charity with its benefit fashion show.

These experiences can help you learn firsthand what it would be like to work in a particular job on a day-to-day basis. You can talk to fellow workers about their responsibilities. You can observe the advantages and disadvantages of certain careers and compare them with your own likes and dislikes. You may discover that a job which appears to be very glamorous is actually filled with routine tasks and long hours.

Talk to Others

Learn as much as you can about jobs that interest you. Talk to relatives, friends, neighbors, and people in your community. What does the person do on an average day? How long are the hours? Is it a standard eight-hours-a-day job or does the person work weekends, evenings, and overtime? Does the job require traveling? Are the trips long or short, frequent or occasional, in the United States or abroad? Where will you find opportunities in this field?

Evaluate what you see and hear. Ask yourself these questions:

School-to-Work Skills

Here are some valuable skills that employers seek in potential employees. You can learn these skills while you are still in high school. In what courses have you already learned some of these skills? Which skills do you need to further develop?

decision making	reading and writing
critical thinking	listening and speaking
problem solving	technology
goal setting	management
math applications	leadership
science applications	teamwork

Working part time as a salesperson or stock clerk will help you decide whether you want a merchandising career.

- Would this type of job be satisfying to me?
- What talents do I have that this job requires?
- Could I do it well?
- What education or training would I need?

Research Career Paths

Finding just the right job can be fun, but you must do some research to be successful. Make an appointment to see your school's guidance counselor. Besides giving you some good advice, your counselor may be able to give you tests to help identify your special skills and interests. Some schools have interactive software programs that students can use to discover their own values, skills, and interests. Students can also access specific information about courses and technical programs.

Your research should help you identify various career clusters and the paths to take to reach specific career levels. It should include the education, training, and skills needed for various careers.

Some schools have interactive software programs that students can go through to learn about their own interests and skills.

Education and Training

Many jobs require special training. Some jobs, such as a salesperson or factory worker, require only a high school education. Additional training is given on-the-job by the employer. If this *on-the-job training is part of a formal program*, it is often called an **apprenticeship program**.

Various jobs require a degree from a vocational school, a junior college, or a four-year college. For example, becoming a pattern maker or textile machine technician requires some vocational school training. A general college degree is usually needed to

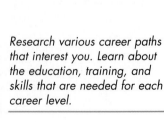

Research various career paths that interest you. Learn about the education, training, and skills that are needed for each career level.

become a copywriter, retail merchandise manager, or public relations specialist. A college degree with specialization in a certain subject is required for a teacher, textile chemist, or plant engineer.

If you are interested in a particular type of job, do some research. For example, talk to a counselor at a vocational school or community college about career paths. Ask where some of their graduates are employed. Also ask what type of job-finding assistance the school offers its graduates.

Many states have special tech-prep programs that link high school and community college courses. The tech-prep programs have also formed partnerships with businesses and industries in their communities. Courses are developed that help students become successful employees within those businesses and industries.

Looking for a Job

Tell everyone you know—friends, relatives, teachers, and parents of friends—that you are looking for a job. "Word of mouth" is sometimes the best way to get one.

Check the "Help Wanted" section of the classified ads in your local newspaper. Sunday is usually the day with the largest number of classified ads. Check the weekly community newspapers. Small local businesses often use these to advertise part-time job opportunities.

Read these ads very carefully, because there can be different ways to list the same job. Watch for clues that will help identify entry-level jobs. Words and phrases such as "trainee," "growth opportunity," "entry-level position," and "must have a desire to learn" are all clues. Part-time jobs may be listed in a separate section or scattered throughout the ads.

Local businesses, particularly stores and factories, often post job notices and "Help Wanted" signs. If they do not, call or write to the human resources department of the local business and ask for an interview.

Technological Skills in the Workplace

Each year, computer skills become more important in the job market. Although a few companies are willing to train new employees, job applicants who have good computer and keyboarding skills will have a big advantage over those who do not.

It is a good idea to know how to use at least one basic program in each of the following computer areas:

- **Word processing.** Anyone who has to write a letter, a report, an article, or a memo should become familiar with the basic principles of word processing.

- **Spreadsheets.** These are programs that involve any type of math calculation. Accounting procedures, inventory control, budgets, sales figures, and expense records are just a few of the ways that businesses use spreadsheet programs.

- **Data bases.** Data base programs have many uses. For example, a mail order company can keep a file on every customer. This file could include information such as where customers live, how often they order, and what they have ordered. The company could use the information in these files to create specialized mailing lists. One list might be based on where the customers live, one on what size  they wear, and another on what type of merchandise they order.

There are many ways to learn about these types of basic programs. Perhaps your school offers computer courses in these areas. Most colleges and adult education programs also offer specialized courses. If you want to specialize in computers, you could take classes at a technical school or community college after graduation.

When looking for a job, check the "Help Wanted" ads in your local newspaper. Some schools have a job board which holds listings of available jobs in the area. Local businesses often post "Help Wanted" signs in their windows.

Employment agencies are another resource for finding full-time jobs. Some agencies will want a fee or a percentage of your salary if they find you a job. Sometimes you are responsible for paying the fee, and sometimes the employer is. Be sure to find out who pays the fee before you take a job that is offered through an agency.

If you are looking for a summer job, you might register with an agency that specializes in temporary jobs. This means you work for the agency, which sends you to work as needed at different companies. One week you could be working as a receptionist in one company, the next week as a typist in another business, and the third week as a mailroom clerk in yet another company. The companies pay the agency, and the agency then pays you.

Applying for a Job

Applying for a job is not always easy. Both first-time applicants and experienced workers are usually nervous about job applications.

To contact an employer about a job, you can write, telephone, or visit the business or company. Which method works best will depend on each situation. Usually you will have to fill out some type of job application form.

Completing an Application Form

An **application form** is *a company document that records information about a person who applies for a job.* The form asks for information about you,

your education, and your work experience. It may also ask for special skills, such as using a computer.

Read the application carefully before you begin to fill it out. Be sure you understand the directions and each of the questions on the application. If you are not sure of any question, ask for assistance.

Unless your handwriting is extremely neat, you should print the information on a job application. It usually helps to bring along a list of

When you apply for a job you may be asked to fill out an application form. Read it carefully before printing the requested information about you, your education, and your work experience.

former jobs so you will have exact names and dates. Also, you will need to list the names, addresses, and telephone numbers of **references**. These are *two or three people who will give you a good recommendation.* They should not be relatives or friends. Instead, list a school official, previous employer, clergy, or life-long adult friend. Be sure to ask permission from these people before you use their names.

Writing a Resumé

A **resumé** (REZ-oo-MAY)is a *detailed summary of your education, work experience, and job-related volunteer activities.* You send or give it to the person you hope will hire you. Since it will represent you when you are not there to speak for yourself, it should be as professional-looking as possible.

A resumé must be typed and single-spaced and preferably only one page long. It should be printed on plain white, 8 x 11 inch paper. If typing is not one of your skills, ask someone to type or print it for you. The resumé should not have any spelling or grammatical errors. Proofread it yourself, and then ask someone else to read it also.

Writing a Cover Letter

Every resumé that you send to a business or company should have a **cover letter** to go with it. The cover letter is *a letter that requests a meeting, or interview, and mentions that you are enclosing your resumé.* It should be typed and, if possible, sent to the person who handles employee applications at the company. If you cannot find the name of such a person, send your letter to the company's human resources director. For smaller businesses, send it to the owner or manager.

Be sure to mention any skills or experiences that would make you particularly valuable to the company. This information is an important part of your cover letter, even if it is already in your resumé.

The Interview

After reading your application form or cover letter and resumé, a company human resources person may want to interview you. A **job interview** is *a meeting to discuss the details of the job and the qualifications of the person seeking the job.*

If you are especially interested in a job, do a little research about the company before your interview. Read the business section of your local daily newspaper. Go to your local library and ask the librarian for assistance. This background information will help you to know what questions to ask during the interview. It will also show that you are interested in the company.

A job interview is an opportunity for you to talk about your qualifications. You also can ask specific questions about the job and its responsibilities.

Points to Remember

- **Relax.** Remind yourself that if the company was not already impressed with you, it would not be giving you an interview.

- **Dress appropriately.** Be sure your clothes are clean and neatly pressed. Do not wear extreme or tightly fitted outfits. Choose colors and styles that flatter you and make you feel good. Avoid wearing too much makeup, perfume or aftershave cologne, and jewelry.

- **Be on time.** There is no excuse for being late. If you do not know where the company is, allow plenty of time to get there. If relatives or friends come with you, ask them to wait outside.

- **Greet the interviewer in a friendly manner.** If the interviewer offers to shake your hand when you meet, return the handshake with a firm grasp. Sit down only when invited to do so. Place any items you may have brought with you on the floor—not on the interviewer's desk.

- **Sit comfortably and speak clearly.** Look directly at the interviewer when talking. Avoid using slang expressions. Do not slump or fidget with your hands or hair.

- **Answer questions with more than a Yes or No.** Always try to tell something about yourself, such as: "Yes, I enjoy working with people. I've worked as a summer camp counselor for two years." Always answer questions honestly.

- **Ask questions about the position.** This shows interest on your part. For example, you might ask about the specific responsibilities of the job and opportunities for advancement.

- **Be interested and enthusiastic.** Have a positive attitude about work opportunities. Avoid criticizing former employers.

- **Thank the interviewer.** As the meeting ends, express appreciation for the time the interviewer has spent with you.

Follow Up

When you get home, type or neatly write a letter to each of the people who interviewed you. Thank them for seeing you and mention that you are very interested in working for the company. Remind them about anything that makes you particularly qualified, such as your previous jobs, your computer skills, or your interest in fashion and sewing. Sometimes the "little extras," such as a follow-up letter or telephone call, will help you get the job.

On-the-Job Success

Once you have been hired, your goals will change. Now your concern should be to do your job well. Success will make you eligible for a raise or even a promotion to a better job.

Personal Qualities

Certain personal qualities, such as the ability to get along well with other people, will help you succeed. Personal qualities are those that reflect your inner self. They influence how other people feel about you and respond to you.

Here are some personal qualities that are valued by all employers:

- **Reliable.** Being **reliable** means that you are *dependable*. The company can be sure that you will do your work. If your employer gives you a task to do, you will do it without constantly being reminded. You will do the best job you can.

- **Punctual.** You should always be at work when you are supposed to be. Being **punctual** means that you *arrive on time* and do not leave early. You don't take extra minutes for lunch or breaks. You don't socialize or loaf on the job. Time is money to your employer. If you are constantly late, you risk being fired.

- **Able to get along with people.** A good employee is friendly, cooperative, and helpful to others. One important aspect of getting along with others is being **courteous**. This means being *polite, considerate toward others, and pleasant to be around.* A person who is rude—whether to the employer, to customers, or to coworkers—is a troublemaker and will not be welcome.

- **Good communication skills.** The basic communication skills of reading, writing, and speaking are important in every job. There are always sales slips to fill out, customers to speak to, reports to write, and instructions to follow. Take the time to develop these skills while you are in school.

- **Willing to learn.** You should take an interest in your job, be willing to learn about new areas, and accept other assignments. Saying "It's not my job" will not make you very popular with your employer. Instead, develop a positive attitude. By trying to do the job better each day, you will become a more valuable employee.

- **Flexible.** Being **flexible** is *the willingness to adapt oneself to new opportunities and situations.* Employers are grateful for employees who will accept new responsibilities, adjust to new schedules, and develop new skills.

Personal qualities, such as being courteous, friendly, and helpful to others, will help you succeed on the job.

Advancement

Most businesses want to promote people who can qualify for other jobs. When you have mastered the job you are doing, find out about other jobs that interest you in the company. What skills do the people in these jobs have? Do you have these skills? If not, think about how you can develop them.

Your employer may be willing to give you on-the-job training if you are interested in more responsibilities. For example, if you are working as a stock clerk, you might want to became a salesperson. If you are a salesperson, you might want to assume some of the responsibilities of an assistant manager.

Perhaps you can take an extra course in school. Some large companies have tuition refund plans that make it possible for you to work and go to school at the same time. If the course you wish to take or the degree you wish to earn meets with the company's approval, the company will pay all or part of the cost of going to school after work.

Employers look for leadership skills in their employees. A good leader can get the job done and help others work together. Leadership skills can be learned and developed. They do not come from a job title. Activities at school and work can help you develop these skills. Learn to organize and manage tasks, listen to other people's ideas and concerns, solve conflicts, help carry out group activities or projects, and build a sense of teamwork within a group.

Leaving a Job

It is best to have another job lined up before you leave your current job. Most employers prefer to hire someone who is already working. Be sure to give your present employer reasonable notice before you resign. Two weeks is standard. Maintain good relations with your employer. He or she may be asked to provide a reference about you to potential employers.

Learn to look at each job as a stepping-stone to your career goal. Examine the job's potential to find out how it can be used to take you where you want to go in the world of work.

REVIEW

Summary

- When deciding on a career, you should consider your own interests and skills.

- You can learn about careers through part-time jobs and talking to others.

- Research career paths and identify the education, training, and skills needed for various careers.

- When looking for a job, use many different resources.

- You may need to fill out an application form or send a resumé and cover letter to obtain an interview.

- An interview is an opportunity for you to learn more about a job and for the employer to learn more about you.

- Certain personal qualities, such as being reliable and able to get along with others, can help you achieve on-the-job success.

Using Vocabulary Terms

On a separate piece of paper, write the vocabulary term that best fits the definition:

1. Polite, considerate toward others, and pleasant to be around.

2. A company document that records information about a person who applies for a job.

3. A detailed summary of your education, work experience, and job-related volunteer activities.

4. Dependable.

5. Willingness to adapt oneself to new opportunities and situations.

Recalling the Facts

1. Why should you analyze your interests and skills when considering job possibilities?

2. What can you learn from a part-time job?

3. Name three ways that you can get additional training for jobs.

4. What are tech-prep programs?

5. Why should you tell as many people as possible that you are looking for a job?

6. What should you find out about employment agency fees?

7. What are references?

8. List at least seven points to remember when interviewing for a job.

9. Why is flexibility an important personal quality of any employee?

10. When leaving a job, what guidelines should you follow?

Thinking Critically

1. **Analysis.** Analyze the school-to-work skills that employers seek in potential employees. How might each one contribute to job success?

2. **Evaluation.** What kind of insights can be learned about a career by working in an entry-level job in a related field?

3. **Synthesis.** Suggest ways that a person could learn about local job opportunities.

4. **Evaluation.** Why do you think good communication skills are important in every job?

Applying Your Knowledge

1. **Want Ads.** Read the want ads in one or more newspapers. Create a display of the listings in the fashion- and clothing-related fields. What education, training, or experience is required?

2. **Resumé.** Write a personal resumé, summarizing your education, activities, and experience.

3. **Dressing Appropriately.** Look through magazines for illustrations that show appropriate and inappropriate clothing for job interviews. Explain the reasons for your choices.

4. **Interviewing.** Working in pairs, write questions that could be asked during a job interview. Then take turns interviewing each other. Discuss ways to improve your skills.

Making the Connection

1. **Math.** Using want ads, compare the salary levels of jobs requiring only a high school education with those requiring additional education.

2. **Language Arts.** Research various career clusters and the paths leading to different job levels. Develop a personal career path, and write a report about the education, training, and skills needed for advancement.

What Is Human Resources?

The human resources department of a company provides a variety of services and support for the company's employees. Human resources is responsible for interviewing prospective employees. For current employees, the department provides career counseling. The staff also answers questions about withholding taxes, vacation days, insurance plans, sexual harassment, and other employee concerns. In some companies, the human resources staff recommends continuing education programs or special counseling services for employees. Many companies have changed the name of their personnel department to human resources. This reflects the expanded employee support provided by the companies.

Try It Yourself

Imagine that you are the director of the human resources department of a company or store. Using library resources, research the roles and responsibilities of a human resources department. What services and benefits are provided? What federal and state regulations must be followed? What are common concerns of today's employees? Then create a reference list of information and services that your department can provide for "employees."

Build Your Portfolio

Place a copy of your reference list for "employees" in your portfolio. If you wish, include an analysis of magazine and newspaper articles on employee benefits and concerns.

Dressmaker

Maria Lopez spends her days surrounded by yards of chiffon, lace, beads, and pearls. She is a custom dressmaker who specializes in bridal and prom dresses. "I started my business when my children were small," says Maria. "At first, it was only part-time. Now I work full-time most of the year. But, when it gets close to prom time, the business takes over my evenings and weekends, too."

Education and Training

As a sophomore in high school, Maria could not find a prom dress that she liked and that fit properly. Her mother took her to a local dressmaker. Together they chose the fabric and combined several patterns to create a style that Maria loved. The finished dress fit her perfectly.

The next semester, Maria added a clothing class to her course schedule. With help from her teacher during the school year and from her neighbor during the summer, Maria's sewing skills developed.

After high school, Maria took courses at a business college. She worked at a bank and then as the office manager for a real estate firm. She married and had two children. "I was trying to juggle everything—work, home, family—and it got to be too much," said Maria. "I kept thinking about starting my own business, but I wasn't sure what to do or how to go about it. Then my sister asked if I would make the bridesmaids' dresses for her wedding. Of course I made them, and they were beautiful! After the wedding, a few people asked if I would sew for them."

"I had no idea what to charge or how to organize myself." Maria continued, "I decided to start looking for information at the library. It was there I saw a notice for a workshop on how to start your own at-home business. I spent the day getting a lot of good advice."

Today Maria has a thriving business. Known for bridal and prom dresses, she also sews other garments. She has made first communion and graduation dresses, outfits for rock bands, and even an adult-size penguin costume—the mascot of one of the local sports teams.

Responsibilities

As an entrepreneur, Maria has responsibilities to her clients and to herself.

- **Provide a quality product and service.** Maria has established a reputation for providing quality. She selects good fabrics and trims, features good workmanship, and seeks the perfect fit for her clients.

- **Keep up-to-date on fashion trends.** Many clients look for Maria for advice on styles, fabrics, and colors. She subscribes to a variety of fashion, bridal, and sewing magazines. She also attends some of the bridal shows in her area.

- **Meet deadlines.** Maria has to have a realistic idea of how much she can accomplish in the amount of time available to sew. No client wants to hear that her wedding or prom dress is not finished because Maria ran out of time.

- **Maintain business records.** Maria uses a computer to keep track of business expenses, such as telephone, sewing equipment, and advertising costs. She is required to charge state sales tax on her finished garments. She also must make quarterly income tax payments to both the state and federal governments.

Knowledge and Skills

Maria's sewing skills are the basis of her business. In addition, she uses other knowledge and skills for every project:

- **Sewing and alterations skills**—for using the proper construction or alterations techniques to create a quality garment that fits properly.

- **Pattern drafting skills**—for adapting patterns or creating original designs for a one-of-a-kind gown.

- **Fashion and fabric knowledge**—to recommend styles, fabrics, trims, and notions to clients.

- **Math skills**—for comparing measurements, computing yardage, making alterations, setting prices, and handling financial records.

- **Marketing skills**—for getting free publicity, creating ads for local newspapers, and receiving recommendations from retail and fabric stores.

- **Interpersonal skills**—for providing professional and courteous service to all clients.

- **Business and computer skills**—for keeping track of income and expenses, sending out invoices, and maintaining financial and tax records.

"As an entrepreneur, I am responsible for all phases of my business. During my first year in business, I struggled with the many responsibilities and challenges—from sewing problems to paying taxes. I now participate in a chat group of professional dressmakers. When I have a sewing problem, I get advice from people all over the world!"

Sewing AND Serging

HANDBOOK

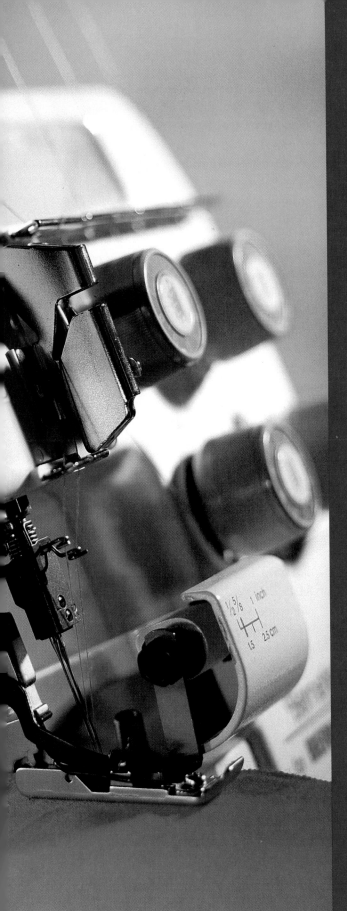

Part 1

Patterns, Fabrics, and Notions

- Lesson 1
  Selecting a Pattern
- Lesson 2
  Selecting Fabric
- Lesson 3
  Selecting Notions

Ask yourself five questions when you decide to sew: who, what, when, where, and why.

- ***Who am I going to sew for?*** *You may sew for yourself because you need something new, or you cannot find what you want in the stores. You might sew for another person because you cannot afford to buy a gift, or because a handmade item would please that person.*
- ***What am I going to sew?*** *You could make something to wear, such as a t-shirt, backpack, or shorts. You could make something for the home, such as pillows or placemats.*
- ***When and where am I going to sew?*** *How much time you have will influence how detailed your sewing project should be. If you do not have a sewing machine at home, perhaps a relative or friend would let you use a machine. Maybe you could use a classroom machine after school or during a study period.*
- ***Why have I selected this particular pattern and fabric?*** *Will the new garment go with other items in your wardrobe? Impulse sewing can be just as bad as impulse buying. Also, when you select a pattern, choose one that will teach you a new sewing technique. For example, if your first project was a t-shirt, your next project might be a simple shirt with a collar. Take time, however, to build your sewing skills. A tailored jacket as your first or second project might lead to frustration.*

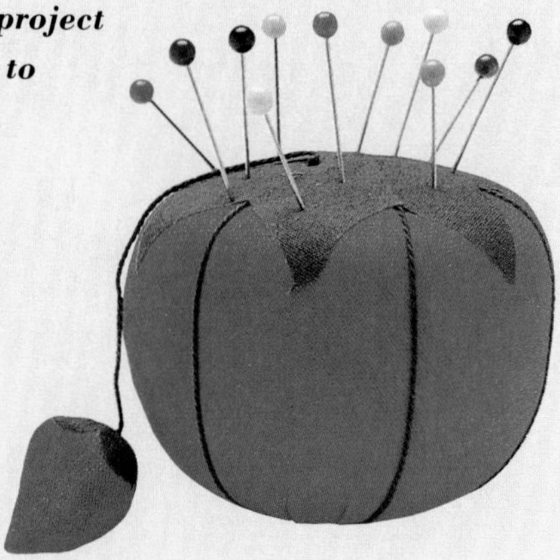

Lesson 1

Selecting a Pattern

When selecting a pattern, you should consider several factors. Be sure the pattern style is flattering to your body shape. Select a pattern that matches your sewing skill level. Finally, choose a pattern in the correct size and figure type in order to get the best fit.

The Pattern Catalog

How do you find a pattern? You start by looking through the pattern catalogs. Each company that manufactures patterns produces its own catalog. Pattern catalogs are divided into sections to make it easy for you to find the styles you want. For example, you will find sections marked for dresses, for sportswear, and for easy-to-sew styles. You also will find sections for special categories such as larger sizes, children and toddlers, men and boys, home decorating, crafts, gifts, and accessories.

Most garments are photographed and sketched in the catalog. By studying both the photograph and the sketch, you will have a good idea of what the finished garment will look like. You will also get ideas for accessories to wear with the garment.

Pattern catalogs are available in stores that sell patterns. Your classroom may have some copies for you to look at. Most of the pattern companies publish a magazine several times a year that features a select-

Pattern catalogs provide information about the style, fit, design details, and sewing difficulty of patterns.

ed group of patterns. You can subscribe to these magazines or buy them at the newsstand.

Selecting the Right Style

How can you tell from a drawing on a catalog page what the finished garment will look like on you? One way is to pay careful attention to the styles of items you already own. Which ones are flattering to your body shape and enjoyable to wear?

Consider all of the information you have learned about line and design. The design principles are important, whether you sew or buy your clothes.

Sewing Tip

If you do not own a garment in the style you are planning to sew, visit a store and try on several versions in ready-to-wear. Look in the mirror and analyze the overall effect. If you are not pleased with the way the garment looks, perhaps the style would be more flattering if it were looser or more fitted, shorter or longer. An advantage of sewing is that you can customize your clothes to suit your own tastes and body proportions.

Sewing Tip

You can use your measurements to interpret the measurements listed on the pattern envelope. Measure the lengths of several different jackets, dresses, or pants in your wardrobe. Also measure the bottom *circumference*, or distance around, of several different styles of pants and skirts. Make a list of these measurements. Use the list to compare your measurements to those listed for the pattern. Then you will know right away, for example, if pants legs that are listed as 20 inches (51 cm) at the lower edge are slimmer or fuller than pants you already own.

Clues on the Pattern Envelope

The pattern envelope will give you information about how the finished garment should look. Carefully examine the sketch or photograph on the front of the envelope. Note the fit of the garment through the shoulders, at the waist, and at the hips. Is it fitted to the curves of the body, or is it full and loose fitting? Also note the type of fabric shown in the photograph or sketch. Is it a heavyweight or a lightweight fabric? Is it a solid color, a print, a plaid, or a stripe? These are clues to help you choose your fabric.

The back of the pattern envelope also has information about the style and the fit of the pattern. Small line drawings show what the back of the garment looks like. A garment description explains whether the style is loose fitting or tight fitting. It also describes design details such as sleeves, pockets, and zippers. The finished garment measurements, such as "width at lower edge" or "finished back length," give you an idea of the proportions of the finished garment. See the illustration of the back of a pattern envelope on page 431.

What information is provided on the front of this pattern envelope?

PATTERN ENVELOPE BACK

The back of the pattern envelope gives you more information per square inch than any other part of the pattern. You will find all of the necessary information for buying the fabric, notions, and sewing supplies needed for the project.

- **Description** mentions the silhouette or fit of the garment, the design features of various parts of the garment, and any special construction details that cannot be shown in the sketch.

- **Number of pattern pieces** indicates the ease of conruction. Usually the fewer the number of pattern pieces, the easier it will be to make the garment.

- **Views** are drawings that show all of the seams, darts, and design details.

- **Body measurements** list all sizes for which the pattern is designed. The actual pattern pieces will measure larger to allow for movement and comfort.

- **Yardage chart** lists the amount of fabric needed for different views, sizes, and fabric widths. The terms *with nap* or *without*

nap appear after each fabric width. **With nap** refers to *fabric with a nap, pile,* or *one-way design.* This means that all pattern pieces must be turned in one direction on the fabric. The *with nap* layouts sometimes require more fabric than cutting the *without nap* layouts.

- **Garment measurements** include the circumference of the hemline at the lower edge and the finished back or side length.

- **Suggested fabrics** are recommended types of fabrics that could be used for this style of garment. Special fabric information will tell you if extra fabric is needed for matching plaids and stripes or if stretch fabric must be used. It will also note if the pattern is not suitable for stripes, plaids, or diagonal fabrics.

- **Notions** list the quantity and recommended sizes of additional sewing supplies such as thread, buttons, tapes, and zippers.

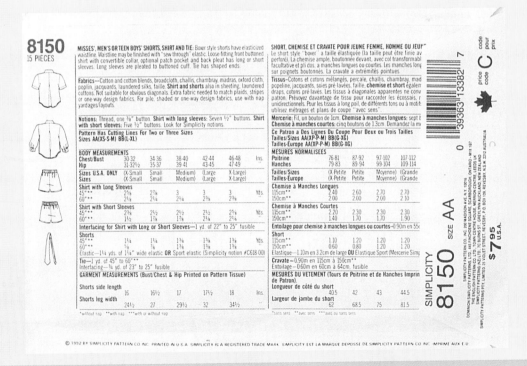

TAKING YOUR MEASUREMENTS

- **Height.** Stand against the wall in bare feet. Have another person make a mark that is level with the top of your head. Measure from this point to the floor. For pants and skirt measurements, it is best to wear shoes.

- **Bust/chest.** The tape measure should be straight across the back and over the fullest part of the bust or chest.

- **Waist.** Tie a length of string around the smallest part of the waistline. It will roll into the natural waistline position. Measure the waistline exactly where the string has settled.

- **Hips or seat.** Measure over the fullest part of the hips in a straight line around the body. For most females, measure 7 to 9 inches (18 to 23 cm) below the waist. For most men, measure 8 inches (20.5 cm) below the waist; for Teen Boys, 7 inches (18 cm) below the waist.

- **Neck** (for males only). Measure around the base of the neck. This measurement plus ½ inch (1.3 cm) is the neck size.

- **Back waist length** (for females only). Bend the head forward to locate a very prominent bone at the base of the neck. Measure from this bone down the center back to the waistline string.

- **In-seam.** Place pants that are the correct length on a flat surface. Measure along inner seam from the bottom of one leg to where the two legs meet.

- **Out-seam.** Measure from the waist to the point where the pants bottom breaks slightly on the shoe.

- **Sleeve.** Bend the arm up for men. Measure from the base of the neck across the center back to the elbow, across the elbow crook, and up over the wrist bone. For women, measure from the top of the shoulder over the bent elbow to the wrist

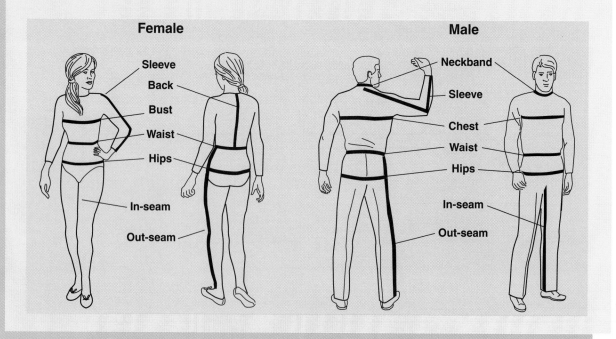

Skill Level

Read the description in the catalog or on the pattern envelope for clues about sewing difficulty. Most of the pattern companies market a special category of easy-to-sew patterns. These categories have special brand names that tell you something about the skill level required to sew the pattern. Look for names such as "Easy," "Fast & Easy," and "It's So Easy."

Easy-to-sew patterns usually have fewer pattern pieces, simple-to-follow layouts, and easier construction techniques. Some easy-to-sew patterns are even marked with a sewing time. This will help you estimate how long it will take you to make the pattern.

Selecting the Correct Size

To determine your correct pattern size, first take your body measurements. Ideally you should take your measurements over your undergarments, not over your clothes. If necessary, you can take them over snug-fitting clothes. Remove sweaters, belts, jackets, or other bulky items.

Use a flexible 60 inch (150 cm) plastic-coated measuring tape. The tape measure should be held snugly, but not tightly, around the body. Be sure that the tape measure is parallel to the floor. For accuracy, have someone help you measure. Write down each measurement as it is taken.

You will want to record your height and your circumference measurements—bust or chest, waist, and hips. Females will need to take their back waist measurement. Males should take their neck and sleeve measurements. For pants, the waist and inseam measurements are needed. See Taking Your Measurements on page 432.

Figure Type

Figure types are *size categories determined by height and body proportions*. In order to determine your figure type, you will need to look at three pieces of information: your height, your back waist length (for females), and your body proportions. Now compare this information with the charts that appear in the back of the pattern catalogs.

Pattern Size

After you have determined your figure type, the next step is to determine your pattern size. Compare your bust or chest, waist, and hip measurements with the ones that are listed on the chart on the pattern

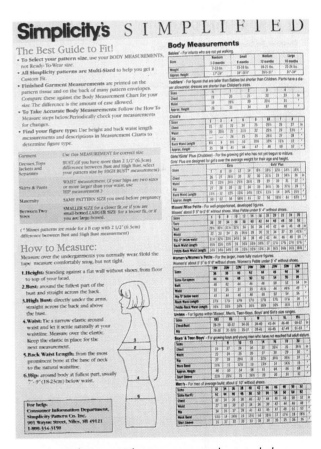

Pattern catalogs provide measurement charts to help you decide what size pattern to buy.

envelope back. Make sure you are looking only at the measurements within your figure type category. Find the measurements that come closest to yours. That is your pattern size.

Since few people are a perfect size, your measurements might not exactly match one of the sizes. If your measurements fall between two sizes: Select the smaller size if the design is full or loose fitting. Select the larger size if the design is closely fitted.

If you are choosing a pattern for pants or a skirt, select the pattern size by your waist measurement. However, if your hips are large in proportion to your waist, choose the pattern by the hip measurement.

Many patterns are **multi-sized,** which means that they are *printed with several sizes on the same pattern tissue.* This is particularly helpful for people who are one size on top and another size on the bottom. Each size range is identified by a letter code printed on the catalog page and on the pattern enve-

lope. Be sure you select the size range that includes your pattern size. See illustration on page 474.

Pattern Ease

All patterns have a certain amount of "ease" built in to them. The garment is larger than your body to give you the space to sit down or bend over in your clothes. This extra space, known as **wearing ease,** is *the amount of fullness needed for movement and comfort.* The only garments that do not have this wearing ease are items made of stretch fabrics, such as bathing suits, body suits, and exercise wear.

There is a second kind of ease that is built into a garment. This is called **design ease.** It is *the extra fullness built into the clothes by the designer to create a particular style or silhouette.* Some designers prefer their clothes to have a very loose-fitting silhouette. Others like their clothes to fit snugly against the body. The picture and the description on the pattern envelope will give you clues as to the amount of ease.

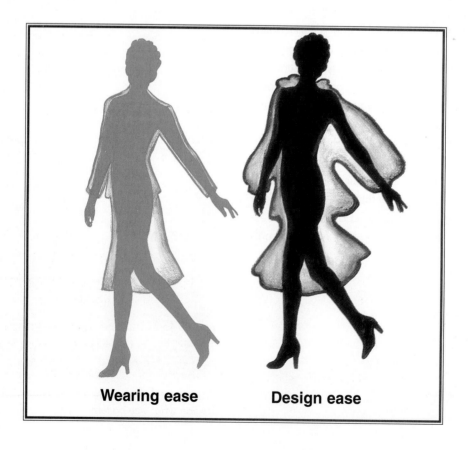

Wearing ease   **Design ease**

Lesson 2

Selecting Fabric

After you have selected a pattern, the next step is to choose a fabric. You will want to select one that is suitable for both the pattern style and your sewing skills.

Fabric Suitable for the Pattern

How do you know which fabrics would be best for your style of garment? Take another look at the back of the pattern envelope. The Suggested Fabric List is a guide for choosing fabric. If the suggested fabrics are denim, poplin, or corduroy, then choose a fabric that is as firm as these. If the suggested fabrics are jersey, tricot, or crepe, then you should choose a soft, drapeable fabric such as these.

The fabric suggestions will also tell you if certain fabrics are not suitable for the design. For example, stripes, plaids, or obvious diagonal fabrics can look very unattractive if made up in certain styles.

Sometimes a pattern is designed only for knit fabrics. You will need to be sure that the knit you are considering has the right amount of stretch for your pattern. All "knits only" patterns have a Stretch Gauge on the pattern envelope. The gauge shows how much the knit must be able to stretch.

If the pattern has gathers, grasp the fabric in your hand to see how it drapes. If the pattern has pleats, crease a small section of the fabric between your fingernails to see if it will hold a pleat.

Check the fabric for any flaws. The color should be even, with no streaks or spots. Any pattern design should be printed on grain. Check for wrinkle resistance and stretchability. For example, squeeze the fabric in your hand to see if it will wrinkle easily. Read the end of the fabric bolt for information about fibers, finishes, and care requirements.

Fabric Suitable for Your Sewing Skills

The type of fabric you should choose depends on your sewing experience. If you are a beginning sewer, you will want to choose a fabric that is easy to sew. Your best choice is a mediumweight, firmly woven or knitted fabric. A small, all-over print is a good choice because any small sewing mistakes often do not show.

Certain fabrics require special sewing techniques. These fabrics are *not good choices* for beginners:

- **Slippery fabrics** are hard to handle as you cut and stitch.

- **Loosely woven fabrics** can ravel easily and require special seam finishes.

- **Sheer fabrics** and **thick, bulky fabrics** are hard to pin, sew, and press.

- **Fabrics with a one-way design** must have all of the pattern pieces laid out in the same direction,

- **Pile fabrics,** such as velvet or corduroy, require special pattern layouts and pressing techniques.

- **Stripes** and **plaids** must be matched at all seamlines and design points, such as collars, cuffs, and pockets.

The pattern envelope will suggest suitable fabrics for the design. Some envelopes have a stretch gauge for checking the stretchability of a knit fabric.

Sewing Tip

To check for color variations and design direction, fold the fabric so that part of it is turned upside-down. Stand back and look carefully at the color and design.

To determine how much extra fabric is needed to match large fabric designs, actually lay out the major pattern pieces on the fabric at the store. Then you will not get home and find that you have too little fabric. Most stores will let you do this, but be sure to ask a salesperson for assistance.

Fabric Suitable for You

The fabric you select should be right for your appearance and your lifestyle. Pick a color and a texture that is flattering to your coloring and body shape. It should coordinate with items you already own.

Choose a fabric that is appropriate for the occasions when you will wear the garment. For example, a

The pattern envelope suggests fabrics that would be suitable for your project. The fabric you select should also be suitable for your appearance, lifestyle, and sewing skills.

pattern envelope says that the dress or shirt can be made in denim. However, a dress or shirt made of denim would not be a suitable choice to wear to a formal wedding.

How Much to Buy

The label or hangtag at the end of the fabric bolt will tell you the width of the fabric. Most fabrics are 36 inches (91.5 cm), 45 inches (115 cm), or 60 inches (150 cm) wide. The Yardage Chart on the back of the pattern envelope will list how much fabric you will need for your size.

Do not buy a fabric that is narrower than the ones listed on your pattern envelope. For example, if the chart lists only 45 (115 cm) or 60 inch (150 cm) fabric, do not buy fabric that is 36 inches (91.5 cm) wide. Some of the pattern pieces for that style are probably too large to fit on a narrower piece of fabric.

The Yardage Chart may indicate that extra fabric is required for fabrics with a nap, pile, shading, or one-way design. With these fabrics, all of the pattern pieces must be cut so the pile or design runs in the same direction. Otherwise the finished garment will look like it has been cut from two different shades of fabric or that part of the fabric's design is upside-down.

Corduroy and velveteen fabrics have a pile, and many knits have a shading. These fabrics need a one-way layout and may require extra yardage. Stripes, plaids, and other designs may need additional fabric in order to match the fabric design at the seams.

Lesson 3

Selecting Notions

Many different items—such as thread, fasteners, interfacing, and trims—may be needed during construction. These *small items that become a permanent part of the garment* are called **notions.**

The notions you need to buy for a project are listed on the back of the pattern envelope. Items listed can include thread, snaps, and hooks and eyes. If a zipper is needed, the length will be given. If buttons are needed, the size and the quantity will be listed.

Some notions, such as lining, interfacing, trim, and elastic, are purchased by the yard or meter. Because the amount you need to buy may depend on the pattern size, these notions will be listed in the Yardage Chart.

Buy the notions when you buy the fabric. Then you will be sure that you have everything you need and that the colors will match. Buttons, tapes, trims, and interfacings should have care requirements that are compatible with the care of the fabric. For example, a cotton shirt cannot be washed if its buttons and trim can only be dry cleaned.

Selecting Colors

Color is very important when choosing notions. Thread should be the same color as the fabric. If you cannot find the exact color, choose one that is a shade darker. Thread looks lighter after it is stitched. Trims should match exactly. If you cannot find trims that match, select a contrasting color instead.

Interfacings and linings should not show through on the right side of the garment. In the store, test the lining and interfacing that you are considering. Drape a piece of your fabric over them.

Thread

Thread is available in a wide assortment of types and colors. A good quality thread is strong and smooth, has even thickness, and resists tangling. The type of thread you select is determined by the type of fabric you are sewing:

- **Polyester** or **polyester/cotton thread** is an all-purpose one that can be used for sewing almost all fabrics. It is strong, flexible, and has less shrinkage than other threads. It is recommended for knits and stretch fabrics because the thread has some give or stretchability. This helps to prevent the seams from breaking as the garment is worn.

- **Mercerized cotton thread** can be used to sew woven fabrics of natural fibers, such as 100 percent cotton or silk. Cotton thread is used mostly for quilting and crafts.

- **Silk thread** can be used on silk or wool fabrics. It is excellent for basting delicate fabrics.

- **Heavy-duty thread** is used to sew heavier fabrics and projects, such as slipcovers, that require strength and durability.

Sewing Tip

Try to match the color of thread as closely as possible to the color of the fabric. If in doubt between two shades of color, choose the darker thread. A single strand of thread will appear slightly lighter in color than it does when wound on the spool. When matching a print or a plaid, select the background or dominant color for the thread.

Choose a color of thread that matches the color of the fabric as closely as possible.

- **Buttonhole twist thread** is thicker than the others. It is used for decorative topstitching and hand-worked buttonholes.

Special threads are available for specific sewing and crafts projects. These include *serger thread, basting thread, quilting thread, rayon machine embroidery thread,* and *carpet thread.* See the Thread Chart on page 448.

Fasteners

Fasteners are any items used to close a garment. They include zippers, buttons, snaps, hooks and eyes, buckles, and hook and loop tape.

Zippers

Zippers are available in a wide variety of colors, lengths, and types. They also come with metal or polyester coils. A lightweight polyester coil zipper is a better choice for a lightweight fabric. The recommended type and length of zipper is listed on the back of the pattern envelope.

Zippers can be purchased in a variety of types:

- **Conventional zipper,** which has a stop at the bottom, is the most common type.

- **Invisible zipper** disappears into the seam when it is closed, so that all you see is the tab at the top of the zipper.

- **Separating zipper** opens at the bottom for use in jackets and coats.

- **Two-way zipper** has sliders at the top and bottom so it can be opened from either end.

- **Trouser zipper** usually has metal teeth and wider tape.

- **Decorative zipper** has large teeth and a pull ring.

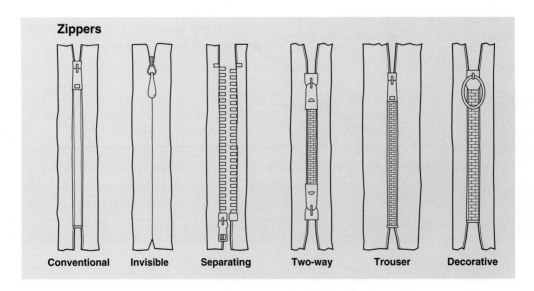

Zippers

Conventional   Invisible   Separating   Two-way   Trouser   Decorative

Buttons

The pattern envelope will recommend the size and number of buttons needed for a project. The size of a button is the measurement of its diameter, stated in fractions of an inch. There are two basic types of buttons:

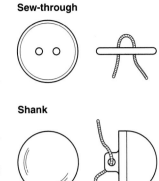

Sew-through

Shank

- **Sew-through buttons** have two to four holes on the face of the button for attaching with thread.

- **Shank buttons** have a metal, plastic, or fabric loop behind the button through which thread is stitched. A shank allows room for the buttonhole to lie smoothly between the button and fabric to which it is stitched.

Snaps

Snaps range in size from 0000 or 4/0 (small) to size 4 (large). The smaller sizes are useful for holding edges together where there is not much strain or pull on the snaps. Larger sizes are good for heavy-duty use. Large covered snaps are available for coats and suits. Snaps preattached to fabric tapes are ideal for sportswear and children's wear.

Hooks and Eyes

Hooks and eyes range in size from 0 (small) to 3 (large). They are packaged with two types of eyes:

- **Curved eye** is used on edges that just meet, such as the edge of a collar or neckline.

- **Straight eye** is used on lapped edges, such as a waistband or cuff.

Large covered hooks and eyes are available for coats and jackets. Specialty waistband fasteners have a large flat hook and bar closure.

Buckles

Buckles are available in a wide variety of shapes, sizes, and materials. They can be purchased separately or in belt kits. There are two basic types:

- **Buckle with a prong** must be used with eyelets. Ready-made metal eyelets can be applied to the belt with special pliers or attaching tool. Eyelets can also be handsewn using a buttonhole stitch.

- **Buckle without a prong** can simply be stitched to the belt end; no eyelets are needed.

Hook and Loop Tape

This fastener consists of two nylon strips, one with tiny hooks and one with looped pile. The hooks and pile intermesh when pressed together. Such tape is often used on jackets, sportswear, and children's clothes. Available by the yard or in precut shapes, it can be stitched by hand or machine.

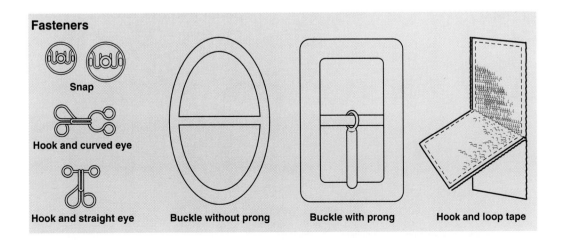

Fasteners

Snap

Hook and curved eye

Hook and straight eye

Buckle without prong

Buckle with prong

Hook and loop tape

Tapes and Trims

Tapes and trims can be functional or decorative. They can be used to reinforce a seam, cover a fabric edge, or create a special design on the outside of a garment. Tapes and trims are available in a variety of types, width, and colors. Some are stretchable; others are not. They may be woven, knitted, braided, or made of lace.

The choice of which type of tape or trim to use depends upon how it will be used in your garment. For areas where you want to prevent stretching, select a firm, nonstretchable tape or trim. For areas that should stretch during wear, such as a knitted cuff, choose a stretchable tape or trim.

Some of the common tapes and trims include:

- **Seam tape** is a woven tape or lace used to finish hem and facing edges.

- **Bias tape** is a single-fold or double-fold tape used for binding curved or straight edges. It can also be used for casings, ties, and trims.

- **Hem facing** is a wide bias tape or lace used for facing hems and binding edges.

- **Foldover braid** is a knitted braid folded in half and used for binding and trimming edges.

- **Ribbing** is a stretchable knitted band used to finish a neckline, armhole, sleeve, pants leg, or lower edge.

- **Twill tape** is a firmly woven tape used for reinforcing seams.

- **Piping** is a narrow, corded bias strip of fabric that is inserted into a seam for a decorative trim.

- **Cable cord** is used as a filler for piping, cording, and tubing.

- **Belting** is a very stiff band used to reinforce belts and waistbands.

Elastics

Elastic is available in several different types and widths. The type of elastic to choose will depend on whether it will be used in a casing or stitched directly to a garment. Read the label when purchasing any type of elastic to be sure it will serve the correct purpose.

Elastics

Woven **Braided** **Clear**

- **Woven elastic** stays the same width when stretched. Thus, it can be stitched directly to a garment or used in a casing.

- **Braided elastic** is recommended only for casings because it narrows when stretched.

- **Clear elastic** is a very stretchy elastic that is stitched directly to the fabric. It is particularly suitable for swimwear and lingerie.

- **Special purpose elastics** are available for lingerie, swimwear, and activewear.

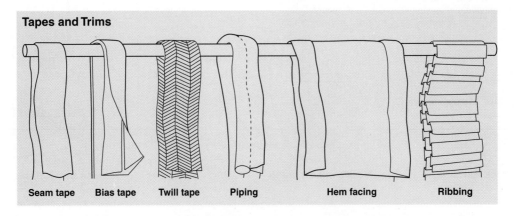

Tapes and Trims

Seam tape   Bias tape   Twill tape   Piping   Hem facing   Ribbing

Interfacings and Linings

Interfacings and linings are fabrics used on the inside of a garment. Both must be able to receive the same care as the outer fabric.

Interfacings

Interfacing is a *piece of fabric placed between the outer fabric and the facing.* It is used to prevent stretching of necklines, front closings, and buttonholes. It adds shape to collars, cuffs, pockets, and hems. Interfacing also can add crispness and stability to waistbands and belts. Each of the three basic types of interfacing has a different method of application:

- **Sew-in interfacing** must be stitched by machine or hand to the garment. It is available in either woven or nonwoven fabrics.

- **Fusible interfacing** has a resin coating on the back of either woven or nonwoven fabric. It will fuse or bond to fabric when pressed with an iron.

- **Combination fusible/sew-in interfacing** is temporarily fused to the fabric with a cool iron so that it acts like a fusible during the sewing process. When the finished garment is washed or dry cleaned, the interfacing loses its bond and becomes a sew-in.

Interfacings are available in a variety of weights, ranging from very lightweight to heavyweight. To select the proper weight of interfacing, choose an interfacing that is the same weight or lighter than your fabric. Heavyweight interfacings are recommended only for accessories and crafts.

Linings

A **lining** is a *fabric used to finish the inside of a jacket, coat, skirt, dress, or pants.* It helps to prevent stretching and to reduce wrinkling. Lining fabrics must be able to receive the same care as the outer fabric. Select one that is firmly woven, slippery, and static-free. The color of a jacket lining can either match or contrast with the outer fabric.

A lining is constructed separately and then inserted into the garment. For skirts and pants, a lining is attached along the waistband and zipper. For coats, jackets, vests, and dresses, a lining is stitched around the facing edges. The hem of a lining can be sewn to the garment hem or hemmed separately. Jacket hems are usually sewn to the garment; coat and skirt hems are hemmed separately.

Fusible Webs

Fusible webs are a special category of sewing supplies. The webs are a *network of bondable fibers used to hold two layers of fabric together.* When heat and/or steam is applied, the web melts and fuses the fabric layers together. Fusible webs can be used to hem, apply trims, and hold facing edges in place.

Fusible webs are sold by the yard in either narrow strips or wider widths. They can be a plain web or have a peel-off  paper backing that makes them easier to cut and use. Before using a fusible web for the first time, read the instructions carefully. Then test the application on a piece of scrap fabric before applying it.

Sewing Tip

To check the final effect of an interfacing, drape the fabric and interfacing together. See how they look and feel together. Remember that even though a fusible and a sew-in interfacing feel the same, the fusible will give crisper results. Always test a fusible interfacing on a scrap of your fabric before fusing it to your garment sections.

Summary

- When selecting a sewing project, consider five questions: who, what, when, where, and why.
- A pattern should be flattering to your body shape and match your sewing skill level.
- Both the pattern catalog and pattern envelope have information about the style and fit of a pattern.
- To determine your correct pattern size, compare your measurements with the pattern charts.
- Select a fabric that is suitable for the pattern style and your sewing skills.
- Certain fabrics require special sewing techniques and are not good choices for beginning sewers.
- Purchase all the notions for a project when you buy the fabric.

Recalling the Facts

1. List the five questions you should ask yourself about a sewing project.
2. What can you learn from the photos and sketches in a pattern catalog?
3. What clues are given on the front of the pattern envelope about how a garment should look?
4. What information is listed on the back of a pattern envelope?
5. Name three characteristics of easy-to-sew patterns.
6. How do you determine your figure type?
7. List the three body measurements that are used to determine your pattern size.
8. What is the advantage of multi-sized patterns?
9. What is the difference between wearing ease and design ease?
10. What is the purpose of the Suggested Fabric List on the back of a pattern envelope?
11. How can you determine if a fabric will wrinkle easily?
12. List at least five types of fabrics that a beginning sewer should avoid using.
13. How should you determine how much fabric to buy?
14. Why might you need to buy extra yardage if you are using a corduroy fabric or a plaid fabric?
15. Why should notions be purchased at the same time as your fabric?
16. What should you do if you cannot find thread the exact color as your fabric?
17. What is the difference between a sew-through button and a shank button?
18. What is the purpose of interfacing?
19. How can you determine what weight of interfacing to buy?
20. What is the purpose of fusible webs?

Thinking Critically

1. **Evaluation.** What advice would you give to someone whose body measurements do not correspond with a pattern size?
2. **Synthesis.** What might happen if a beginning sewer decided to make a corduroy jacket as a second project?

3. **Evaluation.** Why is it important to read all of the information on a pattern envelope before purchasing the pattern, fabric, and notions?

4. **Analysis.** Compare and contrast fusible interfacings and fusible webs.

Practicing Your Skills

1. **Easy-to-Sew.** Look through a pattern catalog and select patterns that would be suitable for beginning sewers. Identify which features make each pattern easy-to-sew.

2. **Pattern, Fabric, and Notions.** Select a pattern style that would be flattering to your body shape. Determine your correct pattern size, using your body measurements. Then list the fabric yardage and notions that are needed to make the garment in your size. Note if any fabrics are not suitable for the design.

Applying Your Knowledge

1. **Garment Descriptions.** Collect illustrations of garments from fashion magazines and catalogs. Write a description of each garment, such as would be found on the back of a pattern envelope. Include style, fit, and design details.

2. **Notions.** Visit a notions department of a store. Research the types and prices of thread, zippers, buttons, snaps, hooks and eyes, tapes, trims, and elastics.

What Is a Pattern Designer?

Pattern designers create the commercial patterns that are shown in pattern catalogs and magazines. The major pattern companies publish new designs almost monthly. The designers create patterns for all types of garments, from sportswear to bridal wear. They also design accessories, costumes, stuffed toys, and home decorating items. The designers must create patterns for various skill levels, from easy-to-sew styles to couture fashions. Patterns for sewing projects are designed similar to ready-to-wear fashions. The garment is constructed from the master pattern, and photographs are taken for the catalog and pattern envelope.

Try It Yourself

Imagine that you are a pattern designer. Sketch several designs for consumers with different levels of sewing skills. Then write a description of the fit and design details of each garment as it would be written on the back of the pattern envelope. List fabrics that would be suitable for each design, as well as any fabrics that would not be suitable. Create a list of notions that would be necessary for the construction of each pattern.

Build Your Portfolio

Place copies of your pattern sketches, garment descriptions, fabric recommendations, and list of notions in your portfolio. If desired, make a doll-size sample in fabric of one of your designs. Add it to your portfolio.

3. **Cost.** Visit a fabric store. Compute how much it would cost for the pattern, fabric, and notions to make a garment.

Sewing Machines, Sergers, and Other Equipment

● ● ● ● ● ● ● ● ● ● ●

The most important and expensive piece of sewing equipment is the sewing machine or the serger. Just like a computer, these machines are highly complex pieces of equipment.

You should understand the parts of the sewing machine or serger that you will be using at school or at home. By becoming familiar with the parts and their use, you will be able to operate the machine more effectively. You also will be able to avoid certain problems that might occur if you are not familiar with the machine.

You will need a variety of tools and equipment for any sewing project. These should be kept together in a special box or basket for easy use. Then you will be able to locate them quickly when you decide to begin a project. Take good care of your sewing tools and equipment, and they will last for many years.

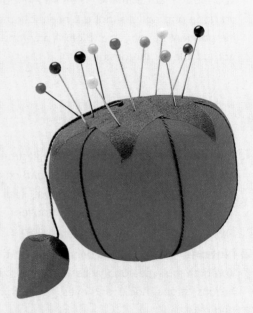

Lesson 1

The Sewing Machine

All sewing machines operate in a similar manner. However, there are differences among various makes and models. Study the illustration on page 446 and then identify the corresponding parts on your machine.

Study the instruction manual that comes with the machine. The manual will show the various parts of the machine and explain what they do. Directions are included for operating the machine and any accessories. Information about caring for the machine is also included. Always refer to the instruction manual when you have a specific question or problem with your machine.

Choosing Machine Needle and Thread

Sewing machine needles are available in a variety of sizes and types. Choose the needle according to the type and weight of fabric that you are sewing.

Always replace a sewing machine needle when it becomes dull, bent, or rough. A damaged needle can cause stitching problems and harm fabric. Some people insert a new needle when they begin a project.

Needle Sizes

Needle sizes range from 9 (for delicate fabrics) to 18 (for heavyweight fabrics). The lower the number, the finer the needle. Some foreign sewing machine manufacturers use a different numbering system for needles. However, the same rule applies: the lighter and finer the fabric, the finer the needle.

- **Size 9** or **11** is used for fine, lightweight fabrics, such as chiffon and voile.

- **Size 14** is used for mediumweight fabrics, such as flannel and corduroy.

- **Size 16** or **18** is for heavier and thicker fabrics.

Types of Needles

Several different types of sewing machine needles are available:

- **Universal** or general-purpose needle has a sharp point and is designed for most woven and knitted fabrics.

- **Ball-point** needle is designed for knits and stretch fabrics. The slightly rounded tip allows the needle to slip between the fabric yarns.

- **Stretch** needle is specially designed to prevent skipped stitches when sewing on synthetic suede and elastic knitwear.

- **Leather** needle has a wedge-shaped point that is designed to pierce leather, vinyl, and heavy nonwoven fabric.

- **Twin** or double needle and **hemstitch** or wing needle are available for decorative stitching.

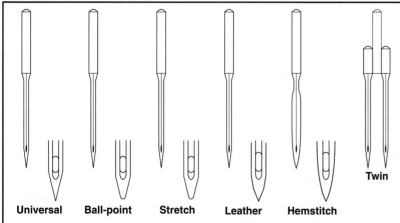

Universal Ball-point Stretch Leather Hemstitch Twin

PARTS OF THE SEWING MACHINE

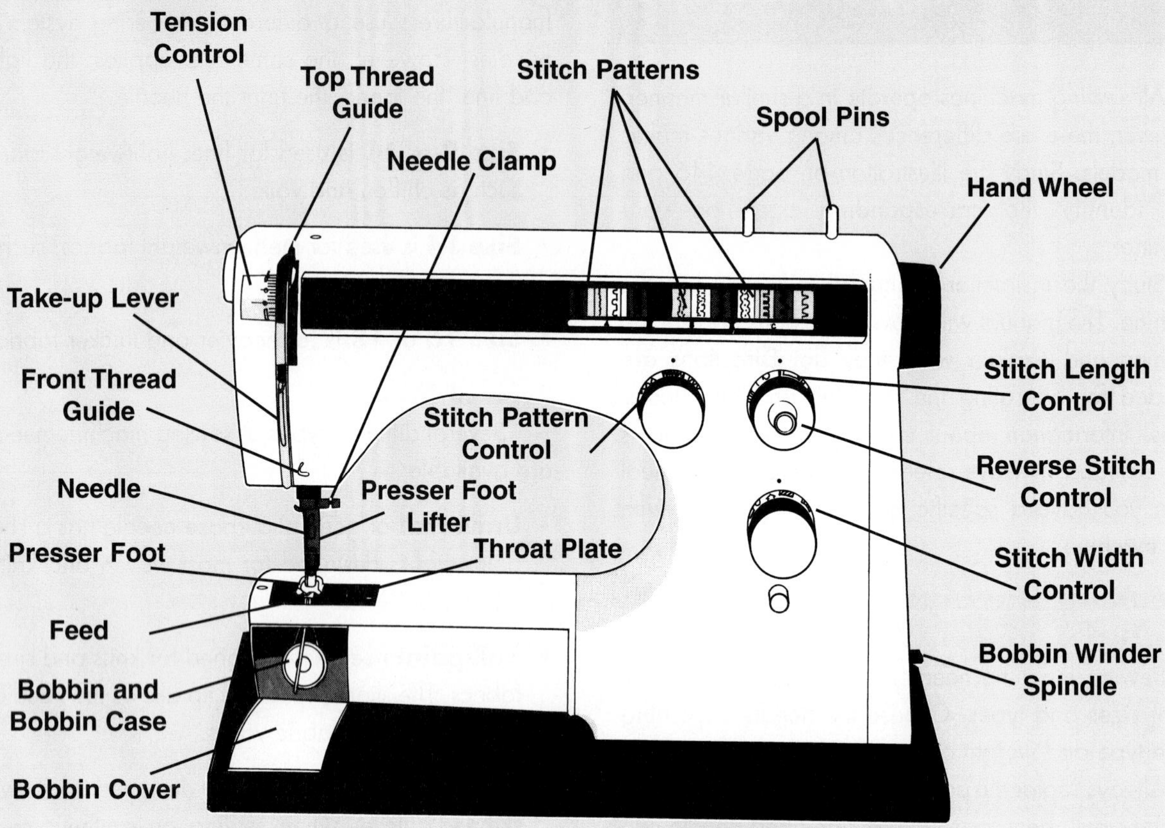

Tension Control

Top Thread Guide

Stitch Patterns

Spool Pins

Needle Clamp

Hand Wheel

Take-up Lever

Front Thread Guide

Stitch Length Control

Stitch Pattern Control

Reverse Stitch Control

Needle

Presser Foot Lifter

Presser Foot

Throat Plate

Stitch Width Control

Feed

Bobbin and Bobbin Case

Bobbin Winder Spindle

Bobbin Cover

Bobbin Holds the bottom, or bobbin, thread.

Bobbin case Holds the bobbin in the machine and regulates the tension of the bobbin thread; may be removable or stationary.

Bobbin cover or slide plate Covers the bobbin and bobbin case in the machine; may be a small hinged cover that flips open or a sliding cover.

Bobbin winder Spindle, latch, and tension discs used to wind thread onto a bobbin.

Feed dog or feed Teeth that move the fabric under the presser foot, advancing the fabric one stitch at a time.

Foot or knee control Regulates the starting, running, and stopping of the machine by the amount of pressure applied to the control (not shown).

Hand wheel Controls the movement of the take-up lever; can be turned by hand to raise or lower needle.

Hand wheel knob Small knob inside the hand wheel which stops the needle from moving while a bobbin is being wound (not shown).

Continued

PARTS OF THE SEWING MACHINE (CONTINUED)

Needle Machine needles come in different types and sizes; must be inserted firmly into the shaft called a needle bar.

Needle clamp Holds the needle firmly in the machine; loosened and tightened by a screw.

Power and light switch Turns on the machine and the light (not shown).

Presser foot Holds the fabric against the feed dog as you stitch.

Presser foot lifter Raises and lowers the presser foot.

Reverse stitch control Button or lever that allows backward stitching.

Spool pins Holds spool of thread.

Stitch length control Regulates the length of the stitch.

Stitch patterns Show the selection of stitches available on the machine.

Stitch pattern control Regulates the selection of different stitching patterns, including zigzag, stretch stitch, and decorative stitches.

Stitch width control Regulates the width of zigzag stitching and positions the needle for straight stitching.

Take-up lever Controls the amount of thread pulled from the spool to the needle for each stitch; moves up and down as you stitch.

Tension control Regulates the tension placed on the needle thread by tightening or loosening the tension discs which the upper thread passes through.

Thread guides Help guide upper thread from the spool to needle without tangling.

Throat or needle plate Located directly under the needle and surrounds the feed dog; usually has seam width guidelines to help keep stitching straight.

Note: Machines vary from model to model. See your owner's manual for the names and locations of the parts and special features of your machine.

Thread

The type of thread is also determined by the type and weight of your fabric. Refer to the chart on page 448 for the recommended thread, needle size, and stitch length for different fabrics.

In general, for lightweight fabrics use a fine needle, fine thread, and short stitches. For heavier fabrics, use a coarser needle, heavier thread, and longer stitches. Except for special decorative stitching, always use the same type of thread in the needle and in the bobbin.

Changing Needles

To change a sewing machine needle:

1. *Raise* needle to highest position by turning hand wheel.
2. *Loosen* thumb screw on needle clamp.
3. *Remove* old needle, being sure to notice the way it is positioned. The long groove on the needle should face the side from which you thread the needle.
4. *Insert* top of needle firmly up in needle clamp.
5. *Tighten* screw securely.

Winding and Inserting the Bobbin

Most bobbins must be removed from the bobbin case in order to be wound. However, some machines have a bobbin winder built into the bobbin case for easy rewinding. Keep extra bobbins in your sewing box to avoid winding one color thread over another.

Winding the Bobbin

Refer to the machine's manual for specific instructions for winding a bobbin. This is a common method for winding bobbins:

1. *Loosen* hand wheel knob to stop movement of needle.
2. *Insert* end of thread through a hole in bobbin.
3. *Wrap* thread securely around bobbin several times.
4. *Place* bobbin on bobbin winder.
5. *Hold* end of thread until bobbin starts winding.

Winding the Bobbin

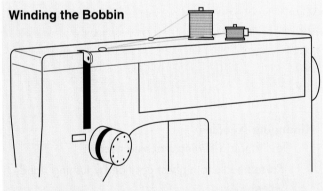

Thread going from spool to bobbin winder tension disc to bobbin

Properly wound

Improperly wound

FABRIC, THREAD, NEEDLE SIZE, STITCH LENGTH

Fabric	Thread	Needle Size	Stitch Length
Delicate: chiffon, fine lace, silk	polyester, polyester/cotton silk	9	4-16
Lightweight: batiste, crepe, organdy, taffeta	polyester, polyester/cotton, silk	11	12-14
Mediumweight: gingham, poplin, linen, fine corduroy, lightweight wool, velveteen	polyester, polyester/cotton, mercerized cotton, silk	14	10-12
Medium-heavy: denim, corduroy, gabardine, woolens, sailcloth	polyester, polyester/cotton, mercerized cotton, silk, heavy-duty	16	10-12
Heavy: canvas, coatings, fake fur, upholstery fabrics	polyester, polyester/cotton, heavy-duty	18	8-10
All knits and stretch fabrics	polyester, polyester/cotton	ball-point or stretch	10-14 or special stretch stitch
Leather and suede	polyester, polyester/cotton, heavy-duty	leather	8-10
Decorative topstitching	any	twin or hemstitch	8-12

It is very important to check that the bobbin winds evenly. It may be necessary to gently guide the thread with your finger. If the bobbin winder does not have an automatic shut-off, wind the bobbin only until it is about three-quarters full. Cut the thread with scissors, and remove the bobbin from the winder. Tighten the hand wheel knob.

Inserting the Bobbin

To insert the bobbin, begin by opening the slide plate that covers the bobbin case. For a built-in bobbin case, simply insert the bobbin directly into the case. For a removable bobbin case, take the case out of the machine and insert the bobbin. Be sure that the thread unwinds in the right direction. Check manual for specific instructions. Insert the bobbin case back into the machine.

Pull the bobbin thread gently to see whether there is a slight tension on it. If it unwinds too easily, check the threading of the bobbin case again. Then close the slide plate.

Threading the Machine

Threading a machine may look difficult at first, but the general procedure is simple. It is the same for all machines: The thread goes from the spool pin through a thread guide to the tension discs. Then it goes to the take-up lever and down to the needle. The thread also must go through the additional thread guides.

Study the illustration on this page and also the one in the manual for your machine.

The Tension Discs

It is important to check the threading of the tension discs. Raise the presser foot and pull the thread gently to see if there is a slight tension on it. If the thread unwinds too easily or without any resistance, you should try once more to pass the thread around the tension discs. The thread should be placed between two of the discs, and then brought up and caught on a hook or spring on the tension discs. Remember to always thread the tension discs before you thread the take-up lever.

The Thread Guides

The location of the thread guides differs from machine to machine. The location of the last thread guide tells you in which direction to thread the needle. If the thread guide is on the right, you thread the needle from the right. If the guide is on the left, you thread the needle from the left. If the guide is on the front of the needle bar, the needle is threaded from front to back.

Pull out at least 3 inches (7.5 cm) of thread from the needle. This will prevent the thread from pulling out of the needle as it is raised and lowered.

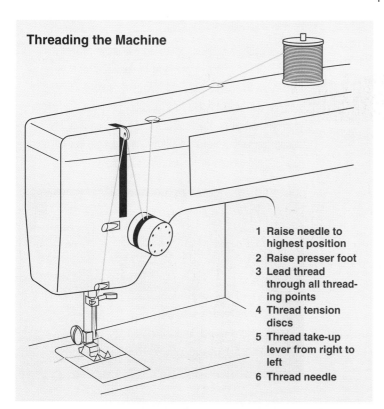

Threading the Machine

1 Raise needle to highest position
2 Raise presser foot
3 Lead thread through all threading points
4 Thread tension discs
5 Thread take-up lever from right to left
6 Thread needle

Raising the Bobbin Thread

After the bobbin and needle have been threaded, bring the bobbin thread up through the hole in the needle or throat plate. To do this, hold the needle thread in your left hand. With your right hand, turn the hand wheel slowly until the needle enters the throat plate. Continue turning until the needle rises and brings up a loop of the bobbin thread. Pull up the loop to bring the end of the bobbin thread out. Pull both thread ends under the presser foot and toward the back of the machine so the threads will not tangle as you start to stitch.

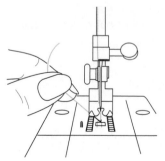

Raising the bobbin thread

COMPUTERIZED SEWING MACHINES

Computerized sewing machines make sewing easier and more creative. Although they are expensive, they can do practically everything but cut out the garment!

Many of these machines feature push-button commands and large, easy-to-read LCD panels. The stitches are displayed on the LCD panel. All you have to do is push a button to select the one you want. The machines also automatically adjust the tension and pressure setting to match your fabric.

A wide range of special stitches and embroidery stitches are built-in or stored in the machine's memory. Some machines offer hundreds of stitch programs, including alphabets, monograms, buttonhole styles, and decorative stitches. The machines can be programmed to combine these stitches into unique patterns or to sew them in single units.

Some machines have sewing advisory LCD panels that provide sewing information and helpful tips. Just press a button and your questions are answered. One machine provides all instructions in eight different languages!

Many computerized sewing machines encourage personalized designs. One machine enables you to draw your own design on the screen, using the command ball as a pencil. Another machine can be connected to a personal computer. You create your own design on the computer and download it to the sewing machine, which then stitches your design. You can store your original designs in the machine's memory.

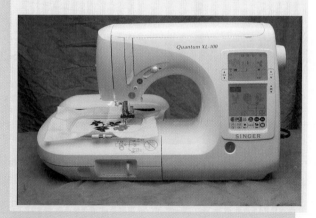

How a Stitch is Formed

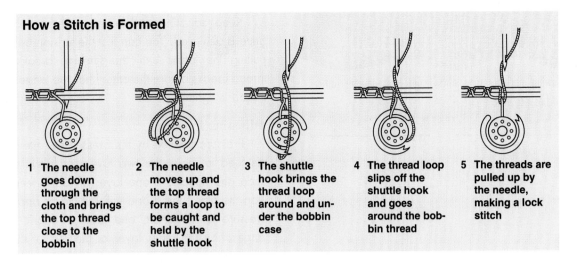

1. **The needle goes down through the cloth and brings the top thread close to the bobbin**

2. **The needle moves up and the top thread forms a loop to be caught and held by the shuttle hook**

3. **The shuttle hook brings the thread loop around and under the bobbin case**

4. **The thread loop slips off the shuttle hook and goes around the bobbin thread**

5. **The threads are pulled up by the needle, making a lock stitch**

Adjusting a Sewing Machine

How does a sewing machine work? As the needle thread intertwines with the bobbin thread, a **lockstitch** is formed. This intertwining of threads creates a *type of stitch that does not pull out or unravel when a loop or loose thread is pulled.*

Different adjustments need to be made to achieve the best type of stitch for each type of fabric. These adjustments include the type of stitch, length of stitch, tension, and pressure.

It is important to always pretest your adjustments by stitching on a scrap of the same fabric. Use a double thickness of fabric to imitate the sewing of actual seams.

Type of Stitch

Although any garment can be constructed with a straight stitch, most machines offer a variety of other stitches. These may include zigzag, stretch, and decorative stitches. The type of stitch is usually regulated by controls on the machine. Sometimes specialty stitches are controlled by separate discs which are inserted into the machine.

Length of Stitch

Stitch length should vary according to the type of fabric and the purpose of the stitching. The numbers on the stitch-length control are based on either the inch or metric measurement. Numbers from 6 to 20 indicate the number of stitches per inch. Numbers from 1 to 5 indicate the length of stitch in millimeters. For example, the number 4 indicates that each stitch is 4 mm long; that is the equivalent of 6 stitches per inch.

- **For regular stitching,** a medium-length stitch is recommended for most fabrics. This is 10 to 12 stitches per inch (or a stitch length of 2 to 2.5 mm). For lightweight fabrics, use a shorter stitch. For heavier fabrics, use a longer stitch.

- **For machine basting,** use the longest stitch possible so it can be easily removed. Basting is 6 to 8 stitches per inch (3 to 4 mm stitch length).

- **For reinforcement stitching,** use very short stitches to prevent stretching or pulling in certain areas. This is 15 to 20 stitches per inch (1 to 1.5 mm stitch length).

STITCH LENGTH CONVERSION

Some sewing machines show stitch length in millimeters rather than stitches per inch:

Stitches per Inch	MM Equivalent
24	1
13	2
9	3
6	4
5	5

Adjusting Tension

A properly balanced stitch has two threads locking in the center between the two layers of fabric. Tension must be adjusted if the stitches are too tight or too loose. Check the tension by sewing sample stitches on a double layer of fabric. Examine the stitching.

If the top thread lies flat on the surface of the fabric and loops show on the top, then the top tension is too tight. Turn the tension dial to a lower number.

If the bottom row of stitching is flat along the bottom layer of fabric with loops showing on the surface, then the top tension is too loose. Turn the dial to a higher number.

Keep adjusting and testing until the proper balance is achieved. You can test the tension balance by pulling the fabric until the stitching breaks. If one thread breaks before the other, then the tension on that thread is tighter.

Adjusting Pressure

Pressure applied by the presser foot interacts with the feed to move the two layers of fabric smoothly under the needle. If one layer of fabric feeds faster than the other, the fabric will bubble or ripple. If the pressure is too great, one layer of fabric may be longer than the other layer at the end of the seam. When the pressure is correct, both layers of fabric feed smoothly under the needle. The result is an an evenly stitched seam.

Some machines have a pressure regulator that can be adjusted; others do not. Refer to your manual.

Using the Sewing Machine

It takes practice to learn to control the speed of a sewing machine. Use light pressure on the knee or foot control. Experiment with slowly increasing and decreasing the speed. Learn how to start slowly, build up speed when stitching a long row of stitching, and then slow down as you approach the end.

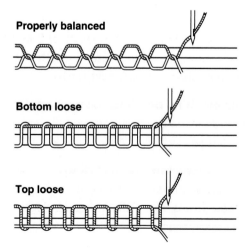

Properly balanced

Bottom loose

Top loose

Safety TIP

- Use a slow speed when learning how to use the machine.
- Keep your fingers away from the needle.
- Do not lean your face too close when stitching in case the needle breaks.
- Do not stitch over pins. Carefully remove them as you sew.
- Unplug the cord from the outlet when the machine is not in use.

Guidelines on Stitching

1. *Before you start to stitch,* raise the take-up lever and the needle to the highest position. This will prevent the upper thread from pulling out of the needle when you start stitching. Be sure both threads are pulled back behind the presser foot to prevent any tangled stitches.

2. *Place* the fabric under the presser foot with the bulk of fabric to the left of the needle.

3. *Line up* the stitching line directly under the needle.

4. *To begin stitching,* turn the hand wheel to lower the needle into the fabric. Then lower the presser foot. Gradually apply pressure on the knee or foot control to stitch at a slow, even speed.

5. *When you stop stitching,* turn the hand wheel to raise the take-up lever and needle to the highest point. Raise the presser foot. Gently slide the fabric toward the back of the machine. Do not pull the fabric forward because you could bend the needle. Clip the threads.

Stitching Straight

It takes practice to learn how to guide the fabric with your hands as you stitch. Your first rows of stitching may not be perfectly straight. Do not pull or push the fabric. Instead, keep one hand in front and one hand behind the presser foot to guide the fabric smoothly.

Use the guideline markings on the needle or throat plate to help keep the rows of stitching straight. Line up the edge of the fabric with the ⅝-inch (1.5 cm) guideline. Keep your eyes on this marking. Do not watch the needle.

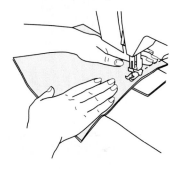

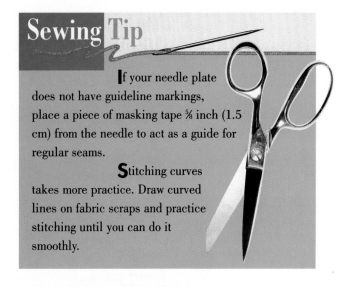

Sewing Tip

If your needle plate does not have guideline markings, place a piece of masking tape ⅝ inch (1.5 cm) from the needle to act as a guide for regular seams.

Stitching curves takes more practice. Draw curved lines on fabric scraps and practice stitching until you can do it smoothly.

Correcting Stitching Problems

Frequently the cause of stitching problems is incorrect threading. If rethreading the machine does not correct the problem, check the needle and the tension setting. Refer to the chart on page 454 for solutions to specific stitching problems.

Sewing Machine Accessories

A variety of accessories are available for most machines:

- **Straight stitch foot** has a narrow opening and is used for sewing straight stitches.

- **Zigzag foot** has a wide opening to allow for sideways movement of the needle for zigzag and special stitches, as well as straight stitches.

- **Zipper foot** can be adjusted to the right or left side of the needle for stitching close to zipper teeth or cording.

- **Buttonhole foot** has markings for measuring buttonhole stitches.

- **Blindstitch hem** foot guides the fabric for a blindstitch hem.

CORRECTING STITCHING PROBLEMS

Problem	Possible Solutions
Skipped Stitches	Replace dull or bent needle Rethread machine Check size and type of needle for fabric Loosen upper thread tension Check needle position
Bunching of thread	Pull thread ends behind presser foot and hold when starting to stitch Rethread machine
Puckering	Loosen upper tension Replace dull or bent needle Use same type thread in needle and bobbin Loosen pressure on presser foot Shorten stitch length
Thread breaks	Check threading of machine Replace needle Check size of needle Check thread for knots or unevenness Begin stitching at a slower speed
Needle breaks	Carefully guide the fabric through the machine, do not pull Check needle position Tighten presser foot Too many layers of fabric
Machine jams under	Check for loops of matted thread under stitching Check bobbin for caught thread Check needle position Check machine threading
Machine does not sew	Check on/off switch Tighten hand wheel knob Check electrical cord Check knee or foot control

Sewing Machine Care

A sewing machine needs routine care so it is always in top working condition. How often do you need to clean your machine? It depends on how often it is used. Lint from fabric gathers around the bobbin and the needle bar and can eventually clog the machine. Many people clean their machine before starting a new project. In the sewing laboratory, your instructor will give you guidelines.

Always disconnect the plug before cleaning the machine. Use a soft cloth to remove lint or fuzz from the machine base and needle bar. Use a soft brush to gently clean the bobbin and bobbin case. If possible, remove the entire bobbin case mechanism, following directions in the manual. Wipe away old oil with a cloth.

Many new machines are designed to never need additional oil. The oil is permanently imbedded in the machine. Never oil these types of machines.

If your machine does require oil, the manual will show the specific areas to be oiled. Use only high-grade sewing machine oil. Wipe the machine carefully with a cloth to remove any drips or excess oil. Then plug it in and stitch on a swatch of fabric to be sure all excess oil is removed. Machine oil stains fabric and is very difficult to remove.

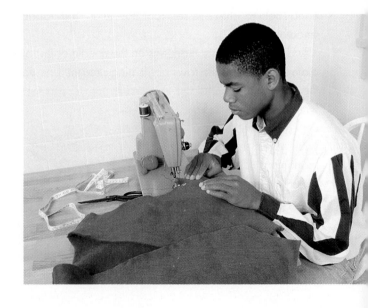

Lesson 2

The Serger or Overlock Machine

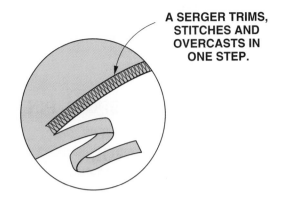

A SERGER TRIMS, STITCHES AND OVERCASTS IN ONE STEP.

The **serger,** also called an **overlock machine,** is a *special sewing machine that can stitch, trim, and overcast a seam all at the same time.* It does this while sewing twice as fast as the conventional machine.

Because a serger can handle thicker threads than a conventional machine, it can be used to create special effects on seams and edges. It also does a special edge finish, called a *narrow rolled hem.*

Sergers are described by the number of threads they use. There are three-thread, four-thread, and five-thread machines. A serger may have one or two needles. Each needle thread has its own knob or dial to control the tension. Only the needle thread penetrates the fabric when serging.

Instead of a bobbin, the serger has two *loopers,* called the upper looper and the lower looper. The two looper threads come up from underneath the needle plate. Each looper has its own tension adjustment. The upper looper thread appears on the top of the fabric; the lower looper thread on the underside. The two looper threads interlock at the fabric edge.

On the right side of the needle plate, there are moveable and stationary *knives.* These trim off the excess fabric before the stitch is formed. Most machines have knives that are retractable, so you can serge without cutting the fabric.

Some sergers have a *differential feed,* which is two sets of feed dogs that move the fabric through the machine at different speeds. This can be used to gather one layer of fabric to a straight piece of fabric. It also can prevent puckered seams on lightweight, silky fabrics and prevent wavy seams on stretchy knits.

The overlock machine is not a replacement for the conventional machine. For example, it cannot make buttonholes, insert a zipper, or do embroidery. However, using both machines allows you to make clothes using the same sewing techniques that are used for ready-to-wear.

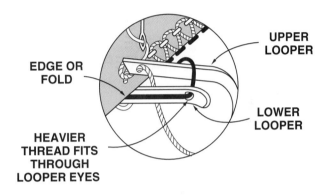

UPPER LOOPER

EDGE OR FOLD

LOWER LOOPER

HEAVIER THREAD FITS THROUGH LOOPER EYES

Serger stitches are formed over the edge of the fabric.

Safety TIP

Never sew over pins with a serger. The knives will cut through a pin, which dulls the blades. The pin fragments can cut your face, hurt your eyes, or damage the inner workings of the machine. If pins are needed to hold the fabric pieces together, place the pins 1 inch (2.5 cm) away from the edge. A glue stick or basting stitches can also be used.

Serger or Overlock Machine

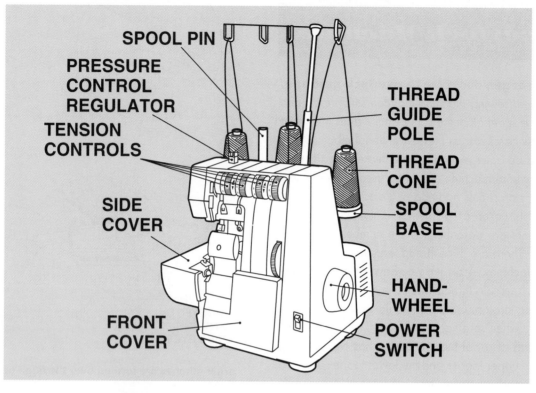

SPOOL PIN

PRESSURE CONTROL REGULATOR

TENSION CONTROLS

SIDE COVER

FRONT COVER

THREAD GUIDE POLE

THREAD CONE

SPOOL BASE

HAND-WHEEL

POWER SWITCH

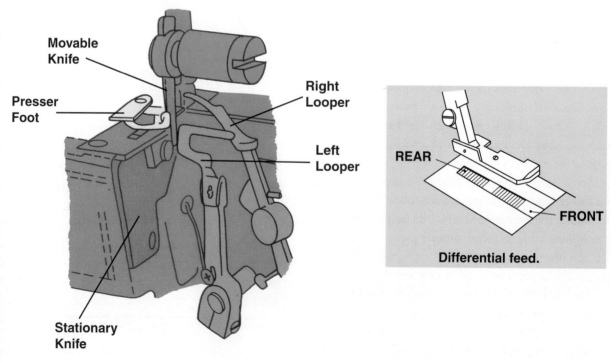

Movable Knife

Presser Foot

Right Looper

Left Looper

Stationary Knife

REAR

FRONT

Differential feed.

Stitch Variations

Some sergers can create only one or two variations of overlock stitches; others can perform several. A five-thread machine can create all of the stitches. Here are different types of overlock stitches:

- **Three-thread overlock stitch** is the basic overlock stitch. It is formed by one needle and two looper threads. All three threads interlock at the edge of the fabric. It is used to stitch and overcast a seam and to finish the fabric edges of a conventional seam. It can also be used for hemming.

- **Four-thread overlock stitch** is more durable than the three-thread stitch because it adds an extra row of stitches. It uses two needles and two loopers. The *four-thread safety stitch* consists of a two-thread overlock stitch and a two-thread chain stitch. It is recommended for woven fabrics, because the chain stitch may break if the fabric is stretched. The *four-thread mock safety stitch* can be used for both knits and wovens.

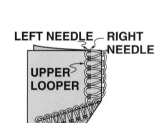

Three–thread overlock stitch

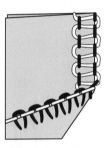

Four–thread overlock stitch

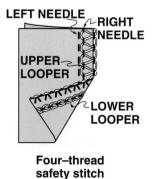

Four–thread safety stitch

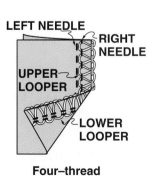

Four–thread mock safety stitch

- **Two-thread overlock stitch** is created by one needle and one looper thread. The two threads interlock at the edge of the fabric. The needle thread forms a V on the underside of the fabric. This stitch is used mainly as a seam finish on a conventional seam or as an edge finish.

- **Two-thread chain stitch** is formed by one needle and one looper. This stitch does not overcast the edge, so it can be used to make a conventional seam. If the cutter can be disengaged, the chain stitch can be used for decorative topstitching. Only a few sergers offer this stitch.

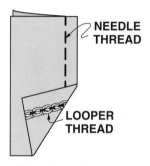

Two–thread overlock stitch

Two–thread chain stitch

- **Five-thread overlock stitch** is a two-thread chain stitch in combination with a three-thread overlock stitch. The more threads involved in the stitch, the more durable the seam.

- **Rolled hem stitch** is a variation of the three-thread overlock stitch. It creates a narrow row of short, dense stitches. The result is a bulk-free hem. This edge finish is often used on placemats, napkins, ruffles, scarves, and garment hems. On some

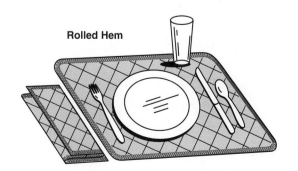

Rolled Hem

overlocks, you can switch to the rolled hem stitch by changing the dials. On others, it is necessary to change the needle plate and/or the presser foot.

is formed on the underside after the fabric is pulled flat. The stitch is reversible because you can plan to have either the loops or the ladder stitches show on the outside of the fabric.

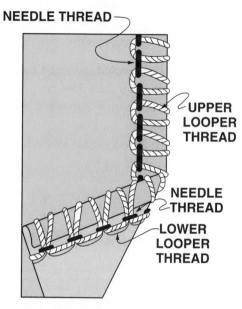

Rolled hem stitch

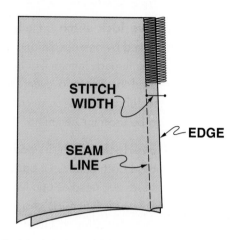

1. Guide fabric under serger so stitches overhang edge of fabric.

- **Flatlock stitch** is used to create a decorative outside seam. It can be done with two threads or three threads, depending on the machine. The stitch forms loops on the top of the fabric; a ladder stitch

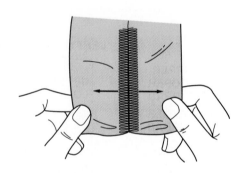

2. Gently pull seam flat.

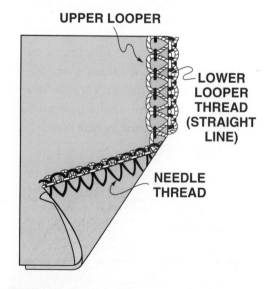

Three-thread flatlock stitch.

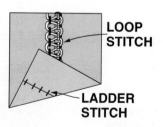

3. Finished flatlock seam has loops on one side, ladders on other side.

Serger Tension

There is one tension control for each thread used in forming the overlock stitch. Thus, you can adjust the tension separately for each looper and each needle. In general, the heavier the thread, the looser the tension.

To create a balanced stitch, you need to adjust the tension whenever you change fabric, thread, stitch width, or stitch length. The upper and lower looper threads should hug the top and bottom of the seam and meet exactly at the edge. If one thread is pulled to the other side of the fabric or overhangs the fabric edge, the tension must be adjusted.

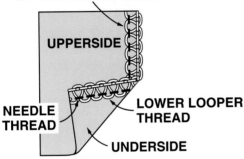

A balanced serger stitch.

The needle thread should look like a line of straight stitching on the top of the fabric, with only tiny loops on the underside. If the tension is too tight, the seam will pucker. If too loose, the seam will spread apart when gently pulled. Always check the tension by serging on a fabric swatch before starting a project.

CORRECTING SERGING PROBLEMS

Problem	Possible Solutions
Skipped Stitches	Replace dull or bent needle Check size and type of needle Loosen upper looper tension Rethread machine
Thread breaks	Check threading sequence Check thread spool or cone Loosen tension of thread Replace dull or bent needle Try a different thread
Loops form at edge of fabric	Check threading at tension discs, take-up lever, thread guides Increase looper tension Check knife alignment
Stitches pull through to right side of fabric	Increase needle thread tension Check threading at tension discs and thread guides Replace dull or bent needle Use wider stitch width Check knife alignment
Machine jams	Serge a thread chain at end of seam so thread will not get caught under presser foot Insert fabric in front of needle and knife

WHAT CAN A SERGER DO?

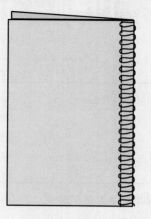

Overlock seam.

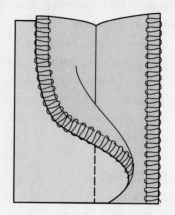

Conventional seam with overlock finish.

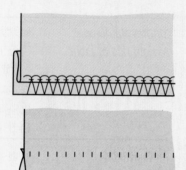

Blindstitch hem.

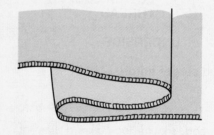

Narrow rolled hem.

Decorative seams.

Stretchable seams.

Serger Threads and Accessories

Conventional polyester or polyester/cotton thread can be used for general sewing. However, because the overlock machine sews faster and uses more threads in each seam, some special threads are helpful.

- **Polyester or polyester/cotton serger thread** is similar to conventional all-purpose thread. It is slightly finer and comes on large cones or tubes.

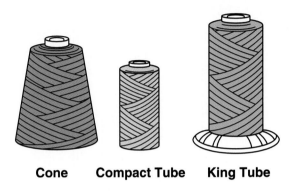

Cone   Compact Tube   King Tube

- **Woolly nylon thread** is a soft, fuzzy thread that stretches when sewn. It is a good choice for serging swimwear and lingerie. It also gives the narrow rolled hem an attractive, "filled in" appearance. Woolly nylon thread is used in the loopers; all-purpose serger thread is used in the needles.

- **Decorative threads** can be used in the loopers to create special effects. These threads include metallic thread, pearl cotton thread, 1/16-inch (1 to 2 mm) wide silk or rayon ribbon, and crochet cotton. Because the loopers have large eyes, it is possible to use a wider range of decorative threads on the overlock than on the conventional sewing machine. A regular serger thread is used in the needles.

Some special notions help ensure smooth stitching:

- **Adapter cones** fit over the spool holder pins. These cones prevent the large thread cones from vibrating when the machine is in operation.

- **Spool caps** fit over the top of standard spools of thread to hold them in place on the spool pin holders. Always place the spool with the notch down to prevent the thread from catching in the notch and breaking.

SPOOL CAP

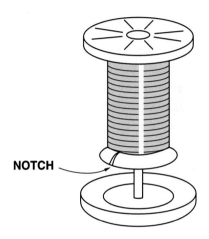

NOTCH

- **Thread nets** fit over the thread spools to keep the thread from unwinding too quickly.

- **Tweezers** and a **loop threader** are helpful for threading the machine.

Overlock Machine Care

As the knife trims the fabric, it creates a great deal of lint. For good performance, it is important to keep the overlock machine lint-free. Use the small brush that comes with the machine to remove lint from the area around the knife and loopers. Canned compressed air also can be used for cleaning. This can be purchased at fabric, sewing machine, and camera stores. Follow the instructions in the machine's manual for how to oil the machine.

Lesson 3

Sewing Equipment

Check with your instructor to learn what basic equipment is needed in your class work. Some tools are necessary to have; others are designed for very specialized tasks. These items can be added to your basic equipment as your skills and interest grow.

Sewing equipment can be divided into six groups according to their use: measuring, pinning, cutting, marking, stitching, and pressing.

Measuring Tools

Measuring tools are among the most important items in your sewing box. Most will include both standard and metric measurements. The three essential measuring tools are a tape measure, a sewing gauge, and a yardstick or meterstick.

- **Tape measure** is a flexible measuring tape 60 inches (150 cm) long to use for taking body measurements; keep neatly rolled in your sewing box. (1)

- **Sewing or seam gauge** is a 6 inch (15 cm) ruler with an adjustable marker to use for measuring short lengths, such as hems and seam widths; set marker for the width you are measuring. (2)

- **Yardstick or meterstick** is a 36 inch (91.5 cm) rigid measuring stick of wood, metal, or plastic to use for checking grain lines and marking hemlines. (3)

- **Transparent ruler** is useful for measuring and marking buttonholes, pleats, tucks, and bias strips. (4)

- **Hem gauge** is a metal or plastic tool to mark straight or curved hems. (5)

- **Skirt marker** is a device used to measure and mark hemlines of garments with either pins or chalk. (6)

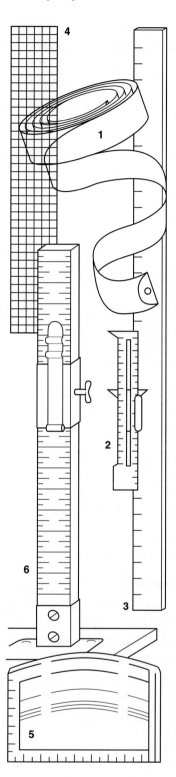

Pinning Tools

Pins are necessary for many stages of sewing—from laying out the pattern, to holding two layers of fabric together while stitching, to marking the hemline. Pins should be sharp, slender, and smoothly finished to avoid damaging the fabric.

- **Silk pins** are made of stainless steel or brass; used with most fabrics. (1)

- **Ball-point pins** have rounded points to slip between the yarns and help prevent snagging the fabric; used for knitted fabrics. (1)

- **Ball-headed pins** have colorful round plastic or glass heads to make them easier to see and to pick up. (2)

- **T-pins** have a large T-shaped head for use with loosely woven, bulky, or pile fabrics. (3)

- **Pin cushions** are available in many different styles; some have an elastic or plastic band so they can be worn around your wrist. *Magnetic pin cushions* hold pins securely even when tipped over. One type is shaped like a shallow bowl and can be turned upside down to pick up pins off a table. Another type has adhesive backing and can be attached to the sewing machine. A third type can be worn as a wrist pin cushion. (4)

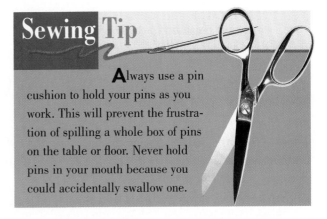

Sewing Tip

Always use a pin cushion to hold your pins as you work. This will prevent the frustration of spilling a whole box of pins on the table or floor. Never hold pins in your mouth because you could accidentally swallow one.

Safety TIP

- Keep pins in a pin cushion, never in your mouth or clothes.
- Keep shears and scissors closed when not using them.
- Pass a sharp object handle first to another person.
- Keep all tools in your sewing box when not in use.

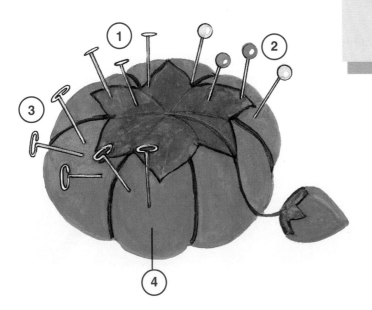

Cutting Tools

Cutting tools are used for cutting out fabric pieces, trimming, clipping, and other detail work. **Shears** *have long blades and two handles that are shaped differently.* They are used for cutting out fabric. **Scissors** *are smaller than shears and both handles are the same shape.* They are used for trimming, clipping, and cutting threads. You will need a pair of shears and a pair of scissors.

Be sure your sewing scissors and shears are sharp. Dull blades make it very difficult to cut accurately.

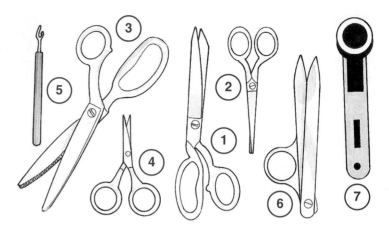

- **Dressmaker's shears** have bent handles so the fabric can lie flat on the table as you cut. This results in better accuracy than lifting up the fabric while cutting. Shears have two differently shaped handles—one fits your thumb and the other handle fits several fingers. Blades are usually 7 to 8 inches (18 to 20 cm) in length. Quality shears have an adjustable screw so you can adjust the cutting action of the blades. (1)

- **Sewing scissors** have small round handles and shorter blades 4 to 6 inches (10 to 15 cm) in length. The blades are different widths. Sewing scissors are easier to handle than shears for detail work. Use scissors to trim seams, clip curves, and cut into corners. (2)

- **Pinking** or **scalloping shears** are used to finish a seam edge or other raw edge on firmly woven fabrics. The zigzag or scallop design helps to prevent raveling. Do not use pinking or scalloping shears to cut out fabric pieces because the uneven

edge is difficult to follow when stitching. Instead, pink or scallop the seam edges after the seams are stitched. (3)

- **Embroidery scissors** are small scissors, only 3 to 4 inches (7.5 to 10 cm) in length, with very pointed blades. Use embroidery scissors for detail work such as cutting buttonholes and ripping stitches. (4)

- **Seam ripper** is a pen-shaped gadget with a small blade at one end for removing stitches. Use the blade to lift the thread away from the fabric before cutting. Be careful not to cut the fabric. (5)

- **Thread clipper** has spring-action blades to clip thread ends or stitching. (6)

- **Rotary cutter** looks like a pizza cutter with a round, retractable blade. Crafters and quilters like it because you can make a straight, clean cut through multiple layers of fabric. The cutter must be used with a special "self-healing" mat. (7)

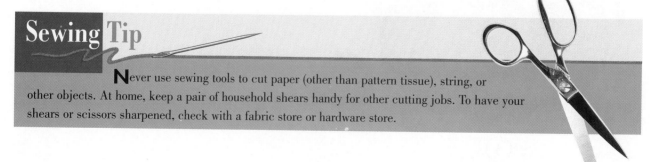

Sewing Tip

Never use sewing tools to cut paper (other than pattern tissue), string, or other objects. At home, keep a pair of household shears handy for other cutting jobs. To have your shears or scissors sharpened, check with a fabric store or hardware store.

Sewing Tip

Ironing over the marks made by some fabric marking pens may permanently set the ink. Be sure to remove the marks before pressing the area.

Marking Tools

Marking tools are needed to transfer symbols and lines from the pattern pieces to the fabric. Accurate markings help make construction easier. The type of marking equipment you use depends on the type of fabric you are marking.

- **Fabric marking pen** contains disappearing ink that makes it possible to mark on the right or wrong side of the fabric. With some pens, the ink marks will disappear when treated with water. With other pens, the ink will evaporate from the fabric, usually in less than 48 hours. (1)

- **Tracing wheel** is used to transfer markings to fabric by running the wheel over dress-maker's tracing paper, a special waxed carbon paper. A saw-toothed wheel can be used for most fabrics. A smooth-edge wheel is recommended for delicate fabrics. The tracing paper is available in several colors. The tracing marks can be removed by washing or dry cleaning the fabric. (2,3,4)

- **Tailor's chalk** is available in small squares or in pencil form to mark fabrics. The markings can be brushed away or will disappear when pressed with an iron. (5, 6)

- **Ordinary thread** can be used to mark construction lines on the fabric.

SPECIAL SEWING ITEMS

Here are some special items for faster and easier sewing:

- **Disappearing basting thread** dissolves in the wash or when you iron over it with a damp press cloth.

- **Liquid seam sealant** is a colorless liquid which can be applied to fabric or ribbon to prevent the cut edges from fraying.

- **Stabilizers** add temporary body and support to your fabric. They are particularly useful for machine embroidery and machine applique work. One type of stabilizer can be torn away after the work is finished. Another type dissolves when washed or sprayed with water.

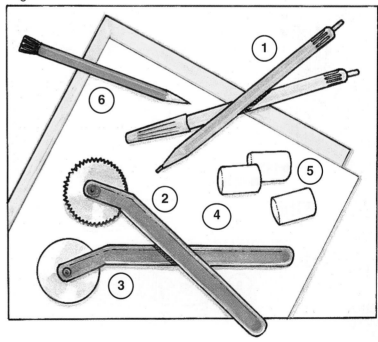

Stitching Tools

Although most projects can be made almost entirely by machine stitching, some hand sewing may be needed to complete the project. All sewing boxes need a variety of needles and at least one thimble:

- **Needles** should have sharp points and smooth eyes to avoid snagging the fabric or splitting the thread. They are available in a variety of sizes and types. Sizes range from 1 (coarse) to 12 (fine). The smaller the number, the larger and coarser the needle. For most hand-sewing tasks, use a size 7 or 8 needle. For delicate fabrics, use a finer needle. For heavy fabrics, use a coarser needle. Some packages contain only one size; others contain a variety.

    Different types of needles have different lengths and shapes of the eye. *Sharps* are all-purpose, medium-length needles with a small eye and sharp point. *Embroidery* and *crewel needles* have larger eyes and are easier to thread. *Specialty needles* are available for heavy-duty fabrics and crafts. (1)

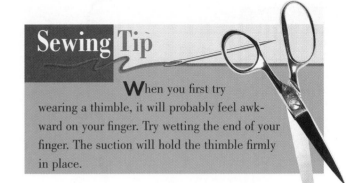

Sewing Tip

When you first try wearing a thimble, it will probably feel awkward on your finger. Try wetting the end of your finger. The suction will hold the thimble firmly in place.

- **Thimble** will help protect your finger when sewing by hand. Made of metal or plastic, thimbles are available in different sizes. Small indentations on the top and sides help hold the end of the needle as you push it through the fabric. (2)

- **Needle threader** is a small device with a thin metal wire that helps thread a needle. (3)

- **Glue stick** is a fast, easy way to temporarily hold two layers of fabric together. Be sure the glue is thoroughly dry before you stitch through it. (4)

- **Basting tape** is a narrow, double-faced tape used to hold two layers of fabric together or a zipper in place for stitching. (5)

- **Bodkin** resembles a large, blunt needle. It is used to pull cord, elastic, or tape through casings. (6)

- **Loop turner** is a long metal rod with a hook. It is used to turn bias tubing right side out. (7)

- **Pointer** is a wooden tool with one pointed end for pushing out sharp corners. The other end is rounded for holding seams open for pressing. (8)

- **Sewing tape** has measured markings to use as a stitching guide. (9)

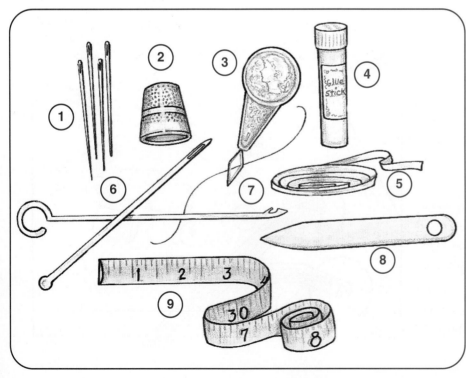

466

Handle an iron carefully. If you drop it, the thermostat control that regulates the temperature can be damaged. Avoid ironing over pins since they can scratch the *soleplate*, or bottom of an iron. Take care when using fusible interfacings or fusible webs so the adhesive does not touch the iron. Irons should be stored empty of water.

- **Press cloth** protects certain fabrics from developing a *shine,* or *glossy* marking, and from scorching. Dampen a press cloth to create steam for special pressing techniques. You can use a clean cloth or handkerchief as a press cloth. (2)

- **Tailor's ham** is a firm, round cushion used to press curved areas of a garment, such as darts and curved seams. (3)

- **Sleeve board** is a small ironing board about 20 inches (51 cm) long. It is used to press narrow areas, such as sleeves, which cannot fit over the end of a regular ironing board. (4)

- **Seam roll** is a long, firm tubular cushion used to press long seams and small curved areas. A seamline can be pressed without having the imprint of the seam allowances showing through on the right side of the fabric. (5)

- **Point presser** has a narrow wooden surface with a pointed end used to press collar points. Other edges can be used for pressing curved and straight edges. (6)

Pressing Equipment

Pressing equipment helps to give a professional finish to a garment. It is very important to press as you sew. Three essential items are an iron, ironing board, and press cloth:

- **Iron** should have a wide temperature range to use with all fabrics. A combination steam-dry iron gives best results. (1)

- **Ironing board** should be level and sturdy with a tight-fitting cover and smooth padding. A silicone-treated cover helps to prevent scorching and sticking.

Part 2 REVIEW

Summary

- All sewing machines operate in a similar manner. Refer to the instruction manual when you have a question or problem.
- Choose the correct needle and thread according to the type and weight of fabric being stitched.
- Replace the needle when it becomes dull, bent, or rough.
- Different adjustments may be necessary to achieve the best type of stitch.
- It takes practice to learn to control the speed of a sewing machine.
- The serger, or overlock machine, can stitch, trim, and overcast a seam at the same time.
- A serger creates different stitches with three, four, or five threads.
- Special equipment and tools are used for measuring, pinning, cutting, marking, stitching, and pressing.

Recalling the Facts

1. What should you do if you have a specific question or problem with your sewing machine or serger?
2. What type of sewing machine needle is designed for knits and stretch fabrics?
3. When choosing a sewing machine needle and thread for a sewing project, what should you consider?
4. What are at least three features of computerized sewing machines?
5. What stitch length is recommended for regular stitching on most fabrics?
6. What type of stitches are used for reinforcement stitching?
7. In a properly balanced stitch, where do the two threads interlock?
8. Before you start to stitch, what two things should you do to prevent any tangled stitches?
9. Where should you place your hands when you are stitching with a conventional sewing machine?
10. What can you use to help you stitch straight?
11. What is a frequent cause of stitching problems?
12. What three tasks does a serger do at the same time?
13. What does a serger have instead of a bobbin?
14. Why should you never sew over pins with a serger?
15. How many threads does the basic overlock stitch have?
16. Name the three essential measuring tools.
17. What is the difference between scissors and shears?
18. List at least three items that can be used to mark fabrics.
19. What is the purpose of a thimble?
20. Name the three essential items needed for pressing.

Thinking Critically

1. **Analysis.** Compare a conventional sewing machine to an overlock machine. What are the advantages and disadvantages of each?

2. **Synthesis.** Summarize the things that a person should check before starting to sew on a conventional sewing machine.

3. **Evaluation.** Make a list of the essential sewing equipment and tools that would be needed to complete a project.

4. **Evaluation.** If you could purchase either a conventional sewing machine or a serger, which would you choose? Support your answer.

Practicing Your Skills

1. **Sewing Machine.** Demonstrate how to wind the bobbin and then thread a conventional sewing machine. Stitch a row of regular stitches, basting stitches, and reinforcement stitches.

2. **Serger.** Demonstrate how to thread an overlock machine and adjust the tension for each looper and needle. Then sew the various types of stitches that the machine can create.

Applying Your Knowledge

1. **Identification.** Working with a partner, name and describe the various parts of a sewing machine or an overlock machine to the other person. Then reverse roles.

What Is an Educational Representative?

Educational representatives are employed by sewing machine and sewing equipment manufacturers. They demonstrate the use of sewing products at conventions and stores. They also write instruction manuals and sewing leaflets. Some educational representatives design special projects and patterns that highlight the use of the manufacturer's products.

Try It Yourself

Imagine that you are an educational representative for a sewing machine or sewing equipment manufacturer. Develop a five-minute demonstration of the company's product(s). Discuss the features and demonstrate the proper use of the product(s).

Build Your Portfolio

Write an outline of your demonstration and place it in your portfolio. If possible, make a tape or video of the presentation and add it to your portfolio.

2. **Safety.** Create a poster of safety tips for using sewing machines, sergers, and equipment.

3. **Equipment.** Visit a store that sells sewing equipment. Research the price of various tools and equipment. Determine the total cost of the basic tools that a beginning sewer would need.

Part 3

Getting Ready to Sew

● ● ● ● ● ● ● ● ● ● ● ●

Take a few minutes to get organized before you begin a project. You will end up saving time and effort along the way:

- **Be sure you have all of the necessary notions and supplies.** The recommended size and quantity of fasteners and trims are listed on the back of the pattern envelope.

- **Read the pattern guide sheet thoroughly.** It is important to understand the various steps of layout and construction. This helps prevent having to rip out and redo stitches.

- **Press after each step of construction.** It may be impossible to carefully press a certain area after other seams have been stitched.

- **Fit as you go along.** It is much easier to make a few minor adjustments during construction than to make a major alteration in the end.

- **Always take a moment to double-check your steps.** Ask yourself some questions: Are all of the pattern pieces properly laid out before starting to cut? Are the fabric pieces pinned together correctly before starting to stitch? Are the seams and darts pressed smoothly before stitching the other seams? Does each section fit properly before continuing on?

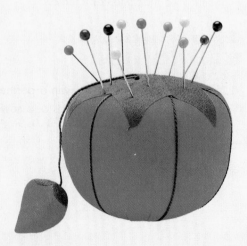

Lesson 1

Understanding the Pattern

A **pattern** is just like a blueprint. It *contains all of the instructions you will need for constructing a sewing project.* Every pattern consists of an envelope, a guide sheet, and tissue pattern pieces.

Always take time to read all parts of the pattern before beginning a project. Each item contains valuable information to help make your sewing easier and more successful.

Pattern Envelope

On the front of the envelope, you will find a drawing or photograph of the fashion design. Several different views may be shown to give you a wider selection of styles. From the illustrations, you will be able to see how the garment fits—whether it is slim or full on the body.

The envelope front will list the pattern number, figure type, size, and price. Sometimes a label will indicate that the pattern is "Easy" or "Includes an Estimated Sewing Time." Special features of the pattern—such as a designer fashion, a sewing lesson, or a crafts project—may be mentioned on the envelope.

The back of the pattern envelope describes the design of the garment. It also lists the amount of fabric and type of notions needed for the project. See page 431.

Guide Sheet

The **guide sheet** gives you *step-by-step information for cutting, marking, and sewing the fabric pieces together.* General information and cutting layouts are printed on the front side of the guide sheet. A diagram of all of the pattern pieces will make it easier to recognize and sort the various pieces. Information about how to lengthen and shorten pattern pieces is given. Sewing directions are printed on the reverse side and may extend to two or more pages.

The guide sheet provides information about cutting, marking, and stitching the fabric pieces together.

The three main parts of a pattern are the envelope, the guide sheet, and the pattern pieces.

Sewing Tip

Circle the correct cutting layout for easy reference. Double-check that it matches your design view, pattern size, fabric width, and "with nap" or "without nap" layout.

Always keep your sewing guide handy so you can refer to it throughout construction. Compete each step. Then go on to the next step.

Cutting Layouts

The diagrams show how to arrange the different size pattern pieces on various widths of fabric. Select the diagram that matches your particular design view, pattern size, fabric width, and "with nap" or "without nap" layout. A separate cutting layout may be included for interfacing or lining.

Sewing Directions

Step-by-step sewing directions appear on the reverse side of the guide sheet. For patterns with several garments or views, the directions may continue on another sheet.

A fabric key will show how shading and texture is used to indicate the right and wrong side of fabric and any interfacing or lining. Some construction details may be enlarged to clearly show the specific sewing procedure.

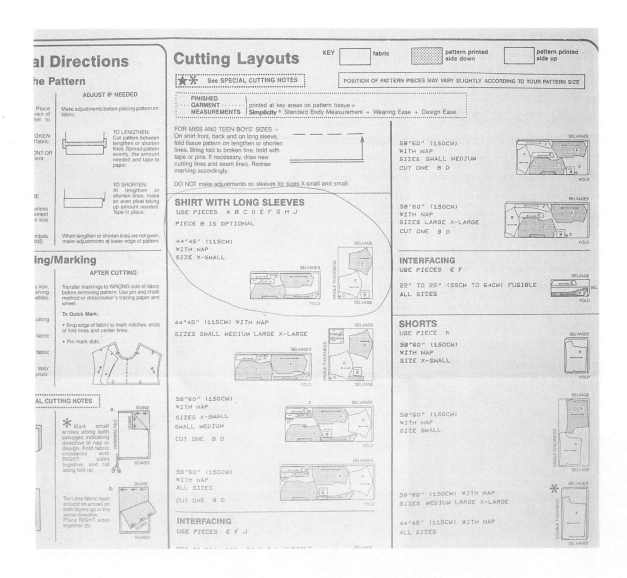

Pattern Pieces

Each pattern piece is marked with a number or letter and with a specific name, such as collar or sleeve. The number of fabric pieces to be cut will also be printed on the pattern piece.

The various lines and symbols on the pattern pieces serve as guides during cutting and sewing. Some pattern pieces will have many markings and symbols; others will have only a few. Learn to recognize and understand these symbols. See Pattern Symbols on pages 374-375.

Pattern Preparation

Remember to handle pattern pieces carefully because they are fragile and can tear. Follow these simple steps:

1. *Remove* entire pattern from envelope.
2. *Circle* layout diagram on guide sheet that you will be using.
3. *Select* pattern pieces that are needed for the view you are sewing.
4. *Fold* rest of pattern pieces and put back into envelope.
5. *Cut apart* any pattern pieces printed on one large piece of tissue paper. Do not trim away extra tissue paper from around pieces. This will be cut off as you cut out the fabric.
6. *Write* your name on the guide sheet, the pattern envelope, and all of the pattern pieces.
7. *Smooth out* pattern pieces. Press with a cool dry iron, if necessary. Wrinkled pattern pieces make it very difficult to cut fabric accurately.
8. *Mark* cutting lines for your size on a multi-sized pattern with a felt-tip pen.

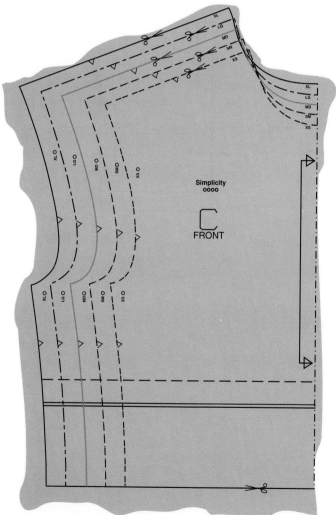

Mark the desired cutting lines on a multi-sized pattern with a felt-tip pen to make them easier to follow.

PATTERN SYMBOLS

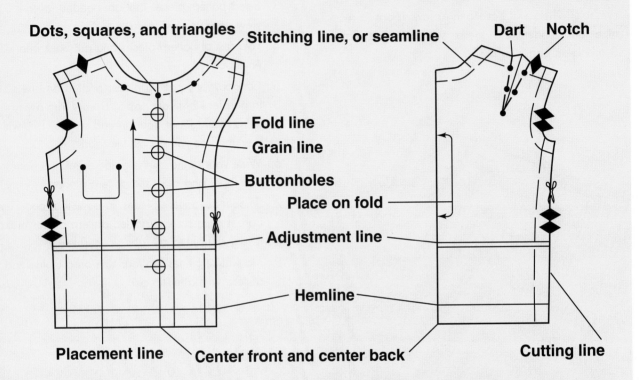

Dots, squares, and triangles

Stitching line, or seamline

Dart

Notch

Fold line

Grain line

Buttonholes

Place on fold

Adjustment line

Hemline

Placement line

Center front and center back

Cutting line

Continued

PATTERN SYMBOLS (CONTINUED)

Grain line A heavy solid line with an arrow at each end. It appears on all pattern pieces that are not cut on a fold. The grain line indicates how to place the pattern piece on grain. To do this, the grain line arrow must be placed exactly parallel to the selvage (unless otherwise noted).

Cutting line A heavy line that outlines the pattern pieces. Sometimes a symbol of a scissors is printed on the line to show the proper direction for cutting. Occasionally a cutting line appears within the pattern. This indicates a shorter hemline, a lower neckline, or a lining cut from the same pattern piece. If the pattern is multi-sized, the major pattern pieces will have several cutting lines. Each cutting line will be marked to indicate the corresponding size. To avoid confusion, use a felt-tip pen to mark the cutting lines for your size.

Notches Diamond-shaped symbols that extend beyond the cutting line. They are used for matching seams and joining garment pieces. Always cut around notches so they are clearly marked. When two or more notches are grouped together, cut them as one large block.

Stitching line or seamline A broken line usually ⅝ inch (1.5 cm) inside the cutting line. Sometimes it is marked by the symbol of a sewing machine presser foot or arrows to show in which direction to stitch. If the pattern is multi-sized, the stitching lines will not be marked. However, the width of the seam allowances will be listed in the general directions on the front of the guide sheet.

Center front and center back A solid line indicating where the center of the garment is located. If brackets appear on this line, then it should be placed on a fold.

Place on fold A bracketed grain line that indicates the pattern edge is to be placed exactly on the fold.

Fold line A solid line showing where fabric will be folded to form a finished edge, such as a hemline or cuff.

Dots, squares, and triangles Symbols used to help match and join garment sections, especially areas that are gathered or eased.

Dart Triangular or diamond shape indicated by dots and two broken lines.

Buttonholes A solid line that shows the exact location and length of each buttonhole.

Placement line A single solid or broken line showing the exact location of pockets, pleats, zippers, and trims.

Adjustment line Double parallel lines showing where the pattern piece can be lengthened or shortened.

Hemline A solid line indicating the finished edge of the garment and the depth of the hem.

Lesson 2

Adjusting the Pattern

Few people have the exact same measurements as those listed for the pattern sizes. Therefore, some minor adjustments may be necessary.

For loosely fitted garments, minor differences in measurements can be overlooked. For fitted garments, your measurements should correspond very closely to the body measurements for your pattern size.

Before you lay out the pattern pieces on the fabric, always check to see if any adjustments are needed in the pattern. After the fabric is cut, it is too late to add any extra inches to any part.

Understanding Ease

Pattern sizes are designed for the body measurements listed on the pattern envelope. However, only garments such as bodysuits or swimsuits will measure exactly the same as those body measurements. Most garments will have wearing ease added to the pattern.

Wearing ease is *the amount of fullness added to a pattern to allow for movement and comfort.* For fitted garments, most patterns have the following amount of ease:

- About 1 inch (2.5 cm) at the waistline.

- 2 to 2 ½ inches (5 to 6.5 cm) at the hips.

- 2 ½ to 4 inches (6.5 to 10 cm) at the bust or chest.

For fuller garments, designers have added *extra fullness to create a particular style or silhouette.* This ease is called **design ease.**

Comparing Measurements

Compare your own personal measurements with the body measurements listed on the pattern envelope. Make a chart listing your own measurements and the pattern size measurements for bust or chest, waist, hip, and back or side length. If any measurements are not the same, mark the plus or minus difference on your chart. Now you know where you have to make adjustments and how much to take in or let out. For example, if your waistline is 1 inch (2.5 cm) larger than the pattern size, you will have to increase the pattern pieces at the waistline a total of 1 inch (2.5 cm).

Some measurements are not listed on the pattern envelope. For these you will have to measure the actu-

PERSONAL MEASUREMENTS CHART

	My Own Measurements	Pattern Measurements	+ or -
Bust/Chest			
Waist			
Hip			
Back/Side Length			

al pattern pieces. Be sure to measure only from seamline to seamline. Do not include any darts, pleats, tucks, or overlapping edges. For total width, measure both the front and back sections and then double the amount. For length, measure only from seamline to hemline. Do not include the hem allowance.

Pattern Adjustments

Adjustments for length and for width must be done on both the front and back pattern pieces. It is very important to be accurate. If you make an error of just ¼ inch (6 mm) at the side seam of a pants pattern, it will become a 1 inch (2.5 cm) error when all four seam allowances are added up.

For all adjustments, follow these steps for best results:

1. *Adjust length* by shortening or lengthening pattern at the hemline or adjustment line.
2. *Adjust width* by increasing or decreasing pattern at side seams.
3. *Check* that grain lines remain straight.
4. *Redraw* any darts or design details.
5. *Complete* same adjustments on both front and back pattern pieces.
6. *Blend sizes* by drawing a new cutting line that tapers from the smaller size to the larger size.

Adjusting Length

Many patterns have adjustment lines printed on the pattern pieces. Other patterns are lengthened or shortened at the lower edge.

- **To lengthen a pattern at the adjustment line:** Cut pattern apart at the adjustment line. Place paper under opening and spread pieces the necessary amount. Keep cut edges parallel across entire opening. Check edges with a ruler. Also check that center front line and grain line are straight. Tape pattern pieces in place. Redraw cutting line along outer edge. Redraw any darts or design details. For pants, first adjust crotch length and then adjust overall length.

- **To lengthen a pattern at the lower edge:** Tape paper to edge of pattern. Measure down the necessary amount and draw a new cutting line parallel to lower edge. Extend cutting lines along side edges.

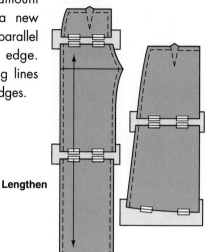

Lengthen

- **To shorten a pattern at the adjustment line:** Measure up from the adjustment line the necessary amount to be shortened and draw a line. Fold pattern along adjustment line and bring fold up to exactly meet new line. Check grain line. Tape fold in place. Redraw cutting lines and any darts or design lines.

Shorten

- **To shorten a pattern at the lower edge:** Draw a new hemline above the original line. Redraw cutting lines.

Adjusting Width

An adjustment of 2 inches (5 cm) or less can be made along the side seams of a garment. Because a garment has two side seams and four side seam allowances, the amount to be adjusted on the front pattern piece is ¼ of the total amount.

For example: To increase the waistline by 2 inches (5 cm), you will add ½ inch (1.3 cm) to the side

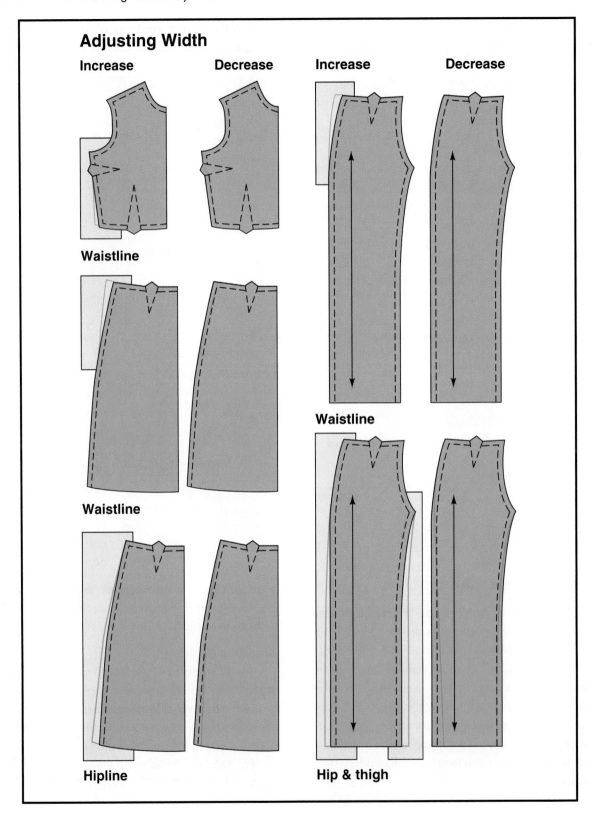

Adjusting Width

Increase   **Decrease**   **Increase**   **Decrease**

Waistline

Waistline

Waistline

Waistline

Hipline   **Hip & thigh**

seam of the front pattern piece and ½ inch (1.3 cm) to the side seam of the back pattern piece. Thus, each side seam will be increased 1 inch (2.5 cm), and the total waistline will be increased 2 inches (5 cm).

Width adjustments larger than 2 inches (5 cm) require cutting and spreading or overlapping the pattern pieces. For these, please refer to an alterations book or a detailed sewing book.

- **To increase the pattern width:** Tape paper along pattern piece edge. Measure out ¼ of the necessary amount at area to be widened. Redraw cutting lines and seam lines, tapering gradually. For a *waistline*, taper side seams up to armhole or down to hipline. Be sure to make same adjustments on waistband pattern. For *hipline*, continue adjustments down to hemline to retain original shape of pants or skirt. Above hipline, taper side seams in to meet original waistline. For *pants thigh*, add ¼ of the amount to each inseam and side seam, extending lines straight down to hem edge.

- **To decrease the pattern width:** Measure in ¼ of the necessary amount on each pattern piece. Redraw cutting lines and side seams, tapering gradually. For a *waistline*, taper side seams up to armhole or down to hipline. For a *waistband*, fold out ½ of the necessary amount at each side seam markings. For *hipline*, taper cutting lines and side seams up to original waistline and straight down to hemline. For *pants thigh*, take in ¼ of the amount on inside seam and side seam, redrawing lines straight down to hemline.

Blending Sizes

Multi-sized patterns are helpful to people who are a different size on top and bottom. For example, a person might have a size 10 bust and a size 12 hips. To blend two sizes, draw a new cutting line that gradually tapers out from the smaller size to the larger size.

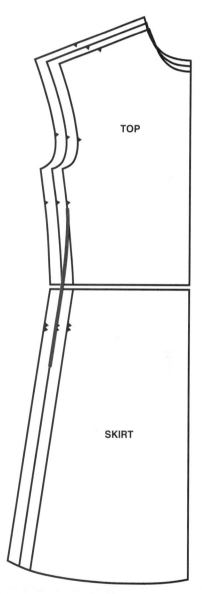

When blending two sizes of a multi-sized pattern, draw a new cutting line, tapering gradually from one size to the other.

Lesson 3

Preparing the Fabric

Although you may be eager to start cutting out the pattern pieces, it is very important to do some preparation steps. These steps are necessary for the fabric pieces to go together easily. They also help to guarantee that the garment will fit properly when it is finished and after it has been worn and laundered.

Straightening Fabric Ends

When fabric is cut from the bolt in a store, it is often not cut straight. Uneven edges make it difficult to check the straightness of the grain.

If you can clearly see the individual crosswise yarns, cut along one yarn from selvage to selvage. If not, clip the selvage and pull one crosswise yarn, gently pushing the fabric along the yarn. The pulled yarn will leave a mark that you can use as a cutting line. 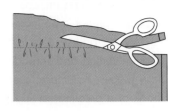 If the yarn breaks in the middle of the fabric, cut up to the broken point, then pick up the end of the yarn and continue pulling.

For knitted fabrics, straighten the ends by cutting along one crosswise row of loops. Knits do not have a  thread that can be pulled. Instead, baste across the fabric, following one row of loops. Use the basting as a cutting line.

FABRIC TERMINOLOGY

Selvages are *the two finished lengthwise edges of the fabric. They are usually stiffer than the rest of the fabric. Avoid placing pattern pieces over the selvage when laying out the pattern.*

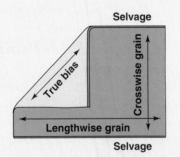

Lengthwise grain
runs in the same direction as the selvage. It is usually the strongest and sturdiest direction of the fabric. Most garments are cut with the lengthwise grain running vertically, or up and down, for more strength and durability during wear. Directions referring to straight grain or grain line mean the lengthwise grain.

Crosswise grain *runs across the fabric from one selvage to the other. In most fabrics, the crosswise grain usually has a slight amount of give or stretch.*

Bias grain *runs diagonally across the fabric. Bias is any direction other than lengthwise or crosswise grain. Fabric cut on bias grain has more stretchability than fabric cut on straight grain. True bias is created by folding the fabric at a 45° angle so the crosswise grain is parallel to the selvage. True bias has the most stretch.*

Wales or ribs are *the lengthwise chains of loops in knitted fabric. They correspond to the lengthwise grain of woven fabrics.*

Courses are *the crosswise rows of loops in knitted fabrics. In most knits, the crosswise loops have the most stretch.*

Preshrinking Fabric

Preshrinking means to *shrink a fabric by washing or dry cleaning to prevent or minimize shrinkage after the fabric is sewn into a finished garment.* Preshrinking also helps to remove some fabric finishes that cause stitching problems on lighter-weight woven and knitted fabrics. The method you choose depends upon how you plan to clean your finished garment. Check the fabric care instructions.

- **For washable fabrics:** Simply wash the fabric in the machine with other clothes. (For fabrics that may ravel easily, first machine zigzag the raw edges.) Dry either in a tumble dryer or lay flat, being sure to keep the edges square.

- **For hand-washable fabrics:** Fold the fabric and place in hot or warm water for 30 minutes.

- **For fabrics to be dry cleaned:** Take the fabric to a professional dry cleaner or a self-service dry cleaner for preshrinking.

Straightening Fabric Grain

Fabric is said to be **off-grain** when *the crosswise yarns are not at right angles to the lengthwise yarns.* This may happen during the finishing process or when the fabric is rolled onto the bolt. If the fabric is not straightened before the pieces are cut out, the garment may pull or twist to one side of your body. The hemline may hang unevenly if the fabric is off-grain.

Check to see if your fabric needs to be straightened. Fold the fabric in half lengthwise and match the selvages accurately. If the crosswise ends match exactly and are at right angles to the selvage, the fabric is straight. The fold will be smooth and wrinkle-free. If the edges do not match or the fabric puckers when you try to line up the edges, the fabric is not straight.

Straight

Off-grain

To straighten the fabric, pull the fabric on the true bias. Open up the fabric and pull the two opposite corners that are too short. Ask someone to help you since two people can do it more easily than one. Refold the fabric to check if you have pulled enough.

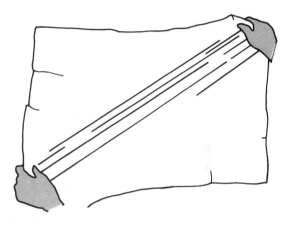

Fabrics that were pulled slightly off-grain when rolled on the bolt can be easily realigned by pulling. However, if the yarns became off-grain during the finishing process, the grain may be locked in position permanently by the finish. The fabric will have to be used as is.

Pressing Fabric

Press your fabric to remove all wrinkles. Fabric that is wrinkled cannot be cut accurately. Check to be sure the center fold can be pressed out of the fabric. If the fold does not press out with a steam iron and a damp press cloth, the fold will not come out with washing or dry cleaning. This sometimes occurs with knits and permanently finished fabrics. You will have to plan a special cutting layout to avoid the fold line.

Lesson 4

Laying Out the Pattern

Locate and circle the cutting layout for your particular view, size, and fabric width. Be sure to use the "with nap" layout if your fabric has a nap, pile, shading, or one-way design.

The cutting guide will show you exactly how to lay out the pattern pieces so all of the pieces will fit on the minimum amount of fabric.

Finding the Right Side

For many fabrics, the right side is very obvious due to the nap, pattern, or print. However, the right side may be difficult to determine on other fabrics. One clue is the way the fabric is folded or rolled on the bolt. Cottons and linens usually have the right side out on the bolt. Wools and most other fabrics are folded with the right side toward the inside.

Fold back one edge and compare the two surfaces. The right side may have a more pronounced weave, more nap, a brighter and clearer print, or be shinier. However, some plain weave fabrics are the same on both sides. For knitted fabrics, stretch a crosswise cut edge. The edge will usually roll to the right side of the fabric.

If you are undecided, pick the side that you like best. Then be sure to keep the same side throughout, so the finished garment will not have any differences in color or sheen. To help identify the sides, you can mark the wrong side of the fabric with chalk marks or small pieces of masking tape.

Folding the Fabric

The cutting layout will show exactly how to fold your fabric. For most layouts, the fabric is folded with the right side in. The pattern pieces are placed on the wrong side of the fabric so it will be easier to transfer markings. This also helps to protect the fabric from soil or dirt as you handle the fabric pieces.

However, stripes, plaids, and prints should be folded with the right side out. This makes it easier to match the fabric design. When cutting a single layer of fabric, place the fabric right side up.

Your fabric may need to be folded lengthwise, crosswise, double, or partial:

- **Lengthwise fold.** Fold fabric in half lengthwise with right sides together. Match selvages and ends.
- **Crosswise fold.** Fold fabric in half crosswise with right sides together. Match cut ends and keep the two layers of selvage even along each side. For napped fabrics, the nap must run in the same direction on both layers. Cut the fabric along the crosswise fold and turn the top layers around end to end. Match all edges.
- **Double fold.** Fold fabric twice along the lengthwise grain, right sides together. Usually the selvages meet in the center. This layout is often used for knitted fabrics.
- **Partial fold.** Fold fabric on the lengthwise grain, right sides together, only wide enough to fit the widest pattern piece.

Lengthwise fold

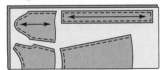

Crosswise fold

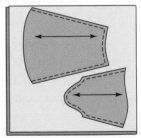

Partial fold   **Double fold**

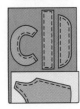

SPECIAL LAYOUTS

Special pattern layouts may require extra fabric depending on the size of the fabric design. Always place the largest pattern pieces on the fabric first. Visualize how the dominant lines or designs will be placed on the body.

- **Napped fabrics.** Place all pattern pieces facing in the same direction. For a richer color in corduroy and velvet, lay out the pattern so the nap or pile runs up the garment. Use a "with nap" layout.

- **Plaids.** Plaids can be even or uneven, depending on the repeat of the lines. *Even plaids* are the same in both the vertical and horizontal directions. Use a "without nap" layout. For *uneven plaids,* use a "with nap" layout so all of the pattern pieces are laid in the same direction. Use the dominant line of the plaid for the center front and center back. Match plaids at side seams and sleeves.

- **Stripes.** For *even stripes,* use a "without nap" layout. For *uneven stripes,* use a "with nap" layout. For *vertical stripes,* place the dominant stripe at center front and center back. Match stripes at side seams and sleeves. Stripes will *chevron,* or meet, on bias seams.

- **Directional prints.** Use a "with nap" layout. Match designs at seamlines.

- **Border prints.** Place all of pattern pieces on the crosswise grain. Match hemline markings to the lower edge of the border design. Place other pieces in the space available above the design.

Match stripes, plaids, and prints by placing corresponding notches of the pattern pieces on the same line or design of the fabric. Be sure to match at the seamline, not at the cutting line.

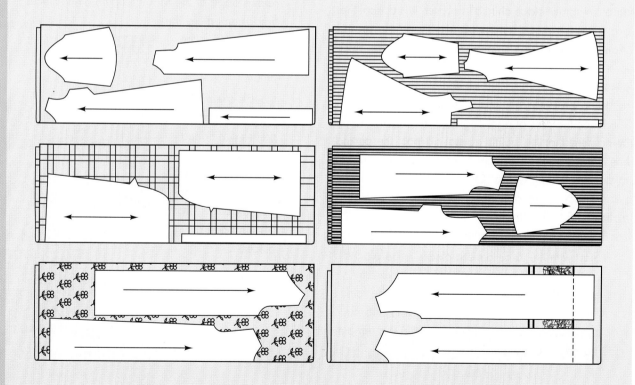

After folding the fabric, smooth out any wrinkles by pulling both layers of fabric at the ends or at the sides. Do not try to smooth only the top layer with your hand. This will cause the two layers to be off-grain. When the grain lines are straight, pin the two layers together along the edges. This prevents the fabric from shifting as you lay out the pattern pieces.

Always work on a large hard surface so the full width of the fabric can be laid out without any fabric hanging over the sides. In school, use a long cutting table. At home, work on a large table, folding cutting board, or the floor. Do not use a bed because the fabric can easily shift on a soft surface.

Pinning the Pattern Pieces

Lay out all of the pattern pieces in the same position as shown on the cutting layout you have circled. Most pattern pieces are placed printed side up on the fabric. Pattern pieces that are shaded on the layout should be placed with the printed side down.

Each pattern piece has the grain line indicated by an arrow or a "place on fold" bracket. It is critical that every pattern piece be placed exactly on the proper grain line. Never try to tilt or angle any pattern piece in order to fit into a smaller space. The result will be a great mistake because that section of the garment will not hang properly.

Place the pins at right angles to the pattern edge, being sure that the points do not go past the cutting line. Pin every 6 to 8 inches (15 to 20.5 cm) along folds and straight edges. On curved edges and slippery fabrics, place pins closer together—every 3 to 6 inches (7.5 to 15 cm).

Follow these steps for pinning the pattern pieces:

1. *Start* with the large pattern pieces to be placed on the fold. Place the pattern fold line exactly along the fabric fold. Place pins along the fold. Smooth the pattern away from the fold and pin diagonally into the corners. Then pin the remaining edges of the pattern.

2. *Next,* pin the pattern pieces that have a grain line arrow. Place a pin at the end of each arrow, pinning through all of fabric layers. Measure carefully from the point of each arrow to the edge of the fabric. If the measurements are not exactly the same, unpin one end and shift the pattern. Repin and measure again. Repeat until the grain line is straight. Smooth out the pattern in all directions from the grain line arrow and pin diagonally into the corners. Finish pinning along all edges of the pattern.

3. *Count* the number of pieces on the circled cutting layout. Then count the pieces pinned to the fabric to be sure you have not forgotten any pieces. If any pattern pieces are to be cut more than once to create four or more layers, be sure that you have left the proper amount of space. If two pieces are to be cut from a single fabric layer, you must reverse the pattern when cutting the second piece. If a piece extends beyond the folded edge of the fabric, cut the other pieces first. Then unfold the fabric and cut the remaining pattern piece.

4. *Double-check* your layout. Are all of the pieces positioned correctly? Are the grain lines straight? Are there any special instructions for certain pattern pieces?

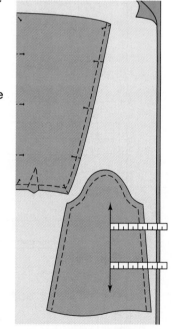

Lesson 5

Cutting and Marking the Fabric

After you have pinned all of the pattern pieces to the fabric, you can begin to cut. Then the lines and symbols on the pattern pieces must be transferred to the fabric. These markings will help you to assemble the garment.

Cutting Accurately

Follow these guidelines when cutting out the fabric pieces:

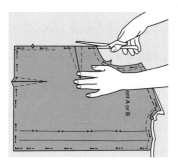

- **Use bent-handled shears.** Cut with long, even strokes without closing the blades completely. Hold the fabric flat on the cutting surface with your other hand. Cut slowly and accurately. Never use pinking shears.
- **Cut directionally with the grain line.** Some patterns have a symbol printed on the cutting line or stitching line to show in which direction to cut and stitch. If in doubt, cut from the widest point to the narrowest point.
- **Follow the correct cutting line on a multi-sized pattern.** Mark the cutting lines for your own size with a felt-tip pen to make them easier to follow, or trim the pattern pieces before laying out.

- **Cut carefully around notches.** Use the tip of the shears for greater accuracy. Cut double and triple notches together with one long edge across the top.
- **Leave pattern pieces pinned to the fabric until you are ready to sew.** You will need to transfer the construction markings to the fabric before the pattern is unpinned.
- **Save all fabric scraps.** You will need them for testing marking methods, type and length of stitches, and pressing temperatures.

What to Mark

The lines and symbols marked on the pattern pieces are important guides used during construction. They should be transferred to the fabric before the pattern is unpinned.

Mark all construction markings such as darts, pleats, tucks, and dots. Placement lines for buttonholes, buttons, pockets, and any trims should be marked. You may also want to mark fold lines and center front and back lines.

There is no need to mark seam allowances or hemlines. Seam allowances can be measured as you stitch by using the guides marked on the sewing machine. Hems are measured and turned under after the garment is made.

Sewing Tip

Before stitching your project together, you may want to finish your seam allowances on the serger. If so, remember that the serger will trim off the notches. Therefore, mark each notch with a line that extends from the tip of the notch to the stitching line.

Sewing Tip

Before using a marking pen on a project, always test the removal procedure on a scrap of your fabric. Do not use evaporating ink if it leaves an oily residue. Do not use water soluble ink if the fabric waterspots or is "dry clean only."

Marking Methods

Markings must be visible as you sew, but they should never show on the outside of the finished garment. Different marking methods may be used for different fabrics and types of marks.

Fabric Marking Pens

Fabric marking pens contain ink that either can be removed with water or will evaporate from the fabric. Because the ink is removable, you can use these pens to mark on the right side of the fabric.

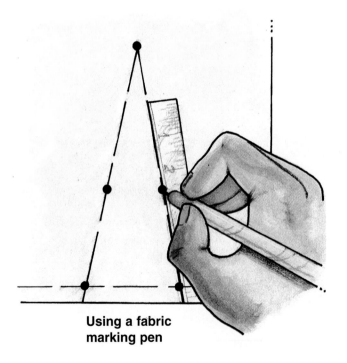

Using a fabric marking pen

1. *Stick* pins straight through pattern and both fabric layers at all marking points.

2. *Start* at an outside edge of the pattern piece, and carefully separate the layers of fabric just enough to place an ink dot where the pin is inserted. Mark both layers of fabric.

3. *Repeat,* working toward the center of the garment section until all symbols are marked.

Tracing Wheel and Dressmaker's Tracing Paper

This method of marking is quick and useful for most fabrics. Use a *saw-toothed wheel* for most fabrics and a *smooth-edged wheel* for delicate fabrics. Tracing paper has a waxy surface on one side and is available in several colors.

1. *Choose* a color of tracing paper that is similar to the fabric color but will still show. Test on a scrap of fabric to be sure markings do not show through on right side. Use caution with light-colored and lightweight fabrics.

2. *Place* waxy side of paper against wrong side of fabric. Two layers of paper are needed to mark a double layer of fabric. For small areas, fold a paper in half.

3. *Mark* all symbols by guiding the tracing wheel over each line or symbol only once. Press down lightly on tracing wheel. Mark dots with an X. Mark the end of a dart with a short line. For longer lines, use a ruler to keep lines straight.

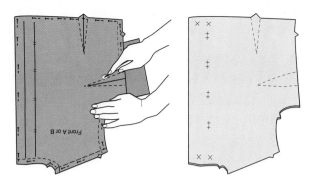

Marking with a tracing wheel and dressmaker's tracing paper

Chalk markings can be easily brushed off some fabrics, so handle carefully until all construction is completed.

1. *Push* a pin through both layers of fabric at each symbol. Carefully loosen paper pattern and slip it over pins. Be careful not to pull out any pins.

2. *Make* a chalk mark at each pin on top layer of fabric.

3. *Turn* fabric over and mark other layer at each pin.

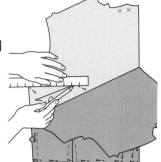

Marking with tailor's chalk

Tailor's Chalk

Chalk markings can be used on most fabrics. Mark only the wrong side of the fabric with either a flat square of chalk or a chalk pencil. Be sure that the edge or point is sharp so the markings are accurate.

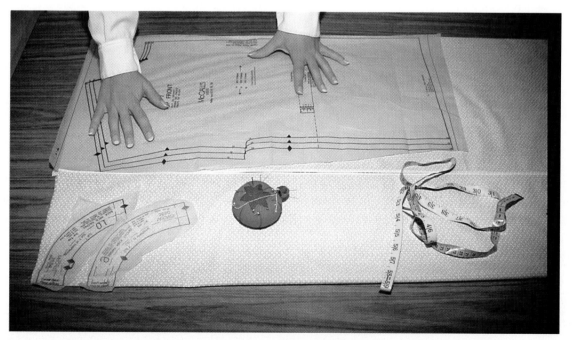

Each step of the preparation process is important for the success of a project.

Summary

- Before you begin a project, take a few minutes to get organized.
- Pattern information and instructions are provided on the envelope, guide sheet, and tissue pattern pieces.
- Compare your measurements with the body measurements on the pattern envelope to see if any adjustments are needed.
- The fabric may need straightening, preshrinking, or pressing.
- The cutting guide shows how to lay out the pattern pieces on the fabric.
- Place each pattern piece exactly on the proper grain line and pin in place.
- Use bent-handled shears to cut out the pattern pieces.
- Mark the construction lines and symbols with a fabric marking pen, tracing wheel and dressmaker's tracing paper, or tailor's chalk.

Recalling the Facts

1. What information is included in the pattern guide sheet?
2. What is the purpose of the notches on pattern pieces?
3. What are the two methods for adjusting the length of a pattern piece?
4. In a multi-sized pattern, how should you blend two different sizes?
5. What are selvages?
6. Why are most garments cut with the lengthwise grain running vertically, or up and down?
7. How can you preshrink washable fabric?
8. What does "off-grain" mean?
9. How can fabric grain be straightened?
10. How can you determine the right side of a fabric?
11. Why do most layouts have the fabric folded with the right side in?
12. Why should stripes, plaids, and prints be folded with the right side out for layout?
13. Name at least four types of fabrics that may require special pattern layouts.
14. Why should you never tilt or angle a pattern piece in order to save fabric?
15. How can you know in which direction to cut out a pattern piece?
16. Describe how to cut around notches.
17. Why should you save the fabric scraps?
18. List at least five construction lines or symbols that should be marked.
19. What two types of construction lines or symbols do not need to be marked?
20. List three types of marking methods.

Thinking Critically

1. **Analysis.** Compare and contrast the information found on a pattern envelope, guide sheet, and tissue pattern pieces.
2. **Evaluation.** When adjusting the length of a pattern, when might it be best to make the

adjustment at the lower edge? at the adjustment line?

3. **Synthesis.** What might be the result of not taking the time to press out any wrinkles in the pattern pieces or fabric before laying out?

4. **Analysis.** Compare the three methods of marking fabric. What are the advantages and disadvantages of each?

Practicing Your Skills

1. **Pattern Preparation and Adjustment.** Complete the following steps on your pattern: circle layout diagram, select needed pattern pieces, write your name on all pattern parts, smooth out or press pattern pieces, mark cutting lines on multi-sized pattern. Make any needed length or width adjustments on the pattern pieces.

2. **Layout, Cutting, and Marking.** Demonstrate the proper techniques for laying out, pinning, cutting, and marking the fabric.

Applying Your Knowledge

1. **Pattern Symbols.** Identify the various lines and symbols found on pattern pieces. Explain the purpose of each symbol.

2. **Measurements.** Compare your own measurements with the body measurements listed on a pattern envelope. Indicate any differences.

3. **Marking Techniques.** Use the three marking methods on different types of fabrics. Compare the results.

What Is an Instructions Writer?

Some writers specialize in writing sewing instructions and directions. They write the guide sheets for patterns, as well as the instructions for sewing projects in magazines, newspapers, and brochures. Sewing writers must be able to describe each step-by-step procedure needed to complete a project successfully. Their writing must be very clear, precise, and detailed. Today most pattern companies have standard sewing procedures and illustrations stored on computer programs. Thus, a writer can pull up generic sketches and directions on the computer and put them in the proper sequence for a particular project. The writers can also use computer programs to create the fabric layouts for the guide sheets.

Try It Yourself

Imagine that you are a writer of sewing instructions for a pattern company. You have been asked to write the directions for making an accessory item, such as a tote bag, backpack, sports bag, belt pack, or duffle bag. Examine a finished item, and write the step-by-step instructions for making the item. Then try creating the item by following your own step-by-step directions.

Build Your Portfolio

Place a copy of your sewing instructions, along with a photo or sketch of the finished item in your portfolio. Write a critique of your directions, describing any steps that were unclear or omitted.

The unit construction method is the simplest way of sewing garments. Unit construction means that everything is completed on the smallest unit possible before you begin to sew the separate units together.

This method allows you to work on smaller areas that are easier to handle. It also guarantees that areas are pressed before being crossed by another seam.

First, all staystitching is completed. Next, any darts, gathers, tucks, or pleats are stitched on each separate piece. Details such as buttonholes and plackets can be completed on small sections. Interfacing can be applied. Then all of the pieces can be carefully pressed before being sewn to each other.

Try to finish a completed stage of construction each time you sew. For example, you can complete a sleeve, attach a pocket, or stitch a waistband. Then the next time you begin to sew, you can start a new step instead of trying to finish a half-completed one.

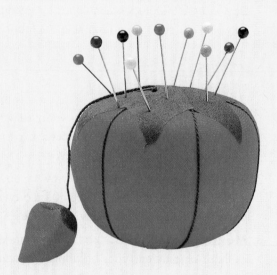

Lesson 1

Machine Stitching

Sewing is a combination of machine and hand stitches. Machine stitches are used for stitching seams, darts, and facings. Machine stitches can also be used to finish seam edges, insert zippers, create buttonholes, and attach trims.

Stitching Guidelines

Always check the machine before you begin sewing. Practice stitching on two layers of scrap fabric to check stitch length and tension.

- Stitch length
- Stitch width
- Tension
- Needle is smooth, straight, and inserted properly
- Presser foot is firmly tightened
- Bobbin is inserted properly into bobbin case
- Hand wheel knob is tightened after winding bobbin

Length of Stitches

The length of the stitches depends upon the purpose of the machine stitching. Most stitching uses a medium length stitch. Basting stitches are very long; reinforced stitches are very short.

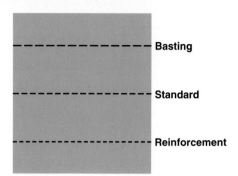

Basting

Standard

Reinforcement

- **Standard stitching.** This is *used to permanently stitch most seams and construction details.* Use 10 to 12 stitches (2 to 2.5 mm in length) per inch for most fabrics. Finer fabrics require a shorter stitch of 12 to 15 stitches (1.5 to 2 mm in length) per inch. Heavy fabrics need a longer stitch of 8 to 10 stitches (2.5 to 3 mm in length) per inch.

- **Basting stitching.** Machine basting is *used to temporarily hold two or more pieces of fabric together until the permanent stitching is completed.* It can also be used on a single layer of easing, gathering, and marking guidelines. Use a very long stitch, 6 stitches (2.5 cm in length) per inch. Decrease the upper tension 1 or 2 settings to make it easier to remove the basting stitches.

Sewing Tip

As you stitch, keep your eyes on the fabric edge and guideline markings—not on the needle. Guide the fabric with your fingers. Do not push or pull the fabric. Control the speed of your stitching. Always slow down as you come to a corner, curve, or end of a seam.

If you are having trouble with the tension or quality of the stitches, try a new needle. A good guideline to follow is to use a new needle with every new project.

Sewing Tip

When sewing on a conventional machine, the top layer of fabric always feeds slightly faster than the bottom layer. As a result, you should stitch with the grain whenever possible.

With a serger, you can stitch a seam in any direction you want. Its presser foot has a firmer pressure and the loopers interlock the threads across the fabric and along the length of the fabric. Therefore, shifting is eliminated on most fabrics.

- **Reinforcement stitching.** This is *used to permanently stitch fabric areas that will be trimmed or clipped close to the stitching.* Use a very short stitch, 15 to 20 stitches (2.5 cm in length) per inch to hold the fabric yarns in place.

Types of Machine Stitching

Machine stitching can be used for many different construction techniques. Specific terms are used to describe each method of stitching. These terms are used frequently in sewing directions. You should learn how to do each of these techniques:

- **Staystitching.** This is *used along bias and curved edges to prevent stretching as you handle the fabric.* It is done after the fabric is marked and before pinning, basting, and permanent stitching. Staystitch on a single layer of fabric ⅛ inch (3 mm) away from the seamline in the seam allowance. Use standard machine stitching and stitch directionally.

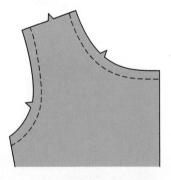

Staystitching can act as a guideline for clipping and joining curved edges.

- **Directional stitching.** This is *stitching with, or in the same direction, as the fabric grain.* It helps to prevent a seam from stretching or changing shape as you stitch. To determine grain direction, run your finger along the fabric edge. The direction that smoothes the yarns against the fabric is with the grain. This is the direction in which to stitch.

Some patterns may indicate grain with an arrow or an illustration of a presser foot on the seamline. If you stitch from the wide part of a fabric section to the narrow part, you will be stitching with the grain in most situations. Seams on straight grain can be stitched in either direction.

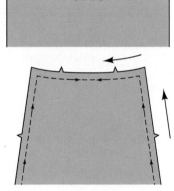

- **Stitching a standard seam.** A standard seam is ⅝ inch (1.5 cm) wide. Almost all patterns are designed with standard seams. If another seam width is used, it will be marked on the pattern piece.

- **Backstitching.** This is *used to secure the ends of a row of stitching.* To backstitch, begin stitching ½ inch (1.3 cm) in from the beginning of the stitching line. Stitch backward to the edge of the fabric, then stitch forward over the stitches you have just made.

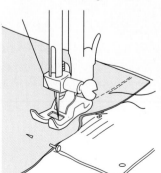

Serging Techniques

Stitching

For a smooth start, serge a 3 to 4 inch (7.5 to 10 cm) long thread chain. Then place the fabric in front of the presser foot with the seamline aligned with the needles. The presser foot can be left in the down position because the feed dogs will pull the fabric under the presser foot.

To end the stitching, serge off the fabric for about 5 to 6 inches (12.5 to 15 cm). This is called *chaining off*. Without raising the presser foot, bring the chain and the fabric around so the chain crosses in front of the knife. Stitch for a few more seconds so that the knives automatically cut the thread chain.

Always remove pins before the knife reaches them. For long seams, place the pins at least 1 inch (2.5 cm) from the cut edge and parallel to the seamline. Then the pins will not come near the cutting blades.

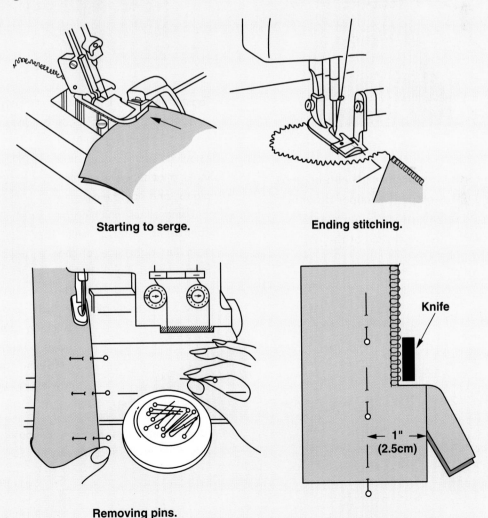

Starting to serge.

Ending stitching.

Removing pins.

Knife

1"
(2.5cm)

Serging Techniques

Remove Stitching

Most serging involves more than two threads. A seam ripper can be used to cut through the looper threads so the other threads will pull free.

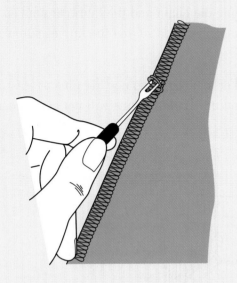

Sometimes the needle threads can be gently pulled out, freeing the looper threads. A serger chain stitch can be unraveled by pulling on the looper thread at the end of the stitching line.

Continue stitching the seam and backstitch at the other end for ½ inch (1.3 cm) exactly over the first stitching.

- **Understitching.** This is *a row of stitching used to keep a facing or bottom layer of fabric rolled out of sight.* Use standard stitching. Stitch from the right side, through the facing and seam allowances, ⅛ inch (3 mm) from the seamline.

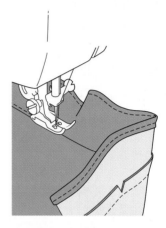

- **Topstitching.** This is *a row of stitching done on the outside of a garment.* It can be decorative or functional. Topstitching is used to outline seams, secure facings, attach pockets, stitch pleats, and hold hems.

  Using either matching or contrasting thread, stitch from the right side of the fabric. Use a slightly longer stitch length, 8 to 10 stitch-es (2.5 cm in length) per inch. To keep the top-  stitching even, use the edge of the presser foot, guideline markings, or sewing tape as a guide.

- **Edgestitching.** This is *a row of topstitching placed very close to the finished edge.*

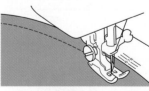

494

- **Stitch-in-the-ditch.** This is *a row of stitching done on the outside of a garment in the groove of a seamline.* It is used to hold two or more layers of fabric together when finishing facings, collars, cuffs, and waistbands. Use standard machine stitching. On the outside, stitch directly in the seam groove through all layers of fabric.

- **Zigzag stitching.** This is available on most machines. It can be used to finish seams, stitch buttonholes, attach cording and elastic, and create decorative designs. Both the length and the width of a zigzag stitch can be adjusted. The stitch can range from very narrow and closely spaced for a satin stitch to very wide and far apart for a seam finish.

- **Specialty stitches.** Some machines also offer a variety of specialty stitches. Refer to your sewing machine manual for specific directions.

Removing Stitches

Mistakes do happen. To rip out stitches, use a seam ripper, thread clipper, or small scissors. Cut threads about every 2 inches (5 cm) along one side of the fabric. Pull the thread out on the other side, and then remove the short threads from the clipped side.

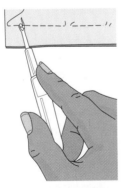

Lesson 2

Handstitching

Handstitches are used primarily for finishing steps, such as hemming or sewing on fasteners. Handstitches are also used for basting, reinforcement, and decorative stitching.

Threading a Needle

Unwind no more than 24 inches (61 cm) of thread. Longer lengths may tangle or knot as you sew. Use scissors to cut the thread at an angle so the end will slide through the eye of the needle easily. Biting or breaking the thread will cause it to fray and make it difficult to thread the needle.

Most hand sewing is done with a single thread. A knot is made in just one thread end. If you need a double thread, hold two ends together as you tie the knot.

Sewing Tip

For easy needle threading, hold the needle up against a white background so you can see the eye clearly. Or use a needle threader. Push the wire through the eye of the needle, then insert the thread through the wire. Pull the wire back out of the needle, drawing the thread through the eye.

Types of Handstitching

For most handstitches, hold the fabric so that you will sew from right to left if you are right-handed. Left-handed sewers will reverse this and sew from left to right.

To secure the beginning and end stitches, make a small knot or take two small stitches, one on top of the other, on the wrong side of the garment.

Tying a Knot

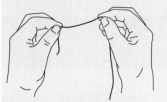
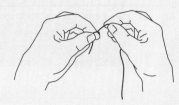

1 *Place* the end of the thread across the tip of your index finger and hold in place with thumb.

2 *Wrap* the thread around your fingertip, over-lapping the thread slightly.

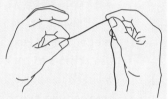

3 *Roll* the thread off your index finger with thumb. The thread will twist and a loop will form as it slides off your finger.

4 *Hold* the loop against the thumb with your middle finger and pull on the thread with your other hand to make the knot.

- **Basting stitch.** Hand basting is temporary stitching used to mark or to hold fabric layers together. Basting should be removed from the garment as soon as the permanent stitching is completed and it is no longer needed. There are two types of basting stitches:

  Even basting is used to hold seams together for

fitting or permanent stitching, such as bast-ing sleeves into arm-holes. Make stitches about ¼ inch (6 mm) long and even on both sides of fabric.

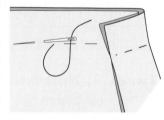

  Uneven basting is used for marking or for hold-ing hems in place for stitching. Make 1 inch (2.5 cm) stitches on top side of fabric and short ¼ inch (6 mm) stitches on the

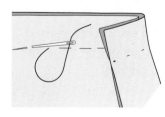

underside. To save time, take several stitches with the needle before pulling thread through.

- **Running stitch.** This is the simplest type of handstitching. It is used for gathering, easing, tucking, quilting, and sewing seams that have little or no strain. Make tiny, even stitches ¼ to ¹⁄₁₆ inch (6 to 1.5 mm) in length.

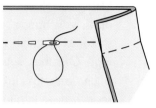

- **Backstitch.** This is one of the strongest hand stitches. It is used to repair machine-stitched seams and to fasten thread ends securely. Begin with a tiny running stitch. Then insert the needle back at the beginning of the first stitch. Bring it out again one stitch length in front of the thread. Keep inserting the needle in the end of the last stitch and bring-ing it out one stitch ahead. The stitches on the underside will be twice as long as those on the upper side.

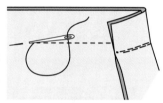

- **Pickstitch.** This is a variation of the backstitch. It is used for the application of zippers by hand and as a decorative stitch. The needle is brought back only one or two threads to form a very tiny stitch on the upper side.

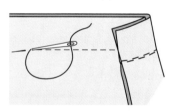

- **Slipstitch.** This is an almost invisible stitch. It is used to attach one folded edge to another piece of fab-ric, such as patch pockets, hems, linings, and trims.

  Slip the needle inside the fold of the upper fab-ric for ¼ inch (6 mm). Then pick up one or two threads of the under fabric directly below. Continue to take a stitch through the fold and then in the other fabric.

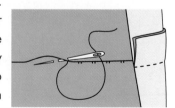

- **Overcast stitch.** This stitch is used to prevent raw edges from raveling. Make diagonal stitches over the edge of the fabric, spacing them evenly apart.

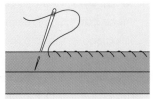

- **Hemming stitch.** This slanted stitch is used for finishing different types of hems, especially ones with seam binding or a folded edge.

  Make a tiny stitch in the garment. Then bring the needle diagonally up through the folded edge of the fabric or the seam binding. Space stitches about ¼ inch (6 mm) apart.

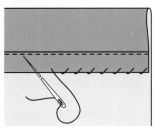

- **Blindstitch.** This is an excellent stitch for hemming and for holding facings in place. It is barely visible from the right side of the garment. It also allows movement without pulling.

  Fold back the hem or facing edge about ¼ inch (6 mm). Take a small stitch in the garment, catching only one or two threads. Then take a tiny stitch diagonally above in the hem or facing. Do not pull the stitches tight. Continue to form a very narrow zigzag stitch.

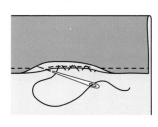

- **Catchstitch.** This criss-cross stitch is used to hold two layers of fabric together with flexibility. It can be used to hem stretchy fabrics or to attach interfacings.

  Stitch from left to right if you are right-handed. Make a small horizontal stitch from right to left in one layer of fabric a short distance from the edge. Then make another horizontal stitch, just over the edge and diagonally to the right, on the other layer of fabric. The threads will cross each other between stitches.

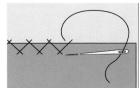

- **Blind catchstitch.** This stitch is concealed between the two layers of fabric. Fold back the hem edge about ¼ inch (6 mm). Make catchstitches between the two layers.

- **Cross-stitch.** This decorative stitch is used to hold layers of fabric together. A series of cross-stitches is often used at the center back pleat of a jacket lining.

  Make a series of horizontal stitches about ¼ to ⅜ inch (6 to 9 mm) wide, spaced as far apart as they are long, to form a diagonal design. Then reverse direction and continue making horizontal stitches at the same location as the previous stitches to form an X design.

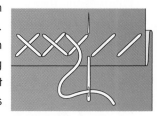

  A *cross-stitch tack* is used to hold a facing edge in place at a seamline. Make a cross-stitch over the edge, being sure that stitches do not show on the outside. Continue making several cross-stitches over the first one.

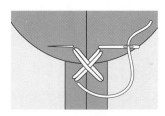

- **Buttonhole stitch.** This stitch is used to make hand-worked buttonholes and to attach hooks and eyes. It can also be used as a decorative finish along the edge of a garment by placing stitches farther apart.

  Use a double thread. Begin by inserting the needle through the buttonhole slash and bringing it out on the right side of the fabric. Then loop the thread under the eye of the needle and under the point. Pull the needle out of the fabric and draw up the loop to form a knot along the buttonhole edge.

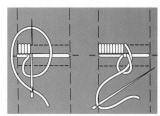

Serging Techniques

Belt Carrier

To make belt carriers, set your serger for a narrow rolled hem stitch. Without any fabric in the machine, serge a long chain of stitches. Thread the chain onto a hand sewing needle. Working from the outside of the garment, insert the needle in a seamline. Gently pull the tail of the chain to the inside of the garment and tie a knot. Repeat for the other end of the chain.

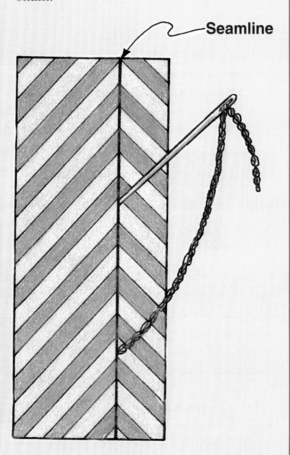

Seamline

- **Blanket stitch.** This stitch is used for making thread loops, eyes, and belt carriers. It can also be used to make bar tacks, French tacks, and a decorative finish along a fabric edge.

  Stitch from left to right, holding the fabric edge toward you. Point the needle toward you and insert through the fabric from the right side. Keep thread under the needle as the stitch is pulled up.

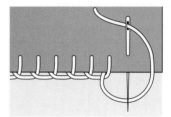

A *thread loop, eye,* or *belt carrier* can be made by working blanket stitches over longer base stitches. Use a double thread. Take two or three stitches the desired length of the loop, eye, or carrier.

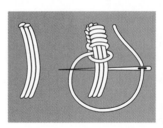

Secure the ends with small backstitches. Be sure the base stitches are long enough for the button, hook, or belt to pass through. Then with the same thread, make closely spaced blanket stitches over the entire length of the base stitches. Secure with several small stitches on the underside of the fabric.

A *French tack* is used to hold a lining hem to a skirt hem or a coat hem at a seamline. Form by working blanket stitches over several long stitches.

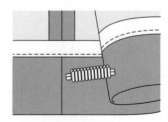

- **Chain stitch.** This stitch can also be used to form thread loops, eyes, and carriers. Use a double thread to form a series of loops.

  Secure thread with several overlapping stitches on the underside. Then take a short stitch to form a loop on the right side. Slip your thumb and first two fingers through the loop. Reach through the loop with a finger and catch the thread to form a new loop. Pull the new loop through the first loop and tighten so that the first loop forms a knot at the base of the thread chain. Keep forming new loops and sliding them down the thread evenly until the desired length. Slip the needle and thread through the last loop to end the chain. Stitch into the fabric and secure with small stitches on the underside.

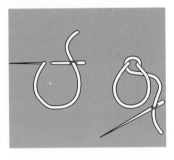

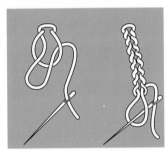

Lesson 3

Pressing

Good pressing techniques are as important as good sewing skills. Pressing is used throughout the sewing process. At the start, pressing insures that your pattern and fabric are wrinkle-free for accurate cutting. Through every step of construction, pressing helps to smooth and shape your garment.

You should keep your pressing equipment near your sewing machine so that you will not be tempted to skip pressing as you sew. You will need an ironing board, a steam iron, and a press cloth. A tailor's ham should be used for pressing curved areas. Other types of pressing equipment can make the job easier but are not necessary. (See page 467).

Pressing Basics

- **Press; do not iron.** Pressing differs from ironing. When you iron, you slide the iron back and forth across the fabric. This may cause wrinkling and stretching of the fabric. In **pressing,** *the iron is lowered to the place to be pressed, then raised off the fabric, and lowered again at the next spot.* The heat and steam do most of the work so

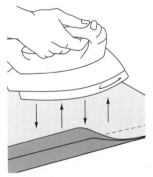

  that heavy pressure is not necessary. This helps to prevent stretching.

- **Use the correct temperature setting for your fabric.** Set the temperature according to the fiber content of your fabric. However, do not use the cotton and linen settings for pressing as there is danger of scorching the fabric. If your fabric is a blend, use the setting for the most heat-sensitive fiber in the blend.

- **Always test your fabric for any reaction to heat, steam, and pressure.** Use a scrap of fabric to check that it is not damaged or marked by the iron. If the fabric sticks, puckers, or melts, then the iron is too hot. Check to see if the fabric waterspots. Too much pressure can crush napped fabrics or create press marks on the right side.

- ***Press on the wrong side of the fabric whenever possible.*** Pressing on the inside prevents shine on the right side of the fabric. Also, seams can be seen clearly and pressed correctly.

- ***If pressing on the right side of the fabric, always use a press cloth.*** Some areas, such as pleats and pockets, may have to be pressed on the outside of the garment. A press cloth will prevent a shiny mark being left on the fabric.

- **Never press over pins.** Pins will leave an impression on the fabric and may scratch the iron.

- **Always press seams and darts before other seams are stitched across them.** This helps to reduce bulk and prevent any lumps in your finished garment.

- **Press directionally with the grain of the fabric.** This will prevent stretching.

- **Press seams flat before you press them open.** Press one side, then turn the seam over and press on the other side. This allows the stitches to settle into the fabric. It also eliminates puckers and creates a smoother seam after it is pressed open.

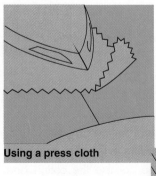
Using a press cloth

Using strips of paper

- **Press curved areas over a curved surface.** Use a tailor's ham to maintain the curved shape of the fabric.

- **Prevent press marks on the right side of the fabric.** Slip strips of paper or an envelope under the edges of seam allowances, darts, and pleats when they are pressed. This will prevent any imprints or press marks on the outside of the garment.

- **Check the fit of the garment before you press any sharp creases, such as pleats.**

- **Do not overpress.** Avoid heavy pressure and let the steam do the work. Use the tip of the iron in small places. Never press the fabric completely dry.

- **When pressing an entire garment, start with the small areas.** First press the collar, cuffs, and other detail areas. Then press the small areas, such as sleeves and yokes. Finally, press the large flat areas of the garment.

Safety TIP

Use special care when using an iron. Don't touch a hot iron except on the handle. Keep your fingers and face away from the steam. Do not overfill the iron or the water can boil out. Use distilled water, if recommended by the manufacturer. Always rest the iron on its heel, not flat down on the soleplate. Turn off and unplug the iron after each use. Some irons should be drained of water before storing.

Pressing Techniques

Which pressing method to use depends upon whether the garment area is flat, curved, enclosed, gathered, or eased.

Flat Areas

Flat areas, such as straight seams, can be pressed flat on the ironing board.

1. *Place* garment on ironing board with both seam allowances to one side. Press seamline to blend stitches into fabric.
2. *Open up* fabric and place it over ironing board. Press seam allowances open, using your fingers and tip of iron to open seam completely. Check on right side to be sure seam is perfectly smooth.

If a seam is to be pressed to one side, such as for a yoke or waistline, first press seam flat. Then press seam allowances open. Finally, press seam allowances toward one side.

Curved Areas

Darts and curved seams should be pressed over a curved tailor's ham to maintain their shape.

1. *Press* dart or seam flat to blend stitches into fabric. Press darts only up to the point, and not beyond, to prevent pressing in a crease.
2. *Place* fabric wrong side up over a tailor's ham. Press seams open; press darts to one side. (See page 503).

Enclosed Seams

Enclosed seams are found on the edge of a collar, facing, or cuff. They should be pressed flat and then pressed open. This will give the seam a sharper edge when the piece is turned to the right side.

1. *Press* seam flat to blend stitches.
2. *Press* seam open. Use only tip of iron near the point or corner.
3. *Turn* right side out. Gently push out corner or point.
4. *Press* piece flat on ironing board, slightly rolling seam to the underside. This helps to prevent the seam from showing at edge of completed garment.

Serging Techniques

Pressing Seams

To press a serged seam, press the seam allowance flat on both sides. Then press the seam allowance to one side.

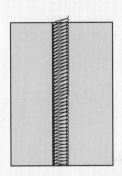

Gathered Areas

Gathers and ruffles should ripple softly below the seamline. They should not be pleated or crushed by the iron.

1. *Press* seam allowances together to flatten fabric above seamline.
2. *Slip* garment over end of ironing board. Turn seam allowance away from fullness.
3. *Press* directly up into the gathers with point of iron. Hold seam allowance taut above the gathers by using your other hand to lift it slightly up from ironing board. This will help to prevent folds being pressed into the gathers at the seamline.

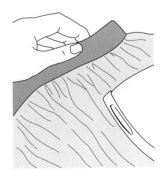

Shrinking in Fullness

Sometimes it is necessary to shrink in fullness of a hem or sleeve cap.

1. *Hold* iron above fabric to allow steam to penetrate before pressure is applied.

2. *Use* your fingers to pat out any folds and flatten fabric.

3. *Press* edge of fabric to shrink in fullness. Check to be sure sleeve or hem looks smooth on right side of garment.

Final Pressing

If you do a good job of pressing throughout the construction of your garment, then only a light pressing will be needed to remove any final wrinkles caused by handling. This final pressing should be merely a touch-up job. It should never be a cure-all for poor pressing during the construction.

Lesson 4

Darts

Darts are *triangular folds of fabric stitched to a point.* They are used to control fullness and give shape to fitted clothing. Darts should point to the fullest part of the body and end about 1 inch (2.5 cm) from the body curve to which they point. The two basic types of darts are the *single-pointed dart* and the *double-pointed dart*.

Stitching Darts

There are four basic steps in stitching single-pointed darts:

1. *Fold* dart with right sides of fabric together matching stitching lines. Place one pin exactly at the point and other pins at small dot markings.

2. *Stitch* from wide end of dart to point.

3. *Stitch* last two or three stitches as close to fold line as possible. This will create a sharp point without any bubbles. Do not backstitch because it can cause puckering at point.

4. *Tie* thread ends in a knot. Or simply leave 1 inch (2.5 cm) thread ends, which will not pull out.

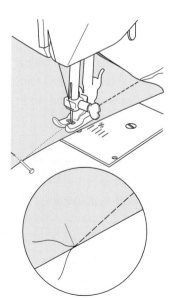

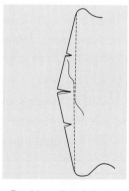

Double-pointed dart

For *double-pointed darts,* start at the center and stitch to each point. Overlap stitching lines in the center about 1 inch (2.5 cm). Make one or more clips in dart along the fold so it can be flat.

Pressing Darts

Always press a dart before crossing it with another seam. *Horizontal darts* are pressed with the fold downward. *Vertical darts* are pressed with the fold toward center front or center back.

1. *Press* dart flat, as stitched.
2. *Place* dart over a tailor's ham and press it to one side.

Wide darts or *darts in heavy fabric* should be pressed open. Refer to your pattern guide sheet. Slash dart along fold line to within 1 inch (2.5 cm) of point. Trim the slash to ½ inch (1.3 cm) from stitching line, as shown. Press dart flat, as stitched. Then press the trimmed edges open and press point flat.

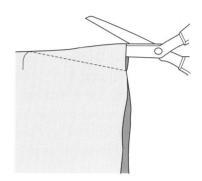

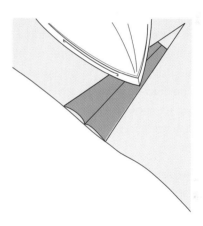

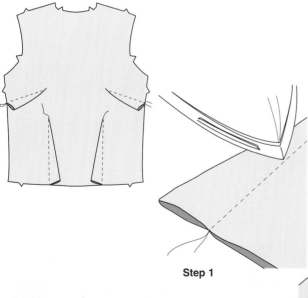

Step 1

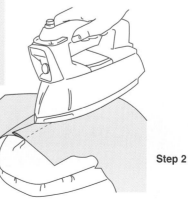

Step 2

Lesson 5

Gathering and Easing

Gathering and easing are methods used to control fullness along a seamline. **Gathers** are *soft folds of fabric* formed by pulling up basting stitches to make the fabric fit into a smaller space. **Easing** *allows fabric to be shaped over a curved area of the body.* It is used when one edge of fabric is only slightly larger than the other. Easing should not create any visible folds or gathers.

Gathering

An area to be gathered will be marked on the pattern with "gather" or "gathering line" on the seamline. The beginning and end of the gathered area will be marked by notches or dots. Usually fabric is gathered into ½ or ⅓ of its original width. It takes more yardage to create full gathers in lightweight fabrics than in heavier ones.

How to Gather

Gathers start with two rows of machine basting. Then the bobbin threads are pulled from both ends to draw up the fabric. Finally the gathered fabric is stitched to the shorter length of fabric.

1. *Adjust* stitch length for 6 to 8 stitches (3 to 4 mm in length) per inch. Loosen upper thread tension.

2. *Stitch* first row of basting next to seamline in seam allowance. Leave long thread ends. For large areas, start and stop stitching at the seams.

3. *Stitch* second row ¼ inch (6 mm) away in seam allowance. Leave long thread ends.

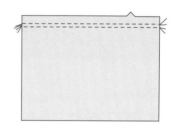

4. *Pin* fabric edges, right sides together, matching notches, seams, and markings.

5. *Pull up* both bobbin threads from one end. Gently slide fabric along thread to gather half the section. Repeat at other end until gathered section is the proper length.

Sewing Tip

When gathering fabric by machine, use a contrasting color of thread in the bobbin. This will make it easy to see which thread to pull.

Trim the ends of the seam allowances before stitching the gathers. If the fabric is bulky, stitch only up to the seams, keeping the seam allowances free.

6. *Wrap* threads in a figure 8 around a pin to secure.

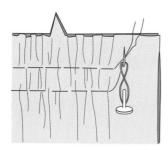

7. *Distribute* gathers evenly and pin in place about every ½ inch (1.3 cm).

8. *Stitch* with standard stitching along seamline, gathered side up. Use your fingers to hold gathers evenly on both sides of the needle to prevent any folds catching in seam.

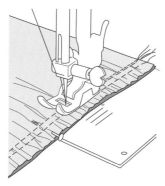

For *heavy fabrics,* use a zigzag stitch over a narrow cord for easier gathering. Place a thin cord on the seam allowance, ¼ inch (6 mm) from the seamline. Zigzag over the cord, being careful not to catch the cord. Pull the cord ends to form gathers. Stitch along the seamline with gathered side up. Remove cord.

Pressing Gathers

To press gathers:

1. *Press* seam allowances flat.

2. *Lay* garment flat on ironing board with seam allowances turned away from gathers.

3. *Press* carefully up into the fullness with tip of iron on wrong side of fabric. Hold seam allowances taut above gathers to prevent folds being pressed into the gathers at seamline. (See page 501.)

Serging Techniques

Gathering

To gather lightweight to mediumweight fabrics:

1. *Adjust* serger for a wide three-thread stitch.

2. *Serge* a thread chain at least 6 inches (15 cm) longer than the edge to be gathered. Do not cut chain. Gently run your fingers along chain to smooth it out.

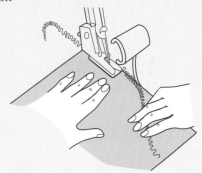

3. *Raise* presser foot. Bring chain under presser foot and around to front, then up and over toe of presser foot to the left of the knife. Lower presser foot.

4. *Serge* along edge of fabric, encasing thread chain in stitches. Do not serge off fabric at end. Instead, stop stitching. Raise needle and presser foot. Turn hand wheel several times and gently ease fabric away from presser foot. Cut threads.

5. *Pull up* on thread chain to gather.

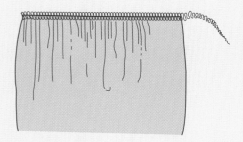

Shirring

Shirring is formed by *several rows of gathering.*
Use only on soft or lightweight fabrics. Stitch as many
rows of gathering as
desired and secure each
row with a knot. Then
stitch over the knots in
the seam allowance.

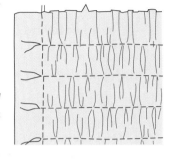

Elasticized shirring
is made by using elastic
thread in the bobbin.
Wind elastic thread on
the bobbin by hand, stretching slightly. Use a long
stitch, 6 to 8 stitches (3 to 4 mm in length) per inch.
Stitch on right side of fabric, stretching the previously
stitched rows as you sew each new row.

Easing

Easing is used most often at shoulder seams,
sleeves, yokes, and waistbands. The most common
eased seam is a set-in sleeve. The finished seam
should look smooth, without any gathers or tucks.

Pinbasting

If one fabric edge is only slightly longer than the
other, pinbaste right sides of fabric together with
longer side on top. Place pins every ½ inch (1.3 cm)
to keep fullness from shifting. Stitch with the longer
seam on top and gently ease in extra fullness as you
stitch.

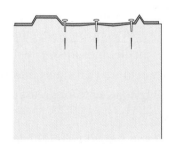

Ease Stitching

To ease a greater amount of fullness, use one or
two rows of ease stitching. Follow the techniques as
for gathering.

1. *Stitch* close to seamline with long machine stitches, extending stitching slightly beyond markings.
2. *Stitch* a second row ¼ inch (6 mm) away in
   seam allowance for set-in sleeves.
3. *Pin* fabric, right sides together, with eased side
   up.
4. *Pull up* thread between markings and distribute
   fullness evenly.
5. *Stitch* along seamline, being careful not to stitch
   in any folds or gathers.

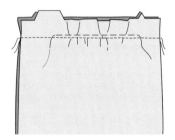

Lesson6

Plain Seams

A **seam** is *a line of stitching used to hold two layers of fabric together.* A plain seam is the standard seam used for most sewing. It is ⅝ inch (1.5 cm) deep and is stitched with the standard stitch length for your fabric. Patterns are designed with standard seams unless stated otherwise. (For special types of seams, see pages 533-536.)

Stitching a Seam

For best results, always follow these steps:

1. *Staystitch* any bias or curved areas ½ inch (1.3 cm) from cut edge.

2. *Pinbaste* fabric layers along seamline, with right sides together. Match fabric ends and notches, then pin. Place additional pins 6 inches (15 cm) apart to keep edges of fabric even. Insert pins at a right angle to stitching line, with heads toward seam allowance.

3. *Raise* needle and take-up lever to their highest point by turning the hand wheel. Be sure thread ends are back behind presser foot to prevent thread from pulling out or jamming when you start to stitch.

4. *Position* fabric under needle. Line up fabric edge with ⅝ inch (1.5 cm) marking on right side of needle plate. Place fabric about ½ inch (1.3 cm) in from the end for backstitching. Turn hand wheel to lower needle into fabric. Lower presser foot.

5. *Backstitch* for ½ inch (1.3 cm) to beginning of seamline.

6. *Stitch* forward slowly and evenly to end of seam. Remove pins as you stitch. Or if your machine allows, stitch slowly over the pins.

7. *Backstitch* ½ inch (1.3 cm) to secure the seam.

8. *Remove* fabric by turning hand wheel to raise take-up lever and needle to their highest position. Lift presser foot. Slide fabric toward back of machine.

9. *Clip* threads at both beginning and end of seam.

10. *Finish* seam edges if necessary. (See page 511.)

11. *Press* seam open.

Safety TIP

When using a conventional sewing machine, take extra care when sewing over pins. Place them at right angles to the stitching line. Stitch slowly so the machine needle will slide over the pin. At a faster speed, the needle might bend or break if it hits a pin. To be safe, remove each pin just before the presser foot reaches it. Never place pins on the underside of the fabric. The pins might become caught in the feed dog and break the machine needle or tear the fabric.

When using a serger, never try to sew over a pin. This will damage the knives and the needle. Plus, there is the danger of pin fragments flying into your eyes or face. Place the pins at least 1 inch (2.5 cm) from the edge, parallel to the stitching line, or remove each pin before it reaches the knives.

Keep a pin cushion next to your sewing machine for pins as you stitch. This will prevent pins falling on the floor. Never place pins in your mouth or clothes as you sew.

Serging Techniques

Plain Seams

With a serger, a seam can be stitched, trimmed, and overcast in one step.

1. *Pin* seam.

2. *Position* fabric in front of presser foot. Match stitching line on fabric to the appropriate mark on the seam guide.

3. *Serge* a 4 to 5 inch (10 to 12.5 cm) thread chain. Then gently feed fabric under presser foot.

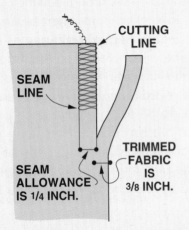

CUTTING LINE

SEAM LINE

SEAM ALLOWANCE IS 1/4 INCH.

TRIMMED FABRIC IS 3/8 INCH.

4. *Serge off* the fabric for 5 to 6 inches (12.5 to 15 cm). Bring thread chain around to front so knife can cut it.

5. *Secure* thread ends. Run fingers along thread chain to smooth it out. Tie thread in a loose loop knot. Insert a pin through center of loop so tip of pin is next to edge of fabric. Pull thread chain until loop tightens into a knot at tip of pin. Remove pin and clip thread tails.

Turning a Corner

To turn a corner in the middle of a seam, pivot the fabric. Stitch to within ⅝ inch (1.5 cm) of the corner and stop with the needle down in the fabric. Lift presser foot and turn fabric on the needle. Lower presser foot and continue stitching in the new direction.

Turning a Sharp Point

To turn a sharp point, such as the point of a collar, take one or two diagonal stitches across the corner. The extra stitch makes a thinner, neater corner when the point is turned to the right side. Stitch to the corner and leave the needle down in the fabric. Raise presser foot and turn fabric diagonally. Lower presser foot and make one or two stitches by turning the hand wheel. Leave needle in fabric, raise presser foot, and turn fabric to complete the corner. Lower foot and continue stitching.

Reinforcing

To reinforce a sharp corner or point, such as a V-neckline or placket, use reinforcement stitches. Stitch for about 1 inch (2.5 cm) on either side of the point. This will help prevent fabric yarns from pulling out of the seam after the fabric is trimmed and turned.

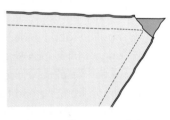

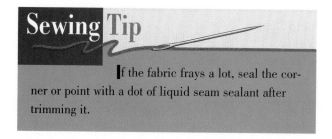

Sewing Tip

If the fabric frays a lot, seal the corner or point with a dot of liquid seam sealant after trimming it.

Special Seam Treatments

Some seams may need special treatment to reduce bulk in the seam allowance. Enclosed seams, such as those in necklines, collars, and cuffs, should lie flat and smooth. Curved seams and corners also need special treatment. There are several different ways to reduce the bulk of a seam: *trimming, grading, clipping, and notching.*

Trimming

Seam allowances of enclosed seams should be trimmed to an even width, usually ¼ inch (6 mm). The corner of a seam allowance should be trimmed diagonally to remove extra thickness when the corner is turned. If the corner is very pointed, make an additional diagonal cut on each side of the point, trimming to ⅛ inch (3 mm).

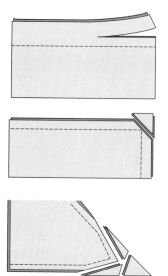

Curved seams, such as the lower part of an armhole and the center back seam of pants, are usually trimmed. These areas can be reinforced with two rows of stitching ¼ inch (6 mm) apart, and then trimmed close to the second row of stitching.

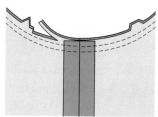

Grading

Grading means *to trim each layer to a different width to reduce bulk.* Enclosed seams in heavier fabrics should be graded. Seams with three layers of fabric, such as a collar stitched to a neckline, should also be graded.

Always grade a seam so that the widest seam allowance is next to the outside of the garment. This reduces press marks on the right side. To grade, trim the seam allowances in half. Then trim the seam allowance toward the inside of the garment in half again. For three layers, trim each one slightly narrower.

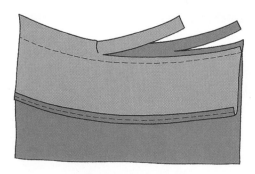

Clipping

On a curved seam, the seam allowances should be clipped to allow the curve to lie flat when pressed. **Clipping** means *making a tiny clip or snip in the seam allowance* every ¼ to ½ inch (6 to 13 mm). Using the point of the scissors, clip to within ⅛ inch (3 mm) of the seamline or up to the staystitching line. The sharper the curve, the closer together the clips should be made. Clipping is done after the seam is trimmed or graded.

Sometimes an inward curve or corner must be clipped before stitching the seam. Stitch a row of reinforcement stitches just inside the seamline in the seam allowance. Clip up to the reinforcement stitches to allow the fabric to lie flat for stitching the seam.

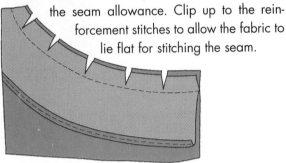

Notching

Some curved seams have too much fabric in the seam allowance after being trimmed or graded. The extra fabric forms ripples and does not allow the seam to lie flat. These are usually outward curves, such as the outer edge of a collar, that are then turned and pressed to form an inward curve.

Notching means *cutting tiny wedge-shaped pieces of fabric from the seam allowances*. Notch no closer than ⅛ inch (3 mm) to the seamline. When the seam is turned and pressed, the sides of the notches should meet.

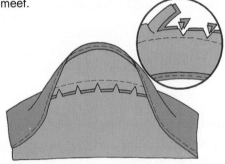

Pressing Seams

Seams should be pressed after they are stitched and before they are crossed by another seam. Check your pattern guide sheet to see if the seam is to be pressed open or to one side.

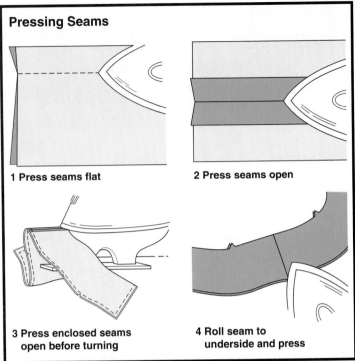

Pressing Seams

1 Press seams flat

2 Press seams open

3 Press enclosed seams open before turning

4 Roll seam to underside and press

First, press all seams flat to blend in the stitches. Then open the seam allowances and press again. If necessary, press both seam allowances to one side. Curved seams should be pressed over a tailor's ham.

Enclosed seams in a collar or cuff should be pressed open before turning. Use a point presser or sleeve board and press with tip of iron. Then turn fabric to right side and lay flat on ironing board with underside up. Roll edge in just until the seam shows and press lightly. This helps to prevent the underside or facing from showing along the edge.

Seam Finishes

A **seam finish** is *any method of sewing or trimming seam edges to prevent raveling or fraying*. They are needed on woven fabrics but not on most knitted fabrics. Seam finishes are done after the seams of the garment are stitched and pressed. The method to use depends upon the type of fabric and the reason for finishing the seams. Zigzag stitching and serging are the easiest and quickest methods to do.

Types of Finishes

- **Machine zigzag finish.** This is a fast and easy method for finishing fabrics that ravel. Set the zigzag setting for medium width and length. For loosely woven or heavy fabrics, use a wide stitch width. Zigzag along edge of each seam allowance.

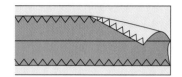

- **Pinked finish.** Most firmly woven fabrics can be trimmed with pinking shears. However, pinking does not prevent raveling entirely. For more protection, stitch ¼ inch (6 mm) from each edge before pinking. Press seam open.

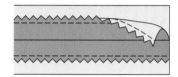

- **Hand overcast finish.** This method is very time-consuming but is sometimes used for sheer or delicate fabrics. Make overcast stitches by hand over the edge of the seam allowances.

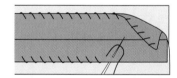

- **Hemmed finish.** This method forms a narrow, single-fold hem along the edges of the seam allowances. It is also called a *clean finish or a turned and stitched finish.* This method can be used on lightweight to mediumweight fabrics. It makes an attractive finish for unlined jackets. Turn edge under ¼ inch (6 mm) and press. Stitch close to folded edge.

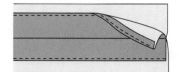

Seam Finishes

To finish a conventional seam, use a two-thread or three-thread overlock stitch. As you serge, the knife should skim the edge of the fabric so nothing is trimmed off the seam allowance except a few loose threads. Finish the edges of the fabric before stitching the seam.

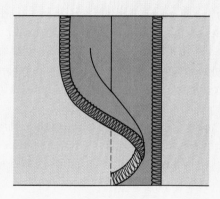

- **Bound finish.** This finish is suitable for mediumweight to heavyweight fabrics. It also is an attractive finish for unlined jackets and coats. Trim notches. Slip double-fold bias tape over raw edge of seam allowances and stitch in place.

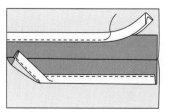

Lesson 7

Facings

A **facing** is *used to finish a raw edge, such as a neckline or armhole.* It may be a separate piece of fabric or cut in one with the garment. It is then turned to the inside for a smooth finish. Facings should not be visible from the outside.

There are three general types of facings:

- **Shaped facing.** A separate pattern piece is given for a shaped facing. It is cut the same shape as the area it will cover. It is stitched, then turned to the inside of the garment. A shaped facing is also called a *fitted facing.*
- **Extended facing.** This facing is cut in one piece with the garment and folded to the inside. It is used along a front or back opening.
- **Bias facing.** This is a strip of bias fabric stitched to the garment and turned to the inside. It is used mostly for very bulky or sheer fabrics. Purchased bias tape or bias strips cut from fabric can be used.

Stitching Shaped and Extended Facings

Both shaped facings and extended facings are attached to a garment in the same way. The facing pieces must first be stitched together. Then the facing is attached to the garment. Next, the facing is understitched. **Understitching** is *a row of stitches used to prevent a facing from rolling to the outside of a garment.* Finally, the edge of the facing should be fastened at each seam allowance.

Construct Facing

1. *Staystitch* notched edge.
2. *Pin* right sides of facing pieces together, matching notches.
3. *Stitch* seams, trim, and press open.
4. *Finish* outside edge of facing with a zigzag, hemmed, or serged finish. (See Seam Finishes, page 511.)

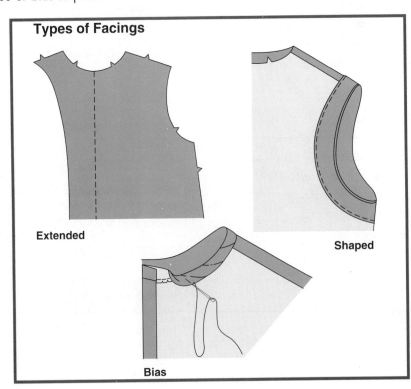

Types of Facings

Extended

Shaped

Bias

Sewing Tip

For a hemmed finish, first stitch a row of staystitching ¼ inch (6 mm) from outside unnotched edge of the facing. This will make it easier to turn under the hem along the staystitching line.

Knitted fabrics do not require a finish. However, a row of staystitching around the outer edge will help the facings to hold their shape better.

Attach Facing to Garment

1. *Pin* facing to garment edge, right sides together. For an extended facing, turn facing to right side along fold line.
2. *Stitch seams.* Trim or grade seam allowances; trim corners. Clip curved areas.
3. *Press* seam allowances open, then press toward facing.
4. *Turn* facing to inside of garment. Press along seamline, rolling seam slightly toward facing side.

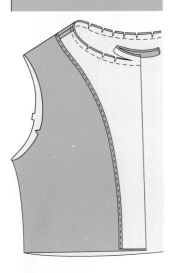

Understitch Facing

1. *Open* facing out flat, with seam allowances toward facing.
2. *Machine stitch* close to seamline from right side of facing through all seam allowances. Gently pull on the fabric on either side of seamline to keep it flat.
3. *Turn* facing to inside and press.

An alternative is to *topstitch* garment edge from the outside, instead of understitching.

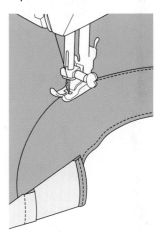

Sewing Tip

If you have clipped the seam allowance, check frequently as you understitch to make sure that the small wedges of fabric don't get folded under during the stitching.

If the garment edge will be topstitched, there is no need to tack the facing in place.

Facings

Use the serger to finish the edges of the facing. If the faced edge is a straight edge or a gradual curve, use the serger to attach the facing to the garment. The overlock stitch creates very narrow seam allowances that need no trimming, grading, notching, or clipping.

1. *Serge* facing sections together at shoulder seams. To reduce bulk, press seams in opposite direction of garment shoulder seams.
2. *Serge-finish* outer edge of facing.
3. *Pin* facing to garment edge. If faced edge has an opening, fold both garment and facing to inside at opening edge and pin.

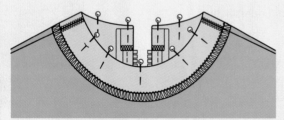

4. *Serge* along neckline seam.

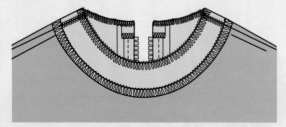

5. *Press* seam allowances toward facing.
6. *Understitch* with a conventional sewing machine.

Tack Facing at Seams

The edge of the facing should be tacked, or fastened, at each seam allowance. Use a hemming stitch, a blindstitch, a cross-stitch tack, or the stitch-in-the-ditch

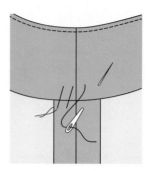

method. (See pages 495 and 497.) Another method is to fuse the facing and garment seam allowances together with a small piece of fusible web, following manufacturer's directions.

Stitching Bias Facings

For a bias facing, open out one long edge of bias tape.

1. *Pin* crease line of tape along seamline of garment, right sides together.
2. *Stitch* seamline. Trim, grade, and clip seam allowances.

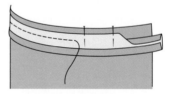

3. *Fold* bias tape to inside of garment and press.
4. *Slipstitch* edge in place.

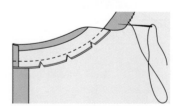

Lesson 8

Casings

A **casing** *is a closed tunnel of fabric that holds a piece of elastic or a drawstring inside.* Casings are used at sleeve edges, necklines, waistlines, and hemlines to help control fullness. The elastic or drawstring makes the garment adjustable. A casing is much easier to construct than a waistband or a cuff and thus is used in many beginner or easy-to-sew patterns.

There are two basic types of casings:

- **Self-casing.** This is formed by folding over the edge of the garment and stitching in place.
- **Applied casing.** This is made by sewing a separate strip of fabric or bias tape to the garment. An applied casing can be sewn to the edge of a garment or inside a garment, such as a waistline casing in a jumpsuit.

Casings can also be sewn with headings. A **heading** is *a width of fabric between the casing and the edge of the garment.* A narrow heading has a more tailored appearance. A wider heading creates a ruffle edge.

Self-Casing

A self-casing is made similar to a hem:

1. *Turn* raw edge under ¼ inch (6 mm) and press.

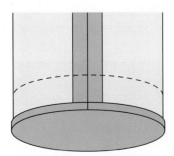

2. *Turn* casing to inside of garment along fold line and pin in place. Press outer edge of casing.
3. *Stitch* close to inner pinned edge of casing. Leave a 2 inch (5 cm) opening at a side seam or center back to insert elastic. If casing has a header, stitch around the heading line.

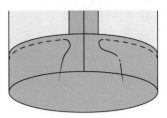

Applied Casing

Either a single-fold bias tape or a strip of fabric can be used for an applied casing. The length of the tape or fabric strip should be ½ inch (1.3 cm) longer than the finished casing. The width of the strip should be 1 inch (2.5 cm) wider than the width of the elastic. The pattern guide sheet should include cutting instructions or a separate pattern piece for the casing. Fold in the long edges of the fabric strip ¼ inch (6 mm) and press before you begin.

At Edge of Garment

1. *Pin* one edge of casing to garment, with right sides together. Fold back ends.
2. *Stitch* a ¼ inch (6 mm) seam. Trim.
3. *Turn* casing to inside of garment and press.
4. *Edgestitch* other edge of casing to garment.

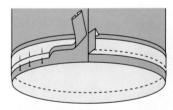

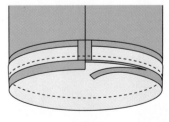

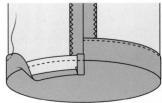

Elastic

Lingerie usually has the elastic exposed rather than hidden inside a casing. The serger applies it in a fast, one-step application with the flatlock stitch. Use special lingerie elastic which is soft and has one decorative edge.

1. *Leave* one garment seam open.

2. *Divide* and mark garment edge into quarters or eighths. Divide and mark elastic into quarters or eighths.

3. *Pin* elastic to right side of fabric, with straight edge of elastic along fold line.

4. *Position* straight edge of elastic next to knife. Serge a couple of stitches to anchor elastic. Be careful not to cut elastic.

5. *Continue serging,* using the flatlock stitch. Hold elastic up against toe of

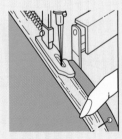

presser foot, slightly off the fabric. As you stitch, stretch elastic to fit between the pins. Remember to remove pins as you come to them.

6. *Pull* on elastic until decorative edge is turned up and seam is flat.

7. *To finish,* serge remaining seam with an overlock stitch.

Within Garment

1. *Pin* casing to garment, using placement markings on pattern. Turn under casing ends so folds meet without overlapping.

2. *Edgestitch* along both long edges of casing.

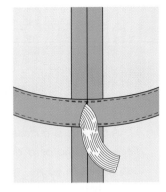

Elastic

Several different types of elastic are available, including special elastics for swimwear and lingerie. The pattern will recommend the proper width of elastic to use. The elastic should be about ⅛ inch (3 mm) narrower than the finished casing so it can be pulled through the casing easily. If the casing is too wide, the elastic may twist and roll inside the casing as the garment is worn.

The guide sheet will give directions for cutting the right length of elastic for your needs. If not, measure your body at the casing position and add 1 inch (2.5 cm) for overlapping the elastic ends.

To insert elastic:

1. *Pull* elastic through casing with a safety pin, being careful not to twist it. Leave ends extending several inches at opening.

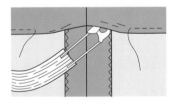

2. *Overlap* the ends ½ inch (1.3 cm) and pin together. Try on garment to check fit and adjust elastic if necessary.

3. *Stitch* overlapped ends securely by machine.

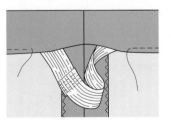

4. *Finish* opening of self-casing by completing the edgestitching, stretching the elastic as you stitch. Finish opening of an applied casing by slipstitching along folded ends.

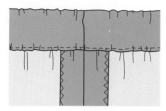

Drawstrings

Drawstrings can be made from cord, tubing, braid, and ribbon. You will need an opening in the garment to pull the drawstring through to either the outside or the inside. The opening can be either two buttonholes or a slit in a seam. It should be reinforced with a small piece of fabric or fusible interfacing.

Make buttonhole openings in outer fabric before casing is stitched. A seam opening is made as you

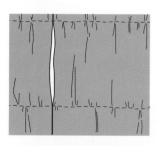

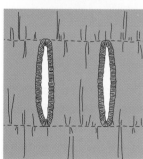

stitch the seam. Leave seam open between markings, and reinforce opening with backstitching. Use a safety pin to pull drawstring through casing. Ends of the drawstring can be knotted to prevent it from pulling out of the casing during wearing or washing.

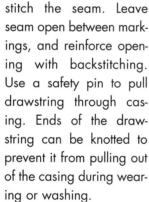

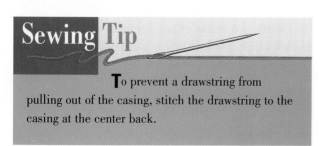

Sewing Tip

To prevent a drawstring from pulling out of the casing, stitch the drawstring to the casing at the center back.

Lesson 9

Fasteners

Fasteners are used to help close garments securely. They include hooks and eyes, snaps, special nylon tapes, buttons, and zippers. There is a wide variety of fasteners for many different purposes. Some are decorative as well as functional. Sometimes a combination of fasteners will be used on the same closing of a garment—such as a hook and eye above a zipper or a snap with a button.

The pattern envelope will recommend which type of fastener is needed for your garment. Usually snaps, hooks and eyes, and buttons are attached by hand. Use a double strand of thread. Always secure the stitches with a knot or tiny backstitches.

Hooks and Eyes

Hooks and eyes are available in a variety of sizes and types. Small hooks and eyes are used most often at necklines. Large covered hooks and eyes are available for jackets and coats. Special heavy-duty hooks and bars are designed for waistbands on pants and skirts.

Hooks are sold with two kinds of eyes—a *round eye* for edges that meet, and a *straight eye* for edges that overlap. A thread eye may be used in place of a metal eye for a less noticeable one. Use either a blanket stitch or a chain stitch.

Edges That Meet

A hook and round eye are used for edges that meet. To attach the hook:

1. *Position* hook ⅛ inch (3 mm) from edge.
2. *Stitch* around each loop with a buttonhole or overcast stitch. Sew only to the facing fabric. No stitches should show on right side of garment.

3. *Slide needle between fabric layers to end of hook*. Take three or four stitches across end of hook to hold it flat against fabric. Secure threads.

   To attach a round eye:

1. *Match* garment edges.

2. *Position* eye so loop extends ⅛ inch (3 mm) beyond edge. When hook and eye are attached, garment edges should meet exactly.

3. *Stitch* around each loop with buttonhole or overcast stitches. Sew only to facing fabric. Secure threads.

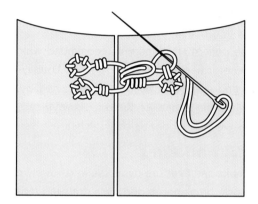

Edges That Overlap

A hook and a straight eye are used for edges that overlap. The hook is placed on the overlap side:

1. *Place* hook on underside of overlap at least ⅛ inch (3 mm) from edge.

2. *Stitch* around each loop with buttonhole or overcast stitches. Be sure no stitches show on right side of garment.

3. *Stitch* across end of hook to hold it flat against fabric. Secure threads.

   Use a straight eye on the underlap side:

1. *Overlap* edges.

2. *Mark* position of eye by placing a pin in the fabric under bend of hook.

3. *Stitch* eye in place with buttonhole or overcast stitches around each loop. Secure threads.

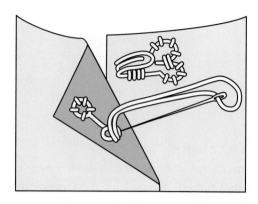

Heavy-duty hooks and bars are used on waistbands. The hooks are strong and flat so they will not slide out of the eye.

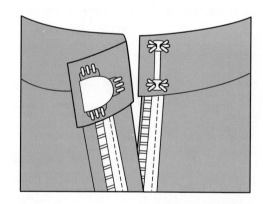

Snaps

Snaps are used to hold overlapping edges together where there is not much strain. They are available in a variety of sizes. Small snaps are used at necklines or cuffs. Heavy gripper snaps are used for children's clothes and sportswear. Large covered snaps are available for jackets and coats.

Snaps are made of two sections—a ball half and a socket half. The ball half is sewn to the overlap. The socket half is sewn to the underlap.

Sewing Tip

When sewing on snaps, first stitch the ball half in place. Then rub tailor's chalk on the ball. Overlap the fabric and press the ball against the fabric to mark the position of the socket half of snap.

1. *Center* ball half of snap over marking on underside of overlap. Be sure it is at least ⅛ inch (3 mm) from edge.

2. *Sew* three or four stitches through each hole. Use either overcast stitch or buttonhole stitch. Carry thread under snap from one hole to the next. Stitch only through facing, being careful not to have any stitches show on right side of garment. Secure threads.

3. *Mark* position of socket half of snap. Overlap edges and push a pin through ball of snap to underlap.

4. *Place* socket half over marking. Hold in place by inserting a pin through center hole of socket and into fabric.

5. *Stitch* in place in same manner as ball half, except stitch through all layers of fabric.

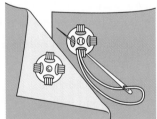

Hook and Loop Tape

Hook and loop tape is a special nylon-tape fastener. It is available in strips or precut into round or square shapes. One side has tiny hooks, the other has a looped pile. When pressed together, the two sides interlock until pulled apart. Hook and loop tape can be used on overlapping edges. It is excellent for sportswear, children's clothes, home furnishings, and craft items.

To stitch hook and loop tape:

1. *Cut* strips to desired length.

2. *Place* loop half on underside of overlapping edge.

3. *Position* hook half directly underneath on the underlap.

4. *Machine stitch* around both tapes.

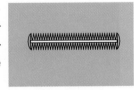

Buttonholes and Buttons

Buttons and buttonholes can be used on all types of overlapping edges, such as collars, cuffs, center fronts and backs, pockets, and waistbands. They are a very strong fastener and are able to withstand much pulling and strain. Besides being functional, buttons and buttonholes can add a decorative accent to a garment.

Buttonholes should always be completed first; then the buttons are sewn in place. Traditionally, buttonholes are made on the right front side in girls' and women's garments. On boys' and men's clothing, buttonholes are made on the left front side.

Buttonholes

There are three types of buttonholes:

- **Machine-stitched buttonholes.** These are stitched with a zigzag machine stitch. They are made after the garment is completed. Machine-worked buttonholes can be used on almost all fabrics.

- **Handworked buttonholes.** These are made with a buttonhole stitch. They are used primarily on fabrics that are too lightweight or too loosely woven to machine stitch.

- **Bound buttonholes.** These are finished with strips of fabric. They are made in the garment before the facing is attached. Bound buttonholes used to be very popular on tailored garments. Today even expensive ready-to-wear garments feature machine-stitched buttonholes. Some couture designers still use bound buttonholes on their garments.

Buttonhole Placement

The location of each buttonhole is indicated on the pattern pieces. If you have adjusted the length of your pattern, then changes may have to be made. Re-space the buttonholes evenly between the top and the bottom buttonholes on the pattern. Sometimes a buttonhole may have to be added or subtracted.

Buttonholes should extend a little beyond the button placement marking to allow for the shank of the button.

- **Horizontal buttonholes** begin ⅛ inch (3 mm) beyond the button marking toward the fabric edge.

- **Vertical buttonholes** begin ⅛ inch (3 mm) above the button marking. Vertical buttonholes are often used on shirt bands or for a row of small buttons.

If you choose a larger size button than the pattern recommends, double check the buttonhole placement. Be sure the buttonholes are placed far enough from the edge of the garment so the buttons will not extend beyond the edge when the garment is buttoned.

Buttonhole Length

Buttonhole length is determined by adding the following three measurements: the diameter of the button; the thickness of the button; and ⅛ inch (3 mm) to allow for the thickness of the fabric. The pattern piece has buttonhole markings that match the recommended button size and fabric type. If you choose a different size button, you will have to adjust the length of the buttonhole.

Buttonhole Markings

Machine-stitched buttonholes are stitched on the right side of the fabric. It is important to choose a marking method that will not leave a permanent line on the outside of your garment.

Several lines should be marked:

- **Center lines**—must meet when the garment is fastened.

- **Short lines**—indicate ends of each buttonhole.

- **Long lines**—indicate length of each buttonhole.

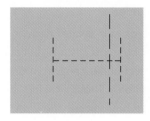

Machine-Stitched Buttonholes

Before making any buttonholes on a garment, always make a sample buttonhole on a piece of scrap fabric. Many sewing machines have a built-in buttonhole attachment. Others are operated manually by changing the zigzag-stitch width. Check to be sure there is plenty of thread on the bobbin. It is difficult to rethread in the middle of a buttonhole.

1. *Mark* location of buttonhole on right side of garment.

2. *Stitch* buttonhole, following instructions in the sewing machine manual.

3. *Place* a pin across each end of the buttonhole to prevent cutting through end stitching.

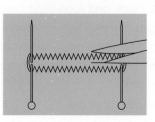

4. *Cut* buttonhole opening, using small, sharp scissors. Insert scissors blade in center of buttonhole and cut from the center in both directions.

Buttons

Buttons are available in a wide variety of sizes, shapes, and designs. The pattern envelope will list the size of button to be used, stated in fractions of an inch. The size of a button is the measurement of its diameter.

Button Placement

Mark the placement of the buttons through the buttonhole openings, rather than from the pattern. This will assure that each button will be in the correct position.

1. *Overlap* fabric edges with buttonhole on top. Match center lines or overlap lines.
2. *Place* a pin through the buttonhole, ⅛ inch (3 mm) from end, along center line.
3. *Slip* buttonhole over head of each pin and separate garment sections. Be careful when doing this step.

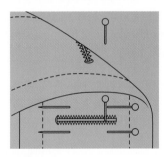

Attaching Buttons

Buttons should be sewn with a double strand of thread. Heavy-duty thread can be used for extra strength on heavier garments. The two basic types of buttons are *sew-through buttons* and *shank buttons*. They are attached differently.

Sew-Through Buttons

These have holes or "eyes" in the face of the button. Buttons used only for decoration can be sewn flat against the fabric. Buttons used with a buttonhole should be attached with a thread shank. The shank allows the buttonhole to fit smoothly between the button and the under fabric. The length of the thread shank is determined by the thickness of the fabric.

1. *Secure* thread at button marking with small backstitches.
2. *Place* a toothpick, heavy pin, or matchstick on top of button.
3. *Bring* needle up through one hole, over toothpick or other object, and down through second hole. Continue to make several stitches through button and fabric. If button has four holes, repeat stitching at other pair of holes. End stitches with needle and thread under button.

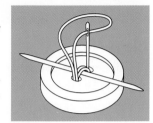

4. *Remove* object and pull button to top of thread loop.
5. *Wind* thread tightly around stitches under button to form a thread shank. Fasten thread securely in fabric under button.

Shank Buttons

These have a metal or plastic loop on the back of the button. Thread is stitched through the shank to attach the button to the fabric.

1. *Secure* thread at marking with backstitches.
2. *Stitch* through shank and fabric with four or five small, even stitches.
3. *Fasten* thread securely in fabric under button.

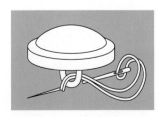

Sewing Tip

Sometimes buttons on heavy fabric or in areas of extra strain need reinforcement. Sew a small, flat button to the wrong side of the garment as you are stitching the sew-through or shank button in place.

Zippers

Zippers are available in different types, weights, and lengths. The most common type of zipper is the conventional zipper, which has a stop at the bottom. Specialty zippers, such as separating, invisible, decorative, and heavy-duty zippers, are also available. The pattern envelope will recommend the type and length of zipper to choose for your project.

Zippers can be stitched in a variety of ways. The methods are known as *applications*. Refer to your pattern guide sheet for which application to use. You will also find instructions for applications in the zipper package.

Zipper Applications

The three most common zipper applications are: centered, lapped, and fly front.

Centered Zipper Application

1. *Machine baste* seam and press open.
2. *Place* zipper face down on open seam allowance. Center zipper teeth or coils exactly on top of basted seam. Hold zipper in place with hand basting or sewing tape.

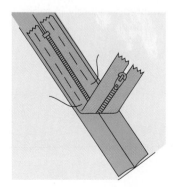

ZIPPER GUIDELINES

For a smooth zipper application, follow these general guidelines:

- Check the zipper package. If the zipper tape is 100 percent polyester, press the tape to remove any folds. If the tape is not 100 percent polyester, preshrink zipper.

- Staystitch any curved or bias seamlines to prevent stretching.

- If seam allowances are less than $\frac{5}{8}$ inch (1.5 cm), stitch seam tape to edge for extra width.

- Check pattern guide sheet to see if zipper should be stitched before or after any facing is attached.

- Check length of zipper opening. Place zipper teeth or coil $\frac{3}{4}$ inch (2 cm) from top edge of fabric. If some type of fastener will be sewn above zipper, place zipper 1 inch (2.5 cm) below top edge. Mark fabric where teeth or coils end at bottom of zipper.

- To shorten a zipper, machine zigzag or whipstitch across teeth or coil in one place to form a new bottom stop. Cut away zipper $\frac{1}{2}$ inch (1.3 cm) below stitching.

- Stitch seam below zipper marking, using a regular machine stitch. Backstitch $\frac{1}{4}$ inch (6 mm) to secure seam.

- Machine baste zipper opening. Clip basting every inch (2.5 cm) to make it easier to remove after application is finished. Be sure to match plaids and stripes carefully. Press seam open.

- If sewing zipper by machine, use a zipper foot attachment so you can stitch close to zipper.

- If sewing zipper by hand, use a pickstitch.

- Always stitch both sides of zipper in same direction to prevent any wrinkles or puckers in zipper placket.

3. *Spread* garment flat, right side up. Mark bottom stop of zipper with a pin. Attach zipper foot.

4. *Begin stitching* at lower end of zipper on right side of fabric. Stitch across end, pivot, and up along one side ¼ inch (6 mm) from basted seam.

5. *Begin* again at lower end and stitch other side in same manner.

6. *Pull* thread ends at bottom to wrong side of fabric and knot.

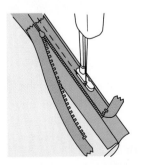

7. *Remove* machine basting. Press.

Lapped Zipper Application

1. *Machine baste* seam and press open.

2. *Open* zipper. Place it face down on back seam allowance with teeth or coil at seamline. Pin, baste, or tape in place.

3. *Machine stitch* through zipper tape and seam allowance only, from bottom to top of zipper. Use zipper foot to stitch close to edge of zipper.

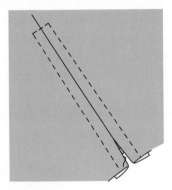

4. *Close* zipper and turn it face up. Smooth fabric away from zipper, forming a narrow fold between zipper coil and basted seam.

5. *Machine stitch* close to fold, beginning at lower end of zipper. Sew through folded seam allowance and zipper tape only.

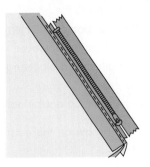

6. *Open* out fabric and place zipper face down on front seam allowance. Turn tab up. Pin in place.

7. *Machine baste* through tape and seam allowance only, starting at top of zipper. This will hold zipper in place for final stitching.

8. *Stitch* from right side of garment, beginning at lower end of zipper. Stitch across bottom, pivot, and go up side of lap. Stitching should be ⅜ to ½ inch (1 to 1.3 cm) from seam.

9. *Pull* thread ends to wrong side of fabric and knot.

10. *Remove* basting stitches and press.

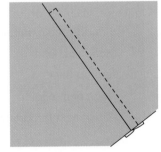

Fly Front Application

Follow the same steps as for the lapped zipper application.

Lesson 10

Hems

A **hem** is *used to finish the bottom edge* of a shirt, jacket, sleeve, skirt, or pants leg. Hem lengths vary according to fashion trends. However, it is important to select a hem length that is flattering to your own body proportions.

A well-made hem should not be noticeable:

- Stitches should not show on the outside of the garment.

- Hem edge should be flat and smooth.

- Garment should hang evenly around your body.

Hems can also be an important part of the garment design. A decorative binding or topstitching can add special interest to a hemline.

Hems can be made in a variety of ways, depending upon the type of fabric and the design of the garment. However, most hems are made by turning the raw edge of fabric to the inside of the garment. Then the edge of the hem is held in place by hand stitching, machine stitching, or fusing.

To finish a hem, follow these four basic steps:

1. *Mark* hem length.
2. *Turn* up hem.
3. *Finish* hem edge.
4. *Attach* hem to garment.

Marking Hem Length

Your garment should hang on a hanger for at least 24 hours before the hem is marked. This allows any bias areas of the garment to stretch and prevents the hemline from sagging.

Put on the garment with the same clothes and shoes that you will wear with it. Fasten all openings and any belt. Stand in your normal posture with your weight on both feet. For complete accuracy, have someone else mark the hem for you. You should remain standing still, and the person doing the marking should move around you.

- **Skirts and dresses.** Use a yardstick, meterstick, or skirt marker. Be sure to keep marker at right angles to floor. Place pins or mark with chalk every 3 or 4 inches (7.5 or 10 cm) around hemline. Turn hem to inside along markings and pin to check length. Readjust if necessary.

- **Pants.** Fold under edge of fabric and pin. Front of pants should just touch top of shoe; back should be about ½ inch (1.3 cm) longer than top of shoe.

- **Jackets.** Fold under fabric along hemline markings and pin. Adjust length according to own body proportions. Be sure hem is even around entire body.

- **Sleeves.** Bend arm so hand is in the center of waistline. Fold under sleeve edge until it just covers wristbone. Pin in place.

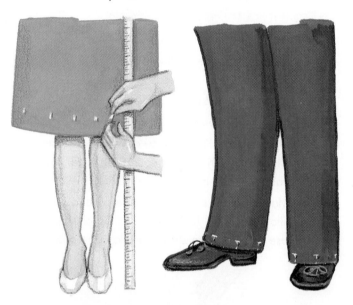

Turning Up Hem

After the hemline is marked, the hem must be trimmed to the proper width and any extra fullness eliminated.

Trim Hem Width

Your pattern will recommend the proper width of the finished hem. Most hems are 2 to 3 inches (5 to

7.5 cm) in depth. This gives added weight to the hemline and helps it to fall evenly.

However, the width of the hem will depend on the flare of the garment and the weight of the fabric. A curved edge will have a narrower hem than a straight edge. Knitted or heavier weight fabrics may have a narrower hem. Sheer fabrics usually have a narrow rolled hem or a very deep hem.

To trim a hem width:

1. *Fold* hem up along marked line.
2. *Measure* an even distance from folded edge with a sewing gauge or small ruler.
3. *Mark* desired hem width with chalk.
4. *Trim* away excess fabric.
5. *Remove* any pins and lightly press fold of hem.

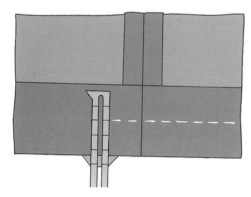

Eliminate Hem Fullness

If the garment is flared, the turned up hem will be wider at the upper edge than the garment. This fullness must be eased in to fit flat against the garment:

1. *Machine baste* ¼ inch (6 mm) from upper edge of hem.
2. *Turn* hem up and pin at each seam and at the center.
3. *Use* a pin to pick up a stitch of the bobbin thread. Gently pull thread toward a seam to ease in extra fabric.
4. *Press* hem allowance to shrink out fullness.

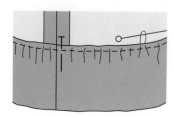

On fabrics that cannot be eased, remove the extra fullness by tapering the seamline below the hem. Take the same amount off each seam. Remove original stitching and trim seam allowances to remove bulk. Press seam open.

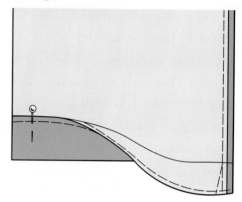

Finishing the Hem Edge

The type of hem finish to use depends upon the fabric and the type of garment. The same finishes used for seams can also be used for hems. (See Seam Finishes, page 511.)

If the fabric ravels, some type of finish must be used to prevent fraying and raveling. Most knits do not need a finish. If you want to cover the edge of the hem, you can use seam tape, bias tape, lace, or other decorative trim.

- **Machine zigzag finish.** This finish can be used for all weights of fabrics. Zigzag close to edge of fabric, or serge the edge with an overlock stitch.

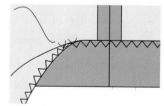

Zigzag finish with blindstitch

- **Seam tape, bias tape, or lace finish.** These can be used on all fabrics. Place tape or trim ¼ inch (6 mm) over raw edge and stitch, overlapping ends.

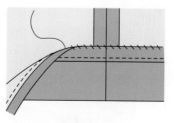

Seam tape finish with hemming stitch

Serging Techniques

Hems

The serger can be used to finish the raw edges of a hem that will be stitched to the garment by hand or machine.

1. *Plan* hem allowance so there is at least 1/16 inch (1-2 mm) of extra fabric that can be trimmed off during serging.
2. *Serge* along raw edge of hem allowance, and secure thread chains.
3. *Complete* hem by folding up hem allowance and using handstitches or topstitching on the conventional machine.

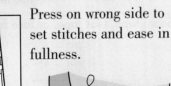

A blind hem can be stitched, using an overlock stitch. Some sergers have a special blind hemming foot to help guide the fabric.

1. *Turn* up hem allowance as for a hand-sewn hem.
2. *Fold* garment back 1/4 inch (6 mm) from raw edge of hem allowance and pin in place. Press hem.
3. *Serge* along raw edge so needle just catches fold of fabric.
4. *Open* out garment until stitches lie flat. Press on wrong side to set stitches and ease in fullness.

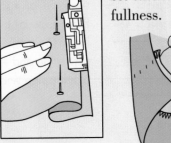

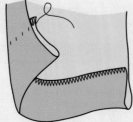

- **Pinked finish.** This can be used for more firmly woven fabrics. Pink edge or stitch 1/4 inch (6 mm) from edge and then pink.

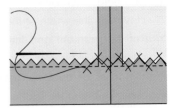

Pinked finish with catchstitch

- **Hemmed finish.** This can be used for lightweight to mediumweight fabrics. Turn under raw edge 1/4 inch (6 mm) and stitch.

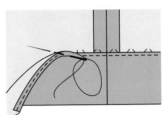

Hemmed finish with slipstitch

Attaching Hem to Garment

The hem can be attached to the garment by *hand stitching, machine stitching, or fusing.* Each method has certain advantages and disadvantages.

Handstitching a Hem

To hem by hand, use a single thread. Make sure stitches do not show on outside of garment. Keep stitches slightly loose so fabric does not pull or ripple. (See Hand stitches, pages 496-497, for specific directions for making each of the stitches.)

- **Blindstitch.** This stitch can be used with all types of fabrics and hem finishes. It shows less than any other type of stitch and allows for movement without pulling.
- **Hemming stitch.** This is used to stitch a hem with seam tape or lace finish.
- **Catchstitch.** This is good for hemming knits and stretch fabrics. It can be done at edge of hem or as a blind catchstitch inside hem.
- **Slipstitch.** This can be used to join a folded edge, such as a hemmed finish, to garment. Excellent for narrow, hand-rolled hems.

Machine Stitching a Hem

Machine stitching can be used for both invisible and decorative stitching. It is a fast, easy way to complete a garment or other type of sewing project.

Some machines have a built-in blindstitch. Fold garment back ¼ inch (6 mm) below hem edge. Machine stitch so straight stitches fall on hem allowance and single zigzag stitch just catches garment along fold line.

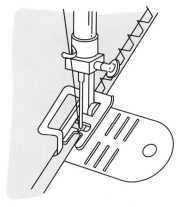

Topstitching can be used to attach the hem and decorate the garment at the same time. Fold hem to desired width. For woven fabrics, turn under raw edge ⅜ inch (1 cm) and press. Stitch close to upper edge. Knitted fabrics can be stitched single thickness and then trimmed close to stitching. Use two or more rows of stitching for a more decorative finish. Be sure to keep rows straight and parallel.

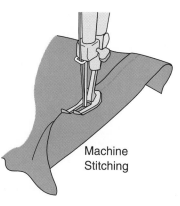

Machine Stitching

Fusing a Hem

Fusible web can be used to fuse two layers of fabric together. Place fusible web between garment and hem about ¼ inch (6 mm) below top of hem. This helps to prevent hem outline from showing on right side of garment. Also, it prevents any web from accidentally touching iron and sticking to it. Press to fuse, following manufacturer's directions.

To alter a fused hem, press area with steam until the two fabric layers can be gently pulled apart.

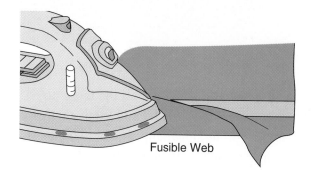

Fusible Web

Special Hem Techniques

Some hems require special hemming techniques. These include a rolled hem, a faced hem, and a hem with a pleat.

Rolled Hem

A narrow, rolled hem can be used for lightweight to mediumweight fabrics. It is often used to hem scarves, ruffles, sashes, blouses, evening clothes, lingerie, tablecloths, napkins, and curtains. It can be stitched by hand or by machine.

Hand-Rolled Hem

1. *Machine stitch* ¼ inch (6 mm) from raw edge and trim close to stitching.

2. *Roll edge* under between your thumb and forefinger until stitching is concealed.

3. *Slipstitch* hem in place, completing one small section at a time.

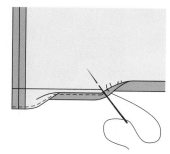

Machine-Rolled Hem

1. *Mark* hemline ⅛ inch (3 mm) longer than desired finished length. Fold up fabric along hemline. Do not press.

Serging Techniques

Rolled Hem

The serger is able to roll the fabric to the underside as the hem is stitched, creating a professional appearance. The lower looper tension is tightened to produce the rolled edge. Use a rolled hem presser foot, if needed.

1. *Plan* at least a ½ inch (1.3 cm) hem allowance.

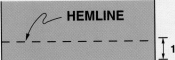

HEMLINE

1/2 INCH (1.3 cm)

2. *Do* a test swatch, and adjust tension settings until hem rolls properly. Tighten lower looper tension and loosen upper looper tension if lower looper thread forms large loops on underside.

3. *Serge* along hemline with garment right side up.

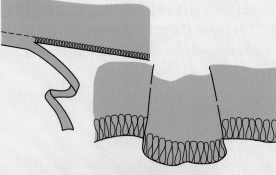

LOWER LOOPER THREAD **NEEDLE THREAD** **UPPER LOOPER THREAD** **NEEDLE THREAD**

2. *Stitch* as close as you can to fold. Trim hem allowance close to stitching, using embroidery scissors.

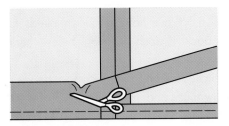

3. *Press* hem allowance up along stitching line. As you press, roll stitching line just to the inside of garment.

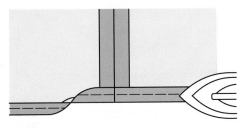

4. *Stitch* again, close to first fold.

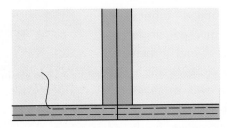

Faced Hem

A hem may be faced if there is not enough fabric for the hem allowance. Facings are also used if the hem edge is an unusual shape, such as scallops, or if the fabric is very heavy or bulky. Purchase bias hem facing or cut your own fabric facing.

1. *Pin* facing to garment, right sides together, overlapping ends.

2. *Stitch* a ¼ inch (6 mm) seam.

3. *Turn* facing to inside of garment and slip-stitch in place.

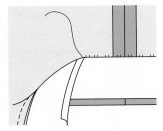

Hem with Pleat

This technique helps create sharp pleats:

1. *Clip* seam allowance above hem area.
2. *Press* seam allowance open below clip and trim to reduce bulk.

3. *Complete* hem.
4. *Press* pleat with seam on edge of fold.
5. *Edgestitch* along fold through all thicknesses of hem.

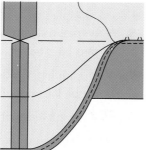
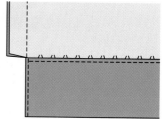

FITTING GUIDELINES

Don't wait until your garment is completed before you try it on. By then it may be too difficult or impossible to make necessary changes. Instead, take time to check the fit as you sew.

Try on the garment as soon as the major seams are joined. Stand in front of a full-length mirror and analyze the fit according to the following guidelines. Begin at the top and work your way down. The fit at the top affects the fit of the lower part of the garment. A wrinkle or a break line in the fabric indicates a problem.

Make any necessary fitting changes. Try on the garment again to be sure the problem has been corrected before you go on to finish the details.

- Does the neckline lie smooth with no pulling or gapping?
- Does the collar roll evenly and are the points identical?
- Do the shoulder seams rest smoothly over the shoulders?
- Do the darts taper toward the fullest part of the body?
- Do the sleeves hang straight from the shoulders to the elbow?
- Are the center front and center back seams in the center of the body and perpendicular to the floor?

- Do the side seams hang straight?
- Does the buttoned closing lie flat without any gapping?
- Is the waistline seam at the natural waistline or just above the hip bone and not too snug?
  - Is the crotch length comfortable for sitting?
  - Do the pants or skirt fit smoothly through the hips and thigh area with no wrinkles or extra fabric?
- Are hemlines even and parallel to the floor?
- Can you stand, sit, stretch, and bend comfortably?

Part 4 REVIEW

Summary

- Machine stitching is used for the major seams of a garment. Handstitching is used for basting, hemming, and sewing on fasteners.
- Pressing should be done after each step of construction.
- Darts, gathers, and easing are used to control fullness.
- Curved and enclosed seams may need to be trimmed, graded, clipped, or notched.
- Facings are used to finish necklines, front openings, and armholes.
- Casings are used to hold elastic or a drawstring.
- Fasteners can be both functional and decorative.
- Hems must be marked, turned up, finished along the edge, and attached to the garment.

Recalling the Facts

1. What is directional stitching?
2. On what parts of a garment should staystitching be used?
3. What is the width of a standard seam?
4. What is the difference between pressing and ironing?
5. Why should curved areas be pressed over a tailor's ham?
6. In what directions should horizontal darts and vertical darts be pressed?
7. What is the difference between easing and gathering?
8. When pinbasting a seam, how far apart should the pins be placed?
9. When grading a seam, which seam allowance should be the widest?
10. Why are curved seams often clipped?
11. When stitching a seam with a serger or overlock machine, what two tasks are done simultaneously?
12. What is the difference between a shaped facing and an extended facing?
13. Why are self-casings easier to make than applied casings?
14. When applying hooks and eyes to edges that overlap, should a straight eye or round eye be used?
15. What are two advantages of machine-worked buttonholes?
16. When can a sew-through button be sewn flat against the fabric? When should it be sewn with a thread shank?
17. On a side seam, should you use a centered zipper application or a lapped zipper application?
18. Why should you stitch both sides of a zipper in the same direction?
19. List the four basic steps in finishing a hem.
20. Name three handstitches that can be used for hemming.

Thinking Critically

1. **Analysis.** If you had access to both a sewing machine and an overlock machine, which one would you use to do the following construction

tasks: stitch a straight seam, stitch darts, gather, attach a neckline facing, finish a hem edge?

2. **Synthesis.** Some people think it is not worth the time to press after each construction step. What could you say to change their opinion?

3. **Evaluation.** If you wanted to shorten a hem but no one was available to mark the length for you, how could you mark it by yourself?

Practicing Your Skills

1. **Samples.** Make samples of the following techniques: types of stitches, darts, gathering and easing, seams and seam finishes, facings, casings, fasteners, and hems. Use handstitching, machine stitching, and overlock stitching where appropriate. Mount samples on heavy paper and write a description of each technique.

2. **Project.** Construct a simple garment, accessory, or home decorating item. Evaluate each of the construction techniques used in the project.

Applying Your Knowledge

1. **Construction Features.** Collect photos of garments from fashion magazines and catalogs. Identify different construction features, such as darts, gathers, seams, facings, casings, fasteners, and hems. Prepare a classroom display

2. **Evaluate Quality.** Select three garments from your wardrobe. Compare several construction features, such as seams, hems, and fasteners,

What Is a Sewing Instructor?

Sewing instructors teach sewing and serging techniques for constructing garments, accessories, and home furnishings. Sometimes they conduct a series of classes taught over several weeks or months. At other times, they may teach a short one- or two-hour workshop on a topic, such as "Sewing on Stretch Fabrics" or "Pillows and Placemats." The sewing classes may be offered by an adult education program or by a fabric or sewing machine store.

Try It Yourself

Imagine that you are a sewing instructor. Prepare samples of the step-by-step techniques used to make a shaped facing and a hem. Mount each sample on heavy paper, along with a description of the construction step. Place the samples of each construction technique in two separate folders for your "students" to use as references.

Build Your Portfolio

Make a list of workshops that you could "offer" on sewing and serging techniques. Place a copy of the workshop titles, along with the step-by-step samples of construction techniques, in your portfolio.

that are used in the garments. Describe any differences. Then rate the quality of construction for each garment.

3. **Compare Time.** Record the amount of time to make a garment detail, such as a facing or finished hem, using an overlock machine and a conventional sewing machine. Which method is faster for each step?

531

Part 5

Special Sewing Techniques

○ ○ ○ ○ ○ ○ ○ ○ ○ ○ ○ ○

The following lessons show special sewing techniques that are used when constructing many garments. Collars, sleeves, and cuffs can be found on shirts, blouses, dresses, jackets, and coats. Many garments have pockets. Some may be hidden in a side seam, while others accent the front of a shirt or jacket.

The waistline of a garment can be finished in several ways. Some designs use a waistband; others are finished with a facing or casing.

Some garments are trimmed with bindings or ruffles. Others are decorated with rickrack, braid, lace, or fabric paints. You can use your creativity to sew a garment that is special and original.

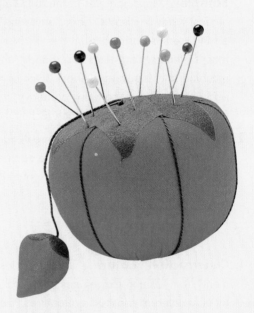

Lesson 1

Special Seams

Different types of seams are used for a variety of purposes in sewing. Some are used to enclose the seam allowance or to create a decorative effect. Other techniques are needed for stitching special areas.

Self-Finished Seams

Self-finished seams *enclose the seam allowances as the seam is stitched.* They are used for a more attractive appearance or to strengthen the seam. Self-finished seams include the French seam, flat-felled seam, double-stitched seam, and narrow overlocked seam.

French Seam

The French seam is used on sheer fabrics because no raw edges show through the fabric. It looks like a plain seam on the outside of the garment and a narrow tuck on the wrong side. It can be used on straight seams, but it is not flexible enough for curved seams.

1. *Pin* wrong sides of fabrics together.
2. *Stitch* ⅜ inch (9 mm) from raw edges. Trim seam allowances to ⅛ inch (3 mm). Press seam allowances open.
3. *Fold* fabric along seamline with right sides together; press.
4. *Stitch* ¼ inch (6 mm) from folded edge. The two seams, ⅜ inch and ¼ inch (9 mm and 6 mm), combine to make a ⅝ inch (1.5 cm) seam.

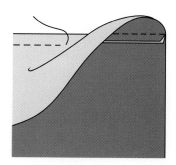

Serging Techniques

Narrow Rolled Seam

This seam is used on sheer and light-weight fabrics. It is especially good for lingerie fabrics and laces.

1. *Pin* wrong sides of fabric together.
2. *Adjust* overlock for a narrow rolled hem with a 1.5 to 2.5 mm stitch length and a balanced tension.
3. *Serge* seam.

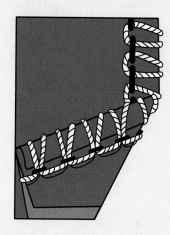

Flat-Felled Seam

This is a very sturdy and durable seam used for shirts, jeans, sportswear, pajamas, and other garments. Two rows of stitching show on the outside of the garment. Contrasting thread can be used as an accent.

1. *Pin* wrong sides of fabric together.
2. *Stitch* ⅝ inch (1.5 cm) standard seam. Press open.
3. *Press* both seam allowances to one side.
4. *Trim* the under-seam allowance to ⅛ inch (3 mm).

Serging Techniques

Reinforced Seam

In areas of stress, a stronger seam can be created by combining the serger and the conventional seam.

1. *Stitch* seam on a conventional machine, using a straight stitch.

2. *Press* seam allowances flat as they were stitched.

3. *Serge* edges together, using the two-thread overlock stitch, ⅛ inch (3 mm) from seamline.

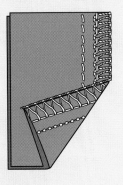

5. *Fold* in edge of upper seam allowance ¼ inch (6 mm). Place it over trimmed seam allowance; press.

6. *Stitch* close to folded edge through all thicknesses.

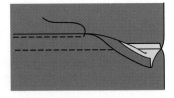

Double-Stitched Seam

This seam can be used for curved seams, such as armhole or crotch seams.

1. *Stitch* ⅝ inch (1.5 cm) standard seam, with right sides of fabric together.

2. *Stitch* again about ⅛ inch (3 mm) from seamline in seam allowance. Narrow zigzag stitch can be used for this second row of stitching.

3. *Trim* seam allowances close to stitching.

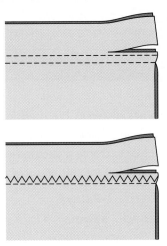

Decorative Seams

Decorative seams *use topstitching or cording to create special effects.* They can give a sporty, tailored, or contrasting finish to a garment. Decorative seams include the topstitched seam, welt seam, lapped seam, and piped or corded seam.

Topstitched Seam

Topstitching can be used to hold bulky seam allowances flat and to emphasize the seams of a garment. Topstitching can be done on one side or on both sides of the seam.

1. *Stitch* ⅝ inch (1.5 cm) standard seam. Press seam allowances open.

2. *Topstitch* along each side of seam, through both layers of fabric. Keep stitching straight and equal distance from seamline.

An alternative: *Press* both seam allowances to one side as indicated on pattern. *Topstitch* through all three layers of fabric.

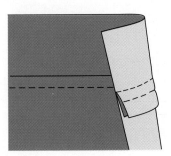

Welt Seam

This seam is used for a tailored finish on heavier fabrics. It is less bulky than the flat-felled seam.

1. *Stitch* ⅝ inch (1.5 cm) standard seam, with right sides of fabric together. Press seam open.
2. *Press* both seam allowances to one side.
3. *Trim* seam allowance against garment to ¼ inch (6 mm).
4. *Stitch* from outside through garment and wider seam allowance. Keep stitching an even distance from seamline.

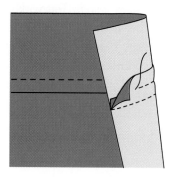

Lapped Seam

This seam is used when one piece is lapped over the other and topstitched in place. It is often used with natural or synthetic leather and suede.

1. *Turn* under seam allowance on section to be lapped; press. For leather and suede, trim away seam allowance.
2. *Lap* folded or trimmed edge over other piece at seamline, wrong side to right side.
3. *Edgestitch* along folded or trimmed edge.
4. *Topstitch* again ¼ inch (6 mm) from edge.

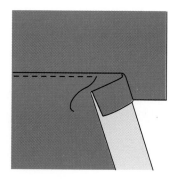

Serging Techniques

Topstitched Seam

A serged seam can be topstitched once or twice for a sporty look. Press serged seam to one side, then topstitch on a conventional machine.

Piped or Corded Seam

Piping or cording covered with bias strips of fabric can be inserted into a seam while it is stitched.

1. *Pin* piping or cording to right side of one fabric section along seamline. Be sure piping or cording is facing garment, and seam allowance is toward edge of fabric.
2. *Stitch* close to seamline in seam allowance, using a zipper foot.
3. *Pin* second piece of fabric over piping or cording, with right sides together.
4. *Stitch* along seamline through all thicknesses, using a zipper foot.

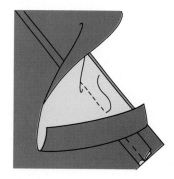

Serging Techniques

Flatlock Seam

A flatlock seam is a good choice for straight seams on knit fabric.

- The traditional flatlock seam is formed by using the two-thread overlock stitch.

- A mock flatlock seam is created with the three-thread overlock stitch. Loosen the needle tension almost as much as possible, and tighten the lower looper tension. When the overlock is properly adjusted, the needle thread will form a V on the underside of the fabric. The lower looper thread will form a straight line along the edge of the fabric.

- For both types of flatlock seams, serge the seam. Then gently pull on the layers until the fabric lies flat and the cut edges meet. The stitch will have a ladder-like appearance on one side of the garment and loops on the other.

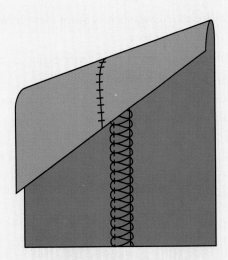

Lesson 2

Tucks and Pleats

Tucks and pleats are folds of fabric used to control fullness or add design interest. They are folded and then pressed or stitched in place.

Tucks

Tucks are *narrow folds of fabric that are stitched part-way or the entire length.* The width of the tucks and the spacing between the tucks can vary depending upon the design. Narrow pin tucks are indicated on the pattern by a series of fold lines. Wide tucks usually have both fold and stitching lines indicated. Follow your pattern guide for stitching directions.

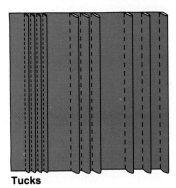

Tucks

1. *Mark* stitching and fold lines of each tuck. To save time, use clips to mark ends of stitching lines, and notches to mark ends of fold lines.
2. *Fold* fabric along fold lines, matching stitching lines.
3. *Stitch* each tuck from the side that will be seen after the tuck is pressed flat. Keep stitching straight and even.
4. *Press* each tuck flat, as stitched. Then press each tuck to one side, as shown on guide sheet.

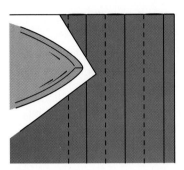

Tucks

Tucks can be stitched on the overlock machine. Mark and fold the fabric the same as for conventional tucks.

- For pin tucks, adjust the overlock for the narrow rolled hem stitch.

- For wider tucks, use the three-thread or four-thread overlock stitch. Disengage the knife, or keep the fold slightly to the left of the knife so the fabric is not cut.

- For decorative tucks, use metallic thread, embroidery floss, pearl cotton, or narrow ribbon in the upper looper.

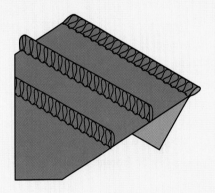

Sewing Tip

You can add your own tucks to a garment by tucking the fabric before cutting out the pattern pieces. Be sure to purchase extra fabric to allow for the tucks.

Pleats

Pleats are *folds of fabric, wider than tucks, that are stitched or pressed in place.* One single pleat or an entire series of pleats can be used in a garment. Pleats can be pressed sharp along the edges or fall in soft folds. They can also be stitched for a more tailored look.

Various effects can be created by the way pleats are turned. *Knife pleats* have the folds turned in one direction. *Box pleats* and *inverted pleats* are made by turning two pleats toward each other. Follow the guide sheet for specific instructions for folding, pressing, and stitching each type of pleat.

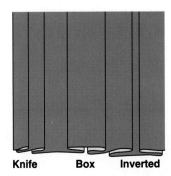

Knife   **Box**   **Inverted**

Folding Pleats

1. *Mark* fold line and placement line for each pleat. If pleats are to be made from the right side, clip and notch ends of lines. Or mark with a fabric marking pen.

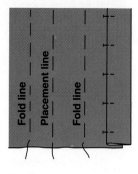

2. *Fold* fabric, matching fold and placement lines, and pin. An arrow on the pattern piece will show direction in which to fold.

3. *Staystitch* pleats along upper seamline.

Pressing Pleats

1. *Press* pleats gently from inside of garment. If pleats leave an impression on fabric, slip strips of paper under each fold before pressing.

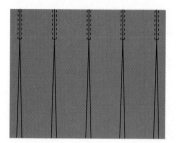

2. *Turn* garment to right side.

3. *Press* pleats in place, using a press cloth. For soft pleats, press lightly. For sharp pleats, use lots of steam and a damp press cloth.

4. *Let* pleats dry on ironing board.

Stitching Pleats

Pleats may be topstitched or edgestitched for a smoother appearance. Stitching also holds the pleats in place. For pleats that are both edgestitched and topstitched, do the edgestitching first.

Edgestitching gives a sharper crease along the outer or inner fold of a pleat.

1. *Complete* hem.

2. *Stitch* from bottom of pleat to top as close to fold as possible.

3. *Repeat* on other fold of pleat, if desired.

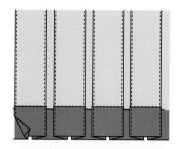

Topstitching is stitched only part way, usually between the waist and hip areas.

1. *Topstitch* from right side through all thicknesses. Begin at hip; do not backstitch. Stitch to top of pleat.

2. *Pull* threads to under side and tie.

Lesson 3

Interfacings and Linings

Interfacings and linings are inner construction fabrics. They do not show on the outside of a garment, but they help to shape and support the outer fabric.

- **Interfacing** is *a layer of fabric placed between the facing and the outer fabric.*

- **Lining** is *a layer of fabric constructed separately from the outer garment and then joined at one or more major seams.*

When choosing an interfacing or lining fabric, always drape the garment fabric over the inner con-

struction fabric. Check to see how the two fabrics look and feel together.

- Is it too soft or too crisp for the shape you want?

- Does the color show through or change the color of the outer fabric?

- Is the fiber content of the two fabrics compatible?

- Can both fabrics be washed or dry cleaned in the same manner?

- Do they require pressing?

Interfacing

Interfacing can be used to give shape to collars, cuffs, and waistbands. It can prevent edges, such as a neckline or front closing, from stretching. It can give added body to a belt, bag, or hat. Sometimes a separate pattern piece will be provided for the interfacing. If not, the interfacing is cut from the facing, collar, cuff, or waistband pattern piece.

Special woven, knitted, and nonwoven interfacing fabrics are available in many different types and weights. Sew-in interfacings are stitched by machine or by hand to the garment. Fusible interfacings are pressed and fused directly to the fabric with an iron.

Sew-In Interfacing

Cut the interfacing pieces following the directions on the guide sheet. Lightweight to mediumweight interfacing can be stitched into the seam of a garment.

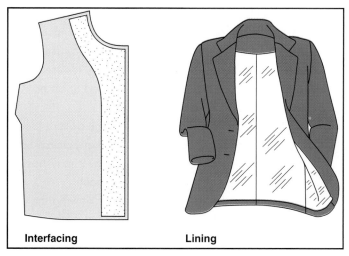

Interfacing   **Lining**

Sewing Tip

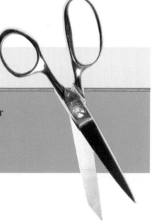

Usually the interfacing should be slightly lighter in weight than the outer fabric. Remember that some fusible interfacings are crisper after they are fused. Always pretest on a scrap of your fabric to be sure you like the results.

1. *Pin* interfacing to wrong side of garment or facing.
2. *Machine baste* ½ inch (1.3 cm) from fabric edge.
3. *Trim* interfacing close to stitching.
4. *Catchstitch* interfacing by hand along a folded edge, such as an extended facing or cuff.

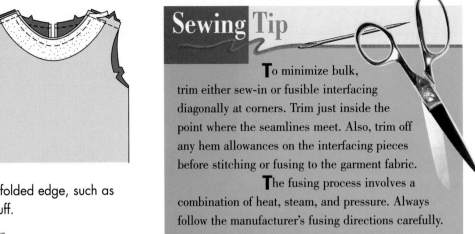

Fusible Interfacing

Before applying a fusible interfacing to garment sections, test the fusing process on a scrap of your fabric. If the interfacing leaves an outline along the edge, then fuse it to the facing rather than to the garment.

1. *Trim* any corners or hem allowances. For mediumweight interfacings, trim away all seam allowances.
2. *Place* adhesive side of interfacing on wrong side of fabric, matching cut edges of interfacing to seamlines.
3. *Fuse* in place, following fusing directions.

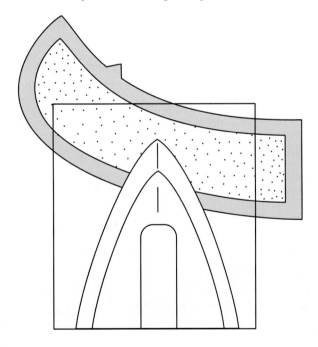

Sewing Tip

To minimize bulk, trim either sew-in or fusible interfacing diagonally at corners. Trim just inside the point where the seamlines meet. Also, trim off any hem allowances on the interfacing pieces before stitching or fusing to the garment fabric.

The fusing process involves a combination of heat, steam, and pressure. Always follow the manufacturer's fusing directions carefully.

Lining

A lining is used to give an attractive appearance to the inside of a garment. It also helps to prevent stretching and wrinkling of the outer fabric. Use a firmly woven fabric with a smooth, slippery texture. Some coat linings are backed with a napped finish or insulation for added warmth.

A lining may be cut from the same pattern pieces as the outer fabric. Some coat or jacket patterns have separate pattern pieces for the lining. It may have a center back pleat to allow for movement.

Stitch the lining pieces together following the pattern guide sheet. Seam finishes are not necessary on either the outer fabric or on the lining unless the fabric ravels easily. Use machine or hand stitching to attach the lining to the garment along the facing or the waistline seam.

Some linings are hemmed separately; others are sewn to the garment. Coat, skirt, and dress linings are usually hemmed separately. Make the lining hem ½ to 1 inch (1.3 to 2.5 cm) shorter than the outer garment. (See Hems, page 524.) For coats, use French tacks to hold the hems together at the seamlines.

Jacket, sleeve, and pants linings are usually attached to the garment hem. The hem should be at least ½ inch (1.3 cm) above the edge of the garment. The lining should form a small tuck at the hemline to allow for movement.

1. *Match* folded hem edges of lining and garment.

2. *Pin* folded edge of lining at least ½ inch (1.3 cm) above garment edge, creating a tuck.

3. *Slipstitch* edge of lining to garment hem.

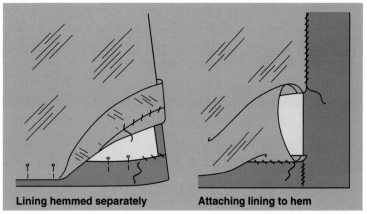

Lining hemmed separately   **Attaching lining to hem**

Lesson 4

Collars

Collars come in many different sizes and shapes. However, there are four basic types of collars.

- **Flat collar** lies flat against the garment. Both the upper and lower collar are cut from the same pattern piece.

- **Rolled collar** stands up at the back of the neck and then turns down to created a rolled edge around the neck. It can be cut with a one-piece upper collar and a two-piece under collar that is slightly smaller. Another way is to cut the entire collar as one piece and fold it at the outer edge.

- **Shirt collar** has a separate *stand*, or band, that attaches the collar to the neckline.

- **Standing collar** is a band that stands straight up or folds over to create a turtleneck.

Because a collar is close to your face, it attracts attention and should be well made. The collar should circle the neck smoothly without rippling. The front points or curves should be identical in shape. The under collar should not show along the edge. A rolled collar and a shirt collar should cover the neck seam in back. The collar should be carefully pressed.

Types of Collars

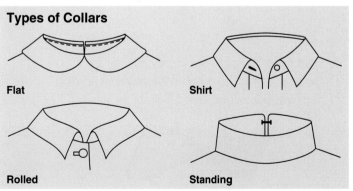

Flat   Shirt

Rolled   Standing

Interfacing is used in collars to give added shape and support. It is usually stitched or fused to the under collar. However, if the outer fabric is lightweight, the interfacing can be stitched to the upper collar to prevent the seam allowances from showing.

There are two basic steps to making a collar:

1. *Construct* collar.
2. *Attach* collar to garment.

Constructing the Collar

Cut out the collar and any facings. The upper and under collar may be cut from the same pattern piece or from separate pieces. Or the collar may be cut from one piece of fabric and folded lengthwise.

1. *Stitch or fuse* interfacing to wrong side of under collar. For a one-piece collar, catchstitch interfacing along fold line. Stitch center back seam of under collar, if necessary. Press seam open and trim.

2. *Pin* collar sections with right sides together. Follow pattern guide sheet for specific directions.

3. *Stitch* outer seam of collar. Reinforce corners or points with short reinforcement stitches.

4. *Trim and grade* seam allowances. Trim corners close to stitching for crisp, sharp points. Clip or notch curved areas. Press seam open, using a point presser.

5. *Turn* collar to right side. Gently pull out the points. (Don't push out with the points of scissors because you might poke a hole in the fabric.)

6. *Press* outer seam, rolling slightly to underside of collar.

7. *Understitch* under collar to seam allowances to help prevent it from showing at edge. Or topstitch around edge of collar.

For a shirt collar, stitch the collar band to the upper collar and the under collar at the inner edge. Trim, grade, clip, notch, and press the seams.

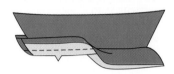

Attaching Collar to Garment

A collar may be stitched to a garment with no facing, a partial neckline facing, or a complete facing. Follow the directions in your pattern guide sheet.

Collar without Facing

This method is used for shirt collars and standing collars:

1. *Staystitch* garment neckline, and clip.

2. *Pin* under collar or band to neckline, right sides together, matching all markings.

3. *Stitch* seam, trim, and clip. Press seam toward collar.

4. *Turn* in seam allowance of upper collar or band; press. Trim seam allowance to ¼ inch (6 mm).

5. *Pin* folded edge over neckline seam. Machine stitch close to edge, or slipstitch by hand.

Collar with Partial Facing

This method is used for flat collars and rolled collars:

1. *Staystitch* garment neckline and clip.
2. *Pin* collar to neckline, matching notches and markings.
3. *Machine baste* collar to neck edge between front openings and shoulder markings. Machine baste under collar only to back neck edge between shoulder markings.

4. *Pin* front facings to neckline, with right sides together. Match all markings. Clip neck edge through all layers at both shoulder markings.
5. *Stitch* neck seam as basted, being careful not to catch the free edge of collar back. Trim, grade, and clip seam allowances.
6. *Turn* facing to inside and press.
7. *Understitch* facing to neckline seam allowances.
8. *Turn under* ⅝ inch (1.5 cm) on raw edge of collar back; press. Trim to ¼ inch (6 mm).
9. *Slipstitch* folded edge of collar over back neck seam. Tack facing to shoulder seam allowances.

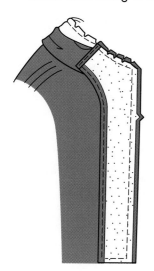
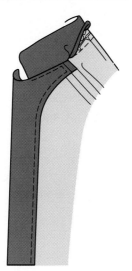

Collar with Neckline Facing

1. *Stitch* facing sections together. Trim and press seams. Finish outer unnotched edge of facing.
2. *Staystitch* garment neckline and clip.
3. *Pin* collar to neckline, matching notches and markings.
4. *Machine baste* collar to neck edge.

5. *Pin* facing to neckline, with right sides together. Match markings and seamlines.
6. *Stitch* neckline seam. Trim, grade, and clip seam allowances.

7. *Turn* facing to inside and press.
8. *Understitch* facing to neckline seam allowances.
9. *Tack* edge of facing to shoulder seam allowances.

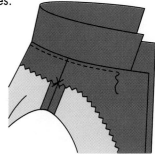

Serging Techniques

Collar

Use this method for a collar with a partial or full neckline facing:

1. *Follow* Steps 1 to 5 for Collar with Neckline Facing to prepare facing, baste collar to neckline, and pin facing to neckline.

2. *Serge* neckline seam.

3. *Follow* Steps 7 to 9 to turn, understitch, and tack facing.

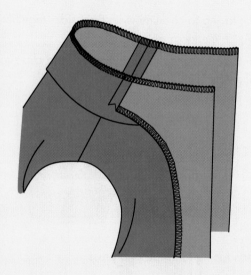

Lesson 5

Sleeves

Sleeves come in many different lengths and shapes. From a short cap sleeve to a long shirt sleeve with cuffs, sleeves require a variety of sewing techniques. Sleeves can be finished at the bottom edge with a hem, facing, casing, or cuff.

There are three basic types of sleeves:

- **Set-in sleeve** is joined to a garment by an armhole seam that circles the arm near the shoulder.

- **Raglan sleeve** has a front and back diagonal seam that extends from the neckline to the underarm.

- **Kimono sleeve** is cut in one piece with the front and back of the garment.

Set -in

Raglan

Kimono

Set-in Sleeve

A set-in sleeve is the most common type of sleeve, but it is also the most difficult. A set-in sleeve almost always measures more than the armhole into which it must fit. The extra fullness in the sleeve is needed so the sleeve will fit over the top curve of your arm and allow movement.

Some set-in sleeves will be very full across the *cap,* or top, of the sleeve. This fullness must be eased into the seam without any gathers or puckers. Other sleeves, such as a tailored shirt, will have a short sleeve cap and will be only slightly larger than the armhole.

There are two methods for sewing a set-in sleeve:

- **Open-sleeve method.** The sleeve is stitched to the armhole. Then the side seam and underarm seam are stitched in one continuous seam.
- **Closed-sleeve method.** The underarm seam of the sleeve and the side seam of the garment are stitched first. Then the sleeve is attached to the armhole.

Open-Sleeve Method

This method is also called the *flat construction method* because the sleeve is stitched to the armhole, while both the sleeve and garment seams remain open. This method is fast and easy. However, the open-sleeve method can only be used for sleeves that require little easing, such as tailored shirts, sports shirts, and shirts with dropped shoulders.

1. *Match* sleeve to garment, right sides together, and pin.
2. *Stitch* seam with sleeve side up. Ease in any fullness with your fingers as you sew.
3. *Stitch* second row of stitching ⅜ inch (1 cm) from outer edge. Trim close to stitching. Press seam allowances toward garment. Alternatives: Topstitch on outside of garment ¼ to ⅜ inch (6 to 9 mm) from seam on the body side, or serge to finish seam.
4. *Match and pin* side seam and underarm sleeve seam.
5. *Stitch* seam from bottom of garment to end of sleeve in one continuous line of stitching. Press seams open. Alternatives: Trim seam allowances and zigzag together, or serge seam.

Closed-Sleeve Method

This method is also called the *unit method* of construction because the sleeve is completed before it is stitched to the armhole. This method is used for sleeves that have extra fullness across the sleeve cap. Use one or two rows of machine basting, about 8 stitches per inch (3 mm in length) to ease or gather in the fullness of the sleeve. Follow the directions in your pattern guide sheet.

1. *Machine baste* close to ⅝ inch (1.5 cm) seamline within seam allowance. Stitch around top of sleeve between notches. (If sleeve cap is full, the pattern guide sheet will recommend a second row of machine basting ⅜ inch or 1 cm from outer edge.)
2. *Stitch* underarm seam of sleeve; press open.
3. *Pull up* bobbin thread ends of machine basting until sleeve cap fits armhole. Adjust fullness evenly between notches.
4. *Turn* garment wrong side out. Turn sleeve right side out and slip inside armhole.

Serging Techniques

Sleeves

For sweatshirts and similar sportswear knit garments, use the two-thread flatlock or three-thread mock flatlock stitch to join the sleeve to the garment. (See Steps 3 and 4 for the Raglan Sleeve.) Use the three-thread or four-thread overlock stitch to serge the underarm seam.

8. *Press* seam allowances together from sleeve side, using side of iron. Do not press seam from right side of garment. An armhole seam is supposed to be gently curved. Turn seam allowances toward sleeve.

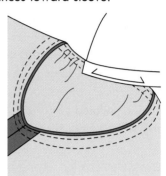

5. *Pin* sleeve to garment, with right sides together. Match underarm seams, shoulder markings, and notches. Adjust fullness. Place pins at right angles to seamline so they can be easily removed as you sew.

6. *Stitch* sleeve to armhole with sleeve side up. This allows you to control fullness and prevents tucks or puckers from forming.

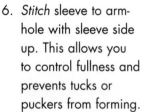

7. *Reinforce* armhole seam with second row of stitches ⅜ inch (1 cm) from outer edge. Trim close to stitching. Or serge to finish seam. (Some armhole seams are reinforced only in the underarm section. Stitch from notch to notch.)

Raglan Sleeve

A raglan sleeve is loose fitting and comfortable to wear. It has a shoulder dart or seam to shape the sleeve over the shoulder area.

1. *Stitch* shoulder dart or seam. Slash and press open.
2. *Pin* diagonal seams of sleeve to garment, with right sides together. Match notches, markings, and underarm seams.

3. *Stitch* seams.
4. *Reinforce* underarm section between notches by stitching again, ⅜ inch (1 cm) from outer edge. Or serge to finish seam.

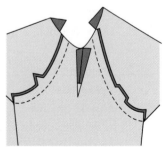

5. *Clip* at end of second row of stitching. Trim underarm close to stitching. Press seams open between notches and neckline.

6. *Stitch* underarm seam of sleeve and side seam, and press open. Alternatives: Trim seam allowances and zigzag together, or serge underarm seam of sleeve and side seam.

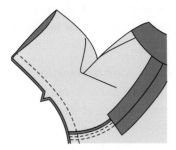

Kimono Sleeve

This is the easiest sleeve for a beginner to make. it is simply an extension of the garment front and back.

1. *Stitch* shoulder seam, right sides together. Press open.

2. *Stitch* underarm seam.

3. *Reinforce* underarm seam with second row of stitching ⅜ inch (1 cm) from outer edge. To give seam extra strength, sew a piece of seam tape over curved underarm seam, stitching through all layers.

4. *Clip* curve of seam, but do not clip seam tape. Press seam open. Or trim seam and zigzag seam allowances together. Or serge to finish seam.

Lesson6

Cuffs

Cuffs give a tailored finish to the end of a sleeve. There are three basic types of cuffs: *fold-up cuff, band cuff, and buttoned cuff.* Some cuffs are interfaced. Follow your pattern guide sheet and the information on Interfacings, page 539.

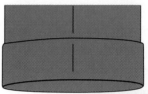

Fold-up Cuff

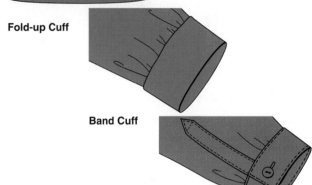

Band Cuff

Buttoned Cuff

Fold-Up Cuff

A *fold-up cuff* is actually a deep hem at the bottom of a sleeve or pants leg that is folded to the right side of the garment.

1. *Finish* lower edge of fabric with zigzag, hemmed, or bound finish. (See Seam Finishes, page 511.)

2. *Turn* cuff to inside along fold line and pin.

3. *Hem* by hand or machine stitching.

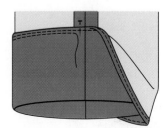

4. *Turn* lower edge of garment to right side along hemline to form cuff.

5. *Tack or stitch-in-the-ditch* to hold cuff in place at each seam.

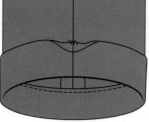

Band Cuff

A *band cuff* has no opening and must be large enough for your hand to slip through easily.

1. *Interface* cuff, if desired.

2. *Fold* unnotched seam allowance of cuff to inside, and press. Trim seam allowance to ¼ inch (6 mm).

3. *Pin* notched edge of cuff to bottom edge of sleeve, right sides together, matching markings. Adjust fullness.

4. *Stitch* seam with sleeve side up. Trim, grade, and press seam allowances toward cuff.

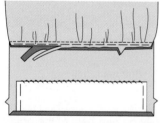
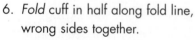
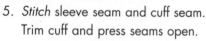

5. *Stitch* sleeve seam and cuff seam. Trim cuff and press seams open.

6. *Fold* cuff in half along fold line, wrong sides together.

7. *Pin* folded edge of cuff over seamline. Topstitch from right side or slipstitch edge in place.

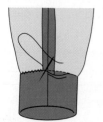

Buttoned Cuff

A *buttoned cuff* fits snugly around the wrist and fastens with a button or some other fastener. There must be some type of opening in the sleeve to allow the cuff to slide over your hand. The opening, called a *placket,* is sewn before the cuff is attached.

Sewing Sleeve Plackets

A **placket** is *a slit at the wrist, neck, or waist of a garment to make it easier to put on and take off.* The three most common types of sleeve plackets are *faced placket, continuous lap,* and *banded placket.* The pattern guide sheet will give complete directions for making the placket.

Faced Placket

This type of placket forms a split opening that can be used for a sleeve or neckline placket.

1. *Finish* edge of placket facing.

2. *Center* placket over opening, with right sides together.

3. *Stitch* along stitching lines, using short reinforcement stitches. Take one small stitch across the point.

4. *Slash* carefully up to the point.

5. *Turn* facing to inside and press.

Continuous Lap

This is a narrow binding that overlaps at the opening. It can be used for a sleeve placket or a waistline placket on pants, skirts, or shorts. Cut a fabric strip 1 ½ inches wide (3.8 cm) and twice the length of the slash.

1. *Staystitch* placket opening along stitching lines, using reinforcement stitches. Take one small stitch across the point.

Sleeve Plackets

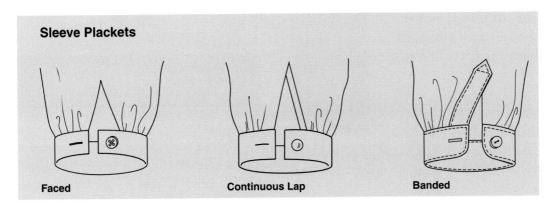

Faced   Continuous Lap   Banded

2. *Slash* carefully up to the point. Open slash until line of stitching is almost straight.

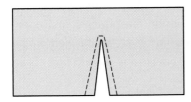

3. *Pin* fabric strip to slashed edge, matching right side of strip to wrong side of sleeve, so stitching line is ¼ inch (6 mm) from edge of strip. Fabric edges will not match.

4. *Stitch* along first row of stitching. Press seam allowances toward fabric strip.

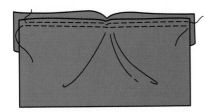

5. *Turn* in raw edge of fabric strip ¼ inch (6 mm) and pin over seam. Topstitch in place.

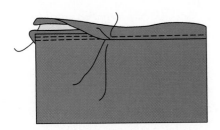

6. *Press* front portion of lap to inside and baste in place across lower edge of opening.

Banded Placket

This placket gives a tailored finish to a sleeve. It is similar to the neckline placket used on the front of a shirt. The banded placket can be one or two pieces.

1. *Reinforce* opening with stitching.
2. *Slash and clip* into corners.
3. *Stitch* underlap to back edge of opening, following directions in guide sheet.

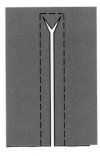

4. *Stitch* overlap to front edge of opening.

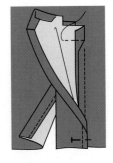

5. *Overlap* placket and stitch at upper edge. Stitch through all thicknesses across point and around edges.

Sewing Buttoned Cuff

Some buttoned cuffs are cut in one piece and folded lengthwise. Others are cut in two pieces and stitched along the outer edge.

1. *Complete* sleeve opening.

2. *Interface* cuff, if desired.

3. *Fold* long unnotched edge of cuff to inside and press. Trim to ¼ inch (6 mm).

4. *Stitch* ends of cuffs, right sides together. Or stitch cuff sections together along outer edge. Trim and grade seams; press. Turn cuff to right side.

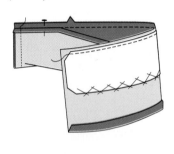

5. *Pin* cuff to gathered sleeve edge, right sides together, matching notches and markings. For a shirt sleeve, cuff edges will be even with placket edges. For other sleeve openings, cuff will extend beyond back edge of placket.

6. *Stitch* seam. Trim, grade, and clip seam allowances. Press seam allowances toward cuff.

7. *Place* folded edge of cuff over seam and extension end. Topstitch in place from right side. If desired, topstitch outer edge of cuff.

8. *Make* machine buttonholes and attach buttons.

Lesson 7

Pockets

Pockets can be functional, decorative, or both. A pocket concealed in a side seam is purely functional, while a patch pocket is both functional and decorative. Check the location of the pocket to be sure the placement is correct for your height and body shape. You may have to raise or lower it for convenience or for better proportion.

There are many different types of pockets. Some are located inside the garment and open through a seam or a slash. Others are stitched on the outside of the garment. Some may have a flap covering the top of the pocket.

Three types of pockets that are easy to make are the *in-seam pocket,* the *patch pocket,* and the *front hip pocket.*

In-Seam Pocket

This is the easiest type of pocket to make. The pocket is attached to the side seam of the garment. It can be cut as part of the garment front and back. Or it can be cut from a separate pattern piece and stitched to the seam. If the outer fabric is bulky or heavy, cut the pocket pieces from lining fabric. All of the construction is done on the inside of the garment.

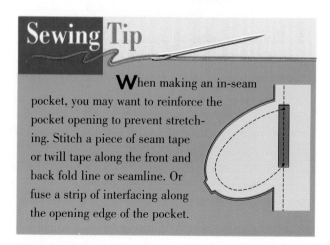

Sewing Tip

When making an in-seam pocket, you may want to reinforce the pocket opening to prevent stretching. Stitch a piece of seam tape or twill tape along the front and back fold line or seamline. Or fuse a strip of interfacing along the opening edge of the pocket.

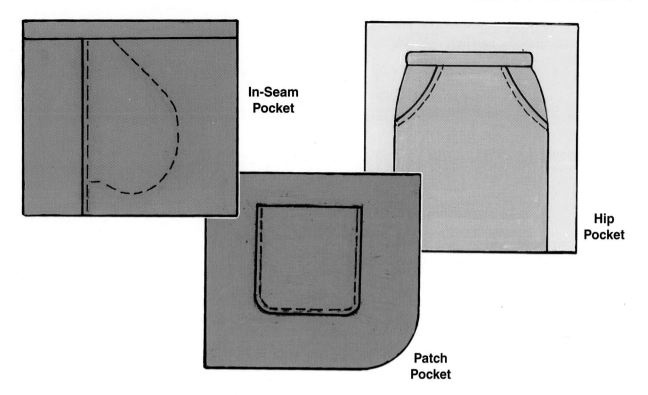

In-Seam Pocket

Hip Pocket

Patch Pocket

1. *Stitch* pocket pieces to front and back opening, right sides together, if pocket is cut separately. Press seam allowances toward pocket pieces.

2. *Pin* garment front to garment back, matching markings at seamline and pocket.

3. *Stitch* directionally along seam and around pocket in one step. Use reinforcement stitches at corners. Press seam allowances flat.

4. *Turn* pocket toward front of garment. Clip back seam allowance above and below pocket so seam allowances of garment can be pressed open.

5. *Finish* seam allowances, if necessary.

Patch Pocket

These are made from the same fabric as the garment and stitched to the outside by machine or hand. If using a plaid, stripe, or printed fabric, match the pocket to the garment. Or cut the pocket on the bias for a special design effect.

When making a pair of patch pockets, be sure both pockets are the same size and shape. Attach the pockets to the garment evenly.

Patch pockets may be lined or unlined. A lining is needed for fabrics that stretch or sag. Fabrics that are firm enough to hold their shape can be used without a lining. Sometimes a flap is stitched above the pocket.

Unlined Patch Pocket

1. *Turn* under top edge of pocket hem ¼ inch (6 mm), press, and stitch.

2. *Turn* hem to right side of pocket along fold line, and pin.

3. *Staystitch* around pocket on seamline, beginning at fold line of hem. Staystitching will act as a guide for turning and pressing edges and corners.

4. *Trim and grade* seam allowances. Trim upper corners diagonally. Turn hem right side out and press.

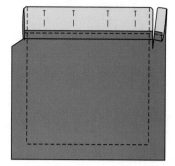

5. *Fold in* seam allowances along stitching and press. Square corners must be mitered; round corners must be notched.

6. *Stitch* edge of hem to pocket by hand, or top-stitch from right side.

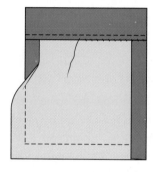

7. *Pin* pocket to garment. Topstitch around edge of pocket, or slipstitch in place. Reinforce corners by backstitching or by stitching a small triangle or square.

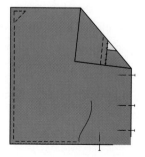

Sewing Tip

Use a blind hem foot to help keep topstitching straight and even.

Square or Rectangular Pocket

Miter the corners to eliminate bulk and form flat, square corners:

1. *Open* out seam allowances.
2. *Trim* each corner diagonally to ¼ inch (6 mm) from fold.
3. *Fold* in corner diagonally and press.
4. *Refold* seam allowances on both sides of corner to form square edge, and press again.

Curved Pocket

Follow these steps:

1. *Machine baste* around curved edges ½ inch (1.3 cm) from outer edge.
2. *Pull* on bobbin thread until seam allowance curves in and lies flat.
3. *Trim and notch* seam allowance to eliminate bulk and puckers.
4. *Press.*

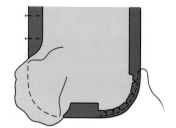

Lined Patch Pocket

1. *Pin* upper edge of lining to upper edge of pocket, right sides together.
2. *Stitch* on seamline, leaving 1 inch (2.5 cm) opening in center for turning. Press seam toward lining.

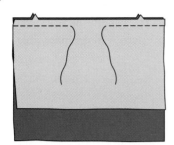

3. *Fold* pocket, right sides together, along upper fold line.
4. *Pin and stitch* lining to pocket around all three sides. Trim and grade seam allowances. Clip corners and notch curved areas.

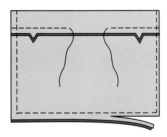

5. *Turn* pocket right side out through opening. Roll seam slightly toward lining and press.
6. *Slipstitch* opening closed.

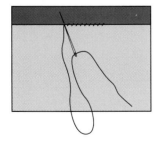

7. *Pin* pocket to garment, and topstitch or slipstitch in place.

Curved Patch Pocket

This technique makes the seam allowances curl to the inside of the pocket:

1. *Set* machine for the widest three-thread overlock stitch. Adjust tensions so that needle is normal, upper looper is slightly tight, and lower looper is slightly loose.
2. *Serge* around outside edge of pocket with needle just inside the seamline. When you reach the curved area, tighten the needle tension. When you are past it, set the needle tension back to normal.

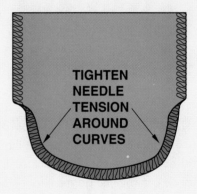

TIGHTEN
NEEDLE
TENSION
AROUND
CURVES

Pocket Flap

1. *Interface* outer half of flap.
2. *Fold* flap in half, right sides together, and stitch end seams. Or pin two flap sections together and stitch around outer edge. Trim and grade seam allowances. Notch any curved areas.

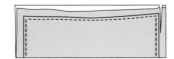

3. *Turn* flap right side out and press.

4. *Pin* flap above pocket, with outer side of flap against outside of garment. Match seamline of flap to placement line on garment.

5. *Stitch* through all thicknesses. Trim seam allowance next to garment close to stitching.

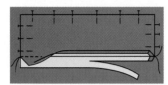

6. *Fold* under long edge of upper seam allowance, turning ends in diagonally. Pin over trimmed edge, and edgestitch.

7. *Turn* flap down and press.

8. *Slipstitch* upper corners of flap to garment to hold in place.

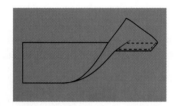

Front Hip Pocket

This style of pocket is often used on pants and shorts. It is a diagonal or curved pocket that attaches to the waist and side seams. The back section of the pocket must be cut from the garment fabric because it is part of the main garment at the front of the hip. The inside front section of the pocket can be cut from the same fabric or a lining fabric.

1. *Reinforce* upper edge of pocket with interfacing or seam tape to prevent stretching.

2. *Pin* front edge of garment to front pocket section, right sides together. Stitch, trim, and grade seam. Press.

3. *Understitch or topstitch* seam to prevent pocket from rolling to right side of garment.

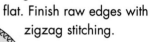

4. *Pin* back section of pocket to front section, right sides together. Stitch around seamline being careful not to catch in garment front. Press seam flat. Finish raw edges with zigzag stitching.

5. *Pin and stitch* side seams, catching in back section of pocket as part of garment front.

6. *Finish* waistline according to pattern directions.

Lesson 8

Waistlines

The waistline of a garment can be finished with a waistband, a facing, or a casing. Most waistlines fall at the natural waistline. However, some garments may have a raised or lowered waistline, depending upon the design.

Waistbands

A waistband is a strip of fabric attached to the waistline of pants, skirts, or shorts. It can be cut straight or curved. Both types of waistbands are attached to the garment in the same way. However, a straight waistband usually has a fold along the upper edge while a curved or shaped waistband has a seam.

The waistband should be about 1 inch (2.5 cm) larger than your actual waistline to allow for movement and comfort. It should not fit too tight. The garment is eased or gathered onto the waistband to allow for the curve of your body below the waistline.

Usually the zipper is stitched before the waistband is applied. A side opening is always on the left side, and the waistband laps from front to back. If the opening is in the front, the waistband overlaps in the same direction as the lapped zipper application. If the opening is in the center back, the waistband laps left over right.

Interface a waistband to prevent stretching or wrinkling. Usually the side that will be on the outside of the garment is interfaced. Follow your pattern directions.

There are two methods of applying a waistband. Your pattern guide sheet will state which method is best for your garment.

- **Plain waistband** is stitched to the right side of the garment, turned to the inside, and stitched by hand.

- **Topstitched waistband** is stitched to the wrong side of the garment, turned to the outside, and topstitched in place.

Plain Waistband

1. *Interface* waistband.
2. *Turn in* seam allowance on unnotched edge of waistband and press. Trim seam allowance to ¼ inch (6 mm).

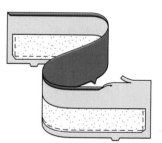

Sewing Tip

A *stay*, or support, can be stitched over the waistline seam to prevent stretching. The stay can be made from seam tape, twill tape, or grosgrain ribbon. To attach a stay, cut tape or ribbon the same length as the waistline measurement of the garment. Pin stay to seam allowance on the bottom section of the garment, with one edge along the waistline seam. Machine stitch just above the waistline seam through stay and seam allowances. Trim seam allowances even with stay. Zigzag upper edge of stay and seam allowances together.

Serging Techniques

Plain Waistband

With heavyweight or bulky fabrics, it may be helpful to eliminate a layer of fabric at the waistline seam of a plain waistband. Serge along the unnotched edge of the waistband, trimming off the ⅝ inch (1.5 cm) seam allowance. When turning the waistband right side out, place the serged edge so that it meets the waistband seam on the inside of the garment.

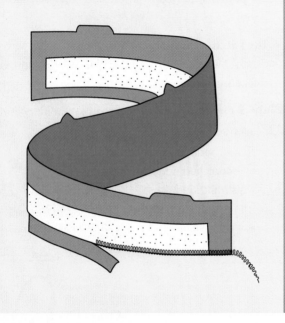

3. *Pin* waistband to garment, right sides together. Match notches and ease garment to waistband between markings. Check that extension is on correct side of opening.

4. *Stitch* waistband to garment along seamline. Trim interfacing close to stitching. Trim and grade seam allowances; clip if necessary. Press seam flat and then up toward waistband.

5. *Fold* ends of waistband, right sides together. Pin carefully, being sure folded edge exactly meets seamline.

6. *Stitch* both ends. Trim and grade seam allowances. Clip corners, and press.

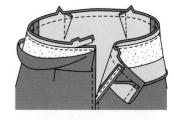

7. *Turn* waistband right side out. Pin folded edge over seam.

8. *Slipstitch* waistband in place, continuing across extension.

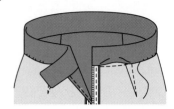

9. *Attach* fasteners.

Topstitched Waistband

1. *Interface* waistband.

2. *Turn in* unnotched edge of waistband along seamline and press. Trim to ¼ inch (6 mm).

3. *Pin* right side of waistband to wrong side of garment, matching notches and markings. Check to be sure waistband will flip over so right side will be on outside of garment.

4. *Stitch* seam. Grade seam allowances so widest layer will be toward outside of garment. Clip if necessary. Press seam allowances up toward waistband.

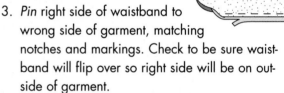

5. *Stitch* ends of waistband, with right sides together. Trim, grade, clip corners, and press.

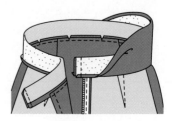

6. *Fold* waistband over seamline to right side of garment. Press and pin.

7. *Topstitch* along bottom edge of waistband close to fold.

8. *Attach* fasteners.

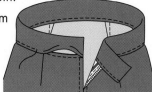

Waistline Facing

A facing can be used to finish a waistline edge. it allows the finished edge of a garment to rest right at the natural waistline. Prevent stretching by interfacing the waistline seam according to the pattern directions.

1. *Apply* fusible interfacing to facing sections or sew-in interfacing to garment edge.

2. *Prepare* facing, and finish outer edge with overlock stitching, zigzag stitching, or a hem.

3. *Stitch* facing to garment, right sides together. Match seams, notches, and markings. Trim, grade, and clip seam allowances. Press seam allowances toward facing.

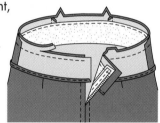

4. *Understitch* facing to seam allowances.

5. *Turn* facing to inside of garment, and press. Tack at seams with small cross stitches.

6. *Turn* under ends of facing at garment opening. Slipstitch to zipper tape.

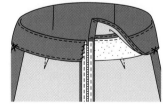

Waistline Casing

A casing can be made at the waistline edge of a garment or within a garment. It can be used with either elastic or a drawstring. (See Casings, page 515.)

Serging Techniques

Waistband

Use the serger to attach a waistband and finish the raw edges in one step. This is especially suitable for knits.

1. *Fold* waistband in half lengthwise, with right sides together.

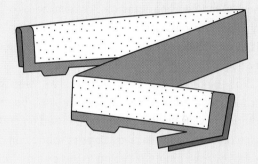

2. *Stitch* across the ends, using a conventional machine. On the underlap side, pivot and stitch along the waistline seam, ending at the dot. Clip at the dot, and trim ends.

3. *Turn* waistband right side out, and press.

4. *Pin* both edges of waistband to outside of garment, matching notches and markings.

5. *Serge* waistline seam, with garment side up. Press seam toward garment.

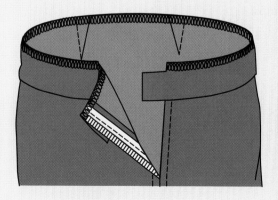

Lesson9

Bias Bindings

Bindings are *narrow trims made from a bias strip of fabric.* They are used to cover the raw edge of fabric, as well as create a decorative trim around an edge. Bias bindings can be used instead of a facing or hem at the neckline, armhole, or hemline of a garment. They are also used to finish the edge of placemats, pillows, backpacks, wallhangings, and many other items.

Bias bindings are cut on the true bias and attached to the edge of the garment or item. Because bindings are very flexible, they can be used on curved as well as straight edges. Bias strips of fabric can also be used to make piping or tubing to use as trim, loops, ties, shoulder straps, and belts.

Your pattern guide sheet will give cutting and stitching directions for self-fabric bindings. The pattern envelope may list single-fold or double-fold bias tape to use as binding. Sometimes fold-over braid trim can also be used. Ready-made bindings come in several widths and a variety of colors to match or contrast with your fabric.

Cutting Bias Strips

There are two methods for cutting bias strips, depending on the amount you need.

Continuous Bias Strip Method

Use this method for cutting a large amount of bias strips:

1. *Cut* a square or rectangular piece of fabric.
2. *Fold* one corner on true bias by matching crosswise grain to lengthwise grain. Cut fabric along fold line.

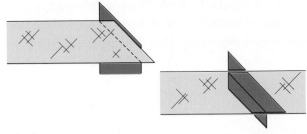

3. *Mark* parallel lines the desired width of bias strip on wrong side of fabric. Unless pattern states otherwise, use 1 ½ inch (3.8 cm) width. Cut away remaining fabric.

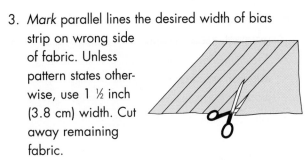

4. *Pin* fabric, right sides together, to form tube. Be sure one strip width extends beyond edge at each end of tube.
5. *Stitch* ¼ inch (6 mm) seam and press open.
6. *Cut* along marked line at one end to create a continuous bias strip of fabric.

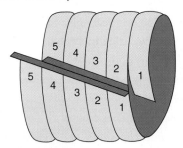

Cut and Piece Bias Strip Method

For smaller lengths, you can cut and stitch individual strips together:

1. *Fold* fabric diagonally, matching crosswise grain to lengthwise grain, to find true bias.
2. *Mark* bias strips on wrong side of fabric. Cut apart.

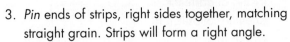

3. *Pin* ends of strips, right sides together, matching straight grain. Strips will form a right angle.
4. *Stitch* ¼ inch (6 mm) seam along straight grain of fabric. Press seam open.

Attaching Binding

Bias strips can be attached using either a one-step or a two- step method. Always follow the directions in the pattern guide sheet for the best method to use for your particular design. Special techniques are needed to create smooth curves and sharp corners.

One-Step Method

Use for attaching double-fold bias tape and fold-over braid, which have one edge folded slightly wider than the other. The binding is slipped over the edge of the fabric and stitched in place with one row of machine stitching.

1. *Trim away* seam allowance from edge to be bound.
2. *Slip* binding over raw edge with wider edge on wrong side of garment. Turn under ends, overlapping if necessary, and pin.
3. *Machine stitch* close to edge of binding through all layers.

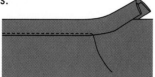

Two-Step Method

Use for single-fold bias tape or for bias strips you cut yourself. The pattern will give directions for cutting self-fabric strips. Usually the bias strip is four times the finished binding width. One edge of the binding is stitched to the fabric. Then the binding is folded over the fabric edge and stitched again by machine or hand.

1. *Trim* away seam allowances from fabric edge.
2. *Pin* edge of binding to fabric, with right sides together.
3. *Stitch* equal distance from edge, according to pattern directions. For single-fold bias tape, stitch along crease line of binding.

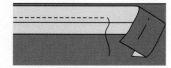

4. *Turn* bias over seam allowance and pin.
5. *Slipstitch* or machine stitch in place.

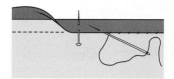

Alternative: Stitch binding to wrong side of garment. Flip binding to right side of garment and edgestitch in place.

Stitching Curves

Preshape binding with steam iron before stitching to fabric.

1. *Lay* tape on top of pattern piece, shaping to fit curve.
2. *Press* with steam to shrink out excess fullness and prevent puckers.

Stitching Outward Corners

1. *Stitch* binding to one edge, ending exactly where seamlines meet.
2. *Fold* binding diagonally at corner and pin to other edge. Start at corner and continue stitching edge.

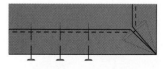

3. *Form* a neat **miter,** or *diagonal fold,* on both sides of binding at corner.
4. *For the two-step method,* finish by stitching inside edge of binding in place. For wider bindings, edgestitch or slipstitch along mitered fold to secure.

Stitching Inward Corners

1. *Reinforce* corner with small machine stitches.
2. *Clip* into corner.

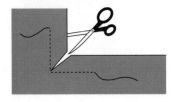

3. *For the one-step method,* slip binding over one edge and stitch to clip. Form neat miter at corner. Slip binding over other edge and continue stitching. Edgestitch along mitered fold if necessary.

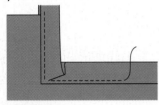

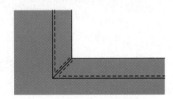

4. *For the two-step method,* stitch binding to edge up to clip. Spread fabric at clipped corner to form a straight edge and continue stitching. Fold binding over edge, forming a miter on both sides at corner. Finish by stitching inside edge by hand or machine.

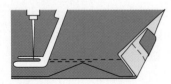

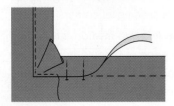

Piping

Piping is *a narrow band of fabric stitched into a seam to accent the seamline or outer edge of a garment.* It is sometimes used around a neckline, at the edge of a collar or cuff, or along a yoke seam.

1. *Cut* bias strip of fabric twice as wide as finished piping, plus 1 ¼ inches (3.2 cm) for seam allowances.
2. *Fold and press* strip lengthwise, with wrong sides together.
3. *Pin* piping to right side of garment, with cut edges even.
4. *Machine baste* just inside seamline in seam allowance. Clip seam allowance of piping around curves.
5. *Pin and stitch* seam.

Corded Piping

Corded piping is stitched over cable cord for a thicker trim.

1. *Fold* bias strip over cording, with cording on inside of fabric.
2. *Stitch* as close as possible to cording, using a zipper foot.
3. *Pin* corded piping to right side of garment so stitching rests on top of seamline.
4. *Machine baste* just inside stitching line in seam allowance. Clip around curves.

5. *Pin and stitch* seamline, working with the corded section on top so you can see the basting stitches. Use a zipper foot. Place the stitches up close to the cord so the basting stitches are in the seam allowance.

Tubing

Tubing is *a strip of fabric stitched and turned right side out so the seam allowances are inside the tube.* It can be used for straps, loops, and belts.

1. *Cut* bias strip of fabric two times finished width of tubing plus seam allowances.

2. *Fold* fabric in half lengthwise, with right sides together.

3. *Stitch,* stretching bias slightly as you sew. At end, slant stitches out toward raw edge to make tube easier to turn.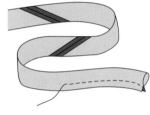

4. *Trim* seam allowances the same width as tubing. For heavier fabrics, trim seam allowances closer to stitching.

5. *Turn* tubing by attaching heavy thread to wide end of seam. Pull, using a large needle or bodkin. Or use a loop turner.

Corded Tubing

Corded tubing is filled with cable cord for added fullness and strength.

1. *Cut* bias strip wide enough to fit around cord plus seam allowances.

2. *Cut* cording twice the length of bias strip plus 1 inch (2.5 cm).

3. *Fold* bias over one end of cord, with right sides together and edges even.

4. *Stitch* across cord and bias at center of cording.

Serging Techniques

Tubing

Tubing can be made easily on the overlock machine.

1. *Serge* a thread chain at least 2 inches (5 cm) longer than bias strip. Run your fingers along chain to tighten stitches.

2. *Pull* chain around to front of presser foot and center it lengthwise on right side of bias strip. Fold strip so cut edges meet and chain is next to fold.

3. *Serge* raw edges together, being careful not to cut the inside chain. Remove strip from serger.

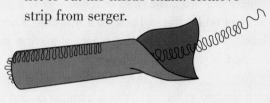

4. *Pull* gently on thread tail to turn tubing right side out.

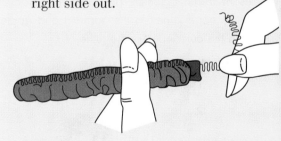

5. *Stitch* long edge close to cord, stretching bias slightly, using a zipper foot. Trim seam allowances.

6. *Turn* right side out by gently pulling fabric down over cord and working fabric along with your hands. Trim off excess cording.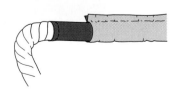

Lesson 10

Ruffles and Trims

Many different types of ruffles and trims can be used to decorate garments, accessories, and home decorating items. They can be bold and colorful or soft and subtle. It is important to coordinate the type of trim to your fabric and project design.

Ruffles

Ruffles can be used around the edge of a neckline, collar, cuff, or hem. They can decorate curtains, dust ruffles, and pillows.

There are two basic types of ruffles:

- **Straight ruffle.** This is made from a straight strip of fabric. It can be gathered along one edge and stitched in a seam or to the edge of the fabric. Or it can be gathered down the center or off-center and stitched to the outside of a garment or curtain.
- **Circular ruffle.** It is created by stitching two or more circles of fabric together. The ruffle fits smoothly along the edge joined to the garment and ripples softly on the outer edge of the ruffle.

The amount of fullness in a ruffle depends on the width of the ruffle. Wide ruffles should have more fullness than narrow ruffles to keep them from looking skimpy. Straight ruffles should be two to three times the length of edge or area to which they will be stitched.

Straight Ruffle

The outer edge of the ruffle can be finished with a narrow hem stitched by hand or machine. On lightweight and sheer fabrics, the ruffle may be cut twice the desired width and folded lengthwise to create a double thickness.

1. *Gather* ruffle along upper edge.

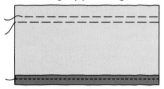

2. *Pin* ruffle to edge of garment, adjusting fullness evenly.

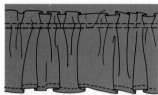

3. *Stitch* ruffle in place, with ruffle on top to prevent stitching tucks into seam.

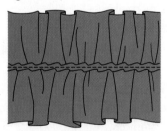

Double-edge ruffle can have trim, such as rickrack, stitched on top of gathering stitches to cover them.

Circular Ruffle

1. *Cut out* circles, following pattern directions.
2. *Stitch* circles together, with narrow seam, to form ruffle. Finish outer edge of ruffle with narrow hem. (Sometimes ruffle is cut as two layers and stitched together at outer edge. Trim, clip, and turn ruffle right side out.)

3. *Staystitch* inner edge of ruffle ½ inch (1.3 cm) from edge. Clip up to staystitching.

4. *Staystitch* garment edge to prevent stretching.

5. *Pin and stitch* ruffle to garment, right sides together. Press seam allowances flat, and trim.

6. *Finish* inside edge with facing or double row of stitching.

Serging Techniques

Ruffles

Use the serger to finish the outer edge of a ruffle with a narrow rolled hem. Then use an overlock stitch to attach a straight ruffle or a circular ruffle to the garment.

Sewing Tip

If the gathers will be hidden in a seam, try this easy gathering technique for ruffles.

1. Cut a piece of strong, thin cord, such as pearl cotton or lightweight packing string, slightly longer than the ruffle.

2. Set sewing machine for a zigzag stitch that is wide enough to cover cord without catching it.

3. Position cord inside seam allowance so left side of zigzag stitch will be just inside the seamline. Stitch over cord.

4. Insert a straight pin at one end of ruffle, and wrap end of cord around pin in a figure eight.

5. Pin ruffle to garment edge, matching markings. Hold loose end of cord taught, and gather fabric by sliding it along cord.

6. Straight stitch along seamline, with gathered side up. Be careful not to catch cord.

7. Pull out cord.

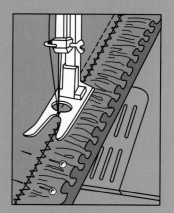

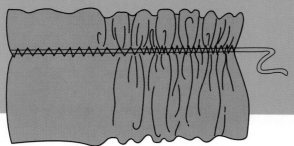

Serging Techniques

Trims

You can use the serger to apply a straight-edge trim, such as lace, to the edge of a garment.

1. *Trim* edge of garment so there is a ⅝ inch (1.5 cm) seam or hem allowance.

2. *Place* lace and fabric right sides together, with straight edge of lace ½ inch (1.3 cm) from raw edge of fabric. Pin or use glue stick to hold lace in place.

3. *Serge,* with lace side up, using an overlock stitch, a flatlock stitch, or a rolled hem stitch. Keep edge of trim slightly to the left of knife. Press seam allowance toward garment.

A serger also can be used to insert lace with two straight edges. Use either a flatlock stitch or a rolled hem stitch. For the flatlock method, place the lace and fabric right sides together. For the rolled hem method, place them wrong sides together. After serging, open out the garment section so the lace lies flat; press.

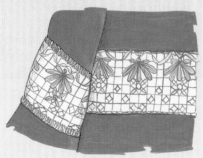

Trims

Trims are available in a wide variety of types, shapes, sizes, and colors. Rickrack, braid, ribbon, lace, eyelet, piping, and fringe are different types of trims. Fabric appliqués can also be used.

Be sure the trim you select can be washed or dry cleaned in the same manner as the outer fabric to which it will be stitched. Preshrink washable trims by placing them in hot water for 30 minutes. You can leave them wrapped around the cardboard, which should be bent slightly to allow for any shrinkage. Let them dry.

Three basic methods are used to apply trim: *flat method, edging method, and inserted method.*

Flat Method

This method can be used for any trim that is finished on both sides, such as braid, ribbon, and rickrack. Use narrow trims for curved areas. Press with a steam iron to shape before stitching in place.

1. *Pin* trim along placement line.

2. *Stitch* along one edge, both edges, or through center. Rickrack should be stitched with a straight row of stitching down the center.

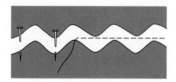

3. *Miter* corners by stitching outside edge up to corner. Lift presser foot, pivot, and continue stitching in new direction. Fold trim diagonally at corner and pin.

4. *Stitch* inside edge of trim. Stitch mitered fold, if necessary.

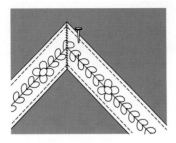

Edging Method

Use this application for trims that have only one finished edge, such as piping, gathered lace, gathered eyelet, and fringe. The trim can be stitched to the edge of a garment or inserted into a seam.

To stitch trim to edge of garment:

1. *Pin* trim along edge or seamline, with right sides together. Be sure trim is toward garment.

2. *Stitch* close to trim, using a zipper foot if necessary.

3. *Finish* edge by turning seam allowance to inside and topstitching through all thicknesses. Or finish edge with a facing.

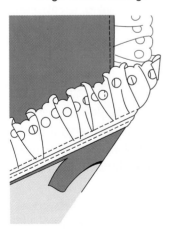

To stitch trim into a seam, place other section of fabric on top of trim, with right sides together. Stitch seam and trim in one step.

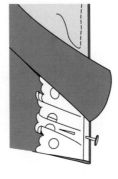

Inserted Method

This application can be used on any straight section of a garment, such as down the front of a shirt or blouse, or around the bottom of a jacket or skirt. It cannot be used for curved areas. Choose flat trims, such as lace or eyelet.

1. *Cut* fabric along placement line.

2. *Turn under* each fabric edge ½ the width of exposed trim. Press edges.

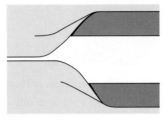

3. *Place* flat trim under folded edges of fabric.

4. *Edgestitch* through all thicknesses.

Finish Ends

There are several different ways to finish the ends of trims to create a neat appearance:

• Stitch trim to fabric before stitching seams so ends will be hidden in seam.

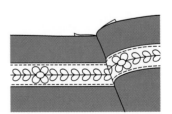

- Turn ends to wrong side and slipstitch.

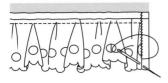

- Taper ends into seamline.

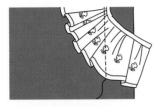

- For overlapping ends, fold one end under ¼ inch (6 mm). Overlap folded end and stitch in place.

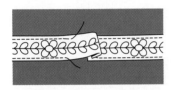

- For heavy trims, fold both ends under ¼ inch (6 mm), so ends just meet. Stitch in place.

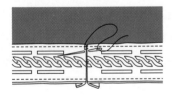

Lesson 11

Decorative Art

Today machines can weave, knit, print, dye, and decorate fabric. There is special satisfaction, however, in doing these things yourself. The result is a special beauty that cannot be duplicated by a machine. **Handicrafts** are *forms of art that are created by using your hands.* The term literally means "crafted by hand."

There are many ways you can express creativity in your clothing, accessories, and home furnishings. You can be creative with the garments that you sew. You can also give ready-to-wear garments your own distinctive touch. These decorated garments are sometimes called *wearable art.*

Some patterns include instructions for wearable art applications. This is a good way to learn a little bit about a new craft. Then, if you want to learn more, there are books and magazines available on almost every handicraft subject. Your local craft store, bookstore, or public library can help you find them.

The following sections describe a variety of decorative arts that can be applied to clothing, accessories, home furnishings, or crafts projects. They are fun to do—as well as a way to express your own originality and creativity.

Painting Fabric

Painting on fabric is similar to painting on any other surface. The color can be applied with a brush, a pen, or a marker. Designs or words can be painted on items such as t-shirts, sweatshirts, caps, canvas bags, and pillows.

There are many different types of fabric paints. These include flat paints, glitter paints, glow-in-the-dark paints, and paints that have a three-dimensional surface.

Here are some helpful guidelines for painting on fabric:

- Choose brush-on paints for a soft look. Squeeze-tube paints provide an outline effect.

- Check the paint instructions to see what type of fabric is recommended. Many paints work best on fabrics that are a cotton/polyester blend.

- Wash the fabric first to remove any finishes that might interfere with the paint's ability to stick. Do not use fabric softener.

- Cover a piece of cardboard with plastic, such as a trash bag or a dry cleaner's bag, to use as a work surface. Place the covered cardboard inside a shirt to prevent the paint from seeping through to the reverse side. Secure garment with tape to hold cardboard in place. Use freezer paper for small areas.

- Begin at the top of the design and work down.

- Use a toothpick or a pin to assist in applying paint in sharp corners of a design.

- Be sure the paint is thoroughly dry before handling the project.

- Follow the paint manufacturer's instructions for garment care. As a general rule, launder in warm water. Washing in cold water can cause some fabric paints to crack. Most paint manufacturers recommend waiting a minimum of 48 hours before laundering newly painted fabric. This allows the paint to "cure."

Tie Dyeing

Dyes can be applied to an entire piece of fabric so that it is all one color. They can also create special patterns and effects on fabric. A special technique, called *tie dyeing,* is fun to use for shirts and scarves. It is a very old method that became popular in the 1970s and again in the 1990s.

Tie dyeing is *a method of tightly tying fabric in certain places, then dipping the fabric into dye.* The dye will not penetrate in the spots where the fabric is held tightly together with rubber bands. The fabric can then be retied and dipped in a different color of dye. This can be repeated again and again to create more complicated designs.

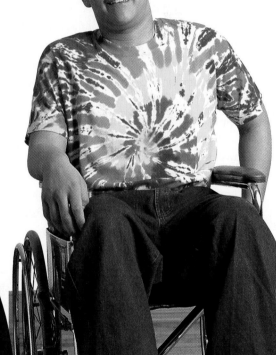

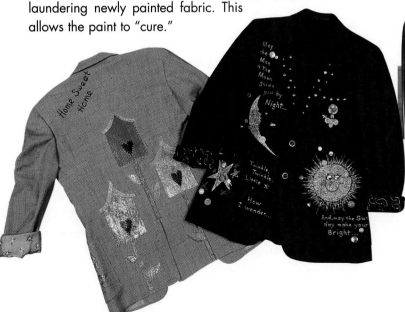

Embroidery

Embroidery is *the art of stitching a pattern or design on fabric.* It includes many different types of decorative stitches that can be done by hand or by machine.

Throughout history, embroidery skills have been highly admired. During Colonial times, young girls made *samplers* to practice and display their skill. Often they embroidered their name and the date at the bottom. Today these old samplers are bought by collectors.

Embroidery kits are available in stores for all levels of difficulty. Fabric, yarn, and craft shops also sell preprinted designs on fabric and embroidery supplies.

Hand Embroidery

Hand embroidery is done with silk or cotton thread, called embroidery floss. It comes six-ply, which means there are six strands of thread twisted together. For a thicker effect, all six strands can be used. For a lighter or more delicate effect, separate the floss and use only one or two strands. Embroidery can also be done with heavy threads, yarns, and silk ribbon for a bolder effect.

There are hundreds of hand embroidery stitches. However, most can be separated into four basic types: flat, looped, crossed, and knotted. These can be used to create almost any type of design. Some stitches outline a shape; others fill it in solidly with stitches placed close together. The *chain stitch* forms a series of loops. The *stroke stitch* is a single stitch that is used for flowers and leaves. The *outline stitch* creates tiny diagonal stitches close together, such as for a flower stem. The *French knot* is made by twisting the thread around the needle, such as for a flower center. Embroidery stitches are also used to monogram garments and linens.

An embroidery hoop is used to hold the fabric taut as you embroider. This is a set of two metal, wooden, or plastic rings. One ring fits inside the other. Using an embroidery hoop helps prevent puckering as you create the stitches.

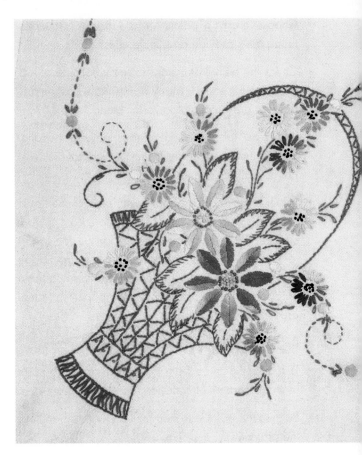

Some of the many different types of embroidery include:

- **Counted cross-stitch embroidery** is a series of small "x's" carefully combined to form a picture or a design.

- **Silk ribbon embroidery** uses silk ribbons to decorate garments, pillows, and wallhangings.

- **Crewel embroidery** is done with wool yarns. It is used on wall hangings, pillows, and chair seats.

- **Needlepoint** is done with embroidery thread or wool yarn on a special open-weave fabric called canvas. The stitches are pulled in and out of the holes in the canvas until the canvas is totally covered. Needlepoint is used to make pillows, chair coverings, and rugs.

Machine Embroidery

Machine embroidery can be created by using the decorative stitches that are built into many sewing machines. By combining different types of stitches, you can create a wide variety of designs. Some machines have the letters of the alphabet so you can even do monogramming. Use machine embroidery to decorate clothes, towels, napkins, stuffed animals, and many other items.

A special type of machine embroidery, called *free motion embroidery,* is like painting with thread. It can be done on any conventional sewing machine. The design is first traced onto the fabric. Then the fabric is secured in an embroidery hoop. As the hoop is moved back and forth by hand under the needle, the stitches fill in the design.

Different types of threads can be used for machine embroidery. Rayon or cotton machine embroidery threads have a slight sheen that is particularly attractive for machine embroidery. Metallic threads can also be used successfully. These special threads are used in the needle.

For the bobbin thread, a regular thread is used in a color that matches or blends with the fabric. If the back of the project will not show, you might want to use a special bobbin thread that is designed for machine embroidery. This type of thread is available in black or white.

Unless you are embroidering on a very heavy fabric, some type of stabilizer is necessary:

- **Tear-away stabilizers** are pinned or ironed to the wrong side of the fabric. The stabilizer is gently ripped off when the embroidery is finished.

- **Iron-away stabilizers** are pinned to the wrong side of the fabric. The stabilizer will completely disappear when a dry, hot iron is applied to the back of the finished embroidery.

- **Wash-away stabilizers** are pinned to the right or wrong side of the fabric. Some stabilizers are removed by dipping the project in water. Others must be washed or simmered in hot water for several minutes.

- **Spray-on stabilizers,** including spray starch, work well on lightweight, sheer, or stretchy fabrics. This type of stabilizer is best for small detail areas.

Your sewing machine manual will include directions for doing machine embroidery. Computerized sewing machines can be programmed to embroider complicated designs that use several different colors of thread. Some machines can even be connected to a personal computer so you can create your own original designs. Other machines have separate scanners. These are able to scan or "read" your original design and then duplicate the design.

Appliqué

Appliqué is *the process of applying one or more cutout pieces of fabric to a larger background for decoration.* The fabric pieces can be cut in different shapes to create a design.

You can create your own fabric shapes, or you can cut out shapes from fabrics with large printed motifs. Paper-backed fusible web makes it easy to create both types of appliqués.

1. *Trace* the outline of an original design or a design from a pattern on the paper backing of fusible web. If using a fabric motif, cut a piece of paper-backed fusible web that is at least 1 inch (2.5 cm) larger than the motif.

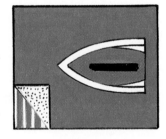

2. *Apply* paper-backed fusible web to wrong side of fabric with an iron. Follow the manufacturer's suggestions for temperature selection.

3. *Cut out* appliqué shape.

4. *Peel off* paper backing.

5. *Fuse* appliqué to background fabric.

6. *Machine zigzag* around edges of appliqué. Using a *satin stitch*. Adjust sewing machine for a narrow- to medium-width zigzag stitch and a very short stitch length (almost 0). Position appliqué so right swing of needle goes just off the edge of the appliqué and into the background fabric. Stitch slowly, following the shape of the appliqué.

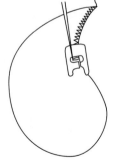

Alternatives: Use a blanket stitch around edges, or outline edges with a three-dimensional fabric paint.

Patchwork

Patchwork is *the technique of cutting out small shapes of fabric and sewing them together to form larger shapes.* Because fabric was scarce, early American settlers used patchwork as a way to utilize all the valuable scraps. These patchwork designs were fashioned into quilts that are famous throughout the world as a uniquely American craft.

The early designs were called "crazy" quilts because they were made up of many different sizes, shapes, and colors of fabrics. Later on, as fabric became more available, the fabric scraps were cut into simple shapes and joined together to create interesting squares, called blocks. These blocks were given names, such as *Log Cabin, Turkey Trot, Baby's Blocks, Lone Star,* and *Dresden Plate.*

Another type of patchwork was created by the Seminole Indians of Florida. Seminole patchwork is an easy strip-piecing technique that has been traditionally done on the sewing machine. After strips of two different fabrics are stitched together, they are cut into rectangles or squares. The strips are then rearranged to create either a *checkerboard* or *diagonal* pattern.

Today patchwork patterns are used for jackets, vests, skirts, pants, pillows, placemats, and wallhangings, as well as quilts. The shapes of a patchwork design fit together like the pieces of a puzzle. In order for the pieces to fit together smoothly, they must be carefully cut out and accurately stitched together.

Most patchwork patterns are designed with a ¼ inch (6 mm) seam allowance. Always press each seam open before crossing it with another seam.

If you are creating many patchwork blocks with the same design, your work will go faster if you piece them assembly-line style. Stitch the first seam for all the blocks. Then stitch the second seam for all the blocks. Follow this procedure until all the seams in each block are stitched.

Patchwork can also be done on the serger. After serging long strips of fabric together, cut the strips into shorter lengths. Then serge the shorter strips together to form the blocks.

Appliqué

Seminole Patchwork

Quilting

Quilting is *the process of stitching together two layers of fabric with a soft material in between.* The stitches can be sewn by hand or by machine. They can form straight lines, create patterns, or outline the design of the fabric.

The top layer is the fashion fabric. The middle layer is the batting. The bottom layer, called the backing, can be a fashion fabric, muslin, or batiste.

Years ago, women would gather together to sew the layers of a quilt together with tiny stitches. Then they would bind the quilt edges with bias strips of fabric. Today antique quilts have become collector's items and are very valuable.

Machine stitching can be used to stitch the layers of a quilted fabric together. It also can be used to create the patchwork design for the top layer. Quilt your own fabrics for jackets, vests, robes, pillows, bed coverings, table runners, and wallhangings.

Because the process tends to "shrink up" the fabric, quilt the fabric first, before cutting out the project.

1. *Choose* a simple quilting pattern. Parallel rows of stitches are called *channel quilting.* Intersecting rows form squares or diamonds. Outline stitching can be used on large, simple fabric designs.

2. *Mark* quilting pattern on right side of top fabric. Use chalk or water-soluble fabric marking pen.

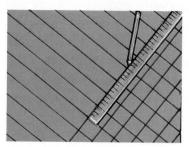

3. *Spread* bottom layer out on a large, flat surface. Place batting directly on top of bottom layer. Then cover batting with top layer. Be sure each layer is flat and smooth.

4. *Hand baste* layers together with long, diagonal stitches.

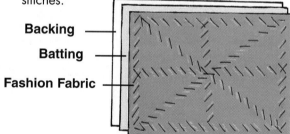

Backing

Batting

Fashion Fabric

5. *Stitch* along marked lines, using a slightly longer stitch length. Reduce pressure on machine's presser foot. (If puckers occur try a *walking foot.* This foot allows both layers of fabric to feed through the machine at the same time.)

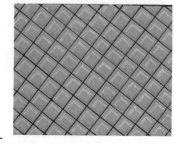

Embellishments

Many fabric items can be decorated with buttons, bows, rhinestones, jewels, nailheads, beads, or other embellishments. There are a variety of techniques that can be used to attach these decorations to fabric. Be sure to read the manufacturer's directions and follow them accurately.

- **Stitching.** Buttons, bows, sequins, beads, and other trims can be stitched in place by hand. Use regular or clear thread.
- **Fabric glue.** Special fabric adhesives provide a permanent, yet flexible bond when dry. They also remain crystal clear and do not stain the fabric. Some work best for fabric, wood, and leather. Others can bond beads, pearls, and other jewels to fabrics. Use fabric glue for wearable art, appliqué work, crafts, and no-sew projects.
- **Glue gun.** Hot-melt glue guns provide bonding for a wide variety of materials. Glue guns use solid glue sticks that melt when passed through a heating chamber. Be sure the surfaces are clean before applying any hot-melt glue. After applying the glue,

press the surfaces together within 15 to 20 seconds to ensure a strong bond. Use special care when operating hot glue guns. Safety glasses and light cotton gloves can provide protection from accidental burns.

- **Nailheads.** These decorations have metal prongs on the back. Just push the prongs through the fabric to the back side. Then bend the prongs securely, using a blunt metal or wooden tool.
- **Fabric paint.** Sparkle can be sprinkled on wet fabric paint to accent special areas. Rhinestones and other jewels can be set in a "puddle" of fabric paint. Allow them to dry on a flat surface for four hours or more.

Use your creativity whenever you sew. Whether you are making something for yourself or others, you can create items that are special and original. Have fun with your own ideas!

Summary

- Special types of seams are used to enclose the seam allowance or to create a decorative effect.
- Tucks and pleats are used to control fullness or add design interest.
- Interfacings and linings help to shape and support the outer fabric.
- The four basic types of collars are the flat collar, rolled collar, shirt collar, and standing collar.
- The three basic types of sleeves are the set-in sleeve, raglan sleeve, and kimono sleeve. They can be finished with a hem, facing, casing, or cuff.
- Three popular styles of pockets include the in-seam pocket, patch pocket, and front hip pocket.
- A waistline can be finished with a waistband, a facing, or a casing.
- Some garments are trimmed with bias binding. Others are decorated with ruffles or trims.
- Decorative arts include fabric painting, tie dyeing, embroidery, appliqué, patchwork, quilting, and other embellishments.

Recalling the Facts

1. List at least three types of self-finished seams.
2. What are two techniques for creating special effects on a seam? Name one decorative seam for each technique.
3. What is the difference between tucks and pleats?
4. What can be done to pleats to give them a smoother appearance or hold them in place?
5. What is the purpose of interfacing?
6. What should you do before applying a fusible interfacing to garment sections?
7. Describe the four basic types of collars.
8. To which side of a collar is interfacing usually applied?
9. What are three methods of attaching a collar to a garment?
10. Describe the three basic types of sleeves.
11. What is the open-sleeve method of sewing a set-in sleeve?
12. Describe the three basic types of cuffs.
13. What is a placket?
14. What type of pocket is purely functional?
15. What are three methods of finishing the waistline of a garment?
16. What are bias bindings?
17. What is the difference between piping and tubing?
18. Describe the two basic types of ruffles.
19. Describe the three methods used to apply trims.
20. What are at least five techniques that you could use to decorate a garment?

Thinking Critically

1. **Analysis.** Compare and contrast the open-sleeve method and the closed-sleeve method for sewing a set-in sleeve.

2. **Evaluation.** How could you use an overlock machine when stitching the collar, sleeves, pockets, and waistband of a garment?

3. **Synthesis.** Suggest a variety of ways that you could accent the design lines of a garment.

4. **Evaluation.** If you were to design a line of decorative t-shirts, what method of decorative art would you use?

Practicing Your Skills

1. **Samples.** Make samples of the following techniques: self-finished seams, decorative seams, tucks, pleats, bias bindings, tubing, and trims. Make mini-samples of a flat or rolled collar, set-in sleeve, cuff, in-seam pocket, patch pocket, waistband, and ruffle.

2. **Project.** Construct a garment that has a collar, sleeves, and pockets. Evaluate each of the special sewing techniques used in the project.

Applying Your Knowledge

1. **Construction Features.** Look at actual garments or photos from magazines and catalogs. Identify special construction features, such as tucks, pleats, collars, sleeves, plackets, cuffs, pockets, waistbands, and bias bindingss.

2. **Decorative Trims.** Collect photos from fashion magazines and catalogs that show different types of decorative trims used on garments. Then describe the construction method used to apply the trimming.

3. **Handicrafts.** Research a craft that was popular with the early pioneers. Explain why the craft developed and how the technique is being used by modern craftspersons.

What Is a Craft Shop Owner?

Craft shops provide a wide selection of supplies, ranging from textile paints and embroidery threads to needlepoint kits and glue guns. The owners of these shops must have knowledge about products, equipment, and techniques used for many types of crafts. Some shops offer special classes on craft techniques, such as quilting or painting on fabric. They also stock books, magazines, and leaflets on almost every handicraft subject.

Try It Yourself

Imagine that you are the owner of a local craft shop. Create a flyer that promotes craft products or special classes in your "store." Then prepare a small display of craft items that would appeal to potential customers.

Build Your Portfolio

Take a photo of the craft display and write a brief explanation of each craft item. Place these, along with a copy of the promotional flyer, in your portfolio.

Glossary

A

abrasion—a worn spot that can develop when fibers rub against something. (12)

absorbent—able to take in moisture. (12)

adornment—decoration. (1)

analyze—to examine carefully and in detail so as to identify causes, factors, and possible results. (16)

application form—a company document that records information about a person who applies for a job. (28)

appliqué—the process of applying one or more cutout pieces of fabric to a larger background for decoration. (S5)

apprenticeship program—on-the-job training that is part of a formal program. (28)

appropriate—suitable. (2)

arbitration—the settlement of a dispute by a person or panel that listens to both sides and issues a decision. (23)

assembly line—each worker specializes in a certain task as the product moves along a planned route. (7)

atelier (at-el-YAY)—designer's workroom. (8)

avant garde (ah-vahn-GARD)—being ahead of fashion. (5)

B

backstitching—used to secure the ends of a row of stitching. (S4)

balance—how the internal spaces of a shape work together. (11)

barter—trading without the use of money. (6)

basting—used to temporarily hold two or more pieces of fabric together until the permanent stitching is completed. (S4)

bias grain—runs diagonally across the fabric. (S3)

bindings—narrow trims made from a bias strip of fabric. (S5)

blazer—a classic, solid-color jacket that may be single- or double-breasted. (9)

blends—different fibers combined into one yarn. (13)

body language—facial expressions, eye contact, posture, position of arms and legs, and even the distance that the person stands or sits from others. (3)

boutique—a type of specialty store featuring very fashionable or unique designs that are higher priced. (20)

branch—a separate operating division of a store that is overseen by the main, or flagship, store. (25)

budget—an estimate of income and expenses for a given period in the future. (16)

C

cardigan—a collarless jacket or sweater that buttons down the front. (9)

casing—a closed tunnel of fabric that holds a piece of elastic or a drawstring inside. (S4)

cellulose—the main component of plants such as cotton and flax. (6)

certification—official approval. (26)

chain—a group of stores that are owned and managed by a central office. (20)

classic—a traditional style that stays in fashion for a very long time. (5)

client—customer. (26)

clipping—making a tiny clip or snip in the seam allowance. (S4)

C.O.D.—cash on delivery. (20)

collection—the clothes produced by a designer for a specific season. (8)

colorfast—the color in the fabric will not change. (14)

color scheme—the way you use a color or combination of colors when planning an outfit or decorating a room. (10)

commission—a percentage of the purchase price on every sale. (25)

comparison shopping—looking at quality, price, and design to compare value. (19)

complementary colors—colors that are directly opposite each other on the color wheel. (10)

compromise—a settlement or give-and-take between two points. (21)

conformity—agreeing or going along with current standards, attitudes, or practices. (3)

consideration—thoughtfulness, or helpfulness toward others. (23)

consignment store—one that will pay you a percentage of the selling price after the store sells your clothes. (18)

contractors—companies or individuals who specialize in sewing certain types of garments for a certain price. (24)

converters—companies or individuals who buy or handle fabric for finishing. (24)

copy—words and sentences that will be used in advertising. (26)

cost per wearing—adding cleaning costs to the purchase price, then dividing by the number of wearings. (21)

costume jewelry—made of nonprecious metals, often set with imitation stones, and relatively inexpensive. (22)

courses—crosswise rows of loops in knitted fabric. (S3)

courteous—polite, considerate toward others, and pleasant to be around. (28)

couture (koo-TOOR)—dressmaking. (8)

couturiers (koo-TOOR-ee-ays)—designers who make fashionable, custom-made clothes. (8)

cover letter—a letter that requests a meeting, or interview, and mentions that you are enclosing your resumé. (28)

cowl—softly draped, hoodlike. (9)

creativity—the ability to use your imagination and make something original or unique. (16)

croquis (kro-KEY)—a rough preliminary drawing. (8)

crosswise grain—runs across the fabric from one selvage to the other. (S3)

culottes—pants that are cut to look like a skirt. (9)

culture—the collection of ideas, skills, beliefs, and institutions of a society at a particular time in history. (1)

curator—person in charge of a collection. (26)

customize—to modify according to individual preference. (16)

customs—established ways of doing things. (2)

D

darts—triangular folds of fabric stitched to a point. (S4)

decorative seams—use topstitching or cording to create special effects. (S5)

design ease—the extra fullness built into clothes by the designer to create a particular style or silhouette. (S1)(S3)

directional stitching—stitching with, or in the same direction, as the fabric grain. (S4)

direct mail—advertising matter sent to large numbers of people. (27)

disability—some type of condition that hampers a person in some way. (22)

distributor—a person or firm who sells a line of merchandise within a given territory. (27)

draping—arranging fabric into graceful folds or attractive lines. (8)

dry cleaning—a process that uses special liquids containing organic solvents to clean fabrics. (17)

dyes—compounds that penetrate and color fibers. (14)

E

easing—allows fabric to be shaped over a curved area. (S4)

economical—inexpensive. (15)

economics—the way that a society produces, distributes, and spends its wealth. (5)

edgestitching—a row of topstitching placed very close to the finished edge. (S4)

elements of design—line, shape, space, texture, and color. (11)

embroidery—the art of stitching a pattern or design on fabric. (S5)

emphasis—the focal point, or center of interest, of a garment. (11)

entrepreneur (AHN-trah-prah-NUR)—a person who organizes and manages his or her own business. (27)

expectations—thoughts about what is reasonable or justified. (2)

F

facing—used to finish a raw edge, such as a neckline or armhole. (S4)

factory—a building or group of buildings in which goods are manufactured. (7)

fad—a fashion that is very popular for only a short time. (5)

family structure—the number, ages, and relationships of the family members. (4)

fashion—the particular style that is popular at a given time. (5)

fashion babies—small dolls about a foot high that were carefully dressed in the latest styles. (6)

fashion merchandising—all phases of buying and selling clothes and accessories. (7)

fashion promotion—all efforts made to inform people about what is new in fashion and to convince them to buy it. (7)

fiber—the basic unit from which fabric is made. (12)

figure types—size categories determined by height and body proportions. (S1)

filament fibers—long continuous fibers that are measured in yards or meters. (13)

filling yarns—croswswise yarns. (13)

finance charge—the cost imposed for the use of credit. (20)

fine jewelry—made with superior workmanship from gold, silver, or platinum and may contain precious and semiprecious stones. (22)

finishes—any special treatments that are applied to fabrics. (14)

flexible—willingness to adapt oneself to new opportunities and situations. (28)

fluctuate—go up and down. (16)

forecasting services—predict color, fabric, and fashion trends. (24)

freelance—selling work or services without receiving a regular salary from one employer. (27)

fusible webs—a network of bondable fibers used to hold two layers of fabric together. (S1)

G

gathers—soft folds of fabric. (S4)

generic name—a general classification of fibers of similar composition. (12)

grading—trimming each layer to a different width to reduce bulk. (S4)

gray goods—fabric that first comes from the loom. (14)

guide sheet—step-by-step information for cutting, marking, and sewing fabric pieces together. (S3)

H

handicrafts—forms of art that are created by using your hands. (S5)

harmony— the pleasing arrangement of all parts of a garment. (11)

haute couture (oht-koo-TOOR)—the most fashionable, expensive, and exclusive designer clothing. (8)

hem—used to finish the bottom edge of a shirt, jacket, sleeve, skirt, or pants leg. (S4)

heritage—the body of culture and tradition that has been handed down from one's ancestors. (4)

hidden costs—expenses for consumer carelessness, theft, and returns. (23)

hue—the name given to a specific color. (10)

I

image ads—designed to appeal to your fantasies, to make a fashion statement, or to promote a designer's or manufacturer's name. (19)

imitate—copy. (3)

impression—an image that is transferred from one place to another. (3)

impulse—sudden. (19)

individuality—the characteristics that make you unique or distinctive from others. (3)

Industrial Revolution—the changes in society that resulted from the invention of power tools and machinery and the growth of factories. (7)

information ads—those that tell you many details about the product. (19)

inseam—the inside leg measurement, from the crotch to the hem edge of pants. (21)

insignias—badges or emblems that show membership in a group. (1)

intensity—the brightness or dullness of a color. (10)

interfacing—a piece of fabric placed between the outer fabric and facing. (S1)(S5)

intermediate color—created when a primary color is combined with a secondary color. (10)

inventory—counting all of the merchandise. (15)

ironing—a back and forward motion of the iron. (17)

irregulars—garments that do not pass inspection because they have a small imperfection. (20)

J

job interview—a meeting to discuss the details of the job and the qualifications of the person seeking the job.(28)

jumpsuit—a one-piece garment that combines a bodice and pants. (9)

K

kimono sleeve—cut in one piece with the front and the back of the garment. (9)

kleptomania—abnormal and persistent impulse to steal. (23)

knitting—a method of looping yarns together. (13)

knock-offs—less expensive copies. (24)

L

lapel—the front part of a shirt or jacket that is folded back on the chest. (9)

laundering—washing fabric by hand or by machine with a soil removing product. (17)

layaway—a small down payment to reserve an item for you. (20)

lengthwise grain—runs in the same direction as the selvage. (S3)

licensing—giving legal permission to use your name to promote a product. (8)

lifestyle—typical way of living. (1)

line—a series of points connected together to form a narrow path. (11)

lines—collections (7)

lining—a fabric used to finish the inside of a garment; constructed separately from the outer garment and then joined at one or more major seams. (SI)(S5)

lockstitch—type of stitch that does not pull out or unravel when a loop or loose thread is pulled. (S2)

logo—symbol. (19)

luster—gloss and sheen. (12)

M

mail-order—takes orders and ships goods through the mail. (27)

mandatory—required by law. (19)

manufactured fibers—fibers made from substances such as wood pulp, petroleum, natural gas, air, and water. (12)

market—the place where designers' and manufacturers' showrooms are located. (25)

marketing—all of the various ways to advertise, promote, and distribute a product. (24)

market research—the study of consumer needs and attitudes. (24)

mass-produced—many garments made at the same time. (7)

maternity clothes—clothes suitable for wear by pregnant women. (22)

media—the means used to communicate messages to a large number of people. (19)

merchandising—all the decisions that go into the selling of a product. (25)

modesty—what people feel is the proper way for clothing to cover the body. (1)

money order—a form stating that money is to be paid to the person or store named on the form. (20)

multi-sized—printed with several sizes on the same pattern tissue. (S1)

N

nap—a soft, fuzzy surface. (14)

natural fibers—fibers that come from natural sources, such as plants and animals. (12)

nonverbal messages—communication without words. (3)

notching—cutting tiny wedge-shaped pieces of fabric from the seam allowances. (S4)

notions—small items that become a permanent part of the garment. (S1)

O

off-grain—crosswise yarns are not at right angles to the lengthwise yarns. (S3)

old fashioned—any style that is no longer in fashion. (5)

outlet—sells only the brands of merchandise that are produced by the manufacturer or the factory that owns it. (20)

overlock machine—a special sewing machine that can stitch, trim, and overcast a seam all at the same time; also called a serger. (S2)

overlock seam—a special combination of stitches that joins the fabric and finishes the edges in one operation. (21)

overruns—excess merchandise. (20)

P

patchwork—a method of sewing together small fabric shapes to create a new, decorative piece of fabric. (18)(S5)

pattern—contains all the instruction you will need for constructing a sewing project. (S3)

pattern grading—the art of converting a pattern from one size into many other sizes. (24)

peer group—people who have a similar background, social status, and age. (1)

peer pressure—pressure by the peer group to conform.(1)

personality—the combination of all your unique qualities. (2)

piecework—being paid so much per piece or per garment. (7)

pile—a raised surface of loops or yarn ends. (13)

pill—form tiny balls of fiber on the fabric. (12)

piping—a narrow band of fabric stitched into a seam to accent the seamline or outer edge of a garment. (S5)

placket—a slit at the wrist, neck, or waist of a garment to make it easier to put on and take off. (S5)

pleats—folds of fabric, wider than tucks, that are stitched or pressed in place. (S5)

ply—the number of yarn strands twisted together. (13)

portfolio—collection of work to show to prospective clients. (26)

preshrinking—to cause a fabric to contract in order to prevent or minimize shrinkage after the finished garment is washed or dry cleaned. (S3)

pressing—raising and lowering the iron from one area to the next. (17) (S4)

pret-a-porter (PRET-a-por-TAY) —deluxe ready-to-wear. (8)

primary colors—red, yellow, and blue. (10)

princess—a close-fitting, flared dress that is shaped by seams. (9)

principles of design—artistic guidelines for using the various design elements within a garment. (11)

printing—transferring color to the surface of a fabric to form a pattern or design. (14)

priorities—preferences. (4)

prioritize—rank. (15)

profit—the amount of money left over after all the expenses have been paid. (27)

proportion—the size relationship of each of the internal spaces within a garment to one another and to the total look. (11)

publicity—any information in the media which brings attention to someone, something, or some event. (26)

public relations—all the actions used to promote goodwill with the public. (26)

punctual—arrive on time. (28)

Q

quality—superior characteristics. (21)

quilting—process of stitching together two layers of fabric with a soft material in between. (S5)

R

raglan sleeve—has a front and back diagonal seam that extends from the neckline to the underarm. (9)

ready-to-wear—clothing made in advance for sale to any purchaser. (7)

recycle—to reclaim items for another use. (18)

redesign—change an existing garment to better meet your needs. (18)

references—two or three people who will give you a good recommendation. (28)

regulations—laws. (27)

reinforcement stitching—used to permanently stitch fabric areas that will be trimmed or clipped close to the stitching. (S4)

reliable—dependable. (28)

resilient—able to spring or bounce back into shape after crushing or wrinkling. (12)

resources—money, time, and skills. (2)

resumé (REZ-oo-MAY)—a detailed summary of your education, work experience, and job-related volunteer activities. (28)

retail—the sale of goods in small quantities to consumers. (25)

retailing—all of the activities connected with the direct selling of items to consumers. (25)

retro—styles of an earlier time. (5)

rhythm—the flow of the lines, shapes, space, and texture of a garment. (11)

ribs—lengthwise chains of loops in knitted fabric; also called wales. (S3)

royalty—a percentage of the profits. (8)

S

sales analysis—the study of what has sold in the past in order to predict what will sell in the future. (24)

sales promotion—a very subtle form of advertising. (19)

scissors—smaller than shears and both handles are the same shape. (S2)

seam—a line of stitching used to hold two layers of fabric together. (S4)

seam finish—any method of sewing or trimming seam edges to prevent raveling or fraying. (S4)

secondary color—created by combining equal amounts of two primary colors. (10)

seconds—garments with more serious flaws. (20)

self-concept—the image you have of yourself. (3)

self-finished seams—enclose the seam allowances as the seam is stitched. (S5)

self-motivated—do not need direction from other people in order to work and do a good job. (27)

selvage—a self-edge formed by the filling yarn when it turns to go back in the other direction; the two finished lengthwise edges of fabric. (13) (S3)

seminar—workshop. (26)

serger—a special sewing machine that can stitch, trim, and overcast a seam all at the same time; also called an overlock machine. (S2)

set-in sleeve—joined to the garment by an arm-hole seam that circles the arm near the shoulder. (9)

shade—a color that is darkened by the addition of black. (10)

shape—the outline, or silhouette, of an object. (11)

shears—have long blades and two handles that are shaped differently. (S2)

sheath—a close-fitting dress that is shaped by darts. (9)

shift—a loose-fitting dress. (9)

shirring—several rows of gathering. (S4)

shuttle—an instrument that is used to weave the crosswise threads in and out, back and forth, on a loom. (7)

silhouettes—outer shapes. (11)

society—a group of individuals who live together in a particular area. (1)

solvent—a substance used to dissolve another substance. (17)

space—the area inside the shape, or outline, of an object. (11)

spreadsheet—a specialized software program used for financial planning. (27)

standards—ethics or customs that are generally regarded as acceptable (1); specific measurements or models to which similar products are compared. (23)

staple fibers—short fibers that are measured in inches or centimeters. (13)

status—position or rank within a group. (1)

status symbols—clothes or other items that offer a sense of status for the ordinary person. (1)

staystitching—used along bias and curved edges to prevent stretching. (S4)

stereotype—a simplified and standardized image of a person or group. (3)

stitch-in-the-ditch—a row of stitching done on the outside of a garment in the groove of a seam-line. (S4)

style—the shape of a particular item of clothing that makes it easy to recognize. (5)

stylist—a designer or consultant who is responsible for determining the look of a product. (24)

sumptuary laws—regulations controlling what each social class could wear. (6)

sweatshops—dark, airless, uncomfortable, and unhealthy places to work. (7)

symbol—something visible that represents something else. (4)

T

tanned—converted into leather by treating with tannic acid made from tree bark. (6)

target audience—a specific group of potential customers. (27)

technology—the way a society uses its scientific knowledge to produce things. (5)

tensile strength—ability to withstand tension or pulling. (12)

texture—the surface characteristics, or feel, of an object. (11)

texturing—process that uses chemicals, heat, or special machinery to turn the straight, rod-like filaments into coiled, looped, or crimped yarns. (13)

tie dyeing—a method of tightly tying fabric in certain places, then dipping the fabric into dye. (S5)

tint—a color combined with white. (10)

topstitching—a row of stitching done on the outside of a garment. (S4)

toxic—poisonous. (23)

trademark—a symbol, design, word, or letter that is used by manufacturers or retailers to distinguish their products from those of the competition. (19)

trade name—registered as a trademark and protected by law. (12)

trade-off—an exchange of one thing for another. (21)

trend—fashion cycle that happens quite slowly. (5)

tubing—a strip of fabric stitched and turned right side out so the seam allowances are inside the tube. (S5)

tucks—narrow folds of fabric that are stitched partway or the entire length. (S5)

U

understitching—a row of stitching used to keep a facing or bottom layer of fabric rolled out of sight. (S4)

unit construction—everything is completed on the smallest unit possible before beginning to sew the separate units together. (S4)

V

value—the lightness or darkness of a color. (10)

values—beliefs about what is important, worthwhile, or desirable. (1)

verbal messages—choice of words and tone of voice. (3)

versatile—able to be worn or combined in a variety of ways. (15)

vintage—classics from the past. (16)

vocational training—provides instruction in a particular occupation. (26)

W

wage—a certain amount of money per hour or per day of work. (7)

wales—lengthwise chains of loops in knitted fabric; also called ribs. (S3)

wardrobe plan—a guide for buying and maintaining the clothes and accessories that are appropriate for you and your lifestyle. (15)

warp yarns—yarns that run the length of the fabric. (13)

warranty—a pledge or assurance that the product or fabric will meet certain standards. (19)

wearing ease—the amount of fullness needed for movement and comfort. (S1) (S3)

weaving—interlacing two sets of yarns at right angles to each other. (13)

wholesale—the sale of goods in quantity for resale. (25)

with nap—fabric with a nap, pile, or one-way design. (S1)

X-Y-Z

yarns—fibers twisted together or laid side by side. (13)

Credits

Cover Design: DesignNet

Cover Photography: Mark Romine

Interior Design: Design 5 and Circle Design

Special thanks to Marshall Greenberg, Art MacDillo's/Gary Skillestad, and Jeff Stoecker for their assistance in updating and revising the art in the Sewing and Serging Handbook.

AFP/Bettmann, 120
Ahmed, David R. Frazier Photolibrary, 23
Arnold & Brown, 72, 73, 110, 124, 152, 153, 186, 187, 228, 229, 284, 285, 354, 355, 424, 425
Bill Aron/PhotoEdit, 65
Art MacDillo's/Gary Skillestad, 213, 572
Bill Bachmann/PhotoEdit, 40, 330
Jim Ballard, 348
Bettmann, 127
Shirley Bortoli, 527
Comstock, 230-231, 286-287, 356-357
Cotton Inc., 194
Myrleen Ferguson/PhotoEdit, 360
David R. Frazier Photolibrary, 21, 24, 60, 61, 64, 67, 97, 334
Tony Freeman/PhotoEdit, 67
Ann Garvin, 20, 66, 111, 115, 124, 172, 178, 247, 251, 252, 258, 265, 274, 275, 276, 278, 279, 280, 281, 296, 297, 303, 306, 307, 311, 316, 317, 319, 322, 323, 331, 346, 350, 367, 375, 376, 379, 380, 383, 389, 394, 397, 403, 404, 407, 415, 429, 436, 438, 454, 471, 487
Gerber Garment Technology, Inc., 111, 113, 364, 365, 368
Steve Greiner, 39, 84, 281, 402
Linda Henson, 123, 166, 178, 207, 251, 253, 276, 292, 293, 295, 303, 304, 321, 323, 324, 345, 395, 567

Richard Hutchings/PhotoEdit, 39
Images Inc.
    Peter Gould, 74-75, 112, 114, 120, 123, 125, 127, 360, 361, 392
    Barbara Rosen, 82, 121
Ken Lax, Photography/Gail Fell, Stylist, 5, 7, 9, 16, 17, 30, 31, 46, 47, 58, 59, 76, 77, 90, 91, 104, 105, 118, 119, 132, 133, 156, 157, 170, 171, 190, 191, 204, 205, 218, 219, 232, 233, 244, 245, 256, 257, 272, 273, 288, 289, 300, 301, 314, 315, 328, 329, 342, 343, 358, 359, 372, 373, 386, 387, 400, 401, 412, 413
Erich Lessing/Art Resource, 96
Linda Matlow/Pix International, 85
Cathy Melloan/Tony Stone Images, 121
Jon McIntosh, 49, 114, 122, 178, 225, 264, 280, 292, 306, 319, 346, 366, 376, 403, 417
Ted Mishima, 12, 13, 18, 63, 78, 125, 142, 158, 161, 221, 225, 396, 428, 429, 430, 435, 436, 437, 441, 444, 450, 453, 459, 463, 464, 465, 466, 467, 470, 471, 472, 486, 490, 491, 492, 504, 513, 532, 537, 539, 540, 555, 567, 568, 569, 570, 571, 572, 573
Morgan-Cain, 42-43, 51, 100-101, 112-113, 126-129, 160, 167, 174, 176, 177, 183, 199, 210, 224, 239, 249, 259, 262-263, 269, 277, 294, 309, 320, 351, 364-365
North Wind Picture Archives, 20, 107, 108, 109
Jonathan Nowrok/PhotoEdit, 68
Tom Pantages, 112, 192, 210, 220, 221, 362, 363
Scott Pease, 223, 240, 241, 258, 338, 383, 408
Brent Phelps, 113
Photo Researchers/Stephen Dalton, 195
Liz Purcell, 62, 79, 83, 92, 93, 94, 95, 98, 100-101, 173, 196, 206, 207, 208, 209, 211, 212, 275, 339, 434, 456, 457, 460, 463, 466, 467, 524, 544, 551, 562, 564, 570

Special thanks to the following individuals, schools, businesses, and organizations for their assistance with photographs in this book. **In Chicago, Illinois**--Jean Van Koughnett, AlyoChildren's Dance Theatre, Singer Factory Distributor on Irving Park, Vogue Fabrics of Evanston. **In Normal, Illinois**--Vanity. **In New Hampshire**--L. W. Packard Company, Ashland; Dorr Woolen Company, Guild. **In Southern California**--Adventure 16, West Los Angeles; The Broadway Department Stores; Boulevard Camera of Santa Monica; Classic Tailors; Executive Dry Cleaners, Santa Monica; Carol Jago; Martin Minkardo; Deborah Rodney; Santa Monica High School; St. Monica's High School; Carl Terzian & Associates; Venice Family Clinic; Windward School. **In Denton, Texas**--Russel's Department Store, Texas Woman's University.

Models and fictional names have been used to portray characters in stories and examples in this text.

Index